AN ENGLISH-PERSIAN DICTIONARY

DARIUSH B. GILANI is a native of Iran spending most of his life in the United States studying and teaching languages. He received his B.A. in 1976 from San Jose State University and he completed his M.S. studies in Linguistics at the same university in 1978. After graduating he was hired by SJSU and taught Persian language and Iranian history for the next twelve years. In 1997 he was invited to teach Persian at Stanford University for several terms. He spent three years compiling this dictionary.

AN
ENGLISH-PERSIAN
DICTIONARY

DARIUSH GILANI

IBEX Publishers
Bethesda, Maryland

An English-Persian Dictionary
Compiled by Dariush Behnam Gilani

فـرهنگ انگلیسی- فارسی

گرداوری داریوش بهنام گیلانی

Graphics: Farideh Esfandi
Illustrations: Ali Dowlatshahi, Simone Porfekr
Computer: Hamid Daroui

Manufactured in the United States of America

The paper used in this book meets the minimum requirements of the American National Standard for Information Services — Permanence of Paper for Printed Library Materials, ANSI Z39.48-1984

Ibex Publishers, Inc.
Post Office Box 30087
Bethesda, Maryland 20824
Telephone: 301-718-8188
Facsimile: 301-907-8707
www.ibexpub.com

Library of Congress Cataloging-in-Publication Information

Gilani, Dariush.
An English-Persian dictionary / Dariush Gilani.
p.   cm.
Introd. also in Persian.
Added title page title: Farhang-i Ingilisi-Fārsi.
ISBN 0-936347-95-3 (alk paper)
1. English language — Dictionaries — Persian.   2. Persian language — Transliteration into English — Dictionaries.   I. Title.   II. Title: Farhang-i Ingilisi-Fārsi.
PK6379.G55   1999
423'.9155—dc21   98-46946
CIP

AN ENGLISH PERSIAN DICTIONARY

The Language of Iran is the legacy of the long and glorious history of that country and its people. Its grammar points to its linguistic link with European languages; its vocabulary represents the contacts Iranians have had with others; and its literature, "the soul of Iran," embodies the feelings of Iranians toward their fellow men and the world around them. The primary aim of this dictionary is to introduce to English speakers the language and, through it ultimately, the culture of Iran.

Persian language spoken in Iran, or "Farsi" as Iranians call it, is the modern version of an ancient language, "Parsi," which has experienced centuries of abuse and hostility by the invasion of thousands of armies of aggressors as well as the linguistic invasion of thousands of foreign words, especially from Arabic. Yet throughout its encounters, the Persian language never succumbed to any of the conquerors of Iran or their particular languages and, although it adopted thousands of words, and a new alphabet from these languages it never lost its spirit. With the aid of some of its poets, especially Ferdowsi, Persian rose from the ashes of these conquests having retained intact its Indo-Aryan linguistic structure.

This book does not make an issue of which words in Persian are of Arabic, Turkish or other origin. Neither does it fall prey to the partisan cries of those who wish to cleanse Persian of foreign words. That task is clearly not the aim of this book.

Our ultimate goal, however, is to introduce the English speaking world at large to the culture of Iran and its literature through the Persian language.

There are three basic differences between this dictionary and those published in Iran. First, instead of emphasizing the pronunciation of the English words we have concentrated on the pronunciation of Persian words by transcribing the Persian entries into a phonetic system. In other words we have assumed that the reader is an English speaker who can also read the English alphabet. This system of phonetics enables those readers who do not know the Persian alphabet to read and pronounce the Persian entries correctly.

Second, the presumption that the reader does not know the Persian alphabet and its grammar places a restriction on the part of the translator of these English words. That is, where other dictionaries may define an English word in one or two sentences we have been denied that luxury because of the above presumption. Therefore, finding an exact single word meaning for some of the English words, without the ability to define them, has been a very elaborate task for us.

Third, as the reader may be aware, the English language spoken in Great Britain and the United States have certain differences in meaning and usage. Many words have totally different meanings in these two countries. Most English-Persian dictionaries published in Iran are based on British English. Because of this overemphasis on British English, and to break rank with the conventional dictionaries, we have made a major effort to give prominence to the current most common and frequently used words in American English.

Finally, the dictionary you have in your hands is the product of years of hard work by dedicated people. Obviously the book will contain some typographical or grammatical errors. We invite those reader who wish to assist us in improving future editions to write to us with any suggestions and corrections. Please write to me in care of the publisher.

In conclusion, although I cannot thank all the contributors to this dictionary on an individual basis. One individual stands out. Hamid Daroui was instrumental in the completion of this book. The data in this dictionary was entered into a special Persian language software, "Padideh," developed by him. The program was a major contribution in helping compile this dictionary. I wish to thank him here.

— Dariush B. Gilani
September, 1998

READING THE DICTIONARY

There is no hyphenation in Persian. However, for the ease of pronunciation, a hyphen is inserted in some of phonetic transcriptions to help the reader in better pronouncing the entries. Example: [bi-chiz]. It is also intended to eliminate confusion in the pronunciation of some words; *i.e.* [ez-hâr].

The maximum of four Persian translations are allowed for each English word. If two or more translations are given for a word the first entry is normally the most commonly used term in Persian.

If you observe a phonetic sign of [e´] in Persian meaning it stands for [ezâfeh] which in Persian grammar is a marker for adjectival and possessive phrases (Refer to your Persian grammar books). Its pronunciation, however, is exactly as that of [e].

The tilde symbol [~] placed over a letter signifies "geminization" which simply means "double-pronunciation" of a given letter. This speech phenomenon is exclusively found in Arabic words borrowed by Persian. Not too many truly Persian words are geminized. In order to pronounce a letter with the symbol [~] over it the reader should momentarily pause on that given letter. For example, the name Mohammad [moham~ad] should be read as Moe-Ham-Mad or the name Khayyam [khay´âm] should be pronounced as (Khay-Yom).

The accent mark [´] in the phonetic system used here stands for two letters in Persian; — [hamzeh] (ء) and [eyn] (ع). These sounds are technically called "glottal stops" which are produced by the vocal chords.

Here is a pronunciation guide for these sounds:

1. INITIAL POSITION — if you see a word beginning with [´] you simply ignore it in the pronunciation. For example; the words [´âli] علی and [âli] آلی are pronounced exactly the same (like the English word for Ollie).

2. MEDIAL POSITION — If the sound [´] occurs in the middle of a word then you must completely pause on this sound before going on. For example, in the words; [mas´ud] and [mas´ul] the reader should simply read them respectively as; (Mass-ood) and (Mass-ool).

3. FINAL POSITION — Sometimes these sounds occur at the end of
   a word. Here [´] sounds like a very short sighing sound – a short
   release of air from the mouth. For example the words [sham´] شمع
   or [enshâ´] انشا should be pronounce as (Sham) and (N. Shaw).

There are two sounds in Persian that do not exist in English. One is
[kh] خ and the other is [q] ق / غ. The first one; [kh] is produced in the
back of the mouth exactly were [h] is produced, with one exception,
which is [kh] uses the mouth water or saliva. Thus [kh] could be called a
wet [h].

The second sound is a (velar stop) and it takes place way in the back of
your mouth where your velum is vibrating. Imagine you are swallowing
the saliva in your mouth and are making a sound at the same time.

THE PERSIAN ALPHABET

F	M	I	A				
ـل	ـل	ل	ا	alef	a	1	۱
ـب	ـبـ	بـ	ب	be	b	2	۲
ـپ	ـپـ	پـ	پ	pe	p	3	۳
ـت	ـتـ	تـ	ت	te	t	4	۴
ـث	ـثـ	ثـ	ث	se	s	5	۵
ـج	ـجـ	جـ	ج	jim	j	6	۶
ـچ	ـچـ	چـ	چ	che	ch	7	۷
ـح	ـحـ	حـ	ح	he	h	8	۸
ـخ	ـخـ	خـ	خ	khe	kh	9	۹
ـد	د	د	د	dâl	d	10	۱۰
ـذ	ذ	ذ	ذ	zâl	z	11	۱۱
ـر	ر	ر	ر	re	r	12	۱۲
ـز	ز	ز	ز	ze	z	13	۱۳
ـژ	ژ	ژ	ژ	zhe	zh	14	۱۴
ـس	ـسـ	سـ	س	sin	s	15	۱۵
ـش	ـشـ	شـ	ش	shin	sh	16	۱۶
ـص	ـصـ	صـ	ص	sâd	s	17	۱۷
ـض	ـضـ	ضـ	ض	zâd	z	18	۱۸
ـط	ـطـ	طـ	ط	tâ	t	19	۱۹
ـظ	ـظـ	ظـ	ظ	zâ	z	20	۲۰
ـع	ـعـ	عـ	ع	eyn	´	21	۲۱
ـغ	ـغـ	غـ	غ	qeyn	q	22	۲۲
ـف	ـفـ	فـ	ف	fe	f	23	۲۳

ـق	ـقـ	قـ	ق	qâf	q	24	۲۴
ـک	ـکـ	کـ	ک	kâf	k	25	۲۵
ـگ	ـگـ	گـ	گ	gâf	g	26	۲۶
ـل	ـلـ	لـ	ل	lâm	l	27	۲۷
ـم	ـمـ	مـ	م	mim	m	28	۲۸
ـن	ـنـ	نـ	ن	nun	n	29	۲۹
ـو	ـو	و	و	vâv	v	30	۳۰
ـه	ـهـ	هـ	ه	he	h	31	۳۱
ـی	ـیـ	یـ	ی	ye	y	32	۳۲
ء	ـئـ	ئـ	ء	hamzeh	´	33	۳۳

A = Alone, I = Initial, M = Middle, F = Final

KEY TO PRONUNCIATION

	ENGLISH	PERSIAN	PTS
â	car, father	bâd باد bâr بار	â
a	bad, tab	bad بد tab تب	æ
i	meet, lead	bid بید sib سیب	i
e / e´	mess, bed	mes مس fer فر	ɛ
o	go, hose	gom گم moz مز	o
u	tool, rule	tul طول sut سوت	u
ay	I, my	ay آی chây چای	ai
ey	made, say	pey پی keyk کیک	e
oy	boy, oil	khoy خوی	oi
ch	cheese, check	chiz چیز chek چک	č
sh	sheer, shack	shir شیر shak شک	š
zh	azure, leisure	zhest ژست zhilâ ژیلا	ž
kh		mikh میخ khâk خاک	x
q		qâz غاز / âqâ آقا	q
´		´ali علی / su´ سؤ	´
~		bar~eh بره pel~eh پله	~

PTS = Phonetic transliteration system used by Orientalists.

A A A

a *ia., n., pre.* یک yek یکی yeki
A.D. *n.* بعد از مسیح ba'd az masih
abacus *n.* چرتکه chortkeh
abandon *n., vt.* ترک کردن tark kardan
abandoned *adj.* متروکه matrukeh
abandonment *n.* ترک tark واگذاری vâgozâri
abase *vt.* پست کردن past kardan تحقیرکردن tahqir kardan
کم کردن kam kardan فرونشاندن foru neshândan
abasement *n.* پست past تحقیر tahqir
abash *vt.* شرمنده کردن sharmandeh kardan
abashment *n.* شرمندگی sharmandegi
abatement *n.* منع man' موقوفی moqufi
abbey *n.* دیر deyr خانقاه khâneqâh
abbreviate *vt.* مختصرکردن mokhtasar kardan
abbreviation *n.* مختصر mokhtasar اختصار ekhtesâr
abdicate *vi., vt.* کناره گیری کردن kenârehgiri kardan
abdication *n.* کناره گیری kenârehgiri استعفاء este'fâ'
abdomen *n.* شکم shekam معده me'deh
abdominal *adj.* شکمی shekami
abduct *vt.* ربودن robudan دزدیدن dozdidan
abductor *n.* دزد dozd آدم ربا âdam-robâ
aberration *n.* انحراف enherâf گمراهی gomrâhi
abet *vt.* حمایت کردن hemâyat kardan ترغیب کردن tarqib kardan
abetment *n.* حمایت hemâyat ترغیب tarqib
abhor *vt.* تنفرداشتن tanaf~or dâshtan نفرت داشتن nefrat dâshtan
abhorence *n.* تنفر tanaf~or انزجار enzejâr
abhorent *n.* متنفر motenaf~er منزجر monzajer
abide *v.* صبرکردن sabr kardan قبول کردن qabul kardan
abide *n.* صبر sabr قبول qabul
abiding *adj., v.* همیشگی hamishegi مطیع moti'
ability *n.* توانایی tavânâyi تاب tâb توان tavân استطاعت estetâ-'at
abject *adj.* پست past فلاکت بار felâkat-bâr
abjection *n.* فلاکت felâkat پستی pasti
abjure *vt.* سوگند شکستن sogand shekastan
ablaze *adj.* شعله ور sho'lehvar سوزان suzân
able *adj., n.* قادر qâder توانا tavânâ
able-bodied *adj.* تندرست tandorost

abloom *adv., adj.* شكوفا shekufâ
ablution *n.* شتستشو shosteshu غسل qosl وضوء vozu'
abnormal *adj.* غیرعادی qeyr-e' 'âd~i
aboard *adv., pre.* سوار savâr-e' (توی) tu(ye')
abode *n., v., vi., vt.* مسكن maskan جا jâ سكنی soknâ
abolish *vt.* موقوف كردن moquf kardan منسوخ كردن mansukh kardan
abolished *adj.* منسوخ mansukh' لغوشده laqv-shodeh ملغی molqâ
abolished *adj.* منسوخ mansukh ملغی molqa
abolition *n.* لغو laqv الغاء elqâ'
abominable *adj.* بد bad مكروه makruh شنیع shani'
abominate *adj.* نكبت زده nekbat-zadeh كریه karih
abomination *n.* كراهت kerâhat نكبت nekbat
aborigines *n.* بومی bumi
abort *vi., vt., n.* سقط كردن saqt kardan ول كردن vel kardan
abortion *n.* سقط جنین saqt-e' janin كورتاژ kur-tâzh
abortive *adj.* بی نتیجه bi-natijeh
abound *v.* فراوان بودن farâvân budan وفورداشتن vofur dâshtan
abound *adj.* فراوان farâvân
about *pre., adv., adj.* درحدود dar hodud-e' تقریباً taqriban
about *pre.* دور dor-e' در اطراف dar atrâf-e'
about *pre.* دربارهٔ dar bâreh-ye' راجع به râje' beh
about-face *n., vi.* عقب گرد aqab-gard
above *adv., pre., adj., n.* بالای bâlâ-ye' روی ru-ye' فراز farâz
above *adv., pre., adj., n.* نامبرده nâm-bordeh مذكور mazkur
above-mentioned *n.* نامبرده nâm-bordeh مذكور mazkur
above-named *n.* نامبرده nâm-bordeh مذكور mazkur
aboveboard *adv., adj.* آشكار âshkâr رو ی میز ru-ye' miz
abrasion *n.* خراش kharâsh سایش sâyesh
abrasive *n., adj.* ساینده sâyandeh سایش sâyesh
خراش دهنده kharâsh-dahandeh
abreast *adv., adj.* پهلو به پهلو pahlu be-pahlu برابر barâ-bar
abreast *adv., adj.* آگاه âgâh درجریان dar jaryân
abridge *vt.* مختصركردن mokhtasar kardan
خلاصه كردن kholâseh kardan
abridgement *n.* اختصار ekhtesâr
abroad *adv.* خارج khârej به خارج beh khârej خارجه khârejeh
abrogate *v.* لغو كردن laqv kardan
abrogation *n.* الغاء elqâ' نسخ naskh

abrupt *adj.* ناگهانی nâgahâni به تندى beh tondi
abruption *n.* قطع qat′
abruptly *adv.* ناگهانی nâgahâni به تندى beh tondi
abscess *n.* دمل domal غده qod~eh
abscond *v.* دررفتن dar raftan گریختن gorikhtan
absence *n.* غیبت qeybat نقدان feqdân غیاب qiab
absent *adj., vt.* غایب qâyeb
absent-minded *adj.* کم حافظه kam hâfezeh گیج gij
absentee *n.* غایب qâyeb
absolute *adj., n.* مطلق motlaq قطعی qat′i تام tâm
absolution *n.* بخشودگی bâkhshudegi آمرزش âmorzesh
مغفرت maqferat
absolve *vt.* تبرئه کردن tabra′eh kardan آمرزیدن âmorzidan
absorb *vt.* جذب کردن jazb kardan
absorbed *adj.* مجذوب majzub غرق qarq مستغرق mostaqraq
absorbent *adj., n.* جذب کننده jazb konandeh
absorption *n.* جذب jazb
abstain *v.* خودداری کردن khod-dâri kardan پرهیزکردن parhiz kardan
مضایقه کردن mozâyeqeh kardan
امساک کردن emsâk kardan
abstain *v.* رأى ممتنع دادن ra′ye momtane′dâdan
خودداری کردن khod-dâri kardan
abstention *n.* خودداری khod-dâri پرهیز parhiz
abstention *n.* رأى ممتنع ra′-ye′ momtane′
abstinence *n.* پرهیز parhiz امساک emsâk زهد zohd
abstinent *adj.* پرهیزکار parhiz-kâr زاهد zahed
abstract *adj., n., vt.* انتزاعی entezâ′i مجرد mojar~ad خلاصه kholaseh
abstract noun *np.* اسم معنی esm-e′ ma′nâ
abstraction *n.* تجرد tajar~od تجرید tajrid
absurd *adj.* مسخره maskhareh مزخرف mozakhraf
absurdity *n.* مسخرگی maskhâregi
abundance *n.* وفور vofur فراوانی farâvâni
abundant *adj.* فراوان farâvân به حد وفور beh had~-e′ vofur
abuse *n.* سوء استفاده su′-e′ estefâdeh بدرفتاری bad-raftâri
abuse *v.* سوء استفاده کردن su′-e′ estefâdeh kardan
بدرفتاری کردن bad-raftâri kardan
abusive *adj.* اهانت آمیز ehânat-âmiz فحش دهنده fohsh-dahandeh
کتک زن kotak-zan

abysmal *adj.* عميق 'amiq ژرف zharf گود god
abyss *n.* گودی godi ژرفا zharfâ ورطه varteh مغاک maqâk
acacia *n.* اقاقیا aqâqiâ
academic *adj., n.* تحصیلی tahsili فرهنگی farhangi
academy *n.* آکادمی âkâdemi فرهنگستان farhangestân
accede *vi.* نائل شدن nâ'el shodan
accelerate *vt., vi.* تسریع کردن tasri' kardan تندترکردن tond-tar kardan
acceleration *n.* تسریع tasri' شتاب shetâb تعجیل ta'jil
accelerator *n.* گاز gâz
accent *n.* لهجه lahjeh
accent *v.* تأکیدکردن ta'kid kardan
accentuate *vt.* تأکید کردن ta'kid kardan
accept *vt., vi.* قبول کردن qabul kardan پذیرفتن paziroftan
acceptable *adj.* قابل قبول qâbel-e' qabul پذیرفتنی paziroftani
acceptance *n.* پذیرش paziresh قبولی qabuli استجابت estejâbat
access *n.* دسترسی dastresi راه râh
accessible *adj.* قابل دسترسی qâbel-e' dastresi دست یافتنی dast-yâftani
accession *n., vt.* جلوس jolus دست یابی dast-yâbi
accessories *pl.* لوازم فرعی lavâzem-e far'i اجزاء ajza'
accessory *n., adj.* همدست ham-dast فرعی far'i
شریک جرم sharik-e' jorm
accident *n.* تصادف tasâdof حادثه hâdeseh سانحه sâneheh
accidental *adj., n.* اتفاقی et~efâqi
accidentally *adv.* اتفاقاً et~efâqan تصادفاً tasâdofan
acclaim *v.* تحسین کردن tahsin kardan
acclaim *v.* تحسین کردن tahsin
acclamation *n.* تحسین tahsin
accomodate *n.* جادادن jâ dâdan منزل دادن manzel dâdan
accompany *vt.* همراهی کردن ham-râhi kardan
accomplice *n.* همدست ham-dast شریک جرم sharik-e' jorm
accomplish *vt.* انجام دادن anjâm dâdan تمام کردن tamâm kardan
accomplishment *n.* انجام anjâm اتمام etmâm
accord *v.* موافقت کردن movâfeqat kardan وفق دادن vefq dâdan
accord *n.* موافقت movâfeqat سازش sâzesh توافق tavâfoq
accordance *n.* مطابقت motâbeqat
according (to) *n.* طبق tebq-e' بنابر banâ-bar
accordingly *adv.* برطبق آن bar tebq-e' ân
accost *vt., n.* مخاطب ساختن mokhâteb sâkhtan

مزاحم شدن .... mozâhem shodan
account v. حساب کردن hesâb kardan جواب دادن javâb dâdan
account n. حساب hesâb شماره shomâreh
accountable adj. جوابگو javâb-gu مسئول mas'ul
accountant n. حسابدار hesâb-dâr
accounting n. حسابداری hesâb-dâri
accumulate v. جمع کردن jam' kardan اندوختن andukhtan
accumulate n. جمع jam' اندوخته andukhteh
accumulation n. جمع آوری jam'-âvari گردآوری gerd-âvari
accuracy n. دقت deq~at درستی dorosti
accurate adj. دقیق daqiq درست dorost
accusation n. تهمت tohmat اتهام et~ehâm
accuse vt., vi. تهمت زدن tohmat zadân متهم کردن mot~aham kardan
accused v. متهم mot~aham
accustomed adj. خوگرفته khu-gerefteh
ace n., vt., adj. آس âs تکخال tak khâl
ache v. دردکردن dard kardan
ache n. درد dard
achieve v. انجام دادن anjâm dâdan بدست آوردن bedast âvardan
achievement n. کاربزرگ kâr-e' bozorg دست آورد dast-âvard
acid n., adj. جوهر johar اسید asid
acknowledge vt. تصدیق کردن tasdiq kardan
اعتراف کردن e'terâf kardan اذعان کردن ez'ân kardan
acne n. جوش صورت jush-e' surat
acorn n. بلوط balut
acoustic adj., n. صوتی soti شنوایی shenavâyi
acoustics n. صوت شناسی sot-shenâsi شنیداری shenidâri
acquaint vt. آشناساختن âshnâ sâkhtan
acquaintance n. آشنا âshnâ آشنایی âshenâyi متعارف mote'âref
acquiesce vi. پذیرفتن paziroftan تسلیم شدن taslim shodan
acquiescence n. پذیرش paziresh رضایت rezâyat
acquire vt. بدست آوردن bedast âvardan گرفتن gereftan
acquired vt. بدست آورده be-dast âvardeh اکتسابی ektesâbi
گرفته gerefteh
acquisition n. کسب kasb اکتساب gereftan اخذ akhz
acquit vt. تبرئه کردن tabra'eh kardan
acquittal n. تبرئه tabra'eh
acre n. هکتار hektâr جریب jarib

acrid adj. گس gas
acrimonious adj. پرسروصدا por sâro sedâ
acrobat n. اکروبات âkrobât بندباز band-bâz
across pre., adv. روبروی ruberu-ye' سرتاسر sar tâ sar
act n. عمل 'amal کار kâr
act v. عمل کردن 'amal kardan بازی کردن bâzi kardan
acting adj., n. هنرپیشگی honar-pishegi
acting adj., n. کفیل kafil نایب nâyeb
action n. عمل 'amal اقدام eqdâm کنش konesh
activate vt. براه انداختن berâh andâkhtan
بکارانداختن bekâr andâkhtan
active adj., n. فعال fa'~âl کاری kâri جدی jed~i
activity n. فعالیت fa'~âliyat
actor n. هنرپیشه honar-pisheh آکتور âktor
actual adj. واقعی vâqe'i
actually adv. درحقیقت dar haqiqat
acupuncture n., vt. طب سوزنی teb~-e' suzani
acute adj., n. تیز tiz حاد hâd~ تند tond
ad n., pre. آگهی âgahi
ad-lib vt., vi., adj. فی البداهه گفتن fel bedâheh goft/an
adam n. آدم âdam
adamant n., adj. یکدنده yek dandeh لجوج lajuj
adapt vt., vi. وفق دادن vefq dâdan
adaptable adj. وفق دادنی vefq-dâdani
adaptation n. توافق tavâfoq اقتباس eqtebâs
add vt., vi., n. جمع کردن jam' kardan اضافه کردن ezâfeh kardan
addendum n. ضمیمه zamimeh
addict n., vt. معتادکردن mo'tâd kardan
addicted adj. معتاد mo'tâd
adding machine np. ماشین حساب mâshin-e' hesâb
addition n. جمع jam' اضافه ezâfeh افزایش afzâyesh
address n., vt., vi. نشانی neshâni آدرس âdres
adept adj., n. ماهر mâher استاد ostâd
adequate adj. کافی kâfi مناسب monâseb
adhere vi. چسبیدن chasbidan اطاعت کردن etâ'at kardan
adherent n., adj. تابع tâbe'
adhesion n. چسبندگی chasbandegi
adhesive adj., n. چسبنده chasbandeh

adhesive tape *np.* نوار چسب navâr chasb
adjacent *adj.* مجاور mojâver همسایه hamsâyeh
adjective *n., adj.* صفت sefat
adjourn *vt., vi.* موکول کردن mokul kardan
adjunct *n., adj.* الحاقی elhâqi
adjust *v.* میزان کردن mizân kardan
adjust *n.* میزان mizân
adjustor *n.* تنظیم کننده tanzim konandeh
adjutant *n.* آجودان âjudân
administer *vt., vi.* اداره کردن edâreh kardan
administration *n.* اداره edâreh
administrator *n.* مدیر modir رئیس ra'is
admiral *n.* ناخدا nâkhodâ دریا سالار daryâ-sâlâr
admiration *n.* تحسین tahsin
admissible *adj.* قابل قبول qâbel-e' qabul مجاز majâz?
admission *n.* تصدیق tasdiq اعتراف e'terâf
admission *n.* ورود vorud ورودیه vorudieh
admit *vt., vi.* پذیرفتن paziroftan اعتراف کردن e'terâf kardan
admittance *n.* ورودی vorudi پذیرش paziresh
admonish *v.* نصیحت کردن nasihat kardan
    سرزنش کردن sar-zanesh kâr/dân
    ملامت کردن malâmat kardan
admonishment *n.* اخطار ekhtâr نصیحت nasihat سرزنش sar-zanesh
    ملامت malâmat
adolescence *n.* دورۀ بلوغ doreh-ye' boluq عنفوان 'onfavân
adolescent *adj., n.* جوان بالغ javân-e' bâleq
adopt *vt.* قبول کردن qabul kardan اقتباس کردن eqtebâs kardan
adoption *n.* فرزند خواندگی farzand khândegi اقتباس eqtebâs
adorable *adj.* شایان ستایش shâyân-e' setâyesh پرستیدنی parastidani
adore *vt., vi.* ستایش کردن setâyesh kardan پرستیدن parastidan
adrift *adj., adv.* شناور shenâvar ول در روی آب vel dar ruye âb
adroit *adj.* زرنگ zerang زیرک zirak
adult *adj., n.* بالغ bâleq سالمند sâlmand
adulterer *n.* مرد زناکار mard-e zenâ-kâr
adulteress *n.* زن زناکار zan-e' zenâ-kâr
adulterous *adj.* زناکارانه zenâ-kârâneh
adultery *n.* زنا zenâ
advance *vt., vi., n., adj.* جلوبردن jelo bordan پیش رفتن pish raftan

advanced *v.* مترقی moteraq~i پیش رفته pish rafteh
advancement *n.* ترقی taraq~i پیشرفت pish-raft
advantage *n., vt.* امتیاز emtiâz مزیت maziy~at آوانتاژ âvântâzh
advantageous *adj.* مزیت دار maziy~at-dâr امتیازدار emtiâz-dâr
adventure *n., vt., vi.* ماجراجویی mâjerâ-juyi
adventurer *n.* ماجراجو mâjerâ-ju
adventurous *adj.* پرماجرا por-mâjerâ مخاطره جو mokhâtereh-ju
adverb *n.* قید qeyd
adversary *n.* رقیب raqib دشمن doshman
adverse *adj.* مخالف mokhâlef منفی manfi
adversity *n.* فلک زدگی falak-zadegi فلاکت felâkat
advertise *vt., vi.* آگهی کردن âgahi kardan
advertisement *n.* آگهی âgahi
advice *n.* نصیحت nasihat پند pand
advisable *adj.* مصلحت دار maslahat-dâr
advise *v.* نصیحت کردن nasihat kardan آگاه کردن âgâh kardan
adviser *n.* مشاور moshâver
advocate *n.* وکیل vakil مدافع modâfe' پشتیبان poshtibân
advocate *v.* پشتیبانی کردن poshtibâni kardan
aeronautics *n.* هواپیمایی havâpeymâyi
aesthetics *n.* زیباشناسی zibâ-shenâsi
affable *adj.* مهربان mehrabân دلجو delju
affair *n.* مطلب matlab موضوع mozu' رابطه râbeteh
affect *vt., n., vi.* اثرگذاشتن asar gozâshtan
affection *n.* محبت' moheb~at علاقه alâqeh
affectionate *adj.* بامحبت bâ-moheb~at خونگرم khun-garm
affiant *n.* استشهاددهنده estesh-hâd dah/ndeh
affidavit *n.* اقرارنامه eqrâr-nâmeh استشهاد estesh-hâd
affiliate *n.* عضو'ozv وابسته vâbasteh
affiliate *v.* عضو شدن'ozv shodan وابسته کردن vâbasteh kardan
affiliation *n.* عضویت'ozviyat وابستگی vâbastegi
affinity *n.* نزدیکی nazdiki وابستگی vâbastegi
affirm *vt., vi.* اثبات کردن esbât kardan
affirmative *adj., n.* مثبت mosbat قطعی qat'i
affix *vt., n.* وصل کردن vasl kardan چسباندن chasbândan
affixed *n.* چسبیده chasbideh الصاق شده elsâq-shodeh
afflict *vt.* غمگین کردن qamgin kardan
affliction *n.* غمزدگی qamzadegi محنت mehnat

affluence *n.* پولداری puldâri وفورنعمت vofur-e' ne'mat
affluent *adj., n.* پولدار puldâr بانعمت bâ ne'mat
afford *vt.* استطاعت داشتن estetâ'at dâshtan
تحمل کردن tahâmol kardan
affront *n.* توهین tohin
affront *v.* توهین کردن tohin kardan
aflame *adj.* شعله ور sho'leh-var آتش گرفته âtash-gerefteh
مشتعل moshta'el
afoot *adv., adj.* توکار tu kâr درجریان dar jaryân
aforementioned *adj.* فوق الذکر foqol-zekr
aforethought *adj., n.* بافکرقبلی bâ fekr-e' qabli عمدی 'amdi
afoul *adv., adj.* بهم خورده be-ham khordeh
afraid *adj.* ترسیده tarsideh ترسان tarsân
Africa *n.* آفریقا âfriqâ
after *pre., adv., adj., con.* بعد از ba'd az پس از pas az
afterbirth *n.* پلا سنتا pelâsentâ
aftermath *n.* نتیجه natijeh پی آمد pey-âmad
afternoon *n., adj.* بعد ازظهر ba'd az zohr
afterthought *n.* پس اندیشه pas- andisheh
again *adv.* دوباره dobâreh باز bâz
against *pre., con.* مخالف mokhâlef برضد bar zed~ برخلاف far khalâf
برغم be-raqm
agate *n.* عقیق 'aqiq
age *n., vi., vt.* سن sen~ سال sâl روزگار ruzegâr عصر 'asr
agency *n.* نمایندگی namâyandegi آژانس âzhâns
agenda *n.* روز 'برنامهٔ barnâmeh-ye' ruz جزئیات بحث joz'iyât-e' bahs
agent *adj.* مأمور ma'mur نماینده namâyandeh کارگزار kâr-gozâr
عامل 'âmel
aggrandize *vt.* بزرگترکردن bozorg-tar kardan
aggravate *vt.* ناراحت کردن nârâhat kardan
شدیدترکردن shadidtar kardan
aggravation *n.* تشدید tashdid بدترشدگی batar shodegi
aggregate *adj., n., vt., vi.* مخلوط makhlut مجموع majmu'
aggression *n.* تعرض ta'ar~oz تجاوز tajâvoz درازدستی derâz-dasti
تعدی ta'ad~i
aggressive *adj.* مهاجم mohâjem تجاوز کننده tajâvoz konandeh
aghast *adj.* مبهوت mabhut گیج gij
agile *adj.* چابک châbok زرنگ zerang فرز ferz

agility n. چابکی châboki چالاکی châlâki

agitate vt., vi. بهم زدن beham zadan مضطرب کردن moztareb kardan
آشفته کردن âshofteh kardan

agitated n. مضطرب moztareb درهم و شوریده dar-ham-o shurideh
آشفته âshofteh مشوش moshav~esh

agitator n. دوبهم زن do-beham zan آشوبگر âshubgar

agnostic n., adj. خداانشناس khodâ-nashnâs

ago adj., adv. پیش pish قبل qabl گذشته gozashteh

agonize vi., vt. دردکشیدن dard keshidan عذاب دادن azâb dâdan

agonizing adj. غصه دار qos~ehdâr ناراحت کننده nârâhat konandeh

agony n. غصه′ qos~eh′ عذاب ′azâb

agree vi., vt. موافقت کردن movâfeqat kardan

agreeable adj. قابل قبول qâbel-e′ qabul پذیرفتنی paziroftani

agreed adj., v. قبول شده qabul shodeh

agreement n. قرارداد qarârdâd پیمان peymân

agressor n. تجاوزکار tajâvoz-kâr متعرض mote′are~z

agricultural adj. زراعتی zera′ati

agriculture n. زراعت zera′at کشاورزی keshâvarzi

aid n. کمک komak مساعدت mosâ′edat مدد madad

aid v. کمک کردن komak kardan

aid n. دستیار dastyâr

ail vt., vi. دردداشتن dard dâshtan

ailing adj. مریض mariz ناخوش nâkhosh

ailment n. مرض maraz بیماری bimâri ناخوشی nâkhoshi

aim v. هدف گرفتن hadaf gereftan مقصودداشتن maqsud dâshtan

aim n. هدف hadaf مقصود maqsud آرمان ârmân

aiming n. هدف گیری hadaf-giri

aimless adj. بی هدف bi-hadaf

air n., adj., adv., vt. هوا havâ

air raid np. حملة′ هوایی hamle-ye′ havâyi

airborne adj. بر هوا bar havâ

aircondition v. تهویه کردن tahvyeh kardan
خنک کردن khonak kardan

aircondition n. تهویه هوا tahvyeh havâ

airforce n. نیروی هوایی niru-ye′ havâyi

airline n. شرکت هواپیمایی sherkat-e′ havâ-peymâyi

airmail n. پست هوایی post-e′ havâ-yi

airplane n. هواپیما havâ-peymâ طیاره tay~âreh

airpocket *n.* چاه هوایی châh-e' havâyi
airport *n.* فرودگاه forud-gâh
aisle *n.* راهرو râhro
ajar *adj., adv.* نیمه باز nimeh-bâz
akin *adj.* هم جنس hamjens هم نسبت hamnesbat
aknowledgement *n.* تصدیق tasdiq اعتراف e'terâf
alarm *n., vt.* زنگ خطر zang-e' khatar هشدار hoshdâr
alas *int.* افسوس که afsus keh وا اسفا vâ-asafâ هیهات hey-hât
albeit *con.* اگرچه agar-cheh باینکه bâ inkeh
albeit *con.* اگرچه agar-cheh
albino *n.* زال zâl
alchemy *n.* کیمیاگری kimiâ-gari
alcohol *n.* الکل alkol
alcove *n.* آلاچیق âlâchiq
alderman *n.* عضو انجمن 'ozv-e' anjoman
alert *adj.* آگاه âgâh هوشیار hoshyâr گوش بزنگ gush be-zang
alert *v.* خبرکردن khabar kardan
alfalfa *n.* یونجه yonjeh
algebra *n.* جبر jabr
alias *n., adv.* نام دیگر nâm-e' digar اسم قلا بی esm-e' qol~âbi
alibi *n., vi., vt.* بهانه نبودن bahâneh-ye' nabudan
دلیل بیگناهی dalil-e' bigonâhi عذرموجه 'ozr-e' movaj~ah
alien *n., adj.* خارجی khâreji بیگانه bigâneh اجنبی ajnabi
alienate *vt.* بیگانه کردن bigâneh kardan
alienation *n.* بیگانگی bigânegi
aligator *n.* سوسمار susmâr تمساح temsâh
align *vt.* هم خط کردن ham- khat~ kardan میزان کردن mizân kardan
alignment *n.* تنظیم tanzim صف بندی saf-bandi
alike *adv., adj.* شبیه shabih مانند mânand یکسان yeksân
alimony *n.* نفقه nafaqeh خرجی زن kharji-e' zan
alive *adj.* زنده zendeh درحیات dar hayât
alkali(ne) *n.* قلیایی qalyâ'i
all *adj., pro., n., adv.* همه hameh تمام tamâm بکلی bekol~i
جمله jomleh
all right *np.* خوب khub عالی 'âli درست dorost
all the time *n.* همیشه hamisheh
all-in *adj.* آزاد âzâd
all-in-all *n.* گرامی gerâmi رویهم رفته ru-ye' ham rafteh

all-out *adj.* باتمام نيرو bâ-tamâm-e' niru

allay *vt.* تسكين دادن taskin dâdan آرام كردن ârâm kardan

allegation *n.* ادعا ed~e'â اتهام etehâm

allege *vt.* ادعاكردن ed~e'â kardan بيدليل گفتن bidalil goftan

alleged *adj.* كذائى kazâ'i

allegiance *n.* وفادارى vafâdâri بيعت bey'at

allegoric *n.* تمثيلى tamsili

allegory *n.* تمثيل tamsil مثل masal

allergic *adj.* حساس به has~âs beh

allergy *n.* حساسيت has~âsiyat آلرژى âlerzhi

alleviate *vt.* كم كردن kam kardan تسكين دادن taskin dâdan

alleviation *n.* تسكين taskin

alley *n.* كوچه kucheh راهرو râhro كوى kuy برزن barzan

alliance *n.* همبستگى ham-bastegi اتحاد et~ehâd

allied *adj.* متفق mot~afeq

alligator *n., vi.* سوسمار susmâr تمساح temsâh

allocate *vt.* اختصاص دادن ekhtesâs dâdan

allocation *n.* تخصيص takhsis اختصاص ekhtesâs

allot *vt.* اختصاص دادن ekhtesâs dâdan

allow *vt., vi.* اجازه دادن ejâzeh dâdan گذشتن gozashtan

allowance *n., vt.* پول جيبى pul jibi

alloy *n., vt.* آلياژ âlyâzh فلز مركب felez~-e' morak~ab ملقمه malqameh

allude *vi.* اشاره كردن eshâreh kardan

allure *v.* اغواكردن eqvâ andâkhtan گول زدن gul zadan كشاندن keshândan

allure(ment) *n.* اغوا eqvâ كشش keshesh

allusion *n.* اشاره eshâreh كنايه kenâyeh

allusive *adj.* اشاره اى eshâreh-i كنايه دار kenâyeh-dâr

alluvial *adj., n.* رسوبى rosubi

ally *n.* هم پيمان ham peymân متحد mot~ahed

ally *v.* هم پيمان شدن ham peymân shodan متحد كردن mot~âhed kardan

almighty *adj., adv., n.* قادر مطلق qader-e' motlag تعالى ta'âlâ

almond *n., adj.* بادام bâdâm

almost *adv.* تقريباً tagriban

alms *n.* صدقه sadaqeh خيرات kheyrât

alone *adj., adv.* تنها tanhâ

along *pre., adv.* همراه hamrâh درطول dar tul-e'
alongside *adv., pre.* درکنار dar kenâr-e'
aloof *adv., adj.* جدا jodâ دور از دنیا dur az donyâ
alopecia *n.* ریزش مو rizesh-e' mu گری gari
aloud *adv.* باصدای بلند bâ sedây-e' boland
alphabet *n.* الفبا alefbâ
already *adv.* درحال حاضر dar hâl-e' hâzer حالا همین hamin hâlâ
جخ jakh
also *adv., con.* هم ham همچنین ham-chenin
altar *n.* محراب mehrâb قربانیگاه qorbâni-gâh
alter *v.* عوض کردن 'avaz kardan تغییر دادن taqyir dâdan
alteration *n.* تغییر taqyir اصلاح eslah
altercate *vi.* دعوا کردن da'vâ kardan نزاع کردن nezâ' kardan
altercation *n.* دعوا da'vâ نزاع nezâ' مشاجره moshâjereh
altered *adj.* دست خورده dast-khordeh مخدوش makhdush
alternate *vi., vt., adj., n.* یک در میان yek-dar miân متناوب motenâveb
alternative *n., adj.* بدیل badeyl آلترناتیو âlternâtiv چاره châreh
alternator *n.* آلترناتور âlternâtor تناوبگر tanâvob-gar
although *con.* اگرچه agar-cheh بااینکه bâ-inkeh
altimeter *n.* ارتفع سنج ertefâ'-sanj فرازسنج farâz-sanj
altitude *n.* ارتفاع ertefâ'
altogether *adv., n.* روی هم رفته ruy-e' ham rafteh
همه با هم hameh bâ-ham
altruism *n.* مراعات no'-garâ'i مورآت morâ'ât نوع گرائی
altruist *n.* مراعات کننده morâ'ât-konandeh نوع گرا no'-garâ
aluminum *n., adj.* آلومینیوم âlumiom
alumni *pl.* فارغ التحصیلان fâreqol-tahsilân
always *adv.* همیشه hamisheh
amalgam *n.* آمیخته âmikhteh ترکیب tarkib
amalgamate *vt., vi.* متحد کردن mot~hed kardan
ادغام کردن edqâm kardan
amass *vt., vi.* جمع کردن jam' kardan گرد آوردن gerd âvardan
amatuer *n.* آماتور âmâtor
amaze *vt., n.* متحیرساختن motehay~er sâkhtan
amazed *adj., v.* متحیر motehay~er بهت زده boht-zadeh
شگفت زده shegeft-zadeh
amazement *n.* حیرت heyrat شگفت shegeft
amazing *adj., v.* شگفت آور shegeft-âvar

ambassador *n.* سفیر کبیر safir-e' kabir
amber *n., adj.* کهربا kahrobâ
ambidextrous *adj.* دو دست do-dast ذوالیمینین zol-yamineyn
ambiguity *n.* ابهام ebhâm
ambition *n., vt.* جاه طلبی jâh-talabi بلند همتی boland hem~ati
ambitious *adj.* جاه طلب jâh-talab بلند همت boland hem~at
amble *vi., n.* راه رفتن râh raftan
ambulance *n.* آمبولانس âmbulâns
ambush *n., vt.* بی خبر حمله کردن bi-khabar hamleh kardan
amen *int., adv., n.* آمین âmin الهی امید elâhi omid
amend *vt., vi.* اضافه کردن ezâfeh kardan اصلاح کردن eslâh kardan
amendment *n.* متمم motam~am
amenity *n.* دلخوشی del-khoshi مفرحی mofar~ahi
amiable *adj.* دوست داشتنی dust dâshtani
amicable *adj.* مسالمت آمیز mosâlemat-âmiz دوستانه dustâneh
amid(st) *n.* درمیان dar miân وسط vasat
amiss *adv., adj.* نادرست nâ-dorost بیموقع bi-moqe'
amity *n.* مناسبات دوستانه monâsebât-e' dustâneh
amnesia *n.* فراموشی farâ-mushi نسیان nesyan
amnesty *n., vt.* عفو عمومی 'afv-e 'omumi
among(st) *n.* درمیان dar miân بین beyn
amorous *adj.* عاشقانه 'âsheqâneh
amortization *n.* وام فرسایی vâm-farsâyi
amortize *vt.* مستهلک کردن mostahlak kardan
amount *n., vi.* مبلغ mablaq مقدار meqdâr
amphibian *n., adj.* دو زیست do-zist آب و خشکی âb va khoshki
amphibious *adj.* دوزیست do-zist
ample *adj.* کافی kâfi فراوان farâvân وافی vâfi
amplification *n.* بزرگی bozorgi افزایش afzâyesh بسط bast
amplifier *n.* تقویه صدا taqvieh-ye' sedâ
amplify *vt., vi.* بزرگتر کردن bozorg-tar kardan
amputate *vt.* قطع کردن qat' kardan بریدن boridan
amputee *n.* چلاق cholâq بریده شده borideh-shodeh
amuck *adv., n.* دیوانه وار divâneh-vâr
amuse *v.* تفریح دادن tafrih dâdan
amuse *v.* سرگرم کردن sar-garm kardan
amused *adj., vt.* سرگرم sar-garm
amusement *n.* سرگرمی sar-garmi تفریح tafrih

amusement park *np.* تفریحگاه tafrih-gâh
an *ia., pre., con.* یک yek
anal *adj.* مقعدی maq'adi
analogize *vi., vt.* قیاس کردن qiâs kardan
analogous *adj.* شبیه shabih مطابق motâbeq
analogy *n.* قیاس qiâs
analysis *n.* تجزیه tajzieh تحلیل tahlil
analyst *n.* تحلیل گر tahlil-gar
analytical *n.* تحلیلی tahlili
analytics *n.* علم تحلیل 'elm-e' tahlil
analyze *vt.* تجزیه و تحلیل کردن tajzieh-o tahlil kardan
anarchism *n.* هرج و مرجی harj-o marji
anarchist *n.* هرج ومرج طلب harj-o marj talab آنارشیست ânârshist
anarchy *n.* هرج و مرج harj o marj آنارشی ânârshi
هرکه هرکه har-keh har-keh اغتشاش eqteshâsh
anathema *n.* شیطانی sheytâni لعنتی la'nati نحش fohsh
anatomic *n.* تشریحی tashrihi
anatomical *adj.* بدنی badani
anatomist *n.* کالبدشناس kâlbod-shenâs
anatomy *n.* تشریح tashrih کالبد شناسی kâlbod- shenâsi
ancestor *n.* جَد jad~ نیا niâ اسلاف aslâf
ancestoral *n.* اجدادی ajdâdi
anchor *v.* لنگر انداختن langar andâkhtan
anchor *n.* لنگر langar
anchorage *n.* لنگرگاه langargâh
anchorman *n.* گوینده اول guyandeh-ye' av~al
ancient *adj., n.* باستانی bâstâni قدیمی qadimi
and *con., n.* و va
anecdote *n.* داستان dâstân
anemic *adj.* کم خون kam-khun
anemic *adj.* کمبود گلبول سرخ kambud-e' golobule' sorkh
anesthesia *n.* داروی بیحسی dâruy-e' bihes~i
anesthetic *n., adj.* بیحس کننده bihes konandeh
anesthetist *n.* پزشک بیهوشی pezeshk-e' bihushi
anew *adv.* از نو az-no
angel *n.* فرشته fereshteh ملک malak سروش sorush
angelica *n.* گلپر gol-par
anger *n., vt., vi.* غضب qazab خشم khashm عصبانیت asabâniyat

.... غيظ qeyz
angle *n., vt., vi.* زاويه zâvieh گوشه gusheh
angry *adj.* عصبانى 'asabâni خشمگين khashmgin
anguish *n., vt.* دلتنگى deltangi غصه qos~eh
anguished *adj.* دلتنگ deltang غصه دار qos~ehdâr
angular *adj.* بازاويه bâzâvieh گوشه دار gushehdâr
animal *n., adj.* حيوان heyvân جانور jânevar
animate *vt., adj.* دادن روح ruh dâdan زنده كردن zendeh kardan
animation *n.* كارتون kârtun جان بخشى jân-bakhshi
animosity *n.* دشمنى doshmani پدركشستگى pedar-koshtegi
ankle *n.* قوزك quzak
annals *n.* تاريخ târikh سالنامه sâl-nâmeh
annex *v.* ضميمه كردن zamimeh kardan
annex *n.* ضميمه zamimeh الحاقى elhâqi
annexation *n.* انضمام enzemâm الحاق elhâq
annihilate *v.* ازبين بردن az beyn bordan نابود كردن nâbud kardan
    كن فيكون كردن kon fayakun kardan
annihilation *n.* نابودى nâbudi فنا fanâ
anniversay *n.* سالگرد sâlgard
annotate *vt., vi.* يادداشت نوشتن yâd-dâsht neveshtan
annotation *n.* يادداشت yâd-dâsht تفسير tafsir
announce *vt., vi.* اعلان كردن e'lân kardan خبردادن khabar dâdan
announcement *n.* اعلانيه e'lânieh آگهى âgahi
announcer *n.* گوينده guyandeh
annoy *vt., vi., n.* اذيت كردن azy~at kardan
    مزاحم بودن mozâhem budan
annoying *adj.* ناراحت كننده nârâhat konandeh
annual *adj., n.* ساليانه sâliâneh يكساله yeksâleh
annuity *n.* سالواره sâl-vâreh پرداخت ساليانه pardâkht-e' sâliâneh
annul *vt.* فسخ كردن fashkh kardan الغاءكردن elqâ' kardan
annulment *n.* فسخ faskh ابطال ebtâl
annulment *n.* فسخ نكاح faskh-e' nekâh
anoint *vt.* روغن مالى كردن roqan-mâli kardan
    تبرك دادن tabar~ok dâdan
anointed *n.* برگزيده bar-gozideh متبرك motebar~ek
anointment *n.* تدهين tadhin مسح mas-h
anomally *n.* برخلاف قاعده bar khalâf-e' qâ'edeh
anonymous *adj.* بى نام binâm بى امضاء bi-emzâ'

another *adj., pro.* دیگر digar دیگری digari
answer *n.* جواب javâb پاسخ pâsokh
answer *v.* جواب دادن javâb dâdan پاسخ دادن pâsokh dâdan
ant *n.* مورچه murcheh مور mur
antagonism *n.* مخالفت mokhâlefat
antagonist *n.* مخالف mokhâlef بدخواه bad-khâh
antagonize *vt., vi.* دشمن کردن doshman kardan
جری کردن jari kardan
antarctic *adj., n.* قطب جنوب qotb-e' jonub
anteater *n.* مورچه خور murcheh-khor
antecedence *n.* تقدم taqad~om پیشی pishi
antecedent *adj., n.* قبلی qabli پیشین pishin
antelope *n.* گوزن کوهی gavazn-e' kuhi
antenna *n.* آنتن ânten موج گیر moj-gir شاخک shâkhak
anterior *adj.* جلویی jelo-yi
anthem *n., vt.* سرود sorud
anthology *n.* گلچین golchin مجموعه majmu'eh جنگ jong
anthrax *n.* سیاه زخم siâh-zakhm
anthropology *n.* مردم شناسی mardom-shenâsi
انسان شناسی ensân-shenâsi
anti- *n.* ضد zed~ مخالف mokhâlef
anti-Christ *n.* مسیح کذاب masih-e' kaz~âb
anticipate *vt., vi.* پیش بینی کردن pishbini kardan
anticipation *n.* پیش بینی pishbini حدس hads
antidote *n.* پادزهر pâd-zahr ضد سم zed~-e' sam~
antiquated *vt.* قدیمی qadimi کهنه kohneh
antique *adj., n., vt.* عتیقه 'atiqeh آنتیک ântik
antiquity *n.* دوران باستانی dorân-e' bâstâni
antiseptic *adj., n.* ضد عفونت zed~ e 'ofunat
antler *n.* شاخ گوزن shâkh-e' gavazn
anus *n.* مقعد maq'ad کون kun ماتحت mâ-taht
anvil *n.* سندان sandân
anxiety *n.* دلواپسی del-vâpasi اشتیاق eshtiâq دلشوره del-shureh
anxious *adj.* دلواپس del-vâpas مشتاق moshtâgh
any *adj., pro., adv.* هر har هیچ hich
anybody *pro., n.* هرکس harkas کسی kasi
anyhow *adv.* بهرجهت behar jahat بهرحال behar hâl
anymore *n.* دیگر digar دیگرنه digar nah

anyone *pro.* هركس har-kas كسى kasi
anything *pro., n., adv.* هرچیز har chiz
anytime هروقت har-vaqt هرزمان har-zamân هرموقع har-moqe'
هرآینه har-âyeneh
anyway *adv.* هرجور harjur بهرحال behar hâl
anywhere *adv.* هرجا harjâ
apart *adv., adj.* جدا jodâ سوا savâ
apartheid *n.* نژاد پرستى nezhâd-parasti
apartment *n.* آپارتمان âpârtemân
apathy *n.* بى علاقگى bi'alâqegi بى احساسى bi-ehsâsi
ape *n., vt.* میمون meymun
aperture *n.* روزنه rozaneh دریچه daricheh
apetite *n.* اشتها eshtehâ
apetizer *n.* اشتها آور eshtehâ-âvar پیش غذا pish-qazâ
apetizer *v.* اشتهادهنده eshtehâ-dahandeh مزه mazeh
apetizing *n.* اشتهاآور eshtehâ-âvar
apocalypse *n.* قیامت qiâmat
apogee *n.* منتهای montehâ-ye'
apolegetic *n.* پوزش آمیز puzesh-âmiz معذرت خواه ma'zerat-khâh
apologetic *adj.* پوزش خواه puzesh-khah طلب بخشش bakhshesh-talab
متعذر mote'az~er
apologize *vi.* عذرخواستن 'ozr khâstan
معذرت خواستن ma'zerat khâstan
apology *n.* معذرت ma'zerat عذر 'ozr پوزش puzesh
apostate *n., adj.* مرتد mortad
apostle *n.* حوارى havâri پیرو peyro
apparatus *n.* دستگاه dastgâh
apparel *n., vt.* لباس lebâs
apparent *adj.* آشکار âshkâr ظاهر zâher نمودار nemudâr
apparently *adv.* ظاهراً zâheran ازقرارمعلوم az qarâr-e' ma'lum
گویا guyâ
appeal *v.* تقاضاکردن taqâzâ kardan
appeal *v.* استیناف کردن estinâf kardan فرجام خواستن farjâm khâstan
appear *vi.* نمایان بودن namâyân budan بنظرآمدن benazar âmadan
ظاهرشدن zâher shodan
appearance *n.* ظاهر zâher حضور hozur نما namâ نمود namud
appease *vt.* آرام کردن ârâm kardan تسکین دادن taskin dâdan
appeasement *n.* تسکین taskin ارضاء erzâ'

appellant n. پژوهش خواه pazhuhesh-khâh
استیناف دهنده estinâf dahandeh
appellate adj. استینافی estinâfi
appellee n. پژوهش خوانده pazhuhesh-khândeh
append vt. تأکید کردن ta'kid kardan فشارآوردن feshâr âvardan
appendix n. ضمیمه zamimeh آپاندیس âpândis
appertain vi. مربوط بودن marbut budan
applaud vi., vt. تحسین کردن tahsin kardan دست زدن dast zadan
applause n. کف زنی kaf zani تشویق tashviq
apple n. سیب sib
appliance n. اسباب asbâb اثاثیه asâsieh
applicant n. درخواست کننده darkhâst konandeh متقاضی moteqâzi
application n. کاربرد kâr-bord اطلاق etlâq
application n. برگ درخواست barg-e' darkhâst
applied adj. عملی 'amali کاربردی kâr-bordi
apply vt., vi. درخواست کردن darkhâst kardan
appoint vt. گماشتن gomâshtan انتصاب کردن entesâb kardan
appointment n. وقت ملاقات vaqt-e' molâqât
appointment n. انتصاب entesâb
apportionment n. قسمت qesmat واگذاری vâ-gozâri
appraisal n. ارزیابی arzyâbi
appraise v. ارزیابی کردن arzyâbi kardan
appreciate v. بالا رفتن bâlâ raftan
appreciate v. قدردانی کردن qadr-dâni kardan
ممنون شدن mamnun shodan
appreciation n. قدردانی qadr-dâni
appreciative adj. قدردان qadr-dân
apprehend vt., vi. دستگیرکردن dast-gir kardan
درک کردن dark kardan
apprehension n. درک تشویش tashvish dark
apprehension n. دستگیری dast-giri
apprehensive adj. نگران negarân دلواپس del-vâpas
apprentice n., vt. شاگرد shâgerd نوآموز no-âmuz
apprised adj. آگاه âgâh باخبر bâ-khabar مطلع mot~ale' واقف vâ-qef
approach v. نزدیک شدن nazdik shodan
approach n. نزدیکی nazdiki تماس tamâs نرود forud
appropriate n. مناسب monâseb مقتضی moqtazi
appropriate v. اختصاص دادن ekhtesâs dâd/ân

appropriation *n.* اختصاص ekhtesâs
approval *n.* تصویب tasvib تأیید ta'yid
approve *vt.* تصویب کردن tasvib kardan قبول کردن qabul kardan
approximate *adj., vt., vi.* نزدیک کردن nazdik kardan تقریبی tâqribi
approximately *adv.* تقریباً taqriban
apricot *n.* زردآلو zardâlu
apron *n., vt.* پیش بند pish-band
apropos *adv., adj.* بجا bejâ مناسب monâseb
apt *adj.* مستعد mosta'ed محتمل mohtamal
aptitude *n.* استعداد este'dâd
aquarium *n.* نمایشگاه آبی namâyeshgâh-e' âbi
Aquarius *n.* دلو dalv بهمن bahman
aquatic *adj., n.* آبی âbi آبزی âbzi
arable *adj., n.* قابل کشت qâbel-e' kesht مزروعی mazru'i
arbitrary *adj., n.* دل بخواه del-bekhâh اختیاری ekhtiâri
arbitrate *vt., vi.* داوری کردن dâv/âri kardan
arbitration *n.* داوری dâv/âri حکمیت hakamiyat
arbitrator *n.* داور dâv/âr حکم hakam
arc *n., vi.* کمان kamân قوس qos
arcade *n., vt.* تیمچه timcheh پاساژ pâsâzh
arch *adj., n., vt., vi.* طاق tâq قوس qos
archaic *adj.* باستانی bâstâni قدیمی qadimi
archeologist *n.* باستان شناس bâstân-shenâs
archeology *n.* باستان شناسی bâstân-shenâsi
archer *n.* کمانگیر kamân-gir تیرانداز tir-andâz
architect *n., vt.* معمار me'mâr
architecture *n.* معماری me'mâri
archives *n.* آرشیو ârshiv بایگانی bâygâni
arctic *adj., n.* قطبی qotbi
ardent *adj.* باحرارت bâ harârat پروپاقرص paro pâ qors
ardor *n.* شوق shoq
arduous *adj.* مشکل moshkel
area *n.* ناحیه nâhyeh منطقه mantaqeh
area *n.* مساحت masâhat
arena *n.* صحنه sahneh گود god عرصه 'arseh
argue *vi., vt.* بحث کردن bahs kardan
مشاجره کردن moshâjereh kardan
arguement *n.* بحث bahs مشاجره moshâjereh بگو ومگو begu-o magu

arid

arid *n.* خشک khoshk بایر bâyar
Aries *n.* حمل hamal فروردین farvardin
arise *vi.* رخ دادن rokh dâdan برخواستن barkhâstan
aristocracy *n.* حکومت اشرافی hokumat-e' ashrâfi
aristocrat *n.* اشراف ashrâf طبقهٔ بالا tabaqeh-ye' bâlâ
Aristotle *n.* ارسطو arastu
arithmatic *n.* حساب hesâb
ark *n.* کشتی (نوح) kashtie'(nuh)
arm *v.* مسلح کردن mosal~ah kardan اسلحه دادن aslaheh dâdan
arm *n.* دست dast بازو bâzu اسلحه aslaheh
armada *n.* ناوگان nâvgân
armadillo *n.* زره پوش zereh-push
armament *n.* تسلیحات taslihât مهمات mohem~ât
armed *adj.* مسلح mosal~ah مجهز moja~haz
armful *n.* یک بغل yek baqal
armistice *n.* صلح solh متارکه motârekeh
armor *n., vt.* زره zereh
armored car *np.* زره پوش zereh-push
arms *n.* تسلیحات taslihât
army *n.* ارتش artesh سپاه sepâh لشگر lashgar قشون qoshun
aroma *n.* بوی خوش buy-e' khosh رایحه râyeheh
aromatic *adj., n.* خوشبو khoshbu
around *adv., pre.* دور dor دراطراف dar atrâf حول hol
arouse *vt., vi.* بیدارکردن bidâr kardan تحریک کردن tahrik kardân
arraign *vt., n.* قرائت جرم کردن qarâ'at-e' jorm kardan
arraignment *n.* قرائت جرم qarâ'at-e' jorm احضار ehzâr
arrange *vt., vi.* ترتیب دادن tartib dâdân چیدن chidan
arrangement *n.* ترتیب tartib قرار qarâr
array *n.* صف saf آراسته شده ârâsteh shodeh
array *v.* آراستن ârâstan
arrears *n.* معوقه mo'av~aqeh عقب مانده aqa'b-mândeh
arrest *n.* دستگیری dast-giri جلب jalb توقیف toqif
arrest *v.* دستگیرکردن dast-gir kardan جلب کردن jalb kardan
    توقیف کردن toqif kardan نگهداشتن negah dâshtan
arrival *n.* ورود vorud مقدم maqd~am
arrive *v.* رسیدن residan واردشدن vâred shodan
arrogance *n.* تکبر takab~or خودبینی khod-bini نخوت nakhvat
arrogant *adj.* متکبر motekab~er مغرور maqrur

arrow *n., vt.* تیر tir خدنگ khadang
arsenal *n.* زرادخانه zar~âd-khâneh انبار اسلحه anbâr-e' aslaheh
arson *n.* آتش گیری عمدی âta sh-giri-e' 'amdi
حریق عمدی hariq-e' 'amdi
arsonist *adj.* آتش زن âtash-zan محرق mohar~eq
art *n., v.* هنر honar
arterial *adj.* شریانی sharyâni
artery *n.* شریان sharyân سرخرگ sorkh-rag
artful *adj.* استاد ostâd حیله گر hileh-gar
arthritis *n.* ورم مفاصل varam-e' mafâsel آرتروز ârteroz
artichoke *n.* انگنار anganâr
article *n., vt., vi.* ماده mâd~eh
article *n., vt., vi.* مقاله maqâleh
articulate *v.* شمرده حرف زدن shemordeh harf zadan
articulate(d) *adj.* شمرده shemordeh نصیح fasih
articulation *n.* شمردگی shemordegi نصاحت fesâhat
artifact *n.* کاردست kâr-dast دست آورد dast-âvard
artificial *adj.* مصنوعی masnu'i ساختگی sâkhtegi
artillery *n.* آتشبار âtashbâr توپخانه tup-khâneh
artisan *n.* صنعتگر san'at-gar
artist *n.* هنرمند honar-mand
artistic *adj.* هنری honari
as *adv., n., con., pro.* مثل mesl-e' بعنوان be'onvân-e'
بمنزله ی be-manzaleh-ye'
as always مثل همیشه mesl-e' hamisheh کماکان kamâ-kân
همچنان ham-chenân
as long as *np.* تازمانیکه tâ zamani keh مادامی که mâdâmi keh
as though *n.* گویا guyâ گفتی gofti مثل اینکه mesl-e' inkeh
ascend *vi., vt.* بالا رفتن bâlâ raftan صعود کردن so'ud kardan
ascension *n.* صعود so'ud جلوس jolus معراج me'râj
ascent *n.* ارتقاء erteqâ' بالا روی bâlâ ravi
ascertain *v.* تحقیق کردن tahqiq kardan ثابت کردن sâbet kardan
ascertain *v.* معلوم کردن ma'lum kardan
ascetic *n., adj.* مرتاض mortâz زاهد zâhed
ascribe *vt.* نسبت دادن nesbat dâdan پیروی کردن peyrovi kardan
ash *n.* خاکستر khâkestar
ash-tray *n.* جاسیگاری jâ sigâri
ashamed *adj.* خجالت زده khejâlat-zadeh شرمنده sharmandeh

ashore *adv.* درساحل dar sâhel
Asia *n.* آسيا âsiâ
aside *adv., n.* بكنار bekenâr به یک طرف beh yek taraf
asinine *adj.* احمق ahmaq نفهم nafahm خر khar
ask *vt., vi.* پرسیدن porsidan سوال کردن so'âl kardan
askew *adv., adj.* کج kaj
asleep *adv., adj.* خواب khâb خوابیده khâbideh
asparagus *n.* مارچوبه mârchubeh
aspect *n.* نظر nazar لحاظ lahâz جنبه janbeh
asperse *v.* هتک کردن hatk kardan هتاکی کردن hat~âki kardan
aspersion *n.* هتاکی hat~âki
asphalt *n., vt., adj.* آسفالت âsfâlt
asphyxia *n.* خفگی khafegi نفس تنگی nafas-tangi
asphyxiated *v.* خفه شده khafeh-shodeh
aspirant *n., adj.* طالب tâleb مشتاق moshtâq
aspirate *vt., n., adj.* تنفس کردن tanaf~os kardan
aspiration *n.* تنفس tanaf~os آرزو ârezu
aspire *vi.* آرزو داشتن ârezu dâshtan
ass *adj.* احمق ahmaq نفهم nafahm خر khar
ass *n.* کون kun
assail *vt.* حمله کردن hamleh kardan
assailant *n., adj.* مهاجم mohâjem حمله کننده hamleh-konandeh ضارب zâreb
assassin *n.* قاتل qâtel جانی jâni آدمکش âdam-kosh
assassinate *vt.* کشتن koshtan ترورکردن teror kardan
assassination *n.* ترور teror آدم کشی âdam-koshi
assault *n., vt.* حمله کردن hamleh kardan
assemble *vt., vi.* جمع شدن jam' shodan سوار کردن savâr kardan مونتاژکردن montâzh kardan
assembly *n.* مجلس majles انجمن anjoman
assert *vt.* ادعاکردن ed~e'â kardan نشارآوردن feshâr âvardan
assertion *n.* ادعا ed~e'â استدلال estedlâl
assess *vt.* ارزیابی کردن arzyâbi kardan
assessment *n.* ارزیابی arzyâbi تشخیص tashkis
assessor *n.* ارزیاب arzyâb
asset *n.* موجودی mojudi دارایی dârâyi مایملک mâ-yamlek
assign *v.* تعیین کردن ta'yin kardan
assign *v.* اختصاص دادن ekhtesâs dâd/ân

assignment n. مشق mashq اختصاص ekhtesâs مأموريت mamuriat
assignor adj. كارگزار kâr-gozâr
assimilate vt., vi. ترکیب کردن tarkib kardan
مستحيل شدن mostahil shodan
assimilation n. ترکیب tarkib استحاله estehâleh
assist v. کمک کردن komak kardan
assist v. مساعدت کردن mosâ'edat kardan
assistance n. کمک komak مساعدت mosâ'edat همراهی ham-râhi
assistant n., adj. دستیار dastyâr معاون mo'âven
associate n. دستیار dastyâr معاون mo'âven همکار hamkâr
associate v. معاشرت کردن mo'âsherat kardan
associate v. ارتباط دادن ertebât dâdan
associate v. معاشرت کردن mo'âsherat kardan
association n. انجمن anjoman معاشرت mo'âsherat
assorted adj. جور شده jur shodeh جور jur
assortment n. یک سری yek seri جورواجور jur-vâjur
assume v. فرض کردن farz kardan
assume v. بعهده گرفتن be'ohdeh gereftan
assumed vt. جعلی ja'li عاریه 'ârieh
assumption n. فرضیه farziyeh
assurance n. اطمينان etminân خاطرنشانی khâter-neshâni
assure v. خاطرنشان کردن khâter-neshân kardan
assure v. اطمينان دادن etminân dâdan
assure v. مطمئن کردن motma'en kardan
aster n. مينا minâ
asterisk n., vt. علامت ستاره 'alâmat-e' setâreh
astern adv. عقب 'aqab
astonish vt. متحير ساختن motahay~er sâkhtan
astonished n. متحير motahay~er درشگفت dar-shegeft
مبهوت mab-hut
astonishment n. حيرت heyrat شگفت shegeft
astride pre., adv., adj. سوار savâr دوپا do-pâ
astrologer n. نجوم بين nojum bin رمال ram~âl منجم monaj~em
astrology n. نجوم بینی nojum-bini
astronaut n. فضانورد fazâ-navard
astronomer n. فضاشناس fazâ-shenâs
astronomical adj. خيلی بالا kheyli bâlâ سرسام آور sarsâm-âvar
astronomy n. فضاشناسی fazâ-shenâsi نجوم nojum

astute *adj.* زیرک zirak تیزنهم tiz-fahm
asunder *adv., adj.* جدا jodâ پاره پاره pâreh-pâreh
asylum *n.* پناهندگی panâhandegi نوان خانه navân-khâneh
at *pre.* در dar به beh بسوی besu-ye'
at last بالاخره beh'akhareh آخرالامر âkherol amr
at least حد اقل had~-e' aqal دست کم dast-e' kam
at once *n.* فوراً foran
atheism *n.* خدانشناسی khodâ-nashnâsi الحاد elhâd
atheist *n.* خدانشناس khodâ-nashnâs بیدین bi-din لامذهب lâmaz-hab
ملحد molhad
athlete *n.* ورزشکار varzesh-kâr
athlete's foot *np.* پاخوره pâ-khoreh
athletic *adj.* ورزشکار varzesh-kâr قهرمانی qahremâni
athletics *n.* ورزش varzesh
Atlantic *adj., n.* اطلس atlas
atlas *n.* نقشه naqsheh
atmoshpere *n.* جو jav~ آتمسفر âtmosfer محیط mohit
atom *n.* اتم atom ذره zar~eh
atonement *n.* کفاره kaf~âreh جبران jobrân غفران qofrân
atrocious *adj.* بیرحم bi-rahm شریر sharir
attach *v.* وصل کردن vasl kardan ضمیمه کردن zamimeh kardan
attache' *n.* وابسته vâ-basteh
attachment *n.* ضمیمه zamimeh وابستگی vâbastegi علاقه 'alâqeh
دلبستگی del-bastegi
attack *v.* حمله کردن hamleh kardan یورش بردن yuresh bordan
attack *n.* حمله hamleh یورش yuresh هجوم hojum
attain *vt., vi.* بدست آوردن bedast âvardan نائل شدن nâ'el shodan
attempt *vt., n.* سعی کردن sa'y kardan کوشش کردن kushesh kardan
attend *v.* حضور پیداکردن hozur peydâ kardan
attend *v.* رسیدگی کردن residegi kardan
attendance *n.* رسیدگی residegi توجه tavaj~oh جمعیت jam'iyat
attendant *n., adj.* مسئول کار mas'ul-e' kâr
attention *n., int.* توجه tavâj~oh دقت deq~at خبردار khabardâr
attentive *adj.* متوجه motevaj~eh ملتفت moltafet
attest *vt., vi., n.* گواهی دادن gavâhi dâdan قسم خوردن qasam khordan
attic *n.* زیرشیروانی zir-shirvâni
attire *vt., n.* لباس lebâs سر و وضع sar o vaz'
attitude *n.* نظر nazar طرز فکر tarz-e' fekr

attorney *n.* وکیل vakil
attract *vt., vi.* جذب کردن jazb kardan جلب کردن jalb kardan
attraction *n.* جذب jazb کشش keshesh جاذبه jâzebeh
attractive *adj.* جذاب jaz~âb جالب توجه jâleb-e' tavaj~oh
attribute *vt., n.* نسبت nesbat صفت sefat
attrition *n.* فرسایشی farsâyeshi بکش بکش bokosh bokosh
aubergine *n.* بادنجان bâdenjân
auburn *n., adj.* خرمایی khormâyi
auction *n.* حراج harâj مزایده mozâyedeh
auction(off) *vt.* حراج کردن harâj kardan
audacity *n.* جسارت jesârat گستاخی gostâkhi جرأت jor'at رو ru
audible *adj.* شنیده شدنی shenideh shodani رسا rasâ
audience *n.* حضار hoz~âr شنوندگان shenavandegân
audio *adj., n.* شنوایی shenavâyi
audit *n., vt., vi.* رسیدگی کردن residegi kardan
audition *n., vt., vi.* معرفی هنر خود mo'ar~efi-e' honar-e khod
auditorium *n.* تالار tâlâr
auger *n.* مته mat~eh
augment *vt., vi., n.* افزودن afzudan اضافه کردن ezâfeh kardan
augmentation *n.* افزایش afzâyesh نزون fozun
augur *n., vt., vi.* پیشگویی کردن pishguyi kardan
augury *n.* پیشگویی pish-guyi فال بینی fâl-bini
August *n.* اوت ut
aunt *n.* عمه am~eh خاله khâleh
aura *n.* مه meh غبار qobâr هاله hâleh
aureole *n.* هاله hâleh
aurora *n.* سپیده دم sepideh-dam فجر fajr
auspice(s) *n.* قیومت qay~umat توجه tavaj~oh
auspicious *adj.* فرخنده farkhondeh مبارک mobârak خجسته khojasteh فرخ far~okh
austerity *n.* سخت گیری sakht-giri مرتاضی mortâzi
Australia *n.* استرالیا ostorâliâ
Austria *n.* اطریش otrish
authentic *adj.* حقیقی haqiqi موثق movas~aq
authenticate *v.* موثق دانستن movas~aq dânestan
authenticate *v.* تصدیق کردن tasdiq kardan
authenticity *n.* صحت seh~at اصلیت asliyat
author *n., vt.* نویسنده nevisandeh مؤلف mo'al~ef

authoritarian *adj., n.* ديكتاتورى diktâtori استبداد estebdâd
authoritative *adj.* مقتدرانه moqtaderâneh آمرانه âmerâneh
authority *n.* توانايى tavânâyi اختيار ekhtiâr
authorization *n.* اجازه ejâzeh اختيار ekhtiâr مجوز mojav~ez
authorize *vt.* اجازه دادن ejâzeh dâdan اختيار دادن ekhtiâr dâdan
authorized *adj.* مجاز mojâz با اجازه bâ-ejâzeh
autobiography *n.* خودزندگينامه khod zendegi-nâmeh
autocracy *n.* حكومت مطلق hokumat-e' motlaq
autocrat *n.* حاكم مطلق hâkem-e' motlaq
autocratic *adj.* مطلق motlaq استبدادى estebdâdi
autograph *n., adj., vt.* امضاء emzâ'
automatic *adj., n.* خودكار khod-kâr
automobile *n., adj.* اتوموبيل otomobil ماشين mâshin
autonomous *adj.* خود مختار khod-mokhtâr
autonomy *n.* خودمختارى khod-mokhtâri
autopsy *n.* كالبدگشايى kâlbod-goshâyi
autumn *n.* پائيز pâ'iz خزان khazân
auxiliary *adj., n.* اضافى ezâfi فوق العاده foqol'âdeh
avail *v.* كمك كردن komak kardan
avail *n.* اثر asar استفاده estefâdeh
availability *n.* موجودبودن mojud budan
avalanche *n., vi., vt.* بهمن bahman
avarice *n.* حرص hers طمع tama' آز âz ولع vala'
avaricious *adj.* حريص haris طمع كار tama'-kâr
avenge *vt., vi.* انتقام گرفتن enteqâm gereftan
avenger *n.* كينه جو kineh-ju
avenue *n.* خيابان khiâbân
average *n., adj., vt., vi.* معدل mo'ad~el متوسط motevas~et
ميانگين miân-gin
averse *adj.* بيزار bizâr متنفر motenaf~er ناموافق nâ-movafeq
aversion *n.* بيزارى bizâri تنفر tanaf~or
avert *vt.* دفع كردن daf' kardan
aviation *n.* هواپيمايى havâ-peymâyi
aviator *n.* هوانورد havâ-navard
avid *adj* مشتاق moshtâq پروپاقرص paropâ qors
avoid *v.* اجتناب كردن ejtenâb kardan
avoid *v.* خوددارى كردن khod-dâri kardan
avoidance *n.* اجتناب ejtenâb خوددارى khod-dâri

avow *vt.* اعتراف کردن e'terâf kardan
avowed *adj.* معترف mo'taref شناخته شده shenâkhteh shodeh
avowedly *adv.* آشکاراً âshkâran
await *vt., vi.* منتظر بودن montazer budan
awake *v.* بیدار کردن bidâr kardan
awaken *adj.* بیدار bidâr
awakening *n.* بیداری bidâri
award *n.* جایزه jâyezeh
award *v.* جایزه دادن jâyezeh dâdan
aware *adj.* آگاه âgâh باخبر bâ-khabar مستحضر mostahzar
  ملتفت moltafet
away *adv., adj.* دور dur کنار kenâr بیرون birun
awe *n., vt.* ترس tars حرمت hormat هیبت heybat
awesome *adj.* هیبت دار heybat-dâr
awful *adj., adv.* خیلی بد kheyli bad ترسناک tarsnâk
awfully *adv.* خیلی خیلی kheyli kheyli
awkward *adj.* ناجور nâjur نادرست nâdorost
awl *n.* درفش derafsh اسکنه eskeneh
awning *n.* سایبان sâyebân
awry *adv., adj.* منحرف monharef کج kaj
ax(e) *n.* تبر tabar تیشه tisheh
axiom *n.* مثال mesâl پند pand
axiom *n.* قاعدهٔ کلی qâ'edeh-ye' kol~i
axis *n.* محور mehvar
axle *n.* محور چرخ mehvar-e' charkh
aye *adv., n.* بله baleh پاسخ مثبت pâsokh-e' mosbat
aye-aye *n.* بله قربان baleh qorbân
azalea *n.* آزاله âzâleh
azure *adj., n.* لاجورد lâjevard

B B B

babble *vi., vt., n.* شر و ور گفتن sher~o ver goftan
من و من men~o men

baboon *n.* بوزینه buzineh عنتر 'antar

baby *n., adj., vt.* بچه bach~eh طفل tefl کودک kudak نی نی nini

baby *n., adj., vt.* عزیزم 'azizam جگر jegar

babysitter *n.* بچه نگهدار bach~eh-negahdâr

bachelor *n.* مجرد mojar~ad عزب 'azab

bachelor degree *n.* لیسانس lisâns

back *n.* پشت posht عقب 'aqab کول kul

back-pay *n.* حقوق عقب افتاده hoquq-e' 'aqab-oftâdeh

backbite *vt., vi.* پشت سرحرف زدن posht-e' sar harf zadan
غیبت کردن qeybat kardan

backdoor *adj.* درپشتی dar-e' poshti

backer *n.* پشتیبان poshtibân حامی hâmi

backgammon *n., vt.* تخته نرد takhteh nard

background *n., adj.* زمینه zamineh سابقه sâbeqeh

backing *n.* پشتیبانی poshtibâni حمایت hemâyat

backlash *n., vi.* عکس العمل 'âksol 'amal

backpack *n., vi., vt.* کوله بار kuleh-bâr پشتواره posht-vâreh
ساک پشتی sâk-e' poshti

backroad(s) *n.* کوره راه kureh-râh

backside *n.* پشت posht عقب 'aqab

backward *adv., adj.* عقب افتاده 'aqab oftâdeh

backwater *n.* آب ساکن âb-e' sâken

backwoods *pl., adj.* دورافتاده dur oftâdeh

bacteria *pl.* میکروب mikrob باکتری bâkteri

bad *adj., n., adv., v.* بد bad

bad-tempered *n.* بد اخلاق bad akhlâq

badge *n., vt.* نشان neshân

badger *n., vt.* موش گورکن mush-e' gurkan

badly *adv., adj.* بدجور bad-jur خیلی بد kheyli bad

baffle *vt., vi., n.* گیج کردن gij kardan شلوغ کردن sholuq kardan

bag *n., vi., vt., int.* کیسه kiseh چمدان chamedân کیف kif پاکت pâkat

baggage *n.* چمدان chamedân بارسفر bâr-e' safar

baggy *adj.* گشاد goshâd

bagman *n.* باج جمع کن bâj jam'-kon

bagpipe *n., vt.* نی انبان ney-anbân

bail *v.* دسته کردن dasteh kardan
bail *n.* ضمانت zemânat وجه الضمانه vajhol-zemâneh
bail *v.* ضمانت کردن zemânat kardan
bail(out) *n.* نجات دادن nejât dâdan
bailiff *n.* پلیس دادگاه polis-e' dâdgâh
bait *v.* دام گذاشتن dâm gozâshtan طعمه کردن to'meh kardan
bait *n.* طعمه to'meh خوراک khorâk
bake *vt., vi., n.* پختن pokhtan
baker *n.* نانوا nânvâ شاطر shâter
balance *v.* میزان کردن mizân kardan موازنه کردن movâzeneh kardan
balance *n.* میزان mizân موازنه movâzeneh
balance sheet *np.* ترازنامه tarâz-nâmeh
balanced *v.* میزان شده mizân shodeh
balas *n.* یاقوت نارنجی yâqut-e' nârenji بدخشان badakhshân
balcony *n.* بالکنی bâlkoni
bald *adj., vi.* طاس tâs کچل kachal بی مو bimu کل kal
balderdash *n.* چرند charand مزخرف mozakhraf
bale *n., vt.* بلا balâ محنت mehnat
balk *vi., vt., n.* سرپیچی کردن sarpichi kardan
balky *adj.* نافرمان nâfarmân متمرد motemar~ed
ball *n.* توپ tup گلوله goluleh گوی guy
ball *n.* مجلس رقص majles-e' raqs جشن jashn
ballad *n.* قصیده qasideh
ballast *n., vt.* وزنه vazneh پاره سنگ pâreh sang
balloon *n., vi., vt., adj.* بادکنک bâdkonak
ballot *n., vi., vt.* ورقۀ رأی varaqeh-ye' ra'y
ballyhoo *n., vt., vi.* سر و صدا sar-o sedâ
balm *n.* بلسان balsân مرهم marham
baloney *n.* کالباس kâl-bâs
baloney! *n.* زرشک zereshk
bamboo *n.* نی ney خیزران khiz-rân
bamboozle *vt., vi.* گول زدن gul zadan
حقه بازی کردن hoq~eh-bâzi kardan
ban *v.* ممنوع کردن mamnu' kardan توقیف کردن toqif kardan
ban *n.* توقیف toqif تحریم tahrim
banal *adj.* پیش پا افتاده pish-e' pâ oftâdeh مبتذل mobtazal
banality *n.* ابتذال ebtezâl
banana *n.* موز moz بنان banân

band *n., vt., vi.* بند band دسته dasteh

bandage *n., vt., vi.* چسب زخم chasb-e' zakhm پانسمان pânsemân باندا ژ bândâzh

bandana *n.* دستمال سر dastmâl-e' sar

bandit *n.* دزد dozd سارق sâreq مشنگ mashang

bane *n.* مزاحم mozâhem سم sam~

baneful *adj.* مضر mozer~ سمی sam~i

banish *vt.* تبعید کردن tab'id kardan طرد کردن tard kardan

banishment *n.* تبعید tab'id اخراج ekhrâj

banister *n.* نرده nardeh

bank *vt., vi.* بانک bânk ساحل sâhel

bank account *np.* حساب بانکی hesâb-e' bânki

banker *n.* بانکدار bânk-dâr

bankrupt *n., adj., vt.* ورشکسته var-shekasteh

bankruptcy *n.* ورشکستگی var-shekastegi

banner *n., adj.* پرچم parcham علم 'alam بیرق beyraq

banquet *n., vt., vi.* میهمانی mih-mâni

bantam *n., adj.* خروس khorus

bantam weight *n.* خروس وزن khorus vazn

banter *n., vt., vi.* شوخی کردن shukhi kardan

baptism *n.* غسل تعمید qosl-e' ta'mid

baptize *vt., vi.* غسل تعمیدکردن qosl-e' ta'mid kardan

bar *n., vt., pre.* میله mileh شمش shemsh قالب qâleb

bar *n., vt., pre.* میخانه meykhâneh پیاله فروش piâleh forush

BAR *n.* کانون وکلا kânun-e' vokalâ

bar-bell *n.* هالتر hâlter

barb *n., vt.* خار khâr نیش nish

barbarian *n., adj.* وحشی vah-shi

barbaric *adj.* وحشیانه vah-shiâneh

barbarity *n.* بربریت bar-bariyat وحشی گری vah-shigari

barbecue *n., vt.* کباب کردن kabâb kardan بریان کردن beryân kardan

barbed wire *np.* سیم خاردار sim-e' khârdâr

barber *n., vt.* سلمانی salmâni

barberry *n.* زرشک zereshk

barbershop *n., adj.* دکان سلمانی dok~ân-e' salmâni

bare *adj., vt.* لخت lokht برهنه berahneh عور 'ur

barefoot *adj., adv.* پابرهنه pâ-berahneh

barely *adv.* بزحمت be-zahmat زورکی zuraki

bargain *n.* معامله mo'âmeleh خرید ارزان kharid-e' arzân
bargain *v.* چانه زدن châneh zadan
barge *n., vt., vi.* قایق بارکش qâyeq-e' bârkesh
barge(in) *n.* باخشونت وارد شدن bâ khoshunat vâred shodan
baritone *n., adj.* صدای کلفت sedâ-ye' koloft
bark *v.* واق واق کردن vâq-vâq kardan پارس کردن pârs kardan
عوعوکردن 'o 'o kardan
bark *n.* پوست درخت pust-e' derakht
barley *n., adj.* جو jo
barn *n., vt.* انبار کاه anbâr-e' kâh طویله tavileh
barometer *n.* هواسنج havâ-sanj
baroque *n., adj.* نامتناسب nâ-motenâseb
barrack(s) *n.* سربازخانه sarbâz-khâneh
barrage *n., vt.* حملهٔ مکرر hamleh-ye' mokar~ar
barrel *n.* لوله luleh
barrel *n.* بشکه boshkeh چلیک chelik
barren *adj., n.* لم یزرع lam yazra' نازا nâzâ
barricade *n.* سنگر sangar
barricade *v.* سنگرگرفتن sangar gereftan
barrier *n.* سد sad~ حصار hesâr
barring *n., v., pre.* بجز bejoz باستثنای be-estesnâ-ye'
barrow *n.* زنبه zanbeh خاک کش khâk-kesh
bartender *n.* می فروش mey-forush
barter *v.* معاوضه کردن mo'âvezeh kardan
barter *n.* دادوستد dâd-o setad پایاپای pâ-yâ-pây معاوضه mo'âvezeh
basalt *n.* سیاه سنگ siâh-sang
base *v.* قراردادن qarâr dâdan
base *adj., n., vt., vi.* پادگان pâdegân ساخلو sâkhlo
base *n.* ته tah پایه pâyeh
base *n.* اصل asl قاعده qâ'edeh اساس asâs
baseless *adj.* بی اساس bi-asâs بی پایه bi-pâyeh واهی vâ-hi
فروهشته foru-heshteh
basemenet *n.* زیرزمین zir-zamin پاشیر pâ-shir
bash *v.* زدن zadan
bash *n.* میهمانی mihmâni پارتی pârti
bashful *adj.* خجالتی khejâlati خجول khajul کمرو kam-ru
bashing *n.* توسرزنی tu sar-zani انتقاد enteqâd
basic *adj., n.* اساسی asâsi اصلی asli

basil *n.* ریحان reyhân
basilica *n.* کلیسا kelisâ
basin *n.* حوضچه hozcheh دستشویی dast-shuyi
basinet *n.* لگن lagan
basis *n.* پایه pâyeh اساس asâs مبنی mabna مأخذ ma'khaz
bask *vi., vt.* آفتاب خوردن âftâb khordan
basket *n.* سبد sabad زنبیل zanbil
bass *adj., n.* بم bam صدای کلفت sedâ-ye' koloft
bassinet *n.* گهواره gahvâreh
bastard *n., adj.* حرامزاده harâmzâdeh
baste *vt.* روغن زدن roqan zadan
bastinado *n., vt.* چوب فلک chub-falak فلکه falakeh
bastion *n.* سر در sar dar قلعه qal'eh
bat *n., vt., vi.* خفاش khaf~âsh چوگان chogân
batch *n., vt., vi.* دسته dasteh
bate *vt., n., vi.* نفس گیری nafas giri
bath *n., vt., vi.* حمام ham~âm شستشو shosteshu
bath-tub *n.* وان حمام vân-e' ham~âm
bathe *vt., vi., n.* حمام گرفتن ham~âm gereftan
bathhouse *n.* حمام ham~âm گرمابه garmâbeh
bathing suit *np.* مایو mâyo
bathrobe *n.* رب دوشامبر rob do shâmbr قطیفه qatifeh
bathroom *n.* حمام ham~âm مستراح mostarâh
baton *n.* باتون bâtun
battalion *n.* گردان gordân
batter *vt., vi., n.* خرد کردن khord kardan کتک زدن kotak zadan
battery *n.* ضرب و جرح zarb-o jarh
battery *n.* پیل pil باطری bâtri
battle *n., vi., vt.* نبرد nabard کارزار kârzâr رزم razm پیکار peykâr
battlefield *n.* نبردگاه nabard-gâh میدان جنگ medan-e' jang
battlefront *n.* میدان جنگ meydân-e' jang رزمگاه razm-gâh
battleship *n.* ناو nâv
bawdy *adj., n.* هرزه harzeh شنیع shani'
bay *n., adj., vi., vt.* خلیج khalij
bay *n., adj., vi., vt.* درخت غار derakht-e' qâr
bayleaf *n.* برگ بو barg-e' bu
bayonet *n., vt.* سرنیزه sar neyzeh
bazaar *n.* بازار bâzâr

be v. باش bâsh
be v. بودن budan
beach n., vt., vi. ساحل sâhel کناردریا kenâr daryâ پلاژ pelazh
beacon n., vt., vi. چراغ دریایی cherâq-e' daryâyi
bead n., vt., vi. مهره mohreh
beak n. منقار menqâr
beam n., vt., vi. تیرآهن tir âhan
beam n., vt., vi. پرتو parto
beaming adj. بشاش bash~âsh
bean n., vt., int. لوبیا lubiâ
bear v. تحمل کردن taham~ol kardan
bear n. خرس khers
bear v. زاییدن zâyidan
beard n. ریش rish
bearded adj. ریشو rishu
bearer n. حامل hâmel حمل کننده haml konandeh
bearing n. یاتاقان yâtâqân
bearing n. موقعیت moqe'iyat
bearskin n. پوست خرس pust-e' khers
beast n. درنده darandeh جانور jânevar چهارپا chahârpâ دد dad
beat n. ضربه zarbeh تپش tapesh
beat vt., vi., n., adj. خسته khasteh فرسوده farsudeh
beat v. زدن zadan شکست دادن shekast dâdan
beaten adj., v. زده zadeh شکست خورده shekast khordeh
beating n., v. کتک کاری kotak-kâri
beau n., vt. نامزد nâmzad دوست پسر dust-e' pesar
beautician n. آرایشگر ârâyesh-gar مشاطه mash~âateh
beautiful adj. زیبا zibâ قشنگ qashang خوشگل khoshgel
beautify vt., vi. زیبا کردن zibâ kardan
beauty n. زیبایی zibâyi وجاهت vejâhat
beaver n. سگ آبی sag-e' âbi
because con., adv. برای اینکه barâ-ye' inkeh
beckon vt., vi., n. طلبیدن talabidan
beckoning n. بازخوانی bâz-khâni فراخوان farâ-khân
become vt. شدن shodan
becoming adj., v., n. زیبنده zibandeh درخور darkhor
bed n., vt., vi. تختخواب takhtekhâb
bedbug n. ساس sâs کک kak

bedecked *n.* مزین mozay˜an آراسته ârâsteh
bedevil *vt.* جادو کردن jâdu kardan گمراه کردن gomrâh kardan
bedfellow *n.* هم خواب ham-khâb هم بستر ham-bastar
bedlam *n.* جنجالخانه janjâl-khâneh
bedridden *adj.* بستری bastari علیل 'alil
bedrock *n., adj.* پایۀ اصلی pâyeh-ye' asli بستر bastar
bedroom *n., adj.* اتاق خواب otâq-e' khâb
bedsheet *n.* ملافه malâfeh
bedside *n., adj.* بالین bâlin
bedspread *n.* روتختی ru-takhti
bedspring *n.* فنر تشک fanar-e' toshak
bedtime *n.* وقت خواب vaqt-e' khâb
bee *n.* زنبور zanbur
beech *n.* آلش âlash
beef *n., vi.* گوشت گاو gusht-e' gâv
beehive *n.* کندوی عسل kandu-ye' 'asal
beer *n.* آبجو âbejo
beet *n., vt.* چغندر choqondar
beetle *adj., n., vi., vt.* سوسک susk
befall *vt.* اتفاق افتادن et˜efâq oftâdan برسرآمدن bar-sar âmadan
befit *vt.* درخور بودن dar-khor budan
before *adv., pre., con.* قبل qabl پیش pish
beforehand *adv., adj.* قبلاً qablan ازپیش az pish
befoul *vt.* کثیف کردن kasif kardan
befriend *vt.* دوست شدن dust shodan
beg *n., vi.* گدایی کردن gedâyi kardan التماس کردن eltemâs kardan
　　تکدی کردن takad˜i kardan
beget *vt.* تولید کردن tolid kardan باعث شدن bâ'es shodan
beggar *n., vt.* گدا gedâ
begin *vt.* شروع کردن shoru' kardan شروع شدن shoru' shodan
beginner *n.* تازه کار tâzehkâr ناشی nâshi مبتدی mobtadi
beguile *vt.* فریب دادن fârib dâdan
beguiled *vt.* فریب خورده fârib-khordeh
behalf *n.* از طرف az taraf خاطر khâter
behave *vt.* رفتار کردن raftâr kardan
behavior *n.* رفتار raftâr حرکت harekat سلوک soluk
behead *vt.* سر بریدن sar boridan
behest *n.* دستور dastur امر amr

behind *pre., adv., adj., n.* پشت posht عقب 'aqab قفا qafâ
نشیمن neshiman
behold *vt., int.* دیدن didan کردن مشاهده moshâhedeh kardan
beige *n., adj.* روشن ای قهوه qahveh-i-e' roshan
being *n.* بودن budan هستی hasti وجود vojud
belated *adj.* دیررسیده dir resideh
belch *v.* زدن آروغ âroq zadan
belch *n.* آروغ âroq
belie *vt.* دادن جلوه دروغی doruqi jelveh dâdân
belief *n.* گمان gamân ایمان imân
believe *vt.* کردن گمان gamân kardan باورکردن bâvar kardan
belittle *vt.* کردن خوار khâr kardan تحقیرکردن tahqir kardan
bell *n., vt., vi.* زنگ zang ناقوس nâqus جرس jaras
bellboy *n.* پادو pâdo
bellicose *adj.* دعوایی da'vâyi جنگجو jangju
belligerence *n.* تهاجم tahâjom
belligerency تهاجم tahâjom وری حمله hamleh-vari
belligerent *adj., n.* مهاجم mohâjem متحارب motehâreb
bellow *vi., vt., n.* کردن غرش qor~esh kardan زدن فریاد faryâd zadan
belly *n., vt., vi.* شکم shekam بطن batn
bellyful *n.* سیر شکم shekâm-e' sir
belong *vi.* بودن متعلق mote'al~eq budan
belonging *n.* متعلق mote'al~eq مال mâl
belongings *n.* متعلقات mote'al~eqât اموال amvâl
beloved *adj., vt., n.* محبوب mahbub عزیز aziz
below *adv., pre.* پایین pâyin درزیر dar zir
belt *v.* زدن zadan
belt *n.* کمربند kamar-band تسمه tasmeh
bench *n., vt.* نیمکت nimkat
bend *v.* کردن دولا dol~â kardan کردن خم kham kardan
bend *n.* گردنه gardaneh پیچ pich خم kham
beneath *adv., pre.* زیر zir پایین pâyin
benediction *n.* نیایش niâyesh
benediction *n.* خیر دعای do'â-ye' kheyr
benefactor *n.* خیر بانی bâni-e' kheyr نعمت ولی vali ne'mat
beneficence *n.* نیکوکاری nikukâri
beneficent *adj.* نیکوکار nikukâr محسن mohsen
beneficial *adj.* سودمند sudmand

beneficiary n. ذینفع zinaf'
benefit v. منفعت کردن manfa'at kardân سودبردن sud bordan
benefit n. منفعت manfa'at سود sud مزیت maziyat
benevolence n. نیکخواهی nik-khâhi
benevolent adj. نیکخواه nik-khâh
benign adj. مهربان mehrabân بی خطر bikhatar خوشخیم khosh-khim
bent adj., n., v. خمیده khamideh
bent(on) n. مصمم mosam~am
bequeath vt. به ارث گذاشتن beh ers gozâshtan
bequest n. میراث mirâs ترکه tarakeh
berate vt. سرکوفت زدن sar-kuft zadan
bereave vt. محروم کردن mahrum kardan
داغدیده کردن dâq-dideh kardan
bereaved vt. محروم mahrum داغدیده dâq-dideh
berry n., vi. توت tut
berserk adj., adv., n. دیوانه divâneh
berth n. خوابگاه khâb-gâh جا jâ
berth v. پهلو گرفتن pahlu gereftan
beseech vt., vi. التماس کردن eltemâs kardan
beset vt. محاصره کردن mohâsereh kardan
beside pre., adv. جدا jodâ غیراز qeyr az
beside pre., adv. درکنار dar-kenâr
besides adv., pre. گذشته ازاین gozashteh az in بعلاوه be'alâveh
besiege vt. احاطه کردن ehâteh kardan
besieged vt. محاصره شده mohâsereh shodeh محصور mah-sur
best adj., adv., n., vt. بهترین behtarin
bestiality n. نزدیکی با حیوانات nazdiki bâ heyvânât
bestman n. ساقدوش sâqdush
bestow vt. بخشیدن bakhshidan
bet n. شرط shart
bet v. شرط کردن shart kardan شرط گذاشتن shart gozâshtân
betray vt. خیانت کردن khiânat kardan
betrayal n. خیانت khiânat
better adj., adv., vt., n. بهتر behtar خوب تر khubtar احسن ah-san
betting v. شرط بندی shart-bandi
between pre., adv. میان miân بین beyn
bevel n., vt., vi., adj. سطح اریب sat-h-e' orib
beverage n. آشامیدنی âshâmidani نوشابه nushâbeh

beware *vt., vi.* حذر کردن hazar kardan
bewilder *vt.* گیج کردن gij kardan
bewilderment *n.* گیجی giji گمراهی gomrâhi
bewitch *vt.* افسون کردن afsun kardan
bewitched *n.* افسون شده afsun shodeh
beyond *pre., adv.* ماورا mâvarâ مافوق mâfoq فراسو farâsu
bias *n., adj., adv., vt.* تعصب ta'as~ob غرض qaraz
biased *adj.* متعصب mote'as~eb مغرض moqrez
bib *n., vt., vi.* پیشبند بچه pishband-e' bach~eh
Bible *n.* انجیل enjil
Biblical *adj.* انجیلی enjili
bibliography *n.* کتاب شناسی ketâb shenâsi
bicentennial *adj., n.* دویست سالگی devist sâlegi
biceps *n.* ماهیچه های بازو mâhicheh-hâ-ye' bâzu
bicycle *n., vi.* دوچرخه docharkheh
bid *v.* پیشنهاد دادن pishnahâd dâdan
bid *n.* پیشنهادمزایده pishnahâd-e' mozâyedeh
bide *vt., vi.* منتظربودن montazer budan
bifocal *adj., n.* دوچشم docheshm عینک 'eynak
big *adj., adv., n., vt.* بزرگ bozorg گنده gondeh
bigamist *n.* شخص دو همسره shakhs-e' do-hamsâreh
bigamy *n.* دوزنی do-zani
bigot(ed) *n.* متعصب mote'as~eb
bigotry *n.* تعصب ta'as~ob
bigwig *n.* متنفذ motenaf~ez کله گنده kal~eh gondeh
bike *n., vi.* دوچرخه docharkheh
biker *n.* دوچرخه سوار docharkheh-savâr
bilateral *adj.* دوجانبه do-jânebeh دوطرفه do-tarafeh
bilingual *adj., n.* دوزبانه do-zâbâneh
bilk *vt., n.* زیرقرض زدن zir-e' qarz zadan
bill *n.* صورتحساب surat-hesâb سیاهه siâheh
bill *n.* اسکناس eskenâs
bill *n.* منقار menqâr نوک nok
bill *n.* لایحه lâyeheh سند sanad
bill *v.* صورتحساب دادن surat-hesâb dâdan
bill of lading *np.* بارنامه bâr-nâmeh
bill of sale *np.* برگ فروش barg-e' forush
billion *n., adj.* میلیارد milyârd

bin *n., vt.* صندوق sandoq تغار taqâr
bind *vt., vi., n.* بستن bastan صحافى كردن sah~âfi-kardan
bind *n.* گرفتارى gereftâri مضيقه maziqeh
binder *n.* جلد jeld
binding *n., v., adj.* واجب الاجرا vâjebol-ejrâ نافذ nâfez
biographer *n.* زندگينامه نويس zendegi-nâmeh nevis
biography *n.* زندگينامه zendegi-nâmeh
biology *n.* زيست شناسى zist-shenâsi
biopsy *n.* بافت بردارى bâft-bardâri
birch *n., adj., vt.* غوشه qusheh
bird *n., vi.* پرنده parandeh
birdseed *n.* ارزن arzan
birth *n.* تولد taval~od زايش zâyesh ميلاد milâd ولادت velâdat
birth certificate *np.* شناسنامه shenâs-nâmeh زايچه zây-cheh
birth-rate *n.* تعدادزايش te'dâd-e' zâyesh
birthday *n.* روز تولد ruz-e' taval~od
birthmark *n.* خال تولد khâl-e' taval~od
birthplace *n.* محل تولد mahal~-e' taval~od زاد گاه zâdgâh
biscuit *n., adj.* بيسكويت biskuyit
bisect *vt., vi., n.* دو قطعه كردن do-qat'eh kardan
bisection *n.* شكافتن shekâftan
bisexual *adj., n.* دوجنس do jens
bishop *n.* اسقف osqof
bishop *n.* فيل fil
bison *n.* گاوميش gâvmish
bit *n., vt.* تكه tek~eh ذره zar~eh مقدار كم meqdâr-e' kam
bitch *n., vi., vt.* سگ ماده sag-e' mâd~eh
bitch *adj.* جنده jendeh ناحشه fâhesheh پتياره patiareh لكاته lak~âteh
bitchy *adj.* قرقرو qorqoru جنده صفت jendeh sefat
bite *vt., vi., n.* گازگرفتن gâz gereftan گزيدن gazidan
bite *n.* گاز gâz گزش gazesh لقمه loqmeh
bitter *adj., n., vt., adv.* تلخ talkh
bittern *n.* بوتيمار butimâr
bivouac *n., vi.* اردو كردن ordu kardan
bizarre *adj.* عجيب و غريب 'ajib-o qarib انتضاح eftezâh
blab *vt., vi., n.* دهن لقى كردن dahan laqi kardân
blabber *n.* دهن لق dahan laq ياوه گو yâveh-gu
black *adj., n., vt., vi.* سياه siâh تاريك târik

black list *n.* لیست سیاه list-e′ siâh

black market *np.* بازارسیاه bâzâr-e′ siâh

blackball *n., vt.* محروم کردن mahrum kardan

blackberry *n.* شاه توت shâh-tut

blackboard *n.* تخته سیاه takhteh siâh

blacken *vt., vi.* سیاه کردن siâh kardan

blackjack *n., vt.* بیست و یک bist-o yek باتون bâtun

blackmail *n., vt.* شانتاژ shântâzh باج سبیل bâj-e′ sebil

blackout *n.* سیاهی تاریکی siâhi târiki

blacksmith *n.* آهنگر âhangar نعلبند na'lband

bladder *n.* مثانه masâneh آبدان âbdân

blade *n.* تیغه tiqeh

blame *vt., n.* سرزنش کردن sarzanesh kardân

blanch *vt., vi., adj.* سفید کردن sefid kardan

bland *adj.* ملایم molâyem نرم narm

blandish *vt., vi.* تملق کردن tamal~oq kardan
چاپلوسی کردن châplusi kardan

blank *adj., n., vt.* خالی khâli سفید sefid

blank check *np.* چک سفید chek-e′ sefid

blanket *n., vt., adj.* پتو patu

blantantly *n.* علناً 'alanan مثل روزروشن mesl-e′ ruz-e′ roshan

blase *n.* زده zadeh بیزار bizâr

blasphemous *adj.* کفرآمیز kofr-âmiz

blasphemy *n.* کفر kofr ناسزا nâsezâ

blast *v.* منفجر کردن monfajer kardan ترکاندن tarekândan

blast *n.* وزش vazesh تندباد tondbâd

blast *n.* انفجار enfejâr

blatant *adj.* آشکار âshkâr واضح vâzeh

blaze *n., vi., vt.* شعله sho'leh زبانه zabâneh

blazer *n.* ژاکت zhâkat

bleach *n.* سفید کن sefidkon

bleach *v.* سفید کردن sefid kardan

bleachers *n.* نیمکت nim-kat

bleak *adj., n.* بیروح biruh سرد sard

bleed *vi., vt., n., adj.* خونریزی کردن khunrizi kardan
رگ زدن rag zadan

blemish *vt., n.* لکه lak~eh عیب 'eyb نقص naqs

blend *vt., vi., n.* آمیختن âmikhtan ترکیب کردن tarkib kardan

bless vt. آمرزیدن âmorzidan
blessed adj., vt., n. مبارک mobârak خجسته khojasteh
blessing n., vt. آمرزش âmorzesh دعای خیر do'â-ye' kheyr
نعمت ne'mat یمن yomn
blimp n. زیپلن ziplan بادکنک bâdkonak خیکی khik~i
blind adj. کور kur نابینا nâbinâ بن بست bonbast
blindfold vt., n., adj. چشم بسته cheshm-basteh
blindly adv. کورکورانه kur-kurâneh
blink vi., vt., n. چشمک زدن cheshmak zadan
bliss n. سعادت sa'âdat برکت barekat
blister n., vt., vi. تاول tâval
blitz(krieg) n. هجوم hojum ایلغار ilqâr
blizzard n. سوز و برف suz-o barf کولاک kulâk
bloated adj. بادکرده bâd-kardeh
bloc n. بلوک belok اتحادیه et~ehâdieh
block v. مسدودکردن masdud kardan سد کردن sad~ kardan
blockade n., vt. سد کردن sad~ kardan
محاصره کردن mohâsereh kardan
blockhead n. بی کله bi-kal~eh
blonde adj. بور bur بلوند belond
blood n., vt. خون khun نسب nasab
blood money np. تقاص taqâs~
blood pressure np. نشارخون feshâr-e' khun
blood test np. معاینهٔ خون mo'âyeneh-ye' khun
bloodless adj. کم خون kam khun بدون خونریزی bedun-e' khun-rizi
bloody adj., vt., adv. خونی khuni
bloom n., vt., vi. شکوفه کردن shekufeh kardan
blooming adj. شکوفا shekufâ
blossom n., vi. شکوفه shekufeh
blot n., vt., vi. لکه lak~eh ننگ nang
blotch n., vt., adj. لکهٔ پوستی lak~eh-ye' pusti
blotter n. خشک کن khoshk-kon
blouse n., vi., vt. پیراهن pirâhan بلوز boluz
blow vi., vt., n. وزش vazesh ضربت zarbat
blow v. خراب کردن kharâb kardan
blow v. وزیدن vazidan دمیدن damidan
blow v. فوت کردن fut kardan
blow(up) n. باد کردن bâd kardan ترکاندن tarekândan

blowgun n. تفنگ بادی tofang-e' bâdi

blowup n. انفجار enfejâr

blubber n., vi., vt., adj. چربی charbi

blue adj. آبی âbi نیل nil

blue n., adj., vt. افسرده afsordeh

blueprint n., vt. طرح اصلی tarh-e' asli کروکی koruki

blues n. افسردگی afsordegi

bluff v. لاف زدن lâf zadan وانمود کردن vânemud kardan

bluff n. پرتگاه pârtgâh

bluff n. لاف bolof

blunder n., vi., vt. اشتباه کردن eshtebâh kardan
خراب کردن kharâb kardan

blunt v. کند کردن kond kardan

blunt adj. گستاخ gostâkh

blunt adj. کند kond

blunt adj. پوست کنده rok pust kandeh

blur vt., vi., n. تار کردن târ kardan

blurry adj. تار târ ناواضح nâvâzeh

blush vi., vt., n. سرخ شدن sorkh shodan

bluster v. تهدید کردن tahdid kardan

bluster v. پرخاش کردن parkhâsh kardan

boa n. بوا boâ اژدر azhdar مار mâr

boar n. خوک وحشی gorâz khuk-e' vahshi گراز

board n. تخته takhteh

board n. هیئت hey'at

board v. سوارشدن savâr shodan

board v. اجاره دادن ejâreh dâdan

boarder n. مستاجر mosta'jer پانسیونی pânsioni

boardwalk n. اسکله eskeleh ساحل چوبی sâhel-e' chubi

boast n. لاف lâf رجز rajaz ادعا ed~e'â

boast v. بالیدن bâlidan لاف زدن lâf zadan نازیدن nâzidan

boat n., vi., vt. قایق qâyeq کشتی kashti کرجی karji

bobbin n. ماسوره mâsureh غرغره qer-qereh

bobcat n. گربۀ وحشی gorbeh-ye' vahshi

bodice n. بالا تنه bâlâ taneh

bodily adj., adv. بدنی badani

body n., vt., adj. بدن badan تن tan جثه jos~eh

bodyguard n. محافظ mohâfez

bogeyman n. لولو lulu
bogus adj., n. بی قلا qol~âbi دروغی doruqi
boil v. جوشاندن jushândan جوشیدن jushidan
boil n. جوش jush کورک kurak دمل domal
boiler n. دیگ بخار dig-e' bokhâr
boisterous adj. رجزخوان rajaz-khân پر سر و صدا por-saro sedâ
bold adj. جسور jasur نترس natars گستاخ gostâkh
boldly adv. جسورانه jasurâneh بی باکانه bi-bâkâneh
bolster n., vt. تقویت کردن taqviat kardan
bolt n. پیچ pich تیر tir
bolt v. قفل کردن qofl kardan
bomb v. بمب انداختن bomb andâkhtan
bomb n. بمب bomb
bombard vt., n. بمباران کردن bombârân kardan
bombardier n. بمب انداز bombandâz
bombastic adj. متکبر motekab~er گزاف گو gazâfgu
bon voyage np. سفربخیر safar bekheyr
bona fide np. رسمی rasmi
bonanza n. اکتشاف طلا ekteshâf-e' talâ گنج ganj
bond n. وابستگی vâ-bastegi رشته reshteh میثاق misâq
bond n. وجه الضمانه vâjhol zemâneh ضمانت zemânat
bond n. قید qeyd نسبت nesbat بند band
bondage n. بندگی bandegi اسارت esârat
bonded adj. ضمانت دار zemânat-dâr تضمین شده tazmin-shodeh
قسم خورده qasam-khordeh مقید moqay~ad
bondsman n. ضامن zâmen
bone n., vt., vi. استخوان ostokhân
bone-setter n. شکسته بند shekasteh-band
bonnet n., vt. کلاه بچه kolâh-e' bach~eh
bonus n. جایزه jâyezeh انعام an'âm
bony adj. استخوانی ostokhâni لاغر lâqar
boo int., n., vi., vt. هو کردن ho kardan
boob n. آدم ساده âdam-e' sâdeh پخمه pakhmeh
boob(s) n. ممه mam~eh پستان pestân
booby trap np. تله taleh دام dâm
book v. رزرو کردن rezerv kardan
book n. کتاب ketâb دفتر daftar
bookbinding n. صحافی sah~âfi

bookcase *n.* جاکتابی jâ-ketâbi
bookie *n.* دلال شرط بندی dal~âl-e' shart bandi
bookkeeper *n.* کتابدار ketâbdâr
bookkeeping *n.* حسابداری hesâbdâri
bookseller *n.* کتاب فروش ketâb forush
bookstore *n.* کتاب فروشی ketâb forushi
boom *n.* غرش qor~esh
boom *v.* غریدن qor~idan
boom *v.* ترقی سریع کردن taraq~i-e' sari'kârdân
boondocks *n.* دهکوره‌ها dehkureh-hâ بیغوله biquleh
boost *vt., n.* بالا بردن bâlâ bordan ترقی دادن taraq~i dâdan
booster *n.* تقویت کننده taqviat konandeh
boot *n.* چکمه chakmeh پوتین putin
booth *n.* غرفه qorfeh
bootleg *n., vt., vi., adj.* قاچاق qâchâq غیرقانونی qeyr-e' qânuni
booty *n.* تاراج târâj غنیمت qanimat
booze *n., vt., vi.* مشروب mashrub
border *n.* مرز marz حد had~
border *n.* حاشیه hâshieh
bore *vt., n., vi.* سوراخ کردن surâkh kardan
boredom *n.* بی حوصلگی bi-hoselegi زده گی zadehgi
born *n.* مولود mulud زائیده شده za'ideh shodeh
borough *n.* قصبه qasabeh
borrow *vt., vi.* قرض کردن qarz kardan قرض گرفتن qarz gereftan
امانت گرفتن amânat gereftan
borrowed *adj.* قرض گرفته شده qarz gerefteh shodeh مستعار mosta'âr
عاریه aâryeh
borrower *n.* قرض گیرنده qarz-girandeh وام گیر vâm-gir
bosom *n., adj., vt.* سینه sineh آغوش âqush بغل baqal
boss *n., vt., vi., adj.* ارباب arbâb رئیس ra'is کارفرما kârfarmâ
bossy *adj., n.* ارباب منش arbâb-manesh دستوریده dastur-bedeh
botanist *n.* گیاه شناس giâh shenâs
botany *n.* گیاه شناسی giâh shenâsi
botch *vt., n.* خراب کردن kharâb kardan سرهم کردن sar-ham kardan
botched-up *n.* خراب کاری kharâb kâri
both *adj., pro., con.* هردو hardo جفتشان jofteshân
bother *vt., vi., n., int.* اذیت کردن azy~at kardan
مزاحم بودن mozâhem budan

bothersome *adj.* دردسردار dard-e' sar-dâr مزاحم mozâhem
bottle *n., vt.* بطری botri شیشه shisheh
bottom *n., vt., vi., adj.* ته tah قعر qa'r
botulism *n.* فاسدشدگی fâsed-shodegi
bough *n.* شاخه shâkheh ترکه tarkeh
boulder *n.* سنگ sang صخره sakhreh
bounce *vi., vt., n., adv.* پریدن paridan جستن jestan
bouncer *n.* بزن بهادر bezan bahâdor
bound *n., vt., vi.* عازم 'âzem
bound *n., vt., vi.* مجبور majbur مقید moqayad
دست وپابسته dast-o pâ basteh
bound *n., vt., vi.* حد had~ محدود mahdud
boundless *adj.* بی پایان bipâyân بیکران bikarân
bountiful *adj.* فراوان farâvân دست ودلباز dast-o del-bâz
bounty *n.* جایزه jâyezeh پاداش pâdâsh
bouquet *n.* دسته گل dasteh gol
bout *n.* مسابقه mosâbeqeh زورآزمایی zur âzmâyi
bovine *adj., n.* گاوی gâvi گاومنش gâvmanesh
bow *n.* کمان kamân قوس qos
bow *n.* کشتی sineh-ye' kashti سینهٔ
bow *v.* تعظیم کردن ta'zim kardan خم شدن kham shodan
کرنش کردن kornesh kardan دولاشدن dol~â shodan
bow *n., adj., vt., vi.* تعظیم ta'zim کرنش kornesh
bow-legged *n.* پاچنبری pâ-chanbari
bowel *n., vt.* روده rudeh شکم shekam
bowl *n., vi., vt.* کاسه kâseh جام jâm طاس tâs قدح qadah
bowtie *n.* پاپیون pâpiyon
box *n.* بوکس boks مشت زنی mosht-zani
box *n.* جعبه ja'beh صندوق sandoq حقه hoq~eh
box office *np.* گیشه gisheh باجه bâjeh
box spring *np.* زیرتشکی zir toshaki
boxer *n.* مشت زن moshtzan بوکسور boksor
boxing *n.* مشتزنی moshtzani
boy *n., int.* پسر pesar
boycott *vt., n.* تحریم کردن tahrim kardan
boyfriend *n.* دوست پسر dust-e' pesar
boyhood *n.* دوران پسری dorân-e' pesari
boysenberry *n.* سیاه توت siâh-tut

brace *v.* مستحکم کردن mostahkam kardan
brace *n.* بست bast جفت joft
bracelet *n.* دستبند dastband
bracket *n.* رتبه rotbeh
bracket *n.* لولا lolâ
brackets *n.* پرانتز parântez
brag *v.* رجز خواندن rajaz khândan لاف زدن lâf zadan
کرکری خواندن korkori khândan
braggart *n., adj.* رجزخوان rajazkhân لاف زن lâfzan
braggart *adj.* لافزن lâf-zan گزاف گو gazâf-gu
مبالغه کن mobâleqeh-kon
braid *n.* گلابتون golâbâtun قیطان qeytân
braid *v.* گیس بافتن gis bâftan قیطان دوختن qeytân dukhtan
brain *vt.* مغز maqz مخ mokh
brainchild *n.* فرضیۀ شخصی farzieh-ye' shakhsi
brainless *adj.* بی مخ bimokh
brainy *adj.* بامخ bâmokh
brake *v.* ترمز کردن tormoz kardan
brake *n.* ترمز tormoz
bran *n., vt.* سبوس sabus
branch *n., vi., vt.* شاخه shâkheh شعبه sho'beh
branch(out) *n.* منشعب شدن monsha'eb shodan
brand *n.* نشان neshân مدل model
brand *v.* داغ کردن dâq kardan علامت گذاشتن alâmat gozâshtan
brand new *n.* نو نو no-ye' no
branding-iron *n.* داغ آهن dâq-âhan
brandish *vt., n.* نشان دادن neshân dâdan جلوه دادن jelveh dâdan
brandishment *n.* بیرون کشی birun keshi اسلحه کشی aslaheh keshi
brash *adj., n.* خرده khordeh
brass *n.* برنج berenj
brass *n.* امیران ارتش amirân-e' artesh
brassiere *n.* سینه بند sineh-band کرست korset
brat *n.* بچۀ شیطون bacheh-ye' sheytun
brave *adj., n., vt., vi.* دلیر dalir شجاع shojâ' باجرأت bâ-jor'at
bravely *adv.* دلیرانه dalirâneh شجاعانه shojâ'âneh
bravery *n.* دلیری daliri شجاعت shojâ'at
bravo *int., n., vt., vi.* مرحبا marhabâ آفرین âfarin احسنت ahsant
brawl *n., vi.* دعوا da'vâ مرافعه morâfe'eh مشاجره moshâjereh

brawl *n.* عضله 'azoleh
brawl *v.* دعواکردن da'vâ kardan
bray *n., vi., vt.* عرعر کردن 'ar'ar kardan
bray *v.* کوبیدن kubidan
braze *vt.* لحیم کردن lahim kardan
brazen *adj., vt.* برنجی berenji بی شرم bisharm
brazier *n.* منقل manqal آتشدان âtash-dân
breach *n.* شکست shekast نقض naqz خلف kholf
breach *v.* شکستن shekastan نقض کردن naqz kardan
خلف کردن kholf kardan
breach of contract *n.* خلف قرارداد kholf-e' qarâr-dâd
bread *n., vt.* نان nân
bread-winner *n.* نان آور nân-âvar خرج دهنده kharj-dahandeh
break *v.* شکستن shekastan پاره کردن pâreh kardan
break *n.* شکستگی shekastegi استراحت esterâhat
break (down) *n.* جزئیات joz'iyât
break (in) *n.* دزدی داخل شدن dozdi dâkhel shodan
break (out) *v.* فرارکردن farâr kardan
break (up) *n.* جدا شدن jodâ shodan
break in *n.* رام کردن râm kardan
breakage *n.* شکستگی shekastegi
breakdown *n.* ازکارافتادگی az-kâr oftâdegi فروپاشی foru-pâshi
breakfast *n., vi., vt.* صبحانه sobhâneh چاشت châsht
breakwater *n.* موج شکن moj-shekan
breast *n., vt.* پستان pestân سینه sineh ممه mam~eh
breast stroke *n.* شنای کرال shenây-e' kerâl
breast-feed *n.* شیردادن shir dâdan
breath *n.* نفس nafas دم dam
breathe *vi., vt.* نفس کشیدن nafas keshidan
breather *n.* نفس راحت nafas-e' râhat نفس کش nafas-kesh
breathless *adj.* بی نفس bi-nafas
breeches *n.* شلوار shalvâr زیرشلواری zir-shalvâri
breed *v.* پرورش دادن parvaresh dâdan
breed *n.* نژاد nezhâd نسل nasl
breeding *n., v.* پرورش parvaresh تربیت tarbiat
breeze *n., vi., vt.* نسیم nasim
breezy *adj.* نسیم دار nasim-dâr
brew *v.* آبجو درست کردن âbejo dorost kardan

brew n. آبجو âbejo نقشه naqsheh
brewery n. آبجوسازی کارخانهٔ kârkhâneh-ye' âbejo Sâzi
bribe v. رشوه دادن roshveh dâdan تطمیع کردن tatmi' kardan
bribe n. رشوه roshveh پول چایی pul-e' châyi
bribery n. تطمیع tatmi' رشوهدهی roshveh-dahi
brick n., vt., adj. آجر âjor
bricklayer n. عمله 'amaleh بنا ban~â
bridal adj., n. مال عروس mâl-e' 'arus
bridal shower n. ولیمه valimeh پاتختی pâ-tâkhti
bride n. عروس 'arus
bridechamber n. حجله hejleh
bridegroom n. داماد dâmâd
bridesmaid n. ندیمه nadimeh
bridge n., vt., vi. پل pol
bridle n., vt., vi. افسار afsâr عنان 'anân لجام lejâm
brief v. درجریان گذاشتن dar-jâryân gozâshtan
brief n. خلاصه kholâseh مجمل mojmal
brief-case n. کیف دستی kif-e' dasti
briefing n. خلاصهٔ گزارش kholâseh-ye' gozâresh
درجریان گذاری dar-jaryân gozâri
briefly adv. بطورخلاصه betor-e' kholâseh
briefs n. زیرشلواری zir shalvâri تنکه tonekeh
brig n., vt. زندان کشتی zendân-e' kâshti
brigade n., vt. تیپ tip
brigadier n. سرتیپ sartip
brigand n. راهزن râhzan یاغی yâqi
bright adj. زرنگ zerang باهوش bâ-hush
bright adj. روشن roshan آفتابی âftâbi درخشان derakh-shân
لامع lâ-me'
brighten vi., vt. روشن کردن roshan kardan
brightness n. روشنی roshani زرنگی zerangi
brilliance n. درخشندگی derakhshandegi
brilliant adj., n. درخشان derakhshân مشعشع mosha'sha'
brim pl., n., vi., vt. لبه labeh
brine n., vt. آب نمک âb-namak
bring vt. آوردن âvardan
brink n. لب lab لبه labeh شرف shorof
briquet(s) n. ذغال zoqâl

brisk *adj., vt., vi.* چابک châbok فرض ferz تند tond
bristle *n., vi., vt.* موی زبر muy-e' zebr
Britain *n.* بریتانیا beritânyâ انگلستان engelestân
British *adj., n.* انگلیسی engelisi
brittle *n.* ترد tord شکستنی shekastani
broach *n., vt., vi.* سنجاق sanjâq
broad *adj.* کلی kol~i جامع jâme'
broad *adj.* پهن pahn وسیع vasi'
broad-minded *adj.* بافهم bâ-fahm
broadcast *v.* پخش کردن pakhsh kardan
broadcast *n.* پخش pakhsh
broaden *vi., vt.* پهن کردن pahn kardan
broil *vt., vi., n.* سرخ کردن sorkh kardan
broiled *n.* سرخ شده sorkh-shodeh
broiler *n.* کباب پز kabâb-paz
broke *v., n.* بی پول bipul
broken *v.* شکسته shekasteh
broker *n.* دلال dal~âl ارز دلال dal~âl-e' arz
bronchitis *n.* برونشیت boronshit
bronze *n., vt., adj.* برنز boronz
brooch *n.* سنجاق سینه sanjâq sineh
brood *v.* کرج کردن korch kardan
brood(over) *n.* توفکررفتن tu-fekr raftan درفکر بودن dar fekr budan
brook *n., vt.* جویبار juy-bâr
broom *n., vt., vi.* جارو jâru
broomstick *n.* دسته جارو dasteh-jâru
broth *n.* آبگوشت âbgusht
brothel *n.* جنده خانه jendeh-khâneh
brother *n., int., vt.* برادر barâdar
brother-in-law *n.* برادرزن barâdar zân
brother-in-law *n.* برادرشوهر barâdar shuhar
brotherly *adj., adv.* برادرانه barâdarâneh
brow *n.* ابرو abru جبین jabin
brown *n., adj., vt., vi.* قهوه ایی qahveh-yi خرمایی khormâyi
bruise *v.* ضربه زدن zarbeh zadan کبودکردن kabud kardan
bruise *n.* ضربه zarbeh ورم varam
bruised *v.* کبودشده kabud shodeh ورم کرده varam-kardeh
brunet *adj., n.* موقهوهای mu qahveh-yi سبزه sabzeh

brunt *n.* لطمه latmeh نشاراصلی feshâr-e' asli
brush *v.* مسواک زدن mesvâk-zadan
brush *n.* برس boros ماهوت پاک کن mâhut pâk kon
brush *n.* قلم مو qalam mu
brutal *adj.* وحشیانه vahshiâneh
brutality *n.* وحشی گری vahshigari
brute *n., vt., adj.* حیوان صفت heyvân-sefat بیرحم birahm
bubble *n., vi., vt.* حباب hobâb
buck *n.* مردسرخ پوست mard-e' sorkh-pust
buck *n.* دلار dolâr چوق chuq
buck *v.* جفتک انداختن joftak andâkhtan
buck *n.* گوزن نر gavazn-e' nar
buck *sl.* مسئولیت mas'uliyat
buckboard *n.* گاری gâri
bucket *n., vt., vi.* سطل satl دلو dalv
buckle *n., vt., vi.* سگک sagak قلاب qol~âb
buckshot *n.* ساچمه sâchmeh
buckskin *n., adj.* پوست آهو pust-e' âhu
buckwheat *n., adj.* گندم سیاه gandom siâh
bud *n., vi., vt.* غنچه qoncheh جوانه javâneh
budding *v.* نوپا no-pâ تازه وارد tâzeh-vâred
buddy *n.* دوست dust جون جونی dust-e' jun juni
رفیق شفیق rafiq-e' shafiq
budge *n., adj., vi., vt.* تکان خوردن takân khordan
budget *n., vt.* بودجه budjeh
buffer *n., vt.* حائل hâ'el ضربگیر zarbgir سپر separ
buffer zone *n.* منطقهٔ حائل mantaqeh-ye' hâ'el
buffet *n., adj., vt., vi.* بوفه bufeh بار bâr
buffoon *n.* مسخره maskhareh دلقک dalqak
bug *n.* حشره hashareh
bug *v.* استراق سمع کردن esterâq-e' sam' kardan
bug *v.* اذیت کردن azyat kardan
bugle *n., adj., vi., vt.* شیپور sheypur
build *vt., vi., n.* ساختن sâkhtan بناکردن banâ kardan
build-up *n.* بالابری bâlâ bari افزایش afzâyesh
builder *n.* خانه ساز khâneh-sâz سازنده sâzandeh
building *n.* ساختمان sâkhtemân بنا banâ
built *v., n.* ساخته شده sâkhteh-shodeh

built-in *adj., n.* داخل ساخت dâkhel-sâkht
bulb *n.* لامپ lâmp پیازگل piâz gol
bulge *n.* قلنبگی qolonbegi برآمدگی bar-âmadegi
bulge *v.* برآمدن bar âmadan قلنبه شدن qolonbeh shodan
bulging *v.* قلنبه qolonbeh
bulk *n.* وزنی vazni کیلوئی kilu'i
bulk *n.* جثه jos~eh قسمت عمده qesmat-e' 'omdeh
bulky *adj.* تنومند tanumand قطور qatur یقر yoqor لندهور landahur
bull *n., adj., vt.* گاو نر gâv-e' nar ورزو varzo
bulldozer *n.* تراکتور terâktor
bullet *n., vi.* تیر tir نشنگ feshang گلوله goluleh
bullet-proof *n.* ضد گلوله zed~-e' goluleh
bulletin *n., vt.* اطلاعیه et~elâ'ieh
bullfight *n.* گاو بازی gâv-bâzi
bullion *n.* شمش shemsh
bullock *n.* گاونراخته gâv-e' nar-e' akhteh
bully *n., vt., vi., adj.* قلدر qoldor گردن کلفت gardan-koloft
bulwark *n., vt.* دیواره divâreh سنگرگاه sangar-gâh
bum *n., vt., vi., adj.* الاف al~âf بیکار bikâr
bump *vt., vi., n.* برآمد گی bar âmadegi ضربت zarbat
bumper *n., adj., vt., vi.* سپر separ
bun *n.* کلوچه kolucheh نان nân
bunch *n., vt., vi.* دسته dasteh گروه goruh
bundle *n., vt., vi.* بقچه boqcheh
bungle *vt., vi., n.* سرهم کردن sar-ham kardan
bungled *v.* شلخته پلخته shelakhteh pelakhteh
bunker *n., vt.* سنگرگاه sangar-gâh
buoy *n., vt., vi.* رهنمای شناور rahnamây-e' shenâvar
buoyancy *n.* شناوری shenâvari سبکی saboki
buoyant *adj.* شناور shenâvar
burden *n., vt.* بار bâr سنگینی sangini سربار sar-e' bâr زحمت zahmat
burden *n., vt.* زحمت دادن zahmat dâdan
سربارشدن sar-e' bâr shodan
burdensome *adj.* پرزحمت por-zahmat سنگین sangin
bureau *n.* کمد komod
bureau *n.* دفتر daftar اداره edâreh
bureaucracy *n.* اداره ای edâreh-i
burgeon *n., vi., vt.* شکوفه کردن shekufeh kardan

burgeoning *n.* شکوفا shekufâ
burglar *n.* دزد dozd سارق sâreq
burglary *n.* دزدی dozdi سرقت serqat
burial *n.* دفن dafn تدفین tadfin
burlap *n.* کنف kanaf کرباس karbâs
burly *adj.* تنومند tanumand ستبر setabr
burn *vi., vt., n.* سوختن sukhtan سوزاندن suzândan
burner *n.* اجاق ojâq
burp *n., vi., vt.* آروغ زدن âroq zadan
burrow *n., vi., vt.* سوراخ کردن surâkh kardan نقب زدن naqb zadan
burst *vi., vt., n.* ترکیدن tarekidan
bury *vt., n.* دفن کردن dafn kardan
bus *n., vt., vi.* اتوبوس otobus
bush *n., vt., vi.* بته bot~eh بیشه bisheh
bushel *n., vt.* واحد وزن vâhed-e′ vazn
bushy *adj.* انبوه anbuh پربته por-bot~eh
business *n., adj.* کار kâr کسب kasb
businessman *n.* کاسب kâseb
buss *n., vt., vi.* بوسه buseh ماچ mâch
bust *v.* خرد کردن khord kardan
bust *n.* نیم تنه nim-taneh سینه sineh
bust *v.* ورشکست کردن varshekast kardan
bustling *v.* شلوغ پلوغ sholuq poluq
busy *adj., vt.* مشغول mashqul
busy-body *n.* فضول fozul
but *con., pre., adv., n.* ولی vali اما am~â لیکن likan بلکه balkeh
butcher *n., vt.* قصاب qas~âb گوشت فروش gusht forush
butler *n.* آبداراباشی âbdâr-bâshi پیشخدمت pish-khedmat
butt *vi., n., vt.* ته tah کپل kapal
butter *n., vt.* کره kareh
butter(up) *n.* تملق کردن tamal~oq kardan
buttercup *n.* آلاله âlâleh
butterfly *n., vt., adj.* پروانه parvâneh
buttock(s) *n.* کفل kafal کون kun
button *n., vt., vi.* دگمه dogmeh
buttress *n., vt.* پشتیبانی کردن poshtibâni kardan
buxom *adj.* چاق و چله châq-o chel~eh
buy *vt., vi., n.* خریدن kharidan ابتیاع کردن ebtiâ′ kardan

buyer *n.* خریدار kharidâr مشتری moshtari
buzz *n., vi., vt.* وزوز کردن vezvez kardan
buzz-off! *n.* بزن بچاک bezan bechâk
buzzard *n., adj.* لاشخور lâsh-khor کرکس karkas
by *pre., adv., adj., n.* بوسیله bevasileh
by the way *n.* راستی râsti
by-law *n.* قانون qânun آئین نامه â'in-nâmeh
bye(-bye) *n.* خداحافظ khodâ hâfez
byegone *n.* گذشته gozashteh
bypass *n.* دورزدن dor zadan فرعی رفتن far'i raftan
byproduct *n.* فرآورده far-âvardeh
bystander *n.* عابر 'âber ناظر nâzer شاهد shâhed

C c c

cab *n., vi.* تاکسی tâksi اطاقک otâqak

cabal *n., vi.* دارودسته dâr-o dasteh گروهک goruhak

cabaret *n., vi.* میخانه meykhâneh کاباره kâbâreh

cabbage *n., vi., vt.* کلم kalam

cabby *n.* تاکسیران tâksirân

cabin *n., adv., vi., vt.* کلبه kolbeh خوابگاه khâbgâh اطاقک otâqak

cabinet *n., adj.* قفسه qafaseh هیئت وزرا hey'at-e' vozarâ

cable *n., vt., vi.* سیم sim کابل kâbl تلگرام telegrâm

caboose *n.* واگن آخر قطار vâgon-e' âkhar-e' qatâr

cache *n., vt.* صندوق sandoq

cackle *vi., vt., n.* قد قد کردن qod-qod kardan

cacophony *n.* ناهنجاری nâ-hanjâri

cactus *n.* کاکتوس kâktus

cadaver *n.* جسد jasad لاشه lâsheh

caddy *n.* پادوی گلف pâdo-ye' golf

cadet *n.* دانشجوی افسری dâneshju-ye' afsari

cadre *n.* کادر kâdr

cafe *n.* کافه kâfeh رستوران resturân

caftan *n.* عبا 'abâ

cage *n., vt.* قفس qafas

cahoots *n.* گاو بندی gâv bandi دست به یکی dast beh yeki

cajole *vt., vi.* گول زدن gul zadan تملق tamal~oq

cake *n., vt., vi.* نان شیرینی nân shirini قالب qâleb کیک keyk

calabash *n.* خربزه kharbozeh

calamity *n.* مصیبت mosibat بدبختی badbakhti

calcium *n.* کلسیوم kalsyom آهک âhak

calculate *vt., vi.* حساب کردن hesâb kardan
محاسبه کردن mohâsebeh kardan

calculator *n.* ماشین حساب mâshin hesâb

calculus *n.* ریاضیات riâziât

calender *n., vt.* تقویم taqvim سالنما sâlnamâ

calf *n.* گوساله gusâleh نرمهٔ ساق پا narmeh-ye' sâq-e' pâ

caliph *n.* خلیفه khalifeh

calisthenics *n.* ورزش سبک varzesh-e' sâbok

calk *n., vt.* سیخک نعل sikhak-e' na'l نعلبندی na'lbandi

call *v.* صدا زدن sedâ zadan نامیدن nâmidan احضار کردن ehzâr kardan

call *n.* ندا nedâ صدا sedâ احضار ehzâr مکالمه mokâlemeh

calligraphy *n.* خطاطی khat~âti خوشنویسی khosh-nevisi
callous *adj., vt., vi.* پینه خورده pineh khordeh بی احساس bi-ehsâs
calm *adj.* آرام ârâm
calm *v.* آرام کردن ârâm kardan آرامش دادن ârâmesh dâdan
calmness *n.* آرامش ârâmesh
calorie *n.* کالری kâlori
camel *n.* شتر shotor
camel-driver *n.* ساربان sârebân
camera *n.* دوربین عکاسی durbin-e' 'ak~âsi
camouflage *n.* پوشش pushesh استتار estetâr
camouflage *v.* پوشاندن pushândan مستترکردن mostater kardan
camp *n., vi., vt.* اردوگاه ordugâh چادر زدن châdor zadan
campaign *n., vi.* فعالیت کردن fa'~âliyat kardan
campground *n.* اردوگاه ordugâh
camphor *n.* کانور kâfur
campus *n.* زمین دانشگاه zamin-e' dâneshgâh
can *n.* قوطی qoti حلبی halabi
can *v.* کمپوت کردن kompot kardan توی قوطی کردن tu-ye' qoti kardan
canal *n., vt.* کانال kânâl ترعه tor'eh تنگه tangeh
canard *n.* قلابی shâye'eh-ye' qol~âbi شایعۀ
canary *n., adj.* قناری qanâri
cancel *vt., vi., n.* باطل کردن bâtel kardan نسخ کردن faskh kardan
canceled *v.* باطل شده bâtel shodeh
cancellation *n.* نسخ faskh القاء elqâ' ابطال ebtâl بطلان botlân
cancer *n.* سرطان saratân
candid *adj., n.* بی خبر bikhabar
candid *adj., n.* رک rok منصف monsef
candidate *n.* نامزد nâmzad داوطلب dâvtalab کاندیدا kândidâ
candidate *v.* نامزد کردن nâmzad kardan
داوطلب شدن dâvtalab shodan
candle *n., vt.* شمع sham'
candlestick *n.* شمعدان sham'-dân
candor *n.* رک گوئی rok guyi
candy *n., vt., vi.* آبنبات âbnabât جوز قند joz-e' qand
cane *n.* عصا 'asâ
cane *n.* نی ney نیشکر neyshekar
canine *adj., n.* ناب nâb نیش nish
canine *adj., n.* سگ sag سگخو sagkhu

canister *n.* قوطی qoti
cannibal *n., adj.* آدمخوار âdamkhâr
cannon *n., vi.* توپ tup
cannonball *n., adj., vi.* سریع کردن sâri' kardan
cannonball *n., adj., vi.* گلولۀ توپ goluleh-ye' tup
canny *adj., adv.* محتاط mohtât
canoe *n., vi., vt.* کانو قایق kânu qâyeq
canon *n.* قانون شرعی qânun-e' shar'i نقه feqh
canonical *adj., n.* شرعی shar'i
canonize *vt.* مقدس کردن moqad~as kardan
canopy *n., vt.* سایبان sâyebân
cantaloupe *n.* طالبی tâlebi
cantankerous *adj.* بد اخلاق badakhlâq دعوا کن da'vâ kon
canteen *n.* تمقمه qomqomeh
cantina *n.* میخانۀ سر راه meykhâne-ye' sar-e' râh
cantor *n.* روضه خوان rozeh-khân
خواننده مذهبی khânandeh-ye' maz-habi
canvas *n.* کرباس karbâs برزنت berezent
canvass *vt., vi., n.* مشتری پیدا کردن moshtari peydâ kardan
canyon *n.* درۀ باریک dareh-ye' bârik
cap *n.* تشتک tashtak
cap *n.* پوشش pushesh
cap *n.* کلاه kolâh
capability *n.* توانایی tavânâyi استعداد este'dâd عرضه 'orzeh
capable *adj.* توانا tavânâ قادر qâder مستعد mosta'ed
capacious *adj.* جادار jâdâr باحجم bâ-hajm
capacity *n.* گنجایش gonjâyesh ظرفیت zarfiyat وسع vos'
cape *n., vi., adj.* شنل shenel دماغه damâqeh
caper *vi., n.* جست و خیز jest-o khiz ماجراجویی mâjerâjuyi
capillary *adj., n.* موئی mu'i
capital *n.* سرمایه sarmâyeh
capital *n.* پایتخت pâyetakht مرکز markaz
capital *n.* حرف درشت harf-e' dorosht سر ستون sar sotun
capitalism *n.* سرمایه داری sarmâyehdâri
capitalist *n.* سرمایه دار sarmâyehdâr
capitalize *vt.* سرمایه (جمع) کردن sarmâyeh(jam') kardan
capitulate *vi.* تسلیم شدن taslim shodan
caprice *n.* تغییر اخلاق taqyir-e' akhlâq

capricious *adj.* آدم متغیر âdam-e' moteqayer دم دمی dam dami
هردم خیال har-dam khiâl
capsize *vi., vt.* چپ کردن chap kardan وارونه شدن vâruneh shodan
capsule *n., vt., adj.* محفظه mahfazeh کپسول kapsul
captain *n., vt.* سروان sarvân ناخدا nâkhodâ کاپیتان kâpitân
caption *n., vt.* عنوان 'onvân زیر نویس zir nevis
captivate *vt.* شیفته کردن shifteh kardan مجذوب کردن majzub kardan
captivating *vt.* شیفته کننده shifteh konandeh
capture *n.* دستگیری dastgiri تسخیر taskhir اسارت esârat
capture *v.* دستگیر کردن dastgir kardan تسخیر کردن taskhir kardan
car *adj., n.* ماشین mâshin اتومبیل otomobil
carafe *n.* تنگ tong
caramel *n.* قند سوخته qand sukhteh
carat *n.* قیرات qeyrât
caravan *n., vi.* کاروان kârevân قافله qâfeleh
caravansary *n.* کاروانسرا kârvânsarâ
carbine *n.* تفنگ لوله کوتاه tofang-e' luleh kutâh
carbon *n.* کاربن karbon ذغال zoqâl
carbon paper *np.* کاغذ کپی kâqaz kopi
carcass *n., vt.* لاشه lâsheh جسد jasad
card *n., vt.* ورق varaq برگ barg کارت kârt
cardamom *n.* هل hel
cardboard *n.* مقوا moqav~â
cardiac *adj., n.* قلبی qalbi
cardinal *adj., n.* کاردینال kârdinâl اصلی asli
care *n.* توجه tavaj~oh علاقه alâqeh نگهداری negahdâri
care *v.* توجه داشتن tavaj~oh dâshtan علاقه داشتن alâqeh dâshtan
careen *vt., vi., n.* ور یک شدن yek var shodan
career *n., vi., adj.* خط مشی khat~-e' mashy حرفه ای herfeh-i
careful *adj.* مواظب mohtât مواظب movâzeb
carefully *adv.* بااحتیاط bâ-ehtiât بدقت be-deq~at
careless *adj.* بی احتیاط biehtiât بی پروا biparvâ لاابالی lâ-obali
لاقید lâ-qeyd
caress *n., vt.* نوازش کردن navâzesh kardan
caretaker *n.* سرایدار sarây-dâr مستحفظ mostah-fez متولی moteval~i
cargo *n.* بار bâr محموله mahmuleh
carnage *n.* آدم کشی âdamkoshi کشتار koshtâr
carnal *adj.* شهوانی shahvâni جسمانی jesmâni

carnation *n., adj.* میخک mikhak
carnival *n.* کارناوال kârnâvâl جشن jashn
carnivore *n.* گوشتخوار gushtkhâr
carol *n., vi., vt.* تصنیف tasnif نغمه سرایی naqmeh sarâyi
carp *pl., vi.* ماهی قنات mâhi-e' qanât
carpenter *vi., vt.* نجار naj~âr چوب بر chub bor درودگر dorud-gar
carpentry *n.* نجاری naj~âri درودگری dorud-gari
carpet *n., vt.* فرش farsh قالی qâli موکت moket
carpetbagger *n.* پست فطرت past fetrat
خریدار مال فقرا kharidar-e' mal-e' foq
carriage *n.* گاری gâri درشکه doroshkeh
carrier *n.* حامل hâmel باربر bârbar
carrot *n., vt.* هویج havij
carry *vt., vi., n.* حمل کردن haml kardan بردن bordan
cart *n., vt., vi.* گاری gâri ارابه arâbeh
cartel *n.* کنسرسیوم konsersiom
cartilage *n.* عضله 'azoleh ماهیچه mâhicheh غضروف qozruf
carton *n.* جعبهٔ مقوایی ja'beh-ye' moqav~â-yi
cartridge *n.* نشنگ feshang لول lul
carve *vt., vi.* تراشیدن tarâshidan کندن kandan
cascade *n., vi., vt.* آبشار کوچک âbshâr-e' kuchak
case *n.* صندوق sandoq
case *n., vt.* مورد mored حالت hâlat
cash *n., pl., vt.* نقد کردن naqd kardan
cash-register *n.* صندوق sandoq باجه bâjeh
cashew *n.* بادام هندی bâdâm hendi
cashier *n., vt.* صندوق دار sândoq-dâr
cashmere *n.* ترمه termeh
casing *n., v.* پوشش pushesh جلد jeld
casino *n.* قمارخانه qomârkhâneh کازینو kâzino
casket *n., vt.* تابوت tâbut
Caspian Sea *np.* دریای خزر daryâ-ye' khazar
cast *n.* بازیگران bâzigarân نقش naqsh
cast *n.* گچ gach
cast *v.* انداختن andâkhtan شرکت دادن sherkat dâdan
cast *n.* قالب qâleb ریخت rikht
cast(off) *n.* لنگر برداشتن langar bardâshtan
castanets *n.* سنج انگشتی sanj-e' angoshti

castaway *n., adj.* كشتى شكسته kashti-ye' shekasteh
caste *n., adj.* طبقه tabaqeh فرقه ferqeh
casterate *n.* اخته كردن akhteh kardan
casterated *n.* اخته akhteh خواجه khâjeh آغا âqâ
castle *n.* قصر qasr دژ dezh
castle *n.* رخ rokh
castor oil *np.* روغن كرچک roqan karchak
casual *adj., n.* معمولى ma'muli
casualty *n.* زخمى zakhmi تلفات talafât
cat *n., vt., vi.* گربه gorbeh پيشى pishi
catacomb *n.* دخمه dakhmeh تونل زير زمينى tunel-e' zirzamini
catalogue *n., v.* رده بندى كردن radeh-bandi kardan كاتالوگ kâtâlog
catalysis *n.* واسطة تركيب vâseteh-ye' tarkib
catapult *n., vt.* منجنيق manjaniq عراده 'ar~âdeh
cataract *n.* آب مرواريد âb morvârid
catastrophe *n.* فاجعه fâje'eh بلا balâ حادثه hâdeseh
catatonic *adj., n.* حالت وحشت hâlat-e' vahshat
catcall *n., vi., vt.* هو كردن ho kardan
catch *v.* گرفتن gereftan
catch *v.* درک كردن dark kardan
catching *adj., v.* واگير vâgir مسرى mosri
catchword *n.* تكيه كلام tekyeh-kalâm ورد verd
مغزكلام maqz-e' kalâm
categorically *adv.* قاطعاً qâte'an صريحاً sarihan
category *n.* طبقه tabaqeh دسته dasteh
cater *vi., vt.* غذاى ميهمانى پختن qazâ-ye' mihmâni pokhtan
caterer *n.* سورسات چى sursât-chi
catering *n.* غذاى ميهمانى qazâ-ye' mihmâni سورسات sursât
caterpillar *n.* كرم درختى kerm-e' derâkhti
catherdral *n.* كليسا kelisâ
catholic *adj.* كاتوليک kâtolik
catnap *vi.* چرت زدن chort zadan
cattle *n.* گله گاو galeh-ye' gâv
caucasian *n.* سفيدپوست sefid-pust
caucus *n., vi.* مجلس رهبران mâjles-e' rahbarân
caught *v.* گير كرده gir kardeh دستگير شده dastgir-shodeh
cauldron *n.* انبيق anbiq پاتيل pâtil
cauliflower *n.* گل كلم gol-kalam

caulk *vt.* درزگیر darzgir
causative *adj., n.* سببی sababi
cause *n.* سبب sabab باعث bâ'es علت el~at
cause *v.* سبب شدن sabab shodan باعث شدن bâ'es shodan
cause *n.* امر amr هدف hadaf
cause of action *n.* تأمین دلیل ta'min-e' dalil
causeway *n., vt.* جاده jâd~eh
cauterize *vt.* سوزاندن suzândan
caution *n., vt., vi.* احتیاط ehtiât
cautious *adj.* محتاط mohtât
cavalcade *n.* دستهٔ سوار dasteh-ye' savâr
cavalier *n., adj., vi.* سوار کار savâr-kâr شوالیه shovâlieh
cavalry *n.* سواره نظام savâreh nezâm
cave *n., int., vt., vi.* غار qâr
caveat *n.* هشدار hoshdâr تذکر tazak~or
cavern *n.* غار بزرگ qâr-'e bozorg
cavity *n.* گودال godâl کرم خوردگی kerm khordegi
cease *vi., vt., n.* بس کردن bas kardan بند آوردن band âvardan
cease-fire *n.* آتش بس âtash-bas
cedar *n.* سرو sarv
cede *vt.* واگذار کردن vâgozâr kardan
cedrate *n.* ترنج toranj
ceiling *n.* سقف saqf طاق tâq
celebrate *vt., vi.* جشن گرفتن jashn gereftan
celebration *n.* جشن jashn
celebrity *n.* آدم مشهور âdam-e' mashhur شهرت shohrat
celery *n.* کرفس karafs
celesital *n.* آسمانی âsemâni بهشتی beheshti
celestial *adj., n.* آسمانی âsemâni سماوی samâvi جبروت jabarut
celibacy *n.* تجرد tajar~od
celibate *n., adj.* بدون زن bedun-e' zan عزب 'azab
cell *n.* یاخته yâkhteh سلول sel~ul زندان zendân گویه guyeh
cellar *n., vt.* زیر زمین zir-zamin
cellular *adj.* سلولی sel~uli
celsius *n.* سانتیگراد sântigrâd
cement *v.* محکم کردن mohkam kardan
cement *n.* سمنت sement سیمان simân
cemetery *n.* گورستان gurestân قبرستان qabrestân

censor *n., vt.* سانسور کردن sânsur kârdan
censorship *n.* سانسور sânsur
censure *n., vt., vi.* انتقاد کردن enteqâd kardan
محکوم کردن mahkum kardan
census *n.* سرشماری sar-shomâri
cent *n.* صد sad صدم یک yek sadom
centennial *adj., n.* سالگی صد sad sâlegi ساله صد sad sâleh
centepede *n.* پا هزار hezâr pâ
center *n., vt., vi.* مرکز markaz وسط vasat
central *adj., n.* مرکزی markazi اصلی asli
centrality *n.* مرکزیت markaziyat
centralization *n.* تمرکز tamarkoz
centrifugal force *np.* مرکز از گریز قوهٔ goveh-ye' goriz az markaz
centurion *n.* رمی فرماندهٔ farmândeh-ye' romi
century *n.* قرن qarn سده sadeh
ceramic *adj., n.* سفال sofâl
ceramics *n.* سازی سفال sofâl-sâzi
cereal *n., adj.* غله qal~eh حبوبات hobubât
cerebral *adj., n.* مغزی maqzi
cerebral palsy *np.* لمسی lamsi
ceremonial *adj., n.* تشریفاتی tashrifâti
ceremonious *adj.* تعارفی ta'ârofi تشریفاتی tashrifâti
ceremony *n.* تشریفات tashrifât جشن jashn
certain *adj.* مطمئن motma'en یقین yaqin حتمی hatmi
certainly *adv.* مطمئناً motma'en~an یقیناً yaqinan مسلماً mosal~aman
certainty *n.* اطمینان etminân یقین yaqin
certificate *n., vt.* نامه گواهی gavâhi-nâmeh
certification *n.* گواهی gavâhi تصدیق tasdiq
certified *v.* شده گواهی gavâhi-shodeh شده تصدیق tasdiq-shodeh
certify *vt., vi.* کردن گواهی gavâhi kardan کردن تصدیق tasdiq kardan
certitude *n.* اطمینان etminân ایقان iqân
cervical *adj.* گردنی gardani
cervix *n.* رحم استخوان ostokhân-e' rahem
cessation *n.* توقف tavaq~of نگهداری دست dast-negahdâri
cession *n.* واگذاری vâgozâri
cesspool *n.* مستراح چاه châh-e' mostarâh
chagrin *n., vt.* اندوه anduh تأسف ta'as~of الم elam کیارا kiârâ
chagrined *v.* رنجور ranjur اندوهناک anduh-nâk

chain *n., vt., vi.* زنجیرکردن zanjir kardan سلسله selseleh
chair *n., vt.* صندلی sandali کرسی korsi
chairman *n., vt.* رئیس ra'is
chalk *n., vt., vi., adj.* گچ gach
challenge *n., vt., vi.* به مبارزه طلبیدن be-mobârezeh talâbidan
challenge *n., vt., vi.* مبارزه mobârezeh برخورد bar-khord
       معارضه mo'ârezeh
challenger *n.* مبارز طلب mobârez-talab نفس کش nafas-kesh
challenging *adj.* سخت sakht
chamber *n., vt.* خشاب khashâb
chamber *n., vt.* اطاق otâq خوابگاه khâbgâh
chamber-maid *n.* کلفت kolfat ندیمه nadimeh
chameleon *n.* مارمولک mâr-mulak
champ(ion) *n.* قهرمان qahremân پهلوان pahlevân
champion *n.* قهرمان qahremân پهلوان pahlevân گرد gord یل yal
championship *n.* قهرمانی qahremâni
chance *n.* بخت bakht فرصت forsat شانس shâns
chance *v.* شانس امتحان کردن shâns-e' emtehân kardan
chancellery *n.* اداره edâreh وزارتخانه vezârat-khâneh
chancellor *n.* رئیس râ'is صدراعظم sad-re' a'zam
chancery *n.* دفترخانه daftar-khâneh
chandelier *n.* شمعدان sham'dân لوستر luster
change *v.* عوض کردن 'avaz kardan تغییرکردن taqyir kardan
change *n.* تعویض ta'viz تغییر taqyir
change *n.* پول خرد pul-e' khord
changeable *adj.* عوض شدنی 'avaz-shodani
channel *n., vt., vi.* مجرا majrâ کانال kânâl دریا daryâ
chant *n., vt., vi.* آواز خواندن âvâz khândan
chaos *n.* هرج و مرج harj-o marj
chap *n.* مردکه mardekeh یارو yâru
chap *v.* خشکاندن khoshkândan ترک دادن tarak dâdan
chapel *n., vt., adj.* کلیسای کوچک kelisâ-ye' kuchek
chaperon *n., vt.* مراقب morâqeb ناظر nâzer
chaplain *n.* کشیش keshish
chapped *v.* خشک شده khoshk-shodeh ترک خورده tarak-khordeh
chapter *n., vt.* فصل fasl باب bâb
char *n., vi., vt.* ذغال کردن zoqâl kardan
character *n., adj., vt.* شخصیت shakhsiyat سیرت sirat سرشت seresht

فطرت .... fetrat

charade *n.* معما mo'am~â

charcoal *n., vt.* ذغال zoqâl

charge *v.* گماشتن gomâshtan عهده دارکردن ohdeh-dâr kardan

charge *n.* اتهام etehâm

charge *v.* حمله کردن hamleh kardan

charge *n.* حساب hesâb هزینه hazineh

charge *v.* پرکردن por kardan شارژ کردن shârzh kardan

charge *v.* متهم کردن motahem kardan

charge *v.* به حساب گذاشتن be-hesâb gozâshtan
حساب کردن hesâb kardan

charge-account *n.* حساب نسیه hesâb-e' nesiyeh

charge-d'affaire *n.* کاردارسفارت kârdâr-e' sefârat

chariot *n., vt., vi.* ارابۀ جنگی arâbeh-ye' jangi

charisma *n.* ابهت ob~ohat جذبه jazabeh

charitable *adj.* خیرخواهانه kheyr-khâhâneh

charity *n.* خیریه kheyriyeh صدقه sadaqeh

charlatan *n.* کلاه بردار kolâh bardâr حقه باز hoq~eh-bâz کلک kalak

charm *n., vt., vi.* افسون کردن afsun kardan
فریفته کردن farifteh kardan

charming *adj.* ملیح malih فریبا faribâ افسونگر afsun-gar
فریبنده faribandeh

chart *n.* نقشه naqsheh جدول jadval

chart *v.* نقشه کشیدن naqsheh keshidan

charter *n.* منشور manshur فرمان farmân

charter *n.* کرایه kerâyeh دربست dar-bast

chase *vt., vi., n.* تعقیب کردن ta'qib kardan دنبال کردن donbâl kardan

chasis *n.* شاسی shâsi

chaste *adj.* پاکدامن pâkdâman نجیب najib عفیف 'afif پارسا pârsâ

chastise *vt.* تنبیه کردن tanbih kardan

chastity *n.* پاکدامنی pâkdâmani عفت 'ef~at عصمت 'esmat

chat *v.* گپ زدن gap zadan پچ و پچ کردن pech-o pech kardan

chat *n.* گپ gap صحبت کوتاه sohbat-e' kutâh

chatter *vi., vt., n.* وراجی کردن ver~âji kardan
دندان ساییدن dandân sâyidan

chauffeur *n.* راننده rânandeh شوفر shufer

chauvinist *n.* پرستش افراطی parastesh-e' efrâti متعصب mote'as~eb

cheap *adj., adv., n.* ارزان arzân

cheapen *vt., vi.* بی ارزش کردن bi-arzesh kardan
cheat *v.* گول زدن gul zadan
cheat *v.* تقلب کردن taqal~ob kardan
cheat *v.* جر زدن jer zadan
cheater *n.* متقلب moteqal~eb جرزن jer-zan
check *v.* کیش کردن kish kardan
check *v.* جلوگیری کردن jelogiri kardan
check *v.* رسیدگی کردن residegi kardan
check *n.* چک check
check-book *n.* دسته چک dasteh chek
check-up *n.* معاینه mo'âyeneh
checker *n., vt.* شطرنجی shatranji
checkmate *n., vt., int.* شاه مات shâh mât
cheek *n.* لپ lop گونه guneh عذار 'ozâr
cheeky *adj.* گستاخ gostâkh پررو por-ru
cheep *vi., vt., n.* جیر جیر کردن jirjir kardan
cheer *n., int., vt., vi.* تشویق کردن tashviq kardan
cheerful *adj.* بشاش bash~âsh با روح bâ-ruh گشاده رو goshâdeh-ru
cheerless *adj.* افسرده afsordeh
cheers! *interj.* بسلامتی be-salâmati نوش nush
cheese *int., vi., vt.* پنیر panir
chef *n.* شف shef سرآشپز sar âsh-paz
chemical *n., adj.* شیمیایی shimiâyi
chemist *n.* شیمیدان shimidân داروساز dârusâz
chemistry *n.* شیمی shimi
cherish *vt.* ارزش گذاشتن arzesh gozâshtan
گرامی داشتن gerâmi dâshtan
cherry *n., adj.* گیلاس gilâs
cherub(ic) *adj.* فرشته ای fereshteh-i کروبی kar~ubi
chess *n.* شطرنج shatranj
chest *n.* صندوق sandoq
chest *n.* سینه sineh
chestnut *n., adj.* شاه بلوط shâh balut
chew *vt., vi., n.* جویدن javidan
chewing-gum *n.* آدامس âdâms
chicanery *n.* دوزوکلک duz-o kalak
chick *n.* جوجه jujeh دختر dokhtar
chicken *n.* جوجه jujeh مرغ morq

chicken *adj.* ترسو tarsu بزدل boz-del
chide *vt.* سرزنش کردن sar-zanesh kardan
chief *adj.* عمده' omdeh اصلی asli
chief *n.* رئیس ra'is ارباب arbâb
child *n.* بچه bach~eh طفل tefl فرزند farzand
childbirth *n.* زایش zâyesh زایمان zâyemân
childish *adj.* بچه گانه bach~egâneh
childlike *adj.* بچه گانه bach~egâneh
children *n., pl.* بچه ها bach~eh-hâ اطفال atfâl فرزندان farzandân
chill *n., adj., vi., vt.* خنک کردن khonak kardan
سرد کردن sard kardan
chilled *n.* خنک khonak سرد شده sard-shodeh
chilly *adj., adv.* خنک khonak تگری tagari
chime *n., vi., vt.* زنگ زدن zang zadan
chimes *n.* زنگ آویز zang-âviz
chimney *n., vi.* دودکش dudkesh لوله luleh
chimpanzee *n.* شامپانزه shâmpânzeh
chin *n., vt., vi.* چانه châneh زنخدان zanakhdân ذقن zaqan
China *n.* چین chin
china *n., adj.* چینی chini
chip *n.* ژتون zheton
chip *v.* خرد کردن khord kardan ترک انداختن tarak dâdan
chipmunk *n.* سنجاب sanjâb
chipped *v.* ترک خورده tarak-khordeh لب پریده lab-parideh
chirp *vi., vt., n.* جیر جیر کردن jirjir kardan
chivalrous *adj.* جوانمرد javân-mard باشهامت bâ-shahâmat
chivalry *n.* جوانمردی javânmardi شهامت shahâmat مروت morev~at
chocolate *n., adj.* شکلات shokolât
choice *n.* انتخاب entekhâb پسند pasand
choice *adj.* ممتاز momtâz برگزیده bar-gozideh به گزین beh-gozin
choir *n., adj., vt., vi.* خواننده های کلیسا khânande-hâ-ye' kelisâ
choke *vt., vi., n.* خفه کردن khafeh kardan
cholera *n.* وبا vabâ
choose *vi.* انتخاب کردن entekhâb kardan برگزیدن bargozidan
chop *vt., vi., n.* خرد کردن khord kardan قطعه کردن qat'eh kardan
chopper *n.* ساطور sâtur
choppy *adj.* متلاطم motelâtem تکه تکه tekeh-tekeh
chops *n.* دندانها dandân-hâ لب و لوچه lab-o lucheh

chord *n.* تار târ
chord *n.* زه zeh وتر vatar
chore(s) *n.* کار روزانه kâr-e' ruzâneh
chorus *n., vt., vi.* سرود جمعی sorud-e' jam'i کر kor
chosen *v., adj.* منتخب montakhab برگزیده bargozideh
chowder *n.* آش ماهی âsh-e' mâhi
chraacteristic *n.* صفت اختصاصی sefat-e' ekhtesâsi
Christ *n.* مسیح masih حضرت عیسی hazrat-e' 'isâ
Christian *adj., n.* مسیحی masihi عیسوی 'isavi نصرانی nasrâni
       ترسا tarsâ
Christmas *n.* کریسمس kerismas
chrome *n., vt.* کروم korom آب نقره âb-noqreh
chronic *adj.* مزمن mozmen باسابقه bâ sâbeqeh
chronological *adj.* بترتیب تاریخ be-tartib-e' târikh
chronology *n.* ترتیب تاریخی tartib-e' târikhi
chrysanthemum *n.* گل داودی gol-e' dâvudi
chubby *adj.* خیکی khik~i گوشتالو gushtâlu توپول topol
chuck *n., vt., vi.* ول کردن vel kardan
       زیر چانه زدن zir-e' châneh zadan
chuckle *vi., n.* پوزخند زدن puz-khand zadan
chump *n., vt., vi.* احمق ahmaq
chunk *n.* قطعه qat'eh تکۀ بزرگ tekeh-ye' bozorg
church *n., vt.* کلیسا kelisâ
churn *n., vt., vi.* بهم زدن beham zadan
chute *n., vi., vt.* چتر chatr کاغذ انداز kâqaz-andâz
cider *n.* شربت سیب sharbat-e' sib
cigar *n.* سیگار برگ sigâr-e' barg
cigarette *n.* سیگار sigâr
cinder *n., vt.* خاکستر khâkestar نیم سوز nimsuz
cinema *n.* سینما sinamâ
cipher *n., vi., vt.* رمز گذاری ramz gozâri صفر sefr
circle *n.* دایره dâyereh محفل mahfel جرگه jargeh
circle *v.* دایره زدن dâyereh zadan حلقه کردن halqeh kardan
circuit *n., vt., vi.* مدار madâr گردش gardesh
circular *adj., n.* دایره ای dâyerehyi گرد gerd بخشنامه bakhshnâmeh
circulate *vi., vt.* گردش کردن gardesh kardan چرخیدن charkhidan
circulation *n.* گردش gardesh جریان jaryân دوران davarân
circulation *n.* انتشار enteshâr تیراژ tirâzh

circumcize *n.* ختنه کردن khatneh kardan
circumcision *n.* ختنگی khatnegi
circumference *n.* محیط mohit پیرامون pirâmun
circumspect *adj.* با احتیاط bâ-ehtiât
circumstance *n., vt.* پیش آمد pish-âmad شرایط sharâyet وضع vaz'
circumstantial *adj.* مبنی برقرائن mabni bar qarâ'en
circumvent *vt.* دورزدن dor zadan پیش دستی کردن pishdasti kardan
circus *n.* سیرک sirk
cistern *n.* منبع manba' آب انبار âb-anbâr
citadel *n.* دژ dezh قلعهٔ شهری qal'eh-ye' shahri
citation *n.* تمجید tamjid تشویق نامه tashviq-nâmeh
citation *n.* جریمه jarimeh احضاریه ehzârieh
cite *n., vt.* ذکر کردن zekr kardan نقل کردن naql kardan
citizen *n.* تبعه taba'eh اهل ahl شهروند shahr-vand
citizenship *n.* تابعیت tâba'iyat
citron *n., adj.* بالنگ bâlang
citrus *n., adj.* مرکبات morak~abât
city *n.* شهر shahr
civic *adj.* شهری shahri اجتماعی ejtemâ'i
civil *adj.* شخصی shakhsi مدنی madani حقوقی hoquqi
civil right(s) *n.* حقوق قانونی hoquq-e' qânuni
civil service *np.* کارمند دولت kârmand-e' dolat
civil war *np.* جنگ داخلی jang-e' dâkheli
civilian *n., adj.* شخصی shakhsi غیر ارتشی qeyr-e' arteshi
civilize *vt.* متمدن کردن motemad~en kardan
civilized *vt.* متمدن motemad~en
clad *v., vt.* لباس پوشیده lebâs-pushideh
claim *vt., n.* ادعا کردن ed~e'â kardan خواستار شدن khâstâr shodan
claimant *n.* مدعی mod~a'i
clam *n., vi.* صدف خوراکی sadaf-e' khorâki
clam(up) *n.* دهن بستن dahan bastan
clamor *n.* سروصدا sar-o seda ولوله vel-veleh
clamor *vi., vt.* فریاد زدن faryâd zadan ولوله کردن vel-veleh kardan
clamp *vi., n., vt.* گیره گذاشتن gireh gozâshtan
clan *n.* دسته dasteh طائفه tâ'efeh خاندان khândân
clandestine *adj.* پنهانی penhâni مخفیانه makhfiâneh
clap *vt., vi., n.* کف زدن kaf zadan
clarification *n.* توضیح tozih وضوح vozuh

clarify *vt., vi.* روشن کردن roshan kardan
واضح نمودن vâzeh nemudan
clarinet *n.* قره نی qarahney
clash *vi., vt., n.* درگیر شدن dargir shodan بهم خوردن beham khordan
clasp *n.* گیره gireh
clasp *v.* جفت کردن cheft kardan
class *n.* کلاس kelâs طبقه tabaqeh زمره zomreh
classic *adj., n.* کلاسیک kelâsik قدیمی qadimi یکتا yektâ
classification *n.* طبقه بندی tabaqeh-bandi
classified *adj., n.* محرمانه mahramâneh کلاسه kelâseh
classify *vt.* طبقه بندی کردن tabaqeh-bandi kardan
classroom *n.* کلاس kelâs
clatter *vi., vt., n.* تق تق کردن teqteq kardan قرچ قرچ qerech qerech
clause *n.* ماده mâd~eh بند band
claustrophobia *n.* ترس از جای تنگ tars az jâ-ye' tang
claw *n., vt., vi.* پنجه زدن panjeh zadan چنگال changâl
clay *n., vt.* گل gel خاک رس khâk-e' ros
clean *adj.* تمیز tamiz پاک pâk پاکیزه pâkizeh طیب tay~eb
clean *v.* تمیز کردن tamiz kardan پاک کردن pâk kardan
clean-cut *adj.* تروتازه tar-o tâzeh
cleanliness *n.* تمیزی tamizi پاکیزگی pâkizegi طهارت tahârat
نظافت nezâfat
cleanse *vt., vi.* تمیز کردن tamiz kardan پاک کردن pâk kardan
cleanser *n.* شوینده shuyandeh
clear *adj., adv., vt., vi.* واضح vâzeh روشن roshan
clear *v.* واضح کردن vâzeh kardan روشن کردن roshan kardan
clear *adj.* صاف sâf باز آنتابی âftâbi bâz
clear-cut *adj.* صریح sarih واضح vâzeh
clear-sighted *adj.* روشن بین roshan-bin بصیر basir
clearance *n.* فروش کلی forush-e' kol~i حراج harâj
clearance *n.* تصفیه tasfiyeh مفاصا mafâsâ
cleared *n.* پاک شده pâk-shodeh مبری mobar~â
clearing *n.* صاف شدگی sâf-shodegi پاک شدگی pâk-shodegi
clearly *adv.* بروشنی be-roshani بوضوح be-vosuh
clearness *n.* روشنی roshani وضوح vozuh
cleat *n., vt.* پیچ کفش pich-e' kafsh
cleavage *n.* شکاف shekâf چاک پستان châk-e' pestân
cleave *vt., vi.* شکاف دادن shekâf dâdan

cleaver *n.* ساطور sâtur

cleft *n., v., adj.* ترک tarak چاله châleh شکاف shekâf

clemency *n.* بخشش bakhshesh رحم rahm عفو 'afv

clench *vt., vi., n.* گره کردن gereh kardan محکم بستن mohkam bastan

clergy *n.* روحانیون ruhâniun علما 'olamâ

clergyman *n.* روحانی ruhâni ملا mol~â

clerical *adj., n.* دفتری daftari انشائی enshâ'i

clerk *n., vi.* دفتر دار daftar-dâr منشی monshi کارمند kâr-mand

clever *adj.* باهوش bâ-hush زیرک zirak

cleverness *n.* زیرکی ziraki ذکاوت zekâvat

click *n., vi., vt.* تیک تیک کردن tik-tik kardan

client(ele) *n.* مشتری moshtari موکل movak~el

cliff *n.* صخره sakhreh پرتگاه part-gâh

climate *n.* آب و هوا âb-o havâ

climax *n., vt., vi.* اوج oj انتهای لذت entehâ-ye' lez~at

climb *vi., vt., n.* رفتن بالا bâlâ raftan بالا روی bâlâ-ravi

clinch *vt., vi., n.* رفع کردن raf' kardan

cling *vi., n.* آویزان شدن âvizân shodan چسبیدن chasbidan

clinical *adj.* بالینی bâlini تمیز tamiz

clip *n., vt., vi.* چیدن chidan کوتاه کردن kutâh kardan

clippers *n.* قیچی qeychi

clique *n., vi.* دسته dasteh دارودسته dâr-o dasteh

cloak *n., vt.* ردا redâ خرقه kherqeh

cloak-and-dagger *adj.* جاسوس بازی jâsus-bâzi

clobber *vt., n., vi.* له و لورده کردن leh-o lavardeh kardan

clock *n., vt., vi.* ساعت sâ'at

clockwise *adv., adj.* مطابق گردش ساعت motâbeq-e' gardesh-e' sâ'at

clockwork *n.* ماشینی mâshini یکسره yek-sareh

clod *n.* احمق ahmaq پخمه pakhmeh

clog *vt., vi., n.* گیر کردن gir kardan مسدود کردن masdud kardan

close *adj.* نزدیک nazdik شبیه shabih

close *v.* بستن bastan تعطیل کردن ta'til kardan

closed *adj., v.* بسته basteh تعطیل ta'til

closely *adv.* ازنزدیک az-nazdik بدقت be-deq~at

closeness *n.* نزدیکی nazdiki قرب qorb

closet *n., adj., vt.* گنجه ganjeh

closure *n., vt., vi.* بستگی bastegi تعطیلی ta'tili خاتمه khâtemeh

clot *n., vi., vt.* لخته lakhteh

cloth *n., adj.* پارچه pârcheh
clothe *vt.* پوشاندن pushândan
clothes *pl.* لباس lebâs رخت rakht
clothing *n., vt.* لباس lebâs رخت rakht تن پوش tan-push
cloud *n., vt., vi.* ابر abr لکه lak~eh
cloudy *adj.* ابری abri تیره tireh تار târ کدر keder
clout *vt.* زور zur قدرت qodrat
clover *n.* شبدر shabdar
clown *n., vi.* دلقک dalqak ملیجک malijak
club *n.* خاج khâj گشنیز geshniz
club *n.* چماق chomâq
club *n.* باشگاه bâsh-gâh کلوب kolub
club-house *n.* باشگاه bâsh-gâh کلوب kolub
cluck *vi., vt., n.* غد غد کردن qod-qod kardan
clue *v.* راهنمایی کردن râh-namâyi kardan
clue *n.* کلید kelid
clump *n., vi., vt.* انبوه anbuh کلوخ kolukh
clumsy *adj.* شلخته shelakhteh دست و پاچلفتی dast-o pâ cholofti
cluster *n., vt., vi.* انبوه کردن ânbuh kardan
clutch *n.* کلاچ kelâch
clutch *v.* به چنگ گرفتن bechang gereftan
clutter *vt., vi., n.* درهم و بر هم darham-o bar ham
ریخته پاشیده rikhteh pâshideh
co-star *n., vi., vt.* هنرپیشهٔ دوم honar-pisheh-y'e dov~om
co-worker *n.* همکار ham-kâr
coach *n.* مربی mor~abi
coach *v.* تعلیم دادن ta'lim dâdan
coach *n.* کالسکه kâleskeh دلیجان delijân
coagulate *vt., vi., adj.* بستن bastan منعقد شدن mon'aqed shodan
coagulation *n.* انعقاد en'eqâd
coal *n., vt., vi.* ذغال سنگ zoqâl sang
coalesce *vi., vt.* بهم پیوستن beham peyvastan
coalescence *n.* پیوستگی peyvastegi ائتلاف e'telâf
coalition *n.* همبستگی ham-bastegi ائتلافی e'telâfi
coarse *adj.* بی ادب bi-adab
coarse *adj.* زبر zebr خشن khashen درشت dorosht
coast *n.* ساحل sâhel کرانه karâneh
coast *v.* خلاص رفتن khalâs raftan

coaster *n.* زيرليواني zir livâni
coat *v.* پوشش دادن pushesh dâdan
coat *n.* نيم تنه nim-taneh كت kot
coat *n.* روكش rukesh
coat *n.* آستر âstar لايه lâyeh
coat of arms *np.* آرم ârm
coat-hanger *n.* چوب رختى chub-rakhti
coax *n., vt., vi.* زيرپانشستن zir-e' pâ neshastan
ترغيب كردن tarqib kardan
cob *n.* چوب بلال chub-e' balâl
cobble(stone) *n.* قلوه سنگ qolveh-sang سنگ فرش sang-farsh
cobweb *n., vt.* تارعنكبوت târ'-ankabut
cockcomb *n.* تاج خروس tâj-e' khorus
cockeye *n.* چشم غره cheshm qor~eh چپ چپ chap-chap
cockpit *n.* كابين خلبان kâbin-e' khalebân
cockroach *n.* سوسك susk
cocktail *n., vt., vi., adj.* نوشابهٔ الكلى nushâbeh-ye' alkoli
coconut *n.* نارگيل nârgil
cocoon *n., vi., vt.* پيله pileh
cod *n., pl.* ماهى روغن mâhi-e' roqan
code *n.* قانون qânun
code *n.* رمز ramz سر ser~
coeducational *adj.* پسرانه دخترانه pesarâneh-dokhtarâneh
coefficient *n., adj.* ضريب zarib
coerce *vt.* مجبوركردن majbur kardan
coercion *n.* اجبار ejbâr زورگويى zur guyi
coexist *vi.* باهم زيستن bâ-ham zistan
coexistence *n.* هم زيستى ham-zisti
coffee *n., adj.* قهوه qahveh
coffin *n., vt.* تابوت tâbut
cognate *adj., n.* شبيه shabih همريشه hamrisheh
cognizance *n.* آگاهى âgâhi درك dark درايت derâyat
cognizant *adj.* آگاه âgâh ملتفت moltafet
cohabit *vi.* هم زيستى كردن hamzisti kardan
cohabitation *n.* هم زيستى hamzisti
coherence *n.* ارتباط ertebât پيوستگى peyvastegi
coherent *adj.* مرتبط mortabet پيوسته peyvasteh
cohesion *n.* چسبندگى chasbandegi هم بستگى ham-bastegi

cohesive *adj.* چسبنده chasbandeh
cohort *n.* هم نشین ham-neshin هم کاسه ham-kâseh دمخور dam-khor
coil *v.* چنبره زدن chanbareh zadan حلقه زدن halqeh zadan
coil *n.* حلقه halqeh سیم پیچ sim-pich
coil *n.* دینام dinâm
coin *n.* سکه sek~eh
coinage *n.* ضرب سکه zarb-e' sek~eh
coincide *vi.* مصادف شدن mosâdef shodan
مطابق شدن motâbeq shodan
coincidence *n.* تصادف tasâdof اتفاق et~efâq انطباق entebâq
coincident *adj.* مصادف mosâdef
coincidently *n.* تصادفا tasâdofan اتفاقا et~efâqan
coitus *n.* جماع jamâ'
cold *adj., n.* بی احساس bi-ehsâs بی اشتیاق bi-eshtiâq
cold *adj., n.* سرد sard سرما sarmâ
cold *adj., n.* سرماخوردگی sarmâ-khordegi
cold sore *np.* تبخال tab-khâl
cold-blooded *adj.* خونسرد khun-sard
cold-hearted *adj.* سنگدل sang-del بی عاطفه bi-'âtefeh
coleslaw *n.* سالاد کلم sâlâd-e' kalam
colic *n., adj.* قولنج qulenj
coliseum *n.* استادیوم estâdiom
collaborate *vi.* همکاری کردن ham-kâri kardan
همدستی کردن ham-dasti kardan
collaboration *n.* همکاری ham-kâri دست بیکی dast beyeki
همدستی ham-dasti تبانی tabâni
collaborator *n.* همکار ham-kâr همدست ham-dast
collapse *vi., vt., n.* فروریختن foru rikhtan غش کردن qash kardan
collar *v.* یقه گرفتن yaqeh gereftan گریبان گرفتن garibân gereftan
خر گرفتن kher gereftan
collar-bone *n.* ترقوه tar-qoveh
collateral *adj., n.* کناری kenâri جنبی janbi
collateral *adj., n.* وثیقه vasiqeh ضمانت zemânat
collateral damage *n.* تلفات غیرنظامی talafât-e' qeyr-e' nezâmi
colleague *n.* همکار ham-kâr همقطار ham-qatâr
collect *v.* وصول کردن vosul kardan
collect *v.* جمع کردن jam' kardan گردآوردن gerd-âvardan
collection *n.* وصول vosul دریافت dar-yâft گردآوری gerd-âvari

collection *n.* مجموعه majmu'eh کلکسیون koleksion
collection agency *n.* اداره وصول مطالبات edâreh-ye' vosul-e' motâlebât

collective *adj., n.* دسته جمعی dasteh jam'i همگانی hamegâni
collectively *adv.* جمعاً jam'an دسته جمعی dasteh jam'i
collector *n.* جمع کننده jam'-konandeh گردآورنده gerd-âvarandeh
college *n.* دانشکده dânesh-kadeh کالج kâlej
collegiate *adj.* دانشکده ای dânesh-kadeh-i کالجی kâlej-i
collide *vi.* تصادم کردن tasâdom kardan بهم خوردن be-ham khordan
collision *n.* تصادف tasâdof
colloquial *adj.* عامیانه 'âmiâneh محاوره ای mohâvereh-i
گفتگویی goftegu-yi
collude *vi.* گاوبندی کردن gâv-bandi kardan تبانی کردن tabâni kardan
collusion *n.* گاو بندی gâv-bandi تبانی tabâni
colon *n.* ویرگول virgul
colonel *n.* سرهنگ sar-hang
colonial *adj., n.* مستعمره ای mosta'mereh-i
colonist *n.* مستعمره نشین mosta'mereh-neshin
colonize *vi.* استعمار کردن este'mâr kardan
colony *n.* مستعمره mosta'mereh کوچ نشین kuch-neshin
color *n.* رنگ rang فام fâm گون gun
color *v.* رنگ زدن rang zadan
color-blind *adj.* کوررنگ kur-rang
colorful *adj.* بانشاط bâ-neshât رنگین rangin
colossal *adj.* بزرگ bozorg غول پیکر qul-peykar عظیم 'azim
colt *n.* کره اسب kor~eh asb
column *n.* ستون sotun ردیف radif رج raj
coma *n.* بیهوشی bihushi اغماء eqmâ'
comb *n., vt., vi.* شانه کردن shâneh kardan
combat *n.* نبرد: nabard رزم razm
combat *v.* نبردکردن nabard kardan مبارزه کردن mobârezeh kardan
combatant *n., adj.* مبارز mobârez رزمجو razm-ju
combative *adj.* رزمی razmi جنگجو jang-ju
combination *n.* مخلوط makhlut ترکیب tarkib مجموع majmu'
combine *vt., vi., n.* ترکیب کردن tarkib kardan
مخلوط کردن makhlut kardan
combustible *adj., n.* آتشزا âtash-zâ محترق mohtareq
come *v.* آمدن âmadan

come(about) *n.* اتفاق افتادن et~efâq oftâdan
come(across) *n.* برخوردن bar khordan
come(around) *n.* بهوش آمدن behush âmadan
قبول کردن qabul kardan
come(back) *n.* برگشتن bar gashtan مراجعت کردن morâje'at kardan
come(through) *n.* موفق شدن movaf~aq shodan
بقول عمل کردن beqol 'amal kardan
comedian *n.* هنرپیشهٔ کمدی honar-pisheh-ye' komedi
comedy *n.* طنز tanz کمدی komedi
comely *adj.* خوبرو khubru
comet *n.* ستارهٔ دنباله دار setâreh-ye' donbâleh-dâr
comfort *v.* آسایش دادن âsâyesh dâdan تسلی دادن tasal~i dâdan
comfort *n.* آسایش âsâyesh تسلی tasal~i راحتی râhati
comfortable *adj., n.* راحت râhat آسوده âsudeh
comforting *n.* تسلی بخش tasal~i-bakhsh
آسایش دهنده âsâyesh-dahandeh
comic *adj., n.* مضحک moz-hek خنده دار khandeh-dâr
coming *n., v., adj.* بعدی ba'di آینده âyandeh
command *v.* فرمان دادن farmân dâdan ریاست داشتن riâsat dâshtan
command *n.* فرمان farmân حکم hokm فرمایش farmâyesh
دستور dastur
commandant *n.* فرمانده farmândeh سرکرده sar-kardeh
commandeer *vt.* بزورگرفتن bezur gereftan
commander *n.* فرمانده farmândeh سرکرده sar-kardeh
commanding *adj.* بااختیار bâ-ekhtiâr آمرانه âmerâneh
commandment *n.* فرمان farmân دستور dastur حکم hokm
commando *n.* کماندو komândo چریک cherik
commemorate *vt.* یادبود کردن yâd-bud kardan
یادگاری نگه داشتن yâdegâri negah-dâshtan
commemoration *n.* یادبود yâd-bud یادگاری yâdegâri اجلال ejlâl
commence *vi., vt.* شروع کردن shoru' kardan آغاز کردن âqâz kardan
commencement *n.* شروع آغاز shoru' âqâz
فارغ التحصیلی fâreqol-tahsili
commend *vt.* ستایش کردن setâyesh kardan
تمجید کردن tamjid kardan ستودن sotudan
commendable *adj.* قابل تمجید qâbel-e' tamjid ستوده sotudeh
قابل ستایش qâbel-e' setâyesh
comment *n., vi., vt.* نظریه دادن nazarieh dâdan

تفسیرکردن .... tafsir kardan
commentary *n.* نظریه nazarieh تفسیر tafsir
commentator *n.* تفسیرکننده tafsir konandeh مفسر mofas~er
commerce *n.* تجارت tejârat بازرگانی bâzargâni
commercial *adj., n.* تجارتی tejârati
commissar *n.* کمیسر komiser مأمور ma'mur کلانتر kalântar
commissary *n.* کلانتری kalântari فروشگاه ارتشی forushgâh-e' arteshi
commission *n.* کارمزد kâr-mozd درجه darejeh کمیسیون komision
commission *n.* مأموریت ma'muriyat کمیسیون komision
commissioner *n.* کمیسر komiser مأمور ma'mur کلانتر kalântar
commit *v.* مرتکب شدن mortakeb shodan
commit *v.* تحویل دادن tah-vil dâdan
commitment *n.* تعهد ta'ah~od
committed *vt.* متعهد mote'ah~ed
committee *n.* کمیته komiteh انجمن anjoman
commode *n.* جارختی jâ-rakhti کمد komod
commodity *n.* کالا kâlâ جنس jens
commodore *n.* ناوسروان nâv-sarvân
common *adj.* مشترک moshtarek
common *n.* عادی 'âd~i عمومی 'omumi معمول ma'mul
متداول motedâvel
common law *np.* عرف 'orf
commoner *n.* عام 'âm~ غیراشرافی qeyr-e' ashrâfi
commonly *adv.* معمولاً ma'mulan
commonplace *adj., n.* معمولی ma'muli
پیش پا افتاده pish-e' pâ oftâdeh
commonwealth *n.* بازارمشترک bâzâr-e' moshtarek
commotion *n.* سروصدا sar-o sedâ شلوغی sholuqi
communal *adj.* اشتراکی eshterâki
commune *n., v., vi.* زندگی اشتراکی zendegi-e' eshterâki
communicate *vt., vi.* درتماس بودن dar tamâs budan
ابلاغ کردن eblâq kardan
communication *n.* ابلاغ eblâq خبر khabar
ارتباط فکری ertebât-e' fekri
communion *n.* سوگند دینی sogand-e' dini
communique' *n.* ابلاغیه eblâqieh پیغام pey-qâm
communism *n.* کمونیستی komonisti
communist *n., adj.* کمونیست komonist

community *n.* جامعه jâme'eh محله mahal~eh
community chest *np.* بيت المال beytol-mâl
commutation *n.* تعويض ta'viz تخفيف جرم takhfif-e' jorm
commute *v.* تخفيف دادن takhfif dâdan
commute *vt., vi.* رفت و آمد روزانه raft-o âmad-e' ruzâneh
ایاب و ذهاب ay~âb-o zahâb
commuter *n.* راننده rânandeh
compact *adj., vt., n.* فشرده feshordeh خلاصه kholâseh
companion *n., vt.* همدم ham-dam همراه ham-râh
همنشین ham-neshin نديم nadim
companionship *n.* همدمى ham-dami همراهى ham-râhi
مصاحبت mosahebat
company *n.* گروهان goruhân
company *n.* مهمان mehmân
company *n.* شركت sherkat
comparable *adj.* قابل مقايسه qâbel-e' moqâyeseh
comparative *adj., n.* تطبيقى tatbiqi
comparatively *adv.* نسبتاً nesbatan
compare *vt., vi., n.* مقايسه كردن moqâyeseh kardan
comparison *n.* مقايسه moqâyeseh تشبيه tashbih سنجش sanjesh
compartment *n., vt.* محفظه mah-fazeh قسمت qesmat كوپه kupeh
compass *n., adj., vt.* پرگار par-gâr قطب نما qotb-namâ
compassion *n., vt.* دلسوزى del-suzi ترحم tarah~om شفقت shafeq~at
compassionate *adj., vt.* رحيم rahim دلسوز del-suz
compatibility *n.* باهم سازى bâham-sâzi سازگارى sâzgâri
compatible *adj.* سازگار sâzgâr
compatriot *n., adj.* هم ميهن ham-mihan
compel *vt., vi.* مجبوركردن majbur kardan تنفيذكردن tanfiz kardan
compelled *adj.* مجبور majbur ناچار nâ-char
compelling *v.* اجبارى ejbâri
compensate *vt., vi.* جبران كردن jobrân kardan
تلافى درآوردن talâfi dar-âvardan
compensation *n.* جبران jobrân تلافى talâfi غرامت qarâmat
compete *vi.* رقابت كردن reqâbat kardan
competence *n.* شايستگى shâyestegi صلاحيت salâhiyat
competency *n.* شايستگى shâyestegi صلاحيت salâhiyat
competent *adj.* شايسته shâyesteh صلاحيت دار sâlâhiyat-dâr
competition *n.* رقابت reqabat مسابقه mosâbeqeh

competitive *adj.* رقابتى reqâbati
competitor *n.* رقیب raqib
compilation *n.* تألیف ta'lif
compile *vt.* انباشتن anbâshtan گردآوردن gerd âvardan
compiled *,,,* گردآورده شده gerd-âvardeh shodeh مدون modav~en
complacence *n.* خودخوشنودى khod-khoshnudi تن آسایى tan-âsâyi
complacency *n.* خودخوشنودى khod-khoshnudi
complacent *adj.* خودخوشنود khod-khoshnud راضى râzi
    تن آسا tan-âsâ
complain *vi.* شکایت کردن shekâyat kardan
    چغلى کردن choqoli kardan گلایه کردن gelâyeh kardan
complainant *n.* شاکى shâki
complaint *n.* شکایت shekâyat گله geleh شکوه shekveh گلایه gelâyeh
complaisance *n.* خوش خدمتى khosh-khedmati
    حاضربخدمتى hâzer be-khedmati
complaisant *adj.* حاضربه اطاعت hâzer beh etâ'at
    حلقه بگوش halqeh begush
complement *n., vt., vi.* مکمل mokam~el متمم motam~am
complete *adj., vt.* کامل کردن kâmel kardan تمام کردن tamâm kardan
completion *n.* تکمیل takmil انجام anjâm اتمام etmâm
complex *adj., n.* پیچیده pichideh غامض qâmez
complex *adj., n.* عقده 'oqdeh
complex *adj., n.* مجموعه majmu'eh
complexion *n.* نما namâ سیما simâ رنگ و رو rang-o ru
complexity *n.* پیچیدگى pichidegi
compliance *n.* اطاعت etâ'at اجرا ejrâ
compliant *adj.* مطیع moti' فروتن forutan
complicate *vt., adj.* پیچیده کردن pichideh kardan
complicated *v.* پیچیده pichideh مشکل moshkel
complication *n.* پیچیدگى pichidegi
complicity *n.* همدستى hamdasti شراکت جرم sherâkat-e' jorm
compliment *n., vt., vi.* تعریف کردن ta'rif kardan
    تعارف کردن tâ'rof kardan
complimentary *adj.* تعارفى tâ'ârofi اهدایى ehdâyi اشانتیون eshântion
comply *vi.* پذیرفتن paziroftan اطاعت کردن etâ'at kardan
component *adj., n.* جزء joz' عنصر 'onsor
compose *v.* ترکیب کردن tarkib kardan
compose *v.* سراییدن sarâyidan تصنیف ساختن tasnif sâkhtan

composed *v.* متكى بخود آرام ârâm mot~aki bekhod
composite *adj., n.* متشكل moteshak~el مركب morak~ab
composition *n.* تركيب tarkib انشاء enshâ' آهنگ سازى âhang sâzi
compost *n.* كود گياهى kud-e' giâhi
composure *n.* آرامش ârâmesh آسودگى âsudegi متانت metânat
compound *adj.* مركب morak~ab
compound *v.* روى هم گذاشتن ruy-e' ham gozâshtân
compound verb *n.* فعل مركب fe'le morak~ab
compound(s) *n.* محوطه mohavat~eh حياط hayât
comprehend *vt.* فهميدن fahmidan دريافتن daryâftan
comprehensible *adj.* فهميدنى fahmidani دريافتنى daryâftani
comprehension *n.* فهم fahm ادراك edrâk
comprehensive *adj., n.* قابل فهم qâbel-e' fahm
اول تا آخر از az av~al tâ âkhar مشروح mashruh
compress *vt., n.* بهم فشردن beham feshordan
compression *n.* فشردگى feshordegi
compressor *n.* كمپرسور kompresor
comprised(of) *n.* مركب morak~ab شامل shâmel-e'
compromise *v.* بخطرانداختن be-khatar andâkhtân
compromise *v.* سازش كردن sâzesh kardan
مصالحه كردن mosâleheh kardan
compromising *v.* رسواآميز rosvâ-âmiz
compulsion *n.* اجبار ejbâr التزام eltezâm
compulsion *n.* اجبارى ejbâri التزامى eltezâmi
compulsive *adj., n.* معتاد mo'tâd
compulsory *adj.* اجبارى ejbâri لزومى lozumi
computation *n.* محاسبه mohâsebeh حساب hesâb
compute *vt., vi., n.* محاسبه كردن mohâsebeh kardan
حساب كردن hesâb kardan
computer *n.* كامپيوتر kâmpiuter
comrade *n.* رفيق rafiq هم رزم ham-razm
comutate *n.* تبديل جريان برق tabdil-e' jaryân-e' barg
con *vt., n.* كلك زدن kalak zadan
كلاه بردارى كردن kolâh-bardâri kardan
con-artist *n.* شياد shay~âd كلاه بردار kolâh-bardâr
concave *adj., n., vt.* مقعر moqa'ar كاو kâv
conceal *vt.* پنهان كردن penhân kardan قايم كردن qâyem kardan
concealed *n.* مخفى makhfi پنهان penhân

concealment *n.* اخفاء ekhfâ' كتمان ketmân
concede *vt., vi.* واگذاركردن vâgozâr kardan قبول کردن qabul kardan
conceit *n., vt.* تكبر takab~ or خودبینی khodbini
conceited *adj.* متكبر motek~aber خودبین khodbin
conceivable *adj.* درک کردنی dark kardani احتمالی ehtemâli
conceive *vt., vi.* تصوركردن tasavor kardan نطفه بستن notfeh bastan
concentrate *vt., vi., n.* تمرکز کردن tamarkoz kardan
concentrated *adj.* متمرکز motemarkez
concentration *n.* تمرکز tamarkoz غلظت qelzat
حواس جمعی havâs jam'i
concentric *adj.* هم مرکز ham-markaz
concept *n.* مفهوم mafhum
conception *n.* تصور tasav~ or مخیله mokhay~eleh
conception *n.* آبستنی âbestani
concern *vt., n.* مربوط شدن marbut shodan ربط داشتن rabt dashtan
concerned *adj.* مربوط marbut علاقمند 'alâqeh-mand دلواپس del-vâpas
concerning *pre.* دربارهٔ dar bâreh-ye راجع به râje' beh
concert *n., adj., vt., vi.* كنسرت konsert هم آهنگی ham-âhangi
concerted *adj.* دسته جمعی dasteh jam'i
concession *n.* امتیاز emtiâz واگذاری vâgozâri گذشت gozasht
conciliate *vt.* فرونشاندن foru neshândan شیفته کردن shifteh kardan
conciliation *n.* دلجویی deljuyi
conciliatory *adj.* دلجویانه deljuyâneh مسالمت آمیز mosâlemat-âmiz
concise *adj.* خلاصه kholâseh مختصر mokhtasar
conclave *n.* اطاق خصوصی otâq-e' khosusi
conclude *vt., vi.* پایان دادن pâyân dâdan
خاتمه دادن khâtemeh dâdan
conclusion *n.* پایان pâyân خاتمه khâtemeh عاقبت âqebat
conclusive *adj.* قطعی qat'i قاطع qâte'
concoct *vt.* جعل کردن ja'l kardan ازخوددرآوردن az khod dar âvardan
concoction *n.* معجون ma'jun
concord *n.* هم آهنگی ham-âhangi توافق tavâfoq
concourse *n.* اجتماع ejtemâ' هم جریان ham-jaryân
concrete *adj., n., vt., vi.* سمنت sement بتون beton
concrete *adj., n., vt., vi.* واقعی vâqe'i غیرخیالی qey-re khiâli
concubine *n.* صیغه siqeh
concur *vi.* موافقت کردن movâfeqat kardan
هم رئی بودن ham-ra'y budan

concurrence *n.* توافق tavâfoq هم جریانی ham-jaryâni

concurrent *adj., n.* در یک زمان dar yek zamân موافق movâfeq
مصادف mosadef

concurrently *adv.* همزمان ham-zamân

concussion *n.* تصادم tasâdom ضربهٔ مغزی zarbeh-ye' maqzi

condemn *vt.* محکوم کردن mahkum kardan تقبیح کردن taqbih kardan

condemnation *n.* محکومیت mahkumiyat

condensation *n.* قطرگی qatregi تقطیر taqtir

condensation *n.* خلاصگی kholâsegi فشردگی feshordegi

condense *vt., vi.* خلاصه کردن kholâseh kardan
غلیظ کردن qaliz kardan

condensed *v.* خلاصه kholâseh فشرده feshordeh

condescend *vi.* فروتنی کردن foru-tani kardan
تمکین کردن tamkin kardan

condescending *adj.* فروتن foru-tan مداراکننده modârâ-konandeh
خاکی khâki

condescension *n.* فروتنی foru-tani تمکین tamkin مماشات momashat

condiment *n.* ادویه advieh چاشنی châshni

condition *n., vt., vi.* وضع vaz' حالت hâlat شرط shart

conditional *adj., n.* شرطی sharti مشروط mashrut

condolence *n.* تسلیت tasliyat

condominium *n.* خانهٔ آپارتمانی khâneh-ye' âpârtemâni

condone *n.* اغماض کردن eqmâz kardan بدندانستن bad nadânestan

condor *n.* لاشخور lâshkhor کرکس karkas

conduce *vi.* منجرشدن monjar shodan

conducive *adj.* موجب mojeb

conduct *v.* جریان دادن jaryân dâdan رهبری کردن rahbari kardan

conduct *n.* جریان jaryân رفتار raftâr عمل 'amal

conduction *n.* انتقال enteqâl

conductor *n.* رهبر rahbar هادی hâdi بلیط چی belit-chi

conduit *n.* آبگذر âbgozar رابط râbet

cone *n., vt.* قیف qif مخروط makhrut

confection *n., vt.* شیرینی shirini

confectionery *n., adj.* شیرینی فروشی shirini forushi قنادی qanâdi

confederacy *n.* اتحادیهٔ ایالتی etehâdieh-ye' ayâlati

confederate *adj., n., vt., vi.* هم پیمان کردن ham-peymân kardan

confederation *n.* کنفدراسیون konfederâsion

confer *vt., vi.* مشورت کردن mashverat kardan

confer(upon) *n.* اعطاء کردن e'tâ' kardan
conference *n.* مذاکره mozâkereh کنفرانس konferâns
مشورت mashverat
confess *vt., vi.* اعتراف کردن e'terâf kardan اقرار کردن eqrâr kardan
confession *n.* اعتراف e'terâf اقرار eqrâr
confessional *adj., n.* اعتراف گاه e'terâf-gâh
confidant *n.* محرم راز mahram-e' râz خودی khodi همراز ham-râz
مقرب moqar~eb
confide *vi., vt.* اعتماد داشتن e'temâd dâshtan
محرمانه گفتن mahramâneh goftan
confidence *n.* اعتماد e'temâd اطمینان etminân وثوق vosuq
confident *adj., n.* مطمئن motma'en وثیق vasiq
confidential *adj.* محرمانه mahramâneh
configuration *n.* ترکیب tarkib شکل shekl
confine *vt., n.* حبس کردن habs kardan
منحصر کردن monhaser kardan
confined *v.* محدود mahdud بستری bastari زندانی zendâni
confinement *n.* حبس habs انحصار enhesâr توقیف toqif
confirm *vt.* تأیید کردن ta'id kardan تصدیق کردن tasdiq kardan
confirmation *n.* تأیید ta'id تصدیق tasdiq
confirmed *adj.* تأیید شده ta'id-shodeh تصدیق شده tasdiq-shodeh
محرز مبرم mobram محرز mohraz
confiscate *vt., adj.* ضبط کردن zabt kardan توقیف کردن toqif kardan
confiscation *n.* ضبط zabt توقیف toqif
conflict *vi., n.* مغایرت moqâyerat
conflict *v.* زدوخورد کردن zad-o khord kardan
نزاع کردن nezâ' kardan
conflict *n.* زدوخورد zad-o khord نزاع nezâ'
conflicting *n.* ضدونقیض zed~-o nâqiz مغایر moqâyer
confluence *n.* هم جریانی ham-jaryâni
confluent *adj., n.* هم جریان ham-jaryân
conform *vi., vt., adj.* سازش کردن sâzesh kardan وفق دادن vefq dâdan
conformation *n.* سازش sâzesh وفق vefq تطبیق tatbiq
conforming *n.* سازشکار sâzeshkâr مطیع moti'
conformist *n., adj.* سازشکار sâzeshkâr مطیع moti'
conformity *n.* مطابقت motâbeqat اطاعت etâ'at
confound *vt.* گیج کردن gij kardan مغشوش کردن maqshush kardan
confront *vt.* مواجه شدن movâjeh shodan

مقابله‌كردن .... moqâbeleh kardan

confrontation *n.* درگیری dargiri رودررو رو ru dar-ru صحبت sohbat-e' ru dar-ru
مواجه movajeheh تقابل taqâbol

confuse *vt.* گیج كردن gij kardan اشتباه كردن eshtebâh kardan

confusion *n.* گیجی giji اغتشاش eqteshâsh
درهم برهمی dar-ham barhami

congenial *adj.* دم خور damkhor هم مشرب ham-mashrab

congenital *adj.* مادرزادی mâdar-zâdi

congest *vt., vi.* انبوه كردن anbuh kardan
پرجمعیت كردن por-jam'iyat kardan

congestion *n.* تراكم tarâkom گرفتگی gereftegi

conglomerate *n., adj., vt., vi.* كمپانی بزرگ kompâni-ye' bozorg

conglomeration *n.* كمپانی بزرگ kompâni-ye' bozorg

congratulate *vt.* تبریک گفتن tabrik goftan

congratulation *n., int.* تبریک tabrik تهنیت tahniyat
شادباش shâd-bâsh

congregate *vi., vt., adj.* گردآوردن gerd âvardan
دورهم جمع كردن dor-e' ham jam' kardan

congregation *n.* جماعت jamâ'at گردهمایی gerd-e' ham-âyi
تجمع tajam~o'

congress *n., vi.* مجلس majles كنگره kongereh

congressman *n.* نمایندهٔ كنگره namâyandeh-ye' kongereh

congruent *adj.* موافق movâfeq مساوی mosâvi

congruous *adj.* متناسب motenâseb

conjecture *n., vt., vi.* حدس hads ظن zan~

conjugal *adj.* ازدواجی ezdevâji نكاحی nekâhi

conjugate *vt., vi., adj., n.* صرف كردن sarf kardan

conjunction *n.* پیوستگی peyvastegi حرف ربط harf-e' rabt

conjure *vt., vi.* تجسم كردن tajas~om kardan قسم دادن qasam dâdan

conjure(up) *n.* ازخوددرآوردن az khod dar âvardan

connect *vt., vi.* وصل كردن vasl kardan

connection *n.* ارتباط ertebât نسبت nesbat پارتی pârti

connivance *n.* دست بیكی dast be-yeki اغماض eqmâz

connive *vi.* دست بیكی كردن dast beh-yeki kardan
نادیده گرفتن nâdideh gereftan

conniving *vi.* حیله گر muzi حیله گر hileh-gar
اغماض كننده eqmâz-konandeh آب زیركاه âb zir-e' kâh

connoisseur *n.* متخصص motekhas~es خبره khebreh

connotation *n.* اشاره eshâreh معنى ma'nâ

conquer *vt., vi.* فتح کردن fat-h kardan

conqueror *n.* فاتح fâteh پیروز piruz

conquest *n.* فتح fat-h پیروزی piruzi سیطره seytareh

conscience *n.* وجدان vejdân

conscientious *n., adj.* باوجدان bâ-vejdân هوشیار hoshyâr
وظیفه شناس vazifeh-shenâs

conscious *adj., n.* ملتفت moltafet هوشیار hoshyâr

consciously *adv.* هوشیارانه hoshyârâneh

consciousness *n.* هوشیاری hoshyâri

conscript *vt., n., adj.* سربازوظیفه sarbâz-e' vazifeh

conscription *n.* سربازگیری sarbâz-giri

consecutive *adj.* پی دریی pey-dar-pey متوالی motevâli

consecutively *adv.* پشت سر هم posht-e' sâr-e' hâm
متوالیاً motevâliyan

consensus *n.* عقیده 'aqideh نظر nazar

consent *vi., n.* رضایت دادن rezâyat dadan
موافقت کردن movâfeqat kardan

consequence *n.* نتیجه natijeh عاقبت 'âqebat

consequently *adv.* درنتیجه dar natijeh عاقبت الامر 'âqebâtol amr
سرانجام sar-anjâm

conservation *n.* صرفه جویی sarfeh-juyi بقاء baqâ'

conservative *adj., n.* محافظه کار mohâfezeh-kâr

conserve *v.* صرفه جویی کردن sarfeh-juyi kardan

conserve *v.* مربا کردن mor~abâ kardan

consider *vt., vi.* ملاحظه کردن molâhezeh kardan

considerable *adj., n.* قابل ملاحظه qâbele molâhezeh
مقدارزیاد meqdâr-e' ziâd

considerate *adj.* باملاحظه bâ-molâhezeh

consideration *n.* ملاحظه molâhezeh توجه tavaj~oh

considering *pre., adv., con.* بادرنظرگرفتن bâ dar-nazar gereftan

consign *vt., vi.* سپردن sepordan امانت گذاشتن amânat gozâshtan

consignee *n.* محمول الیه girandeh گیرنده mahmul elayh

consignment *n.* واگذاری vâgozâri محموله mahmuleh

consist *vi., n.* مرکب بودن morak~ab budan

consistency *n.* پیوستگی peyvastegi ثبات sabât

consistent *adj.* پیوسته peyvasteh ثابت sâbet منظم monaz~am

consistently *adv.* مرتباً morat~aban پیوسته peyvasteh

consolation *n.* تسليت tasliat دلداری del-dâri

console *v.* دلداری دادن deldâri dâdan تسلی دادن tasal~i dâdan
دلجو یی کردن delju-yi kardan

console *n.* محفظه mahfazeh

consolidate *vt., vi., adj.* محکم کردن mohkam kardan
مقتدرکردن moqtader kardan

consolidation *n.* تحکیم tahkim

consonant *n., adj.* حرف گنگ harf-e' gong مصمت mosam~at

consort *n., vi., vt.* هم بستر hambastar

consort *n., vi., vt.* معاشرت کردن mo'âsherat kardan

conspicouous *n.* واضح vâzeh آشکار âshkâr

conspiracy *n.* توطئه tote'eh

conspirator *n.* توطئه چین tote'eh-chin همدست ham-dast

conspire *vi., vt.* توطئه چیدن tote'eh chidan

constable *n.* پاسبان pâsbân

constant *adj., n.* ثابت sâbet پایدار pâydâr دایمی dâ'emi

constipate *vt.* یبس شدن yobs shodan

constipated *vt.* یبس شده yobs-shodeh

constipation *n.* یبسی yobsi

constituency *n.* حوزهٔ انتخابی hozeh-ye' entekhâbi

constitute *vt.* تشکیل دادن tashkil dâdan مشروط شدن mashrut shodan

constitution *n.* قانون اساسی qânun-e' asâsi اساسنامه asâsnâmeh

constrain *v.* درفشارگذاشتن dar feshâr gozâshtan

constraint *n.* فشار feshâr اضطرار ezterâr

constrict *vt.* بهم فشردن beham feshordan

constriction *n.* نشردگی feshordegi

construct *vt., n.* ساختن sâkhtan بناکردن banâ kardan

construction *n.* ساختمان کاری sâkhtemân kâri بنا banâ بنائی ban~â'i

constructive *adj.* متشکل moteshak~el مثبت mosbat سازنده sâzandeh

constructor *n.* سازنده sâzandeh

construe *vt., vi., n.* تعبیرکردن ta'bir kardan

construed(as) *n.* تعبیر شده ta'bir shodeh باین عنوان be-in 'onvân

consul *n.* کنسول konsul قنسول qonsul

consulate *n.* کنسولگری konsulgari

consulate-general *n.* سرکنسولگری sar-konsulgari

consult *vt., vi., n.* مشورت کردن mashverat kardan

consultant *n.* مشاور moshâver رایزن rây-zan

consultation *n.* مشورت mashverat مشاوره moshâvereh

---

rây-zani رایزنی kankâsh کنکاش ....

consulting *n.* مشاور moshâver

consulting *n.* مشورت mashverat مشاوره moshâvereh

consultor *n.* مشاور moshâver

consume *vt., vi.* مصرف کردن masraf kardan سوزاندن suzândan

consumer *n.* مصرف کننده masraf-konandeh

consumption *n.* مصرف masraf استفاده estefâdeh

contact *n., vt., vi., adj.* تماس گرفتن tamâs gereftan ارتباط ertebât

contagious *adj.* واگیر vâ-gir مسری mosri

contain *vt.* شامل بودن shamel budan
درخود نگه داشتن dar-khod negah dasht

container *n.* ظرف zarf

contaminate *vt., adj.* آلوده کردن âludeh kardan
سرایت دادن sarâyat dâdan

contamination *n.* آلودگی âludegi

contemplate *vt., vi.* درنظرداشتن dar-nazar dâshtan
انتظارداشتن entezâr dâshtan

contemplation *n.* تفکر fekr تفکر tafak~ or پندار pendâr

contemporary *adj., n.* همزمان ham-zamân معاصر mo'âser

contempt *n.* اهانت ehânat خواری khâri

contemptuous *adj.* اهانت آمیز ehânat-âmiz خوارکننده khâr-konandeh

contend *vi., vt.* راضی بودن râzi budan مدعی بودن mod~a'i budan

contender *n.* مدعی mod~a'i جدال طلب jedâl-talab

content *adj., vt., n.* محتوی mohtavâ ظرفیت zarfiyat مضمون mazmun

content(ed) *adj.* راضی râzi قانع qâne' خوشنود khosh-nud

contention *n.* مجادله mojâdeleh معارضه mo'ârezeh

contentment *n.* رضایت rezâyat خوشنودی khoshnudi تناعت qanâ'at

contest *n.* مسابقه mosâbeqeh

contest *v.* مسابقه دادن mosâbeqeh dâdan

context *n.* متن matn زمینه zamineh شرایط sharâyet قرائن qarâ'en

contextual *adj.* زمینه ای zamineh-i قرینه ای qarineh-i

continent *n., adj.* قاره qâr~eh خوددار khod-dâr

continental *adj., n.* قاره ای qâr~eh-i شاهانه shâhâneh

contingency *n.* احتمال ehtemâl اضطرار ezterâr

contingent *adj., n.* موکول به mokul-beh
مشروط براینکه mashrut bar inkeh منوط manut

continual *adj.* دائمی dâ'emi مداوم modâvem

continually *adv.* دائماً dâ'eman

continuance *n.* دوام davâm ادامه edâmeh
continuation *n.* ادامه edâmeh دنباله donbâleh
continue *vi., vt.* ادامه دادن edâmeh dâdan دنبال کردن donbâl kardan
continued *v.* دنباله دار donbâleh-dâr موکول شده mokul-shodeh
continuity *n.* پیوستگی peyvastegi ادامه edâmeh
continuous *adj.* پیوسته peyvasteh دائم dâ'em متصل motas~el
continuously *adv.* دائما dâ'eman
contortion *n.* پیچ pich تاب tâb
contour *n., vt., adj.* شکل shekl پیچ و خم pich-o kham
contraband *n., adj.* قاچاق qâchâq
contrabass *n., adj.* ویولون سل violon sel
contraception *n.* جلوگیری ازنطفه بستن jelogiri az notfeh bastan
contraceptive *adj., n.* جلوگیرحاملگی jelogir-e' hâmelegi
contract *n.* قرارداد qarârdâd پیمان peymân
contract *v.* قراردادبستن qarârdâd bastan
contract *v.* مخفف کردن mokhaf~af kardan
contract *v.* مرض گرفتن maraz gereftan
contract *v.* منقبض کردن monqabez kardan
contraction *n.* انقباض enqebâz فشردگی feshordegi
contractor *n.* مقاطعه کار moqâte'eh-kâr پیمانکار peymân-kâr
contradict *vt., vi.* تناقض داشتن tanâqoz dâshtan
ضدو نقیض گفتن zed~-o naqiz goftan
contradiction *n.* نقض naqz تکذیب takzib تناقض tanâqoz
مغایرت moqâyerat
contradictory *adj., n.* متناقض motenâqez متضاد motazâd~
مغایر moqâyer
contraption *n.* اختراع غریب ekhterâ'-e' qarib معجون ma'jun
contrary *adj., n., adv.* معکوس ma'kus مخالف mokhâlef
contrast *n.* فرق farq مباینت mobâyenat
contrast *vt., vi., n.* فرق واضح داشتن farq-e' vâzeh dâsht
contribute *vt., vi.* کمک کردن komak kardan اهداکردن ehdâ kardan
contributing *v.* کمک komak
contribution *n.* کمک komak هدیه hadiyeh اعانه e'âneh
contributor *n.* کمک کننده komak-konandeh
contrite *adj.* پشیمان بودن pashimân budan
contrition *n.* پشیمانی pashimâni ندامت nedâmat
contrivance *n.* تدبیر tadbir
contrive *vt., vi.* تدبیرکردن tadbir kardan

control *vt., n.* جلوگیری jelogiri ممانعت momâne'at
control *vt., n.* نظارت nezârat بازدید bâz-did
control *vt., n.* اختیار ekhtiâr
control *v.* نظارت کردن nezârat kardan جلوگیری کردن jelogiri kardan
controller *n.* ناظر nâzer ممیز momay~ez
controversial *adj.* موردبحث mored-e' bahs مشاجره ای moshâjereh-i
controversy *n.* بحث bahs اختلاف ekhtelâf
contusion *n.* ضربت zarbat کوفتگی kuftegi
convalesce *vi.* بهبودیافتن behbud yâftan
convalescence *n.* نقاهت neqâhat
convalescent *adj., n.* درنقاهت dar neqâhat
convene *v.* جمع کردن jam' kardan احضار کردن ehzâr kardan
convene *v.* بهبود یافتن behbud yâftan
convenience *n.* راحتی râhati آسودگی âsudegi مصلحتی maslahati
convenient *adj.* راحت râhat بی زحمت bi-zahmat
convent *n.* تارک خانه târek-khâneh صومعه some'eh
convention *n.* قرارداد qarârdâd گردهمایی gerd-e' hamâyi
conventional *adj.* معمولی ma'muli قراردادی qarârdâdi
converge *vi., vt.* یک جا جمع کردن yek-jâ jam' kardan
conversant *adj.* خوش صحبت آگاه âgâh khosh-sohbat
conversation *n.* صحبت sohbat مکالمه mokâlemeh
conversational *adj.* مکامه ای mokâlemeh-i محاوره ای mohâvereh-i
converse *adj., n., vi.* معکوس ma'kus
conversely *adv.* برعکس bar-'aks
conversion *n.* تبدیل tabdil
conversion *n.* تغییر مذهب taqyir-e' maz-hâb
convert *v.* تغییر مذهب دادن taqyir-e' maz-hâb dâdan
convert *n.* تازه کیش tâzeh-kish نوآئین no-â'in
convert *v.* تبدیل کردن tabdil kardan
converter *n.* مبدل mobad~el تبدیل کننده tabdil-konandeh
convertible *adj., n.* عوض شدنی 'avaz shodani کروکی koruki
convex *adj., n.* محدب mohad~ab
convey *vt.* بردن bordan رساندن resândan
conveyance *n.* انتقال enteqâl نقل naql
conveyer *n.* تسمهٔ متحرک tasmeh-ye' motehar~ek
conveyer *v.* نقل کننده naql-konandeh
convict *v.* محکوم کردن mahkum kardan
convict *n.* محکوم mahkum مقصر moqas~er مجرم mojrem

conviction *n.* محکومیت mahkumiyat
conviction *n.* ایمان imân عقیدهٔ محکم aqideh-ye' mohkam
convince *vt.* متقاعد کردن moteqâ'ed kardan راضی کردن râzi kardan
مجاب کردن mojâb kardan
convinced *vt.* متقاعد moteqâ'ed قانع qâne'
convincing *vt.* قابل اعتماد qâbel-e' 'etemâd
convocation *n.* جمع آوری jam'âvari
convoluted *v.* بهم پیچیده beham pichideh قاطی پاتی qâti-pâti
convolution *n.* بهم پیچیدگی beham pichidegi
convoy *vt., n.* کاراوان kârâvân قافله qâfeleh
convulse *vt.* تشنج داشتن tashan~oj dâshtan
convulsion *n.* تشنج tashan~oj کش واکش kesh vâ kesh
convulsive *adj.* متشنج moteshan~ej
coo *int., vi., vt., n.* مورمورکردن murmur kardan
cook *v.* پختن pokhtan آشپزی کردن âshpazi kardan
cook *n.* آشپز âshpaz
cook-book *n.* کتاب آشپزی ketâb-e' âshpazi
cookie *n.* شیرینی shirini
cooking *n.* آشپزی âsh-pazi طبخ tabkh پخت pokht
cool *v.* خنک کردن khonak kardan
cool *adj.* خنک khonak
cool-headed *adj.* خونسرد khunsard
cooler *n.* کولر kuler یخچال yakh-châl
coolness *n.* خونسردی khunsardi خنکی khonaki
coop *n.* قفس qafas مرغدان morqdân
coop(erative) *n.* شرکت تعاونی sherkat-e' ta'âvoni
cooper *n., vt., vi.* صفار safâr
cooper(smith) *n.* مسگر mesgar
cooperate *vi.* همکاری کردن hamkâri kardan
cooperation *n.* همکاری hamkâri تشریک مساعی tashrik-e' masâ'i
cooperative *adj., n.* همکاری کن hamkâri-kon
coordinate *adj., n., vt., vi.* یکی کردن yeki kardan
متناسب کردن motenâseb kardan
coordination *n.* هم آهنگی ham-âhangi توازن tavâzon
coordinator *n.* میزان کننده mizân konandeh
cop *n.* پاسبان pâsbân پلیس polis
cop *v.* دزدیدن dozdidan
cope *n., v., vt.* تحمل کردن taham~ol kardan

copula *v.* فعل بودن fe'l-e' budan
copula *n.* واصل vâsel متمم motam~am
copulate *vi., adj.* جماع کردن jamâ' kardan جفت گیری joftgiri
copulation *n.* جماع jamâ' جفت گیری joftgiri
copy *v.* کپی کردن kopi kardan رونوشت گرفتن ru-nevesht gereftan
copy *v.* تقلید کردن taqlid kardan
copy *n.* کپی kopi رونوشت ru-nevesht نسخه noskheh
copycat *n., vt.* مقلد moqal~ed تقلیدکننده taqlid-konandeh
copyright *n., adj., vt.* حق چاپ haq~-e' châp
coquet *v.* نازکردن nâaz kardan عشوه کردن 'eshveh kardan
  قمیش آمدن qamish âmadan اطفاریختن atfâr rikhtan
coquetry *n.* ناز nâaz غمزه qamzeh عشوه 'eshveh کرشمه kereshmeh
coquette *adj.* نازدار nâa-dâr عشوه گر 'eshveh-gar طناز tan~âaz
  اطفاری atfâri
coquettish *adj.* نازدار nâz-dâr اطفاری atfâri کرشمه دار kereshmeh-dâr
  عشوه گر 'eshveh-gar
coral *n., adj.* مرجان marjân
cord , *vt.* ریسمان rismân سیم sim وتر vatar رباط rebât
cordial *adj., n.* صمیمانه samimâneh دوستانه dustâneh
cordiality *n.* صمیمیت samimiyat مودت maved~at
cordon(off) *n.* روبان بستن rubân bastan
core *n., vt.* مرکز markaz هسته hasteh مغز maqz
coriander *n.* گشنیز geshniz
cork *n., vt.* چوب پنبه chub-panbeh
corkscrew *n., adj., vt., vi.* پیچ چوب پنبه pich-e' chub-panbeh
corn *n., vt.* بلال balâl ذرت zor~at میخچه mikh-cheh
cornea *n.* قرنیه qarnieh
corner *n., adj., vt., vi.* گوشه gusheh کنج konj کنار kenâr
cornerstone *n.* پایه pâyeh بنیاد bonyâd
cornfield *n.* مزرعة بلال mazra'eh-ye' balâl
cornflour *n.* آردذرت ârd-e' zor~at
cornmeal *adj.* آردذرت ârd-e' zor~at
cornoil *n.* روغن ذرت roqan-e' zor~at
corny *adj.* لوس lus بی مزه bimazeh جلف jelf
corollary *n.* نتیجه ای natijeh-i استنادی estenâdi
corona *n.* هاله hâleh تاج tâj اکلیل eklil دیهیم deyhim
coronary *adj., n.* رگهای قلبی rag-hâ-ye' qalbi تاجی tâji
coronate *adj.* تاجگذاری کردن tâj-gozâri kardan

coronation *n.* تاج‌گذاری tâj-gozâri
coroner *n.* پزشک قانونی pezeshk-e' qânuni
corporal *n.* سرجوخه sarjukheh
corporal *adj.* بدنی badani جسمی jesmi
corporate *adj.* متحد motah~ed صنفی senfi
corporation *n.* شرکت با مسئولیت محدود sherkat bâ mas'uliat-e' mahdud

corps *n., pl.* هیئت hey'at لشگر lashgar گروه goruh
corpse *n.* جسد jasad نعش na'sh جنازه jenâzeh مردار mordar
corpsman *n.* سپاهی پزشکی sepâhi-e' pezeshki
corral *n., vt.* گله گاه gal~eh gâh دوربست اسب dorbast-e' asb
correct *vt., adj.* صحیح کردن sahih kardan
تصحیح کردن tas-hih kardan
correction *n.* تصحیح tas-hih تأدیب ta'dib
correction *n.* تأدیبی ta'dibi
correctly *adv.* صحیحاً sahihan
correlate *vt., vi., adj., n.* ارتباط دادن ertebât dâdan
نسبت دادن nesbat dâdan
correlation *n.* ارتباط ertebât نسبت nesbat
correspond *vi.* مطابق بودن motâbeq budan
مکاتبه کردن mokâtebeh kardan
correspondence *n.* مکاتبه mokâtebeh نامه نگاری nâmeh-negâri
مراسله morâseleh
correspondent *n., adj.* مطابق motâbeq خبرنگار khabarnegâr
corresponding *n.* مطابق motâbeq متشابه moteshâbeh
corridor *n.* راهرو râhro ایوان eyvân
corrigible *adj.* صحیح شدنی sahih shodani
corroborate *vt., adj.* تأیید کردن ta'yid kardan
تقویت کردن taqviat kardan
corroboration *n.* تأیید ta'yid تقویت taqviat
corrode *vt., vi.* زنگ زدن zang zadan خورده شدن khordeh shodan
corrosion *n.* خرابی kharâbi زنگ zang سائیده گی sâ'idehgi
corrosive *adj., n.* خورنده khorandeh
corrupt *adj.* فاسد fâsed شریر sharir
corrupt *v.* فاسد کردن fâsed kardan
corruptible *adj.* فاسد شدنی fâsed-shodani رشوه گیر roshveh-gir
corruption *n.* فساد fesâd شرارت sherârat
corsage *n.* یک دسته گل yek dasteh gol

corset *n., vt.* كرست korset
cortex *n.* پوست pust
cosignment *n.* كالا kâlâ محموله mahmuleh
cosine *n.* كوسينوس kosinus
cosmetic *n., adj.* آرايشى ârâyeshi
cosmetologist *n.* آرايشگر ârâyesh-gar
cosmetology *n.* آرايشگرى ârâyesh-gari
cosmic *adj.* ستاره يى setâreh-yi
cosmopolitan *adj., n.* دنياوطنى donyâ vatani
شهربزرگ shâhr-e' bozorg
cost *v.* خرج برداشتن kharj bardâshtan ارزيدن arzidan
cost *n.* خرج kharj بها bahâ قيمت qeymat هزينه hazineh
costly *adj.* پرخرج por-kharj گران gerân
costume *n., vt.* لباس lebâs پوشاك pushâk
cot *n.* تختخواب سفرى takhtekhâb-e' safari
cotangent *n.* كتانژانت kotânzhânt
cottage *n.* كلبه kolbeh
cotton *n., vi.* پنبه panbeh كتان katân
couch *n., vt., vi.* مبل mobl نشيمن neshiman
couch-potato *n.* تنبل tanbal راحت طلب râhat-talab
cough *vi., vt., n.* سرفه كردن sorfeh kardan
council *n.* هيئت hey'at شورا shorâ
counsel *n., vt., vi.* وكيل vakil
counsel *v.* مشورت كردن mashverat kardan وكيل بودن vakil budan
counselor *n.* مشاور moshâver وكيل vakil
count *vt., vi., n., adj.* رديف radif اتهام etehâm
count *v.* شمردن shemordan اهميت داشتن aham~iyat dâshtan
count *n.* كنت kont
count *n.* شمارش shemâresh جمع jâm'
counter *v.* خنثى كردن khonsâ kardan
counter *n.* پيشخوان pishkhân
counter- *n.* مخالف mokhâlef-e' ضد zed~-e' برعكس bar-'aks-e'
counterbalance *n., vt., vi.* تعادل vazneh-ye' ta'âdol وزنۀ
counterfeit *v.* جعل كردن ja'l kardan
counterfeit *adj.* جعلى ja'li ساختگى sâkhtegi
counterfeiter *n.* جعل كننده ja'l-konandeh
counterpart *n.* مخالف noqteh-ye' mokhâlef نقطۀ هم رقيب ham-raqib
counterpoint *n., vt.* تكامل آهنگى takâmol-e' âhangi

counterweight n. وزنهٔ برابر vazneh-ye' barâbar
country n. کشور keshvar میهن mihan
country n. بیرون شهر birun-e' shahr ییلاق yeylâq
countryman n. هم میهن ham-mihan
countryside n. بیرون شهر birun-e' shahr حومه homeh
county n. بخش bakhsh استان ostân حوزه hozeh
coup(d'e'tat) n. کودتا ku-detâ
couple v. جفت کردن joft kardan دونفره کردن donafareh kardan
couple n., vt., vi. دونفر do-nafar
coupon n. کوپن kopon
courage n. جرأت jor'at
courageous adj. باجرأت bâ-jor'at باشهامت bâ-shahâmat
courier n. حامل hâmel پیک peyk چاپار châpâr
course n. جریان jaryân
course n. خط سیر khat~-e' seyr
course n. دوره doreh رشته reshteh
course n. غذا ghazâ پرس pors
court n. بارگاه bârgâh دربار darbâr
court v. نامزد بازی کردن nâmzad-bâzi kardan
court n. دادگاه dâdgâh محکمه mahkameh
court-martial n., vt. محاکمهٔ نظامی mohâkemeh-ye' nezâmi
courteous adj. مودب mo'ad~ab بااحترام bâ-ehterâm
courtesy n. ادب adab وقار veqâr
courthouse n. دادگاه dâdgâh محضر mahzar
courtly adj., adv. مودب mo'ad~ab بااحترام bâ-ehterâm
cousin n. پسر دائی pesar dâ'i
cousin n. دختردائی dokhtar dâ'i
cousin n. پسرعمو pesar 'amu
cousin n. پسر عمه pesar 'am~eh
cousin n. دخترعمو dokhtar 'amu
cousin n. دخترعمه dokhtar 'âm~eh
cove n., vt., vi. خلیج khalij طاقچه tâqcheh
covenant n. پیمان peymân عهد 'ahd وثاق vesaq
covenant v. هم قسم شدن ham-qasam shodan
سوگند دادن sogand dâdan
cover n. جلد jeld
cover v. پوشانیدن pushânidan
cover n. پوشش pushesh

cover v. اشاره کردن eshâreh kardan
cover charge np. ورودیه vorudiyeh
cover girl np. مدل مجله model-e' majal~eh
cover letter n. سرنامه sar-nâmeh
cover(up) n. سرپوش گذاشتن sar-push gozâshtan
پنهان کردن penhan kardan
cover-up n. سرپوشی sar-pushi اختفاء ekhtefâ'
coverage n. دربرگیری darbar-giri مقداربیمه meqdâr-e' bimeh
coverall n. لباس تمام قد lebâs-e' tamâm qad
covered v. ترتیب داده شده tartib-dâdeh shodeh
covered adj. پوشیده pushideh مخفی makhfi
covert adj. مخفیانه makhfiâneh پوشیده pushideh
covet v. طمع کردن tama' kardan سوء نظرداشتن su'e nazar dâshtan
covetous adj. آزمند âz-mand طمع کار tama'-kâr
cow v. ترساندن tarsândan
cow n. گاو ماده gâv-e' mâd~eh
coward n., adj. ترسو tarsu بزدل boz-del نامرد nâ-mard
cowardice n. ترسویی tarsuyi بزدلی boz-deli
نامردی nâ-mardi ناجوانمردی nâ-javân-mardi
cowboy n. گاوچران gâv-charân کابوی kâboy
cower vi. ازترس جا زدن az tars jâ zadan
coy v. نازکردن nâz kardan
coy adj. خجول khajul محجوب mahjub
coyote n. شغال shoqâl
cozy adj., n. راحت râhat دنج denj دلپذیر delpazir
crab n., vi., vt. خرچنگ kharchang
crabby adj. بداخلاق bad-akhlâq
crack adj. شوخ shukh بامزه bâ-mazeh خنده دار khandeh-dâr
crack n. ترک tarak شکستگی shekastegi شکاف shekâf چاک châk
crack v. ترک دادن tarak dâdan شکستن shekastan
خرد کردن khord kardan
crack(down) n. سرکوب کردن sar-kub kardan
سخت گیری کردن sakht-giri kardan
crack-down n. سرکوب sar-kub سخت گیری sakht-giri
cracker n. ترقه taraq~eh
cracker n. نان خشک nân khoshk
crackle vi., vt., n. ترق و تروق کردن taraq-o toruq kardan
crackpot n., adj. دیوانه divâneh خل khol

cradle *n., vt., vi.* گهواره gahvâreh مهد mahd ننو nanu
craft *n.* سفینه safineh قایق qâyeq
craft *n.* پیشه pisheh مهارت mahârat استادی ostâdi
craftsman *n.* صنعتگر san'at-gar
crafty *adj.* حیله گر hileh-gar موذی muzi آب زیر کاه âb-zir-e′ kâh
cram *vt., vi., n.* چپانیدن chapânidan
cramp *n., vt., adj.* گرفتگی عضله gereftegy-e′ 'azoleh
crane *n.* جرثقیل jaresaqil
crane *n.* درنا dornâ
crank *v.* چرخاندن charkhândan
crank *adj.* مزاحم mozâhem
crank *n.* هندل hendel
crank-call *n.* تلفن مزاحم telefon-e′ mozâhem
crankshaft *n.* میل لنگ mil-lang
cranky *adj.* دمدمی dam-dami غرغرو qor-qoru بدعنق bad-'onoq
cranny *n.* شکاف shekâf چاک châk
crap *n., vi., vt., v.* گه goh
crape *n., vt.* کرپ kerep
crash *vt., vi., n., adj.* بهم زدن beham zadan سقوط کردن soqut kardan
crash course *n.* دورۀ کوتاه doreh-ye′ kutâh
crass *adj.* زمخت zomokht خرفت khereft
crate *n., vt.* صندوق sandoq
crater *n., vt., vi.* دهانۀ آتشفشان dahâne-ye′ atash-feshân
cravat *n., vt.* کراوات kerâvât
crave *vt., vi.* ویارکردن viâr kardan آرزو کردن ârezu kardan
craving *n., v.* آرزو ârezu اشتیاق eshtiâq
craw *n.* گلو galu
crawl *vi., n.* خزیدن khazidan سینه خیز رفتن sineh-khiz raftan
crayon *n., vt.* مدادرنگی medâd rangi
craze *vt., vi., n.* دیوانه کردن divâneh kardan
craziness *n.* دیوانگی divânegi
crazy *adj.* دیوانه divâneh مجنون majnun
creak *vi., vt., n.* قژقژکردن qezh-qezh kardan
cream *n., vi., vt., adj.* خامه khâmeh سرشیر sarshir کرم kerem
crease *n., vt., vi.* چین دادن chin dâdan تاه کردن tâh kardan
create *vt., vi., adj.* بوجودآوردن bevojud âvardan آفریدن âfaridan
creation *n.* آفرینش âfarinesh خلقت khelqat کون ومکان kon-o makân
creative *adj.* خلاق khal~âq آفریننده âfarinandeh

creativity *n.* خلاقیت khal~âqiyat آفرینندگی âfarinandegi
creator *n.* آفریدگار âfaridegâr خالق khâleq جهان آفرین jahân âfarin
creature *n.* آفریده âfarideh جانور jânevar
credence *n.* اعتبار e'tebâr باور bâvar
credential *n., adj.* استوار نامه ostovâr-nâmeh
credibility *n.* اعتبار e'tebâr
credible *adj.* معتبر mo'tabar باورکردنی bâvar-kardani
credit *n., vt.* اعتباردادن e'tebâr dâdan نسیه دادن nesyeh dâdan
credit-card *n.* کارت اعتباری kârt-e' e'tebâri
creditable *adj.* معتبر mo'tabar باورکردنی bâvar-kardani
creditor *n.* طلبکار talab-kâr بستانکار bestân-kâr
credulity *n.* زودباوری zud-bâvari
credulous *adj.* زودباور zud-bâvar
creed *n.* عقیده 'aqideh آیین â'in
creek *n.* جویبار juybâr نهر nahr
creep *v.* لغزیدن laqzidan
creep *adj.* آدم پست âdam-e past
creepy *adj.* وحشت انگیز vahshat-angiz
cremate *vt.* سوزاندن suzândan خاکستر کردن khâkestar kardan
crematory *adj., n.* کوره kureh تون tun
crescent *n., adj.* هلال helâl ماه نو mâh-e' no
cress *n.* شاهی shâhi
crest *n., vt., vi.* سر sar نوک nok تاج tâj
crevasse *n., vt.* شکاف shekâf
crew *n., vt., vi.* کارکنان kârkonân جاشویان jâshuyân
crib *n., vt., vi.* تختخواب بچه takhtekhâb-e' bach~eh
cricature *n.* کاریکاتور kârikâtor
cricket *n., vi.* سوسک susk جیرجیرک jir-jirak
crime *n.* جنایت jenâyat جرم jorm
criminal *adj., n.* جنائی jenâ'i
criminal *adj., n.* جانی jâni تبهکار tabah-kâr
crimp *n., vt.* چین دادن chin dâdan
crimson *adj., n., vt., vi.* سرخ sorkh لاکی lâki
cringe *vi., n.* از ترس دولا شدن az tars dol~â shodan
crinkle *vt., vi., n.* چین خوردن chin khordan
cripple *n., vt., adj.* علیل کردن 'alil kardan فلج کردن falaj kardan
crippled *n.* فلج falaj مفلوج mafluj معلول ma'lul
crisis *n.* بحران bohrân

crisp *adj., vt., vi., n.* خشک کردن khoshk kardan
crisp(y) *n.* تازه tâzeh ترد tord
crisscross *adj., n., adv., vt.* متقاطع moteqâte'
criteria *n.* معیارها me'yâr-hâ ها ملاک melâk-hâ
criterion *n.* معیار me'yâr ملاک melâk محک mahek
critic *n.* انتقادکننده enteqd konandeh منتقد montaqed نقاد naq~âd
critical *adj.* انتقادی enteqâdi
critical *adj.* بحرانی bohrâni وخیم vakhim
criticism *n.* انتقاد enteqâd
criticize *vi., vt.* انتقاد کردن enteqâd kardan
critique *n.* انتقاد enteqâd نقد naqd
croak *vi., vt., n.* قارقارکردن qârqâr kardan مردن mordan
crochet *n., vt., vi.* قلابدوزی qol~âb-duzi
crock *n., vt., vi.* کوزه kuzeh
crock-pot *n.* اجاق سنگی ojâq-e' sangi
crockery *n.* بدل چینی badal chini کوزه گری kuzeh gari
crocodile *n.* سوسمار susmâr تمساح temsâh
croft *n.* باغچه bâqcheh
crony *n.* رفیق rafiq دوست صمیمی dust-e' samimi هم پیاله ham-piâleh
crook *adj., n., vt., vi.* شارلاتان shârlâtân حقه باز hoq~eh-bâz
crooked *adj.* کج kaj کج بین kajbin
crooner *n.* آوازه خوان âvâzeh-khân
crop *n., vt., vi.* محصول mahsul بار bâr
cross *n.* تقاطع taqâto'
cross *v.* پیوند زدن peyvand zadan
cross *n.* صلیب salib چلیپا chalipâ خاج khâj
cross *v.* قطع کردن qat' kardan
cross section *np.* نمونه nemuneh برش مقطعی boresh-e' maqta'i
cross-bar *n.* تیرافقی tir-e' ofoqi
cross-breed *n.* دورگه do-rageh
cross-examine *vt.* بازپرسی کردن bâzporsi kardan
cross-eyed *adj.* چپ chap لوچ loch
cross-legged *adj.* پا پاروی pâ ru-ye' pâ
crossing *n.* تقاطع taqâto' عبور obur
crossroad *n.* تقاطع taqâto' نقطۀ عطف noqteh-ye' 'atf
crosswalk *n.* پیاده رو piâdeh-ro
crosswise *adv.* ازوسط az vasat
crossword puzzle *np.* جدول متقاطع jadval-e' moteqâte'

crotch *n.* عصا 'asâ
crotch *n.* لای پا lâ-ye' pâ
crouch *v.* دولا شدن dol~â shodan
crow *vi., n.* کلاغ kalâq صدای خروس sedâ-ye' khorus
crowbar *n.* دیلم deylam
crowd *n.* جمعیت jam'iyat
crowd *v.* شلوغ کردن sholuq kardan ازدحام کردن ezdehâm kardan
crowded *adj.* شلوغ sholuq پرجمعیت por-jam'iyat
crown *n.* تاج tâj
crown *v.* تاج گذاری کردن tâj gozâri kardan
crown-prince *n.* ولیعهد vali'ahd
crucial *adj.* قاطع qâte' حایطی hayâti
crucifixion *n.* صلیب کشی salib keshi تصلیب taslib
crucify *vt.* بصلیب کشیدن be-salib keshidan
crude *n.* خام khâm
crude *adj.* خشن khashen
crude oil *np.* نفت خام naft-e' khâm
cruel *adj.* بیرحم birahm ظالمانه zâlemâneh
cruelty *n.* بیرحمی birahmi ظلم zolm
cruise *vi., vt., n.* گشت زدن gasht zadan
cruiser *n.* گشتی gashti رزمناو razm-nâv
crumb *n., vt.* خرده khordeh
crumble *vt., vi., n.* خردکردن khord kardan
crummy *adj., n.* کثیف kasif بد bad
crunch *vt., vi., n.* قرچ قرچ کردن qerech qerech kardan
crusade *n., vi.* جنگ کردن jang kardan جهد کردن jahd kardan
crusader *n.* مجاهد mojâhed
Crusades *n.* جنگهای صلیبی jang-hâ-ye' salibi
crush *v.* له کردن leh kardan
crush *n.* علاقۀ شدید 'alâqeh-ye' shadid
crust *n., vt., vi.* پوست pust قشر qeshr
crutch(es) *n.* عصای زیربغل 'asây-e' zir-baqâl
crux *n.* مغزکلام maqz-e' kalâm اصل مطلب asl-e' matlab
لب مطلب lob~-e' matlab
cry *vi., vt., n.* گریه کردن geryeh kardan فریادزدن faryâd zadan
cry-baby *n.* نی نی nini گریه کن geryeh-kon
crypt *n.* دخمه dakhmeh سرداب sardâb
cryptic *adj., n.* رمزی ramzi

crystal *n., adj., vt.* بلور bolur
crystal ball *np.* حباب بلوری hobâb-e' boluri
جام جهان بین jâm-e' jahân-bin
crystalize *n.* متبلور کردن motebalver kardan
شکل گرفتن shekl gereftân
cub *n.* توله tuleh
cube *n., vt.* کعبه ka'beh مکعب moka'ab
cube root *np.* ریشۀ سوم risheh-ye' sev~om
cube sugar *n.* قند qand
cubic(al) *n.* مکعب moka'ab
cuckoo *n., vi., vt., adj.* فاخته fâkhteh کوکو kuku
cucumber *n.* خیار khiâr
cuddle *vt., vi., n.* درآغوش گرفتن dar âqush gereftan
cue *n., vt.* اشاره دادن eshâreh dâdan ندا دادن nedâ dâdan
cue ball *np.* گوی سفیدبیلیارد guy-e' sefid-e' biliârd شار shâr
cuff *n., vt.* سرآستین sarâstin
cuisine *n.* آشپزی âshpazi
cul-de-sac *n.* کوچۀ بن بست kuche-ye' bon-bast
culinary *adj.* آشپزخانه ای âshpaz-khâneh-i
culminate *vi., vt.* منجرشدن monjar shodan
culpability *n.* مجرمیت mojremiyat قصور qosur
culpable *adj.* مجرم mojrem مقصر moqas~er
culprit *n.* مقصر moqas~er
cultivate *vt.* زراعت کردن zerâ'at kardan پروراندن parvarândan
cultivation *n.* پرورش parvaresh کشت kesht
cultural *adj.* فرهنگی farhangi
culture *n.* فرهنگ farhang
culture *n.* نمونه nemuneh کشت kesht
cultured *adj.* بافرهنگ bâ-farhang موقر movaq~ar
culvert *n.* جوی سرپوشیده juy-e' sar pushideh
cumbersome *adj.* پرزحمت por-zahmat
cuneiform *adj., n.* میخی mikhi سنگی sangi
cunning *n., adj., v.* حیله گر hilehgar چرب زبان charb-zabân
cup *n., vt.* فنجان fenjân جام jâm پیاله piâleh ساغر sâghar
cupboard *n.* قفسه qafaseh گنجه ganjeh
curable *adj.* علاج پذیر 'alâj-pazir بهبودیافتنی behbud-yâftani
curator *n.* متصدی motesad~i موزه دار muzeh-dâr
curb *n., vt.* جلوگیری کردن jelogiri kardan

curb(side) *n.* جدول jadval
curd(le) *n.* شیردلمه شده shir-e' dalameh shodeh
cure *n.* دوا davâ شفا shafâ
cure *v.* خشک کردن khoshk kardan نمک زدن namak zadan
cure *v.* شفادادن shafâ dâdan
cureless *adj.* غیرقابل شفا qeyr-e' qâbel-e' shafâ
curfew *n.* قدغن زمانی qadeqan-e' zamâni
curiosity *n.* کنجکاوی konjkâvi
curious *adj.* کنجکاو konjkâv غریب qarib
curl *v.* فردادن fer dâdan حلقه شدن halqeh shodan
curl *n.* فر fer حلقه halqeh طره tor~eh
curly *adj.* فری feri پیچیده pichideh مجعد moja'ad
currant *n.* مویز maviz کشمش keshmesh
currently *adv.* درحال حاضر dar hâl-e' hâzer اخیراً akhiran
curriculum *n.* لیست درسها list-e' dars-hâ
curry *n., vt.* کاری kâri
curry favor *v.* چاپلوسی کردن châp-lusi kardan
خودشیرینی کردن khod-shirini kardan
curse *v.* نفرین کردن nefrin kardan لعنت کردن la'nat kardan
curse *n.* نفرین nefrin لعنت la'nat کفر kofr
cursed *adj., v.* نفرین شده nefrinshodeh ملعون mal'un
cursive *adj., n.* پیوسته pey-vasteh روان ravân
cursor *n.* مکان نما makân-namâ
cursory *adj.* شتابزده shetâb-zadeh سردستی sar-dasti
curt *adj.* خشک و کوتاه khoshk-o kutâh
curtail *n., vt.* کوتاه کردن kutâh kardan کم کردن kam kardan
curtailment *n.* کم شدگی kam-shodegi کوتاهی kutâhi
curtain *n., vt.* پرده pardeh
curtly *adv.* کوتاه و بی ادبانه kutâh-o bi-adabâneh
curtness *n.* شدت لحن shed~at-e' lahn
curve *n., vt., vi., adj.* منحنی monhani خم kham پیچ pich اریب orib
cushion *n., vt.* بالش bâlesh متکا motak~â
cusp *n.* لبه labeh مابین mâbeyn
cuss *n., vt., vi.* فحش دادن fohsh dâdan ناسزادادن nâ-sezâ dâdan
دشنام دادن doshnâm dâdan
custard *n.* فرنی تخم مرغ ferni-e' tokhm-e' morq
custodian *n.* سرایدار sarâydâr قیم qay~em متولی moteval~i
custody *n.* حفاظت hefâzat نگهداری negahdâri حبس habs

حضانت .... hezânat
custody *n.* حبس habs توقيف toqif
custom *n., adj.* رسم rasm سنت son~at
custom-built *adj.* ساخت سفارشى sâkht-e' sefâreshi
customary *adj., n.* مرسوم marsum عادى 'âd~i
customer *n.* مشترى moshtari
customs *n.* گمرک gomrok
cut *v.* بريدن boridan
cut *n.* سهم sahm
cut *v.* کوپ کردن kup kardan
cut *v.* چيدن chidan
cut *n.* برش boresh بر bor
cut(back) *n.* کم کردن kam kardan قطع کردن qat' kardan
cut(down) *n.* کم کردن kam kardan خوارکردن khâr kardan
cut(off) *n.* قطع کردن qat' kardan
cut(out) *n.* بس کردن bas kardan
cut(through) *n.* ميان بر زدن miânbor zadan
cut-rate *adj.* ارزان arzân تخفيف takhfif
cut-throat *n.* آدم کش âdam-kosh
cute *adj.* بانمک bâ-namak بامزه bâ-mazeh مليح malih
cuticle *n.* پوست اضافى pust-e' ezâfi
cutlery *n.* کارد و چنگال kârd-o changâl
cutter *n.* برنده borandeh
cyanide *n., vt.* سيانويد siânoyd
cybernetics *n.* علم عصب شناسى 'elm-e' 'asab shenâsi
cycle *n., vi.* دور dor گردش gardesh
cyclic *adj.* گردش کننده gardesh konandeh
cyclone *n.* گردباد gerdbâd
cylinder *n., vt.* استوانه ostovâneh سيلندر silandr
cymbal *n.* سنج sanj
cynic *n., adj.* مظنون maznun بدگمان bad-gamân
cynicism *n.* بدگمانى bad-gamâni ظن zan~
cypress *n.* سرو sarv
Cyprus *n.* قبرس qebres
Cyrus *n.* کوروش kurosh
cyst *n.* غده qod~eh کيسه kiseh
czar *n.* سزار sezâr قيصر qeysar

D D D

dab *vt., vi., n.* زدن آهسته âhesteh zadan کم یک yek-kam ذره zar~eh
daddy *n.* بابا bâbâ
daffy *adj.* احمق ahmaq
dagger *n., vt.* خنجر khanjar
daggle *vt., vi.* شدن گلی geli shodan
daily *adj., n., adv.* روزانه ruzaneh یومیه yomieh روزمره ruz-mar~eh
dainty *adj., n.* پسند مشکل moshkel-pâsând ظریف zarif
dairy *n., adj.* لبنیات labaniyât شیرفروشی shirforushi
dairy products *n.* لبنیات labaniyât
daisy *n.* مروارید گل gol-e' morvârid
dam *n., vt.* کردن سد sad~ kardan بند band
damage *v.* زدن ضرر zarar zadan زیان آوردن بار be-bâr âvardan زیان ziân رساندن آسیب âsib resândan زدن خسارت khesârat zadan
dame *n.* بانو bânu خانم khânom ضعیفه za'ifeh
damn *vt., vi., int., n.* کردن لعنت la'nat kardan
damnation *n., int.* لعن la'n درک darak
damned *adj., n., adv.* لعنتی la'nati ملعون mal'un رجیم rajim
damp *adj., n., vt.* نم nam رطوبت rotubat نمور namur
dampen *vt., vi.* کردن خیس khis kardan
damper *n.* کن خفه khafeh-kon اجاق دریچهٔ daricheh-ye' ojâq
damsel *n.* دختر dokhtar دوشیزه dushizeh
dance *vi., vt., n.* کردن رقص raqs kardan رقصیدن raqsidan
dancer *n.* رقاص raq~âs
dandelion *n.* قاصد گل gol-e' qâsed
dandruff *n.* شوره shureh
dandy *n., adj.* لباس خوش khosh-lebâs راحت râhat
danger *n.* خطر khatar
dangerous *adj.* خطرناک khatarnâk
dangle *vi., vt., n.* کردن آویزان âvizân kardan
dare *vi., vt., n.* کردن جرأت jor'at kardan
daredevil *adj.* ماجراجو mâjerâju
daring *n., adj.* جرأت و بادل bâ del-o jorat
dark *adj., n., vt., vi.* تیره tireh تاریک târik سبزه sabzeh
darn *adj., adv., vt., n.* کردن رفو rofu kardan لعنتی la'nâti
dart *n., vi., vt.* تیر tir میخک mikhak رفتن تند tond raftan
dash *vt., vi., n.* کردن پرت part kardan کردن عجله ajaleh kardan
dashboard *n.* داشبورت dâshbort

dassle *n.* درد سر dard-e' sar
dastard *adj.* ترسو tarsu نامرد nâ-mard بزدل boz-del
dastardly *adv.* نامردانه nâ-mardâneh بزدلانه boz-delâneh
data *n., pl.* اطلاعات et~elâ'ât ها دانسته dânesteh-hâ
date *n.* تاریخ târikh راندوو rândevu
date *v.* تاریخ گذاشتن târikh gozâshtan
datepalm *n.* نخل nakhl
dates *n.* خرما khormâ
daughter *n.* دختر dokhtar صبیه sabieh
daughter-in-law *n.* عروس 'arus زن پسر zan-e' pesar
dauntless *adj.* بی محابا bi-mohâbâ
dawn *n., vi.* طلوع کردن tolu' kardan
dawn *n.* سحر sahar پگاه pegâh سپیده دم sepideh-dam فجر fajr
day *n.* روز ruz
daylight *n., adj.* روز روشن ruz-e' roshan
daytime *n.* روز ruz
daze *vt., n.* خیره کردن khireh kardan گیج کردن gij kardan
dazzle *vt., vi., n.* مفتون کردن maftun kardan
dazzling *v.* خیره کننده khireh konandeh
deactivate *vt., vi.* از کار انداختن az kâr andâkhtan
dead *adj., n., adv.* مرده mordeh
dead heat *np.* درست مساوی dorost mosâvi
dead pan *np.* سیمای بی حالت simây-e' bi-hâlat
dead-end *adj.* بن بست bonbast
deadline *n.* مهلت زمانی mohlat-e' zamâni
deadlock *n., vt., vi.* گیر کرده gir-kardeh
deadly *adj., adv.* مرگ آور marg âvar
deaf *adj.* کر kar اطروش otrush
deaf-mute *n.* کر و لال kar-o lâl
deal *v.* معامله کردن mo'âmeleh kardan طرف شدن taraf shodan
deal *n.* معامله mo'âmeleh مقدار meqdâr
dealer *n.* فروشنده forushandeh دلال dal~âl قمارچی qomârchi
معامله گر mo'âmeleh-gar
dean *n.* ناظم nâzem ریش سفید rish-sefid
dear *adj., n., adv., int.* عزیز 'âziz جان jân گران gerân
dearth *n.* ندرت kam-yâbi کمیابی nodrat
death *n.* مرگ marg فوت fot درگذشت dargozasht رحلت rehlat
deathbed *n.* بسترمرگ bastar-e' mârg

deathblow *n.* ضربت کشنده zarbat-e' koshandeh
debacle *n.* ریزش rizesh خرابکاری kharâbkâri
debase *v.* توسرزدن tu-sar zadan
debase *v.* کم ارزش کردن kam-arzesh kardan
debasement *n.* پستی pasti خواری khâri زبونی zabuni
debate *n., vi., vt.* مباحثه کردن mobâheseh kardan
     اندیشیدن andishidan
debauchery *n.* نسادگری fesâdgari فسق و فجور fesq-o fojur
debilitate *vt.* ناتوان کردن nâtavân kardan
debility *n.* ناتوانی nâ-tavâni عجز 'ajz
debit *n., vt.* بدهی bedehi کسرکردن kasr kardan
debris *n.* خرده سنگ khordeh-sang خرابه ها kharâbeh-hâ
debt *n.* بدهی bedehi قرض qarz دین deyn منت men~at
debtor *n.* بدهکار bedehkâr مقروض maqruz مدیون madyun
decade *n.* دهه daheh ده سال dah sâl
decadent *adj., n.* فاسد fâsed هرزه harzeh
decant *vt.* بطری به بطری ریختن botri be-botri rikhtan
decapitate *vt.* سربریدن sar boridan
decay *vi., vt., n.* فاسد کردن fâsed kardan خراب شدن kharâb shodan
decease *n., vi.* مرگ marg مقتول کردن maqtul kardan
deceased *v.* مرده mordeh متوفی motev~afâ
deceit *n.* فریب farib تقلب taqal~ob مکر makr حیله hileh
deceitful *adj.* فریب آمیز fârib-âmiz مزور mozav~er مکار mak~âr
deceive *vt., vi.* فریب دادن farib dâdan گول زدن gul zadan
decency *n.* نجابت nejâbat
decent *adj.* درستکار dorost-kâr تمیز tamiz
deception *n.* حقه hoq~eh فریب farib نیرنگ nirang
     دوزوکلک duz-o kalak
decide *vt., vi.* تصمیم گرفتن tasmim gereftan
decision *n.* تصمیم tasmim رأی ra'y
decisive *adj.* مصمم mosam~am قطعی qat'i
deck *n.* عرشه arsheh کف kaf
deck *v.* آراستن ârâstan
declarant *n.* اظهارکننده ez-hâr konandeh
declaration *n.* اظهار نامه ez-hâr-nâmeh اعلان e'lân ابراز ebrâz
declare *vt., vi.* اظهار کردن ez-hâr kardan اعلان کردن e'lân kardan
     ابرازکردن ebrâz kardan
declension *n.* انزوال enzevâl تنزل tanaz~ol

decline *vt., vi., n.* تنزل کردن tanaz~ol kardan رد کردن rad kardan
decompose *vt., vi.* فاسد شدن fâsed shodan
decorate *vt.* آذین بستن âzin bastan مدال دادن medâl dâdan
decoration *n.* دکوراسیون dekorâsion آذین âzin
decoy *n., vt., vi.* طعمهٔ دام to'meh-ye' dâm
پلیس مخفی polis-e' makhfi
decrease *v.* کاهش یافتن kâhesh yâftan
decrease *v.* کم کردن kam kardan کم شدن kam shodan
decree *n., vt., vi.* حکم کردن hokm kardan دستور dastur امر amr
decry *vt.* تقبیح کردن taqbih kardan
dedicate *vt., adj.* اهدا کردن ehdâ kardan
اختصاص دادن ekhtesâs dâdan
deduce *vt.* استنباط کردن estenbât kardan
استنتاج کردن estentâj kardan
deduct *vt.* کم کردن kam kardan
deductible *adj., n.* کم کردنی kam kardani
deduction *n.* استنباط estenbât قیاس qiâs استنتاج estentâj
deduction *n.* کاست kâst کسر kasr کاهش kâhesh
deductive *adj.* قیاسی qiâsi لمی lemi
deed *n., vt.* سند sanad قباله qabâleh عمل 'amal
deep *adj., n., adv.* گود god عمیق 'amiq
deer *n.* آهو âhu گوزن gavazn
deface *v.* بد شکل کردن bad-shekl kardan
deface *v.* شکل خراب کردن shekl kharâb kardan
defame *vt.* رسوا کردن rosvâ kardan آبروبردن âberu bordan
default *v.* حاضرنشدن hâzer nashodan
default *v.* پرداخت نکردن pardâkht nakardan
نکول کردن nokul kardan
defeat *vt., n.* شکست دادن shekast dâdan
defecate *vi., vt.* ادرارکردن edrâr kardan ریدن ridan
defect *n.* پناهنده panâhandeh
defect *n.* عیب 'eyb نقص naqs
defection *n.* عیب 'eyb نقص naqs پناهندگی panâhandegi
defective *adj., n.* عیب دار 'eybdâr ناقص nâqes
defend *vt., vi.* دفاع کردن defâ' kardan حمایت کردن hemâyat kardan
defendant *n., adj.* متهم mot~aham
defender *n.* مدافع modâfe'
defense *n.* دفاع defâ' حمایت hemâyat

---

defensible *adj.* قابل دفاع qâbel-e' defâ'

defensive *adj., n.* دفاعی defâ'i

defer *vt., vi.* بتعویق انداختن be-ta'viq andâkhtan

deference *n.* حرمت hormat احترام ehterâm تمکین tamkin

deferential *adj.* محترمانه mohtaramâneh

deferment *n.* تعویق ta'viq

defiance *n.* مخالفت mokhâlefat

defiant *adj.* جنگجو jang-ju

deficiency *n.* کمبود kambud نقصان noqsan

deficient *adj.* ناقص nâqes ناکامل nâkâmel

deficit *n.* کسری kasri

defile *vt., n., vi.* آلوده کردن âludeh kardan

define *vt.* معین کردن mo'ay~an kardan

definite *adj.* معین mo'ay~an قطعی qat'i

definition *n.* معنی ma'nâ

definitive *adj., n.* قاطع qâte'

definitude *n.* دقت deq~at

deflate *vt., vi.* باد خالی کردن bâd khâli kardan

deflect *vt., vi.* منحرف کردن monharef kardan

deflection *n.* انحراف enherâf

deform *adj., vt.* ناقص کردن nâqes kardan

deformed *adj.* ناقص nâqes

deformity *n.* نقص naqs

defraud *vt.* کلاه برداری kolâh-bardâri

defray *vt.* پرداختن pardâkhtan

deft *adj.* ماهر mâher

defunt *adj.* ازمیان رفته az miân rafteh ازبین رفته az beyn rafteh منقرض monqarez

defy *v.* بمبارزه طلبیدن bemobârezeh talabidan

defy *v.* بی اعتنایی کردن bi-e'tenâyi kardan

degenerate *vi., adj., n.* فاسد شده fâsed shodeh

degradation *n.* پستی pâsti

degrade *vt., vi.* پست کردن past kardan پایین بردن pâyin bordan

degree *n.* درجه darejeh اندازه andâzeh مدرک madrak

dehydration *n.* کم آبی kam-âbi

deity *n.* خدایی khodâyi الوهیت olo-hiyat

dejected *adj.* افسرده afsordeh

delay *-vt.* دیر کردن dir kardan معطل کردن mo'at~al kardan

delegate *n., vt.* نماینده فرستادن namâyandeh ferestâdan
بکارگزاردن ma'mur kardan مأمورکردن be-kâr gozârdan
delegation *n.* هیئت hey'at گروه نمایندگان goruh-e' namâ-yandegân
delete -*vt.* حذف کردن hazf kardan
deliberate *v.* مشورت کردن mashverat kardan اندیشیدن andishidan
صلاح اندیشی کردن salâh-andishi kardan
deliberation *n.* صلاح اندیشی salâh-andishi کنکاش kankâsh
delicate *adj., n.* ظریف zârif لطیف latif
delicatessen *n.* اغذیه فروشی aqzieh forushi
delicious *adj., n.* خوشمزه khoshmazeh لذیذ laziz
delight *n., vt., vi.* خوشی دادن khoshi dâdan, لذت دادن lez~at dâdan
delighted *adj.* خوشوقت khosh-vaqt مشعوف mash'uf
delinquency *n.* کوتاهی kutâhi قصور qosur
عدم پرداخت 'adam-e' pardâkht
delirious *adj.* هذیانگو hazyân-gu
delirium *n.* هذیان hazyân
deliver *v.* تحویل دادن tahvil dâdan
deliver *v.* تحویل دادن tahvil dâdan رهایی دادن rahâyi dâdan
deliverance *n.* تحویل tahvil رهایی rahâyi وارستگی vâ-rastegi
delivery *n.* وضع حمل vaz'-e' haml
delivery *n.* تحویل tahvil عرضه 'arzeh
delta *n.* مصب mas~ab
delusion *n.* خیال باطل khiâl-e' bâtel دلخوشی del-khoshi
delve *vi., vt.* سوراخ کردن surâkh kardan
demagogue *n.* عوام فریب 'avâm-farib دجال daj~âl
demand *vt., vi., n.* خواستن khâstan تقاضا کردن taqâzâ kardan
demarcate *vt.* خط کشی کردن khat-keshi kardan
demarcation *n.* علامت گذاری 'alâmat gozâri
demeaning *n.* پست past خوارکننده khâr-konandeh
demise *n., vt., vi.* مرگ marg ازبین رفتن az beyn raftan
demo *n.* نمایشی nâmâyeshi
democracy *n.* مردم سالاری mardomsâlâri دمکراسی demokrâsi
demolish *vt.* ویران کردن veyrân kardan
demon *n., adj.* شیطان sheytân ابلیس eblis
demonstrate *vt., vi.* نشان دادن neshân dâdan
تظاهرات کردن tazâhorât kardan
demonstration *n.* تظاهرات tazâhorât نمایش namâyesh
demonstrative *adj., n.* نشان دهنده neshân dahandeh

esm-e' eshâreh اسم اشاره ....

demoralize *v.* نااميدكردن nâ-omid kardan

demoralize *v.* روحيه خراب كردن ruhieh kharab kardan

demotion *n.* تنزل tânaz~ol

demur *vi., n.* اعتراض كردن e'terâz kardan

den *n., vi.* مخفيگاه makhfigâh اطاق فراغت otâq-e' farâqat

denial *n.* انكار enkâr تكذيب takzib

denomination *n.* واحد vâhed گروه goruh نام گذارى nâmgozâri

denominator *n.* مخرج makhraj

denotation *n.* معنى مستقيم ma'ni-e' mostaqim

denote *vt.* علامت گذاشتن 'alâmat gozâshtan

denounce *vt.* متهم كردن mot~ahem kardan
تقبيح كردن taqbih kardan

dense *adj.* غليظ qaliz فشرده feshordeh

density *n.* غلظت qelzat چگالى chagâli

dental *adj., n.* دندانى dandâni

dental floss *np.* نخ دندان nakh-e' dandân

dentist *n.* دندان پزشك dandân pezeshk دندانساز dandân-sâz

dentistry *n.* دندانپزشكى dandân pezeshki

denture *n.* دندان مصنوعى dandân masnu'i

denude *vt.* لخت كردن lokht kardan

denunciation *n.* تقبيح taqbih بد گويى bad-guyi

deny *vt.* انكار كردن enkâr kardan تكذيب كردن takzib kardan

depart *vi., vt., n.* خارج شدن khârej shodan
روانه شدن ravâneh shodan

department *n.* اداره edâreh قسمت qesmat

departure *n.* حركت harekat عزيمت 'azimat خروج khoruj

depend *vi.* وابستگى داشتن vâbastegi dâshtan

dependence *n.* وابستگى vâbastegi توكل tavakol

dependent *adj., n.* وابسته vâbasteh تابع tâbe' متعلق mote'al~eq
نانخور nân-khor

depending *n.* بستگى bastegi

depict *vt.* عرضه كردن 'arzeh kardan رسم كردن rasm kardan

deplete *vt.* خالى كردن khâli kardan تهى كردن tohi kardan

deplorable *adj.* رقت انگيز req~at-angiz تاسف آور ta'as~of-âvar
فلاكت بار felâkat-bâr

deplore *vt.* متأسف بودن mote'as~ef budan

deploy *vt., vi.* پخش كردن pakhsh kardan

deport *vt., n.* اخراج کردن ekhrâj kardan
deportation *n.* اخراج ekhrâj
depose *v.* خلع کردن khal' kardan
depose *v.* گواهی دادن gavâhi dâdan استشهاد دادن estesh-hâd dâdan
deposed *adj.* معزول ma'zul مخلوع makhlu'
deposit *vt., vi., n.* بحساب ریختن behesâb rikhtan
رسوب کردن rosub kardan
deposition *n.* گواهی gavâhi استشهادیه esteshhâdieh
deposition *n.* خلع khal'
depositor *n.* ودیعه گذار vadi'eh-gozâr
depot *n.* انبار anbâr ایستگاه istgâh
depravation *n.* فساد fesâd
deprave *vt.* فاسد کردن fâsed kardan
depravity *n.* تباهی tabâhi
depreciate *vt., vi.* تنزل کردن tanaz~ol kardan
depreciation *n.* تنزل tanaz~ol
depress *vt.* پایین فشار دادن pâyin feshâr dâdan افسردن afsordan
depressant *adj., n.* حال گیر hâl-gir
depressed *adj.* افسرده afsordeh پریشان parishân محزون mah-zun
ملول malul
depressing *n.* ناراحت کننده nârâhat konandeh
depression *n.* کساد اقتصادی kesâd-e' eqtesâdi
depression *n.* افسردگی afsordegi اندوه anduh دلتنگی del-tangi
حزن hozn
depression *n.* گودی godi فرورفتگی foru-raftegi
deprivation *n.* محرومیت mahrumiyat
deprive *vt.* محروم کردن mahrum kardan
deprived *vt.* محروم mahrum مهجور mahjur
depth *n.* عمق 'omq ورطه varteh گودی godi
deputy *n., adj.* معاون mo'âven نماینده namâyandeh نایب nâyeb
derange *vt.* دیوانه کردن divâneh kardan برهم زدن barham zadan
deranged *adj.* دیوانه divâneh قاطی پاتی qâti pâti مختل mokhtal~
derelict *adj., n.* متروک matruk ولگرد velgard
derivation *n.* اشتقاق eshteqâq
derivative *adj., n.* مشتق moshtaq
derive *vi.* مشتق شدن moshtaq shodan
derived *adj.* مشتق moshtaq مأخوذ ma'khuz
derrick *n., vt., vi.* برج چاه کنی borj-e' châh-kani

derriere *n.* باسن bâsan کون kun

descend *vi., vt.* پایین آمدن pâyin âmadan فرودآمدن forud âmadan نازل شدن nâzel shodan هبوط کردن hobut kardan

descendant *n., adj.* وارث vâres نسل nasl

descent *n.* نرود forud نسل nasl نزول nozul هبوط hobut

describe *vt.* شرح دادن sharh dâdan توصیف کردن tosif kardan

description *n.* شرح sharh توصیف tosif تشریح tâshrih

descriptive *adj.* مشروح mashruh ترسیمی tarsimi وصفی vasfi

desease *n.* مرض maraz ناخوشی nâkhoshi بیماری bimâri

desert *n.* بیابان biâbân صحرا sahrâ برهوت barahut

desert *v.* فرارکردن farâr kardan
ازسربازی دررفتن az sar-bâzi dar raftan

desertion *n.* فرارازخدمت farâr az khedmat

deserve *vt., vi.* شایسته بودن shâyesteh budan
سزاواربودن sezâvâr budan

deserving *adj.* مستحق mostahaq~ شایان shâyân سزاوار sezâvâr

design *n.* قصد qasd نیت niyat عمد 'amd

design *v.* طرح کردن tarh kardan

designate *v.* منتخب کردن montakhab kardan

designate *v.* تایین کردن ta'yin kardan

designation *n.* تخصیص takhsis انتخاب entekhâb

designee *n.* منتصب montasab

desirable *adj., n.* مطلوب matlub

desire *v.* میل داشتن meyl dâshtan هوس کردن havas kardan

desire *n.* میل meyl آرزو ârezu رغبت reqbat

desk *n., adj.* میزتحریر miz-e' tahrir

desolate *v.* ویران کردن virân kardan

desolate *adj.* متروک matruk ویران virân

despair *n., vi., vt.* یأس داشتن ya's dâshtan ناامیدی nâ-omidi
حرمان hermân

desperado *n.* دزد dozd

desperate *adj., n.* مأیوس ma'yus پاک باخته pâkbâkhteh

despicable *adj.* پست past

despise *vt.* متنفر بودن motenaf~er budan

despite *pre., n., vt.* علیرغم 'alâraqm بااینکه bâ-inkeh

despiteful *adj.* کینه توز kineh-tuz

despond *vi., n.* دلسرد شدن delsard shodan

despondence *n.* دلسردی delsardi

despondent *adj.* دلسرد delsard افسرده afsordeh
despot *n.* مستبد mostabed ستمگر setam-gar
despotic *adj.* مستبدانه mostabedâneh مطلق motlaq
dessert *n.* دسر deser
destabilize *n.* بی ثبات کردن bi-sabât kardan
destination *n.* مقصد maqsad
destine *vt.* درنظرگرفتن dar nazar gereftan تقدیرداشتن taqdir dâshtan
destined *adj.* تقدیرشده taqdir shodeh
destiny *n.* سرنوشت sarnevesht تقدیر taqdir قسمت qesmat
destitute *adj., vt.* بی چیز bi-chiz مستضعف mostaz'af بدبخت bad-bakht
فلکزده falak-zadeh
destitution *n.* تهی دستی tohi-dasti
destroy *vt., vi.* ازبین بردن az beyn bordan خراب کردن kharâb kardan
destroyer *n.* مخرب mokhar~eb ناوشکن nâv-shekan
destruct *adj., n., vt.* خراب کردن kharâb kardan
destruction *n.* خرابی kharâbi انهدام enhedâm ویرانی virâni
ازاله ezâleh
destructive *adj.* مخرب mokhar~eb
detach *vt.* جدا ساختن jodâ sâkhtan
detached *adj.* جدا jodâ مجزا mojaz~â
detachment *n.* جدائی jodâ'i تجرد tâjar~od
detail *n., vt.* گروه اعزامی goruh-e' e'zâmi
detail *v.* تمیز کاری tamiz-kâri
detail *n.* جزء joz'
detail *v.* به تفصیل گفتن beh tafsil goftan
detailed *n.* بتفصیل be-tafsil مفصل mofas~al مشروح mashruh
details *n.* جزئیات joz'iyât
detain *vt.* نگهداشتن negah dâshtan حبس کردن habs kardan
detect *vt.* کشف کردن kashf kardan بو کشیدن bu keshidan
detection *n.* کشف kashf آشکاری âshkâri
detective *n., adj.* کارآگاه kârâgâh
detector *n.* یابنده yâbandeh
detent *n.* صلح solh مسالمت mosâlemat
detention *n., adj.* نگهداری negahdâri بازداشت bâzdâsht
deter *vt.* جلوگیری کردن jel-o giri kardan بازداشتن bâz dâshtan
detergent *adj., n.* شوینده shuyandeh
پودر رخت شویی pudr-e' rakht shuyi
deteriorate *vt., vi.* بدتر کردن badtar kardan

خرابتر شدن .... kharâb-tar shodan
deterioration n. خرابی kharâbi زوال zavâl
determinant n. تأیین کننده ta'yin konandeh
determinate adj., vt. مصمم mosam~am معین mo'ay~an
determination n. تصمیم tasmim تأیین ta'yin
determine vt., vi. معین کردن mo'ay~an kardan
تشخیص دادن tashkhis dâdan
determined adj. مصمم mosam~am
deterrent adj., n. مانع mâne' بازدارنده bâz-dârandeh
detest vt. تنفر داشتن tanaf~or dâshtan
dethrone v. خلع کردن khal' kardan
dethrone v. از پادشاهی انداختن az pâdeshâhi andâkhtan
dethroned vt. مخلوع makhlu'
detonate vi., vt. منفجر کردن monfajer kardan
detonation n. انفجار enfejâr
detour n., vi., vt. جادهٔ موقتی jâd~eh-ye' movaq~ati
دورگشت dor-gasht
detract vt., vi. کم کردن kâm kardân کسر کردن kasr kardan
detraction n. کسر kasr
detriment n. زیان ziân
detrimental adj. مضر mozer~ زیان آور ziân-âvar ضرر دار zarar dâr
devalue vt. تنزل دادن tanaz~ol dâdan
devastate vt. منهدم کردن monhadem kardan
devastation n. انهدام enhedâm ویرانی veyrâni
develop vt., vi. توسعه دادن tose'eh dâdan مبتلاشدن mobtalâ shodan
developer n. توسعه دهنده tose'eh dahandeh
development n. توسعه tose'eh پیشرفت pishraft
development n. تکامل takâmol پیشامد pishâmad
deviate v. منحرف شدن monharef shodan
deviate v. منحرف کردن monharef kardan
deviation n. انحراف enherâf
device n. وسیله vasileh اختراع ekhterâ' تدبیر tadbir
devil n., vt. شیطان sheytân
devise vt., vi., n. اختراع کردن ekhterâ' kardan
تدبیر کردن tadbir kardan
devoid adj. خالی khâli تهی tohi عاری 'âri
devote vt., adj. وقف کردن vaqf kardan اختصاص دادن ekhtesâs dâdan
devoted adj. فداکار fadâ-kâr علاقمند alâqemand

devotee *n.* مرید morid ندائی fadâ'i
devotion *n.* علاقه 'alâqeh نداکاری fadâ-kâri هواخواهی havâ-khâhi
devour *vt.* بلعیدن bal'idan دریدن daridan
devout *adj.* دیندار dindâr بااعتقاد bâ-e'teqâd پارسا pârsâ
dew *n., vt.* شبنم shabnam ژاله zhâleh
dew melon *n.* گرمک garmak
dexterity *n.* مهارت mahârat زبردستی zebardasti
diabetes *n.* مرض قند maraz-e' qand
diagnose *vt., vi.* تشخیص دادن tashkhis dâdan
diagnosis *n.* تشخیص tashkhis
diagonal *adj., n.* مایل mâyel مورب movar~ab
diagram *n., vt.* طرح tarh عکس 'aks
dial *v.* شماره گرفتن shomâreh gereftan
dial *n.* صفحهٔ ساعت safheh-ye' sâ'at
dialect *n.* لهجه lahjeh
dialogue *v.* گفتگو کردن goftegu kardan
dialogue *n.* گفتگو goftegu
diameter *n.* قطر qotr
diamond *n., adj., vt.* الماس almâs
diaper *n., vt.* کهنهٔ بچه kohneh-ye' bach~eh
diaphragm *n., vt.* حجاب حاجز hejâb-e' hâjez دیافراگم diâfrâgm
diarrhea *n.* اسهال es-hâl
diary *n.* روزنوشت ruznevesht سفرنامه safarnâmeh
diatribe *n.* انتقاد شدید enteqâd-e' shadid
dice *n., vt., vi.* تاس tâs خردکردن khord kardan
dichotomy *n.* تقسیم مقایسه‌ای taqsim-e' moqâyeseh-i
dicker *vi., vt., n.* چانه زدن châneh zadan
dictate *vt., vi., n.* دیکته کردن dikteh kardan دستور دادن dastur dâdan
dictator *n.* دیکتاتور diktâtor حاکم مطلق hâkem-e' motlaq
dictatorship *n.* استبداد estebdâd دیکتاتوری diktâtori
dictionary *n.* دیکسیونر diksioner فرهنگ لغات farhang-e' loqât
قاموس qâmus
didactic *adj.* تعلیمی ta'limi یاددهنده yâd dahandeh
die *n.* تاس tâs سرسکه sar-sek~eh قالب qâleb
die *v.* مردن mordan فوت کردن fot kardan هلاک شدن halâk shodan
diet *n., vt., vi.* رژیم گرفتن rezhim gereftan غذای ویژه qazâ-ye' vizheh
dietary *adj., n.* رژیمی rezhimi
differ *vi.* فرق داشتن farq dâshtan اختلاف داشتن ekhtelâf dâshtan

difference *n., vt.* فرق farq اختلاف ekhtelâf تفاوت tafâvot
تفاضل tafâzol
different *adj.* متفاوت motefâvet
differential *adj., n.* مختلف mokhtalef
differentiate *vt., vi.* فرق گذاشتن farq gozâshtan
تشخیص دادن tashkhis dâdan
difficult *adj.* مشكل moshkel سخت sakht
difficulty *n.* اشكال eshkâl سختی sakhti زحمت zahmat
diffidence *n.* خجالت khejâlat کمرویی kam-ruyi
diffident *adj.* کمرو kam-ru خجالتی khejâlati خجول khajul
diffuse *v.* افشاندن afshândan رفع انفجار raf'e enfejâr
diffuse *adj.* پراکنده parâkandeh پخش pakhsh
diffusion *n.* اضافه ezâfeh پخش pakhsh پرحرفی por-harfi
dig *v.* کندن kandan حفر کردن hafr kardan چال کردن châl kardan
dig *v.* دوست داشتن dust dâshtan
digest *vt., vi., n.* هضم کردن hazm kardan
digestible *adj.* هضم شدنی hazm-shodani گوارا govârâ
digestive *adj., n.* هضمی hazmi هاضمه hâzemeh
digit *n.* رقم raqam عدد 'adad انگشت angosht
digital *adj., n.* رقمی raqami نمره دار nomreh-dâr
dignified *adj.* باشخصیت bâ-shakhsiyat متشخص moteshakh~es
موقر novaq~ar
dignify *vt.* با ارزش کردن bâ-arzesh kardan
dignitary *n.* مقام دار maqâm-dâr معروف ma'ruf
dignity *n.* شأن sha'n شرف sharaf
digress *vi.* منحرف شدن monharef shodan
dike *n., vt.* سد sad~ خاک ریز khâkriz
dilapidated *adj.* خراب kharâb نکسنی fakas~ani
dilemma *n.* مخمصه makhmaseh بی تکلیفی bi-taklifi
diligence *n.* کوشش kushesh
diligent *adj.* کوشا kushâ ساعی sâ'i مجد mojed~
dilute *vt., vi., adj.* رقیق کردن raqiq kardan
dim *adj., vt., vi.* کم نور کردن kamnur kardan تارکردن târ kardan
dim *adj.* کم نور kam-nur کم سو kam-su
dime *n.* ده سنتی dah senti
dimension *n.* اندازه andâzeh بعد bo'd
diminish *vt., vi.* کم کردن kam kardan تقلیل یانتن taqlil yâftan
diminutive *adj., n.* کوچک kuchek نسقلی fesqeli مصغر mosaq~ar

dimple *n., vt., vi.* چال châl

dine *vi., vt., n.* غذا خوردن qazâ khordan شام خوردن shâm khordan

dingbat *n.* خرئت کودن kodan khereft

dinghy *n.* قایق پارویی qâyeq-e' pâruyi

dingy *adj., n.* چرک cherk خل khol

dinky *adj., n.* خل khol

dinner *n.* شام shâm

dip *v.* درآب فروبردن dar âb foru bordan

dip *v.* فرورفتگی foru raftegi

dip *n.* آبتنی âbtani

dip *v.* آبتنی کردن âbtani kardan

diphteria *n.* دیفتری difteri

diploma *n., vt.* دیپلم diplom مدرک madrak

diplomacy *n.* دیپلماسی diplomâsi سیاستمداری siâsatmadâri

diplomat *n.* دیپلمات diplomât سیاستمدار siâsatmadâr

dipper *n.* ملاقه malâqeh ملاغه malâqeh

dire *adj.* اسفناک asaf-nâk ترسناک tars-nâk

direct *vt., vi., adj., adv.* مستقیم mostâqim بی واسطه bi-vâseteh
یک راست yek-râst

direct *v.* هدایت کردن hedâyat kardan

direct *v.* راهنمایی کردن râhnamâyi kardan

direction *n.* دستور dastur

direction *n.* هدایت hedâyat راهنمایی râhnamâyi جهت jahat

directive *adj., n.* دستوریه dasturieh

directly *adv., con.* مستقیما mostaqiman یک راست yek-râst

director *n.* هدایت کننده hedâyat-konandeh کارگردان kârgardân

dirt *n.* خاک khâk چرک cherk

dirty *adv., adj., vt., vi.* خاکی khâki چرک cherk کثیف kasif
ملوث molav~as

disable *v.* ازکارانداختن az kâr andâkhtan

disable *v.* فلج کردن falaj kardan

disabled *vt.* فلج falaj ناتوان nâtavân معلول ma'lul عاجز 'âjez

disadvantage *n.* زیان ziân نامطلوبی nâ-matlubi
نکتهٔ منفی nokteh-ye' manfi

disadvantageous *adj.* بی صرفه bi-sarfeh زیان آور ziâan-âvar
نامساعد nâ-mosa'ed

disaffected *adj.* ناراضی nâ-râzi نامایل nâ-mâyel
زده شده zadeh-shodeh

disaffection *n.* نارضایتی nâ-rezâyati عدم تمایل 'adam-e' tamâyol زدگی zadegi

disagree *vi.* ناموافق بودن nâmovâfeq budan مخالف بودن mokhâlef budan

disagreement *n.* اختلاف ekhtelâf ناموافقت nâ-movâfeqat

disallow *vt.* اجازه ندادن ejâzeh nadâdan

disappear *vt.* ناپدیدشدن nâ-padid shodan غیب شدن qeyb shodan محوشدن mahv shodan آب شدن âb shodan

disappearance *n.* ناپدیدی nâ-padidi غیب شدگی qeyb-shodegi محو mahv

disappoint *vt.* مأیوس کردن ma'yus kardan

disappointed *adj.* مأیوس ma'yus

disappointing *adj.* یأس آور ya's-âvar ناامیدکننده nâ-omid konandeh

disappointment *n.* ناامیدی nâ-omidi یأس ya's

disapproval *n.* ناقبولی nâ-qabuli تقبیح taqbih

disaprove *n.* مخالفت کردن mokhâlefat kardan

disarm *vt., vi.* خلع سلاح کردن khal'-e' selâh kardan

disarray *vt., n.* بهم ریختن beham rikhtan

disassociate *vt.* جدا کردن jodâ kardan

disaster *n.* مصیبت mosibat بلا balâ بدبختی badbakhti

disavow *vt.* رد کردن rad kardan انکار کردن enkâr kardan

disavowal *n.* انکار enkâr

disband *vt., vi.* منحل کردن monhal kardan

disbar *vt.* اخراج از وکالت ekhrâj az vekâlat

disbelief *n.* ناباوری nâ-bâvari

disbelieve *v.* باورنکردن bâvar nakardan

disbelieve *v.* بی اعتقادبودن bi-e'teqâd budan

disburse *v.* پرداخت کردن pardâkht kardan خرج کردن kharj kardan

disbursemnt *n.* پرداخت pardâkht خرج kharj

disc jockey *np.* آهنگ گذار âhang-gozâr

discard *vt., vi., n.* دورانداختن dur andâkhtan

discern *vt., vi.* تشخیص دادن tashkhis dâdan

discerning *adj.* فهمیده fahmideh

discernment *n.* تشخیص tashkhis

discharge *vt., vi., n.* خالی کردن khâli kardan آزاد کردن âzâd kardan

disciple *n., vt.* پیرو peyro ندیم nadim اصحاب as-hâb

disciplinarian *n., adj.* انظباطی enzebâti

discipline *n., vt.* انضباط دادن enzebât dâdan

disclaim *vt., vi.* ازخود ندانستن az khod nadânestan
disclose *v.* افشاءکردن efshâ' kardan گفتن goftan
disclosure *n.* افشاء efshâ'
discolor *vt., vi.* بیرنگ کردن birang kardan
discomfort *n., vt.* ناراحتی nârâhati
discomfort *n.* ناراحتی nâ-râhati
disconnect *vt.* جدا کردن jodâ kardan
disconnected *adj.* قطع شده qat' shodeh
discontent *adj., n., vt.* نارضایتی nâ-rezâyati
discontinue *vt., vi.* ادامه ندادن edâmeh nadâdan
discord *n., vi.* ناسازگاری nâ-sâzegâri اختلاف ekhtelâf
discordant *adj.* ناساز nâ-sâz ناسازگار nâ-sâzgâri
discount *vt., vi., n.* تخفیف دادن takhfif dâdan
discourage *vt.* ناامید کردن nâ-omid kardan
دلسرد کردن delsard kardan
discouraged *vt.* ناامید nâ-omid دکوراژه dekorâzheh
discourse *n.* سخنرانی sokhanrâni گفتار goftâr
discourtesy *n.* بی ادبی bi-adabi بی احترامی bi-ehterâmi
discover *vt.* کشف کردن kashf kardan
discoverer *n.* کاشف kâshef
discovery *n.* کشف kashf اکتشاف ekteshâf
discredit *v.* بی اعتبارکردن bi-e'tebâr kardan
discredit *v.* بد نام کردن bad-nâm kardan
discreet *adj.* محتاط mohtât سری ser~i
discrepancy *n.* اختلاف ekhtelâf
discrete *adj.* جدا jodâ
discretion *n.* صلاحدید salâh-did دلخواه del-khâh
discretionery *n.* صلاحدیدی salâh-didi دلبخواهی del-bekhâhi
discriminate *vi., vt., adj.* فرق گذاشتن farq gozâshtan
تبعیض کردن tab'iz kardan
discrimination *n.* تبعیض tab'iz
discus *n.* دیسک disk مهره mohreh
discuss *vt.* بحث کردن bahs kardan مذاکره کردن mozâkereh kardan
discussion *n.* بحث bahs مذاکره mozâkereh
disdain *v.* پست شماردن past shemârdan تکبر کردن takob~ or kardan
disdain *n.* پست شماری past shemâri تکبر takab~ or
disdainful *adj.* متکبر motekab~ er اهانت آمیز ehânat-âmiz
disect *v.* دوقسمت کردن do-qesmat kardan دونیم کردن do-nim kardan

تجزیه کردن .... tajzieh kardan شکاف دادن shekâf dâdan
disection *n.* تجزیه tajzieh شکاف shekâf
disembark *vt., vi.* پیاده شدن piâdeh shodan
disengage *vt., vi.* رهاکردن rahâ kardan درآوردن dar âvardan
disfavor *n., vt.* غضب داشتن qazab dâshtan
disfigure *vt.* ناقص کردن nâqes kardan
disgorge *vt., vi.* ازگلودرآوردن az galu dar âvardan
disgrace *v.* لکه دار کردن lak~eh-dâr kardan
disgrace *v.* شرمنده کردن sharmandeh kardan
disgrace *n.* ننگ nang رسوائی rosvâ'i فضاحت fezâhat
disgraceful *adj.* ننگ آمیز nang-âmiz شرم آور sharm-âvar
disgruntled *vt.* عصبانی 'asabâni
disguise *vt., n.* لباس مبدل lebâs-e' mobad~al
disguise *v.* پنهان کردن penhân kardan
disguised *v.* درلباس dar lebâs-e'
disgust *vt., n.* بیزارکردن bizâr kardan
disgusted *n.* بیزار bizâr منزجر monzajer
disgusting *adj.* انزجار آور enzejâr âvar
dish *n., vt.* ظرف zarf بشقاب boshqâb خوراک khorâk
dishearten *vt.* دلسرد کردن delsard kardan
dishonest *adj.* نادرست nâ-dorost متقلب moteqal~eb
dishonesty *n.* نادرستی nâ-dorosti
dishonor *n.* ننگ nang عار 'âr
dishonor *n., vt.* بی احترامی کردن bi-ehterâmi kardan
dishonorable *adj.* ننگین nangin شرم آور sharm-âvar
dishonored *n.* بی آبرو bi-âberu
dishwasher *n.* ظرف شور zarf-shur
disillusioned *n.* وازده vâzadeh
disinfect *v.* ضد عفونی کردن zed~-e' 'ofuni kardan
گندزدایی کردن gan-zedâyi kardan
disinfectant *adj.* ضد عفونی zed~-e' 'ofuni گندزدا gand-zedâ
disinformation *n.* جعلیات ja'liyât
disinherit *vt.* ازارث محروم کردن az ers mahrum kardan
عاق کردن 'âq kardan
disintegrate *vi., vt.* خرد شدن khord shodan
متلاشی کردن motelâshi kardan
disinterested *adj.* بی علا قه bi-'alâqeh
disk *n., vt.* مهره mohreh دیسک disk کمردرد kamar dard

dislikable *adj.* دوست نداشتنی dust nadâshtani
dislike *vt., n.* دوست نداشتن dust nadâshtan
dislocation *n.* دررفتگی dar-raftegi
dislodge *vt., vi.* درآوردن dar âvardan
disloyal *adj.* بیوفا bi-vafâ
disloyalty *n.* بیوفایی bi-vafâ'i
dismal *adj., n.* رقت انگیز req~at-angiz
dismantel *n.* پیاده کردن piâdeh kardan بهم پاشیدن beham pâshidan
dismay *n.* یأس ya's ناامیدی nâ-omidi
dismay *v.* ترساندن tarsândan مأیوس کردن ma'yus kardan
dismember *v.* تکه تکه کردن tek~eh-tek~eh kardan
dismember *v.* قطعه قطعه کردن qat'eh qat'eh kardan
dismiss *vt.* اخراج کردن ekhrâj kardan مرخص کردن mor-khas kardan
dismissal *n.* اخراج ekhrâj
dismount *vi., vt., n.* پیاده شدن piâdeh shodan
disobedience *n.* نافرمانی nâ-farmâni تمرد tamar~od
disobedient *adj.* نافرمان nâfarmân سرپیچ sarpich متمرد motemar~ed
disobey *vt., vi.* سرپیچی کردن sâr-pichi kardan
disorder *n., vt.* بی نظمی binazmi ناامنی nâ-amni
disorderly *adj., adv.* بی نظم bi-nazm درهم و بر هم dar ham-o bar-ham
ریخته پاشیده rikhteh pâshideh مغشوش maqshush
disorganized *vt.* نامنظم nâ-monaz~am
disorient *vt.* مغشوش کردن maqshush kardan
disown *vt.* عاق کردن 'âq kardan
disparage *vt.* حقیرکردن haqir kardan
dispatch *v.* اعزام کردن e'zâm kardan
گسیل دادن gosil dâdan مخابره کردن mokhâbereh kardan
dispatcher *n.* مخابر - تلفنچی mokhâber- telefonchi
dispensable *adj.* چشم پوشیدنی cheshm pushidani
dispensation *n.* ترخیص tarkhis توزیع tozi'
dispense *v.* صرف نظرکردن sarf-e' nazar kardan
dispense *v.* توزیع کردن tozi' kardan
disperse *vt., vi., adj.* پراکنده شدن parâkandeh shodan
dispersion *n.* پراکندگی parâkandegi
displace *vt.* بیجا کردن bijâ kardan تعویض کردن ta'viz kardan
displacement *n.* جابجاشدگی jâ-bejâ-shodegi
display *vt., n.* نمایش دادن namâyesh dâdan نشان دادن neshân dâdan
displease *vt., vi.* رنجاندن ranjândan

displeasure *n.* رنجش ranjesh آزردگى âzordegi نارضايتى nâ-rezâyati کدورت kodurat

disposable *adj.* دورانداختنى dur andâkhtani

disposal *n.* توزيع tozi' اختيار ekhtiâr بيرون ريز birun-riz

dispose *vt., vi., n.* مستعد کردن mosta'ed kardan دورانداختن dur andâkhtan

disposed *adj.* متمايل motemâyel

disposition *n.* حالت hâlat اخلاق akhlâq استقرار esteqrâr

disspossess *vt.* نخواستن nakhâstan خلع يد کردن khal'e' yad kardan

disprove *vt.* رد کردن rad kardan

disputable *adj.* قابل بحث qâbel-e' bahs مشاجره اى moshâjereh-i

dispute *v.* مشاجره کردن moshâjereh kardan گفتگو کردن goftegu kardan منکر شدن monker shodan

dispute *n.* گفتگو goftegu عدم توافق 'adam-e' tavâfoq يک و دو yek-o do مشاجره moshâjereh

disqualify *vt.* سلب صلاحيت کردن salb-e' salâhiyat kardan

disregard *vt., n.* اهميت ندادن ahamiyat nadâdan

disreputable *adj.* بدنام bad-nâm

disrespect *n., vt.* بى احترامى کردن bi-ehterâmi kardan

disrespectful *adj.* بى احترام bi-ehterâm

disrobe *vt., vi.* لباس در آوردن lebâs dar âvardan لخت شدن lokht shodan

disrupt *vt., adj.* قطع کردن qat' kardan بهم زدن beham zadan

disruptive *adj.* دوبهمزن do-behamzan

dissatisfied *adj.* ناراضى nâ-râzi

dissatisfy *vt.* ناراضى کردن nârâzi kardan

dissect *vt.* تشريح کردن tashrih kardan

dissection *n.* کالبد شکافى kâlbod-shekâfi

dissension *n.* اختلاف ekhtelâf

dissent *vi., n.* نا قبولى کردن nâ qabuli kardan

dissenting *n.* مخالف mokhâlef

disservice *n.* زيان ziân

dissident *adj., n.* مخالف mokhâlef

dissimilate *vt.* ناجور کردن nâjur kardan

dissipate *v.* تلف کردن talaf kardan

dissipate *v.* پراکنده کردن parâkandeh kardan

dissolution *n.* جدايى jodâ'i

dissolve *vt., vi., n.* حل کردن hal~ kardan

منحل كردن .... monhal~ kardan

distance *n., vt.* فاصله fâseleh مسافت masâfat

distant *adj.* فاصله دار fâseleh-dâr دور dur

distaste *n., vt.* بی میلی bi-meyli بی مزه گی bi mazegi

distill *vt., vi.* تقطیر كردن taqtir kardan

distiller *n.* تقطیر كننده taqtir konandeh

distinct *adj.* مجزا mojaz~â واضح vâzeh متمایز motemâyez
متباین motebâyen

distinction *n.* فرق farq برتری bartari تباین tabâyon

distinctly *adv.* بطورواضح be-tor-e' vâzeh

distinguish *vt., vi.* تمیز دادن tamiz dâdan
تشخیص دادن tashkhis dâdan

distinguished *adj.* برجسته barjesteh موقر movaq~ar

distort *vt.* بدشکل كردن bad-shekl kardan تغییردادن taqyir dâdan

distorted *adj.* کج شده kaj-shodeh

distortion *n.* تحریف tahrif تغییرشکل taqyir-e' shekl

distract *vt., adj.* حواس پرت كردن havâs part kardan

distress *n., vt.* پریشان كردن parishân kardan خطر khatar

distressful *adj.* پریشان parishân

distribute *vt.* پخش كردن pakhsh kardan توزیع كردن tozi' kardan

distribution *n.* توزیع tozi'

distributor *n.* پخش كننده pakhsh konandeh

district *n., vt.* بخش bakhsh ناحیه nâhiyeh برزن barzan

district attorney *np.* دادستان dâdsetân

distrust *vt., n.* ناباوری nâ-bâvari

distrust *v.* بی اعتماد بودن bi-e'temâd budan

distrustful *adj.* بدگمان bad-gamân

disturb *vt., vi.* مزاحم شدن mozâhem shodan

disturbance *n.* ناراحتی nârâhati مزاحمت mozâhemat غائله qa'eleh

disturbed *n.* ناراحت شده na-râhat shodeh مضطرب moztareb

ditch *n., vt., vi.* گودال godâl دور انداختن dur andâkhtan

dither *n., vi.* هیجان hayajân آشفتگی âshoftegi لرزیدن larzidan

dithery *n.* دودل do-del

ditto *n., adv., vt.* همانطور hamântor کپی kopi

divan *n.* نیمکت راحتی nimkat râhati

dive *pl.* شیرجه زدن shirjeh zadân

diver *n.* غواص qav~âs

diverge *vi., vt.* ازهم دور شدن az-ham dur shodan

واگراییدن .... vâ-garâyidan

divergence n. ازهم دوری az-ham duri واگرایی vâ-garâyi

divergent adj. دورازهم dur az-ham واگرا vâ-garâ

diverse adj. متعدد mote'ad~ed گوناگون gunâgun

diversify vt. متنوع کردن motenav~e' kardan

diversion n. انحراف enherâf رد گم کن rad gom-kon

diversity n. گوناگونی gunâguni تنوع tanav~o'

divert vt. برگردانیدن bar gardânidan منحرف کردن monharef kardan

divest vt. بیچیزکردن bi-chiz kardan بی چیز کردن bichiz kardan

divestment n. محرومیت mahrumiyat

divide v. تفرقه انداختن tafreqeh andâkhtan

divide v. تقسیم کردن taqsim kardan

divided adj. تقسیم شده taqsim shodeh

dividend n. سود سهام sud-e' sahâm بهره bahreh

divider n. جداکننده jodâ konandeh مقسم moqas~em

divine adj., n., vt., vi. الهی elâhi خدایی khodâyi لاهوت lâhut

divinity n. الوهیت oluhiyat لاهوت lâhut

division n. تقسیم taqsim بخش bakhsh

division n. لشگر lashgar

divorce n., vt., vi. طلا ق دادن talâq dâdan

divorced v. طلا ق گرفته talâq gerefteh مطلقه motal~aqeh

divorcer n. طلا ق دهنده talâq dahandeh

dizzy adj., vt. گیج gij

do v. کردن kardan انجام دادن anjâm dâdan

do (away) n. کنارگذاشتن kenâr gozâshtan کشتن koshtan

do (in) n. کشتن koshtan

do (over) n. دوباره انجام دادن dobâreh anjâm dâdan

do (without) n. بدون چیزی سرکردن bedun-e' chizi sar kardan

docile adj. رام râm اهلی ahli مطیع moti'

dock n., vt., vi. بارانداز bârandâz لنگر انداختن langar andâkhtan

docket n., vt. خلا صه kholâseh اجرایی ejrâyi

doctor n., vt., vi. پزشک pezeshk طبیب tabib دکتر doktor

doctorate n. دکترا doktorâ

doctrine n. تعلیم ta'lim نلسفه falsafeh

document n., vt. سند sanad مدرک madrak

dodge v. اززیر دررفتن az zir dar raftan

dodge v. جا خالی دادن jâ khâli dâdan

dodger n. جاخالی کن jâ khâli-kon نرارکن farâr-kon

dodo *n.* خرفت khereft
dog *n.* سگ sag کلب kalb
dog-gone *n.* لا مصب lâ-mas~ab لعنتی la'nati
dogberry *n.* ذغال اخته zoqâl-akhteh
dogfight *n., vt.* جنگ تعقیبی jang-e' ta'qibi
dogma *n.* عقیده 'aqideh ایمان imân
dogmatic *adj.* سخت گیر sakht-gir متعصبانه mote'as~ebâneh
dole *np., vt.* خیرات kheyrât صدقه دادن sadaqeh dâdan
doll *n., vt., vi.* عروسک 'arusak
dollar *n.* دلار dolâr
dolly *n., vt., vi.* بارکش چرخ دار bârkesh-e' charkh-dâr
domain *n.* قلمرو qalamro ملک molk
dome *n., vt., vi.* گنبد gonbad
domestic *adj., n.* اهلی ahli وطنی vatani خدمتکار khedmatkâr
domicile *n., vt.* مکان makân اقامتگاه eqâmatgâh مقر maqar~
dominant *adj., n.* مسلط mosal~at حکمفرما شدن hokm-farmâ shodan
dominion *n.* ملک molk قلمرو qalamro پادشاهی pâdeshâhi
don *con., n., vt.* پوشیدن pushidan
donate *vt., vi.* بخشیدن bakhshidan اهدا کردن ehdâ kardan
donation *n.* دهش dahesh صدقه sadaqeh
donkey *n., adj.* خر khar الاغ olâq
doodle *vt., vi., n.* بی هدف نوشتن bi-hadaf neveshtan
doom *n., vt.* محکوم کردن mahkumm kardan
doomed *n.* محکوم بفنا mahkum be-fanâ
doomsday *n.* روزقیامت ruz-e' qiâmat
door *n.* در dar باب bâb
doorkeeper *n.* دربان darbân
dope *n., vt.* مخدرات mokhad~arât احمق ahmaq
dormant *adj.* خوابیده khâbideh
dormi(tory) *n.* خوابگاه khâbgâh
dosage *n.* مقدار دوا meqdâr-e' davâ
dot *n., vt., vi.* نقطه چین کردن noqteh-chin kardan نقطه noqteh
dotted *adj.* نقطه چین noqteh-chin
double *adj., n., vt., vi.* دوتا dotâ دوبرابرکردن dobarâbar kardan
     دوبل dubl مضاعف mozâ'af
double cross *np.* خیانت کردن khiânat kardan نارو زدن nâro zadan
double-decker *n.* دو طبقه do-tabaqeh
double-faced *adj.* دو رو doru

doubletalk *n.* زدن دوپهلوحرف do-pahlu harf zadan
doubt *vt., vi., n.* کردن شک shak~ kardan کردن تردید tardid kardan
doubt *n.* شک shak~ تردید tardid شبهه shobheh
doubtless *adv., adj.* شک بدون bedun-e' shak~
dough *n.* خمیر khamir مایه mâyeh پول pul
dour *adj.* عبوس 'abus سرسخت sarsakht
douse *vt., vi., n.* کردن خاموش khâmush kardan ریختن آب âb rikhtan
dove *n., v.* کبوتر kabutar قمری qomri
dowel *n., vt.* چوبی میخ mikh-e' chubi
down *adv., pre., adj., n.* پایین pâyin
down *adv., pre., adj., n.* افسرده afsordeh
down *adv., pre., adj., n.* پر par
downfall *n.* سقوط soqut ریزش rizesh
downhill *adv., adj.* سرازیری sarâziri
downright *adj., adv.* کاملا kâmelan رک rok
downstairs *adv., adj., n.* پایین طبقهٔ tabaqeh-ye' pâyin
dowry *n.* جهیزیه jahiziyeh کابین kâbin
dozen *vt., n., adj.* دوجین dojin
drab *n., adj., vi.* یکنواخت yek-navâkht کننده خسته khasteh konandeh
draft *v.* کردن نویس پیش pishnevis kardan
draft *v.* بردن سربازی sarbâzi bordan کردن انتخاب entekhâb kardan
draft *n.* سربازی sarbâzi انتخاب entekhâb
draft dodger *np.* فرارکرده ازسربازی az sarbâzi farâr kardeh
draftsman *n.* طراح tar~âh کش رسم rasm-kesh
drafty *adj.* دار باد bâd dâr کوران kurân
drag *n.* مسابقه mosâbeqeh
drag *n.* کشش keshesh
drag *n.* زحمت اسباب asbâb-e' zahmat
drag *v.* کشیدن keshidan دادن کش kesh dâdan
dragnet *n.* دستگیرنامه dastgirnâmeh جلب برگ barg-e' jalb
dragon *n.* اژدها ezhdehâ
drain *vt., vi., n.* کردن آبکش âbkesh kardan
کردن خشک khoshk kardan
drainage *v.* آبکشی âbkeshi
drainage *n.* آب فاضل fâzel-âb
drama *n.* انگیز غم نمایش namâyesh qam-angiz درام derâm
dramatize *vt.* کردن عرضه درام derâm 'arzeh kardan
drape *vt., vi., n.* زدن پرده pardeh zadan

drastic *adj.* فوق العاده foqol-'âdeh باشدت bâshed~at
draw *vt., vi., n.* عکس کشیدن 'aks keshidan رسم کردن rasm kardan
drawbridge *n.* پل متحرک pol-e' motehar~ek
drawers *n.* کشوها keshohâ زیرشلواری zir-shalvâri
dread *vt., vi., n., adj.* ترس داشتن tars dâshtan
dreadful *adj., n.* ترسناک tars-nâk بیمناک bim-nâk
dream *n., vi., vt.* رویا دیدن royâ didan خواب دیدن khâb didan
dredge *n., vt., vi.* لا روبی کردن lârubi kardan لجن کش lajan-kesh
drench *vt., n.* خیس کردن khis kardan
dress *n., adj., vt., vi.* لباس پوشیدن lebâs pushidan
پانسمان کردن pânsemân kardan
dresser *n.* جالباسی jâlebâsi کمد komod
dressing *n.* سس sos تزئین taz'in پانسمان pânsemân
dribble *vi., vt., n.* چکیدن chekidan دریبل کردن deribl kardan
drift *n., vi., vt.* شناور بودن shenâvar budan باباد رفتن bâ-bâd raftan
drill *v.* سوراخ کردن surâkh kardan تمرین دادن tamrin dadan
drill *n.* مته mat~eh تمرین tamrin مشق mashq
drink *v.* نوشیدن nushidan آشامیدن âshâmidan
drink *n.* نوشابه nushâbeh مشروب mashrub
drip *vi., vt., n.* چکه کردن chek~eh kardan قطره qatreh
drive *vt., vi., n., adj.* رانندگی کردن rânandegi kardan
جلو بردن jelo bordan
driver *n., adj.* راننده rânandeh شوفر shufer
drizzle *vt., vi., n.* باران ریز آمدن bârân-e' riz âmadan
نم نم آمدن nam nam âmadan
droll *adj., n., vi.* دلقک بازی کردن dalqak bâzi kardan
مسخره maskhareh
drone *vi., vt., n.* هواپیمای بی خلبان havâpeymâ-ye' bi-khalabân
drool *vi., n.* له له زدن lahlah zadan آب افتادن âb oftâdan
drop *n.* قطره qatreh سقوط soqut نشست neshast
drop *v.* انداختن andâkhtan افتادن oftâdan ول کردن vel kardan
dropping *n.* تاپاله tâpâleh پشکل peshkel
drought *n.* خشک سالی khoshksâli
drown *vi., vt.* غرق کردن qarq kardan
drudge *n., vi.* بیگاری کردن bi-gâri kardan
حمالی کردن ham~âli kardan
drug *n., vt.* داروخوراندن dâru khorândan دوادادن davâ dâdan
druggist *n.* داروساز dâru-sâz

drugstore *n.* داروفروشی dâru-forushi دواسازی dâvâ-sâzi
drum *n.* طبل tabl کوس kus
drum up *v.* دست وپاکردن dast-o pâ kardan جمع کردن jam' kardan
drummer *adj.* طبل زن tabl-zan طبال tab~âl دهل زن dohol-zan
drunk(ard) *n.* مست mast
dry *adj., vt., vi., n.* خشک کردن khoshk kardan
dry cleaner *np.* خشک شویی khoshk-shuyi
dual *adj., n.* دوتایی dotâyi
dub *vt., n., vi.* لقب دادن laqab dadan دوبله کردن dubleh kardan
dubious *adj.* مشکوک mashkuk
duck *vi., vt., n.* اردک ordak جاخالی دادن jâ-khâli dâdan
dud *n.* بی مصرف bimasraf نترکیده natarekideh
dude *n.* ژیگول zhigul یارو yâru
due *adj., n., adv.* قابل پرداخت qâbel-e' pardâkht بدهی bedehi
due (to) *n.* بنابر banâbar
duel *n., vt., vi.* جنگ تن بتن jang-e' tan-be-tan
dues *n.* حقوق عضویت hoquq-e' 'ozviyat بدهکاری bedehkâri
duet *n.* دونفره do-nafareh
dugout *n.* حفاری haf~âri سنگر sangar
dulcimer *n.* سنتور santur
dull *v.* کند کردن kond kardan
dull *adj.* خسته کننده khasteh-konandeh گرفته gerefteh کسل kesel
dull *adj.* کند kond
dull-minded *adj.* کندذهن kond-zehn
dumb *adj.* نفهم nafahm گنگ gong لال lâl
dumbell *n.* دمبل dambel هالتر hâlter
dumfound *vt.* مبهوت کردن mabhut kardan
dumfounded *n.* مبهوت mabhut
dummy *n., adj., vt.* آدمک âdamak آدم مصنوعی âdam-e' masnu'i کهنگ kheng
dump *vt., vi., n.* آشغال دانی âshqâldâni زباله ریختن zobâleh rikhtan
dump truck *np.* کامیون خاکروبه kâmion-e' khâkrubeh
dunce *n.* کودن kodan
dune *n.* تپه شنی tap~eh-ye' sheni
dungeon *n.* دخمه dakhmeh
dungeon *n.* کود kud تاپاله tâpâleh
duo *n.* دونفره do-nafareh
dupe *n.* هالو hâlu

duplex *adj., n.* دوجزئی dojoz'i دوتایی dotâyi
دوآپارتمانه do-âpârtemaneh
duplicate *adj., n., vt.* کپی گرفتن kopi gereftan المثنی almosan~â
durability *n.* استقامت esteqâmat
durable *adj., n.* بادوام bâ-davâm
duration *n.* طی tey مدت mod~at طول tul
duress *n.* اجبار ejbâr نشار feshâr
during *pre.* درحین dar-heyn-e' در مدت dar mod~at-e'
دراثنای dar asnâ-ye'
dusk *adj., n., vt., vi.* غروب qorub شفق shafaq
dust *n., vt., vi.* خاک khâk غبار qobâr گرد gard
dust *v.* گردگیری کردن gard-giri kardan
duster *n.* گردگیر gard-gir
dustpan *n.* خاک انداز khâk-andâz
duties *n.* گمرکی gomroki مالیات گمرک mâliât-e' gomrok
dutiful *n.* وظیفه شناس vazifeh-shenâs
duty *n.* وظیفه vâzifeh سر کار sar-e' kâr
duty *n.* گمرکی gomroki
dwarf *n., adj., vt., vi.* کوتوله kutuleh قدکوتاه qad kutâh
dwell *vi., n.* ساکن بودن sâken budan
dwindle *vi., vt.* کم شدن kam shodan کوچک شدن kuchak shodan
dye *n., vt., vi.* رنگ زدن rang zadan
dying *adj., vi., n.* مردنی mordani
dynamic *adj.* باحرکت bâ-harekat با انرژی bâ-enerzhi
dynamics *n.* علم حرکت اجسام 'elm-e' harekat-e' ajsâm
dynamite *n., vt.* دینامیت dinâmit
dynasty *n.* سلسله selseleh دودمان dudmân
dysentery *n.* اسهال خونی es-hâl-e' khuni

E E e

elan *n.* نشاط neshât شوق shoq
each *adj., pro., adv.* هر یک har yek هر کدام har kodâm
eager *adj., n.* مشتاق moshtâq
eagle *n., vt.* عقاب 'oqâb شاهین shâhin هما homâ
ear *n.* گوش gush
ear *n.* خوشه khusheh
eardrum *n.* پردۀ گوش pardeh-ye' gush
early *adv., adj.* قدیمی qadimi
early *adv., adj.* زود zud
earmark *n., vt.* تخصیص دادن takhsis dâdan
earn *v.* بدست آوردن bedast âvardan
earn *v.* سزاوار بودن sezâvâr budan
earnest *adj., n.* جدی jed~i واقعی vâqe'i
earnings *n.* درآمد darâmad کارمزد kârmozd
earth *n., vt.* زمین zamin
earthliness *n.* فروتنی forutani
earthquake *n.* زلزله zelzeleh
earthy *adj.* فروتن forutan خاکی khâki
earwax *n.* موم گوش mum-e' gush
earwig *n., vt.* گوش خزک gush khazak
ease *n., vt., vi.* آسانی âsâni راحتی râhati سهولت sohulat
ease *v.* آسوده کردن âsudeh kardan
easel *n.* سه پایه seh-pâyeh
easily *adv.* براحتی berâhati به آسانی be-âsâni
east *n., adj., adv.* شرق sharq خاور khâvar مشرق mashreq
Easter *n.* عید پاک 'eyd-e' pâk
easy *adj., adv., n.* آسان âsân راحت râhat
easy chair *np.* صندلی راحتی sandali râhati
easy-going *n.* آسان گیر âsân-gir
eat *vt., vi., n.* خوردن khordan
eatable *adj., n.* خوردنی khordani خوراکی khorâki
eavesdrop *vi., vt., n.* استراق سمع esterâq-e' sam'
eavesdrop *vi., vt., n.* دزدکی گوش دادن dozdaki gush dâdan
ebb *n., vi.* فروکشیدن foru keshidan جزر jazr
ebony *n., adj.* آبنوس âbnus
ebulient *n.* خروشان khorushân با هیجان bâ-hayajân
eccentric *adj., n.* دور از مرکز dur az markaz جنجالی janjâli

echelon *n., vt., vi.* دسته dasteh طبقه tabaqeh
echo *v.* منعکس شدن mon'akes shodan
echo *n.* انعکاس en'ekâs
eclips *n.* کسوف kosuf
eclipse *n., vt.* خسوف khosuf
ecology *n.* محیط شناسی mohit-shenâsi
economic *adj.* اقتصادی eqtesâdi
economical *adj.* کم مصرف kam-masraf کم خرج kam-kharj
مقرون بصرفه sarfeh-ju صرفه جو maqrun-e' be-sarfeh
economy *n., adv.* اقتصاد eqtesâd
ecstasy *n.* وجد vajd خلسه khalseh نشئه nash'eh سکر sokr
edge *n., vt., vi.* لبه labeh کنار kenâr تیزی tizi
edgy *adj.* عصبی 'asabi
edible *adj., n.* خوردنی khordani خوراکی khorâki مأکول ma'kul
edict *n.* فرمان farmân دستور dastur
edifice *n.* ساختمان sâkhtemân بنا banâ
edit *vt.* تصحیح کردن tashih kardan مونتاژ montâzh
editical *n.* موضعی moze'i مربوط بهجراحی marbut beh jar~âhi
edition *n.* چاپ châp
editor *n.* سردبیر sar-dabir
editorial *n., adj.* سرمقاله sar-maqâleh
editpathy *n.* بی علاقگی bi'alâqegi تنفر tanaf~ or
educate *vt., vi.* تحصیل کردن tahsil kardan
educated *vt.* تحصیل کرده tahsil kardeh
education *n.* تحصیل tahsil تحصیلات tahsilât
آموزش و پرورش 'muzesh-o parvaresh
تعلیم و تربیت ta'lim-o tarbiat
educator *n.* مربی morab~i
eel *pl.* مارماهی mâr mâhi
eerie *adj.* ترسناک tars-nâk
effect *n., vt.* اثرگذاشتن asar gozâshtan
effective *adj., n.* موثر mo'as~er قابل اجرا qâbel-e' ejrâ کاری kâri
effeminate *adj.* زن نما zan-namâ مخنث mokhan~as
effervescent *adj.* گازدار gâz-dâr
efficiency *n.* کفایت kefâyat کارکرد kârkard کارآیی kâr-âyi
efficient *adj.* باکفایت bâ-kefâyat باعرضه bâ-'orzeh کاربر kâr-bor
کار پیش بر kâr pish-bar
effigy *n.* تمثال temsâl پیکر peykar مجسمه moj~asâmeh

efflorescent *adj.* باشكوفه bâ-shekufeh

effort *n.* كوشش kushesh سعى sa'y اهتمام ehtemâm عنايت 'enâyat

effusive *adj.* بيرون ريز birun-riz متظاهر motezâher

egg *n., adj., vt.* تخم tokhm تخم مرغ tokhm-e' morq

egg (on) *n.* تيركردن tir kardan

eggplant *n.* بادنجان bâdenjân

egis/ aegis *n.* قيوميت qayumiyat مسئوليت mas'uliyat

ego *n.* خود khod غرور qorur

egocentric *adj., n.* خودبين khod-bin

egotism *n.* خودشيفتگى khod-shiftegi

egotist *n.* خودشيفته khod-shifteh

egotistical *n.* خودشيفته وار khod-shifteh-vâr

egress *n., vi.* بيرون رفتن birun raftan دررو dar-ro

eight *n., adj.* هشت hasht

eighteen *n., adj.* هجده hej-dah

eighty *n., adj.* هشتاد hashtâd

either *adj., pro., con., adv.* يا yâ هركدام har-kodâm هريك har-yek

eject *vt.* بيرون كردن birun kardan بيرون پريدن birun paridan

elaborate *v.* پيچيده pichideh

elaborate *v.* تفكر كردن tafak~or kardan

elapse *vi., n.* زمان گذشتن zamân gozashtan

elastic *adj., n.* كشدار keshdâr قابل كشش qâbel-e' keshesh

elate *vt., adj.* باروحيه كردن bâ ruhieh kardan نشاط دادن neshât dâdan

elated *adj., v.* سرافراز sar-afrâz

elation *n.* سرافرازى sar-afrâzi

elbow *n., vt., vi.* آرنج ârenj

elder *adj., n.* بزرگتر bozorgtar ارشد arshad ريش سفيد rish sefid

elderly *adj.* مسن mosen

eldest *adj.* بزرگترين bozorgtarin

elect *vt., vi., adj., n.* انتخاب كردن entekhâb kardan
برگزيدن bargozidan

elections *n.* انتخابات entekhâbât برگزيدگى bargozidegi

elective *adj., n.* انتخابى entekhâbi

elector *n.* انتخاب كننده entekhâb konandeh

electric *adj., n.* برقى barqi

electrician *n.* برق كار barq-kâr سيم كش simkesh

electricity *n.* الكتريسيته electriciteh برق barq

electrify *vt.* به هيجان آوردن be-hayajân âvardan

elegant *adj.* باشكوه bâ-shokuh با زرق و برق bâ zarq-o barq
مجلل mojal~al

element *n.* جزء joz' ركن rokn عنصر 'onsor دليل dalil

elementary *adj.* ابتدايى ebtedâyi مقدماتى moqadamâti اصلى asli

elementary school *np.* دبستان dabestân

elephant *n.* نيل fil

elevate *vt., adj.* بالا بردن bâlâ bordan بلند كردن boland kardan

elevation *n.* ارتفاع ertefâ' ارتقاء erteqâ' بلندى bolandi

elevator *n.* آسانسور âsânsor بالابر bâlâ-bar

eleven *n., adj.* يازده yâz-dah)

elf *n.* كوتوله kutuleh بچه شيطان bach~eh sheytân

elicit *vt.* بيرون آوردن birun âvardan

eligible *adj., n.* شايسته shâyesteh واجد شرايط vâjed-e' sharâyet

eliminate *vt.* حذف كردن hazf kardan برطرف كردن bartaraf kardan

elite *n., adj.* نخبگان nokhbegân اشراف ashrâf

elixir *n.* اكسير eksir

elk *n.* گوزن gavazn

ellipse *n.* بيضى beyzy

elm *n.* نارون nârvan

elocution *n.* هنرسخنرانى honar-e' sokhanrâni

elongate *vt., vi., adj.* درازكردن - شدن derâz kardan/shodan

eloquence *n.* فصاحت fesâhat بلاغت belâqat

eloquent *adj.* روان سخن ravân-sokhan بليغ baliq فصيح fasih
روان سخن ravân-sokhan

else *adj., adv.* ديگر digar والا vaelâ

elucidate *vt.* روشن كردن roshan kardan تشريح كردن tashrih kardan

elude *v.* گريز زدن goriz zadan

elude *v.* درنتن dar raftan

elusive *adj.* گريزان gorizân دست نيافتنى dast-nayâftani

emaciate *vt.* لاغر كردن lâqar kardan

emanate *vi., vt.* تجلى كردن tajal~i kardan بيرون ريختن birun rikhtan

emancipate *vt.* آزاد كردن âzâd kardan

emancipation *n.* آزادى âzâdi اعتاق e'tâq

emasculate *vt., adj.* ازمردى انداختن az mardi andâkhtan

embalm *vt.* موميايى كردن mumiâyi kardan

embankment *n.* خاك ريز khâkriz تپه tap~eh

embargo *n., vt.* محاصرۀ اقتصادى mohâsereh-ye' eqtesâdi
منع كردن man' kardan

embark *vt., vi.* سوارکردن savâr kardan
embark(upon) *n.* مبادرت کردن mobâderat kardan
embarrass *v.* خجالت دادن khejâlat dâdan
embarrass *v.* شرمنده کردن sharmandeh kardan
embarrassed *adj.* شرمنده sharmandeh خجل khajel شرمسار sharm-sâr
embarrassment *n.* خجالت khejâlat شرمندگی sharmandegi
embassy *n.* سفارت خانه sefârat khâneh
embattle *vt.* مستحکم کردن mostahkam kardan
درگیربودن dargir budan
embedded *vt.* جاگرفته jâ-gerefteh
embellish *vt.* تزیین دادن taz-yin dâdan
آب و تاب دادن âb-o tâb dâdan
ember *n.* اخگر akhgar عنبر 'anbar
embezzle *v.* اختلاس کردن ekhtelâs kardan
embitter *vt.* اوقات تلخ کردن oqât talkh kardan
emblazon *vt.* تزیین کردن taz'in kardan
emblem *n., vt.* علامت 'alâmat نشان neshân
embodiment *n.* مظهر maz-har تجسد tajas~od
embody *vt.* متشکل شدن moteshak~el shodan
emboss *vt.* برجسته کردن barjesteh kardan
embrace *vt., vi., n.* بغل کردن baqal kardan
درآغوش گرفتن dar âqush gereftan
embroider *vt., vi.* سوزنکاری کردن suzan-kâri kardan
embroidery *n.* قلا بدوزی qol~ âb-duzi
embroil *vt.* گرفتار کردن gereftâr kardan
embryo *n., adj.* جنین janin
emcee *n., vt., vi.* معرفی کننده mo'ar~efi konandeh شو من sh-oman
emerald *n., adj.* زمرد zomor~od
emerge *vi.* پدیدارشدن padidâr shodan بروز آمدن boruz âmadan
emergency *n.* اضطراری ezterâri اورژانس urzhâns
emersed *adj.* در آب فرو رفته dar âb foru-rafteh
emigrant *n., adj.* مهاجر mohâjer
emigration *n.* مهاجرت mohâjerat
eminence *n.* بلندی bolandi برتری bartari عالیجناب 'âlijenâb
eminent *adj.* برجسته barjesteh
emir *n.* امیر amir
emissary *n., adj.* فرستاده ferestâdeh سفیر safir
emission *n.* خروج khoruj بیرون ریز birun-riz

emit *vt.* بیرون ریختن birun rikhtan
emotion *n.* احساس ehsâs
emotional *adj.* احساساتی ehsâsâti
emotionless *adj.* بی احساس bi-ehsâs
empathic *adj.* تأکید شده ta'kid shodeh
empathy *n.* همدردی کردن hamdardi kardan
emperor *n.* امپراطور emperâtur شاهنشاه shâhanshâh
emphasis *n.* تأکید ta'kid
emphasize *vt.* تأکید کردن ta'kid kardan
emphatic *adj., n.* تأکیدی ta'kidi جدی jed~i مؤکد mo'akad
emphysema *n.* خش خشه khesh khesheh تنگی نفس tangi-ye' nafas
empire *n., adj.* امپراطوری emperâturi
empiric *n., adj.* تجربه‌ای tajrobeh-i غیرعلمی qeyr-e' 'elmi
emplacement *n.* نصب nasb
employ *vt., n.* استخدام کردن estekhdâm kardan
بکاربردن bekâr bordan
employee *n.* مستخدم mostakhdem کارمند kâr-mand
employer *n.* کارفرما kâr-farmâ
employment *n.* استخدام estekhdâm
empower *vt.* مختار کردن mokhtâr kardan وکالت دادن vekâlat dâdan
empress *n.* شهبانو shahbânu
empty *adj., vt., vi., n.* خالی کردن khâli kardan تهی tohi
empty-handed *adj.* دست خالی dast-khâli
emulate *vt., adj.* رقابت برتری کردن reqâbat-e' bartari kardan
emulsion *n.* شیره shireh
en masse *np.* همه با هم hameh bâ ham
en route *np.* در راه dar râh-e'
enable *vt.* قادرکردن qâder kardan
enact *vt.* مقرر داشتن moqar~âr dâshtan وضع کردن vaz' kardan
enamel *n., vt.* مینا minâ لعاب la'âb
enamored *adj.* فریفته fârifteh شیفته shifteh دلباخته del-bâkhteh
enchant *vt.* شیفته کردن shifteh kardan
enchantment *n.* شیفتگی shiftegi
encircle *vt.* محاصره کردن mohâsereh kardan احاطه ehâteh
enclave *n.* محصورشده mahsur-shodeh متصرفه motesar~efeh
enclose *v.* درلفافرستادن dar lafâ ferestâdan
enclose *v.* ضمیمه کردن zamimeh kardan
enclosed *vt.* در جوف dar jof پیوست peyvast سرپوشیده sar-pushideh

enclosure n. محصورشده mahsur shodeh ضمیمه zamimeh
encore int., n., vt. دوباره dobâreh تکراری tekrâri
encounter vt., vi., n. مواجه شدن movâjeh shodan
encourage vt. امیدوارکردن omidvâr kardan
تشویق کردن tashviq kardan
encroach vi. تجاوز کردن tajâvoz kardan تخطی کردن takhat~i kardan
encroachment n. تجاوز تدریجی tajâvoz-e' tadriji
encumbrance n. مانع شدن mâne' shodan
اسباب زحمت asbâb-e' zahmât
encyclopedia n. دائرةالمعارف dâ'eratol ma'âref
end n., vt., vi. پایان دادن pâyân dâdan
end n. پایان pâyân انتها entehâ نهایت nahâyat غایت qâyat
end(in) n. منجر شدن monjar shodan
endanger vt. درخطر انداختن dar khatar andâkhtan
endeavor vi., n. کوشش کردن kushesh kardan
endemic adj., n. محلی mahal~i همگانه hamegâneh
ending n. پایان pâyân خاتمه khâtemeh
endive n. هندباء hendabâ'
endless adj. بی پایان bi-pâyân
endless adj. بی انتها bi-entehâ
endorse v. پشتیبانی کردن poshtibâni kardan
endorse v. پشت نویسی کردن posht-nevisi kardan
endorsement n. امضا emzâ پشتیبانی poshtibâni
endow vt. اعطا کردن e'tâ kardan
endowed n. بااستعداد bâ-este'dâd
endowment n. اعطا e'tâ استعداد este'dâd
endurance n. دوام davâm تحمل taham~ol
endure vt., vi. دوام کردن davâm kardan
تحمل کردن taham~ol kardan
enema n. تنقیه کردن tanqieh kardan
enemy n., adj. دشمن doshman
energetic adj. فعال fa'âl باحرارت bâ-harârat
energy n. نیرو niru انرژی enerzhi توان tavân یارا yaârâ
enforce vt. اجراکردن ejrâ kardan
enforcement n. اجرا ejrâ
engage vt., vi. نامزد کردن nâmzad kardan گیر کردن gir kardan
engagement n. قرار qarâr تعهد ta'ah~od نامزدی nâm-zadi
engagement n. نامزدی nâmzadi توسل tavas~ol

engine *n.* موتور motor
engineer *n., vt.* مهندس mohandes
England *n.* انگلستان engelestân
English *adj., n., vt.* انگلیسی engelisi
engorge *vt., vi.* پرخوری کردن porkhori kardan
engrave *v.* حکاکی کردن hak~âki kardan
کنده کاری کردن kondeh-kâri kardan
engraver *adj.* کنده کار kondeh-kâr حکاک hak~âk
engulf *vt.* فرا گرفتن farâ gereftan
enhance *vt.* بالا بردن bâlâ bordan اضافه کردن ezâfeh kardan
enigma *n.* معما mo'am~â راز râz
enjoin *vt.* مقرر داشتن moqar~ar dâshtan
ممنوع کردن mamnu' kardan
enjoy *vt.* لذت بردن lez~at bordan
بهره مند شدن bahreh-mand shodan
enlarge *vt., vi.* بزرگ کردن bozorg kardan
افزایش دادن afzâyesh dâdan
enlighten *vt.* فهماندن fahmândan شیرفهم کردن shirfahm kardan
enlightenment *n.* چشم گشایی cheshm goshâyi
enlist *vi., vt.* نام نویسی کردن nâm nevisi kardan
اسم نویسی کردن esm-nevisi kardan
enlisted *n.* داوطلب dâvtalab اسم نوشته esm-neveshteh
enmity *n.* دشمنی doshmani کینه kineh عداوت 'edâvat
enormous *adj.* هنگفت hengoft بسیار بزرگ besyâr bozorg کلان kalân
enough *adj., n., adv., int.* کافی kâfi بس bas مکفی mokfi
enrage *vt.* خشمگین کردن khashmgin kardan
enrich *vt.* پولدار کردن puldâr kardan غنی کردن qani kardan
enroll *vt., vi.* اسم نویسی کردن esm nevisi kardan
enrollment *n.* اسم نویسی esm nevisi
enrollment *n.* ثبت sabt تعداد شاگردان te'dâd-e' shâgerdân
ensemble *n., adv.* باهم bâham یک نما yek namâ
ensign *n.* پرچم parcham
enslave *vt.* برده کردن bardeh kardan
ensue *vi.* بدنبال آوردن bedonbâl âvardan متعاقب mote'âqeb
entail *vt., n.* موجب شدن mojeb shodan
entangle *vt.* گیر کردن gir kardan
entente *n.* حسن تفاهم hosn-e' tafâh~om
enter *vi., vt.* داخل شدن dâkhel shodan وارد شدن vâred shodan

enterprise *n.* کمپانی kompâni شیرین کاری shirinkâri
enterprising *adj.* با دل و جرأت bâ del-o jor'at
entertain *v.* در فکر بودن dar fekr budan
entertain *v.* پذیرایی کردن pazirâyi kardan
entertainer *n.* مهماندار mehmândâr میزبان mizbân
هنرمند honar-mand
enthrone *vt.* برتخت نشاندن bar takht neshândan
enthusiasm *n.* اشتیاق eshtiâq شوق shoq
enthusiastic *adj.* با علاقه bâ-'alâqeh اشتیاق دار eshtiâq-dâr
entice *vt.* اغفال کردن eqfâl kardan اغوا کردن eqvâ kardan
entire *adj., n.* قاطبه qâtebeh همه hameh تمام tamâme بکلی bekol~i
entitle *vt.* حق دادن haq~ dâdan اجازه دادن ejâzeh dâdan
entity *n.* حقیقت ذات hâqiqat-e' zât وجود vojud هستی hasti
entomology *n.* حشره شناسی hashareh shenâsi
entourage *n.* ملتزمین moltazemin دور و بر dor-o bar
entrance *n., vt.* مدخل madkhal دخول dokhul ورود vorud
entrance *vt.* مات کردن mât kardan مشعوف کردن mash'uf kardan
entrap *vt.* بدام انداختن bedâm andâkhtan
entrench *vt., vi.* سنگرگیری کردن sangar-giri kardan
entrepreneur *n.* دل به دریا زن del beh daryâ-zân
همه کاره hameh kâreh
entrust *vt.* درامانت گذاشتن dar amânat gozâshtan سپردن sepordan
entry *n.* درگاه dargâh ورود vorud
enunciate *vt., vi.* اعلان کردن e'lân kardan
enuncuate *n.* واضح تلفظ کردن vâzeh talaf~oz kardan
envelop *vt., n.* دربرگرفتن dar bar gereftan
envelope *n.* پاکت pâkat
environment *n.* طبیعت tabi'at محیط mohit
envisage *vt.* مواجه شدن movâjeh shodan
تصور کردن tasav~or kardan
envoy *n.* سفیر safir فرستاده ferestâdeh
envy *n., vt., vi.* غبطه خوردن qabteh khordan رشک بردن rashk bordan
epaulet(te) *n.* سردوشی sardushi سرشانه sarshâneh
epic *adj., n.* اشعار رزمی ash'âr-e' razmi حماسه hemâseh
epidemic *adj., n.* همه گیری hameh-giri شیوع shoyu' عمومی 'omumi
epilepsy *n.* صرع sar' غشی qashi
epileptic *n.* مصروع masru'
epilog(ue) *n.* باب آخر bâb-e' âkhar پی نویس pey nevis

episode *n.* حادثه hâdeseh اتفاق et~efâq
epitaph *n., vt.* گور نوشت gur nevesht یادبود yâdbud مرثیه marsieh
epitome *n.* منتهای montahâ-ye' عرش 'arsh
epoch *n.* دوران dorân زمان zamân عصر 'asr
equal *n.* مساوی mosâvi برابر barâbar یکسان yeksân همتا ham-tâ
equality *n.* برابری barâbari تساوی tasâvi
equalizer *n.* مساوی کننده mosâvi konandeh
equally *adv.* بطور مساوی betor-e' mosâvi
equate *vt.* مساوی دانستن mosâvi dânestan
equation *n.* معادله mo'âdeleh تعدیل ta'dil
equator *n.* خط استوا khat~-e' ostovâ نصف النهار nesfon~ahâr
equatorial *adj., n.* استوایی ostovâyi گرمسیری garmsiri
equestrian *adj., n.* اسب سواری asb savâri پرش با اسب paresh bâ-asb
equilateral *adj., n.* متساوی الاضلاع motesâviol azlâ'
equilibrium *n.* موازنه movâzeneh تعادل ta'âdol
equinox *n.* تعدیل شب و روز ta'dil-e' shab-o ruz
equipment *n.* اسباب asbâb وسایل vasâyel لوازم lavâzem
equipped *adj.* مجهز mojah~az وسیله دار vasileh-dar
equitable *adj.* باعدالت bâ-'edâlat باارزش bâ-arzesh
equity *n.* ارزش مستقل arzesh-e' mostaqel عدالت 'edâlat
equivalent *adj., n.* معادل mo'âdel برابر barâbar همچند ham-chand
equivocate *vi.* دو پهلو جواب دادن dopahlu javâb dâdan
era *n.* زمان zamân دوران ' dorân عصر asr
eradicate *vt.* ازریشه کندن az risheh kandân
erase *vt., vi.* پاک کردن pâk kardan
eraser *n.* پاک کن pâk-kon
erect *adj.* راست râst رشید rashid سهی sahi شق shaq~
erect *v.* شق کردن râst kardan شق کردن shaq kardan
erection *n.* تأسیس ta'sis kardan شق شده گی shaq-shodegi نعوظ no'uz
erode *vt., vi.* فرسوده کردن farsudeh kardan پوساندن pusândan
erosion *n.* فرسایش farsâyesh خوردگی khordegi
erotic *adj., n.* سکسی seksi
err *vi.* خطا کردن khatâ kardan گمراه شدن gomrâh shodan
errand *n.* پادو گری pâdo-gari کار kâr
errant *adj.* سرگردان sargardân گمراه gomrâh
errata *n.* اشتباهات eshtebâhât
erratic *adj., n.* ناثابت nâsâbet متغیر moteqayer
erroneous *adj.* اشتباه eshtebâh نادرست nâ-dorost

error v. اشتباه کردن eshtebâh kardan
error n. اشتباه eshtebâh خطا khatâ
ersatz adj., n. بدل badal جانشین jâneshin
erst adv. اول av~al اصلی asli
erstwhile adj., adv. سابق sâbeqi پیشین pishin
erupt vi., vt. ترکیدن tarekidan
eruption n. انفجار enfejâr
escalator n. پله برقی pel~eh barqi
escapade n. گریز از مسئولیت goriz az mas'uliyat
escape vi., vt., n. فرارکردن farâr kardan دررفتن dar raftan گریز goriz
escape goat n. سپربلا separ-e' balâ بهانه bahâneh
escargot n. حلزون پخته halazun-e' pokhteh
eschew vt. پرهیز کردن parhiz kardan
escort n., vt. مشایعت کردن moshâye'at kardan محافظ mohâfez
escrow n. قولنامه qol-nâmeh
esophagus n. مجرای گلو majrây-e' galu
esoteric adj. شخصی shakhsi خصوصی khosusi
especially adv. مخصوصا makhsusan بخصوص bekhosus
علی الخصوص 'alal-khosus بویژه bevizheh
espionage n. جاسوسی jâsusi
espouse vt. همسر گرفتن hamsar gereftan
حمایت کردن hemâyat kardan
esquire n., vt. جناب jenâb عالیجناب 'âlijenâb
essance n. اصل asl جوهر johar وجود vojud لپ lop~
essay n., vt. آزمایش کردن âzmâyesh kardan مقاله maqâleh
essence n. وجود vojud ذات zât جوهر johar اصل asl
essential adj., n. واجب vâjeb ضروری zaruri اصلی asli
establish v. تأسیس کردن ta'sis kardan
establish v. برقرار کردن barqarâr kardan
establishment n. موسسه mo'aseseh پایه گذاری pâyeh gozâri
estate n., vt. ملک melk دارایی dârâyi ماترک mâtarak
esteem v. احترام گذاشتن ehterâm gozâshtan
esteem v. گرامی داشتن gerâmi dâshtan
esteemed n. گرامی gerâmi محترم mohtaram ارجمند arjomand
معزز mo'az~ez
estimate vt., vi., n. تخمین زدن takhmin zadan
estow n. کنار هم چیدن kenâr-e' ham chidan
estrange(d) n. جدا شده jodâ shodeh مجزا mojaz~â

estrogen *n.* ماهی خاویار mâhi-e' khâviâr
estuary *n.* مصب masab~
etch *vt., vi., n.* سیاه قلم کردن siâh qalam kardan
eternal *adj., n.* ابدی abadi جاویدان jâvidân پایا pâyâ
همیشگی hamishegi
eternity *n.* ابدیت abadiyat ابدالدهر abadol-dahr
ethical *adj.* اخلاقی akhlâqi
ethics *pl.* آداب رفتار âdâb-e' raftâr نزاکت nezâkat
ethnic *adj.* بومی bumi اقلیت aqaliyat
ethos *n.* سیرت sirat
etiquette *n.* آداب معاشرت âdâb-e' mo'âsherat
etymology *n.* لغت شناسی loqat shenâsi اشتقاق eshteqaq
eulogy *n.* مدح madh مداحی mad~ahi
eunuch *n.* خواجه khâjeh اخته akhteh
euology *n.* مدح کردن madh kardan ستایش setâyesh
euphemism *n.* حسن تعبیر hosn-e' ta'bir
euphoria *n.* حالت وجد و نشاط hâlat-e' vajd-o neshât
Europe *n.* اروپا orupâ
evacuate *vt., vi.* تخلیه کردن takhlieh kardan
evade *vt., vi.* فرار کردن farâr kardan گریز زدن goriz zadan
evaluate *vt.* ارزشیابی کردن arzeshyâbi kardan سنجیدن sanjidan
evaluation *n.* ارزیابی arz-yâbi
evangelical *adj., n.* انجیلی enjili
evangelist *n.* کشیش سیار keshish-e' say~âr
evaporate *vi., vt.* تبخیر کردن tabkhir kardan
بخار شدن bokhâr shodan
evasion *n.* فرار farâr گریز goriz طفره tafreh
Eve *n.* حوا hav~â
even *adj., n., adv., vt.* حتی hat~â ولو valo
even *adj., n., adv., vt.* هموار hamvâr
evenhanded *n.* بیطرفانه bitarafâneh
evening *n., adj.* عصر 'asr غروب qorub شامگاه shâm-gâh
event *n.* رویداد ruydâd حادثه hâdeseh واقعه vâqe'eh عارضه 'ârezeh
eventful *adj.* پرحادثه por-hâdeseh
eventually *adv.* بالاخره bel-akhareh درنتیجه dar-natijeh
ever *adv.* هرگز hargez همیشه hamisheh
everglade *n.* مرداب mordâb
evergreen *n.* همیشه سبز hamisheh sabz

everlasting *adj., n.* با دوام bâ-davâm ابدی abadi ماندگار mâandegar
پایدار pâaydar

every *adj.* هر har همه hameh

every other day یک روز در میان yek ruz dar miân

every other one یک درمیان yek dar miân

everybody *pro.* هرکس har-kas همه کس hameh-kas

everyday *adj.* هرروز har-ruz

everything *pro., n.* هرچیز har-chiz

everytime *n.* هروقت har-vâqt

everywhere *adv.* هرجا har-jâ

evict *vt.* بیرون کردن birun kardan اخراج کردن ekhrâj kardan

evidence *n., vt.* گواه gavâh مدرک madrak

evident *adj.* بدیهی badihi معلوم ma'lum واضح vâzeh عیان 'ayân

evidently *adv.* ازقرار معلوم az qarâr-e' ma'lum ظاهراً zâheran

evil *adj., n., adv.* شیطان sheytân

evil *adj., n., adv.* شرور sharur

evitable *adj.* اجتناب پذیر ejtenâb-pazir

evolution *n.* تکامل takâmol

evolve *vt., vi.* بوجود آمدن bevojud âmadan
تکمیل شدن takmil shodan

ewe *n.* میش mish

exacerbate *vt.* شدت دادن shed~at dâdan بدترکردن badtar kardan

exact *adj.* درست dorost صحیح sahih دقیق daqiq

exact *v.* بزور گرفتن bezur gereftan

exactly *adv.* دقیقاً daqiqan عیناً 'eynan

exaggerate *v.* مبالغه کردن mobâleqeh kardan
گزاف گفتن gazâf goftan اغراق کردن eqrâq kardan

exaggeration *n.* مبالغه mobaleqeh اغراق eqrâaq غلو qolov~

exalt *vt.* ستایش کردن setâyesh kardan تجلیل کردن tajlil kardan

exalted *adj.* بالا برده bâlâ bordeh متعال mot~a'âl

examine *vt.* معاینه کردن âzmâyesh kardan
امتحان کردن mo'âyeneh kardan

examiner *n.* ممتحن momtahen

example *n., vt.* مثال mesâl نمونه nemuneh

example *n., vt.* عبرت ebrat

exasperate *vt., adj.* پریشان کردن parishân kardan

excel *vt., vi.* بهتر کردن behtar kardan مافوق کردن mâfoq kardan

excellent *adj.* عالی 'âli بسیار خوب besyâr khub

except *pre., vt., con., vi.* بجز bejoz غيراز qeyr-az مگر magar غير qeyr
exception *n.* استثنا estesnâ فرق farq
exceptional *adj.* استثنايى estesnâyi بى مانند bi-mânand
excerpt *n., vt.* عبارت برگزيده ebârat-e' bargozideh
excess *n., adj.* افراط efrât اضافى ezâfi زياده روى ziâdeh-ravi فرط fart
excessive *adj.* افراطى efrâti زياده رو ziâdeh-ro
exchange *vt., vi., n.* معاوضه کردن mo'âvezeh kardan بورس burs مبادله mâbâdeleh
excise *n., vt.* ماليات تجملى mâliât-e' tajam~oli
excitation *n.* هيجان hayajân تحريک tahrik
excite *vt.* هيجان دادن hayajân dâdan برانگيختن bar angikhtan
excitement *n.* هيجان hayajân تحريک tahrik شادى shâdi
exciting *vt.* مهيج mohay~ej شادآور shâd-âvar جالب jâleb
exclaim *vi., vt.* بتندى گفتن betondi goftan
exclamation mark *n.* علامت تعجب 'alâmat-e' ta'aj~ob
exclude *vt.* کنارگذاشتن kenâr gozâshtan حذف کردن hazf kardan
exclusive *adj., n.* خصوصى khosusi ويژه vizheh منحصر monhaser
excommunicate *vt., n., adj.* تکفير کردن takfir kardan
excrement *n.* مدفوع madfu' نجاست nejâsat
excrete *vt.* تجزيه کردن tajzieh kardan
excruciating *adj.* دردناک dardnâk جانگداز jân-godâz
excursion *n.* مسافرت کوتاه mosâferat-e' kutâh گشت gasht
excuse *v.* بخشيدن bakhshidan
excuse *n.* بهانه b/âhâneh عذر 'ozr
excused *adj.* بخشيده شده bakhshideh shodeh معذور ma'zur
execrate *vt., vi.* نفرين کردن nefrin kardan
execute *vt.* اعدام کردن e'dâm kardan اجرا کردن ejrâ kardan
execution *n.* اعدام e'dâm
execution *n.* اجرا ejrâ
executioner *n.* جلاد jal~âd ميرغضب mir-qazab
executive *n., adj.* اجرائى ejrâyi رياستى riâsati
executor *n.* مجرى mojri وصى vasi
exemplary *adj.* نمونه nemuneh عبرت آميز ebrat-âmiz
exemplify *vt.* مثال زدن mesâl zadan
exempt *vt., adj., n.* معاف کردن mo'âf kardan
exemption *n.* معافى mo'âfi
exercise *v.* بکاربردن bekâr bordan
exercise *v.* ورزش کردن varzesh kardan تمرين کردن tamrin kardan

exert *vt.* نشار آوردن feshâr âvardan
exhale *vi., vt.* نفس بیرون دادن nafas birun dâdan
exhaust *v.* بکلی تمام کردن bekol~i tamâm kardan
مستهلک کردن mostahlak kardan تحلیل رفتن tahlil raftan
exhaust *v.* خسته کردن khasteh kardan
exhausted *adj.* خسته و کوفته khasteh-o kufteh خالی شده khâli-shodeh
مستهلک شده mostahlak shodeh واماندہ vâ-mândeh
exhaustion *n.* خستگی khastegi تحلیل tahlil استهلاک estehlâk
کوفتگی kuftegi
exhibit *vt., vi., n.* نمایش دادن namâyesh dâdan
نشان دادن neshân dâdan
exhilarate *vt.* نشاط دادن neshât dâdan
exhilarated *vt.* شاد shâd
exhilarating *adj.* مفرح mofar~ah فرحبخش farah-bakhsh
فرحناک farah-nâk
exhilaration *n.* نشاط neshât
exhilirating *adj.* نشاط بخش neshât-bakhsh مفرح mofar~ah
exhort *vt., vi.* ترغیب کردن tarqib kardan
متقاعد کردن moteqâed kardan
exhume *vt.* نبش کردن nabsh kardan
exigent *adj.* اضطراری zaruri ضروری ezterâri
exile *n., vt.* تبعید کردن tab'id kardan دور از وطن dur az vatan
exise *n.* بریدن boridan
exist *vi.* وجود داشتن vojud dashtan زیستن zistan
existence *n.* وجود vojud هستی hasti
exit *n., vi.* بیرون رفتن birun raftan در خروجی dar-e' khoruji
exodus *n.* مهاجرت قومی mohâjerat-e' qomi
exonorate *n.* تبرئه کردن tabra'eh kardan
exorbitant *adj.* خیلی زیاد kheyli ziâd گزاف gazâf
exorcise *vt.* شیطان بیرون کردن sheytân birun kardan
exorcism *n.* جن گیری jen-giri
exorcist *n.* جن گیر jen-gir پریخوان pari-khân
exoteric *adj.* خارجی khâreji عمومی 'omumi
exotic *adj., n.* خارجی khâreji باشکوه bâ-shokuh
expand *vt., vi.* توسعه دادن tose'eh dâdan
منبسط کردن monbaset kardan
expanded *adj.* توسعه یافته tose'eh yafteh مبسوط mabsut
expanse *n.* وسعت دار vos'at-dâr عریض 'ariz

expansion *n.* توسعه tose'eh انبساط enbesât گسترش gostaresh
expatiate *vi.* منحرف شدن monharef shodan زیادگویی ziâdguyi
expatriate *v.* بیوطن کردن bi-vatan kardan
expatriate *v.* تبعید کردن tab'id kardan
expect *vt., vi.* انتظار داشتن entezâr dâshtan
منتظربودن montazer budan
expectant *adj., n.* منتظر montazer خواهان khâhân آبستن âbestan
expectation *n.* انتظار entezâr توقع tavaqo'
expected *n.* انتظاررفتنی entezâr raftani مترتبه moteraq~ebeh
expecting *adj.* منتظر montazer متوقع motevaq~e'
expedience *n.* مصلحت maslahat اقتضاء eqtezâ'
expediency *n.* مصلحت maslahat اقتضاء eqtezâ'
expedient *adj., n.* مقتضی moqtazi اجباری ejbâri مصلحتی maslahati
expedite *vt., adj.* تسریع کردن tasri' kardan تندتر کردن tondtar kardan
expedition *n.* تسریع tasri' سفر اعزامی safar-e' e'zâmi
expel *vt.* اخراج کردن ekhrâj kardan
expend *vt.* خارج کردن kharej kardan مصرف کردن masraf kardan
expense *n.* مخارج makhârej مصارف masâref
expense *n.* خرج kharj هزینه hazineh
expensive *adj.* گران gerân پرخرج por-kharj
experience *n., vt.* تجربه کردن tajrobeh kardan
experienced *adj.* باتجربه bâ-tajrobeh کارآزموده kâr-âzmudeh
مجرب mojar~ab کاردیده kâr-dideh
experiment *n., vi.* آزمایش کردن âzmâyesh kardan
تجربه کردن tajrobeh kardan
expert *n., adj., vt.* کارشناس kârshenâs متخصص motekhas~es
نخبه nokhbeh
expiate *v.* جزا دادن jazâ dâdan کفاره دادن kaf~âreh dâdan
غفران خواستن qofrân khâstan
expiation *n.* کفاره kaf~âreh غفران qofrân
expire *vi., vt.* تمام شدن tamâm shodan سپری شدن separi shodan
explain *vt., vi.* توضیح دادن tozih dâdan تشریح کردن tashrih kardan
explained *n.* واضح vâzeh بیان شده bayân-shodeh مبین mobin
explanation *n.* توضیح tozih معنی ma'ni تبیین tabyin
explanatory *n.* توضیح دهنده tozih-dahandeh
بیان کننده bayân-konandeh مبین mobay~en
expletive *adj., n.* زیادی ziâdi بیخودی bikhodi
explicate *vt.* واضح کردن vâzeh kardan

explicit *adj.* واضح vâzeh رک گو rok-gu پوست کنده pust-kandeh
explode *vi., vt.* منفجر کردن monfajer kardan ترکاندن tarekândan
exploit *v.* استثمارکردن estesmâr kardan
exploit *v.* بهره برداری کردن bahreh bardâri kardan
exploitation *n.* بهره برداری bareh bardâri استثمار estesmâr
exploration *n.* اکتشاف ekteshâf جستجو josteju پیگردی peygardi
explore *v.* جستجو کردن josteju kardan
explore *v.* اکتشاف کردن ekteshâf kardan
explosion *n.* انفجار enfejâr
explosive *adj., n.* منفجره monfajereh ترکیدنی tarekidani
export *vt., n., adj.* صادر کردن sâder kardan
exporter *n.* صادرکننده sâder konandeh
exports *n.* صادرات sâderât
expose *vt.* افشاء کردن efshâ' kardan مواجه کردن movâjeh kardan
exposed *adj.* فاش شده fâsh-shodeh آشکار âshkâr نوردیده nur-dideh
exposition *n.* افشا گری efshâ gari نمایش namâyesh
exposure *n.* مواجهت movâjehat افشاء efshâ'
expound *vt.* مفصل توضیح دادن mofas~al tozih dâdan
express *v.* بیان کردن bayân kardan اظهار کردن ez-hâr kardan
ابرازداشتن ebrâz dâshtan
express *adj.* تندرو tond-ro سریع sari'
expression *n.* بیان bayân اظهار ez-hâr اصطلاح estelâh حالت hâlat
expressive *adj.* گویا guyâ بیانگر bayân-gar
expropriate *vt.* زمین تصاحب کردن zamin tasâhob kardan
expulsion *n.* اخراج ekhrâj
expunge *vt.* پاک کردن pâk kardan
exquisite *adj., n.* عالی âli ماهرانه mâherâneh دلپسند delpasand
extemporaneous *adj.* خارج از نوبت khârej az nobat
فی البداهه felbedâheh
extend *vt., vi.* تمدید کردن tavil kardan طویل کردن tamdid kardan
extension *n.* تمدید tamdid طول tul امتداد emtedâd الحاقی elhâqi
extent *n.* اندازه andâzeh حد had~ وسعت vos'at
exterior *adj., n.* نما namâ ظاهر zâher
exterminate *vt.* ازبین بردن az beyn bordan
exterminate *vt.* نسل برانداختن nasl barandâkhtan
extermination *n.* نابودی nâ-budi قلع و قمع qal'-o qam'
external *adj., n.* خارجی khâreji بیرونی biruni
extinct *adj.* ازبین رفته az beyn rafteh ناموجود nâ-mojud

extinguish *vt.* خاموش کردن khâmush kardan
extort *vt.* بزور گرفتن bezur gereftan باج گرفتن bâj gereftan
extortion *n.* باج bâj غصب qasb اخاذی ekhâzi
extra *adj., n., adv.* اضافی ezâfi فوق العاده foqol'âdeh زیادی ziâdi
extract *vt., n.* درآوردن dar âvardan استخراج کردن estekhrâj kardan
extract *n.* شیره shireh عصاره 'osâreh آسانس esâns
extract *n.* رونوشت ru-nevesht مدرک madrak
extradite *vt.* مجرم پس دادن mojrem pas dâdan
بازپس فرستادن bâz-pas ferestâdan
extradition *n.* تسلیم taslim استرداد esterdâd بازپسی bâz-pasi
extramarital *adj.* خارج از ازدواج khârej az ezdevâj
extraneous *adj.* بی ربط bi-rabt خارجی khâreji سخت sakht
extraordinary *adj.* فوق العاده foqol'âdeh
extrapolate *vt., vi.* حدس زدن hads zadan
پیش بینی کردن pishbini kardan
extrasensory *adj.* ماوراء حواس mâvarâ'-e' havâs
extravagance *n.* زیاده روی ziâdeh-ravi افراط efrât
extravagant *adj.* زیاده رو ziâdeh-ro افراطی efrâti گزاف gazâf
extreme *adj., n.* منتهی الیه montahâ elayh در انتها dar entehâ
extremely *adv.* بی نهایت bi-nahâyat
extremist *n., adj.* افراطی گرا efrâti-garâ
extremities *pl.* اعضاء a'zâ'
extremity *n.* نهایت hahâyat انتها entehâ افراط efrât
منتها الیه monteha elayh
extricate *vt.* خلاص کردن khalâs kardan رها کردن rahâ kardan
extrinsic *adj.* خارجی khâreji
extrovert *n., adj., vt.* خارج بین khârej-bin باشناخت bâ-shenâkht
extrude *vt., vi.* سر در آوردن sar dar âvardan بیرون زدن birun zadan
extrusion *n.* بیرون آمدگی birun âmadegi
exuberant *adj.* با نشاط bâ neshât بشاش bash~âsh
exude *vi., vt.* بیرون دادن birun dâdan تراوش کردن tarâvosh kardan
exult *vi.* وجد کردن vajd kardan خوشحالی کردن khosh-hâli kardan
eye *v., n., vt., vi.* چشم cheshm نگاه کردن negâh kardan
eyeball *n.* تخم چشم tokhm-e' cheshm
eyebrow *n.* ابرو abru
eyeful *n.* یک نگاه yek negâh دیدنی didani
eyeglass *n.* عینک 'eynak
eyelash *n.* مژه mozheh مژگان mozhgân

eyelet *n., vt.* حلقه halqeh سوراخ surâkh
eyelid *n.* پلک چشم pelk-e′ cheshm
eyesight *n.* بینایی binâyi دید did

F F F

fable *n.* افسانه afsâneh

fabric *n.* بافته bâfteh ساختمان sâkhtemân فابریک fâbrik

fabricate *vt.* ساختن sâkhtan بافتن bâftan جعل کردن ja'l kardan

facade *n.* نما namâ ظاهر zâher جلوه jelveh

face *n.* صورت surat رو ru سطح sat-h

face *v.* مواجه شدن movâjeh shodan روبروشدن ruberu shodan

face card *np.* عکس 'aks

face lifting *np.* پوست برداری pust bardâri

face value *np.* ارزش ظاهری arzesh-e' zâheri

face(down) *n.,vt.* دمرو damaru غلبه کردن qalabeh kardan

face(to face) *n.* روبرو ruberu

face(up to) *n.* طرف شدن taraf shodan مواجه شدن movâjeh shodan

facet *n., vt.* برش boresh جنبه janbeh

facetious *adj.* هزل گو hazl-gu مزه انداز mazeh-andâz
شوخ بیمزه shukh-e' bi-mazeh

facial *adj., n.* صورتی surati صورت مالی suratmâli

facile *adj.* آسان âsân

facilitate *vt.* آسان کردن âsân kardan

facility *n.* آسانی âsâni سهولت sohulat وسیله vasileh

facing *n., v.* نما namâ

facsimile *n., vt.* رونوشت runevesht عین 'eyn فاکس fâks

fact *n.* حقیقت haqiqat امرمسلم amr-e' mosal~am

faction *n.* جناح jenâh دسته بندی dasteh bandi

factor *n., vt.* عامل 'âmel

factory *n.* کارخانه kâr-khâneh فابریک fâbrik

factual *adj.* حقیقی haqiqi واقعی vâqe'i

faculty *n.* قوه qov~eh توانایی tavânâyi دبیر dabir

fad *n.* مد mod

fade *adj., vi., vt.* محو شدن mahv shodan
ناپدید شدن nâ-padid shodan

fag *vt., vi., n.* خرکاری کردن khar-kâri kardan کونی kuni

fagot *n., vt.* خرده چوب khordeh chub فاسد fâsed

fail *vi., vt., n.* شکست خوردن shekast khordan رد شدن rad shodan

failure *n.* شکست shekast ناتوانایی nâtavânâyi

fain *n., adv., adj.* مشتاق moshtâq

faint *adj., vi., n.* غش کردن qash kardan
رنگ پریدن rang paridan کمرنگ شدن kam-rang shodan

fair *adj., adv., n., vt.* بیطرف bitaraf بور bur روشن roshan
fair *adj., adv., n., vt.* نمایشگاه namâyeshgâh
بازارمکاره bâzâr-e' mak~ âreh
fair and square *n.* بطور مساوی betor-e' mosâvi
fair ground *n.* جشن بازار jashn bâzâr
fair play *np.* باصداقت bâ-sedâqat
fair trade *np.* قیمت معین qeymat-e' mo'ay~ an
fair-minded *adj.* منصف monsef بیطرف bitaraf
fairly *adv.* نسبتاً nesbatan منصفانه monsefâneh
fairway *n.* شعبۀ آبی sho'beh-ye' âbi
fairy *n., adj.* پری pari فرشته fereshteh
fairyland *n.* سرزمین افسانه‌ای sarzamin-e' afsâneh-yi
fait accompli *np.* عمل انجام شده 'amal-e' anjâm shodeh
faith *n.* ایمان imân عقیده 'aqideh دین din
faithful *adj., n.* باوفا bâ-vafâ باایمان bâ-imân مؤمن mo'men
faithless *adj.* بی دین bi-din بی وفا bi-vafâ خائن khâ'en
fake *n., vt., vi., adj.* کلک زدن kalak zadan قلابی بودن qol~ âbi budan
falcon *n.* شاهین shâhin قرقی qerqi قوش qush
fall *v.* افتادن oftâdan سقوط کردن soqut kardan
پایین آمدن pâ-yin âmadan
fall *n.* سقوط soqut تنزل tanaz~ ol
fall *n.* آبشار âbshâr
fall *n.* پاییز pâyiz برگ ریزان barg-rizân
fall(away) *v.* بهم پاشیدن beham pâshidan
متلاشی شدن motelâshi shodan
fall(back) *v.* عقب کشیدن 'aqab keshidan
fall(behind) *v.* عقب افتادن 'aqab oftâdan
fall(for) *v.* گول خوردن gul khordan عاشق شدن 'âsheq shodan
fall(in with) *v.* ملاقات و ملحق شدن molâqât va molhaq shodan
fall(in) *v.* صف کشیدن saf keshidan
fall(off) *v.* افت کردن oft kardan
fall(on/upon) *v.* حمله کردن hamleh kardan
fall(out) *v.* دعواکردن da'vâ kardan
fall(short) *v.* کم آوردن kam âvardan ناکام شدن nâ-kâm shodan
fall(through) *v.* بهم خوردن beham khordan
شکست خوردن shekast khordan
fall(under) *v.* مشمول شدن mashmul shodan
افسون شدن afsun shodan

fallacy *n.* اشتباه eshtebâh خطا khat~â سفسطه safsateh
fallen *v., adj.* افتاده oftâdeh بی آبرو bi-âberu
fallible *adj.* جایزالخطا jâyezol khat~â
fallout *n.* ریزش rizesh
false *adj., adv.* دروغ doruq مصنوعی masnu'i عاریه 'ârieh کاذب kâzeb
false bottom *np.* زیربندی مصنوعی zirbandi-e' masnu'i
false pretenses *np.* تظاهر غیر قانونی tazâhor-e' qeyr-e' gânuni
false step *np.* خطای پا khatâ-ye' pâ قدم اشتباه qadam-e' eshtebâh
false teeth *np.* دندان عاریه dandân 'âryeh
falsehood *n.* عدم صحت 'adam-e' seh~at دروغ doruq
falsely *adv.* بدروغ be-doruq کاذبانه kâzebâneh
falsies *n.* پستان مصنوعی pestân-e' masnu'i
falsification *n.* تحریف tahrif دروغ بافی doruq-bâfi تکذیب takzib
falsify *vt., vi.* تحریف کردن tahrif kardan دروغ بافتن doruq bâftan
falter *n.* تأمل ta'am~ol لکنت loknat
falter *v.* تلوتلو خوردن telo telo khordan
fame *n., vt.* شهرت shohrat معروفیت ma'rufiyat آوازه âvâzeh
familiar *adj., n.* آشنا âshnâ خودمانی khodemâni
familiarize *vt., vi.* آشنا کردن âshnâ kardan
family *n., adj.* خانواده khânevâdeh خاندان khândân فامیل fâmil
طایفه tâyefeh
family circle *np.* جمع خانوادگی jam'-e' khânevâdegi
family name *np.* نام خانوادگی nâm-e' khânevâdegi
اسم فامیل esm-e' fâmil
family tree *np.* ریشهٔ اجدادی risheh-ye' ajdâdi
شجره نامه shajareh-nâmeh
famine *n.* قحطی qahti گرسنگی gorosnegi
famish *vt., vi.* گرسنگی کشیدن gorosnegi keshidan
famous *adj.* مشهور mash-hur معروف ma'ruf نامدار nâmdâr
fan *v.* باد زدن bâd zadan تحریک کردن tahrik kardan
fan *n., adj.* دوستدار dust-dâr علاقمند 'alâqeh-mand پیرو peyro
fan *n.* بادبزن bâd-bezan
fan mail *np.* نامهٔ دوست دار nâmeh-ye' dust-dâr
fanatic *n., adj.* متعصب mote'as~eb غیرتی qeyrati
fancier *n.* خیالباف khiâlbâf
fancy *n., adj., vt., int.* هوس کردن havas kardan
خیال کردن khiâal kardan
fane *n.* معبد ma'bad

fanfare n. سروصدا sar-o sedâ قیل و قال qil-o qâl
fang n., vt. دندان ناب dandân-e' nâb نیش nish
fanny n. کپل kapal کون kun
fantail n., adj. کبوتر دم پهن kabutar-e' dom-pahn
fantastic adj. عالی âli عجیب 'ajib
fantasy n., vt., vi. آرزوی خیالی ârezu-ye' khiâli افسانه afsâneh
far adv., adj. دور dur
far-reaching n. وسیع vasi' جامع jâme' شدید shadid
faraway adj. دور رس dur-ras رویایی royâyi
farce n., vt. مسخره maskhareh چرت chart کمدی komedi
fare n. کرایه kerâyeh
farewell int., n., adj. وداع vedâ' خداحافظی khodâ hâfezi
farfetched n. بدست نیاوردنی bedast nayâvardani
farflung n. پهناور pahnâvar
farm v. زراعت کردن zerâ'at kardan کشاورزی کردن keshâvarzi kardan
farmer n. کشاورز keshâvarz دهقان dehqân برزگر barzegar کدیور kadivar
farmhouse n. دهقان خانه dehqân-khâneh کلبه kolbeh
farrier n. نعل بند na'l-band آهن‌کار âhan-kâr
farrow adj., n., vt., vi. گاو نازا gâv-e' nâzâ توله خوک tuleh khuk
farseeing adj. دوربین durbin آینده بین âyandeh-bin
farsighted adj. دوربین durbin مآل اندیش maâl-andish
fart n., vi. گوز دادن guz dâdan تیزدرکردن tiz dar kardan
farther adv., adj. دورتر durtar فراتر farâ-tar
farthermost adj. دورترین حد durtarin had~
farthest adj., adv. دورترین durtarin اقصی aqsâ
farthing n. یک چهارم yek chahârom
fraud adj. شیاد shay~âd دغلکار daqal-kâr حقه باز hoq~eh-bâz مکار mak~âr
fascinate vt., vi. مجذوب کردن majzub kardan جلب کردن jalb kardan
fascist n., adj. فاشیست fâshist
fashion n., vt. مد mod سبک sabk طریقه tariqeh طرز tarz
fast adj., n., vi. تند tond تندرو tond-ro سریع sari' چابک châbok
fast adj., n., vi. روزه گرفتن ruzeh gereftan
fasten vt., vi. بستن bastan سفت کردن seft kardan
fastener n. بست bast جفت cheft
fastidious adj. مشکل پسند moshk~el-pasand ایرادگیر irâd-gir
fat adj. چاق châq فربه farbeh پروار parvâr خیکی khik~i

fat *n.* چربی charbi پیه pih
fatal *adj.* کشنده koshandeh مرگ آور marg-âvar مهلک mohlek
fatality *n.* تلفات talafât بلاخیزی balâ-khizi مرگ ومیر marg-o mir
fate *n., vt.* سرنوشت sarnevesht تقدیر taqdir قسمت qesmat
fateful *adj.* سرنوشت انگیز sar-nevesht-angiz
سرنوشت آمیز sar-nevesht-âmiz
fathead(ed) *n.* نفهم nafahm
father in-law *n.* پدرزن pedar zan پدر شوهر pedar shuhar
fatherland *n.* میهن mihan وطن vatan
fatherly *adj.* پدرانه pedarâneh
fathom *n., vt.* عمق یابی کردن 'omq yâbi kardan نهمیدن fahmidan
fathomless *adj.* عمیق 'amiq غیرقابل فهم qeyr-e' qâbel-e' fahm
fatigue *v.* خسته کردن khasteh kardan فرسوده کردن farsudeh kardan
fatso *n.* خیکی khik~i کوپول kopol
fatten *vt., vi.* چاق کردن châq kardan
fatty *adj.* چربی دار charbi-dâr
faucet *n.* شیر shir
fault *n., vi., vt.* گسل gosal زلزله شکاف shekâf-e' zelzeleh
fault *n., vi., vt.* تقصیر taqsir عیب 'eyb
faultless *adj.* بی تقصیر bitaqsir
faulty *adj.* معیوب ma'yub مقصر moqas~er ناقص nâqes
favor *n., vt.* لطف lotf احسان ehsân عنایت 'enâyat
favorable *adj.* موافق movâfegh مناسب monâseb شرطه shorteh
favorite *n., adj.* مطلوب matlub مورد علاقه mored-e' 'alâqeh
favorite son *np.* محبوب نماینده namâyandeh-ye' mahbub
fawn *adj., vi.* بچه آهو bach~eh âhu چاپلوسی کردن châplusi kardan
fay *n., vt., vi.* وصل کردن vasl kardan
faze *vt.* مغشوش کردن maqshush kardan
fear *v.* وحشت داشتن vahshat dâshtan ترس داشتن tars dâshtan
fear *n.* وحشت vahshat ترس tars بیم bim واهمه vâ-hemeh
fearful *adj.* ترسناک tars-nâk ترسان tarsân وحشت زده vahshat-zadeh
fearless *adj.* نترس natars بی باک bibâk بی پروا biparvâ
feasible *adj.* عملی 'amali شدنی shodani
feast *n., vi., vt.* میهمانی mihmâni جشن jashn عید 'eyd
feat *adj., n.* کارمهم kâr-e' mohem~ شاهکار shâh-kâr
feather *n., vt., vi.* پر par
featherweight *n., adj.* پروزن par vazn سبک sabok
feature *n., vt.* شکل shekl سیما simâ قیافه qiâfeh طرح tarh

featured *v.* باشكل bâ-shekl منقوش manqush
feckless *adj.* بی روح bi-ruh بی فكر bi-fekr
fed-up *n.* خسته khasteh ذله zel~eh
federal *adj., n.* دولتی dolati پیمانی peymâni متحد mot~ahed
federate *vt., vi., adj.* متحد شدن mot~ahed shodan
هم پیمان شدن ham-peymân shodan
fee *n., vt.* كارمزد kârmozd حق الزحمه haqol-zahmeh
feeble *adj.* ناتوان nâtavân عاجز 'âjez
feed *vt., vi., n.* غذا دادن qazâ dâdan خوردن علف 'alaf khordan
feed(off) *n.* ازدیگران خوردن az digarân khordan
feed(on/upon) *n.* تغذیه كردن taqzieh kardan
حمایت كردن hemâyat kardan
feedback *n.* برگشت bargasht پاسخ pâsokh
feel *vt., vi., n.* احساس كردن ehsâs kardan لمس كردن lams kardan
feel(like) *n.* هوس داشتن havas dâshtan بنظرآمدن benazar âmadan
feel(out) *n.* تحقیق كردن tahqiq kardan
feel(up to) *n.* توانایی داشتن tavânâyi dâshtan
feeler *n.* شاخک shâkhak امتحان كننده emtehân konandeh
feeling *n., v., adj.* احساس ehsâs حس hes~ عاطفه 'âtefeh
feet *n., pl.* پاها pâhâ قدم qadam
feign *vt., vi.* وانمود كردن vânemud kardan
feint *n., vi.* كلک زدن kalak zadan
felicitate *vt., adj.* تبریک گفتن tabrik goftan
خوشحال كردن khosh-hâl kardan
fell *n.* انداختن andâkhtan
fellow *n., vt., adj.* طرف taraf یارو yâru مردک mardak
fellowship *n., vt., vi.* دوستی dusti همدمی hamdami
بورس تحصیلی burs-e' tahsili
felon *n., adj.* جانی jâni تبهكار tabah-kâr آدمكش âdam-kosh
felony *adj.,n.* جنایی jenâyi جرم سنگین jorm-e' sangin
felt *n., adj., vt., vi.* نمد namad
female *n., adj.* ماده mâd~eh مؤنث mo'an~as
feminine *adj., n.* زنانه zanâneh لطیف latif
fen *n., pl.* مرداب mordâb
fence *v.* حصاركشیدن hesâr keshidan
fence *v.* شمشیربازی كردن sham-shir bâzi kardan
fend *vt., vi.* دفاع كردن defâ' kardan
fend off *n.* دفع كردن daf' kardan

fender *n.* گلگير gelgir محافظ mohâfez
fence *n.* ديوار divâr نرده nardeh چپر chapar پرچين parchin
fenugreek *n.* شنبليله shanbalileh
ferment *n.* بهيجان آمدن be-hayajân âmadan
ferment *n., vt., vi.* تخمير كردن takhmir kardan
fern *n.* سرخس sarakhs
ferret *n., vt., vi.* راسو râsu كنجكاوى كردن konjkâvi kardan
Ferris wheel *np.* چرخ و فلك charkh-o falak
ferry *n., vt., vi.* روى آب حمل كردن ruy-e' âb haml kardan
fertile *adj.* حاصلخيز hâsel-khiz بارور bâr-var
fertilize *vt.* كوددادن kud dâdan حاصلخيز كردن hâselkhiz kardan
fervent *adj.* باحرارت bâ-harârat پروباقرص par-o pâ qors
fervid *adj.* سوزان suzân مشتاق moshtâq
fervor *n.* حرارت شديد harârat-e' shadid التهاب eltehâb
fester *vi., vt., n.* چرك شدن cherk shodan گنديدن gandidan
festival *n., adj.* جشن واره jashn vâreh فستيوال festivâl
festive *adj.* شاد shâd جشنى jashni
festoon *n., vt.* هلال گل helâl-e' gol تزيين دادن taz'in dâdan
fetal *adj.* جنينى janini
fetch *vt., vi., n.* رفتن و آوردن raftan va âvardan
fete *n., vt.* مهمانى دادن mehmâni dâdan
fetid *adj.* بدبو bad-bu بوى گند buy-e' gand متعفن mote'af~en
fetish *n.* علاقة بخصوص 'alâqeh-ye' bekhosus مرض maraz
fetlock *n.* مچ پاى اسب moch-e' pây-e' asb
fetor *n.* بوى بد buy-e' bad
fetter *n., vt.* زنجيرپا zanjir-e' pâ مقيد كردن moqay~ad kardan
fettle *n., vt.* حاضركردن hâzer kardan
fetus *n.* جنين janin
feu *n., vt.* حق الكشت haq~ol kesht
feud *n., vi.* نزاع كردن nezâ' kardan كينه كردن kineh kardan
feudal(ism) *n.* ملوك الطوايفى moluk oltavâyefi
fever *n., vt.* تب tab
fever sore *np.* تبخال tab-khâl
feverish *adj.* تبدار tab-dâr داغ dâq
few *adj., n., pro.* كم kam اندك andak قليل qalil بعضى ba'zi
fiance(e) *n.* نامزد nâmzad
fiasco *n.* شكست باافتضاح shekast bâ eftezâh گندكارى gand-kari
fiat *n.* امر amr حكم hokm

fib *vt., n., vi.* دروغ کوچک گفتن doruq-e' kuchek goftan
fiber *n.* بافت bâft رشته reshteh فیبر fibr لیف lif
fickle *adj.* بی وفا bivafâ نامرد nâmard
fiction *n.* افسانه afsâneh قصه qes~eh
fictitious *adj.* جعلی ja'li ساختگی sâkhtegi
fiddle *v.* ویولن زدن violon zadan
fiddle *v.* وقت تلف کردن vaqt talaf kardan
fiddler *n.* ویولن زن violon-zan
fiddlesticks *int.* مزخرفات mozakhrafât
fidelity *n.* وفاداری vafâ-dâri دقت deq~at صحت seh~at
fidget *vi., vt., n.* وول خوردن vul khordan بی قراری bi-qârâri
fiducial *adj.* اعتقادی e'teqâdi ایمانی imâni
fief *n.* ملک طایفه ای melk-e' tâyefeh-i تیول toyul
field *n., vt., vi., adj.* مزرعه mazra'eh زمین zamin رشته reshteh
میدان meydân
field day *np.* روزنمایشی ruz-e' namâyeshi روزخوب ruz-e' khub
field hand *np.* کارگر kârgar
field mouse *np.* موش صحرایی mush-e' sahrâyi
field trip *np.* سفرآموزشی safar-e' âmuzeshi
fiend *n.* پلید palid معتاد mo'tâd
fierce *adj.* درنده خو dar~andeh khu سهمگین sahmgin
fiery *adj.* آتشین âtashin زودسوز zud-suz
fifteen *n., adj.* پانزده pânzdah
fifth *adj., adv., n.* پنجم panjom
fifth column *np.* جاسوس بیگانه jâsus-e' bigâneh
fifty *n., adj.* پنجاه panjâh
fig *vt., n.* انجیر anjir
fight *n., vi., vt.* دعوا کردن da'vâ kardan جنگ کردن jang kardan
نزاع کردن nezâ' kardan مبارزه کردن mobârezeh kardan
fighter *n.* جنگجو jângju جنگنده jangandeh بکسور boksor
مبارز mobarez
figment *n.* خیال khiâl ساخته و پرورده sâkhteh va parvârdeh
figurative *adj.* مجازی majâzi تحت اللفظی tahtol-lafzi
figure *v.* مجسم کردن mojas~am kardan حساب کردن hesâb kardan
figure *n.* حساب hesâb رقم raqam
figure *n.* شکل shekl اندام andâm شبح shabah
figure of speech *np.* لفظی lafzi مجازی majâzi
figure on *n.* نقشه داشتن naqsheh dâshtan

figure out *n.* حل كردن hal~ kardan نهميدن fahmidan
figured *adj.* باشكل bâ-shekl بانقش bâ-naqsh
figurehead *n.* رئيس ظاهرى ra'is-e' zâheri
figurine *n.* مجسمهٔ كوچك mojasameh-ye' kuchak
filament *n.* رشته reshteh سيم توى لامپ sim-e' tuy-e' lâmp
filbert *n.* فندق fandoq
filch *vt.* جيب برى jib bori آنتابه دزدى âftâbeh-dozdi
file *n.* سوهان suhân رديف radif
file *n.* بايگانى bâygâni پرونده parvandeh
file *v.* بايگانى كردن bâygâni kardan بصف كردن besaf kardan
filial *adj.* فرزندانه farzandâneh
filibuster *n., vi., vt.* وراجى درمجلس كردن ver~âji dar majles kardan
fill *vt., vi., n.* پر كردن por kardan نسخه پيچيدن noskheh pichidan
fill(in) *v.* جا پر كردن jâ por kardan
fill(one in on) *v.* درجريان گذاشتن dar jaryân gozâshtan
fill(out) *v.* پر كردن por kardan چاق كردن châq kardan
filled *n.,adj.* پرشده por shodeh سرشار sa-r shâr
filler *n.* جا پر كن jâ por kon
filling *n.* پرى دندان pori-e' dandân
filling station *np.* پمپ بنزين pomp-e' benzin
filly *n.* ماديان جوان mâdiân-e' javân
film *v.* فيلم برداشتن film bardâshtan
filter *n., vt., vi., adj.* صاف كردن sâf kardan فيلتر filter صافى sâfi
filth *n.* كثافت kesâfat نجاست nejâsat
filthy *adj.* كثيف kasif ناپاك nâ-pâk
fin *n., vt., vi.* پرك parak بال ماهى bâl-e' mâhi پره par~eh
final(e) *n.* نهايى nahâyi قطعى qat'i خاتمه khâtemeh
finalize *vt., vi.* قطعى كردن qat'i kardan
finally *adv.* درخاتمه dar khâtemeh بالا خره bel-akhareh
finance *n., vt., vi.* بودجه دادن budjeh dâdan
 قسطى گرفتن qesti gereftan
financial *adj.* مالى mâli
financier *n., vt., vi.* بودجه گذار budjeh-gozâr
 سرمايه گذار sarmâyeh-gozâr
finch *n.* سهره sohreh
find *vt., vi., n.* پيدا كردن peydâ kardan دريافتن daryâftan
find out *n.* نهميدن fahmidan ملتفت شدن moltafet shodan
finding *n., v.* كشف kashf پيدايش peydâyesh

fine *v.* جریمه کردن jarimeh kardan
fine *adj.* ظریف zarif ریز riz قشنگ qashang
fine *n.* جریمه jarimeh
finesse *n., vi., vt.* مهارت mahârat فن fan~
finger *v.* انگشت کردن angosht kardan
finger tip *n.* نوک انگشت nok-e' angosht سر انگشت sar angosht
fingernail *n.* ناخن انگشت nâkhon-e' angosht
fingerprint *n., vt.* اثر انگشت asar-e' angosht
finicky *adj.* مشکل پسند moshkel-pasand
finish *v.* پایان دادن pâyân dâdan
finish *v.* تمام کردن tamâm kardan
finished *adj.* تمام شده tamâm shodeh کامل kâmel
finite *n.* معین mo'ay~an محدود mahdud متناهی motenâhi
fink *n., vi.* لو دهنده lo-dahandeh جاسوس jâsus
fiord *n.* خلیج تنگ khalij-e' tang
fir *n.* صنوبر sanobar کاج kâj
fire *v.* آتش کردن âtesh kardan شعله ور کردن sho'leh-var kardan
fire *n.* آتش âtash آذر âzar
fire *v.* اخراج کردن ekhrâj kardan شلیک کردن shel~ik kardan
fire alarm *np.* زنگ خطر آتش zang-e' khatar-e' âtash
fire department *np.* ادارهٔ آتش نشانی edâreh-ye' âtesh-neshâni
fire drill *np.* تمرین آتش سوزی tamrin-e' âtesh-susi
fire engine *np.* ماشین آتش نشانی mâshin-e' âtesh neshâni
fire escape *np.* فرارگاه آتش farârgâh-e' âtash
fire extinguisher *np.* پلهٔ آتش سوزی peleh-ye' âtash-susi
fire(away) *n.* شروع کردن shoru' kardan
fire(up) *n.* آتشی شدن âtashi shodan روشن کردن roshan kardan
fire-eater *n.* آتش خوار âtesh-khâr
firearm *n.* اسلحه گرم aslaheh-ye' garm
fireball *n.* گولهٔ آتشین guleh-ye' âtashin
firebird *n.* مرغ آتشین morq-e' âtashin
firecracker *n.* ترقه taraq~eh
firefly *n.* سوسک شب تاب susk-e' shab tâb
fireman *n.* مأمور آتش نشانی ma'mur-e' âtesh neshâni
fireplace *n.* اجاق دیواری ojâq-e' divâri شومینه shomineh
fireproof *adj., vt.* نسوز nasuz
firewood *n.* هیزم hizom
fireworks *n.* آتش بازی âteshbâzi

firing pin *np.* چاشنی châshni
firing squad *np.* جوخهٔ آتش jukheh-ye' âtash
firm *adj.* محکم mohkam راسخ râsekh قایم qâyem واثق vâseq
first *adj., adv., n.* یکم yekom اول av~al نخستین nakhostin
first born *n.* ارشد arshad نخست زاده nakhost-zâdeh
first finger *n.* سبابه sabâbeh
first floor *np.* طبقهٔ اول tabaqeh-ye' av~al
first lady *np.* خانم رئیس جمهور khânom-e' ra'is jomhur
first mate *np.* معاون ناخدا mo'âven-e' nâkhodâ
first offender *np.* مجرم بی سابقه دار mojrem-e' bi-sâbeqeh-dâr
first person *np.* شخص اول shakhs-e' av~al
first-aids *n.* کمک های اولیه komak-hâ-ye' av~alieh
first-class *adj., adv.* درجه یک darejeh yek
first-rate *adj., adv.* درجه یک darejeh yek تراز اول tarâz-e' av~al
firsthand *adv., adj.* مستقیم mostaqim دست اول dast-e' av~al
firth *n.* شاخه رود shâkheh rud
fiscal *adj., n.* مالی mâli
fiscal year *np.* سال مالی sâl-e' mâli
fish *v.* ماهی گرفتن mâhi gereftan
fish *n.* ماهی mâhi
fisherman *n.* ماهیگیر mâhi-gir
fishery *n.* شیلات shilât صید ماهی seyd-e' mâhi
fishhook *n.* قلاب ماهی qol~âb-e' mâhi
fishing *n.* ماهیگیری mâhi-giri
fishpond *n.* حوض ماهی hoz mâhi
fishy *adj.* مشکوک mashkuk
fission *n.* پاشیدگی pâshidegi تکثیر taksir
fissure *n., vt., vi.* شکاف دادن shekâf dâdan
fist *n., vt.* مشت زدن mosht zadan
fistful *n.* مشت پر mosht-e' por
fistula *n.* ناسور nâ-sur
fit *n.* ناراحتی nârâhati
fit *v.* خوردن khordan جا انداختن jâ andâkhtan
fit *v.* اندازه بودن andâzeh budan شایسته بودن shâyesteh budan
fitting *adj., n.* اندازه گیری andâzeh-giri پرو perov
five *n., adj.* پنج panj
fix *v.* تنگنا tangnâ ثابت نگه داشتن sâbet negah dâshtan
fix *v.* درست کردن dorost kardan تعمیر کردن ta'mir kardan

fixate *vt., vi.* چشم دوختن cheshm dukhtan
fixed *adj.* ثابت sâbet درست شده dorost shodeh معین mo'ay~an
fixer *n.* تعمیر کننده ta'mir konandeh کار چاق کن kâr châq-kon
fixture *n.* اثاثیهٔ ثابت asâsiyeh-ye' sâbet
fiz(zle) *n.* فیس فیس کردن fis fis kardan
fizzle *vi., n.* ازبین رفتن az beyn raftan
flabbergast *vt.* مبهوت کردن mabhut kardan
flabby *adj.* سست sost شل shol یبس yobs
flaccid *adj.* سست sost بیجان bijân
flag *n., v., vi.* پرچم parcham بیرق beyraq علم 'alam
flagellate *vt., adj., n.* شلاق زدن shal~âq zadan
زنجیرزدن zanjir zadan
flagrant *adj.* رسوا خیز rosvâ khiz وقیح vaqih
flagship *n.* کشتی دریادار kashtie daryâdâr
flagstaff *n.* میلهٔ پرچم mileh-ye' parcham
flail *vt., vi.* کوبیدن kubidan
flair *n.* شامه shâm~eh استعداد este'dâd
flak *n.* آتشبار ضد هوایی âteshbâr-e' zed~-e' havâyi توبیخ tobikh
flake *n., vi., vt.* پوسته پوسته شدن pusteh pusteh shodan
flaky *adj.* خرد شدنی khord shodani
flam *n., vt., vi.* حقه بازی hoq~eh bâzi کلاه برداری kolâh bardâri
flamboyant *adj., n.* زرق و برقدار zarq-o barq-dâr اغراقی eqrâqi
flame *v.* شعله زدن sho'leh zadan زبانه کشیدن zabâneh keshidan
flame-thrower *n.* آتش انداز âtash andâz
flank *n., vt., vi.* پهلو گرفتن pahlu gereftan کنار kenâr جناح jenâh
flannel *n., vt.* پشم ظریف pashm-e' zarif فلانل felânel
flap *n.* بال bâl zadan لبه labeh تا tâ
flare *v.* شعله ور شدن sho'leh-var shodan برآمدگی barâmâdegi
flare *n.* مشعل هوایی mash'al-e' havâyi
flare-up *n.* آتشی شدن âtashi shodan
flash *v.* برق زدن barq zadan
flash *v.* نور دادن nur dâdan تاباندن tâbândan
flash flood *np.* سیل ناگهانی seyl-e' nâgahâni
flash-back *n.* برگشت خاطرات bargasht-e' khâterât
flashing *n.* خودنمایی khod-namâyi بست شیروانی bast-e' shirvâni
flashlight *n.* چراغ قوه cherâq-qov~eh
flask *n.* قمقمه qomqomeh تنگ tong فلاسک felâsk
flat *adj., n., vt., vi.* پهن pahn صاف sâf پنجر panchar

flat tire *np.* پنچری panchari
flatfoot *n.* پلیس پیاده polis-e' piâdeh
flatten *v.* صاف کردن sâf kardan بدون گاز bedun-e' gâz
flatten *v.* پهن کردن pahn kardan
flatter *v.* تملق گفتن tamal~oq goftan
flatter *v.* چاپلوسی کردن châplusi kardan
flatterer *adj.* چاپلوس châaplus متملق motemal~eq
flattery *n.* تملق tamal~oq چاپلوسی châplusi کاسه لیسی kâseh-lisi
مداهنه modaheneh
flattop *n.* کشتی هواپیمابر kashti-e' havâ-peymâ bar
flaunt *vi., vt., n.* پز دادن poz dâdan بالیدن bâlidan
flavor *n., vt.* مزه دادن mazeh dâdan طعم ta'm
flaw *n., vt., vi.* نقص naqs ترک tarak عیب 'eyb
flawless *adj.* بی نقص bi-naqs بی عیب bi-'eyb بی اشتباه bi-eshtebâh
flax *n.* بذرک bazrak
flay *vt.* پوست کندن pust kandan چاول chapâvol انتقاد enteqâd
flea *n.* کک kak
flea-market *n.* بازار مکاره bâzâr-e' mak~âreh
fleck *n., vt.* ذره zar~eh نقطه گذاری noqteh gozâri
fledge *vt., vi., adj.* پر در آوردن par dar âvardan
fledgling *n.* تازه پر tâzeh par جوجه jujeh ناشی nâshi
flee *vi., vt.* فرار کردن farâr kardan
fleece *n., vt.* پشم چیدن pashm chidan لخت کردن lokht kardan
fleer *vi., vt., n.* باتمسخر خندیدن bâ-tamaskhor khandidan
fleet *adj., n., vi., vt.* ناوگان nâvgân زود گذشتن zud gozashtan
fleeting *adj.* زودگذر zud gozar
flesh *n., vt.* گوشت gusht بدن badan شهوت shahvat
fletcher *n.* پیکان ساز peykân-sâz
flex *vt., vi., n.* بازو گرفتن bâzu gereftan
منقبض کردن monqabez kardan
flexible *adj.* باانعطاف bâ-en'etâf کشی keshi متغیر moteqay~er
flick *n., vt., vi.* تلنگر زدن talangor zadan ضربت zârbat
flicker *vi., vt., n.* سریع بال زدن sari' bâl zadan
سوسو زدن susu zadan
flier *n.* اعلامیه e'lâmieh
flight *n., vi.* پرواز parvâz گریز goriz
flimflam *n., vt.* چرت گفتن chart goftan
حقه بازی کردن hoq~eh-bâzi kardan

flimsy *adj., n.* نازک nâzok ظریف zarif سطحی sat-hi
flinch *vi., vt., n.* عقب کشیدن 'aqab keshidan
fling *vt., vi., n.* پرتاب کردن partâb kardan
    جفتک انداختن joftak andâkhtan
flint *n., vt.* سنگ فندک sang-e' fandak چخماق chakhmâq
flip *vt., vi., n.* چرخاندن charkhândan گرداندن gardândan
flirt *vi., vt., n.* لا س زدن lâs zadân
float *vi., n.* شناور شدن shenâvar shodan
floater *n.* شناور shenâvar سرگردان sargardân
floating *adj.* شناور shenâvar معلق mo'al~âq متحرک motehar~ek
flock *n., vi., vt.* گله gal~eh گروه goruh
flog *vt.* شلاق زدن shal~âq zadan
flood *n., vt., vi.* طغیان کردن toqyân kardan سیل آمدن seyl âmadan
flood-light *n.* نورافکن nur-afkan
floor *n., vt.* زمین زدن zamin zadan کف kaf طبقه tabaqeh
floor plan *np.* نقشهٔ ساختمانی naqsheh-ye' sâkhtemân
floor walker *n.* مدیر modir مراقب morâqeb
floozy *n.* زن هرجایی zan-e' har jâyi
florescent *adj.* درخشان derakhshân شکوفان shekufân مهتابی mahtâbi
florist *n.* گل فروش gol-forush
floss *n.* نخ ابریشمی nakh-e' abrishami
flotation *n.* شروع کردن shoru' kardan
flottila *n.* ناوگان کوچک nâvâgân-e' kuchak
flounce *n., vt., vi.* تقلا کردن taqal~â kardan
flourish *vi., vt., n.* شکوفه کردن shekufeh kardan
    زینت کردن zinat kardan
flow *vi., vt., n.* جریان کردن jaryân kardan جاری شدن jâri shodan
flower *v.* گل دادن gol dâdan گل کردن gol kardan
flower *n.* گل gol
flower pot *n.* گلدان goldân گیرکردن gir kârdan
    دست وپازدن dast-o pâ zadan
flowing *adj.* روان ravân ریزان rizân
flu *n.* سرماخوردگی sarmâ-khordegi
fluctuate *v.* تغییرکردن taqyir kardan
fluctuate *v.* یکدم عوض شدن yekdam 'avaz shodan
fluctuation *n.* نوسان navasân
flue *n., vi.* لوله luleh دودکش dudkesh
fluent *adj.* سلیس salis جریان دار jaryân-dâr مسلط mosal~at

نصیح .... fasih

fluff *n., vt., vi.* پنبه زنی کردن panbeh-zani kardan اشتباه eshtebâh

fluffy *adj.* پرپر par par نرم narm

fluid *n., adj.* روان ravân مایع mâye'

fluke *n., vt.* تیزنوک tiznok خوش شانسی khosh shânsi

flunk *vi., vt., n.* رفوزه کردن rofuzeh kardan

رفوزه شدن rofuzeh shodan

fluorescent *adj.* مهتابی mahtâbi

flurry *n., vt.* بوران burân گیج کردن gij kardan

flush *n.* رنگ rang

flush *v.* آبشویی کردن âb-shuyi kardan سرخ شدن sorkh shodan

fluster *vt., vi., n.* هول کردن hol kardan

سراسیمه شدن sarâsimeh shodan

flute *n., vi., vt.* فلوت زدن folut zadan نی لبک ney labak

flutter *vi., vt., n.* پرپرزدن parpar zadan لرزاندن larzândan

flux *n., vt., vi.* جریان دادن jaryân dâdan جوش دادن jush dâdan

fly *v.* افراشتن afrâshtan هواکردن havâ kardan

fly *v.* پریدن paridan پرواز کردن parvâz kârdan

fly *n.* مگس magas

flycatcher *n.* مگس گیر magas-gir

flying saucer *np.* بشقاب پرنده bosh-qâb parandeh

flytrap *n.* مگس گیر magas-gir حشره خوار hashareh khâr

foal *n., vt., vi.* کره زاییدن kor~eh zâyidan

foam *n., vi., vt.* کف کردن kaf kardan

focalize *vt.* مرکزیت دادن markaziyat dâdan

focus/foci *n.* مرکز markaz کانون kânun

fodder *n., vt.* علف 'alaf علوفه 'olufeh

foe *n.* دشمن doshman مخالف mokhâlef

fog *n., vt., vi.* مه mah مبهم کردن mobham kardan

fog bank *n.* مه غلیظ mah-e' qaliz

foggy *adj.* مه آلود mah-âlud مبهم کردن mobham kardan

foible *n.* ضعف نقطهٔ noqteh-ye' za'f

foil *n.* آلومینیوم ورقهٔ varaqeh-ye' âlminiom

foil *v.* خنثی کردن khonsâ kardan

foist *vt.* کف رفتن kaf raftan دروغی جا دادن doruqi jâ dâdan

fold *n.* گوسفند آغل âqol-e' gusfand گروه goruh برابر barâbar

fold *v.* تا کردن tâ kardan دولا کردن dol~â kardan

folder *n.* تا کن tâ kon پوشه pusheh

folds *n.* تا لابلا lâ-belâ tâ
foliage *n.* شاخ و برگ shâkh-o barg
foliate *v.* برگ دادن barg dâdan
foliate *v.* صفحه صفحه کردن safheh safheh kardan
folio *n., adj., vt.* کاغذ تا شده kâqaz-e' tâ-shodeh
folk dance *np.* رقص محلی raqs-e' mahal~i
folk song *np.* آواز محلی âvâz-e' mahâl~i
folklore *n.* عقاید' رسوم شناسی 'aqâyed rosum shenâsi
folks *n.* مردم mardom خویشاوند khishâvand
follicle *n.* کیسه kiseh غده qod~eh
follow *vt., vi., n.* پیروی کردن peyrovi kardan
دنبال کردن donbâl kardan
follow out *v.* بپایان رسانیدن be-pâyân resânidan
follow out *v.* انجام دادن anjâm dâdan
follow-through *n.* تاآخررفتن tâ âkhar raftan
follow-up *n., adj.* تعقیب کردن ta'qib kardan مکمل mokam~al
follower *n.* پیرو peyro مرید morid تعقیب کننده ta'qib konandeh
following *n., adj.* پیروی peyrovi متعاقب mote'âqeb بعدی ba'di
ذیل zeyl
folly *n.* حماقت hemâqat
foment *vt.* برانگیختن bar angikhtân
fond *adj., n.* شیفته shifteh دوستدار dustdâr
fondle *vt., vi.* نازکردن nâz kardan نوازش کردن navâzesh kardan
دستمالی کردن dast-mâli kardan
font *n.* کاسهٔ سنگی kâseh-ye' sangi
food *n.* غذا qazâ خوراک khorâk طعام ta'âm مائده mâ'edeh
fool *v.* گول زدن gul zadan
fool *adj.* احمق ahmaq نادان nâdân لوده lodeh ابله ablah
fool's errand *np.* کار بی ثمر kâr-e' bi-samar
foolhardy *adj.* شجاعت ابلهانه shojâ'at-e' ablahâneh
foolish *adj.* ابلهانه ablahâneh نادان nâdân
foolproof *adj.* خراب نشدنی kharâb nashodani بی نقص bi nâqs
foot *n., vi., vt.* پا pâ قدم qadam دامنه dâmaneh
foot soldier *np.* سرباز پیاده sarbâz-e' piâdeh
footage *n.* اندازهٔ فیلم andâzeh-ye' film
football *n.* فوتبال آمریکایی futbâl-e' âmrikâyi
foothill *n.* دامنهٔ تپه dâmaneh-ye' tap~eh
footing *n.* جاپا jâ-pâ زمینه zamineh

---

footlocker *n.* صندوق پاتختی sandoq-e' pâtakhti
footnote *n., vt.* یادداشت yâd-dâsht پانوشت pâ nevesht
footprint *n.* جاپا jâ pâ رد پا rad-e' pâ
footstep *n.* قدم qadam گام gâm
footstool *n.* پاصندلی pâ sandali زیرپایی zir pâyi
footwork *n.* پیاده روی piâdeh-ravi رقص پا raqs-e' pâ
for *pre., con.* برای barây-e' بجای be jây-e' برله bar lah-e'
forage *n., vi., vt.* لاشخوری کردن lâsh khori kardan
امرار معاش emrâr-e' ma'âsh
forasmuch *con.* ازآنجایی که az ânjâyi keh
foray *n., vi., vt.* تاراج کردن târâj kardan غارت کردن qârat kardan
forbear(er) *n.* خودداری کردن khod-dâri kardan جد jad~
forbid *n.* منع کردن man' kardan قدغن کردن qadeqan kardan
forbidden *v., adj.* ممنوع mamnu' حرام harâm
force *v.* مجبور کردن maj-ur kardan
force *n.* نیرو niru زور zur قوت qov~at اجبار ejbâr
forced *adj., v.* مجبور majbur باقوت bâ-qov~at اجباری ejbâri
forceful *adj.* نیرومند niru-mand قوی qav~i
forceps *n.* گیرهٔ جراحی gireh-ye' jar~âhi
forcible *adj.* زوری zuri اجباری ejbâri عدوانی 'odvâni
fore *adj., int., adv., n.* درجلو dar jelo پیشین pishin
forearm *n., vt.* ساعد sâ'ed
forecast *vt., vi., n.* پیش بینی کردن pish-bini kardan
foreclose *vt., vi.* سلب مالکیت کردن salb-e' mâlekiyat kardan
forefather *n.* جد jad~ نیا niâ
forefinger *n.* انگشت سبابه angosht-e' sabâbeh
forefront *n.* جلو jelo جلوی jelo-ye' jelo
forego *v.* دست کشیدن dast keshidan
forego *v.* صرف نظرکردن sarfe-nazar kardan
foregoing *adj., vi.* قبلی qabli ذکرشده zekr shodeh
foregone *vt.* ازقبل تعیین شده ta'yin shodeh az gabl
foreground *n.* پیش منظره pish manzareh
forehand *adj., n., adv.* جلو دست jelo dast
forehead *n.* پیشانی pishâni جبین jabin ناصیه nâsieh
foreign *adj., adv.* بیگانه bigâneh خارجی khâreji
foreign affairs *np.* امورخارجی omur-e' khâreji
foreigner *n.* بیگانه bigâneh خارجی khâreji اجنبی ajnabi
forejudge *v.* پیش داوری pishdâvari

forejudge *v.* بيجا قضاوت كردن bijâ qezâvat kardan
foreknowledge *n.* آگاهی قبلی âgâhi-e' qabli علم غيب 'elm-e' qeyb
foreman *n.* سركارگر sar kâr-gar
foremost *adj., adv.* اولين av~alin مهمترين mohemtarin
forensic *adj., n.* بحثی bahsi گلوله شناسی goluleh shenâsi
forerunner *n.* پيشرو pish-ro پيش قدم pish-qadam نشانه neshâneh
foresee *vt., vi.* پيش بينی كردن pishbini kardan
foresight *n.* پيش بينی pishbini شناخت shenâkht فهم fahm
عاقبت انديشی 'âqebat-andishi
foreskin *n.* ختنه پوست khatneh pust
forest *n., vt.* جنگل jangal
forestall *vt.* ازقصد مانع شدن az qasd mâne' shodan
forestry *n.* جنگل بانی jangal-bâni
foreswear *n.* سوگند دروغی sogand-e' doruqi
foretell *vt., vi.* پيش گويی كردن pishguyi kardan
foreteller *n.* پيشگو pish-gu
forethought *n.* دور انديشی dur-andishi
forever *adv.* برای هميشه barây-e' hamisheh جاودانی jâvdâni
foreword *n.* پيش گفتار pish-goftâr
forfeit *n., vt., adj.* باختن bâkhtan دست كشيدن dast keshidan
forge *n., vt., vi.* ساختن sâkhtan جعل كردن ja'l kardan كوره kureh
forget *vt., vi.* فراموش كردن farâmush kardan
forgetful *adj.* فراموشكار farâmush-kâr
forgive *vt., vi.* بخشيدن bakhshidan عفو كردن 'afv kardan
forgiveness *n.* بخشش bakhshesh عفو 'afv آمرزش âmorzesh
مغفرت maqferat
forgiving *adj.* بخشنده bakhshandeh رحيم rahim
fork *n.* چنگال changâl
fork *n., vt., vi.* دو شاخه do shâkheh منشعب شدن monsha'eb shodan
forlorn *adj.* ناميدی nâ-omidi بيچاره bichâreh فلاكتبار felâkat-bâr
form *v.* شكل دادن shekl dâdan تشكيل دادن tashkil dâdan
form *n.* شكل shekl ساخت sâkht ورقه varaqeh قسم qesm
formal *adj., n., adv.* رسمی rasmi اداری edâri مودبانه mo-a'd~abâneh
formality *n.* تشريفات tashrifât
formalize *vt., vi.* رسمی كردن rasmi kardan
formally *adv.* رسماً rasman
format *n., vt.* نقشه naqsheh طرح tarh برنامه barnâmeh
formation *n.* تشكيل tashkil دسته dasteh نظم nazm

formative *adj., n.* تشکیل دهنده tashkil dahandeh
former *adj., n.* سابق sâbeq اسبق asbaq قبلی qabli پیشین pishin
formerly *adv.* سابقاً sâbeqan قبلاً qablan
formidable *adj.* قوی qav~i سخت sakht سهمگین sahm-gin
formula(te) *n.* درست کردن قاعده qâ'edeh dorost kardan
فرمول formul
fornicate *v.* جنده بازی کردن jendeh bâzi kardan زناکردن zenâ kardan
fornication *v.* زنا zenâ جنده بازی jendeh-bâzi
forsake *vt.* ترک کردن tark kardan ول کردن vel kardan
forswear *vt., vi.* قسم توبه خوردن qasam-e' tobeh khordan
fort *n.* قلعه qal'eh دژ dezh قوی qavi
forte *adj., adv., n.* هنر honar مهارت mahârat
forth *adv., pre.* بیرون از خفا birun az khafâ جلو jelo پیش pish
forthcoming *adj., n.* نزدیک آینده' âyandeh-ye' nazdik
forthright *adj., adv., n.* رک گو rok-gu
forthwith *adv.* فوراً foran بیدرنگ bi-derang
fortification *n.* محکم کاری mohkam-kâri تقویت taqviat
استحکام estehkâm
fortify *vt., vi.* محکم کردن mohkam kardan
تقویت کردن taqviat kardan
fortitude *n.* صبر sabr بردباری bord-bâri طاقت tâqat
fortress *n., vt.* دژ dezh قلعه' نظامی qal'eh-ye' nezâmi
fortuitous *adj.* اتفاقی et~efaqi تصادفی tasâdofi
fortuity *n.* بخت bakht اتفاق et~efaq
fortunate *n.* خوشبخت khosh-bakht خوش شانس khosh-shans
نیک اختر nik-akhtar
fortunately *adv.* خوشبختانه khosh-bakhtâneh
fortune *n., vt., vi.* بخت bakht اقبال eqbâl شانس shâns دارایی dârâyi
fortuneteller *n.* فالگیر fâl-gir طالع بین tâle' bin
forty *n., adj.* چهل chehel
forum *n.* بحث bahs نظرخواهی nazar khâhi
forum *n.* میزگرد miz-e' gerd جلسه jaleseh
forward *adv., adj., n., vt.* جلو jelo پیش pish
نشانی دادن neshâni dâdan
forwardness *n.* رک گویی rok-guyi گستاخی gostâkhi
fossil *n., adj.* سنگواره sangvâreh فسیل fosil
fossilize *vt., vi.* محجر کردن mohaj~ar kardan
foster *vt., n.* پروراندن parvarândan پرورش دادن parvaresh dâdan

foster child *np.* فرزند خوانده farzand khândeh

foul *adj., adv., n., vt.* خطا کردن khat~â kardan ناپاک nâ-pâk بد bad فول fol

foul play *np.* عمل نادرست 'amal-e' nâ-dorost

found *vt., adj., n., vi.* پایه گذاشتن pâyeh gozâshtan تأسیس کردن ta'sis kardan

foundation *n.* پایه pâyeh بنیاد bonyâd پی ریزی peyrizi شالوده shaludeh

founder *vi., vt., n.* بنیانگذار bonyân-gozâr مؤسس mo'as~es بانی bâni

foundling *n.* سرراهی bach~eh-ye' sar-e' râhi

foundry *n.* کارخانه ذوب فلز kârkhâneh-ye zobe' felez

fountain *n.* چشمه cheshmeh فواره favâreh

fountain pen *np.* قلم خودنویس qalam khodnevis

four *n., adj.* چهار chahâr

four-letter word *np.* حرف رکیک harf-e' rakik

foursome *n., adj.* چهارنفره chahâr nafareh

fourteen *n., adj.* چهارده chahâr-dah

fowl *adj., n., vi.* گوشت مرغ gusht-e' morq

fox *n., vt., vi.* روباه rubâh گول زدن gul zadan

foxy *adj.* روباه منش rubâh manesh فریبنده faribandeh

foyer *n.* سالن sâlon جلوگاه jelogâh

fracas *n.* جنگ و جدال دعوا da'vâ jang-o jedâl

fraction *n., vt.* کسر kasr شکست shekast خرده khordeh

fractional *adj.* کسری kasri جزیی joz'i

fracture *n., vt., vi.* شکستن shekastan شکستگی shekastegi ترک tarak

fragile *adj.* شکستنی shekastani ظریف zarif ترد tord

fragment *n., vi., vt.* پاره pâreh تکه tek~eh قطعه qat'eh

fragrant *adj.* خوشبو khoshbu معطر mo'at~âr

frail *adj., n.* ضعیف za'if سست sost خرد شدنی khord shodani

frame *v.* قاب گرفتن qâb gereftan

frame *n.* قاب qâb چهارچوب chahâr-chub هیکل heykal

frame *v.* دروغی مقصر کردن doruqi moqas~er kardan

frame - up *n.* پاپوش دوختن pâ-push dukhtan

frame of mind *n.* حالت فکری hâlat-e' fekri حالت ذهنی hâlat-e' zehni

framework *n.* ساختمان sâkhtemân استخوان بندی ostokhân-bandi

France *n.* فرانسه farânseh

franchise *n., vt.* حق توزیع و تجارت haq~-e' tozi' va tejârat

frank

frank *adj., n., vt.* صاف و پوست کنده sâf va pust kandeh
بیریا رک گو rok gu biriâ
frantic *adj.* جنون آمیز jonun âmiz هراسان hârâsân عصبانی 'asabâni
frater(nal) *n.* برادروار barâdar-vâr
fraternity *n.* برادری barâdari اخوت انجمن anjoman-e' okhov~at
fratricide *n.* برادر کشی barâdar koshi
fraud *v.* کلاه برداری کردن kolâh bardâri kardan
fraudulent *adj.* قلابی qol~âbi جعلی ja'li حقه باز hoq~eh-bâz
fraught *adj., n.* پر por مملو mamlo سرشار sarshâr
fray *vi., n., vt.* نزاع nezâ' ساییدن sâyidan
freak *vt., adj., n.* عجیب الخلقه 'ajib ol-khelqeh
freak *vt., adj., n.* غریب qarib نامعمولی nâma'muli
freckle *n., vt., vi.* کک و مک kak-o mak
free *v.* آزاد کردن âzâd kardan رها کردن rahâ kardan
free *adj., adv., vt.* آزاد âzâd مجانی majâni رایگان râyegân
freedom *n.* آزادی âzâdi رهایی rahâyi
freelance *n., vi., adj., adv.* آزاد قلم âzâd qalam مستقل mostaqel
freely *adv.* آزادانه âzâdâneh
Freemason *n.* فراماسون ferâmâson
freeway *n.* شاهراه shâhrâh بزرگراه bozorg-râh
freewill *adj.* داوطلبانه dâv-talabâneh
freeze *v.* منجمد شدن monjamed shodan
freeze *v.* یخ بستن yakh bastan منجمد کردن monjamed kardan
freezer *n.* یخچال yakhchâl
freezing point *np.* نقطه انجماد noqteh-ye' enjemâd
freight *n., vt.* باری بارکشی bâr keshi باری فرستادن bâri ferestâdan
freighter *n.* بارکش bârkesh کشتی باری kashti-e' bâri
French *n.* فرانسوی farânsavi
frenzy *n., vt.* جنون آنی jonun-e' âni دیوانه کردن divâneh kardan
frequency *n.* تکرر takaror بسامد basâmad فرکانس ferekâns
frequent *adj., vt.* حضور یافتن hozur yâftan
frequent(ly) *n.* غالباً qâleban مکرراً mokararan بارها bâr-hâ
fresh(en) *n.* تازه کردن tâzeh kardan
freshman *n., adj.* دانشجوی سال اول dâneshjuy-e' sâl-e' av~al
freshness *n.* تازگی tâzegi طراوت tarâvat شادابی shâdâbi
fret *n., vt., vi.* خرده شدن khordeh shodan ساییدن sâyidan
friar *n.* راهب râheb
fribble *vi., vt., n., adj.* وقت تلف کردن vaqt talaf kardan

fricative adj., n. اصطکاکی estekâki لرزان larzân
friction n. اصطکاک estekâk ساییدگی sâyidegi کدورت kodurat
friday n. جمعه jom'eh
friend n., vt. دوست dust رفیق rafiq یار yâr
friendship n. دوستی dusti رفاقت refâqat مودت maved~at ولاء vela'
frigate n. کشتی جنگی kashti-e' jangi
fright n. ترس tars وحشت vah-shat خوف khof هراس harâs
frighten v. ترساندن tarsândan وحشت زدن vashat zadan
هراسانیدن harâsânidan
frightened n. هراسان harâsân ترسیده tarsideh
وحشت زده vah-shat-zadeh
frigid adj. یخ زده yakhzadeh سرد sard زن بی احساس zan-e' bi-ehsâs
fringe n., vt. سرحد ریشه کردن risheh risheh kardan سرحد sar-had~
fringe benefit(s) n. مزایا mazâyâ
frisk vi., vt., n. دستمالی کردن dastmâli kardan گشتن gashtan
شاد shâd
frizzle vi., vt., n. جزو وز کردن jez-o vez kardan وزوزی vezvezi
fro adv. عقب 'aqab پس pas
frock vt. عبا 'abâ نیم تنه nim-taneh
frog n., vi. قورباغه gurbâqeh وزغ vazaq غوک quk
frogman n. غواص qav~âs
from pre. از az
front n., adj., vt., vi. جلو jelo پیش pish جبهه jebheh بنا banâ
front-page adj., vt. صفحهٔ اول safheh-ye' av~al
frontage n. جلوگاه jelogâh جادهٔ کناری jâd~eh-ye' kenâri
frontal adj., n. ازجلو az jelo جلویی jeloyi
frontier n., adj. سرحد sar-had~ مرز marz
frost n., vt., vi. یخ بندان yakh bandân سرمازدن sarmâ zadan
frostbite n., vt. سرمازدگی sarmâ zadegi
froth n., vt., vi. کف کردن kaf kardan
frown vi., vt., n. اخم کردن akhm kardan
ترش رویی کردن torsh ruyi kardan
frozen v., adj. یخ بسته yakh basteh منجمد monjamed بلوکه belokeh
فریزه ferizeh
frugal adj. صرفه جو sarfehju زودباور zudbâvar
fruit n. میوه miveh ثمره samareh بار bâr
fruitcake n. کیک میوه دار keyk-e' miveh-dâr قاطی پاتی qâti-pâti
fruition n. وصال vesal

fruity *adj.* میوه ایی miveh-yi آبدار âbdâr
frustrate *vt., vi., adj.* مغشوش کردن maqshush kardan
frustrate *vt., vi., adj.* کفر درآوردن kofr dar-âvardan
frustrated *n.* ازکوره دررفته za kureh dar rafteh مستأصل mosta'sal
fry *vt., vi., n.* سرخ کردن sorkh kardan نیمرو کردن nimru kardan
frying-pan *n.* ماهی تابه mâhitâbeh
fuchsia *n., adj.* گل آویز gol âviz
fuddle *vt., vi., n.* سست کردن sost kardan گیج کردن gij kardan
fuddy-duddy *n., adj.* وسواسی vasvâsi قرقرو qorqoru
fudge *v.* سرهم و برهم کردن sarham-o barham kardan
fudge *n.* شکلات shokol~ât چرت chart
fuel *v.* سوخت گیری کردن sukht giri kardan
fuel *v.* تحریک کردن tahrik kardan
fugitive *n., adj.* فراری farâri گریزان gorizân آواره âvâreh
fulfill *vt.* اجرا کردن ejrâ kardan ارضاء کردن erzâ' kardan
full *adj., adv., vt., vi.* پر por مملو mamlo تام tâm آکنده âkandeh
full house *np.* فول ful
full moon *np.* ماه شب چهارده mâh-e' shab-e' chahârdah
full-blooded *adj.* اصیل asil غیور qayur پاک نژاد pâk nezhâd
full-length *adj.* تمام قد tamâm qad دراز derâz
fumble *v.* کورمالی کردن kurmâli kardan
سرهم بندی کردن sar-ham bandi kardan
fume *n., vt., vi.* دود دادن dud dâdan عصبانی شدن asabâni shodan
fumigate *vt.* ضدعفونی کردن zed~-e' 'ofuni kardan
fun *n., vi., vt., adj.* خوشی khoshi تفریح tafrih کیف keyf
function *v.* کارکردن kâr kardan
function *v.* وظیفه بودن vazifeh مفید بودن mofid budan
functional *adj., n.* کارکن kâr-kon عملی 'amali سالم sâlem مفید mofid
fund *n., vt.* سرمایه sarmâyeh پس انداز pasandâz
قرض دادن qarz dâdan
fundamental *adj., n.* ابتدایی ebtedâyi اساسی asâsi اصلی asli
funds *n.* وجوه vojuh موجودی mojudi پول pul مایه mâyeh
funeral *n., adj.* دفن dafn تشییع جنازه tashyi'-e' jenâzeh
fungus/fungi *n.* قارچ qârch کپک kapak
funnel *n., vt.* قیف qif بزور رد کردن bezur rad kardan
funny *adj., n.* بامزه bâ-mazeh خنده دار khandeh-dâr مضحک moz-hek
fur *n., adj., vt.* خز khaz پوست pust
furious *adj.* عصبانی 'asabâni

furl *vt., vi., n.* سفت پیچیدن seft pichidan
furlough *n., vt.* مرخصی دادن morkhasi dâdan
furnace *n., vt.* کوره kureh تنور tanur بخاری bokhâri
furnish *n.* مجهز کردن mojahaz kardan دارا کردن dârâ kardan
furnished *n.* مبله mobleh
furniture *n.* اثاثه asâseh مبلمان moblemân
furor *n.* خشم khashm علاقهٔ شدید 'alâqeh-ye' shadid
furrow *n., vt., vi.* شخم زدن shokhm zadan شیار دادن shiâr dâdan چروک choruk
further *n., adv., adj., vt.* بیشتر bish-tar دورتر dur-tar ثانوی sânavi
furthermore *adv.* بعلاوه be'alâveh وانگهی vân-gahi
fury *n.* خشم khashm خشونت khoshunat جنون jonun
fuse *n., vi., vt.* گداختن godâkhtan جوش دادن jush dâdan فتیله fetileh
fuselage *n.* بدنهٔ هواپیما badaneh-ye' havâ-peymâ
fusion *n.* گداز godâz جوش jush
fuss *n., vi., vt.* قرقر کردن qor qor kardan هیاهو hayâ hu
fussy *adj.* وسواسی vasvâsi
fusty *adj.* کپک زده kapak zadeh
fusty *adj.* بوی رطوبت buy-e' rotubat نمدار nam-dâr
futile *adj.* بی اثر bi-asar بیهوده bi-hudeh بی فایده bi-fâyedeh عبث 'abas
futility *n.* بی اثری bi-asari بیفایدگی bi-fâyedegi
future *n., adj.* آینده âyandeh آتیه âtieh عاقبت âqebat آجل âjel
fuzz *n., vt.* کرک kork پشم pashm پلیس polis
fuzzy *adj.* کرکی korki پشمالو pashmâlu تار târ مکدر mokad~ar

G G g

gadfly *n.* خرمگس khar-magas مردم آزار mardom âzâr
gadget *n.* اسباب asbâb دستگاه dast-gâh
gaff *n., vi., vt.* گاف gâf اشتباه eshtebâh خرابکاری kharâb-kâri
gag *pl., vi., vt., n.* خفه کردن khafeh kardan دهان بندی dahân bandi
gage *n., vt.* گذاشتن گرو gero gozâshtan وثیقه vasiqeh ضمانت zemânat
gain *n., vt., vi.* آوردن بدست bedast âvardan پیشرفت pish-raft سود sud
gait *n., vt.* قدم برداشتن qadam bardâshtan
gala *adj., n.* جشن jashn باشکوه bâ-shokuh
galactic *adj.* شیری shiri کهکشانی kahkeshâni
galaxy *n.* کهکشان kahkeshân
gale *n.* تندباد tond-bâd
galena *n.* آرامش ârâmesh نوش دارو nush-dâru
gall *vt., vi., n.* زهره zahreh رو ru گستاخی gostâkhi
gall-bladder *n.* کیسه صفرا kiseh-ye' safrâ
gallant *adj., n., vt., vi.* دلاور delâvar شجاع shojâ' عشقباز 'eshq-bâz
gallery *n.* تالار tâlâr سرسرا sarsarâ گالری gâlori
galley *n.* کشتی پارویی kashti pâruyi آشپزخانه âshpaz-khâneh
gallon *n.* گالن gâlon
gallop *v.* چهارنعل رفتن chahâr na'l raftan
gallop *n.* تاخت و تاز tâkht-o tâz
gallows *n.* تیراعدام tir-e' e'dâm دارچوب dâr chub
gallstone *n.* سنگ صفرا sang-e' safrâ
galosh *n.* گالش gâlesh کفش لاستیکی kafsh-e' lâstiki
galvanize *vt.* لعاب روی دادن la'âb-e' ruy dâdan
galvenize *n.* به جنب وجوش آوردن be-jonb-o jush âvardan
gambit *n.* حرکت حساب شده harekat-e' hesâb shodeh
gamble *vi., vt., n.* قمار کردن qomâr kardan
gambler *n.* قمارباز qomâr-bâz
gambol *vi., n.* جست و خیز کردن jest-o khiz kardan
game *n.* شکار shekâr آماده âmâdeh
game *n.* بازی bâzi مسابقه mosâbeqeh
gander *n.* غاز نر qâz-e' nar
gang *n., vt., vi.* گروه goruh دسته dasteh
gangrene *n., vt., vi.* سیاه زخم siâh zakhm قانقرایا qânqrâyâ
gangster *n.* تبه کار tabah kâr دزد dozd گانگستر gângester
gangway *n., int.* راهرو râhro
gap *n., vt.* شکاف دادن shekâf dâdan روزنه rozaneh اختلاف ekhtelâf

gape v. بهت زدن boht zadan
gape v. دهن دره کردن dahan-dar~eh kardan
garage n., vt. گاراژ gârâzh تعمیرگاه ta'mir-gâh
garb n., vt. لباس ویژه lebâs-e' vizheh
garbage n. آشغال âshqâl زباله zobâleh
garbage can np. آشغال دانی âshqâl-dâni زباله دانی zobâleh- dâni
garble vt., n. مغلطه کردن maqlateh kardan تحریف tahrif
garden n., adj., vi., vt. باغ bâq روضه rozeh
gardener n. باغبان bâq-bân
gardening n. باغبانی bâqbâni
gargantuan adj. غول پیکر qul-peykâr کلان kalân
gargle vt., vi., n. غرغره کردن qerqereh kardan
gargoyle n. چشمهٔ سنگی cheshmeh-ye' sangi
garish adj. زرق و برق دار zarq-o barq dâr
garland n. تاج گل tâj-e' gol دیوان divân گلبند gol-band
garlic n., adj. سیر sir
garment n., vt. جامه jâmeh لباس lebâs رخت rakht البسه albaseh
garnish vt., n. تزیین کردن taz'in kardan
garret n., vt. زیرشیروانی zir-shirvâni
garrison vt. پادگان pâdegân
garter n., vt. کش جوراب kesh-e' jurâb
gas n., vt., vi. گاز gâz بخار bokhâr بنزین benzin
gas(oline) n. بنزین benzin
gash n., adj., vt. شکاف دادن shekâf dâdan زخم عمیق zakhm-e' 'amiq
gasket n. کاسکت kâsket شکاف گیر shekâf-gir
gaslight n. چراغ گاز cherâq-gâz
gasp n., vi. نفس نفس زدن nafas nafas zadan
gassy adj. گاز دار gâz-dâr
gate n., vt., vi. دروازه darvâzeh درعقب dar-e' 'aqab
gateway n. دروازه darvâzeh
gather vt., vi., n. جمع کردن jam' kardan
استنباط کردن estenbât kardan
gathering n. جمعیت jam'iyat گردآوری gerd-âvari
gaud(y) n. زرق و برق ظاهری zarq-o barq-e' zâheri
gauge vt., n. اندازه گرفتن andâzeh gereftan درجه سنج darejeh-sanj
gaunt adj. لاغر lâqar استخوانی ostokhâni
gauntlet n. دستکش آهنین dastkesh-e' âhanin
gavel n. چکش چوبی chakosh-e' chubi

gawk *n., vi.* زل زل زدن zol-zol zadan
gay *adj., n.* شاد shâd خوشدل khoshdel
gay *adj., n.* هم جنس باز hamjens-bâz
gaze *vi., n.* خیره نگاه کردن khireh negâh kardan
gazebo *n.* آلاچیق âlâchiq
gazelle *n.* غزال qazâl آهو âhu
gazette *n., vt.* روزنامه ruznâmeh
gear *n.* دنده dandeh
gear *n.* لوازم lavâzem پلاس palâs
gearbox *n.* جعبه دنده ja'beh dandeh گیربوکس girboks
gee *int., vi., vt.* عجب ! 'ajab!
geezer *n.* پیرمرد اهل حال pir-mard-e' ahl-e' hâl
gelatin *n.* ژلاتین zhelâtin
geld *n., vt.* اسب اخته شده asb-e' akhteh shodeh
gelding *n., vt.* خواجه اخته akhteh khâjeh
gem *n., vt., adj.* جواهر گوهر javâher gohar
geminization *vt., vi., adj.* دوتایی کردن dotâyi kardan تثنیه tasnieh
gendarmerie *n.* ژاندارمری zhândâr-meri
gender *n., vt., vi.* جنس jens
gene *n.* ژن zhen
genealogy *n.* شجره نامه shajareh nâmeh نسل شناسی nasl shenâsi
general *adj., n.* سرتیپ sartip
general *adj., n.* عمومی 'omumi کل kol~
generalize *vt., vi.* یکسان گرفتن yeksân gereftân
عمومی کردن 'omumi kardan
همگانی کردن hamegâani kardan
تعمیم دادن ta'mim dâdan
generally *adv.* کلاً kol~an
generate *vt.* تولید کردن tolid kardan بوجود آوردن bevojud âvardan
generation *n.* تولید tolid نسل nasl
generative *adj.* تولیدی tolidi زایا zâyâ
generator *n.* زاینده zâyandeh تولید کننده tolid konandeh دینام dinâm
generic *adj.* نسلی nasli گروهی goruhi جنسی jensi
بدون مارک bedun-e' mârk
generosity *n.* بخشندگی bakhshandegi بذل bazl سخاوت sekhâvat
کرم karam
generous *adj.* بخشنده bakhshandeh دست ودل باز dast-o del bâz
جواد javâd کریم karim

genesis *n.* پيدايش peydâyesh تكوين takvin
genetic *adj.* نسلى nasli ارثى ersi
genial *adj.* خوش مشرب khosh-mashrab دوستانه dustâneh
genie *n.* جن jen پرى pari
genital *adj.* عورت 'orat آلت تناسلى âlat-e' tanâsoli
genitive *adj., n.* نسبتى nesbati مالكيت mâlekiyat
genius *n.* نابغه nâbeqeh نبوغ nobuq
genocide *n.* كشتار نژادى koshtâr-e' nezhâdi
genre *n., adj.* نوع no' سبك sabk
genteel *adj.* باوقار bâvaqâr مهربان mehrabân
gentile *adj., n.* غيركليمى qeyr-e' kalimi
gentle *adj., vt.* ملايم molâyem نجيب najib باتربيت bâ-tarbiat
gentleman *n.* آقا âqâ رادمرد râd-mard
gentlewoman *n.* خانم khânom بانو bânu
gently *adv.* بنرمى benarmi بالطافت bâ-letâfat
gentry *n.* نيمه اشرافى nimeh ashrâfi
genuine *adj.* اصلى asli خالص khâles حقيقى haqiqi بيريا biriâ
geocentric *adj.* زمين مركزى zamin markazi
geography *n.* جغرافيا joqrâfiâ
geology *n.* زمين شناسى zamin shenâsi
geometric *adj.* هندسى hendesi
geometry *n.* هندسه hendeseh
geranium *n.* گل شمعدانى gol-e' sham'dâni
germ *n., adj.* جرم jerm
german *adj.* آلمانى âlmâni
german measles *n.* سرخك sorkhak
germany *n.* آلمان âlmân
germinate *vi., vt.* جوانه زدن javâneh zadan
gerrymander *n., vt.* رأى سازى كردن ra'y-sâzi kardan
gerund *n.* اسم مصدر esm-e' masdar
gest(e) *n.* قيافه qiâfeh ژست zhest ماجراجويى mâjerâ juyi
gesture *n., vi., vt.* حركت harekat اشاره eshâreh
gesundheit! *n.* عافيت باشه 'âfiat bâsheh!
get *vt., vi., n.* گرفتن gereftan بدست آوردن bedast âvardan
get (back) *n.* تلا فى درآوردن talâfi dar âvardan
get together *n.* باهم جمع شدن bâ-ham jam' shodan
get up *n.* بلند كردن boland kardan
get up *n.* بالا رفتن bâlâ raftan

get(across) *n.* حالی کردن hâli kardan آنطرف رفتن ântaraf raftan
get(ahead of) *n.* پیش رفتن pish raftan
get(along) *n.* باهم ساختن bâham sâkhtan بسربردن besar bordan
get(around) *n.* همه جا رفتن hameh jâ raftan گشتن gashtan
get(away with) *n.* دررفتن dar raftan
get(away) *n.* در رفتن dar raftan دور شدن dur shodan
get(back) *n.* برگشتن bar-gashtan
get(by) *n.* رد شدن rad-shodan زندگی گذراندن zendegi gozarandan
get(down)/(to) *n.* سرموضوع رفتن sar-e' mozu' raftan
get(in) *n.* تو آمدن tu âmadan وارد شدن vâred shodân
get(it) *n.* نهمیدن fahmidan تنبیه شدن tanbih shodan
get(nowhere) *n.* بنتیجه نرسیدن benatijeh naresidan
get(off) *n.* پیاده شدن piâdeh shodan درآوردن dar âvardan
get(on) *n.* ادامه دادن edâmeh dâdan جلو رفتن jelo raftan
get(on) *n.* سوارشدن savâr shodan
get(out of) *n.* خلاص شدن khalâs shodan
get(over) *n.* خوب شدن khub shodan
get(over) *n.* ازناراحتی درآمدن az nârâhati dar âmadan
get(through) *n.* تمام کردن tamâm kardan
get(to) *n.* دسترسی یافتن رسیدن residan dastresi yâftan
get(together) *n.* فراهم آوردن farâham âvardan
get(up) *n.* پاشدن pâ shodan
get-together *n.* جمع jam' محفل mahfel دوره doreh
get-up *n.* لباس پوشی lebâs pushi
geyser *n.* آب فشان âb-feshân
ghastly *adj., adv.* ترسناک tarsnâk رنگ پریده rang parideh
مخوف mokhof
ghetto *n.* منطقه فقرا mantaqeh-ye' foqarâ زاغه zâqeh
ghost *n., vt., vi.* روح ruh
ghoul *n.* غول qul مرده خوار mordeh-khâr
giant *n., adj.* غول پیکر qul peykar بزرگ بدن bozorg-badan
gibberish *n.* نامفهوم حرف زدن nâ-mafhum harf zadan
gibbet *n., vt.* دار زدن dâr zadan چوبهٔ دار chubeh-ye' dâr
gibe *vi., vt., n.* مسخره کردن maskhareh kardan استهزاء estehzâ'
ونق vefq
giblet *n.* جغوربغور jaqur baqur
giddy *adj., vt., vi.* سرگیجه آور sargijeh-âvar گیج gij
giddy *adj., vt., vi.* گیج کننده gij konandeh ناپایدار nâ-pâydâr

gift *n., vt.* هديه hadiyeh پيشكش pishkesh عيدى 'eydi
gifted *adj.* بااستعداد bâ-este'dâd
gig *n., vi., vt.* نيزه neyzeh برنامهٔ موسيقى barnâmeh-ye' musiqi
gigantic *adj.* غول پيكر qul-peykar عظيم الجثه azim-ol jos~eh
giggle *vi., n.* كركرخنديدن ker-ker khandidan
gigolo *n.* ژيگول zhigul
gild *n., vt.* مطلا كردن motal~â kardan خوش نما khosh namâ
gilding *n., vt.* مطلا كارى motal~â-kâri آب طلا âb-talâ
gill *n., vt.* گوشك gushak شش ماهى shosh-e' mâhi
gimlet *n., vt., adj.* متهٔ كوچك mat~eh-ye' kuchek
gimmick *n.* كلك kalak چشم بندى cheshm bandi
gin *n., vi., vt.* ماشين پنبه پاك كنى mâshin-e' panbeh pâk koni جين jin
ginger *n., vt., adj.* زنجبيل zanjebil
gingerbread *n., adj.* نان زنجبيلى nân-e' zanjebili
gingerly *adv., adj.* با احتياط bâ ehtiât
giraffe *n.* زرافه zarâfeh
gird *vi., vt., n.* كمر بند بستن kamar band bastan
girder *n.* تيرآهن tirâhan
girdle *n., vt.* كمرگير kamar-gir شكم بند shekam band
girl *n.* دختر dokhtar
girth *n.* زين بند zinband قطر كمر qotr-e' kamar
gist *n.* نقطهٔ مركزى noqteh-ye' markazi اصل موضوع asl-e' mozu'
give *v.* دادن dâdan فرو ريختن foru rikhtan
give *v.* بخشيدن bakhshidan
give(and take) *n.* اينور و آنور invar-o ânvar
give(away) *n.* تقديم كردن taqdim kardan لو دادن lo dâdan
give(back) *n.* پس دادن pas dâdan
give(forth) *n.* بيرون دادن birun dâdan
give(in) *n.* تسليم شدن taslim shodan
give(it to) *n.* تنبيه كردن tanbih kardan
خدمت رسيدن khedmat residan
give(off) *n.* بيرون دادن birun dâdan
give(out) *n.* بيرون دادن birun dâdan تمام شدن tamâm shodan
give(up) *n.* تسليم شدن taslim shodan ول كردن vel kardan
give-and-take *n.* رد و بدل rad-o badal
giveaway *n.* هديهٔ مجانى hadiyeh-ye' maj~âni
gizzard *n.* سنگدان sangdân
glacier *n.* توچال tochâl يخ كوه yakh-kuh

glad *n., adj., vt.* خوشحال khoshhâl شاد shâd

gladiator *n.* گلادیاتور gelâdiâtor اسیر شمشیرزن asir-e' shamshir zan

glamor *n.* شکوه shokuh تجمل tajam~ol

glance *vi., vt., n.* زیرچشمی نگاه کردن zir-e' cheshmi negâh kardan

gland *n.* غده qod~eh

glare *n., vi., vt.* نورزننده nur-e' zanandeh

glare *v.* خیره نگاه کردن khireh negâh kardan

glasnost *n.* علنیت 'alaniyat

glass *adj., vt.* شیشه shisheh لیوان livân

glasses *n.* عینک 'eynak

glasses *n.* دوربین durbin

glaze *vt., vi., n.* لعاب دادن la'âb dâdan براق کردن bar~âq kardan

gleam *n.* برق barq انعکاس en'ekâs

gleam *v.* روشنایی دادن roshanâyi dâdan

glee *vi., n.* خوشی khoshi شادی shâdi

glib *adj.* فصیح fasih واضح vâzeh خوش زبان khosh zabân

glich *n.* قلق qeleq

glide *vi., vt., n.* سر خوردن sor khordan سبک پری sabok pari

glim(mer) *n.* چراغ cherâq روشنایی ضعیف roshanâyi-e' za'if

glimpse *n., vt., vi.* نگاه آنی negâh-e' âni

glint *n., vi., vt.* برق barq انعکاس en'ekâs

glisten *vi., n.* برق زدن barq zadan

glitter *vi., n.* زرق و برق zarq-o barq درخشیدن derakhshidan

gloat *vi., n.* پیش خود بالیدن pish-e' khod bâlidan غلو qolov

globe *n., vt., vi.* کره koreh گوی guy

globetrotter *n.* جهانگرد jahân-gard کره koreh گوی guy

globule *n.* گلبول golobul گوی چه guycheh

gloom *n., vi., vt.* افسردگی afsordegi تیرگی tiregi

gloomy *adj.* تیره tireh تاریک târik

glorify *vt.* تجلیل کردن tajlil kardan بزرگ کردن bozorg kardan

glory *n., vi., int.* شکوه shokuh افتخار eftekhâr عزت 'ez~at جلال jalâl

gloss *n., vt., vi.* جلا دادن jalâ dâdan لعاب دادن la'âb dâdan

glossary *n.* فهرست لغات fehrest-e' loqât

glottal *adj., n.* گلویی galuyi حنجره ایی hanjarehyi

glove *n., vt.* دستکش dastkesh

glow *n., vi.* تابیدن tâbidan درخشیدن derakhshidan تابش tâbesh

glowworm *n.* کرم شب تاب kerm-e' shab-tâb

glucose *n.* گلوکز golukoz قند انگور qand-e' angur

glue *v.* سریش serish چسباندن chasbândan
glue *v.* چسب زدن chasb zadan
glum *adj.* کدر keder افسرده afsordeh پژمرده pazhmordeh
glut *vt., vi., n.* اشباع کردن eshbâ' kardan پر کردن por kardan
glutton *n.* شکمو shekâmu پرخور por-khor
gluttony *n.* شکموئی shekamu'i پرخوری porkhori
gnarl *n., vi., vt.* غرغرکردن qor qor kardan
gnash *vt., vi., n.* (دندان) بهم فشردن (dandân) beham feshordan
gnaw *vt., vi.* دندان زدن dandân zadan جویدن javidan
gnosis *n.* عرفان 'erfân
gnostic *adj., n.* عارف 'âref
gnosticism *n.* عرفان 'erfân
go *vi., vt., n., int.* رفتن raftan
go (at) *n.* طرف شدن taraf shodan
go along *n.* قبول کردن qabul kardan
go back on *n.* بی وفا بودن bi-vafâ budan
go down *n.* تنزل tanaz~ol ثبت شدن sabt shodan
go into *n.* دربرداشتن darbar dâshtan
go(about) *n.* اقدام کردن eqdâm kardan گردش کردن gardesh kardan
go(after) *n.* دنبال کردن donbâl kardan
go(against) *n.* بر خلاف عمل کردن bar-khalaf 'amal kardan
go(along) *n.* همراهی کردن hamrâhi kardan
go(around) *n.* دور زدن dor zadan
go(at) *n.* فعالیت کردن fa'âliyat kardan
go(back on) *n.* بدقولی کردن bad qoli kardan
go(beyond) *n.* افراط کردن efrât kardan
متجاوز شدن motejâvez shodan
go(by) *n.* گذشتن gozashtan شناخته شدن shenâkhteh shodan
go(down) *n.* پایین رفتن pâyin raftan
go(halves) *n.* نصف کردن nesf kardan
go(in with) *n.* شریک شدن sharik shodan
go(into) *n.* رسیدگی کردن residegi kardan
go(off) *n.* دور شدن dur shodan دررفتن dar raftan
go(on) *n.* ادامه دادن edâmeh dâdan اتفاق افتادن et~efâq oftâdan
go(out) *n.* بیرون رفتن birun raftan خاموش شدن khâmush shodan
go(over) *n.* مرور کردن morur kardan جستجو کردن josteju kardan
go(through with) *n.* تحمل کردن taham~ol kardan
go(together) *n.* باهم مناسب بودن bâ-ham monâseb budan

go(under) *n.* غرق شدن qarq shodan خوردن شکست shekast khordan
go(up) *n.* بالا رفتن bâlâ raftan ترقی کردن taraq~i kardan
go(with) *n.* بهم خوردن be-ham khordan همراهی hamrâhi
go(without) *n.* بدون چیزی سرکردن bedun-e' chizi sar kardan
go-between *n.* واسطه vâseteh میانجی miânji
go-getter *n.* پشتکاردار poshtekâr-dâr
goad *v.* تحریک کردن tahrik kardan تیرکردن tir kardan
goad *v.* سیخونک زدن sikhunak zadan
goal *n.* مقصد maqsad دروازه darvâzeh
goal *n.* هدف hadaf آرمان ârmân آماج âmâj
goalie *n.* دروازه بان darvâzeh-bân
goalkeeper *n.* دروازه بان darvâzeh-bân
goat *n.* بز boz هوسباز havas-bâz
goatee *n.* ریش بزی rish bozi
gob *n., vt.* گوله guleh انبوه anbuh ملوان malevân
gobble *n.* صدای بوقلمون sedây-e' buqalamun
gobble *v.* باحرص خوردن bâ-hers khordan
gobbler *n.* بوقلمون نر buqalamun-e' nar
goblet *n.* جام jâm
goblin *n.* جن jen
God *n., vt., int.* خدا khodâ ایزد izad الله al~âh
God-fearing *adj.* متدین moted~ayen خداشناس khodâshenâs
godchild *n.* فرزند خوانده farzand-khândeh
goddamned *adj., adv.* ملعون mal'un خدا لعنتی khodâ la'nati
goddess *n.* الهه elâheh
godfather *n., vt.* پدرخوانده pedar khândeh
Godforsaken *adj.* متروک matruk نفرین شده nefrin shodeh
Godgiven *n.* خدادادی khodâ-dâdi
godliness *n.* حالت خدایی hâlat-e' khodâyi دین داری din-dâri
godmother *n., vt.* مادر خوانده mâdar khândeh
godsend *n.* نعمت خدایی ne'mat-e' khodâyi
goggles *n.* عینک محافظی 'eynak-e' mohâfezi
goiter *n.* گواتر goâtr
gold *n., adj.* طلا talâ زر zar
gold digger *np.* زن پول تیغ زن zan-e' pul-tiq zan
golden *adj.* طلایی talâyi زرین zar~in
goldfish *n.* ماهی طلایی mâhi talâyi
goldsmith *n.* طلا ساز talâ sâz زرگر zargar

golf *n., vi.* گلف بازی کردن golf bâzi kardan
golly! *n.* ای وای ey vây!
goner *n.* رفتنی raftani مردنی mordani
gong *n., vt.* ناقوس پهن nâqus-e' pahn
gonorrhea *n.* سوزاک suzâk
goo(ey) *n.* نوچ nuch
good *adj., n., int., adv.* خوب khub نیک nik خیر kheyr
good day *np.* روزبخیر ruz bekheyr
good morning *n.* صبح بخیر sobh bekheyr
good news *h* خبرخوب khabar-e' khub مژده mozhdeh
مژدگانی mozhdegani
good night *np.* شب بخیر shab bekheyr
good-fornothing *n.* بی ارزش bi-arzesh بی فایده bi-fâyedeh
good-hearted *adj.* مهربان mehrabân بخشنده bakhshandeh
good-looking *np.* خوش قیافه khosh qiâfeh
good-natured *adj.* خوش طبع khosh tab'
goodbye *int., n.* خداحافظ khodâ hâfez خدانگهدار khodâ negah-dâr
goodness *n., int.* خوبی khubi برای خاطرخدا barây-e' khâter-e' k
goods *n.* کالا kâlâ اجناس ajnâs اموال amvâl متاع matâ'
goodwill *n.* رضایت rezâyat برکت barekat سرقفلی sar-qofli
goody *adj., n., int.* قاقا qâqâ تحفه tohfeh
آخ جون âkh jun!
goof(y) *n.* چلفتی chelofti دست و پا dast-o pâ cholofti خل khol
gook *n.* ژاپنی zhâponi
goon *n.* لات lât اوباش obâsh چاقوکش châqu-kesh
goose *n., vt.* غاز qâz انگشت کردن angosht kardan
gopher *n., vi.* موش سوراخ کن mush-e' surâkh kan
gorge *n.* تنگ دره tang dar~eh
gorge *v.* حریصانه غذا خوردن harisâneh qazâ khordan
gorgeous *adj.* باشکوه bâ-shokuh مجلل mojal~al قشنگ qashang
gorilla *n.* گوریل guril
gory *adj.* خونین khunin
gospel *n., adj.* انجیل enjil
gossamer *n., adj.* تارعنکبوت târ'ankabut
پارچهٔ نازک pârcheh-ye' nâzok
gossip *n., vi., vt.* شایعه shâye'eh دری وری dari-vari
gouge *n., vt.* درآوردن dar âvardan شکاف دادن shekâf dâdan
gourd *n.* گیاه کدو قلیانی giâh-e' kadu qalyâni

gourmet *n.* متخصص motekhas~es آشپز زبده âshpaz-e' zobdeh
gout *n.* نقرس neqres
govern *vt., vi.* حکومت کردن hokumat kardan
governess *n., vt., vi.* معلم زن سرخانه mo'al~em-e' zan-e' sar-khâneh
government *n.* حکومت hokumat دولت dolat
governor *n.* حاکم hâkem فرماندار farmândâr حکمران hokmrân
والی vâli
governor-general *n.* استاندار ostândâr
governorship *n.* فرمانداری farmândâri
gown *n., vt., vi.* لباس بلند lebâs-e' boland لباس شب lebâs-e' shab
grab *vt., n.* گرفتن gereftan ربودن robudan
grab bag *np.* ندیده خریدن nadideh kharidan
grace *v.* زیبایی دادن zibâyi dâdan
grace *n.* وقار veqâr شکوه shokuh جلال jalâl حشمت heshmat
grace *n.* شکرگزاری shokr gozâri سپاس sepâs حمدوثنا hamd-o sanâ
graceful *adj.* زیبا zibâ باوقار bâ-veqâr باشرافت bâ-sherâfat
gracious *adj., int.* مهربان mehrabân باادب bâ-adab موقر movaq~âr
gradation *n.* درجه بندی darajeh-bandi تبدیل tabdil
grade *v.* درجه دادن darajeh dâdan نمره دادن nomreh dâdan
grade *n.* پایه pâyeh رتبه rotbeh درجه darajeh
gradual *adj., n.* تدریجی tadriji کم کم kam-kam
gradually *adv.* بتدریج be-tadrij متدرجاً motedar~ejan
graduate *n., adj., vi., vt.* فارغ التحصیل شدن fâreq-ol tahsil shodan
graduation *n.* فارغ التحصیلی fâreq-ol tahsili
graduation *n.* درجه بندی darajeh-bandi
graft *n., vt., vi.* پیوند زدن peyvand zadan پول دزدی pul dozdi
grain *n., vt.* دانه dâneh حب hab بافت bâft ذره zar~eh
gram *n.* گرم geram
grammar *n.* دستورزبان dastur-e' zabân
grammatical *adj.* دستوری dasturi باقاعده bâ-qâ'edeh
granary *n.* انبار غله anbâr-e' qal~eh
grand *adj.* عالی 'âli بزرگ bozorg کل kol~ هزار hezâr
grand larceny *np.* دزدی سنگین dozdi-e' sangin
grandchild *n.* نوه naveh
granddaughter *n.* نوهٔ دختر naveh-ye' dokhtar
grandeur *n.* عظمت 'azemat شکوه shokuh کبریاء kebriâ'
grandeur *n.* شرافت sherâfat شأن sha'n
grandfather *n.* پدربزرگ pedar bozorg

grandiose *adj.* باعظمت bâ-'azemat پرافتخار por eftekhâr
grandmother *n.* مادربزرگ mâdar bozorg ننه naneh
grandson *n.* نوهٔ پسر naveh-ye' pesar
grandstand *n., vi., adj.* شاهکارهنری shâhkâr-e' honari جلوگاه jelogâh
granite *n.* گرانیت خارا gerânit سنگ خارا sang-e' khârâ
granite *n.* سنگ خارا sang-e' khârâ
granny *n.* مادربزرگ mâdar bozorg ننه naneh
grant *vt., n.* عطا کردن 'atâ kardan بخشیدن bakhshidan بورس burs
granulate *vt., vi.* دانه دانه کردن dâneh-dâneh kardan
grape(s) *n.* انگور angur
grapefruit *n.* توسرخ tusorkh
grapevine *n.* درخت مو derakht-e' mo شایعه shâye'eh
graph *n., vt.* منحنی monhani نمودار nemudâr
graphic *adj.* شکلی shekli ترسیمی tarsimi روشن roshan
graphite *n.* سرب سیاه sorb-e' siâh گرافیت gerâfit
grapnel *n.* چنگک changak قلاب qol~âb
grapple *v.* دست به یخه شدن dast beh-yakheh shodan
گلاویزشدن galâviz shodan کلنجاررفتن kalanjâr raftan
grasp *vt., vi., n.* محکم گرفتن mohkam gereftan
درک کردن dark kardan
grass *n., vt., vi.* سبزه sabzeh چمن chaman علف 'alaf
grass-roots *adj.* خلقی khalqi عامی 'âm~i
grasscutter *n.* چمن زن chaman zan
grasshopper *n.* ملخ malakh
grate *n., vt., vi.* رنده کردن randeh kardan ساییدن sâyidan نرده nardeh
grateful *adj.* سپاسگزار sepâsgozâr ممنون mamnun
نمک شناس namak-shenâas
grater *n.* رنده randeh
gratification *n.* حظ haz~ کیف keyf پاداش pâdâsh لذت lez~at
gratify *vt.* لذت دادن lez~at dâdan راضی کردن râzi kardan
grating *adj., n., v.* در نرده ایی dar-e' nardehyi
گوش خراش gush kharâsh
gratis *adv., adj.* رایگان râyegân مجانی maj~âni
gratitude *n.* سپاسگزاری sepâsgozâri حق شناسی haq~ shenâsi
gratuity *n.* انعام an'âm
grave *adj., adv., n.* گور gur قبر qabr مزار mazâr لحد lahd
grave *adj., adv., n.* وخیم vakhim سخت sakht
gravedigger *n.* گورکن gur kan قبرکن qabr-kan

gravel *n., vt., adj.* ريگ rig ماسه mâseh ريزه سنگ sang rizeh
graveyard *n.* گورستان gurestân قبرستان qabrestân
gravitation *n.* كشش keshesh جاذبه jâzebeh گرايش gerâyesh
gravity *n.* وخامت vekhâmat خطر khatar
gravity *n.* جاذبه jâzebeh سنگينى sangini
gravy *n.* شيرهٔ گوشت shireh-ye' gusht
gray *adj., n., vt., vi.* خاكسترى khâkestari
graze *vi., vt., n.* چريدن charidan خراشيدن kharâshidan
grease *n., vt.* روغن roqan چربى charbi گريس geris
grease monkey *np.* مكانيك mekânik
greaser *n.* روغن زن roqan zan مكزيكى mekziki
greasy *adj.* روغنى roqani چرب charb
great *adj., adv., n.* بزرگ bozorg عظيم 'azim كبير kabir
great *adj., adv., n.* سلام كردن salâm kardan
Great Britain *np.* بريتانياى كبير beritânyâ-ye' kabir
great-grandchild *n.* نبيره nabireh
greatness *n.* بزرگى bozorgi عظمت 'azemat كبرياء kebriâ'
سيادت siâdat
greaves *n.* زرهٔ ساق پا zereh-ye' sâqe-pâ
Greece *n.* يونان yunân
greed *n., vt., vi.* حرص hers آز âz طمع tama' ولع vala'
greedy *adj.* حريص haris طمعكار tama'kâr
green *n., vi., vt.* نارس nâras كال kâl تازه كار tâzeh kâr
green *v.* سبزكردن sabz kardan
green light *np.* چراغ سبز cherâq-e' sabz
دستورحركت dastur-e' harekat
greenback *n.* اسكناس eskenâs
greenhorn *n.* ناشى nâshi تازه كار tâzeh kâr بى تجربه bi-tajrobeh
greenhouse *n.* گرم خانه garm khâneh
greet *n., vi., vt.* خوشامد گفتن khoshâmad goftan
تهنيت گفتن tahniat goftan
greeting(s) *n.* سلام salâm درود dorud تبريك tabrik تهنيت tahniat
gregarious *adj.* گله اىى gal~eh-i اجتماعى ejtemâ'i
gremlin *n.* شيطان كوچولو sheytân kuchulu
grenade *n.* نارنجك nârenjak
grenadine *n.* شربت انار sharbat-e' anâr
greyhound *n.* سگ تازى sag-e' tâzi
grid *n.* در مشبك dar-e' moshab~ak

griddle *n., vt.* سراجاقی sar ojâqi
gridiron *n.* تورسیمی tur-e' simi
grief *n.* غم qam اندوه anduh غصه qos~eh ماتم mâtam
grievance *n.* گله geleh دلخوری delkhori شکایت shekâyat
شکوه shekveh
grieve *vi., vt.* غمگین کردن qamgin kardan
غصه خوردن qos~eh khordan
grieved *adj.* ماتمزده mâtam-zadeh عزادار 'azâ-dâr سوگدار sog-dâr
griffin *n.* شیربالدار shir-e' bâldâr
grifter *n.* حقه باز hoq~eh bâz
grill *n., vt., vi.* اجاق نرده ایی ojâq-e' nardehyi
فشارسؤالی feshâr-e' so'âli
grim *adj.* عبوس 'abus ترشرو torsh-ru اخمو akhmu نامطلوب nâ-matlub
grimace *n., vi.* اخم و تخم کردن akhm-o takhm kardan
grime *n., vt.* دوده dudeh چرک cherk خاک کثیف khâk-e' kasif
grin *n., vt., vi.* نیش وا کردن nish vâ kardan پوزخند puzkhand
grind *vt., vi., n.* آسیاب کردن âsiâb kardan خرد کردن khord kardan
grinder *n.* خردکن khordkon تیزکن tizkon
grinder *n.* دندان آسیاب dandân-e' âsiâb
gringo *n.* آمریکایی âmrikâyi
grip *n.* چنگ chang گیره gireh
grip *v.* محکم گرفتن mohkam gereftan
gripe *vt., n.* دردپیچ dardpich شکایت کردن shekâyat kardan
grisly *adj.* مهیب mohib نجیح fajih
grit *n., vt., vi.* سنگ ریزه sang rizeh سایش sâyesh جرأت jor'at
grizzly *adj., n.* هولناک hol-nak وحشتناک vah-shatnâk
groan *n., vi., vt.* نالیدن nâlidan ناله nâleh قر qor
groaning *adj.* نالان nâlân
grocer *n.* بقال baq~âl
groceries *pl.* مواد غذایی mavâd-e' qazâyi
grocery-store *n.* بقالی baq~âli
groggy *adj.* مست gij گیج mast خواب آلود khâbâlud
groin *n., vt.* زیرشکم zir-e shekam بیضه beyzeh
groom *n., vt.* مهتر mehtar د اماد dâmâd
groom *v.* شانه کردن shâneh kardan
groove *n., vt., vi.* شیار دادن shiâr dâdan
grope *v.* دستمالی کردن dastmâli kardan
grope *v.* کورمالی کردن kurmâli kardan

gross

gross *pl., adj., n., vt.* گنده gondeh غیرخالص qeyr-e' khâles فاحش fâhesh

grotesque *adj., n.* بدشکل bad shekl قناس qenâs نجیه fajih

grouch(y) *n.* ترقرو qorqoru

ground *adj., vt., vi.* چرخ کرده charkh kardeh سبب sabab

ground *n.* زمین zamin

ground *adj., vt., vi.* زمینه zamineh

ground *v.* بگل نشستن be-gel neshastan

ground cover *np.* زمین پوش zamin-push

ground floor *np.* طبقۀ اول tabaqeh-ye' av~a

ground hog *np.* موش کور mush-e' kur

grounds *n.* زمینه zamineh میدان meydân پایه pâyeh دلیل dalil

group *n., vt., vi.* گروه goruh دسته بندی dasteh bandi جرگه jargeh زمره zomreh

grouse *adj., n., v.* شکایت کردن shekâyat kardan ترقرو qorqoru

grout *n., vt.* دوغاب duqâb سمنت نرم sement-e' narm

grove *n.* درختستان derakhtestân

grovel *vi.* بخاک افتادن bekhâk oftâdan خودخواری khodkhâri

grow *v.* روییدن ruyidan

grow *v.* بزرگ کردن bozorg kardan بزرگ شدن bozorg shodan

grow *v.* پروراندن parvarândan

grower *n.* روینده ruyandeh

growl *vi., vt., n.* غرش کردن qor~esh kardan

grown-up *adj.* بالغ bâleq سالمند sâlmand

growth *n.* رشد roshd ترقی taraq~i نمو nomov~

grub *n., vt., vi.* درآوردن dar-âvardan ریشه risheh dar-âvardan غذا qazâ کرم kerm

grubby *adj., n.* کثیف kasif کرم زده kermzadeh

grubstake *n., vt.* سرمایۀ نسیه sarmâyeh-ye' nesieh

grudge *vt., vi.* لج بودن laj budan غبطه خوردن qabteh khordan

gruesome *adj.* وحشتناک vahshatnâk

gruff *adj.* خشن khashen ناهنجار nâhanjâr

grumble *vi., vt., n.* قرقر کردن qor-qor kardan

grumpy *adj.* غرغرو qor-qoru گوشت تلخ gusht-talkh

grunt *vt., n.* خرخر کردن khor-khor kardan

guarantee *n., vt.* ضمانت کردن zemânat kardan تعهد ta'~ahod

guarantor *adj.* ضامن zâmen پایندان pâyandân ضمانت کننده zemânat konandeh کفیل kafil

guard *vt., vi., n.* نگهبان negahbân کشیک keshik پاسدار pâsdâr

مستحفظ mostah-fez ....

guarded *adj.* محافظت شده mohâfezat shodeh بااحتياط bâ-ehtiât

guardian *n., adj.* سرپرست sarparast قیم qay~em ولی vali

guerrilla *n., adj.* پارتیزان pârtizân چریک cherik

guess *vt., vi., n.* حدس زدن hads zadan گمان کردن gamân kardan

guest *n., vt., vi.* مهمان mehmân

guestroom *n.* مهمان خانه mehmân-khâneh

guidance *n.* هدایت hedâyat رهنمود rahnemud راهنمایی râhnamâyi ارشاد ershâd

guide *v.* هدایت کردن hedâyat kardan راهنمایی کردن râh-namâ-yi kardan

guide *n.* راهنما râhnamâ هادی hâdi

guild *n.* صنف senf

guilt *n.* گناه gonâh تقصیر taqsir جرم jorm

guilty *adj.* گناهکار gonâhkâr مقصر moqas~er مجرم mojrem

guinea pig *np.* خوک هندی khuk-e' hendi تحت آزمایش taht-e' âzmâyesh

guise *n., vt., vi.* لباس lebâs نمای ظاهری namây-e' zâheri لفافه lafâfeh

gulf *n., vt.* خلیج khalij ورطه varteh

gull *vt., n.* زودفریب zudfarib مرغ دریایی morq-e' daryâyi

gullible *adj.* زودباور zudbâvar ساده لوح sâdeh-loh هالو hâlu

gulp *vi., vt., n.* غلپ زدن qolop zadan غورت دادن qurt dâdan جرعه jor'eh

gum *int., n., vt., vi.* آدامس âdâms لثه laseh صمغ samq چسب chasb

gumbo *n., adj.* بتۀ بامیه bot~eh-ye' bâmieh

gumshoe *n., vi.* گالش gâlesh کارآگاه kârâgâh

gun *n., vi., vt.* تفنگ tofang توپ tup گاز دادن gâz dâdan

gunboat *n.* کشتی توپدار kashti-e' tup dâr

gunfire *n.* آتشبار âtash-bâr

gung ho *np.* تمایل سفت و سخت tamâyol-e' seft-o sâkht

gunman *n.* تفنگدار tofangdâr هفت تیر کش haft-tir kesh

gunner *n.* توپچی tupchi تیرانداز tirandâz

gunny *n.* گونی guni جوال jovâl

gunpowder *n.* باروت bârut

gunrunner *n.* قاچاقچی اسلحه qâchâqchi-e' aslaheh

gunshot *n., adj.* صدای تیر sedâ-ye' tir برد bord توپ رس برد tupres

gunsmith *n.* تفنگ ساز tofang-sâz

gurgle *v.* غرغره کردن qer-qereh kardan

gurgle *v.* قل قل کردن qol-qol kardan
gush *vi., vt., n.* جهیدن jahidan بیرون ریختن birun rikhtan
gust(y) *n.* تندباد tond-bâd طغیان toq-yân
gusto *n.* لذت lez~at وجد vajd ذوق zoq
gut *n., vt.* روده rudeh زه zeh دل و جرات del-o jor'at
guts *sl.* دل وجرأت del-o jor'at جربزه jorbozeh شهامت shahâmat
gutter *n., vi., vt.* جوی juy جوب jub آبرو âb-ro
guttural *adj., n.* گلویی galuyi
guy *n., vt.* مرد mard یارو yâru شخص shakhs میزانی mizâni
guzzle *vi., vt.* مثل گاو خوردن mesl-e' gâv khordan
gymnasium *n.* ورزشگاه varzesh-gâh زورخانه zur-khâneh
gymnastic(s) *n.* ژیمناستیک zhimnâstik ورزشی varzeshi
gynecologist *n.* پزشک زنانه pezeshk-e' zanâneh
gypsy *n.* کولی koli
gyrate *vi., adj.* گردیدن gardidan چرخیدن charkhidan
gyroscope *n.* دوران سنج dorân-sanj

H H н

H-Hour *n.* ساعت معین sâ'at-e' mo'ay~an ساعت موعود sâ'at-e' mo'ud
haberdasher *n.* خراز kharâz
haberdashery *n.* خرازی kharâzi
habit *n., vi., vt.* عادت 'âdat خو khu
habitable *adj.* قابل زندگی qâbel-e' zendegi
habitat *n.* جای مسکونی jây-e' maskuni
محیط پرورش mohit-e' parvaresh
habitual *adj.* دائمی dâ'emi عادتی 'âdati
habitually *adv.* برحسب عادت bar-hasb-e' 'âdat
habituate *v.* عادت دادن 'âdat dâdan
habituate *v.* رفت و آمد کردن raft-o âmad kardan
hack *v.* قلمه کردن qalameh kardan خرد کردن khord kardan
hack *vi., n., vt.* اجیر ajir
hack *v.* سخت سرفه کردن sakht sorfeh kardan
hack saw *n.* ارهٔ آهن بر ar~eh-ye' âhan-bor
hacking *n.* خشن khashen خشک khoshk
hackle *n., vt.* پرگذاشتن par gozâshtan
haft *n., vt.* دسته dasteh قبضه qabzeh
hag *n.* عجوزه 'ajuzeh
haggard *adj., n.* فرسوده farsudeh پریشان parishân
haggle *vi., vt., n.* چانه زدن châneh zadan خرد کردن khord kardan
hail *v.* تگرگ آمدن tagarg âmadan
hail *v.* درود گفتن dorud goftan
hair *n.* مو mu
hair trigger *np.* ضامن حساس zâmen-e' has~âs
hair-raising *adj.* مو سیخ کننده mu sikh konandeh
hairbreadth *n., adj.* بنازکی مو benâzoki-e' mu
hairbrush *n.* برس boros
haircut *n.* سلمانی salmâni برش مو boresh-e' mu
hairdo *n.* سبک آرایش مو sabk-e' ârâyesh-e' mu
hairdresser *n.* سلمانی salmâni
hairless *adj.* بی مو bimu کچل kachal طاس tâs
hairline *n.* خط مو khat~-e' mu
hairsplitting *n., adj.* مو شکافی mu shekâfi
hairy *adj.* مودار mu-dâr پرمو por-mu پشمالو pashmâlu
halberd *n.* تبرزین tabar-zin
half *n., adj., adv.* نصف nesf نیم nim

half brother *np.* برادر ناتنی barâdar-e′ nâtani
half sister *np.* خواهر ناتنی khâhar-e′ nâtani
half-and-half *adj., adv., n.* نصف به نصف nesf beh nesf
half-hour *n., adj.* نیم ساعت nim sâ′at
half-mast *n., vt.* نیمه افراشته nimeh afrâshteh
half-moon *n.* نیم هلال nim helâl
half-staff *n.* نیمه افراشته nimeh afrâshteh
half-truth *n.* نادرست nâ-dorost
half-wit(ted) *n.* خل khol
halfback *n.* هافبک hâfbak
halfbreed *n.* دورگه do-rageh
halfway *n.* نصف راه nesf-e′ râh وسط vasat کمرکش kamar-kesh
halfway house *np.* دیوانه خانه divâneh-khâneh
halfway house *n.* دیوانه خانه divâneh-khâneh
دارالمجانین dârol majânin
halidom *n.* مقدس moqad~as
halitosis *n.* نفس گندی nafas gandi
hall *n.* راهرو râhro ایوان eyvân تالار tâlâr سالن sâlon
hall tree *np.* جارختی jâ-rakhti
hallelujah *int., n.* شکر خدا shokr-e′ khodâ
hallmark *n., vt.* نشان neshân انگ ang
halloo *n.* آهای âhây
hallow *int., n., vi., vt.* مقدس کردن moqad~as kardan
hallucinate *vi., vt.* هذیان گفتن hazyân goftan
hallucination *n.* هذیان hazyân هپروت hapârut
hallway *n.* راهرو râhro ایوان eyvân
halo *n., vt., vi.* هاله hâleh
halt *vi., adj., n., vt.* دست نگه داشتن dast negah dâshtan
ایست دادن ist dâdan
halter *n., vt.* جلوبند jelo-band ریسمان rismân
halve *vt.* نصف کردن nesf kardan
ham *n., vi.* خودنما khod-namâ متظاهر motezâher
ham *n., vi.* ژامبون zhâmbon
ham *n., vi.* پشت ران posht-e′ rân
hamlet *n., pl.* دهکده dehkadeh
hammer *n.* چکش chakosh
hammer(away) *v.* سرسختانه کارکردن sar-sakhtâneh kâr kardan
hammer(out) *n.* بازحمت درست کردن bâ-zahmat dorost kardan

hammock *n.* ننو nanu
hamper *n.* سبد sabad
hamper *v.* مانع شدن mâne' shodan
hamster *n.* خوکچه khukcheh
hamstring *n., vt.* پی زیر زانو pi-e' zir-e' zânu
hand *n.* دسته dasteh عقربه 'aqrabeh
hand *n.* دست dast ید yad
hand down *n.* اعلان کردن e'lân kardan
hand grenade *np.* نارنجک nârenjak
hand to hand *n.* تن بتن tan betan
hand(and foot) *n.* ساعیانه sâ'iâneh خدمت khedmat
hand(down) *n.* به ارث گذاشتن beh-ers gozâshtan
hand(in hand) *n.* دست بدست dast bedast
hand(in) *n.* تحویل دادن tahvil dâdan
hand(it to) *n.* ایوال گفتن eyvâl goftan
hand(on) *n.* فرستادن ferestâdan
hand(out) *n.* توزیع کردن tozi' kardan
hand(over fist) *n.* گر و گر gor-o gor مشت مشت mosht mosht
hand(over) *n.* تحویل دادن tahvil dâdan وا گذاردن vâ gozârdan
hand-knit *vt., adj.* دستباف dastbâf
hand-me-down *n.* دست دوم dast-e' dov~om
hand-out *n.* صدقه sadaqeh
hand-picked *n.* دست چین dastchin
hand-to-hand *adj.* تن بتن tan betan
hand-to-mouth *adj.* بخور و نمیر bokhor-o namir
handbag *n.* کیف دستی kif-e' dasti
handbook *n.* راهنما râhnamâ کتاب دستی ketâb dasti
handcart *n.* گاری دستی gâri dasti ارابه دستی arâbeh dasti
handclasp *n.* دست فشردن dast feshordan
handcuff *n., vt.* دستبند dast-band
handfast *n., adj., vt.* باقسم دست دادن bâ-qasam dast dâdan
handful *n.* چندتن chândtan یک مشت پر yek mosht-e' por
handgrip *n.* گیرش giresh دسته dasteh
handicap *n., vt.* آوانس دادن âvâns dâdan
handicapped *adj.* ناتوان nâ-tavân فلج falaj معلول ma'lul
handicraft *n.* کاردستی kâr-e' dasti
handiwork *n.* کاردستی kâr-dasti
handkerchief *n.* دستمال dastmâl

handle *v.* دستمالی کردن dastmâli kardan
handle *n.* دسته dasteh دستگیره dastgireh قبضه qabzeh
handle *v.* ترتیب دادن tartib dâdan
handle *v.* ازپس برآمدن az pas bar âmadan
handle bar *n.* دسته dasteh دستگیره dastgireh فرمان farmân
handler *n.* گرداننده gardânandeh ترتیب دهنده tartib dahandeh
handmade *adj.* دست ساخت dast-sâkht دستی dasti
handrail *n.* نرده nardeh
hands(down) *n.* براحتی be-râhati دست بسته dast basteh
hands(off)! *n.* دست نزن dast nazan!
hands(up)! *n.* دستها بالا dast-hâ bâlâ!
handshake *n.* دست دادن dast dâdan
handsome *adj.* خوش قیافه khosh qiâfeh
سخاوتمندانه sekhâvat-mandâneh
handwork *n.* کاردستی kârdasti
handwriting *n.* دست خط dast-khat~
handy *adj.* دردسترس dar dastres مفید mofid بدردخور bedard-khor
handyman *n.* همه کاره hameh kâreh
hang *vt., vi., n.* آویزان کردن âvizân kardan
بدارکشیدن be-dâr keshidan
hang up *n.* عقده 'oqdeh
hang up *v.* گوشی گذاشتن gushi gozâshtan
hang(around) *n.* پرسه زدن parseh zadan
hang(back) *n.* مردد بودن morad~ad budan
hang(it (up)) *n.* کنار گذاشتن kenâr gozâshtân
hang(on) *n.* ادامه دادن edâmeh dâdan چسبیدن seft chasbidan
hang(out) *n.* معاشرت کردن mo'âsherat kardan
hang(up) *n.* آویزان کردن âvizân kardan
hang-out *n.* پاتوق pâtoq
hangar *n.* آشیانه âshiâneh
hanger *n.* چوب رختی chubrakhti
hanging *n., adj.* آویزان âvizân اعدام e'dâm
hangman *n.* دارزن dâr-zan
hangnail *n.* ناخن ریش nâkhon-rish
hangover *n.* مست گیجه mast gijeh
hanker *vi.* هوس داشتن havas dâshtan
hanky-panky *n.* کاسه زیرنیم کاسه kâseh zir-e' nim kâseh
haphazard *adj., adv., n.* شانسکی shânsaki الله بختی al~âh-bakhti

hapless *adj.* بدبخت bad-bakht
happen *vi.* اتفاق افتادن etef~âq oftâdan رخ دادن rokh dâdan
happening *n.* اتفاق etef~âq
happily *adv.* خوشبختانه khosh-bakhtâneh
happiness *n.* خوشبختی khosh-bakhti سعادت sa'âdat
happy *adj.* خوشبخت khosh-bakht خوشحال khosh-hâl سعید sa'id
happy-go-lucky *adj., adv.* بی غم biqam خوش alaki-khosh
harangue *n., vt., vi.* بافریاد نطق کردن bâ-faryâd notq kârdan
harass *vt.* اذیت کردن azy~at kardan آزار دادن âzâr dâdan
harassment *n.* اذیت و آزار azy~ât-o âzâr
harbinger *n., vt.* نویددهنده navid dahandeh جار زن jâr zan
مبشر mobash~er منادی monâdi
harbor *v.* پناه دادن panâh dâdan
harbor *n.* بندرگاه bandar gâh
hard *adj., adv., n.* سخت گیر sakhtgir دشوار doshvâr سفت seft
hard cash *np.* نقد فوری naqd-e' fori
hard labor *np.* اعمال شاقه a'mâl-e' shâqeh
hard palate *np.* سق دهان saq~-e' dahân
hard to please *n.* مشکل پسند moshkel pasand
hard(and fast) *n.* سفت و سخت seft-o sakht
hard(of hearing) *n.* گوش سنگین gush sangin کر kar
hard(up) *n.* محتاج mohtâj بدون چاره bedun-e' châreh
hard-bitten *adj.* سمج semej پخته کار pokhteh kâr
hard-boiled *adj.* سفت پز seft-paz خشک khoshk
hard-bound/cover *n.* جلد مقوایی jeld-e' moqavâyi
hard-headed *n.* سرسخت sar-sakht
harden *vt., vi.* سفت کردن seft kardan انقباض enqebâz
hardly *adv.* بزحمت bezahmat زورکی zuraki
hardship *n.* سختی sakhti مشقت masheq~ât
hardtop *n.* باسقف bâ-saqf
hardware *n.* سخت افزار sakht-afzâr لوازم فلزی lavâzem-e' felez~i
hardwood *adj.* سنگ چوب sang chub چوب فرش chub farsh
hardy *adj., n.* باشهامت bâ-shahâmat پرطاقت por-tâqat
hare *n., vi.* خرگوش khargush
harem *n.* حرم سرا haram sarâ
haricot *n.* آبگوشت âbgusht
hark *vi., vt., n.* گوش بدهید gush bedahid
harlot *n., adj.* جنده jendeh روسپی ruspi فاحشه fâhesheh

harm *n., vt.* آزار رساندن âzâr resândan آسیب زدن âsib zadan
harm *n.* آزار âzâr آسیب âsib گزند gazand
harmful *adj.* مضر moz~er زیان آور ziân-âvar
harmless *adj.* بی ضرر bizar~ar مظلوم mazlum بی آزار biâzâr
harmonic *adj., n.* هماهنگ hamâhang
harmonica *n.* سازدهنی sâz dahani
harmonious *adj.* مناسب monâseb موافق movâfeq موزون mozun
harmonize *vt., vi.* هماهنگ کردن hamâhang kardan
harmony *n.* هماهنگی hamâhangi
harness *n., vt.* یراق کردن yarâq kardan افسار زدن afsâr zadan
harp *n., vi., vt.* چنگ chang
harpoon *n., vt.* نیزهٔ نهنگ کشی neyzeh-ye' nahang keshi
harrow *n., vt.* مازو کشیدن mâzu keshidan رنج دادن ranj dâdan
harrowing *n.* دردناک dard-nâk زجرآور zajr-âvar
harry *vt., vi.* غارت qârat تاراج کردن târâj kardan
harsh *adj.* خشن khashen تند tond زبر zebr
hart *n.* نر آهوی âhu-ye' nar
harvest *v.* دروکردن dero kardan خرمن برداشتن kharman bardâshtan
harvest *n.* درو dero خرمن kharman
hash *n., vt.* قیمه کردن qeymeh kardan
hasp *n., vt.* چفت cheft
hassle *n., v.* سربسر گذاشتن sar besar gozâshtan
haste *n., vi., vt.* شتاب کردن shetâb kardan عجله 'ajaleh
hastily *adv.* عجولانه 'ajulâneh
hasty *adj.* شتاب زده shetâb zadeh عجول 'ajul
hat *n., vt.* کلاه kolâh
hatch *v.* ازتخم درآوردن az tokhm dar-âvardan
hatch *n.* دریچه daricheh
hatchet *n.* تبرچه tabarcheh
hatchetman *n.* عامل اجرا nocheh نوچه 'âmel-e' ejrâ
hatching *n.* جوجه کشی jujeh keshi
hate *vt., vi., n.* تنفر داشتن tanaf~or dâshtan
hateful *adj.* متنفر motenaf~er
hatpin *n.* سنجاق کلاه sanjâq-e' kolâh
hatrack *n.* جاکلاهی jâ-kolâhi
hatred *n.* تنفر tanaf~or انزجار enzejâr
haughty *adj.* متکبر motekab~er مغرور maqrur
haul *vt., vi., n.* کشیدن keshidan

haunch *n.* باسن bâsan کپل kapal
haunt *vt., vi., n.* عذاب روحی دادن 'azâb-e' ruhi dâdan
haunted *adj.* جنی jeni خانۀ ارواح khâney-ye' arvâh
haunting *adj., n.* فراموش نشدنی farâmush nashodani
hauteur *n.* تکبر takab~ or غرور qorur
have *vt., vi., v., n.* داشتن dâshtan
have-not *n.* ندار nadâr فقیر faqir
haven *n., vt.* پناهگاه panâhgâh بندر bandar
havoc *n., vt., vi.* بلا balâ بی خانگی bi-khânegi
hawk *v.* دوره فروختن doreh forukhtan دست فروشی dast forushi
hawk *n.* قرقی qerqi قوش qush
hay *n., vt., vi.* کاه kâh
hay fever *np.* آلرژی به علف âlerzhi beh 'alaf
haystack *n.* دسته کاه dasteh kâh
haywire *n., adj.* قراطی qar-e' qâti
hazard *n., vt.* خطر khatar مخاطره mokhâtereh
haze *n., vt.* غبار qobâr مه mah خیط کردن khit kardan
hazel *n., adj.* درخت فندق derakht-e' fandoq میشی mishi
hazelnut *n.* فندق fandoq
hazy *adj.* مه آلود mah âlud مبهم mobhâm
he *nom., pro., n., adj.* وی u او vey
head *n., adj., vt., vi.* سر sar کله kal~eh راس ra's رئیس ra'is
head off *n.* جلوگیری کردن jelo-giri kardan
head over heels *n.* بکلی bekol~i عجولانه 'ajulâneh
head-hunter *n.* شکارچی سر shekâr-chi-e' sar
headache *n.* سردرد sar-dard
headed *adj.* سرشکل sar-shekl عازم 'âzem
header *n.* باسر bâ-sar شیرجه shirjeh
headfirst *adv.* باسر bâsar
heading *n.* سرنویس sar-nevis عنوان 'onvân
headlight *n.* چراغ جلو cherâq-e' jelo
headline *n., vt.* سرصفحه sar-safhe تیتر درشت titr-e' dorosht
headlong *adv., adj.* باسر bâsar باکله bâkal~eh
headman *n.* کدخدا kad-khodâ رئیس ra'is
headquarters *n.* ادارۀ مرکزی edâreh-ye' markazi
heads up! *n.* سرهابالا sar-hâ bâlâ! بپا be-pâ
headstand *n.* بالانس زدن bâlâns zadan
headstone *n.* سنگ قبر sang-e' qabr گورنویس gur-nevis

headstrong adj. سرسخت sar-sakht خودرأى khod-ra'y
headway n. پيشرفت pishraft
heal vt., vi. شفا دادن shafâ dâdan بهبود يافتن behbud yâftan
    التيام دادن eltiam dâdan
health n. سلامتى salâmati تندرستى tandorosti مزاج mezaj
healthy adj. سالم sâlem تندرست tandorost سلامت salâmat
heap vt., vi. توده tudeh انبوه anbuh كپه kop~eh
hear vt., vi. شنيدن shenidan گوش كردن gush kardan
hearing n., v. شنوايى shenavâyi دادرسى dâdresi
hearse n. نعش كش na'sh-kesh
heart n., vt. قلب qalb دل del
heart-failure n. سكتهٔ قلبى sekteh-ye' qalbi
heart-rending n. دل آزار delâzâr
heart-to-heart adj. محرمانه mahramâneh
heartache n. درد قلب dard-e' qalb غصه qos~eh
heartbeat n. تپش قلب tapesh-e' qalb
heartbreaking adj. دل شكن del-shekan دردناك dard-nâk
heartburn n. آشوب دلى âshub-deli
hearten vt. تشويق كردن tashviq kardan
hearth n. سكوى جلوى اجاق saku-ye' jelo-ye' ojâq
heartland n. مركز markaz
heartless adj. بى عاطفه bi-'âtefeh
hearty adj., n. گرم garm شديد shadid مفصل mofas~al
heat n., vt., vi. گرم كردن garm kardan حرارت harârat گرما garmâ
heat wave np. گرماى غير معمولى garmâ-ye' qeyr-e' ma'muli
heat-rash n. عرقسوز 'araq-suz
heater n. گرمكن garmkon بخارى bokhâri
heathen pl. كافر kâfar بت پرست bot parast
heather n. بته زار bot~eh-zâr خلنگ khalang
heatstroke n. گرما زدگى garmâ zadegi
heave vt., vi., n. بلند كردن boland kardan باد كردن bâd kardan
heaven n. بهشت behesht پرديس pardis آسمان âsemân جنت jan~at
heavenly adj. بهشتى beheshti آسمانى âsemâni الهى elâhi
    ملكوتى malakuti
heavens n. آسمانها âsemân-hâ سماوات samâvât
heavy adj., n., adv. سنگين sangin زياد ziâd غليظ qaliz
heavy-duty adj. بادوام bâ-davâm قرص qors كت و كلفت kat-o koloft
heavy-footed adj. شل و ول shol-o vel

heavy-handed *adj.* قلدر qoldor خام دست khâm dast
heavyweight *adj., n.* سنگین وزن sangin vazn
hebetate *vt., vi., adj.* کند - خرفت کردن kond/khereft kardan
Hebrew *n., adj.* عبرانی 'ebrâni عبری 'ebri
heck *n.* به درک ! be darak!
heckle *vt., n.* هو کردن ho kardan
hectic *adj., n.* تب‌دار tab-dâr پر درد سر por-dard-e' sar
hedge *n., vt., vi.* شمشاد shemshâd پرچین کردن parchin kardan
hedonism *n.* لذت طلبی lez~at talabi
heed *vt., vi., n.* اعتنا کردن e'tenâ kardan
محل گذاشتن mahal~ gozâshtan
heedless *adj.* بی اعتنا bi-e'tenâ بی محل bi-mahal~
heehaw *n., vi.* عرعر کردن 'ar-'ar kardan
heel *vt., n., vi.* پاشنه pâshneh آدم پست âdam-e' past
heft *n., vt.* وزن vazn سنگینی sangini
hefty *adj.* پروزن porvazn سنگین sangin تنومند tanumand
hegemony *n.* استیلا estilâ چیرگی chiregi تسلط tasal~t سلطه solteh
Hegira *n.* هجره hejreh
height *n.* بلندی bolandi ارتفاع ertefâ' اوج oj
heighten *vt., vi.* بالا بردن bâlâ bordan
heighten *vt., vi.* بلندترکردن boland-tar kardan
زیادترکردن ziâd-tar kardan
heinous *adj.* شنیع shani' شریر sharir
heir *n., vt.* وارث varaseh وارث vâres
heir apparent *np.* وارث مشخص vâres-e' moshakh~as
heiress *n.* ورثه varaseh وارث vâres
heirloom *n.* موروثی moresi ارث خانوادگی ers-e' khânevâdegi
ترکه tarekeh
helicopter *n., vi., vt.* هلیکوپتر helikupter
helium *n.* هلیوم heliom
helix *n.* پیچ پیچ pich-pich منحنی monhani
hell *n., int.* جهنم jahan~am دوزخ duzakh درک darak سقر saqar
hello *int., n., vi., vt.* سلام salâm
helm(s) *n.* سکان sok~ân
helmet *n.* کلاه خود kolâh khud
helmsman *n.* سکان دار sok~ân-dâr
help *v.* کمک کردن komak kardan مساعدت کردن mosâ'edat kardan
help *vt., vi., n., int.* کمک komak یاری yâri

help out *n.* یاری کردن yâri kardan
helpful *adj.* سودمند sudmand مفید mofid
helpless *adj.* عاجز âjez درست نشدنی dorost nashodani
hem *int., n., vi., vt.* لبه تو گذاشتن labeh tu gozâshtan
hemisphere *n.* نیمکره nim-koreh
hemlock *n.* بیخ تفت bikh taft شکران shokarân
hemorrhage *n., vi.* رگ پارهگی rag pârehgi
hemorrhoid *n.* بواسیر bavâsir
hemp *n.* بتۀ شاهدانه bot~eh-ye' shâhdâneh
hen *n.* مرغ morq ماکیان mâkiân
hence *adv., int.* ازاینرو az inru از این پس az in pas
henceforth *adv.* ازاین بعد az in be-ba'd
henceforward *n.* ازاین پس az in pas
henchman *n.* نوچه nocheh پیرو peyro
heptagon *n.* هفت ضلعی haft zel'i
her *pro.* مال او mâl-e' u او را u-râ
herald *n., vt.* نوید دادن navid dâdan مژده دادن mozhdeh dâdan
herb *n.* گیاهمعطر giâh-e' mo'at~ar
herd *n., vi., vt.* گله کردن gal~eh kardan گروه goruh
herdsman *n.* گله دار gal~eh-dâr
here *adv., n., int.* اینجا injâ
hereabout(s) *n.* درهمین نواحی dar hamin navâhi
hereafter *adv., n.* ازاین بعد az in be-ba'd
hereby *adv.* بدین وسیله bedin vasileh
hereditary *adj.* مورثی ارثی ersi moresi
heredity *n.* مشخصات ارثی moshakh~asât-e' ersi
herein *adv.* در اینجا dar injâ
hereinafter *adv.* ازاینجا بعد az injâ be ba'd
hereof *adv.* از این az in مربوط به این marbut-e' beh-in
heresy *n.* رفض rafz
heretic *n., adj.* رافضی râfezi
herewith *adv.* بدینوسیله bedin-vasileh
heritage *n.* میراث mirâs
hermetic *adj.* محکم بسته mohkam basteh هوا بست havâ bast
کیپ kip~
hermit *n.* گوشه گیر gusheh-gir زاهد zâhed
hermitage *n.* تنهاگاه tanhâ-gâh خانگاه khâne-gâh
hernia *n.* باد فتق bâd-e' fatq

hero n. پهلوان pahlevân قهرمان qahremân گرد gord یل yal
heroic adj., n. قهرمانانه qahremânâneh دلیرانه dalirâneh
heroine n. زن قهرمان zan-e' qahremân شیرزن shir-zan
herpes n. مازوس mâzus هرپیز herpiz
hers pro. مال او mâl-e' u
herself pro. خودش khodash
hesitant adj. دودل do-del مردد morad~ad متردد moterad~ed
hesitatation n. تردید tardid تامل ta'am~ol درنگ derang
hesitate vi. تردیدکردن tardid kardan مکث کردن maks kardan
heterosexual adj., n. ازجنس مخالف az jens-e' mokhâlef
hew vt., vi. بریدن boridan تیشه زدن tisheh zadân
hewn v. بریده borideh تراشیده tarâshideh
hex adj., vt., n. طلسم کردن telesm kardan
بد یمن کردن bad yomn kardan
hexagon n. شش ضلعی shesh zel'i
hey int., n. آهای âhây
heyday int., n. دوران خوشی dorân-e' khoshi
hi int. سلام salâm
hiatus pl. وقفه vaqfeh تعطیلات tâ'tilât
hibernate vi. درزمستان خوابیدن dar zemestân khâbidan
hiccup n., vi. سکسکه کردن sek-sekeh kardan هق هق heq-heq
hick n., adj. ساده لوح sâdeh loh هالو hâlu
hickey n. جای گاز jây-e' gâz کبودی kabudi
hickory n. چوب گردو chub-e' gerdu
hidden adj., v. پنهان penhân نهفته nahofteh مخفی makhfi نهانی nahâni
hide v. پنهان کردن penhân kardan پنهان شدن penhân shodan
hide n. چرم charm پوست pust
hide-and-seek n. سکسک sok-sok قایم باشک qâyem-bâshak
hide-out n. پناهگاه panâh-gâh
hideous adj. وحشتناک vahshat-nâk ترسناک tars-nâk
hierarchy n. سلسله مراتب selseleh-ye' marâteb سران sarân
high adj., adv., n. بلند boland مرتفع mortafa'
high adj., adv., n. نشئه nash'eh منگ mang
high school np. دبیرستان dabirestân
high seas n. آبهای آزاد âbhâ-ye' âzâd
high tide np. مد mad
high-brow n. متکبر motekab~er
high-class adj. مجلل mojal~al یک درجه darejeh yek اشرافی ashrâfi

high-frequency *adj.* فرکانس بالا ferekâns-e' bâlâ
high-handed *n.* دلبخواه del bekhâh مستبد mostabed
high-spirited *adj.* دلیر dalir باشرف bâ-sharaf
highball *n., vi., vt.* تند رفتن tond raftan
highbred *adj.* نژاد اصیل nezhâd-e' asil باتربیت bâ-tarbiat
higher education *np.* تحصیلات عالیه tahsilât-e' 'âlieh
higher-up *n.* مقام بالاتر maqâm-e' bâlâtar
highland *n., adj.* بلندی bolandi ارتفاعات ertefâ'ât
highlight *vt., n.* بهترین قسمت behtarin qesmat
highlight *vt., n.* پررنگ کردن por-rang kardan
highly *adv.* بسیار زیاد besyâr ziâd
highness *n.* بلندی bolandi
hight *adj., n., vt.* باسم be-esm-e'
highway *n.* شاهراه shâhrâh اتوبان otoban بزرگراه bozorg-rah
hijack *vt., vi.* ربودن robudan دزدیدن dozdidan
hike *v.* بالا بردن bâlâ bordan
hike *v.* تپه پیمایی tap~eh peymâi کوه نوردی kuh-navardi
hilarious *adj.* خیلی خنده دار kheyli khandeh-dâr
hilarity *n.* خنده داری khandeh-dâri
hill *n., vt.* تپه tap~eh تل tal
hillbilly *n., adj.* دهاتی dehâti پشت کوهی posht kuhi
hilt *n., vt.* دسته dasteh قبضه qabzeh
himself *pro.* خودش khodash
hind *adj., n.* عقب 'aqab پسین pasin
hinder *adj., vt., vi.* جلوگیری کردن jelogiri kardan
بازداشتن bâz dâshtan
hindrance *n.* سرراه sar-e' râh مانع mâne'
hindsight *n.* پیش اندیش pish andish
hinge *n., vi., vt.* لولا lolâ محور mehvar
hint *vt., vi.* اشاره کردن eshâreh kardan
hinterland *n.* سرزمین دور افتاده sarzamin-e' dur oftâdeh
hip *n., adj., vt.* اهل دل ahl-e' del
hip *n., adj., vt.* باسن bâsan کپل kapal
Hippocrates *n.* بقراط boqrât
hippopotamus *n.* اسب آبی asb-e' âbi
hire *vt., n.* استخدام کردن estekhdâm kardan
hiss *vi., vt., n.* فیس فیس fis-fis نش نش fesh-fesh
هیس کردن his kardan

hist! *n.* ساکت sâket هیس his
historian *n.* تاریخدان târikhdân مورخ movar~ekh
history *n.* تاریخ târikh
hit *vt., vi., n.* ضربت zarbat اصابت esâbat
hit *v.* خوردن khordan
hit *v.* زدن zadan
hit(it off) *n.* باهم جور بودن bâ-ham jur budan
hit(of) *n.* خوب تشریح کردن khub tashrih kardan
hit(or miss) *n.* شانسکی shânsaki بختی الله al~âh-bakhti
hit-and-run *adj.* زدن و فرارکردن zadan va farâr kardan
hitch *vt., vi., n.* گره gereh اشکال eshkâl
hitch *vt., vi., n.* جفت cheft گاری بند gâri band
hitchhike *vi.* سواری مجانی گرفتن savâri-e' majâni gereftan
hither *adv., adj.* این طرفی in tarâfi
hitherto *adv.* تاکنون tâ-konun
hive *n., vt., vi.* کندو kandu
hives *n.* کهیر kahir
hoard *n., vt., vi.* احتکار کردن ehtekâr kardan
hoarder *adj.* محتکر mohtaker
hoarse *adj.* صدا گرفته sedâ gerefteh
hoax *n., vt.* کلک kalak کلا شی kal~âshi
hob(nob) *n.* هم پیالگی ham piâlegi
hobble *vi., vt., n.* لنگیدن langidan
hobby *n.* مشغولیت mashquliyat کار سرگرمی kâr-e' sar-garmi
hobo *n.* ولگرد velgard
hock *n., vt.* گرو گذاشتن gero gozâshtan
hocus pocus *n.* حقه بازی hoq~eh bâzi کلک kalak
hoe *n., vt., vi.* کج بیل kaj-bil بیلچه bilcheh
hog *n., vt., vi.* خوک khuk
hoist *vt., n.* بلند کردن boland kardan
hold *vt., vi., n.* نگه داشتن negah dâshtan جا گرفتن jâ gereftan
hold back *n.* پنهان کردن penhân kardan
hold off *n.* دست نگه داشتن dast negah dâshtan
hold on *n.* صبر کردن sabr kardan
hold over *n.* بتعویق افتادن beta'viq oftâdân
hold(back) *n.* جلوی خود گرفتن jelo-ye' khod gereftan
hold(down) *n.* پایین نگه داشتن pâyin negah dâshtan
hold(forth) *n.* سخنرانی کردن sokhan-râni kardan

hold(in) *n.* خودداری کردن khod-dâri kardan
hold(off) *n.* دور نگه داشتن dur negah dâshtan
hold(on) *n.* سفت نگه داشتن seft negah dâshtan
hold(one's own) *n.* ایستادگی کردن istâdegi kardan
hold(out) *n.* ایستادگی کردن istâdegi kardan ندادن nadâdan
hold(over) *n.* موکول کردن mokul kardan
hold(up) *n.* سرقت کردن serqat kardan کردن معطل mo'at~al kardan
holder *n.* دارنده dârandeh نگهدار negah-dâr
hole *n., vt., vi.* سوراخ surâkh حفره hofreh منفذ manfaz
holiday *n., adj., vi.* تعطیلی ta'tili
holiness *n.* تقدس taqad~os
hollow *adj., n., vt., vi.* توخالی tukhâli پوک puk پوچ puch
holocaust *n.* آتش سوزان âtash suzân قتل عام qatl-e' 'âm
holster *n.* غلاف qalâf
holy *adj., n.* مقدس moqad~as
homage *n.* بزرگداشت bozorg-dâsht تجلیل tajlil
home *n., adj., adv., vi.* خانه khâneh منزل manzel میهن mihan
کاشانه kâshâneh
home-bred *n.* خانگی khânegi
home-coming *n.* بازگشت bâz-gasht
homeland *n.* میهن mihan مرز و بوم marz-o bum وطن vatan
homely *adj.* خانگی khânegi بیریخت birikht
homemade *adj.* خانگی khânegi
homemaker *n.* خانه ساز khâneh-sâz کدبانو kad-bânu
homesick *adj.* دلتنگ deltang
homestead *n., vt., vi.* خانۀ زراعتی khâneh-ye' zerâ'ati
homework *n.* مشق mashq
homicide *n.* جنایت jenâyat آدمکشی âdamkoshi
homogeneous *adj.* همجنس ham-jens یکجور yek-jur
متجانس motejânes
homogenize *vt.* یکجور کردن yek-jur kardan
homosexual *adj., n.* همجنس باز ham-jens bâz
hone *vi., n., vt.* تیز کردن tiz kardan چاقوتیزکن châqu tiz-kon
honest *adj.* راستگو râst-qu صدیق sadiq درستکار dorost-kâr
honesty *n.* درستی dorosti صداقت sedâqat
honey *n., adj., vt., vi.* جگر jegar عزیزم 'azizam
honey *n., adj., vt., vi.* انگبین angabin عسل 'asal
honeybee *n.* زنبورعسل zanbur-e' 'asal

honeycomb *n., adj., vt.* شانهٔ عسل shâneh-ye' 'asâ'l
موم پنجره mum panjereh
honeydew *n.* شهد shahd شیره shireh
honeydew *n.* گرمک garmak
honeymoon *n., vi.* ماه عسل mâh-e' 'asal
honeysuckle *n.* گل امین الدوله gol-e' amino-doleh
honk *n., vi., vt.* بوق زدن buq zadan
honky-tonk *np., n., adj.* کافهٔ پایین شهری kâfeh-ye' pâyin shahri
honor *v.* احترام گذاشتن ehterâm gozâshtan
honor *n., vt., adj.* شرف sharaf آبرو âberu پاکدامنی pâk-dâmani
شرافت sharâfat
honor *v.* افتخار دادن eftekhâr dâdan
honorary *adj.* افتخاری eftekhâri
honored *adj.* گرامی gerâmi مفتخر moftakhar مشرف moshar~af
hood *n., vt.* کلاهک kolâhak
hood *n., vt.* کاپوت kâput
hood(lum) *n.* دزد dozd گانگستر gângster
hoof *n., vt., vi.* سم som
hook *n., vi.* قلاب qol~âb چنگک changak بتورزدن be-tur zadan
hook and eye *np.* قزن قفلی qazan qofli
hook up *n.* وصل کردن vasl kardan
hooka(h) *n.* قلیان qalyân
hooked *adj.* قلاب مانند qol~âb mânand گیر افتاده gir oftâdeh
hooker *n.* جنده jendeh فاحشه fâhesheh
hooligan *n., adj.* لات lât جاهل jâhel هوچی ho-chi
hoop *n., vt.* حلقه زدن halqeh zadan بشگه بند boshgeh-band
hooping cough *n.* سیاه سرفه siâh sorfeh
hoopla *n.* سروصدا sar-o sedâ قیل وقال qil-o qâl غوغا qoqâ
الم شنگه alam-shangeh
hoot *int., vi., vt., n.* هو کردن ho kardan صدای جغد sedâ-ye' joqd
hop *n., vt., vi.* لی لی کردن ley-ley kardan جستن jestan
hope *n., vt., vi.* امید داشتن omid dâshtan
hopeful *adj., n.* امیدوار omidvâr
hopeless *adj.* ناامید nâ-omid نومید nomid چاره ناپذیر châreh nâ-pazir
hopscotch *n.* لی لی بازی ley-ley bâzi
horde *n., vi.* گروه goruh گله gal~eh
horizon *n.* افق ofoq
horizontal *adj.* افقی ofoqi

hormone *n.* هورمون hormon
horn *n., vt., adj.* شاخ shâkh
horn *n., vt., adj.* بوق buq شیپور sheypur
horn *n., vt., adj.* دماغه damâqeh
hornet *n.* زنبور درشت zanbur-e' dorosht
horny *adj.* شاخی shâkhi حشری hashari
horoscope *n.* جدول طالع بینی jadval-e' tâle' bini
horrendous *adj.* وحشتناک vahshat-nâk
horrent *adj.* موسیخی mu sikhi
horrible *adj.* ترسناک tarsnâk خیلی بد kheyli bad
horrid *adj.* نفرت انگیز nefrat angiz
horrify *vt.* وحشت انداختن vahshat andâkhtan
horror *n., int.* وحشت vahshat ترس tars
horse *n., vt., vi., adj.* اسب asb خرک kharak
horse around *n.* شوخی خرکی کردن shukhi-e' kharaki
horse radish *n.* ترب torob
horseback riding *n.* اسب سواری asb savâri
horseman *n.* اسب سوار asb savâr
horseplay *n.* شوخی خرکی shukhi-e' kharaki
horsepower *n.* نیروی اسب niru-ye' asb
horseshoe *n., vt., adj.* نعل اسب na'l-e' asb
horticulture *n.* بستان کاری bostân-kâri
hose *pl., n., vt.* شیلنگ آب shilang-e' âb
hose *pl., n., vt.* جوراب jurâb
hosiery *n.* جوراب و کشباف jurâb va keshbâf
hospitable *adj.* مهمان نواز mehmân-navâz غریب نواز q/rib-navâz
hospital *n.* بیمارستان bimârestân مریضخانه mariz-khâneh
hospitality *n.* مهمان نوازی mehmân-navâzi
host *n., vt.* میزبان mizbân اجرا کننده ejrâ konandeh
hostage *n., vt.* گروگان gerogân
hostel *n., vi., vt.* مهمانخانه mehmân-khâneh
مسافرخانه mosâfer-khâneh
hostess *n., vt.* میزبان زن mizbân-e' zan
hostile *adj.* متخاصم motekhâsem دشمن doshman
hostile *adj.* خصومت آمیز khosumat âmiz دشمنانه doshmanâneh
hostility *n.* خصومت khosumat مخاصمه mokhasemeh
hot *adj., adv., vt., vi.* تند tond
hot *adj., adv., vt., vi.* داغ dâq خیلی گرم kheyli garm

hot *adj., adv., vt., vi.* مال دزدی mâl-e' dozdi

hot dog *np.* سوسیس sosis

hot-blooded *adj.* خونگرم khun-garm متعصب mote'as~eb

hot-head(ed) *n.* کله شق kal~eh shaq عجول 'ajul

hotel *n.* هتل hotel مسافرخانه mosâfer-khâneh

hothouse *n., adj.* گرم خانه garm-khâneh

hound *n.* سگ شکاری sag-e' shekâri سگ تازی sag-e' tâzi

hound *v.* تعقیب کردن ta'qib kardan

hour *n., adj.* ساعت sâ'at وقت vaqt

hourglass *n., adj.* ساعت شنی sâ'at-e' sheni

hourly *adj., adv.* ساعت به ساعت sâ'at beh sâ'at

house *n., vt., vi., adj.* خاندان khândân

house *n.* خانه khâneh منزل manzel

house *v.* خانه دادن khâneh dâdan مکان دادن makân dâdan

household *n., adj.* خانواده khânevâdeh خانگی khânegi عائله 'â'eleh

housekeeper *n.* خانه دار khâneh-dâr کلفت kolfat

housewarming *n.* ولیمه valimeh چشم روشنی cheshm roshani

housewife *n.* خانه دار khâneh-dâr کدبانو kad-bânu

housing *n., v.* تهیهٔ جا tahiyeh-ye' jâ قاب qâb

hovel *n., vt.* انباری anbâri

hover *vi., n.* درفراز بودن dar farâz budan پلکیدن palekidan

how *adj., con., n.* چطور chetor چگونه chequneh

however *adv., con.* اگرچه agar-cheh هرچند har-chand ولیکن valikan

howitzer *n.* توپ لوله کوتاه tup-e' luleh kutâh

howl *vi., vt., n.* زوزه کشیدن zuzeh keshidan

hubble-bubble *n.* قلیان qalyân

hubbub *n.* شلوغی sholuqi ولوله velveleh

hubby *n.* شوهر shuhar

huckster *n., vt., vi.* دستفروش dast-forush دوره گرد doreh-gard

huckster *n., vt., vi.* چانه زدن châneh zadan

hue *n.* سایه رنگ sâyeh rang

huff(and puff) *n.* هن و هن کردن hen-o hen kardan
اوقات تلخی oqât talkhi

hug *vt., vi., n.* بغل کردن baqal kardan

huge *adj.* بسیار بزرگ besyâr bozorg عظیم الجثه 'azimol-jos~eh

hulk *n., vi.* لندهور landehur تنومند tanumând

hull *n., vt., vi.* پوست کندن pust kandan
بدنهٔ کشتی badaneh-ye' kashti

hum *v.* زمزمه کردن zamzameh kardan
hum *v.* وزوز کردن vez-vez kardan
human *adj., n.* آدم âdam بشر bashar انسان ensân
human being *n.* بشر bashar انسان ensân
humane *adj.* انسانی ensâni بشری bashari
humanitarian *adj., n.* انسان دوست ensân dust
humanity *n.* انسانیت ensâniyat آدمیت âdamiyat
humble *adj.* فروتن forutan متواضع motevâze'
humble *v.* پست کردن past kardan
humbly *adv.* عاجزانه' âjezâneh مخلصانه mokhlesâneh
humbug *n., vt., vi., int.* چرت و پرت chert-o pert مزخرف mozakhraf
humdinger *n.* ممتاز momtâz
humdrum *adj., n.* یکنواخت yek-nâvâkht کسل کننده kesel konandeh
humid *adj.* مرطوب martub نمدار namdâr
humidity *n.* رطوبت rotubat نمی nami
humiliate *v.* پست کردن past kardan خوارکردن khâr kardan
humiliate *v.* جریحه دار کردن jariheh-dâr kardan
humiliation *n.* پستی pasti خواری khâri سرشکستگی sar-shekâstegi
مذلت mazel~at
humor *n., vt.* خلق kholq طبع tab'
humorous *adj.* شوخ shukh بامزه bâ-maz~eh نکاهی fokâhi
hump *n., vt., vi.* قوز کردن quz kardan کوهان kuhân
humus *n.* خاک کود khâk-e' kud
hunch *vt., vi., n.* قوز کردن quz kardan
بدل برات شدن bedel barât shodan
hunchback *n.* قوز quz گوژپشت guzh-posht
hundred *n., adj.* صد sad
hung *v.* آویزان âvizân
hunger *n., vi., vt.* گرسنگی خوردن gorosnegi khordan
hungry *adj.* گرسنه gorosneh ناشتا nashta
hunk *n.* تکه بزرگ tek~eh-ye' bozorg مرد خوشگل mard-e' khoshgel
hunt *vt., vi., n.* شکار shekâr صید seyd
hunt *v.* جستجو کردن josteju kardan
hunter *n.* شکارچی shekâr-chi صیاد say~âd
hurdle *n., vt., vi.* مانع mâne' جهش jahesh
hurl *vt., vi., n.* پرتاب کردن partâb kardan
hurrah *int., vi., n.* زنده باد zendeh-bâd هورا hurâ
hurricane *n.* طوفان گردباد tufân-e' gerdbâd

hurry *vi., vt., n.* عجله کردن 'ajaleh kardan شتاب کردن shetâb kardan
hurt *v.* آزار رساندن âzâr resândan آسیب زدن âsib zadan
hurt *vt., vi., n., adj.* مجروح majruh مصدوم masdum
hurtle *vi., vt., n.* پرتاب کردن partâb kardan
husband *n., vt.* شوهر shuhar
husbandry *n.* خانه داری khâneh-dâri کشاورزی keshâvarzi
hush *n., vt., vi., adj.* سکوت sokut خاموشی khâmushi
hush *v.* ساکت کردن sâket kardan
hush money *np.* حق السکوت haqol-sokut
husk *n., vt., vi.* پوست کندن pust kandan
husky *adj., n.* پوستدار pust-dâr
husky *adj., n.* گردن کلفت gardan koloft تنومند tanumand
hustle *vi., vt., n.* بزور هول دادن bezur hol dâdan تقلا taqal~â
hustler *n.* فعال fa'~âl ناحشه fâhesheh
hut *n., vt., vi.* کلبه kolbeh آلونک âlunak
hutch *n., vt.* گنجهٔ بشقاب ganjeh-ye' boshqâb
hyacinth *n.* سنبل sonbol
hybird *n.* دورگه do-rageh پیوندی peyvandi
hyena *n.* کفتار kaftâr
hymen *n.* پردهٔ بکارت pardeh-ye' bekârat
hymn *n., vt., vi.* سرود خواندن sorud khândan
hyperbola *n.* قطع زائد qat-e' zâ'ed
hyperbole *n.* مبالغه mobâleqeh
hyphen *n., vt.* خط پیوند khat~-e' peyvand
hypnotize *vt., vi.* خواب کردن khâb kardan
hypocrisy *n.* دورویی doruyi ریا کاری riâ kâri
hypocrite *n.* دورو doru دغل باز daqal-bâz ریاکار riâ-kâr
hypogastric *adj.* زیرشکمی zir shekami
hypothenuse *n.* وتر vatar زه zeh
hypothesis *n.* فرضیه farzieh
hyssop *n.* زوفا zofâ
hysteria *n.* تشنج روحی tashan~oj-e' ruhi

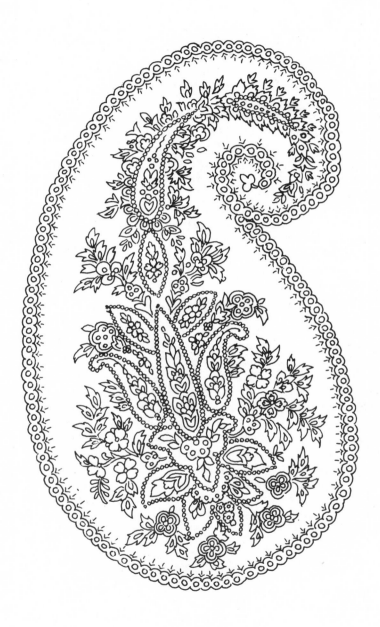

I *nom., pro., n.* من man

ibex *n.* بزکوهی boz-e' kuhi

ibid(em) *n.* درهمان جا dar hamân jâ

ice *n., vt., vi., adj.* یخ yakh

ice cream *np.* بستنی bastani

iceberg *n.* کوه یخ kuh-e' yakh

icebox *n.* جایخی jâyakhi یخچال yakhchâl

icebreaker *n.* یخ شکن yakhshekan

iceman *n.* یخ فروش yakh-forush

icicle *n.* یخ قندیل yakh qandil

icon *n.* بت bot شمایل shamâyel

iconoclast *n.* بت شکن botshekan

icy *adj.* یخی yakhi سرد sard

id est(i.e.) *n.* یعنی ya'ni

idea *n.* عقیده 'aqideh اندیشه andisheh نظر nazar ایده ideh

ideal *n., adj.* کمال مطلوب kamâl-e' matlub نورعلی نور nur-e' 'alâ nur

idealist *n., adj.* معنوی ma'navi تصوری tasav~ori

idealize *vt., vi.* تصور کردن tasav~or kardan

identical *adj.* یک شکل yek Shekl مثل هم mesl-e' ham

identification *n.* تعیین هویت ta'yin-e' hoviyat شناسایی shenâsâyi

identify *vt., vi.* شناسایی کردن shenâsâyi kardan

identity *n.* هویت hoviyat شخصیت shakhsiyat

ideologist *n.* آرمان گرا ârmân-garâ تیوریسین teorisian

ideology *n.* عقیده شناسی 'aqideh shenâsi طرزفکر tarz-e' fekr

idiocy *n.* حماقت hemâqat ابلهی ablahi

idiom *n.* اصطلاح estelâh زبان خودی zabân-e' khodi

idiomatic *adj.* مصطلح mostalah

idiot *n.* نادان nâ-dân احمق ahmaq ابله ablah

idle *adj., vi., vt., n.* درجا زدن dar-jâ zadan بیهوده bi-hudeh
    بیکار bi-kâr

idle away *n.* بیکار گشتن bi-kâr gashtan

idle hours *n.* ساعتهای بیکاری sâ'at-hâ-ye' bikâri

idle rumors *n.* شایعات پوچ shâye'ât-e' puch

idle talk *n.* چرت و پرت chert-o pert مزخرفات mozakhrafât
    یاوه yâveh

idle wheel *np.* میان چرخ miân charkh

idleness *n.* بیکاری bikâri تنبلی tanbali

idler *adj., n.* بیکار bikâr تنبل tanbal الاف alâf
idol *n.* بت bot صنم sanam معبود ma'bud
idolater *n.* بت پرست bot parast
idolatry *n.* بت پرستی bot parasti
if *con., n.* اگر agar هرگاه hargâh
igloo *n.* کلبهٔ برفی kolbeh-ye' barfi
igneous *adj.* آتش نشانی âtashin آتش فشانی âtash feshâni
ignitable *adj.* محترق mohtareq آتشگیر âtash-gir
ignite *vt., vi.* آتش زدن âtash zadan آتش گرفتن âtash gereftan
ignition *n.* سوئیچ su'ich
ignition *n.* آتشگیری âtashgiri افروزش afruzesh
ignoble *adj.* بیشرف bisharaf پست past
ignominious *adj.* بی آبرو bi-âberu بدنام badnâm
ignominy *n.* بی آبرویی bi-âberuyi بدنامی badnâmi
ignoramus *n.* نادان nâdân
ignorant *adj.* نادان nâdân جاهل jâhel
ignore *v.* ندیده گرفتن nadideh gereftan
ignore *v.* محل نگذاشتن mahal~ nagozâshtan
ilk *n., adj., pro.* مانند mânand نوع no'
ill *adj., n., adv.* بیمار bimâr مریض mariz ناخوش nâkhosh
ill fame *np.* بدنامی bad-nâmi
ill will *np.* منظور بد manzur-e' bad
ill-advised *adj.* غیر عاقلانه qeyr-e' 'âqelâneh
ill-being *n.* ناسلامتی nâ-salâmati
ill-bred *adj.* بی تربیت bi-tarbiyat
ill-considered *adj.* بدون ملاحظه bedun-e' molâhezeh
ill-defined *n.* مبهم mobham نامعلوم nâ-ma'lum
ill-desposed *n.* بدنیت bad niyat نا مساعد nâ-mosâ'ed
ill-fated *adj.* بدبخت bad-bakht
ill-favored *adj.* نا مطلوب nâ-matlub زننده zanandeh
ill-founded *adj.* بی اساس bi-asâs پوچ puch
ill-gotten *adj.* نامشروع nâ-mashru
ill-humor(ed) *n.* بی مزه bi-maz~eh
ill-mannered *adj.* بی ادب bi-adab بی تربیت bi-tarbiyat
ill-natured *adj.* بدخو bad-khu کج نهاد kaj-nahâd
ill-reputed *adj.* بدنام bad-nâm
ill-spent *adj.* ولخرجی vel-kharji تلف شده talaf shodeh
ill-suited *adj.* نامناسب nâ-monâseb

ill-tempered *n.* بداخلاق bad-akhlâq
ill-timed *adj.* نابهنگام nâ-behengâm
illegal *adj.* غیرقانونی qeyr-e' qânuni نامشروع nâ-mashru'
illegible *adj.* ناخوانا nâ-khânâ لایقرء lâ-yoqra'
illegitimate *adj., vt., n.* غیرقانونی qeyr-e' qânuni
حرام زاده harâm-zâdeh
illicit *v.* گرفتن gereftan
illicit *adj.* نامشروع nâ-mashru' ممنوع mamnu'
illiteracy *n.* بیسوادی bi-savâdi
illiterate *adj., n.* بیسواد bi-savâd
illness *n.* بیماری bi-mâri ناخوشی nâ-khoshi کسالت kesâlat سقم soqm
illogical *adj.* غیرمنطقی qeyr-e' manteqi
illuminate *vt., vi., adj., n.* روشن کردن roshan kardan
illumination *n.* روشنایی roshanâyi
illusion *n.* خطای بصری khat~â-ye' basari چشم بندی cheshm-bandi
illusionist *n.* شعبده باز sho'badeh-bâz
illustrate *v.* باتصویرشرح دادن bâ tasvir sharh dâdan
illustrate *v.* روشن کردن roshan kardan
illustrated *n.* باتصویر ba-tasvir مصور mosav~ar
illustration *n.* تصویر tasvir روشنایی roshanâyi مثال mesâl
illustrious *adj.* برجسته barjesteh
illwisher *n.* بدخواه bad khâh
image *n., vt.* تصویر tasvir مثال mesâl عکس 'aks وجهه vej-heh
imagery *n.* تصویری tasviri شکلی shekli
imaginary *adj., n.* خیالی khiâli تصوری tasav~ori
imagination *n.* خیال khiâl تصور tasav~or
قوهٔ تخیلی qov~eh-ye' takhay~oli وهم vahm
imaginative *adj.* خیالی khiâli تصوری tasav~ori
imagine *vt., vi.* تصور کردن tasav~or kardan خیال کردن khiâl kardan
imagined *adj.* خیالی khiâli تصورشده tasav~or-shodeh موهوم mohum
imbecile *n., adj.* احمق ahmaq کودن kodan سفیه safih
imbibe *vt., vi.* آب خوردن âb khordan فرو بردن foru bordan
imbroglio *n.* سوء تفاهم su'-e' tafâhom
مسئلهٔ غامض mas'aleh-ye' qâmez
imbrue *vt.* خیس کردن khis kardan
imbue *vt.* اشباع کردن eshbâ' kardan رنگین کردن rangin kardan
imitate *vt.* تقلید کردن taqlid kardan
imitation *n., adj.* تقلیدی taqlidi بدل badal تقلبی taqal~obi

imitation *n.* حد ~had محدودیت mahdudiyat
imitator *n.* تقلید کننده taqlid konandeh مقلد moqal~ed
immaculate *adj.* بی عیب bi-'eyb بدون اشتباه bedun-e' eshtebâh پاک pâk
immanent *adj.* باقی jâv-dâni جاودانی bâqi
immaterial *adj.* غیرمادی qeyr-e' mâd~i بی اهمیت bi-ahamiyat
immature *adj.* نابالغ nâ-bâleq رشد نکرده roshd nakardeh
immeasurable *adj.* بی اندازه bi-andâzeh بیکران bi-karân
immediate *adj.* فوری fori مستقیم mostaqim
immediate family *n.* خانوادهٔ نزدیک khânevâdeh-ye' nazdik
immediately *adv., con.* فوراً foran بیدرنگ bi-derang دفعتاً daf'atan
immemorial *adj.* یاد نیاوردنی yâd nayâvardani باستانی bâstâni
immense *adj.* بسیار بزرگ besyâr bozorg وسیع vasi'
immerse *vt.* فروبردن foru bordan فروکردن foru kardan
immersion *n.* غوطه وری qoteh-vari فروبری foru-bari
immigrant *n., adj.* مهاجر mohâjer
immigrate *vi., vt.* مهاجرت کردن mohâjerat kardan
imminent *adj.* نزدیک به اتفاق nazdik beh-et~efâq مشرف moshref قریب الوقوع qaribol voqu' عنقریب 'anqrib
immobile *adj.* بی حرکت bi-harekat ثابت sâbet
immobilize *v.* بی حرکت کردن bi-harekat kardan
immobilize *v.* فلج کردن falaj kardan
immoderate *adj.* افراطی efrâti نامتعادل nâ-mote'âdel
immodest *adj.* بی حیا bi-hayâ جسور jasur
immolate *vt.* قربانی کردن qorbâni kardan
immoral(ity) *n.* غیر اخلاقی qeyr-e' akhlâqi
immortal *adj., n.* جاودانی jâv-dâni ناپذیر fanâ-napazir لا یموت lâ-yamut امرداد amordâd
immortalize *vt.* جاودانی کردن jâv-dâni kardan
immovable *adj., n.* غیرمنقول qeyr-e' manqul
immune *adj., n.* مصون masun
immunity *n.* مصونیت masuniyat
immunize *vt.* مصون ساختن masun sâkhtan
immure *vt.* دیوار کشیدن divâr keshidan محصور کردن mahsur kardan
immutable *adj.* تغییر ناپذیر taqyir nâpazir
imp(ish) *n.* شیطان sheytân تخم جن tokhm-e' jen~
impact *n., vt., vi.* برخورد barkhord تصادم tasâdom اثر asar
impair *adj., vt., vi., n.* آسیب زدن âsib zadan بدتر کردن badtar kardan

impale

impale *vt.* به ميخ كشيدن beh-mikh keshidan
impalpable *adj.* لمس نشدنى lams nashodani
imparity *n.* نابرابرى nâbarâbari
impart *vt., vi.* سهم دادن sahm dâdan آشكار كردن âshkâr kardan
impartial *adj.* بيطرف bi-taraf
impassable *adj.* گذرناپذير gozar nâ-pazir
impassible *adj.* بى‌عاطفه bi-'âtefeh بى‌حس bi-hes~
impassioned *adj.* پراحساس por-ehsâs
impassive *adj.* بى احساس bi-ehsâs خونسرد khunsard
impatience *n.* بيصبرى bi-sabri بى طاقتى bi-tâqati
impatient *adj.* بيصبر bi-sabr بيطاقت bi-tâqat ناشكيبا nâ-shakibâ
impeach *vt., n.* استيضاح كردن estizâh kardan
impeccable *adj., n.* بى عيب bi-'eyb نجيب najib
impeccant *adj.* بيگناه bi-gonâh
impecunious *n.* بى پول bi-pul
impedance *n.* مقاومت moqâvemat
impede *vt.* جلوگيرى كردن jelogiri kardan مانع شدن mâne' shodan
impediment *n.* مانع mâne' گرفتگى gereftegi لكنت loknat
impel *vt.* وادار كردن vâdâr kardan
impending *adj.* نزديك باتفاق nazdik be-etefâq
قريب الوقوع qaribol voqu'
impenetrable *adj.* نفوذ ناپذير nofuz nâ-pazir
impenetrable *adj.* سوراخ نشدنى surâkh nashodani
imperative *adj., n.* امرى amri دستورى dasturi ضرورى zaruri
imperceptible *adj., n.* درك نشدنى dark nashodani
imperfect *adj., n.* ناكامل nâ-kâmel ناقص nâqes
imperforate *adj., n.* بى سوراخ bi-surâkh لب صاف lab-sâf
imperial *adj., n.* امپراطورى emperâturi
imperialism *n.* امپرياليسم amperiâlizm استعمارطلبى este'mâr talabi
imperil *vt.* بخطر انداختن bekhatar andâkhtan
impermeable *adj.* نفوذ ناپذير nofuz nâ-pazir
impermissible *adj.* غير مجاز qeyr-e' mojâz
impersonal *adj., n.* غير شخصى qeyr-e' shakhsi
impersonate *v.* تقليد كردن taqlid kardan
impersonate *v.* ادا درآوردن adâ dar âvardân
impertinent *adj.* نامربوط nâmarbut بى احترام bi-ehterâm
imperturbable *adj.* ناراحت نشدنى nârâhat nashodani
impervious *adj.* غيرقابل نفوذ qeyr-e' qâbel-e' nofuz

impetuous *adj.* بی باک bi-bâk بی پروا bi-parva متهور motehav~er
impetus *n.* قوّهٔ محرکه qov~eh-ye' moharek~eh
impiety *n.* بی دینی bi-dini بی حرمتی bi-hormati
impinge *v.* برخورد کردن barkhord kardan
impinge *v.* تجاوز کردن tajâvoz kardan
implacable *adj.* آرام نشدنی ârâm nashodani سختگیر sakht-gir
implant *vt., n.* کاشتن kâshtan پیوند کردن peyvand kardan
implausible *adj.* ناجور nâ-jur
implement *n., vt.* انجام دادن anjâm dâdan اجراکردن ejrâ kardan
implicate *vt.* بهم پیچیدن beham pichidan قاطی کردن qâti kardan
implicit *adj.* بی چون و چرا bi-chun-o cherâ مطلق motlaq
implore *vt., vi.* التماس کردن eltemâs kardan
imply *vt.* دربرداشتن dar bardâshtan
impolite *adj.* بی ادب bi-adab
import *vt., vi., n.* وارد کردن vâred kardan
importance *n.* اهمیت ahamiyat
important *adj.* مهم mohem~
importation *n.* ورود vorud
importer *n.* وارد کننده vâred-konandeh
imports *n.* واردات vâredât
importune *vt., vi., adj.* سمج بودن semej budan
مزاحم شدن mozâhem shodan
impose *vt., vi.* تحمیل کردن tahmil kardan
imposition *n.* تحمیل tahmil
impossible *adj.* امکان ناپذیر emkân nâ-pazir
غیرممکن qeyr-e' momken محال mohal
impost *n., vt.* مالیات گمرکی mâliât-e' gomroki
impostor *n.* شیاد shay~âd قلابی qol~âbi
impotent *adj.* ناتوان nâ-tavân بی قدرت bi-qod~rat
impound *vt.* توقیف کردن toqif kardan نگه داشتن negah dâshtan
impoverish *vt.* فقیر کردن faqir kardan
imprecate *vt.* لعنت کردن la'nat kardan نفرین گفتن nefrin goftan
impregnable *adj.* تسخیر ناپذیر taskhir nâ-pazir
impregnate *vt., adj.* آبستن کردن âbestan kardan
impresario *n.* کارگردان اپرا kârgardân-e' operâ
imprescriptible *adj.* بدون برگشت bedun-e' bargasht
impress *v.* اثر گذاشتن asar gozâshtan
impress *v.* تو فشاردادن tu-feshâr dâdan

impression *n.* جا اثر jâ asar برداشت bardâsht
impressive *adj.* موثر moas~er جالب jâleb
imprest *n., v.* مساعده mosâ'edeh
imprint *n., vt.* چاپ کردن châp kardan مهر کردن mohr kardan
imprison *vt.* زندانی کردن zendâni kardan
improbable *adj.* بعید ba'id غیرمحتمل qeyr-e' mohtamal
impromptu *adj., adv., n.* فی البداهه fel-bedâheh
improper *adj.* نادرست nâ-dorost ناشایسته nâ-shâyesteh
impropriate *adj., vt.* واگذاری ملک vâgozâri-e' melk
improve *vt., vi.* بهبود دادن behbud dâdan اصلاح کردن eslâh kardan
improvement *n.* بهبود behbud اصلاح eslâh آبادی âbâdi
improviden *n.* بی احتیاط bi-ehtiât ولخرج velkharj
improvise *vt., vi.* آنا ساختن ânan sâkhtan ابتکار کردن ebtekâr kardan
imprudent *adj.* بی احتیاط bi-ehtiât بی تدبیر bi-tadbir
impudent *adj.* گستاخ gostâkh بی حیا bi-hayâ
impugn *vt.* اعتراض و انتقاد کردن e'terâz va enteqâd kardan
impuissant *adj.* بی قدرت bi-qod~rat ضعیف za'if
impulse *n.* انگیزهٔ ناگهانی angizeh-ye' nâgahâni
impulsion *n.* شتاب shetâb حرکت قوهٔ qov~eh-ye' harekat
impulsive *adj.* بیفکر bi-fekr هوسی havasi
impunity *n.* بخشودگی bakhshudegi
impure *adj.* ناخالص nâ-khâles ناپاک nâ-pâk
impurity *n.* ناپاکی nâ-pâki
impute *vt.* نسبت دادن nesbat dâdan متهم کردن motah~am kardan
in *pre., adv., adj., n.* در dar توی tu-ye' داخل dâkhel مد mod
in a hurry هول هولکی hol holaki عجولانه 'ajulâneh
in absentia *np.* درغیبت dar qeybat
in as much as *n.* ازآنجاییکه az ânjâ'i-keh
in cash *n.* نقداً naqdan
in lieu of *n.* درقبال dar-qebâl-e' درازاء dar-ezâ'-e'
in-and-in *adv.* هم گرایی hamgarâyi
in-and-out *n.* اینور آنور invar ânvar
in-law(s) *n.* خانواده همسر khânvâdeh-ye' hamsar
inability *n.* ناتوانی nâ-tavâni بی عرضگی bi-'orzegi عجز 'ajz
inaccessible *adj.* دست نیافتنی dast nâyâftani
inaccurate *adj.* نادرست nâ-dorost
inaction *n.* بی حرکتی bi-harekâti
inactivate *vt.* ازکارانداختن az kâr andâkhtan

inactive *adj.* بی حرکت bi-harekat بیکار bi-kâr
inadequate *adj.* غیرکافی qeyr-e' kâfi ناکامل nâ-kâmel
inadmissible *adj.* غیرجایز qeyr-e' jâyez ناپذیرفتنی nâ-paziroftani
inadvertent(ly) *n.* غیر عمدی qeyr- e' 'amdi
inadvisable *adj.* ناعاقلانه nâ-'âqelâneh
inalienable *adj.* جدا نشدنی jodâ nashodani
inalterable *adj.* تغییر ناپذیر taqyir nâ-pazir
inane *adj., n.* خالی khâli بی معنی bi-ma'ni
inanimate *adj.* بیجان bi-jân بی روح bi-ruh
inapt *adj.* بی استعداد bi-este'dâd
inattentive *adj.* بی اعتنا bi-e'tenâ
inaudible *adj.* نارسا nâ-resâ کم صدا kam-sedâ
inaugural *adj., n.* گشایشی goshâyeshi قسم خوری qasam-khori
inaugural *n.* گشایشی goshâyeshi افتتاحی eftetâhi
inaugurate *v.* افتتاح کردن eftetâh kardan گشودن goshudan
inaugurate *vt.* افتتاح کردن eftetâh kardan
inauguration *n.* گشایش goshâyesh افتتاح eftetâh آغاز âqâz
تحلیف tahlif
inauspicious *adj.* نحس nahs
inborn *adj.* نهادی nahâdi
inbred *adj.* ذاتی zâti
inbreed *vt.* همگرایی کردن ham-gârâ'i kardan
incalculable *adj.* غیرقابل محاسبه qeyr-e' qâbel-e' mohâsebe
incandescence *n.* افروختگی afrukhteqi
incandescent *adj.* نور پر حرارت nur-e' por harârat
incantation *n.* ورد verd افسون afsun
incapable *adj., n.* عاجز 'âjez ناتوان nâ-tavân
incapacitate *vt.* سلب قدرت کردن salb-e' qod~rat kardan
incapacity *n.* ناتوانی nâ-tavâni بی صلا حیتی bi-salâhiyati
incarcerate *vt., adj.* زندانی کردن zendâni kardan
incarceration *n.* حبس habs
incarnate *adj., vt.* شکل دادن shekl dâdan
incarnation *n.* تشکل tashak~ol شکل یابی shekl-yâbi
incendiary *adj., n.* آتشزا âtashzâ فتنه جو fetneh-ju
incense *n., vt., vi.* عود 'ud خشمگین کردن khashmgin kardan
incentive *n., adj.* باعث bâ'es محرک mohar~ek
incept(ion) *n.* آغاز âqâz پیدایش peydâyesh
incessant *adj.* پیوسته peyvasteh پشت سر هم posht-e' sar-e' ham

لا ينقطع .... lâ-yanqate'

incest *n.* زنا بامحرم zenâ bâ-mahram

inchoate *adj.* نورسیده no-resideh

incident *n., adj.* اتفاق et~efâq رویداد ruydâd عارضه 'ârezeh

incidental(ly) *n.* اتفاقاً et~efâqan ضمناً zemnan

incinerate *vt.* آتش زدن âtash zadan خاکستر کردن khâkestar kardan

incipient *adj.* تازه رس tâzeh ras

incise *vt.* شکاف دادن shekâf dâdan

incision *n.* شکاف shekâf برش boresh

incite *vt.* برانگیختن bar angikhtan تحریک کردن tahrik kardan

inclination *n.* سرازیری sarâziri تمایل tamâyol

incline *V.* تمایل داشتن tamâyol dâshtan

incline *v.* سرازیر کردن sarâzir kardan

inclined *v.* شیبدار shib-dâr مایل mâyel

include *vt.* شامل بودن shâmel budan دربرداشتن dar bar dâshtan

including *n.* شامل شده shamel-shodeh منجمله menjomleh

inclusion *n.* انضمام enzemâm گنجایش gonjâyesh

inclusive *adj.* شامل shâmel کامل kâmel دربردارنده dar bar dârandeh متضمن motezam~en

incognito *adj., adv., n.* مخفی makhfi ناشناس nâ-shenâs

incoherence *n.* بی ربطی bi-rabti

incoherent *adj.* بی ارتباط bi-ertebât

incombustible *adj., n.* نسوز nasuz آتش نگیر âtash nagir

income *n.* درآمد dar âmad

income tax *np.* مالیات بر درآمد mâliât-e' bar-dar âmad

incoming *adj., n.* درحال آمدن dar hâl-e' âmadan

incompatibility *n.* عدم سازش 'adam-e' sâzesh

incompatible *adj., n.* ناسازگار nâ-sâzgâr

incompetent *adj., n.* بی صلاحیت bi-salâhiyat

incomplete *adj.* ناتمام nâ-tamâm

incompliant *adj.* ناساز nâ-sâz لجوج lajuj

incomprehensible *adj.* غیرقابل ادراک qeyr-e' qâbel-e' edrâk

inconceivable *adj.* غیرقابل تصور qeyr-e' qâbel-e' tasâv~or

incondite *adj.* بدساخته شده bad sâkhteh shodeh

incongruent *adj.* نامساوی nâ-mosâvi ناجور nâ-jur

incongruous *adj.* ناجور nâ-jur متباین motebâyen

inconsequential *adj.* بی نتیجه bi-natijeh بی اهمیت bi-ahamiyat

inconsiderable *adj.* ناچیز nâ-chiz جزئص joz'i

inconsistent *adj.* نا ثابت nâ-sâbet متناقض motenâqez مغایر moqayer
inconspicuous *adj.* نا پیدا nâ-peydâ
inconstant *adj.* بی ثبات bi-sabât
incontinent *adj., adv.* نامسلط nâ-mosal~ât
incontrollable *adj.* غیرقابل کنترل qeyr-e' qâbel-e' kontorol
inconvenient *adj.* ناراحت nârâhat
incorporate *vt., vi., adj.* یکی کردن yeki kardan
متشکل کردن moteshak~el kardan
incorporation *n.* شرکت سهامی sherkat-e' sahâmi
incorrigible *adj., n.* اصلاح ناپذیر eslâh nâ-pazir
incorruptible *adj.* رشوه نگیر roshveh-nagir
incrassate *vt., vi., adj.* کلفت کردن koloft kardan
increase *vt., vi., n.* اضافه کردن ezâfeh kardan زیاد کردن ziâd kardan
increase *n.* افزایش afzâyesh اضافه ezâfeh مزید mazid ازدیاد ezdiâd
incredible *adj.* باورنکردنی bâvar nakardani
incredulity *n.* دیرباوری dir-bâvari
increment *n.* افزایش afzâyesh ضریب zarib
incriminate *vt.* گناهکار کردن gonâh-kâr kardan
incubate *vt., vi.* روی تخم خوابیدن ruy-e' tokhm khâbidan
incumbent *n.* خوابیده khâbideh متصدی fe'li وقت motesad~i
سرکار sar-e' kâr
incumbent *adj.* واجب vâjeb لازم lâzem فرض farz
incur *v.* متحمل شدن moteham~el shodan
incur *v.* برخورد کردن bar-khord kardan
incurable *adj., n.* علاج ناپذیر 'alâj nâ-pazir لاعلاج lâ-'alâj
incurrent *adj.* توریزی turizi
incursion *n.* تهاجم tahâjom
indebted *adj.* مقروض maqruz مرهون marhun مدیون madyun
مشغول ذمه mashqul zam~eh
indecency *n.* بیشرمی bi-sharmi
indecent *adj.* ناشایسته nâ-shâyesteh ناپسند nâ-pasand
indecision *n.* بلا تصمیمی belâ-tasmimi
indeed *adv., int.* براستی be-râsti حقیقتاً haqiqatan همانا hamânâ
indefatigable *adj.* خسته نشدنی khasteh nashodani
indefensible *adj.* دفاع ناپذیر defâ' nâ-pazir
indefinite *adj.* نامعلوم nâ-ma'lum نامحدود nâ-mahdud
indefinitely *adv.* بطورنامعلوم betor-e' nâ-ma'lum
indelible *adj.* پاک نشدنی pâk nashodani

indelicate *adj.* بی ظرافت bi-zerâfat خشن khashen
indemnify *vt.* تاوان دادن tâvân dâdan غرامت دادن qarâmat dâdan
indemnity *n.* تاوان tâvân غرامت qarâmat
indentation *n.* تورفتگی tu-raftegi
indenture *n., vt.* قرارداد qarârdâd
independence *n.* استقلال esteqlâl
independent *adj., n.* مستقل mostaq~el
indescribable *adj.* غیرقابل تشریح qeyr-e' qâbel-e' tashrih
indestructible *adj.* خراب نشدنی kharâb nashodan لا یزال lâ-yazâl
indeterminate *adj.* نامصمم nâ-mosamam نامعلوم nâ-ma'lum
index *n., vt.* فهرست fehrest شاخص shakhes
index finger *np.* انگشت نشان angosht-e' neshân
index number *np.* شمارهٔ تطبیق shomâreh-ye' tatbiq
India *n.* هندوستان hendustân
Indian *n., adj.* هندی hendi سرخ پوست sorkh pust
Indian giver *np.* هدیه پس گیر hadiyeh pasgir
Indian Ocean *np.* اقیانوس هند oqiânus-e' hend
Indian summer *np.* پاییز گرم pâyiz-e' garm
indicate *vt.* نشان دادن neshân dâdan علامت دادن 'alâmat dâdan
indicative *adj., n.* علامت دهنده 'alâmat dahandeh اخباری akhbâri
indicator *n.* نشان دهنده neshân dahandeh شاخص shâkhes
مقیاس meqyas
indict *n.* کیفر خواست کردن keyfar-khâst kardan
indiction *n.* فرمان مالیاتی farmân-e' mâliâti
indictment *n.* کیفر خواست keyfar-khâst
indifferent *adj., n., adv.* بی علاقه bi-taraf بی طرف bi-'alâqeh
indifinite article *n.* حرف نکره harf-e' nakareh
indigenous *adj.* بومی bumi
indigent *adj., n.* فقیر faqir مسکین meskin مفلس mofles
indigestion *n.* سوء هاضمه su'-e' hâzemeh
indignant *adj.* دلخور delkhor عصبانی 'asabâni
indignation *n.* دلخوری delkhori
indigo *n., adj.* نیل nil
indirect *adj.* غیرمستقیم qeyr-e' mostaqim
indirect object *np.* مفعول بیواسطه maf'ul-e' bi-vâseteh
indiscreet *adj.* بی احتیاط bi-ehtiât
indiscrete *adj.* بی ملاحظه bi-molâhezeh
indiscriminate *adj.* بدون تبعیض bedun-e' tâb'iz

بدون فرق گذاری .... bedun-e' farq-gozari
indispensable *adj., n.* ضروری zaruri واجب vâjeb
indisputable *adj.* بی چون و چرا bi-chun-o cherâ
indissoluble *adj.* حل نشدنی hal~ nashodani
indistinct *adj.* نامشخص nâ-moshakh~as
indite *vt.* نوشتن neveshtan سرودن sorudan
individual *adj., n.* انفرادی enferâdi فرد fard شخص shakhs
individualism *n.* فردی fardi آزادی âzâdi-e' fardi
individuality *n.* شخصیت انفرادی shakhsiyat-e' enferâdi
indivisible *adj., n.* بخش ناپذیر bakhsh nâ-pazir
indoctrinate *vt.* تلقین عقاید کردن talqin-e' 'aqâyed kardan
indolence *n.* بی دردی bi-dardi تنبلی tanbali
indolent *adj.* تنبل tanbal بی درد bi-dard
indoor *adj.* داخلی dâkheli درونی daruni
induce *vt.* موجب شدن mojeb shodan وادار کردن vâdâr kardan
induct *vt.* وارد کردن vâred kardan معرفی کردن mo'arefi kardan
induction *n.* ورود vorud استدلال estedlâl
inductive *adj.* استدلالی estedlâli ترغیب کننده tarqib konandeh
inductor *n.* واداركننده vâdâr konandeh
indue *vt.* دارا کردن dârâ kardan
indulge *vi., vt.* رو دادن ru dâdan افراط کردن efrât kardan
indulgence *n., vt.* اسراف esrâf زیاده روی ziâdeh-ravi
indulgent *adj.* هوسران havas-rân افراطی efrâti زیاده رو ziâdeh-ro
indult *n.* وظیفه vazifeh
indurate *vt., vi., adj.* سفت کردن seft kardan
سرسخت کردن sarsakht kardan
industrial *adj., n.* صنعتی san'ati
industrialize *vt., vi.* صنعتی کردن san'ati kardan
industrious *adj.* ساعی sâ'i
industry *n.* صنعت san'at
inedible *adj.* ناخوردنی nâ-khordani
ineffable *adj.* نگفتنی nagoftani
ineffective *adj.* بی اثر bi-asar
ineffectual *adj.* بی نتیجه bi-natijeh ناموثر nâ-moas~er
inefficient *adj.* بی کفایت bi-kefâyat بی دست و پا bi-dast-o pâ
ineligible *adj., n.* غیرواجد شرایط qeyr-e' vâjed-e' sharâyet
ineluctable *adj.* غیرقابل اجتناب qeyr-e' qâbel-e' ejtenâb
inept *adj.* نامناسب nâ-monâseb بی کفایت bi-kefâyat

ineptitude n. بیعرضگی bi-'orzegi
inequality n. نابرابری nâ-barâbari
inequitable adj. غیرعادلانه qeyr-e' 'âdelâneh
inerrant adj. اشتباه ناپذیر eshtebâh nâ-pazir
inert adj. بی حرکت bi-harekat
inertia n. بی حرکتی bi-harekati
inescapable adj. فرار ناپذیر farâr nâ-pazir
inessential adj., n. غیرضروری qeyr-e' zaruri
inevitable adj., n. اجتناب ناپذیر ejtenâb nâ-pazir
inexcusable adj. نابخشیدنی nâ-bakhshidani
inexhaustible adj. تمام نشدنی tamâm nashodani
inexhaustible adj. خسته ناپذیر khasteh nâ-pazir
inexorable adj. راضی نشدنی râzi nashodani
inexpedient adj. بی مصلحت bi-mâslahat
inexpensive adj. ارزان arzân کم خرج kam kharj
inexperience n. بی تجربگی bi-tajrobegi
inexperienced adj. بی تجربه bi-tajrobeh
inexplicable adj. غیرقابل توضیح qeyr-e' qâbel-e' tozih
inextricable adj. حل نشدنی hal~ nashodâni
infallible adj., n. اشتباه ناپذیر eshtebâh nâ-pazir
infamous adj. بدشهرت bad shohrat
infamy n. رسوایی rosvâyi
infancy n. کودکی kudaki طفولیت tofuliyat
infant n., adj. کودک kudak طفل tefl
infanticide n. بچه کشی bach~eh-koshi
infantile adj. بچگانه bach~egâneh
infantry n. پیاده نظام piâdeh nezâm
infatuate vt., adj., n. شیفته کردن shifteh kardan
infect vt., vi., adj. آلوده کردن âludeh kardan چرک کردن cherk kardan
infected n. چرک شده cherk shodeh
infection n. چرک cherk عفونت 'ofunat
infectious adj. عفونتی 'ofunati چرک شده cherk shodeh
infer v. استنباط کردن estenbât kardan
infer v. دلالت کردن delâlat kardan
inference n. استنباط estenbât اشاره eshâreh تلویح talvih
inferior adj., n. پست past زیردست zir-dast مادون mâ-dun
نامرغوب nâ-marqub
inferiority n. پستی pasti زبونی zabuni

infernal *adj.* جهنمى jahan~âmi شيطانى sheytâni
inferno *n.* آتش سوزى âtaâsh-suzi حريق hariq جهنم jahan~m
inferno *n.* جهنم jahan~am آتش سوزى âtash-suzi
infertile *adj.* نابارور nâ-bâr-var عقيم 'aqim
infest *vt.* هجوم آوردن hojum âvardan
infestation *n.* هجوم hojum
infidel *n., adj.* كافر kâfar بى وفا bi-vafâ
infidelity *n.* بى وفايى bi-vafâyi خيانت به همسر khiânat beh ham-sar
infiltrate *vt., vi., n.* رخنه كردن rekhneh kardan
infinite *adj., n.* بى پايان bi-pâyân لا يتناهى lâ-yatanâhi لا يزال lâ-yazâl
infinitive *n., adj.* مصدر masdar نامعلوم nâ-ma'lum
infinity *n.* بينهايت bi-nahâyat
infirm *adj., vt.* شل shol بى ثبات bi-sabât ناتوان nâ-tavân
infirmary *n.* پرستارخانه parastâr-khâneh
infirmity *n.* شلى sholi بى ثباتى bi-sabâti سستى sosti
infix *vt., vi., n.* درداخل گذاشتن dar-dâkhel gozâshtan
inflame *vt., vi.* آتش زدن âtash zadan باد كردن bâd kardan
inflammable *adj., n.* آتش گير âtash-gir هيجان انگيز hayajân-angiz
محترق mohtareq اهانت آميز ehânat-âmiz
inflammation *n.* التهاب eltehâb بادكردگى bâd kardegi
inflammatory *adj.* التهابى eltehâbi فتنه انگيز fetneh-angiz
inflatable *adj.* بادشدنى bâd-shodani
inflate *vt., vi.* بادكردن bâd kardan
inflated *adj.* متورم motevar~em باددار bâd-dâr
inflation *n.* تورم tavar~om
inflect *v.* خم كردن kham kardan
inflect *v.* كج و كوله كردن kâj-o koleh kardan
inflection *n.* خميدگى khamidegi
inflexible *adj.* خم نشدنى kham nashodani
inflict *vt.* وارد آوردن vâred âvardan ضربه زدن zarbeh zadan
influence *n., vt.* اثر گذاشتن asar gozâshtan نفوذ كردن nofuz kardan
influential *adj.* بانفوذ bâ-nofuz كت و كلفت kat-o koloft
متنفذ motenaf~ez
influenza *n.* آنفلوانزا ânfolu-ânzâ
influx *n.* ريزش rizesh توريزى turizi
inform *adj., vt., vi.* اطلاع دادن et~elâ' dâdan
آگاهى دادن âgâhi dâdan
informal *adj.* غيررسمى qeyr-e' rasmi

informant *n.* خبردهنده khabar dahandeh
information *n.* آگاهی âgâhi خبر khabar اطلاعات et~elâ'ât
استحضار esteh-zâr
informed *n.* باخبر bâ-khabar مطلع mot~ale' آگاه âgâh
مستحضر mostahzar
informer *n.* خبرچین khabar-chin لودهنده lo-dahandeh
infraction *n.* شکستگی shekastegi تخلف takhal~of
infrared *n., adj.* ماوراء قرمز mâvarâ'-e' qermez
infrequent *adj.* کم وقوع kam-voqu'
infringe *vt., vi.* شکستن shekastan تخلف کردن takhal~of kardan
infuriate *vt., adj.* خشمگین کردن khashm-gin kardan
infuse *vt., vi.* ریختن rikhtan پرکردن por kardan
infusion *n.* ریزش rizesh
ingenious *adj.* بانبوغ bâ-nobuq باابتکار bâ-ebtekâr
ingenuity *n.* نبوغ nobuq ابتکار ebtekâr کیاست kiâsat
ingenuous *adj.* رک گو rok-gu
ingest *n.* خوردن khordan
inglorious *adj.* بی شکوه bi-shokuh
ingot *n., vt.* شمش shemsh قالب qâleb
ingrain *vt., adj., n.* توبافت tu-bâft
ingratiate *vt.* خودشیرینی کردن khod-shirini kardan
ingratitude *n.* ناسپاسی nâ-sepasi ناشکری nâ-shokri
ingredient *n.* جزء joz'
ingress *n.* توروی tu-ravi ورود vorud
ingrown *adj.* درونی daruni رشد داخلی roshd-e' dâkheli
inhabit *vt., vi.* سکونت کردن sokunat kardan
inhabitable *adj.* غیرقابل سکونت qeyr-e' qâbel-e' sokunat
inhabitant *n.* ساکن sâken
inhabited *adj.* مسکونی maskuni
inhalant *adj., n.* نفس کش nafas kesh بخور bakhur
inhalation *n.* نفس کشی nafas keshi
inhale *vt., vi.* نفس کشیدن nafas keshidan
inhere *vi.* باطنی bâteni
inherent *adj.* طبعی tab'i ذاتی zâti
inherit *vt., vi.* به ارث بردن beh-ers bordan
inheritance *n.* وراثت verâsat میراث mirâs ارث ers ماترک mâ-tarak
inhibit *vt.* جلوگیری کردن jelogiri kardan
inhibition *n.* بازداری bâz-dâri

inhospitable *adj.* مهمان نانواز mehmân nâ-navâz
inhuman(e) *n.* ضدبشرى zed~-e' bashari غیرانسانى qeyr-e' ensâni
inhumanity *n.* بى انسانیت bi-ensâniyat
inhume *vt.* دفن کردن dafn kardan
inimical *adj.* دشمنانه doshmanâneh
inimitable *adj.* تقلیدنشدنى taqlid nashodani
initial *adj., n., vt.* امضاى مخفف emzây-e' mokhaf~af
initial *adj., n., vt.* نخستین nakhostin اولیه av~alieh
initially *adv.* درابتدا dar ebtedâ
initiate *vt., adj., n.* وارد کردن vâred kardan آشنا کردن âshnâ kardan
initiation *n.* ورودى vorudi آشنایى âshenâyi
initiative *n., adj.* پیشقدمى pish-qadami ابتکار ebtekâr
inject *vt.* تزریق کردن tazriq kardan آمپول زدن âmpul zadan
injection *n.* تزریق tazriq بمیان آوردن be-miân âvardan
injudicious *adj.* بى تدبیر bi-tadbir
injunction *n.* دستور دادگاهى dastur-e' dâdgâhi
injure *vt.* آسیب زدن âsib zadan زخمى کردن zakhmi kardan
injury *n.* صدمه sadameh زخم zakhm
injustice *n.* بى عدالتى bi-'edâlati
ink *n., vt.* جوهر johar مرکب morak~ab
inkle *n.* نخ نازک nakh-e' nâzok
inkling *n.* آشاره eshâreh برات شدگى barât shodegi
inlaid *adj.* خاتم کارى khâtam-kâri منبت کارى monab~at-kâri
معرق mo'ar~aq
inland *adj., adv., n.* داخلى dâkheli
inlay *vt., n.* خاتم کارى کردن khâtam kâri kardan
inlet *n., vt.* مجراى آبى majrây-e' âbi
inmate *n.* هم اطاق ham-otâq هم زندانى ham zendâni
inn *n.* مسافرخانه mosâfer khâneh
innate *adj.* ذاتى zâti طبعى tab'i فطرى fetri
inner *adj.* درونى daruni باطنى bâteni
innervate *vt.* تحریک کردن tahrik kardan
inning *n.* بازگیرى bâzgiri
innocence *n.* بیگناهى bi-gonâhi
innocent *adj., n.* بیگناه bi-gonâh معصوم ma'sum مبرا mobar~â
innocuous *adj.* بیضرر bi-zar~ar بى آزار bi-âzâr
innovate *v.* ابتکار کردن ebtekâr kardan ابداع کردن ebdâ' kardan
بدعت گذاشتن bed'at gozâshtan

innovation *n.* ابتكار ebtekâr نوآوری no-âvari ابداع ebdâ'
innovator *adj.* نوگرا no-garâ مبتكر mobtaker
innteract *n.* بهم تاثیرکردن beham ta'sir kardan
innuendo *n.* كنایه kenâyeh شایعه shâye'eh
innumerable *adj.* بیشمار bi-shomâr
innumerous *n.* ناشمردنی nâ-shemordani
inobservant *adj.* بی اعتنا bi-e'tenâ
inoculate *vt., vi.* واکسن زدن vâksan zadan مایه کوبی mâyeh-kubi
inoculation *n.* مایه کوبی mâyeh-kubi
inoffensive *adj.* بی منظور bimanzur بی آزار bi-âzâr
inoperable *adj.* عمل نشدنی 'amal nashodani
inoperative *adj.* بدردنخور be-dard nakhor ازکارافتاده az kâr oftâdeh
inordinate *adj.* نامنظم nâ-monaz~am افراطی efrâti
inorganic *adj.* آلی âli
inpatient *n.* بیمار بستری bimâr-e' bastari
input *n., adj., vt., vi.* درون گذاری darun gozâri
inquest *n.* رسیدگی residegi بازجویی bâzjuyi
inquire *vt., vi.* تحقیق کردن tahqiq kardan جویا شدن juyâ shodan
inquiry *n.* بازجویی bâzjuyi رسیدگی residegi پرسش porsesh
استفسار estefsâr
inquisition *n.* رسیدگی residegi تفتیش عقاید taftish-e' 'aqâyed
inquisitive *adj., n.* کنجکاو konjkâv فضول fozul
inquisitor *n.* بازجو bâzju تحقیق کننده tahqiq konandeh
inroad *n.* تاخت و تاز tâkht-o tâz تاثیر بد ta'sir-e' bad
insane *adj.* دیوانه divâneh
insanity *n.* دیوانگی divânegi جنون jonun
inscribe *vt.* نوشتن neveshtan نقش کردن naqsh kardan
inscription *n.* نقش naqsh نوشته neveshteh کتیبه katibeh
insect *n., adj.* حشره hashareh
insecticide *n.* حشره کش hashareh-kosh
insecure *adj.* ناامن nâ-amn نامطمئن nâ-motma'en
insecurity *n.* ناامنی nâ-amni
inseminate *vt.* تلقیح کردن talqih kardan
insensate *adj.* بی احساس bi-ehsâs
insensible *adj.* بیحس bi-hes~ بی عاطفه bi-'âtefeh
insensitive *adj.* بی احساس bi-ehsâs خونسرد khun-sard
inseparable *adj., n.* جدا نشدنی jodâ nashodani لاینفک lâ-yanfak
ناگسستنی nâ-gosastani لا یتجزی lâ-yatajaz~i

insert *vt., n.* فرو کردن foru kardan جا دادن jâ dâdan
inset *v.* عکس درونی 'aks-e' daruni
inside *pre., adv., n., adj.* تو tu داخل dâkhel درمیان dar miân جوف jof
insider *n.* درونی daruni ازتو az tu
insidious *adj.* موذیانه muziâneh موش مرده mush mordeh
insight *n.* شناخت shenâkht ادراک باطن edrâk-e' bâten فراست farâsat
insignia *n.* نشان neshân
insignificant *adj., n.* ناچیز nâ-chiz بی معنی bi-ma'ni ناقابل nâ-qâbel
insincere *adj.* بی صداقت bi-sedâqat نامطمئن nâ-motma'en
insinuate *vt., vi.* منظور داشتن manzur dâshtan جا دادن jâ dâdan
insipid *adj.* بی مزه bi-maz~eh بی نمک bi-namak
insipient *adj.* نادان nâdân
insist *v.* اصرار کردن esrâr kardan پافشاری کردن pâ-feshâri kardan
insistence *n.* پافشاری pâ-feshâri اصرار esrâr ابرام ebrâm
insistent *adj.* مصر moser بااصرار bâ-esrâr
insofar(as) *n.* تا آنجایی که tâ ânjâyi keh
insolate *vt.* درآفتاب خشک کردن dar âftâb khoshk kardan
insolation *n.* آفتاب گیری âftâb giri
insolence *n.* گستاخی gostâkhi
insolent *adj., n.* گستاخ gostâkh جسورانه jasurâneh
insoluble *adj.* حل نشدنی hal~ nashodani لاینحل lâ-yanhal
insolvent *adj., n.* درمانده dar-mândeh ورشکست var-shekast
تنگدست tang-dast
insomnia *n.* بی خوابی bikhâbi شب خیزی shab-khizi
insomniac *n., adj.* بیخواب bi-khâb شب بیدار shab-bidâr
شب خیز shab-khiz
insomuch *adv.* اینقدرکه in-qadr keh
به اندازه یی که beh-andâzehyi keh
insouciant *adj.* بی خیال آرام ârâm bi-khiâl
inspect *vt.* تحقیق کردن tahqiq kardan تفتیش کردن taftish kardan
inspect *v.* معاینه کردن mo'âyeneh kardan
inspection *n.* بازرسی bâzresi تفتیش taftish
inspector *n.* بازرس bazres مفتش mofat~esh
inspectorate *n.* بازرس bâzres
inspiration *n.* نفس گیری nafas-giri الهام elhâm وحی vah-y
inspire *vt., vi.* نفس کشیدن nafas keshidan الهام دادن elhâm dâdan
instability *n.* بی ثباتی bi-sabâti
install *vt.* نصب کردن nasb kardan سرکار آوردن sar-e' kâr âvardan

installation *n.* نصب nasb انتصاب entesâb
installations *n.* تاسیسات ta'sisât
installment *n.* قسطی qesti قسمت qesmat
instance *n., vt., vi.* نمونه nemuneh مورد mored وهله vahleh
instant *n., adj., adv.* لحظه lahzeh فوری fori مورد mored
instantaneous *adj.* آنی âni
instantly *adv., con.* آناً ânan فوراً foran
instead *adv.* درعوض dar-'avaz بجای bejâ-ye'
instigate *vt.* باعث شدن bâ'es shodan تحریک کردن tahrik kardan
instigator *adj.* محرک mohar~ek عامل 'âmel
instil(l) *n.* قطره قطره ریختن qatreh-qatreh rikhtan
instinct *adj., n.* غریزه qarizeh
instinctive *adj.* غریزی qarizi
institute *v.* تأسیس کردن ta'sis kardan
institute *v.* برقرار کردن barqarâr kardan
institution *n.* موسسه moaseseh انجمن anjoman بنگاه bongâh
instruct *vt.* یاددادن yâd dâdan دستور دادن dastur dâdan
instruction *n.* دستور dastur تعلیم ta'lim آموزش âmuzesh
instructive *adj., n.* آموزنده âmuzandeh
instructor *n.* آموزگار âmuzegâr معلم mo'al~em مربی morab~i
instrument *n., adj., vt.* وسیله vasileh آلت âlat
instrumental *adj., n.* کمک کننده komak konandeh آلتی âlati
insubordinate *adj., n.* نافرمان nâ-farmân
insubordination *n.* نافرمانی nâ-farmâni
insubstantial *adj.* بی پایه bi-pâyeh جزیی joz'i
insufferable *adj.* تحمل ناپذیر taham~ol nâ-pazir
insufficient *adj.* ناکافی nâ-kâfi کم kam
insular *adj., n.* مجزا mojaz~â محفوظ mahfuz
insulate *vt.* جدا کردن jodâ kardan عایقدار کردن 'âyeq-dâr kardan
insulated *adj.* عایق دار 'âyeq-dâr
insulation *n.* عایق کاری 'âyeq-kâri
insulator *n.* عایق کننده 'âyeq konandeh
insulin *n.* دوای مرض قند davây-e' maraz-e' qand
insult *vi., n.* توهین کردن tohin kardan
insurance *n.* بیمه bimeh
insure *vt., vi.* بیمه کردن bimeh kardan تضمین کردن tazmin kardan
insured *v.* بیمه شدن bimeh shodeh
insurgency *n.* شورش shuresh یاغیگری yâqi-gari

insurgent *n., adj.* شورشی shureshi یاغی yâqi
insurmountable *adj.* غلبه ناپذیر qalabeh nâ-pazir
insurrection *n.* قیام طغیان qiâm toqyân
intact *adj.* دست نخورده dast nakhordeh
intake *n.* فروکش forukesh دهنده dahandeh
intangible *adj., n.* لمس ناپذیر lams nâ-pazir
integer *n.* عدد صحیح 'adad-e' sahih
integral *adj., n.* جزء مکمل joz'-e' mokam~el
integrate *vt., vi.* کامل کردن kâmel kardan
integrate *vt., vi.* باهم یکی کردن bâ ham yeki kardan
integrity *n.* درستی dorosti تمامیت tamâmiyat
intellect *n.* عقل 'aql فهم fahm هوش hush
intellectual *adj., n.* روشنفکر roshan-fekr فهمیده fahmideh
intelligence *n.* هوش hush زیرکی ziraki آگاهی âgâhi
intelligent *adj.* باهوش bâ-ush آگاه âgâh زیرک zirak
هوشمند hush-mand
intelligentsia *pl.* روشن فکران roshan fekrân
intelligible *adj.* قابل فهم qâbel-e' fahm
intemperate *adj.* افراطی efrâti سهمگین sahmgin
intend *v.* قصد داشتن qasd dâshtan قصد کردن qasd kardan
intend *v.* خیال داشتن khiâl dâshtan
intended *adj., n.* قصدی qasdi نامزد nâmzad
intense *adj.* شدید shadid سخت sakht
intensify *vt., vi.* شدید کردن shadid kardan قوی کردن qavi kardan
intension *n.* تصمیم tasmim
intensity *n.* شدت shed~at غلظت qelzat
intensive *adj., n.* باشدت bâ-shed~at فشرده feshordeh
intent *adj., n.* نیت niyat قصد qasd عزم 'azmg آهنگ âhang
intention *n.* قصد qasd نیت niyat عمد 'amd
intentional *adj.* قصدی qasdi عمدی 'amdi
inter *vt.* دفن کردن dafn kardan
interact *vi.* فعل و انفعال کردن fe'l-o enfe'âl kardan
intercede *vt.* شفاعت کردن shafâ'at kardan
وساطت کردن vesâtat kardan
intercept *v.* قطع کردن qat' kardan
intercept *v.* بین راه گرفتن beyn-e' râh gereftan
interceptor *n.* تقاطع کننده taqâto'konandeh
interchangeable *n.* تعویض شدنی ta'viz-shodani متبادل motebâdel

intercollegiate *adj.* میان دانشکده‌ها miân-e' dânesh-kadeh-hâ
intercom *n.* دستگاه ارتباطی dast-gâh-e' ertebâti
intercourse *n.* آمیزش âmizesh جفتگیری joft-giri
interdependent *adj.* وابسته بهم vâbasteh be-ham
interdict *n., vt.* ممنوع کردن mamnu' kardan
محروم کردن mâhrum kardan
interest *v.* علاقه مند کردن 'alâqehmand kardan
interest *n., vt.* علاقه 'alâqeh اشتیاق eshtiâq تمایل tamâyol
interest *n., vt.* بهره bahreh ربح rebh تنزیل tanzil
interested *adj.* علاقمند 'alâqeh-mand مایل mâyel ذینفع zinaf'
راغب râqeb
interesting *adj.* جالب jâleb
interfere *vi.* دخالت کردن dekhâlat kardan
مزاحم شدن mozâhem shodan
interim *n., adj., adv.* موقتی movaq~âti فاصله fâseleh
interior *adj., n.* داخل dâkhel درون darun
interjacent *adj.* وسطی vasati
interject *vt.* درمیان آوردن dar miân âvardan
interjection *n.* حرف ندا harf-e' nedâ
interlace *vi., vt.* بهم پیچیدن be-ham pichidan
interlocution *n.* گفتگو goftegu بحث bahs
interlope *vi.* مداخله کردن modâkheleh kardan
interlude *n.* میان پرده miân pardeh
intermarry *vi.* غریب ازدواجی qarib ezdevâji هم گرایی ham-garâyi
intermediary *adj., n.* میانجیگر miânjigar وسطی vasati
intermediate *adj., vi., n.* متوسط motevas~et وسطی vasati
interminable *adj.* پایان ناپذیر pâyân nâ-pazir
intermission *n.* میان پرده miân pardeh آنتراک ânterâk
intermittent *adj.* متناوب motenâveb
intermix *vt., vi.* باهم مخلوط کردن bâ-ham makhlut kardan
intern *n., vi.* نگهداری کردن negahdâri kardan
intern *n.* کارورز kâr-varz انترن antern
internal *adj., n.* داخلی dâkheli درونی dâruni
international *adj., n.* بین المللی beyn-ol melali
internship *n.* کارورزی kâr-varzi انترنی anterni
interpose *vt., vi.* جا دادن jâ dâdan مداخله کردن modâkheleh kardan
interpret *v.* ترجمه کردن tarjomeh kardan
interpret *v.* تعبیرکردن ta'bir kardan

interpreter *n.* مترجم motarjem
interrelated *adj.* مربوط بهم marbut-e' be-ham
interrogate *vt., vi.* سؤال کردن so'âl kardan
بازپرسی کردن bâz-porsi kardan
interrogation *n.* بازپرسی bâz-porsi باز جوئی bâz-ju'i استنطاق estentâq
interrogative *adj., n.* سؤالی so'âli استفهامی estefhâmi
interrogator *n.* بازپرس bâz-pors پرسش کننده porsesh-konandeh
interrogatory *adj., n.* پرسشنامه porsesh-nâmeh استعلامیه este'lamieh
interrupt *vt., vi.* قطع کردن qat' kardan
interruption *n.* گسیختگی gosikhtegi وقفه vaqfeh
intersect *vt., vi.* تقاطع کردن taqâto' kardan
دونصف کردن do-nesf kardan
intersection *n.* تقاطع taqâto' چهارراه chahâr-râh
interval *n.* فاصله fâseleh مدت mod~at
intervene *v.* وساطت کردن vesâtat kardan
intervene *v.* مداخله کردن modâkheleh kardan
intervention *n.* مداخله modâkheleh وساطت vesâtat
interview *n., vt.* مصاحبه کردن mosâhebeh kardan
intestine *n., adj.* روده rudeh
intimacy *n.* محرمی mahrami نزدیکی nazdiki
intimate *adj., vt., n.* محرم mahram درونی daruni خصوصی khosusi
مقرب moqar~eb
intimidate *vt.* ترساندن tarsândan اجبار کردن ejbâr kardan
into *pre., adj.* توی tu-ye' داخل dâkhel-e' در dar
intolerable *adj.* غیرقابل تحمل qeyr-e' qâbel-e' taham~ol
intolerant *adj., n.* بی تحمل bi-taham~ol
intonation *n.* زیر و بم zir-o bam
intone *vt., vi.* زیر و بم دادن ziro bam dâdan
intoxicate *vt., vi., adj.* مست کردن mast kardan
از خود بیخود کردن az khod bi-khod kardan
intoxicated *adj.* مست mast
intramural *adj.* داخلی dâkheli تو چهار دیواری tu chahâr divâri
intransigent *adj., n.* ناسازگار nâ-sâz-gâr یک دنده yek-dandeh
intransitive *adj., n.* لازم lâzem
intrepid *adj.* نترس natars بی باک bi-bâk
intricacy *n.* پیچیدگی pichidegi
intricate *adj.* پیچیده pichideh بغرنج boq-ranj
intrigue *vt., vi., n.* دسیسه کردن dasiseh kardan راز و نیاز râz-o niâz

intriguing *v.* مرموز mârmuz
intrinsic *adj.* ذاتى zâti درونى daruni
introduce *vt.* معرفى كردن mo'ar~efi kardan آشنا كردن âshenâ kardan
introduction *n.* معرفى mo'ar~efi مقدمه moqad~ameh
introductory *adj.* مقدمهاى moqâd~âmeh-i
introspect *vi., vt.* خود نگرى كردن khod-negari kardan
introvert *n., adj., vt.* متوجه بخود motevaj~eh be-khod
درون گرا darun-garâ
intrude *vt., vi.* بزور تو رفتن bezur tu raftan
intruder *n.* مزاحم mozâhem
intrusion *n.* تجاوز tajâvoz مزاحمت mozâhem~at
intuition *n.* ادراک ذاتى edrâk-e' zâti درک آنى dark-e' âni برات barât
intuitive *adj.* داراى ادراک ذاتى dârây-e' edrâk-e' zâti
inundate *vt.* غرق كردن qarq kardan سيل آمدن seyl âmadan
inure *vt., vi.* عادت دادن 'âdat dâdan
invade *vt., vi.* هجوم آوردن hojum âvardan تجاوز كردن tajâvoz kardan
invader *n.* مهاجم mohâjem تجاوز كننده tajâvoz konandeh
invalid *n., adj., vt., vi.* عاجز 'âjez عليل 'alil
invalid *n., adj., vt., vi.* بى اعتبار bi-e'tebâr باطل bâtel
invalidate *vt.* بى اعتبار كردن bi-e'tebâr kardan
invalidate *v.* باطل كردن bâtel kardan
invaluable *adj.* گرانبها gerânbahâ
invariable *adj., n.* تغيير ناپذير taqyir nâ-pazir
invasion *n.* هجوم hojum حمله hamleh
invective *n., adj.* پرخاش par-khâsh اعتراض شديد e'terâz-e' shadid
inveigh *v.* پرخاش كردن parkhâsh kardan
inveigh *v.* اعتراض شديدكردن e'terâz-e' shadid kardan
invent *v.* ازخوددرآوردن az khod dar âvardan
invent *v.* اختراع كردن ekhterâ' kardan
invention *n.* اختراع ekhterâ'
inventive *adj.* مبتكر mobtaker
inventor *n.* مخترع mokhtare'
inventory *n., vt., vi.* موجودى mojudi
صورت برداشتن surat bar-dâshtan
inverse *adj., n., vt.* وارونه كردن vâruneh kardan
معكوس كردن ma'kus kardan
inversion *n.* برگردانى bargardâni
invert *vt., vi., adj., n.* وارونه كردن vâruneh kardan

معکوس کردن .... ma'kus kardan

invertebrate *adj., n.* بی استخوان bi-ostokhân بی شهامت bi-shahâmat

inverted *adj.* وارونه vâ-runeh

invest *vt., vi.* سرمایه گذاشتن sarmâyeh gozâshtan

investigate *vt., vi.* تحقیق tahqiq رسیدگی کردن residegi kardan

investigation *n.* تحقیق tah-qiq بازجویی bâz-ju-yi

investigator *n.* رسیدگی کننده residegi konandeh کارآگاه kârâgâh

investiture *n.* اعطا e'tâ خلعت khal'at

investment *n.* سرمایه گذاری sarmâyeh-gozâri

inveterate *adj.* دیرینه dirineh خو گرفته khu gerefteh

invicible *n.* فتح ناپذیر fat-h nâ-pazir رویین تن ru'in-tan

invigorate *vt.* نیرو دادن niru dâdan روح بخشیدن ruh bakhshidan

invisible *adj., n.* نادیدنی nâ-didani نامرئی nâmar'i ناپیدا nâ-peyda

invitation *n., adj.* دعوت da'vat

invite *vt., vi., n.* دعوت کردن da'vat kardan

inviting *adj.* پرجاذبه por jâzebeh کشنده keshandeh

invocation *n.* توسل tavas~ol دعا do'â استدعا ested'â

invoice *n., vt.* فاکتور fâktor صورت حساب surat hesâb فیش fish قبض qabz

invoilable *n.* تخلف ناپذیر takhal~of nâ-pazir

invoke *vt.* توسل کردن tavas~ol kardan احضار کردن ehzâr kardan

involuntary *adj.* غیرارادی qeyr-e' erâdi بی اختیار bi-ekhtiâr

involute *adj., n., vi.* لوله کردن luleh kardan

involve *v.* گرفتار کردن gereftâr kardan

involve *v.* مشغول بودن mashqul budan

involvement *n.* گرفتاری gereftâri

invulnerable *adj.* زخم ناپذیر zakhm nâ-pazir رویین تن ru'in-tan

inward *adv., adj., n.* بطرف تو betaraf-e' tu

iodine *n.* ید yod

Iranian *adj., n.* ایرانی irâni

Iraq *n.* عراق 'arâq

irate *adj.* عصبانی 'asabâni خشمگین khashm-gin

ire *n.* غضب qazab خشم khashm

iris *n., vi.* زنبق zanbaq تارچشم târ-e' cheshm

irk *vt.* خسته khasteh کسل کردن kesel kardan

iron *v.* اطو کردن otu kardan اطو otu

iron *n.* آهن âhan

iron out *n.* صاف کردن sâf kardan ازبین بردن az beyn bordan

ironhanded *adj.* قرص qors مقتدر moqtader

ironic(al) *n.* طعنه آمیز ta'neh âmiz استهزا آمیز estehzâ âmiz جالب jâleb

irony *adj., n.* طعنه ta'neh خنده داری khandeh-dâri

irradiate *vt., vi., adj.* درخشان کردن derakhshân kardan

irrational *adj., n.* غیر منطقی qeyr-e' manteqi

irreconcilable *adj., n.* موافقت نشدنی movâfeqat nashodani

irrecoverable *adj.* علاج ناپذیر 'alâj nâ-pazir باز نیافتنی bâz nayâftani

irredeemable *adj.* جبران ناپذیر jobrân nâ-pazir

irredeemable *adj.* بازخریدنشدنی bâz-kharid nashodani

irrefutable *adj.* تکذیب ناپذیر takzib nâ-pazir

irregular *adj., n.* نامعمولی nâ-ma'muli غیر عادی qeyr-e' 'âd~i

irregularity *n.* بی نظمی bi-nazmi بی قاعدگی bi-qâ'edegi

irrelative *adj.* بی نسبت bi-nesbat

irrelevant *adj.* بی ربط bi-rabt نامربوط nâ-marbut

irresistable *n.* غیرقابل مقاومت qeyre' qâbele' moqâvemat

irresolute *adj.* بی تصمیم bi-tasmim وسواسی vasvâsi

irrespective *adj.* بی توجه bi-tavaj~oh بی اعتنا bi-e'tenâ

irresponsible *adj., n.* نامسئول nâmas'ul

irreverence *n.* بیحرمتی bi-hormati

irreverent *adj.* بی ادب bi-adab

irreversible *adj.* برنگشتنی bar-nagashtani

irrevocable *adj.* بدون برگشت bedun-e' bar-gasht

irrigate *vt.* آبیاری کردن âbyâri kardan

irritant *adj., n.* خارش دهنده khâresh dahandeh

irritant *adj., n.* تحریک کننده tahrik konandeh

irritate *vt., vi.* آزاردادن âzâr dâdan خارش دادن khâresh dâdan

irritation *n.* تحریک tahrik خارش khâresh آزار âzâr

Islam *n.* اسلام eslâm

island *n., vt.* جزیره jazireh سکو sak~u

isle(t) *n.* نیم جزیره nim jazireh ردیف radif

isobar *n.* هواشناسی خط کشی khatkeshi-e' havâ shenâsi

isolate *vt., adj.* جداکردن jodâ kardan مجزا کردن mojaz~â kardan

isolation *n.* جدایی jodâyi انزوا enzevâ

isometric *adj., n.* یک اندازه yek-ândâzeh

isosceles *adj.* متساوی الساقین motesâvi-ol sâqeyn

issuance *n.* صدور sodur

issue *n.* موضوع mozu' جریان jaryân

issue *v.* صادر کردن sâder kardan
isthmus *n.* تنگه tangeh
it *nom., pro., n.* آن ân
italics *n.* حروف کج horuf-e' kaj
itch *vi., vt., n.* خاریدن khâridan خارش داشتن khâresh dâshtan
item *n., adv., vt.* قلم qalam نقره faqareh
itemize *vt.* نقره بندی کردن faqareh bandi kardan
iterate *vt.* تکرار کردن tekrâr kardan
itinerary *n., adj.* خط سیر khat~-e' seyr سفر نقشهٔ naqsheh-ye' safar
itself *pro.* خودش khodash
ivory *n., adj.* عاج 'âj
ivy *n.* پیچک pichak

J J ج

jab *vt., vi., n.* فروکردن foru kardan مشت زدن mosht zadan
jabber *vt., vi., n.* تندوتندحرف زدن tond-o tond harf zadan
jack *n., vt., vi., adj.* جک jak
jack-in-the-box *n.* اکبرجک akbar jak
jack-knife *n.* ازوسط تاشدن az vasat tâ shodan
jack-knife *n.* چاقوی بزرگ châqu-ye' bozorg
jack-o'-lantern *n.* فانوس کدویی fânus-e' kaduyi
jack-of-all-trades *n.* همه کاره hameh kâreh
jackal *n.* شغال shoqâl
jackass *n.* نره خر nar~eh-khar
jackboot *n.* چکمهٔ بلند chakmeh-ye' boland
jackdaw *n.* زاغچه zâqcheh
jacket *n., vt.* ژاکت zhâkat جلد jeld
jackpot *n.* جایزهٔ بزرگ jâyezeh-ye' bozorg
jacks *n.* یقل دوقل yeqol doqol
jactation *n.* بخودبالیدن bekhod bâlidan
jade *n., vt., vi.* یشم سبز yashm-e' sabz خسته کردن khasteh kardan
jaded *adj., v.* خسته khasteh کند kond
jag *n., vt.* دندانه وار بریدن dandâneh-vâr boridan پاره گی pâreh-gi
jaguar *n.* پلنگ palang
jail *n., vt.* زندان zendân حبس کردن habs kardan
jailbird *n.* زندانی zendâni
jailer/jailor *n.* زندانبان zendânbân
jalopy *n.* ماشین قدیمی mâshin-e' qadimi
jam *n.* مربا morab~â
jam *v.* چپاندن chapândan
jam *v.* گیر کردن gir kardan فرو کردن foru kardan
jamb(e) *n.* تیرک tirak پایه pâyeh
jamboree *n.* جمبوری jamburi جشن پیشاهنگی jashn-e' pishâhangi
jangle *v.* جنجال کردن janjâl kardan
jangle *vi., vt., n.* صدای ناهنجار sedây-e' nâ-hanjâr
janitor *n.* رفتگر roftegar
jape *vi., vt., n.* شوخی کردن shukhi kardan کلک زدن kalak zadan
jar *vi., vt., n.* کوزه kuzeh بطری botri
jargon *n., vi.* اصطلاح estelâh
jasmine *n.* یاسمین yâsamin
jasper *n.* یشم yashm

jaundice *n., vt.* يرقان yaraqân

jaunt *vi., n.* سفرگردشی safar-e' gardeshi

jaunty *adj.* سرحال sar-e' hâl شیک shik

javelin *n., vt.* نیزه neyzeh زوبین zubin

jaw *n., vi., vt.* فک fak أرواره ârvâreh

jawbreaker *n.* فک شکن fak shekan دندان شکن dandân-shekan

jay *n.* زاغ کبود zâq-e' kabud

jaywalk *vi.* تخلف پیاده رو takhal~of-e' piâdeh ro

jazz *n., adj., vt., vi.* جاز jâz چرت و پرت chart-o part

jealous *adj.* حسود hasud بخیل bakhil

jealousy *n.* حسودی hasudi حسادت hesâdat رشک rashk

jean *n.* کتان katân-e' نخی nakhi

jeer *vi., vt., n.* هوکردن ho kardan استهزا estehzâ

jell *vi., n.* کرم غلیظ kerem-e' qaliz معلوم شدن ma'lum shodan

jelly *n., vt., vi., adj.* ژله zheleh لرزانک larzânak

jelly fish *n.* بلورماهی bolur mâhi

jeopardize *vt.* به مخاطره انداختن be-mokhâtereh andâkhtan

jeopardy *n.* خطر khatar مخاطره mokhâtereh

jerk *n.* تکان takân هف مچل hachal haf

jerk *v.* تند تکان دادن tond takân dâdan کشیدن keshidan

jerky *adj., n.* پر تلاطم por talâtom خشک گوشت khoshk gusht

jersey *n.* ژاکت کشباف zhâkat-e' keshbâf

jess *n., vt.* پابند عقاب pâ band-e' 'oqâb

jest *v.* شوخی کردن shukhi kardan

jest *v.* مسخره کردن maskhareh kardan

jester *n.* دلقک dalqak ملیجک malijak مزاح maz~âh

jesus *n.* عیسی 'isâ مسیح masih

jet *adj., n., vt., vi.* فواره زدن fav~âreh zadan

jettison *vt.* سبک باری کردن sabok-bâri kardan
خالی کردن khâli kardan

jettison *n.* دور ریختن dur rikhtan سبک باری sabok-bâri

jetty *adj., n., vt.* موج گیر moj-gir اسکله eskeleh

jew's harp *n.* زنبورک zanburak

Jew(ish) *n.* یهودی yahudi کلیمی kalimi

jewel *n., vt.* جواهر javâher گوهر gohar

jewel-studded *adj.* گوهرنشان gohar-neshâan
جواهرنشان javâher-neshân مرصع moras~a'

jeweler *n.* جواهرفروش javâher forush گوهر فروش gohar forush

jewelry *n.* جواهرات javâherât
jibe *v., n., vi., vt.* هماهنگی داشتن hamâ-hangi dâshtan
jiffy *n.* زود zud چشم بهم زدن cheshm-beham-zadan
jig *n., vt., vi.* ورجه وورجه کردن vârjeh vurjeh kardan
jigger *n., adj.* استكانك estekânak
jiggle *vt., vi., n.* تكان تكان دادن takân takân dâdan
jigsaw *vt., adj., n.* اره مویی ar~eh muyi
jigsaw puzzle *np.* معمای عكسی mo'am~â-ye' 'aksi
jihad *n.* جهاد jahâd
jilt *vt., n.* عهدشكستن 'ahd shekâstan جفاكاری jafâ-kâri
jimjams *n.* دلشوره del-shureh
jingle *vi., vt., n.* جلنگ و جلنگ كردن jilang-o jilang kardan
jingo *n., adj.* جنگجو jang-ju
jinn(i) *n.* جن jen~ پری pari
jinx *n., vt.* چشم زدن cheshm zadan نحس nahs
jitter(s) *n.* عصبی بودن 'asabi budan دلشوره del-shureh
jittery *adj.* عصبی 'asabi دلواپس delvâpas
jive *v.* دست انداختن dast andâkhtan
jive *v.* شوخی کردن shukhi kardan
job *n., vi., vt., adj.* كار kâr شغل shoql حرفه herfeh
jockey *n., vt., vi.* سواركار savâr-kâr جابازكردن jâ bâz kardan
jockstrap *n.* تخم بند tokhm-band
jocund *adj.* بجا bejâ دلنشین delneshin
jog *vt., vi., n.* تكان دادن takân dâdan آهسته دويدن âhesteh davidan
joggle *vt., vi., n.* تكان دادن takân dâdan تكان خوردن takân khordan
join *vt., vi., n.* وصل كردن vasl kardan پيوستن peyvastan
joinder *n.* الحاق elhâq پيوست peyvast
joiner *n.* نجار naj~âr هرجايی harjâyi
joint *n., adj., vt., vi.* بند band مفصل mafsal شريكی shariki محل mahal
joint account *np.* حساب شريكی hesâb-e' shariki
joint resolution *np.* تصويب مجلس و سنا tasvib-e' majles va sanâ
joist *n., vt.* تيرآهن tir âhan الوار alâvâr
joke *n., vi., vt.* شوخی كردن shukhi kardan
joke *n.* شوخی shukhi لطيفه latifeh
joker *adj.* شوخ shukh شوخی كن shukhi-kon لطيفه گو latifeh-gu
jolly *adj., vt., vi., n.* سرخوش sarkhosh خوش مشرب khosh-mashrab
jolt *vi., n.* تكان دادن takân dâdan تكان خوردن takân khordan
jonquil *n.* گل نسرين gol-e' nasrin

josh *v.* دست انداختن dast andâkhtan
josh *v.* سربسرگذاشتن sar be-sar gozâshtan
jostle *vt., vi., n.* هول دادن hol dâdan تنه زدن taneh zadan
jot *vt., n.* یکذره yek-zar~eh مختصر یادداشت yâd-dâsht-e' mokhtasar
journal *n.* روزانه یادداشت yâd-dâsht-e' ruzâneh
journalism *n.* روزنامه نویسی ruznâmeh nevisi
journalist *n.* روزنامه نویس ruznâmeh-nevis
journey *n., vi.* سفرکردن safar kardan
journeyman *n.* کارگر باتجربه kârgar-e' bâ-tajrobeh
joust *n., vi.* نیزه سواری جنگیدن neyzeh-savâri jangidan
jovial *adj.* خوش مشرب khosh-mashrab
jowl *n.* نک fak غبغب qab-qab
joy *n., vi., vt.* لذت lez~at bordan خوشی khoshi شادی shâdi
مسرت maser~at
joyful *adj.* شاد shâd شادمان shâdeman مسرور masrur
joyous *adj.* بانشاط bâ-neshât سرورآمیز sorur-âmiz فرخنده farkhondeh
jubilant *adj.* پیروزانه piruzâneh شاد shâd
jubilation *n.* جشن پیروزی jashn-e' piruzi
jubilee *n., adj.* جشن jashn
Judaism *n.* کلیمیت kalimiyat یهودیت yahudiyat
Judas *n., adj.* یهودا اسقریوط yahudâ esqariot خائن khâ'en
judge *n., vt., vi.* قاضی qâzi داور dâvar قضاوت کردن qezâvat kardan
judgement *n.* قضاوت qezâvat داوری dâvari حکم hokm
judgment day *n.* قیامت qiâmat آخرت âkherat
judicial *adj.* قضایی qazâ'i عادل 'âdel
judicious *adj.* باقضاوت bâ-qezâvat عاقل 'âqel
jug *n., vi., vt.* کوزه kuzeh سبو sabu
juggernaut *n.* پرمشقت por masheq~at
juggle *v.* بالا و پایین انداختن bâlâ va pâyin andâkhtan
juggle *n.* تردستی tardasti
juggler *n.* تردست tardat طرار tar~âr عیار 'ay~âr
jugular *adj., n.* شریانی shariâni شاهرگی shâh-ragi
jugular vein *n.* شاهرگ shâh-rag
juice *n., vt.* شیره shireh آب âb عصاره 'osâreh
juicy *adj.* آبدار âb-dâr
jujube *n.* عناب 'an~âb
juke box *n.* آهنگ پخش کن پولی âhang pakhsh-kon-e' puli
jumble *vt., vi., n.* درهم برهم کردن dar-ham bar-ham kardan

jumbo *n., adj.* گنده gondeh بزرگ bozorg
jump *vi., vt., n., adj.* پریدن paridan جستن jastan جهیدن jahidan
jumper *n.* سیم برقی sim-e' barqi رولباسی ru lebâsi
jumper *n.* پرنده parandeh
jumping jack *np.* خرک kharak جست و خیز jest-o khiz
junction *n.* اتصال et~esâl مقطع maqta' تقاطع taqâto'
juncture *n.* مقطع زمانی maqta'-e' zamâni
jungle *n.* جنگل jangal
junior *adj., n.* کهتر kehtar صغیر saqir کوچکتر kuchektar
junior college *np.* دانشکده dâneshkadeh
juniper *n.* اردج ardaj
junk *n., vt., adj.* آشغال âshqâl دور انداختن dur andâkhtan
junket *n., vi., vt.* گردش دسته جمعی gardesh-e' dasteh jam'i
junkman *n.* آشغال فروش âshqâl-forush اوراق چی orâq-chi
junky *n.* معتاد mo'tâd
junkyard *n.* ماشینهای اسقاط mâshin-hâ-ye' asqât
junta *n.* هیئت hey'at کمیته komiteh
Jupiter *n.* مشتری moshtari ژوپیتر zhupiter
jurant *adj., n.* قسم خورده qasam khordeh
jurat *n.* برگ تأییدی barg-e' ta'idi
jurisdiction *n.* حدود اختیارات hodud-e' ekhtiârât
jurisprudent *adj., n.* قانون دان qânun-dân
jurist *n.* قانون شناس qânun shenâs
juror *n.* قضاوت کننده qezâvat konandeh
jury *adj., n.* هیئت منصفه hey'at-e' monsefeh
just *adj., n., vi., adv.* بحق be-haq~ منصفانه monsefâneh
just *adj., n., vi., adv.* درست dorost
just *adj., n., vi., adv.* دادگر dâd-gar عادل 'âdel
justice *n.* عدل 'adl عدالت 'edâlat
justifiable *adj.* موجه movaj~ah بادلیل bâ-dalil
justification *n.* صحه گذاری seh~eh gozâri توجیه tojih
justify *vt., vi.* صحه گذاشتن seh~eh gozâshtan
توجیه کردن tojih kardan
justly *adv.* حقاً haq~an انصافاً ensâfan
jut *vi., n.* پیشرفتگی داشتن pishraftegi dâshtan
jute *n.* چتایی chatâ'i
jutty *n., vi., vt.* برآمدگی bar-âmadegi
juvenile *adj., n.* جوان javân نابالغ nâ-bâleq

juxtapose *vt.* چیدن هم کنار kenâr-e' ham chidan
juxtaposition *n.* پهلویی به پهلو pahlu beh pahluyi

K K к

keen *adj., n., vi.* تیزهوش tiz-hush حساس has~âs
keep *v.* نگه داشتن negah dâshtan
keep *v.* محافظت کردن mohâfezat kardan
keep (to oneself) *n.* پیش خود نگهداشتن pish-e' khod negahdâshtan
keep (up with) *n.* پا بپارفتن pâ be-pâ raftan آگاه بودن âgâh budan
keep (up) *n.* ادامه دادن edâmeh dâdan
keep up *n.* خوب نگهداشتن khub negah-dâshtan
keeper *n.* نگهدارنده negah-dârandeh محافظ mohâfez
keeping *n., v.* نگهداری negah-dâri حفاظت hefâzat
keepsake *n.* یادگاری yâdgâri
keg *n.* چلیک chelik بشگه boshgeh
kelp *n., vi.* علف دریایی 'alaf-e' daryâyi کتانجک katânjak
kennel *n., vt., vi.* سگدانی sagdâni
kern *n., vt., vi.* لبه labeh
kernel *n., vt.* تخم tokhm مغز maqz هسته hasteh
ketchup *n.* سس گوجه فرنگی sos-e' gojeh farangi
kettle *n.* کتری ketri قوری qori
kettledrum *n.* نقاره naq~âreh
key *n., adj., vt.* کلید kelid مفتاح meftâh
keyboard *n.* ردیف ماشه radif-e' mâsheh
keyhole *n., adj.* سوراخ کلید surâkh kelid
keynote *n., vt.* مایه mâyeh اساسی asâsi اصلی asli
keystone *n.* میان سنگ miânsang پایۀ اصلی pâyeh-ye' asli
khaki *n., adj.* خاکی khâki پارچۀ ارتشی pârcheh-ye' arteshi
kibitz *vi.* فضولی کردن fozuli kardan پارازیت دادن pârâzit dâdan
kibitzer *n.* تماشاگر فضول tamâshâgare fozul
kick *v.* لگد زدن lagad zadan
kick *v.* لگد انداختن lagad andâkhtan
kick *v.* شوت کردن shut kardan
kick (back) *n.* لگد اندازی lagad andâzi
kick (up) *n.* آشوب راه انداختن âshub râh andâkhtan
kick-back *n.* رشوه roshveh
kid *n.* بچه bach~eh بزغاله bozqâleh
kid *v.* شوخی کردن shukhi kardan
kidder *n.* شوخ shukh کلک kalak
kidnap *vt.* آدم دزدی کردن âdam dozdi kardan
kidney *n.* کلیه kolieh قلوه qolveh

kidney bean *np.* لوبیا قرمز lubiâ qermez
kidney stone *np.* سنگ کلیه sang-e' kolieh
kier *n.* لگن lagan
kill *vt., vi., n.* کشتن koshtan رساندن بقتل beqatl resândan
kill(off) *n.* ازبین بردن az beyn bordan
kill(time) *n.* وقت گذراندن vaqt gozarândan
killer *n.* قاتل jâni جانی کشنده koshandeh
killing *n., adj.* مرگ آور marg-âvar خوش بیاری khosh-biâri
kiln *n., vt.* کوره kureh تنور tanur
kin *n., adj.* خویشاوند khish-âvand بستگان bastegân
kind *adj., n.* مهربان mehrabân رحیم rahim خوش قلب khosh-qalb
kind *adj., n.* قسم qesm نوع no' جور jur گونه guneh
kindergarten *n.* کودکستان kudakestân
kindle *vt., vi., n.* روشن کردن roshan kardan بر افروختن bar afrukhtan
kindless *adj.* نامهربان nâ-mehrabân بی شفقت bi-shafeq~ât
kindly *adj., adv.* بامهربانی bâ-mehrabâni صمیمانه samimâneh
لطفاً lotfan
kindness *n.* مهربانی mehrabâni محبت moheb~at لطف lotf
kinfolk *pl.* خویش اوند khish âvand بستگان bastegân
king *n., vt., vi.* شاه shâh پادشاه pâdeshâh سلطان soltân ملک malek
king size *n.* بزرگ bozorg
kingdom *n.* پادشاه نشین pâdeshâh-neshin
قلمرو سلطنتی qalamro-e' saltanati ملک molk
kingpin *n.* اصل کاری asl-e' kâri
kink *n., vt., vi.* گره انداختن gereh andâkhtan تاب tâb
گرفتگی gereftegi
kinky *adj.* گره دار gereh-dâr نفرفری ferferi قاطی پاتی qâti-pâti
kismet *n.* قسمت qesmat تقدیر taqdir
kiss *v.* بوسیدن busidan ماچ کردن mâch kardan
kiss *n.* بوس bus ماچ mâch
kiss(off) *n.* کنار گذاشتن kenâr gozâshtan
kisser *n.* ماچ کن mâch kon لب و دهن lab-o dahan
kitchen *n., adj.* آشپزخانه âshpaz khâneh مطبخ matbakh
kite *n., vi., vt.* بادبادک bâdbâdak
kitten *n., vt., vi.* بچه گربه bach~eh gorbeh پیشی pishi
kittle *v.* متحیر کردن motehay~er kardan
kittle *v.* قلقلک دادن qelqelak dâdan
kitty (cat) *n.* پیشی pishi

kleenex *n.* دستمال کاغذی dastmâl kâqazi
kleptomani *n.* مرض دزدی maraz-e' dozdi
knack *n.* قلق qeleq لم lem
knapsack *n.* کوله پشتی kuleh poshti پشتواره posht-vâreh
knave *n.* بچه سرباز bach~eh sarbâz متقلب moteqal~eb
knead *vt.* مالش دادن mâlesh dâdan ورزیدن varzidan
knee *n., vt., vi.* زانو zânu
kneecap *n.* کاسهٔ زانو kâseh-ye' zânu
kneel *vi., n.* زانو زدن zânu zadan
kneepad *n.* زانوبند zânu-band
knicknack *n.* خرده چیز khordeh chiz هله هوله haleh huleh
knife *n.* چاقو châqu کارد kârd گزلیک gazlik
knight *n., vt.* شوالیه shovâlieh سلحشور salah-shur
knit *vt., vi., n.* بافتن bâftan
knitted *adj.* بافته bâfteh کشباف kesh-bâf
knitting *n., v.* بافتنی bâftani
knob *n., vt.* دستگیره dastgireh کپه kopeh
knock *v.* کوچک گرفتن kuchek gereftan
knock *v.* در زدن dar zadan کوبیدن kubidan
knot *n., vt., vi.* گره زدن gereh zadan
knotted *adj., v.* گره دار gereh-dâr پیچیده pichideh
knotty *adj.* پرگره por-gereh
know *vt., vi., n.* دانستن dânestan بلد بودن balad budan
know-how *n.* مهارت mahârat راه و چاه râh-o châh
know-it-all *np., n., adj.* پرمدعا por mod~e'â
know-nothing *n., adj.* نفهم nafahm نادان nâdân
knowing *adj., v.* هوشیار hushyâr فهمیده fahmideh پرمعنی porma'nâ
knowingly *adv.* هوشیارانه hush-yârâneh عمداً 'amdan
knowledge *n.* دانش dânesh معرفت ma'refat علم 'elm فضل fazl
knowledgeable *adj.* دانشمند dânesh-mand عالم 'âlem
فاضل fâzel با اطلاع bâ-'et~elâ'
knuckle *n., vt.* بند انگشت bând-e' angosht
kosher *adj., n., vt.* حلال halâl پاک شده pâk shodeh شایسته shâyesteh
kujube *n.* عناب 'an~âb

L L L

label *v.* علامت گذاشتن 'alâmat gozâshtan
label *v.* برچسب زدن bar-chasb zadan
labial *adj., n.* لبی labi
labor *n., vi., vt.* زحمت کشیدن zahmat keshidan کارکردن kâr kardan
زایمان zâyemân
labor of love *np.* کارلذت بخش kâr-e' lez~at-baksh
laboratory *n., adj.* آزمایشگاه âzmâyesh-gâh
laborer *n.* کارگر kârgar عمله 'amaleh
laborious *adj.* پرمشقت por masheq~at
labyrinth *n.* پیچ پیچک pich pichak
مسئلهٔ بغرنج mas'aleh-ye' boq-ran
lace *n., vt., vi.* بند band نوار navâr حاشیه hâshieh
lacerate *v.* پاره کردن pâreh kardan
lacerate *v.* جریحه دارکردن jâriheh-dâr kardan
laceration *n.* پارگی pâregi دریدگی daridegi
lachrymal *adj., n.* اشکدان ashk-dân اشک آور ashk-âvar
lacing *n., v.* بند اندازی band-andâzi
lack *v.* کمبود داشتن kambud dâshtan
lack *n., vt., vi.* عدم 'adam فقدان feqdân
lackadaisical *adj.* بی قیدوبند bi-qyed-o band بی غم bi-qam'
لاابالی lâ-obâli
lackluster *adj., n.* بینوری binuri
lacky *n.* نوکر nokar پادو pâdo
laconic *adj.* کم حرف و دقیق kam harf va daqiq
lacquer *n., vt.* لاک الکل lâk alkol
lad(die) *n.* پسربچه pesar bach~eh
ladder *n., vt., vi.* نردبان nardebân
lade *vt., vi.* بار کردن bâr kardan
laden *adj., vt.* پربار por-bâr
ladle *n., vt.* ملا قه malâqeh
lady *n., adj.* خانم khânom بانو bânu
lady in waiting *n.* ندیمه nadimeh
lady-killer *n.* زن کش zan-kosh جذاب jaz~âb
ladybug *n.* پینه دوز pineh-duz
lag *vt., n.* کند رفتن kond raftan عقب افتادن 'aqab oftâdan
laggard *n., adj.* کندرو kond-ro
lagoon *n.* خلیجک khalijak مرداب mordab

laid-up *n.* ازکارافتاده az kâr oftâdeh

lair *n., vi., vt.* لانه lâneh آشيانه âshiâneh

laissez-faire *adj.* اختيار آزادی ekhtiâr âzâdi

lake *n.* درياچه daryâcheh

lamb *n., vi.* بره bar~eh

lambast(e) *n.* توبيخ کردن tobikh kardan کتک زدن kotak zadan

lambent *adj.* شعلهٔ ملايم sho'leh-ye' molâyem

lambskin *n.* پوست بره pust-e' bar~eh

lame *n., adj., vt.* لنگ کردن lang kardan

lame duck *np.* بی قدرت bi-qodrat

lament *vt., vi., n.* عزاگرفتن 'azâ gereftan
متاسف بودن moteas~ef budan

lamentable *adj.* اسفناک asafnâk رقت آور req~at-âvar

laminate *vt., vi., adj., n.* ورقه ورقه کردن varaqeh varaqeh kardan

lamp *n., vt.* چراغ cherâq لامپ lâmp

lampoon *n., vt.* هجو کردن hajv kardan انتقاد فکاهی enteqâd-e' fokâhi

lamppost *n.* تير چراغ برق tir-e' cherâq barq

lance *n., vt.* نيزه زدن neyzeh zadan نيشتر زدن nishtar zadan

lancer *n.* نيزه دار neyzeh-dâr

land *v.* نشاندن neshândan فرود آمدن forud âmadan

land *n.* سر زمين sar-zamin خشکی khoshki ملک molk ارض arz

land mine *np.* مين min بمب زيرجاده bomb-e' zir-e' jâd~eh

land-grabber *n.* زمينخوار zamin-khor

land-grant *n.* زمين اعطايی zamin-e' e'tâ'i

landau *n.* درشکه doroshkeh

landholder *n.* صاحب زمين sâheb zamin

landing *n.* نشست neshast ورود به خشکی vorud beh khoshki

landing gear *np.* چرخ هواپيما charkh-e' havâpeymâ

landlady *n.* صاحبخانهٔ زن sâheb-khâneh-ye' zan

landlocked *adj.* زمين بست zamin-bast
محصور در خشکی mahsur dar khoshki

landlord *n.* صاحبخانهٔ مرد sâheb-khâneh-ye' mard

landmark *n.* زمين نشان zamin neshân
واقعهٔ تاريخی vâqe'eh-ye' târikhi

landowner *n.* زميندار zamin-dâr

landscape *n., vt., vi.* چشم انداز cheshm-andâz

landscape *n., vt., vi.* چمن کاری کردن chaman-kâri kardan

landslide *n., vi.* لغزش زمينی laqzesh-e' zamini

lane *n.* باریکراه bârik-râh کوی kuy خط khat‿ ردیف radif
langor *n.* سستی sosti کندی kondi فتور fotur
language *n.* زبان zabân
languid *adj.* بیحالت bi-hâlat ریقو riqu
languish *vi., n.* بیحال شدن bi-hâl shodan
پژمرده شدن pazh-mordeh shodan
languor *n.* سستی sosti ضعف za'f
lanky *n.* دراز derâz بیقواره bi-qavâreh
lantern *n.* فانوس fânus
lap *v.* شلپ کردن sholop sholop kardan
lap *v.* لیس زدن lis-lis zadan
lap *vt., vi., n.* دور کامل dor-e' kâmel
lap *vt., vi., n.* دامن dâman روی زانو ruy-e' zânu
lapel *n.* یقه yaqeh
lapse *n., vi.* لغزش کردن laqzesh kardan گذشتن gozashtan
lapse *n., vi.* گذشت gozasht سپری شدن separi- shodan
larceny *n.* دزدی dozdi سرقت serqat
larder *n.* خوراک خانه khorâk khâneh انباری anbâri
lardy *adj.* چرب charb
lare *n.* مادیان mâdiân
large *adj., n., adv.* بزرگ bozorg وسیع vasi'
دست و دل باز dast-o del bâz
large-minded *adj.* آزادفکر âzâd-fekr
large-scale *adj.* بزرگ شده bozorg shodeh وسیع vasi'
largely *adv.* اصولاً osulan بیشتر bishtar
largess(e) *n.* بخشش bakhshesh بخشندگی bakhshandegi
lark *n., vi.* چکاوک chakâvak
larva *n.* کرم حشره kerm-e' hashareh کرمینه kermineh
laryngal *n.* حنجرهای hanjareh-i
laryngitis *n.* گلو سرخی galu sorkhi
larynx *n.* گلوگاه galugâh حنجره hanjareh
lascivious *adj.* شهوانی shahvâni شهوت انگیز shahvat-angiz
lash *n., vt., vi.* شلاق زدن shal‿âq zadan مژه mozheh زخم zakhm
lash out *n.* توبیخ کردن tobikh kardan ضربت زدن zarbat zadan
lass(ie) *n.* جوان دختر javân dokhtar
lasso *n., vt.* کمند انداختن kamand andâkhtan
last *v.* دوام آوردن davâm âvardan طول کشیدن tul keshidan
last *adj., n., vi.* آخرین âkharin پیش pish گذشته gozashteh

last night *n.* دیشب dishab پرندوش parandush
lasting *adj., n.* بادوام bâ-davâm همیشگی hamishegi پایدار pâydâr
latch *n., vt., vi.* چفت انداختن cheft andâkhtan
late *adj., adv.* فقید faqid مرحوم marhum
late *adj., adv.* اخیر akhir
late *adj., adv.* دیر dir
lately *adv.* اخیراً akhiran تازگی tâzegi
latent *adj.* پنهانی panhâni درنهان dar nahân
later *adj., adv.* بعداً ba'dan دیرتر dirtar سپس sepas
lateral *adj., n., vi.* پهلویی pahluyi ضلعی zel'i
latex *n.* شیره shireh براق bar~âq
lath *n., vt.* توفال tufâl
lathe *n., vt.* دستگاه تراش کاری dastgâh-e' tarâsh kâri
lather *n., vi., vt.* کف کردن kaf kardan صابون زدن sâbun zadan
Latin *n., adj.* لاتین lâtin
latitude *n.* پهنای جغرافیایی pahnâ-ye' joqrâfiâyi آزادی âzâdi
latrine *n.* مستراح mostarâh
latter *adj.* دومی dov~omi نیمهٔ دوم nimeh-ye' dov~om آخری âkhâri مؤخر mo'akh~ar
lattice *n., vt.* داربست مشبک dârbast-e' moshab~ak
laud *vt., n.* حمد کردن hamd kardan ستایش setâyesh
laudable *n.* قابل ستایش qâbel-e' setâyesh ستوده sotudeh
laugh *vi., vt., n.* خندیدن khandidan
laugh (at) *n.* مسخره کردن maskhareh kardan
laugh(off) *n.* باخنده رد کردن bâ-khandeh rad kardan
laughable *adj.* خنده دار khandeh-dâr مسخره mas-khareh
laughing *n., adj.* خنده‌کن khandeh-kon خنده‌آور khandeh-âvar
laughing stock *n.* آلت خنده âlat-e' khandeh
laughingly *adv.* باخنده bâ-khandeh بشوخی beshukhi
laughter *n.* خنده khandeh
launch *v.* پرتاب کردن par tâb kardan
به آب انداختن beh-âb andâkhtan
launch *v.* بکارانداختن be-kâr andâkhtan
launder *vt., vi., n.* شستن و اطو کردن shostan va otu kardan
laundry *n.* رخت شستنی rakht shostani
laureate *adj., n.* برگ تاج barg-tâj عالیقدر 'âliqadr علامه 'al~âmeh
laurel *n., vt.* درخت غار derakht-e' qâr
lava *n.* گدازه godâzeh آتش‌آب âtash-âb

lavatory *n.* دستشویی dast-shuyi

lave *adj., n., v.* شستن shostan غوطه ور کردن quteh-var kardan

lavender *n.* ارغوانی arqavâni

lavish *v.* پرتجمل بودن por tajam~ol budan

lavish *v.* ولخرجی کردن velkharji kardan

law *adj., adv., n., int.* قانون qânun شریعت shari'at

law-abiding *adj.* پیروقانون peyro-e' qânun

lawbook *n.* قانون نامه qânun-nâmeh

lawbreaker *n.* قانون شکن qânun-shekan

lawful *adj.* قانونی qânuni مشروع mashru'

lawgiver *n.* قانون گذار qânun-gozâr

lawless *adj.* بی قانون bi-qânun متمرد motemar~ed

lawlessness *n.* بیقانونی bi-qânuni تمرد tamar~od

lawmaker *n.* قانون ساز qânun-sâz

lawman *n.* مامورقانون mamur-e' qânun

lawn *n.* چمن chaman

lawnmower *n.* چمن زن chaman-zan

lawsuit *n.* دادخواهی da'vâ دعوی dâd-khâhi

lawyer *n.* حقوقدان vakil وکیل hoquqdân

lax *adj.* شل shol سست sost

lax *adj.* شل گیر shol-gir آسان گیر âsân-gir

laxative *n., adj.* ملین molay~en لینت دهنده linat-dahandeh

laxity *n.* شلی sholi سستی sosti لینت آسانگیری linat âsân-giri

lay *v.* خواباندن khâbândan قراردادن qarâr dâdan

lay *v.* گذاشتن gozâshtan

lay (aside) *n.* کنار گذاشتن kenâr gozâshtan

lay (away) *n.* کنارگذاشتن kenâr gozâshtan

lay (down) *n.* فداکردن fadâ kardan اعلان کردن e'lân kardan

lay (it on) *n.* رک گفتن rok goftan

lay (off) *n.* دست برداشتن dast bar dâshtan

lay away *n.* پس اندازکردن pas-andâz kardan

lay off *n.* بیکارکردن bi-kâr kardan

lay(out) *n.* پهن کردن pahn kardan خرج کردن kharj kardan

lay(over) *n.* توقف کردن tavaq~of kardan

lay-off *n.* بیکاری bi-kâri اخراج ekhrâj

layer *n., vt.* ورقه varaqeh لایه lâyeh

layman *n.* عامه 'âm~eh عادی 'âd~i

layout *n.* نقشه naqsheh برنامه barnâmeh طرح tarh

layover *n.* توقف tavaq~ of
laze *vi., vt., n.* تنبل بودن tanbal budan
lazy *adj.* تنبل tanbal
lazy bones *n.* تنبل باشی tanbal-bâshi
lazy bum *n.* تن لش tan-e' lash
leach *vt., vi., n.* آبکشی کردن âb-keshi kardan آب نشست âb-neshast
lead *V.* رهبری کردن rahbari kardan
lead *vt., adj., vi., n.* جلویی jeloyi پیشقدمی pish-qadami
lead *V.* راهنمایی کردن râhnami kardan
lead *vt., adj., vi., n.* سرب sorb
lead *vt., adj., vi., n.* هدایت کردن hedâyat kardan
lead *vt., adj., vi., n.* ردپا rad-e' pâ سرمشق sarmashq
lead(en) *n.* سربی sorbi
lead-off *adj.* مقدمی moqad~ ami
leader *n.* رهبر rahbar پیشوا pishvâ سردسته sar-dasteh
leadership *n.* رهبری rahbari ریاست riâsat
leading *adj., n.* رهنمایی rahnamâyi نخست nakhost مهم mohem
leading article *np.* سرمقاله sar-maqâleh
leaf *n., vi., vt.* برگ barg ورقه varaqeh
leaflet *n.* دست نامه dastnâmeh اعلانیه e'lâniyeh
leafy *adj.* برگدار barg-dâr پربرگ por-barg
league *n., vt., vi.* اتحادیه et~ ehâdieh پیمان peymân فرسنگ farsang
leaguer *vt., n.* انجمنی anjomani
leak *vi., vt.* چکه کردن chek~ eh kardan تراوش کردن tarâvosh kardan
leakage *n.* سوراخ شدگی surâkh shodegi آب پسی âb-pasi نشت nasht
leaky *n.* سوراخدار surâkh-dâr چکه کن chek~ eh-kon رازگو râz-gu
leal *adj.* باوفا bâ-vafâ راستگو râst-gu
lean *v.* تکیه دادن takyeh dâdan تکیه کردن takyeh kardan
lean *adj., n., vi., vt.* لاغر lâqar بی چربی bi-charbi
lean *v.* مایل شدن mâyel shodan
leaning *n.* تمایل tamâyol مایل mâyel
leap *vi., vt., n.* پریدن paridan جستن jestan
leap year *np.* سال کبیسه sâl-e' kabiseh
leapfrog *n., vt., vi.* جفتک چارکش joftak chârkosh
                  شلنگ تخته shelang-takhteh
learn *vt., vi.* یاد گرفتن yâd gereftan آموختن âmukhtan
learned *adj., v.* دانا dânâ عالم 'âlem دانشمند dânesh-mand
learning *n.* یادگیری yâd-giri آموزش âmuzesh

lease

lease *n., vt., vi.* اجاره کردن ejâreh kardan اجاره‌دادن ejâreh dâdan
leaseholder *n.* مستاجر mosta'jer
leash *n., vt.* افسار بستن afsâr bastan
leasing *n., v.* اجاره ejâreh دروغ doruq
least *adj., n., adv.* کمترین kamtarin
leather(y) *n.* چرمی charmi
leave *v.* ترک کردن tark kardan باقی گذاردن bâqi gozârdan
leave *vt., vi.* مرخصی morkhasi اجازه ejâzeh
leave *v.* ول کردن vel kardan
leave of absence *np.* مرخصی morkhasi
leaven *n., vt.* خمیرمایه khamir mâyeh خمیرترش khamir torsh
lecher(ous) *n.* شهوت پرست shahvat-parast فاسق fâseq
lechery *n.* شهوت پرستی shahvat-parast فسق fesq
lectern *n.* تریبون teribun میز خطابه miz-e' khatâbeh
lecture *n., vi., vt.* سخنرانی کردن sokhanrâni kardan
lecturer *n.* سخنران sokhanrân
ledge *n., vt.* لبه labeh طاقچه tâqcheh هره her~eh
ledger *n.* دفترکل daftar-e' kol~
lee *n., adj.* پناهگاه panâh-gâh بادپناه bâd-panâh
leech *n., vt., vi.* زالو zâlu
leek *n.* تره tareh
leer *v.* چشم چرانی کردن cheshm-charani kardan
leer *v.* هیزچشمی کردن hiz-cheshmi kardan
lees *n.* رسوب rosub درد dord
leeway *n.* باد جهتی bâd jahati فرجه forjeh
left *adj., v., n., adv.* چپ chap
left-handed *adj., adv.* چپ دست chap dast
leftist *n., adj.* چپی chapi چپ رو chap-ro
leftover *n., adj.* مانده mândeh بیات bayât
lefty *n., adj., adv.* چپول chapul
leg *n., vt.* پا pâ ساقه sâqeh پایه pâyeh پاچه pâcheh
leg work *n.* پیاده روی piâdeh-ravi سگ دو sag-do
legacy *n.* میراث mirâs بازمانده bâz-mândeh مرده ریگ mordeh rig
legal *adj., n.* قانونی qânuni حقوقی hoquqi مشروع mashru'
legal tender *np.* وجه قانونی vajh-e' qânuni
legality *n.* قانونی بودن qânuni budan
legalization *n.* رسمیت rasmiyat قانونی شدن qânuni-shodan
legalize *vt.* قانونی کردن qânuni kardan

legally *adv.* قانوناً qânunan
legate *n.* نماینده namâyandeh سفیر safir
legation *n.* نمایندگی namâyandegi سفارت خانه sefârat-khâneh

legend *n.* افسانه afsâneh
legendary *adj., n.* افسانه ای afsâneh-i
legendry *n.* افسانه ها afsâneh-hâ
legible *adj.* خوانا khânâ واضح vâzeh
legion *n.* گروه goruh هنگ hang
legionary *adj., n.* هنگی hangi سرباز sarbâz
legislate *vi., vt.* قانون گذاری کردن qânun-gozâri kardan
legislation *n.* قانون گذاری qânun-gozâri
legislator *n.* قانون گذار qânun-gozâr
legislature *n.* هیئت مقننه hey'at-e' moqananeh
legit *adj., n.* قانونی qânuni
legitimacy *n.* قانونی بودن qânuni-budan حلال زادگی halâl-zâdegi
legume *n.* سبزی sabzi نخودلوبیا nokhod lubiâ
lei *n., pl.* حلقه گل halqeh gol
leisure *n., adj.* فراغت farâqat آسودگی âsudegi
leisurely *adj., adv.* خوش خوشک khosh-khoshak
سرفرصت sar-e' forsat
lemon *n., adj.* لیمو limu بنجل bonjol
lemonade *n.* آبلیمو âb-limu لیموناد limunâd
lend *vt., vi.* قرض دادن qarz dâdan وام دادن vâm dâdan
lender *n.* قرض دهنده qarz-dahandeh وام ده vâm-deh
length *n.* درازا derâzâ طول tul مدت mod~at اندازه andâzeh
lengthen *vt., vi.* دراز کردن derâz kardan طولانی کردن tulâni kardan
lengthwise *adv., adj.* از درازا az derâzâ
lengthy *adj.* دراز derâz طویل tavil مفصل mofas~al
leniency *n.* آسانگیری âsân-giri نرمی narmi دلرحمی del-rahmi
lenient *adj.* آسانگیر âsân-gir نرم narm دل رحم del-rahm
lens *n.* عدسی 'adasi
lentil *n.* عدس 'adas
leopard *n.* پلنگ palang
leotard *n.* شلواربالـه shalvâr-e' bâleh
leper *n.* جذامی jozâmi
leprosy *n.* جذام jozâm آکله âkeleh
leprous *adj.* جذامی jozâmi

lesbian *n.* زن همجنس باز zan-e' ham-jens bâz طبق زن tabaq-zan لحاقه lahâqeh

lesion *n.* زخم zakhm زیان ziân

less *adv., adj., n., pre.* کمتر kam-tar منهای menhâ-ye'

lessee *n.* مستاجر mosta'jer

lessen *vi., vt.* کمتر کردن kam-tar kardan

lesser *adj.* کمتر kam-tar کوچکتر kuchek-tar

lesson *n., vt.* درس dars عبرت 'ebrat

lessor *n.* اجاره دهنده ejâreh dahandeh مؤجر mo'jer

lest *con.* مبادا که mabâdâ keh

let *n., v.* اجازه دادن ejâzeh dâdan

let (alone) *n.* بحال خود گذاشتن be-hâl-e' khod gozâshtan

let alone *n.* چه برسد به cheh beresad beh

let(by) *n.* اجازهٔ عبوردادن ejâzeh-ye' 'obur dâdan

let(down) *n.* پایین آوردن pâyin âvardan مایوس کردن mayus kardan

let(in on) *n.* تو آوردن tu âvardan همراز کردن hamrâz kardan

let(off) *n.* بیرون دادن birun dâdan ندیده گرفتن nadideh gereftan

let(on) *n.* وانمود کردن vânemud kardan

let(out) *n.* مرخص کردن morkhas kardan بیرون دادن birun dâdan

let(up on) *n.* دست برداشتن dast bar dâshtan

let(up) *n.* آهسته کرد âhesteh kardan

letdown *n.* کنفی kenefi بزیاری boz-biâri

lethal *adj.* کشنده koshandeh مرگ آور marg-âvar

lethargic *adj.* خمار khomâr بیحال bi-hâl سباتی sobati

lethargy *n.* خماری khomâri بیحالی bi-hâli

letter *n., vt., vi.* نامه nâmeh حرف harf نوشته neveshteh مکتوب maktub

letter carrier *np.* نامه بر nâmeh-bar

lettered *adj.* باسواد bâ-savâd حروفی horufi

letterhead *n.* سرکاغذ sar kâqaz

lettuce *n.* کاهو kâhu

letup *n.* تقلیل taqlil

leucoma *n.* سفید چشمی sefid cheshmi

leukemia *n.* سرطان خون saratân-e' khun

levee *n., vt.* سیلگیر seyl-gir خاکگیر khâk-gir

level *v.* یک سطح کردن yek sat-h kardan

level *adj., n., vt., vi.* هموار hamvâr مسطح mosat~ah تراز tarâz

level *v.* هموار کردن hamvâr kardan

lever *n.* اهرم ahrom ميله mileh دسته dasteh
leverage *n.* نيروی اهرمی niru-ye' ahromi نفوذ nofuz
levis *n.* شلوار كابوی shalvâr kâboyi
levitate *vi., vt.* اززمين بلند كردن az zamin boland kardan
levy *n., vt., vi.* ماليات وضع كردن mâliyât vaz' kardan
lewd *adj.* بيشرم bi-sharm شنيع shani' هرزه harzeh
lewd behavior *n.* حركت وقيحانه harekat-e' vaqihâneh
lewdness *n.* هرزگی harzegi وقاحت veqâhat بيشرمی bi-sharmi
lexical *adj.* واژه ای vâzheh-i
lexicon *n.* واژه‌ها vâzheh hâ
liability *n.* بدهی bedehi مسئوليت mas'uliyat بضرر be-zarar
liable *adj.* مسئول mas'ul موظف movaz~af ممكن momken
liaison *n.* رابط râbet واسطه vâseteh
liar *adj.* دروغگو doruq-gu كاذب kâzeb چاخان châkhân
libel *n., vt.* تهمتی tohmati افترا efterâ
libelous *adj.* آبروبر âberu-bar بدنام كننده bad-nâm konandeh
liberal *adj.* آزادفكر âzâd-fekr آزاديخواه âzâdi-khâh
گشاده دل goshâdeh-del نظربلند nazar boland
liberalize *vt., vi.* آزاديخواه كردن âzâdi-khâh kardan
آزادفكری âzâd-fekri
liberate *vt.* آزاد كردن âzâd kardan
liberated *adj.* آزادشده âzâd-shodeh وارسته vâ-rasteh
liberation *n.* آزادی âzâdi رهايی rahâyi
liberator *n.* آزادكننده âzâd konandeh رهايی بخش rahâyi-bakhsh
libertine *n., adj.* بی بند و بار bi-band-o bâr
liberty *n.* آزادی âzâdi بااجازه bâ-ejâzeh
libido *n.* غريزهٔ جنسی qarizeh-ye' jensi
library *n.* كتابخانه ketâb-khâneh
librate *vi.* توازن داشتن tavâzon dâshtan
lice *n., pl.* شپش shepesh
license *n., vt.* پروانه parvâneh جواز دادن javâz dâdan
licensee *n.* پروانه دار parvâneh-dâr صاحب جواز sâheb-e' javâz
lichen *n., vt.* گل سنگ gol-sang
lick *vt., n.* ليسيدن lisidan غلبه كردن qalabeh kardan
lickety-split *adv.* باسرعت زياد bâ-sor'at ziâd
lid *n.* در dar سرپوش sarpush پلك pelk
lie *v.* واقع شدن vâqe' shodan قراركرفتن qarâr gereftan
lie *v.* دروغ گفتن doruq goftan

lie *n.* دروغ doruq کذب kezb
lie(down) *n.* درازکشیدن derâz keshidan خوابیدن khâbidan
lien *n.* حبس ملکی habs-e' melki
lieu *n.* عوض 'avaz جا jâ
lieutenant *n.* ستوان sot-vân
lieutenant colonel *np.* سرهنگ دو sarhang-do
lieutenant general *np.* سپهبد sepahbod
life *n., adj.* زندگی zendegi جان jân عمر 'omr حیات hayât
life cycle *np.* گردش زندگی gardesh-e' zendegi
life expectancy *np.* طول عمر tul-e' 'omr
life giving *n.* جان بخشی jân-bakhshi
life guard *n.* غریق نجات qariq nejât
life insurance *np.* بیمهٔ عمر bimeh-ye' 'omr
life line *np.* طناب نجات tanâb-e' nejât مسیرحیاتی masir-e' hayâti
life of the party *n.* نقل مجلس noql-e' majles
life perserver *n.* نیم تنهٔ غریق نجات nim-taneh-ye' qariq nejât
life size *n.* هم قد ham-qad
lifeboat *n.* قایق نجات qâyeq nejât
lifeless *adj.* بیجان bi-jân
lifelike *adj.* زندهنما zendeh-namâ
lifelong *adj.* تمام عمر tamâm-e' 'omr
lifer *n.* حبس ابدی habs-e' abadi
lifesaver *n.* ناجی nâji
lifesaving *adj., n.* نجات دهندگی nejât dahandegi
lifetime *n., adj.* مدت زندگی mod~at-e' zendegi
lift *vt., vi., n.* بلند کردن boland kardan بالا بردن bâlâ bordan
ligament *n.* پیوند peyvand غضروف qozruf
ligerie *n.* لباس خواب زنانه lebâs khâb-e' zanâneh
light *adj., n., v., vi.* چراغ cherâq روشن roshan نور nur
light *adj., n., v., vi.* سبک sabok
light *adj., n., v., vi.* روشن کردن roshan kardan
light(up) *n.* آتش زدن âtash zadan نشاط دادن neshât dâdan
light-foot(ed) *n.* سبک پا sabok-pâ
light-handed *adj.* تردست tar-dast سبک دست sabok-dast
light-minded *adj.* بی فکر bi-fekr دمدمی damdami
light-year *n.* سال نوری sâl-e' nuri
lighten *v.* سبک کردن sabok kardan تخفیف دادن takhfif dâdan
lighten *v.* روشن کردن roshan kardan

lighter *n., vt.* فندک fandak
lighthouse *n.* برج فانوس دار borj-e' fânus dâr
lighting *n., vi.* روشنایی roshanâyi
lightly *adv.* نرمک نرمک narmak narmak به غفلت beh-qeflat
lightness *n.* سبکی saboki ظریفی zarifi
lightning *v.* رعدوبرق ra'd-o barq صاعقه sâ'eqeh آذرخش âzarakhsh
lightning rod *np.* صاعقه گیر sâ'eqeh-gir
lightweight *adj., n.* سبک وزن sabok-vazn
ligitimate *n.* قانونی qânuni حلال زاده halâl-zâdeh
ligneous *adj.* چوبی chubi
likable *adj.* دوست داشتنی dust dâshtani
like *v.* دوست داشتن dust dâshtan میل داشتن meyl dâshtan
like *adj., pre., adv., con.* مثل mesl-e' مانند mânand-e' شبیه shabih-e'
like-minded *adj.* هم عقیده ham-'aqideh
likelihood *n.* احتمال ehtemâl امکان emkân
likely *adj., adv.* احتمالی ehtemâli
liken *vt.* تشبیه کردن tashbih kardan
likeness *n.* شباهت shebâhat کپی kopi مانند mânand نظیر nazir
likewise *adv.* همین جور hamin-jur متقابلاً moteqâbelan
liking *n., v.* میل meyl تمایل tamây~ol علاقه 'alâqeh
lilac *n., adj.* نیلک nilak
lily *n., adj.* سوسن susan زنبق zanbaq
Lima bean *n.* باقالی bâ-qâli
limb *n.* عضو 'ozu شاخه shâkheh دست و پا dast-o pâ
limber *adj., n., vt., vi.* باانعطاف کردن bâ-en'etâf kardan نرم narm
limbo *n.* هچل hachal
lime *n.* آهک âhak
lime *n.* لیموترش limu torsh
limelight *n.* نورافکن nur-afkan
limestone *n.* سنگ آهک sang-e' âhak
limit *v.* حد گذاشتن had gozâshtan محدودکردن mahdud kardan
limit *n.* حد had~ اندازه andâzeh
limited *adj., n.* محدود mahdud منحصر monhaser مضیق maziq
limitless *adj.* نامحدود nâ-mahdud بی پایان bi-pâyân
limp *adj., vi., n.* لنگیدن langidan شل shol
limpid *adj.* صاف sâf زلال zolâl
limping *adj.* لنگان langân
limy *adj.* آهکی âhaki

linchpin *n.* میخ محوری mikh-e′ mehvari
line *n.* خط khat~ سطر satr صف saf ردیف radif
line *v.* خط کشیدن khat keshidan یک ردیف کردن yek-radif kardan
line up *n.* صف کشیدن saf keshidan
lineage *n.* خاندان khândân دودمان dudmân نسب nasab
lineal *adj.* خطی khat~i موروثی morusi
linear *adj.* خطی khat~i طولی tuli
lineate *adj.* خط خطی khat-khati
linen *n., adj.* کتان katân رخت rakht
linesman *n.* داورکنار dâvar-e′ kenâr خط بان khat-bân
linger *vi., vt.* فس فس کردن fes-fes kardan
lingo *n.* زبان آمیخته zabân-e′ âmikhteh
linguist *n.* زبان شناس zabân-shenâs
linguistic(s) *n.* زبان شناسی zabân-shenâsi
lining *n., v.* آستر âstar
link *n., vt., vi.* بهم پیوستن be-ham peyvastan حلقه halqeh
linkage *n.* پیوند peyvand تسلسل tasalsol اتصال etesâl
linoleum *n.* مشمع mosham~â′
linseed *n.* تخم کتان tokhm-e′ katân
lint *n.* کرک kork
lion *n.* شیر shir
lioness *n.* شیرزن shirzan ماده شیر mâdeh-shir
lionheart(ed) *n.* شیردل shir-del
lip *n., adj., vt.* لب lab لبه labeh گستاخی gostâkhi
lipreading *n.* لب خوانی lab-khâni
lipstick *n.* ماتیک mâtik
liquid *adj., n.* مایع mâye′ آبکی âbaki نقد شدنی naqd shodani
liquidate *vt., vi.* پاک حسابی pâk hesâbi از بین بردن az beyn bordan
liquor *n., vt., vi.* مشروب mashrub نوشابهٔ الکلی nushâbeh-ye′ alkoli
lisp *n., vt., vi.* نوک زبانی حرف زدن nok zabâni harf zadan
list *n.* صورت surat فهرست fehrest
list *v.* صورت دادن surat dâdan فهرست کردن fehrest kardan
list *v.* یکوربودن yek-var budan کجی kaji
list price *np.* قیمت اصلی qeymat-e′ asli
listen *vi., vt.* گوش کردن gush kardan گوش دادن gush dâdan
listen in (on) *n.* دزدکی گوش کردن dozdaki gush kardan
listless *adj.* بیروح bi-ruh
liter *n.* لیتر litr

literacy *n.* باسوادی bâ-savâdi
literal *adj.* حروفی horufi تحت اللفظی taht-ol lafzi
literal-minded *adj.* بی تجسم bi-tajas~om
literalize *vt.* حروفی کردن horufi kardan
literally *adv.* بمعنای واقعی be-ma'nâ-ye' vâqe'i
literary *adj.* ادبی adabi ادیب adib
literature *n.* ادبیات adabiyât
lithe *adj.* نرم narm باانعطاف bâ-en'etâf
lithography *n.* چاپ سنگی châp-e' sangi
litigant *n.* طرف دعوی taraf-e' da'vâ متداعی motedâ'i
متنازع motenâze'
litmus *n.* تورنسل turnosol
litter *v.* آشغال ریختن âshqâl rikhtan ریخت و پاش rikht-o' pâsh
litter *n.* توله tuleh
little *adj., adv., n.* کوچک kuchek کوچولو kuchulu
little by little *n.* کم کم kam-kam
livable *adj.* قابل زندگی qâbel-e' zendegi
live *adj., adv., vi., vt.* زنده zendeh باحال bâ-hâl روشن roshan
live *v.* زندگی کردن zendegi kardan زیستن zistan
زنده بودن zendeh budan
live(in) *n.* خوابکاری khâb-kâri خانهای khâneh-i
live(out) *n.* تاآخر زندگی کردن tâ-âkhar zendegi kardan
live(through) *n.* جان بدر بردن jân bedar bordan
live(well) *n.* خوب زندگی کردن khub zendegi kardan
livelihood *n.* معاش ma'âsh زندگی zendegi معیشت ma'ishat
liveliness *n.* زنده دلی zendeh-deli سرخوشی sar-khoshi
بانشاطی bâ-neshâti
lively *adj., adv.* زنده دل zendeh-del سرخوش sar-khosh
بانشاط bâ-neshât
liven *vt., vi.* زنده کردن zendeh kardan باروح کردن bâruh kardan
liver *n., adj., vi.* جگر jegar کبد kabed
livery stable *np.* اسطبل اسب establ-e' asb
livestock *n.* دام dâm چارپایان اهلی châr-pâyân-e' ahli
livid *adj.* کبود kabud
living *adj., v., n.* زنده zendeh زندگی zendegi
living death *np.* زندگی فلاکتبار zendegi-e' falâkat-bâr
living picture *np.* عکس زنده 'aks-e' zendeh
living room *np.* مهمان خانه mehmân-khâneh

lixiviate *vt.* آبگیری کردن âb-giri kardan
lizard *n.* مارمولک mârmulak بزمجه boz-mâjeh
load *v.* بار کردن bâr kardan پر کردن por kardan
load *n.* بار bâr سنگینی sangini
loaded *adj.* پربار por-bâr پولدار puldâr
loaf *n.* قرص qors کله قند kal~eh-qand
loaf *v.* الافی کردن alâfi kardan ولگردی کردن velgardi kardan
loafer *n.* الاف al~âf ولگرد velgard ارسی orsi
loam *n., vt.* کود خاک kud khâk
loan *n., vt., vi.* قرض qarz وام vâm عاریه دادن 'âriyeh dâdan
loan applicant *n.* وام خواه vâm-khah
loan shark *np.* کلاش kal~âsh رباخوار rebâ-khâr
loan word *np.* کلمهٔ اقتباسی kalameh-ye' eqtebâsi
loath *adj.* ناراضی nâ-râzi بی میل bi-meyl
loathe *vt.* نفرت داشتن nefrat dâshtan بیزاربودن bi-zâr budan
loathing *n., vt.* تنفر tanaf~or نفرت nefrat بیزاری bizâri
loathsome *adj.* نفرت انگیز nefrat-angiz
lob *vt., vi., n.* هوایی انداختن hâvâyi andâkhtan
lobby *n., vi., vt.* پیش اطاق pish-otâq راهرو râhro سرسرا sarsarâ
lobbyist *n.* رأی گیر ra'y-gir هواخواه لایحه havâ khâh-e' lâyeheh
lobe *n.* نرمه narmeh پره pareh
lobotomy *n.* جراحی مغز jar~âhi-e' maqz
lobster *n.* خرچنگ kharchang کلنجار kalan-jâr
local *adj., n.* محلی mahal~i بومی bumi موضعی moze'i
locality *n.* محل mahal موضع moze' مکان makân
localize *vt., vi.* محلی کردن mahal~i kardan
محدود کردن mahdud kardan
locally *adv.* درمحل dar-mahal
locate *vt., vi.* جا نشان دادن jâ neshân dâdan قرار دادن qarâr dâdan
location *n.* جا jâ محل mahal مکان makân
locative *adj., n.* مکان صرفی makân sarfi
loch *n.* دریاچه daryâ-cheh
lock *v.* قفل کردن qofl kardan
lock *n.* قفل qofl سدچهٔ کانال sadcheh-ye' kânâl
lock(out) *n.* قفل بست کردن qofl bast kardan
lock(up) *n.* بعدازهمه قفل کردن ba'd az hameh qofl kardan
lock(up) *n.* حبس کردن habs kardan
locker *n.* رخت کن rakht-kan صندوق sandoq

locker room *np.* اطاق رختکنی otâq-e' rakht-kani
locket *n.* گردن بند gardan-band
lockjaw *n.* کزاز kozâz
locksmith *n.* قفلساز qofl-sâz چلنگر chalan-gar
loco *n., vt., adj.* خودرو khodro
locomotion *n.* نیروی حرکت niru-ye' harekat
locus *n.* جا jâ دستگاه dast-gâh
locust *n.* ملخ malakh
locution *n.* عبارت سازی 'ebârat sâzi شیوهٔ صحبت shiveh-ye' sohbat
lode *n.* رگه rageh
lodge *n.* منزل manzel کلبه kolbeh
lodge *v.* عرضحال دادن 'arz-e' hâl dâdan
lodge *v.* منزل دادن manzel dâdan
lodge *v.* گیرکردن gir kardan
lodging *n., v.* جا jâ اقامت eqâmat
loft *n., vt., vi.* اطاق زیر شیروانی otâq-e' zir-e' shirvâni
lofty *adj.* بلند boland متکبرانه motekab~erâneh
log *n.* کنده kondeh هیزم hizom تنه taneh
log *v.* یادداشت کردن yâd-dâsht kardan ثبت کردن sabt kardan
logarithm *n.* لگاریتم logâritm
loge *n.* لژ lozh
logger *adj., n.* درخت بر derakht-bor
loggerhead *n.* کودن kodan
logging *n., v.* درخت بری derakht-bori
logic *n.* منطق manteq
logical *adj.* منطقی manteqi
logistic *n., adj.* محاسبهای mohâsebeh-i
logo *n.* علامت ویژه 'alâmat-e' vizheh آرم ârm
loin(s) *n.* گرده gordeh کمر kamar
loiter *vi., vt.* پرسه زدن parseh zadan الاف گشتن al~âf gashtan
loll *vi., vt., n.* لم دادن lam dâdan آویزان بودن âvizân budan
lollipop *n.* خروس قندی khorus qandi
lone *adj.* تک tak تنها tanhâ
lonely *adj.* تنها tanhâ بی کس bikas
loner *n.* تنها tanhâ تکرو takro
lonesome *adj., n.* گوشه گیر gusheh-gir
دلتنگ کننده deltang konandeh
long *v.* درحسرت بودن dar hasrat budan آرزوداشتن ârezu dâshtan

long *n., adv., vi.* دراز derâz طویل tavil طولانی tulâni بلند boland
long jump *np.* پرش طول paresh-e' tul
long shot *np.* بعید ba'id کم احتمال kam ehtemâl ازدور az dur
long-distance *adj.* مسافت دور masâfat-e' dur
long-faced *adj.* دلخور del-khor پریشان parishân
long-range *adj.* بردبلند bord-e' boland درازمدت derâz mod~at
long-standing *n.* سابقه دار sâbeqeh-dâr
longe *n., vt.* افسار تعلیمی afsâr-e' ta'limi
longevity *n.* عمردراز 'omr-e' derâz
longing *n., adj.* حسرت hasrat اشتیاق eshtiâq
longitude *n.* مدارطولی madâr-e' tuli
longshore *adj.* باراندار bâr-andâz
longshoreman *n.* کارگرباراندار kârgar-e' bâr andâz
lonliness *n.* تنهایی tanhâyi تکی taki
loofah *n.* لیف lif
look *v.* بنظر آمدن be-nazar âmadan
look *v.* نگاه کردن negâh kardan تماشاکردن tamâshâ kardan
look(after) *n.* مواظبت کردن movâzeb~at kardan
look(alive) *n.* حواس جمع داشتن havâs-e' jam' dâshtan
look(back) *n.* بیاد آوردن be-yâd âvardan
look(daggers) *n.* چشم غره رفتن cheshm qor~eh raftan
look(down on/upon) *n.* حقیرشمردن haqir shemordan
پست دانستن past dânestan
look(for) *n.* تعقیب کردن ta'qib kardan جستجو josteju
look(forward to) *n.* مشتاق بودن moshtâq budan
look(in on) *n.* سرزدن sar zadan
look(into) *n.* رسیدگی کردن residegi kardan
look(on) *n.* تماشا کردن tamâshâ kardan
look(out) *n.* مواظب بودن movâz~b budan
look(over) *n.* براندار کردن bar-andâz kardan
look(to) *n.* مواظبت کردن movâzeb~at kardan
منتظر بودن montazer budan
look(up & down) *n.* براندار کردن bar-andâz kardan
look(up to) *n.* احترام گذاشتن ehterâm gozâshtan
look(up) *n.* دنبال گشتن donbâl gashtan بهترشدن behtar shodan
look-in *n.* دید مختصر did-e' mokhtasar تک پا tok-pâ
looker *n.* خوشگل khoshgel
looker-on *n.* تماشاکننده tamâshâ konandeh ناظر nâzer

looking glass *n.* آئینه âyineh

lookout *n.* دیده بان dideh-bân بپا be-pâ

loom *n.* دستگاه بافندگی dast-gâh-e' bâfândegi قاب فرش qâb-e' farsh

loom *v.* نمودارشدن nemudâr shodan پدیدارشدن padidâr shodan

loon *n.* مرغ غواص morq-e' qav~âs

loony *adj., n.* خل khol

loop *n., vt., vi.* حلقه halqeh پیچ pich

loophole *n., vt.* جاسوراخی jâ-surâkhi دررو dar-ro

loose *adj., adv., vt., vi.* لق laq~ شل shol هرز harz گشاد goshâd

loose ends *n.* خرده کاری khordeh-kâri

loose-jointed *adj.* باانعطاف bâ-en'etâf تابشو tâ-besho

loose-tongued *adj.* دهن لق dahan-laq

loot *n., vt., vi.* غارت کردن qârat kardan تاراج کردن târâj kardan

lop *vi., vt., adj., n.* بریدن boridan

loquacious *adj.* ورّاج ver~âj پرحرف por-harf

loquat *n.* گلابی وحشی golâbi-e' vahshi

Lord *n.* خداوند khodâvand

lord *n.* ارباب arbâb لرد lord

lore *n.* دانش dânesh علم 'elm

lorn *adj.* از دست رفته az dast rafteh

lorry *n.* بارکش bâr-kesh کامیون kâmion

lose *v.* گم کردن gom kardan

lose *v.* باختن bâkhtan ازدست دادن az dast dâdan

loser *n.* بازنده bâzandeh بازب bebâz

losing *adj., v., n.* بازنده bâzandeh باخت bâkht

loss *n.* زیان ziân خسارت khesârat

loss *n.* باخت bâkht

loss *n.* ازدست رفتگی az dast raftegi

lost *adj., vt., vi.* گم شده gom shodeh گم گشته gom- gashteh

lot *n., vt., vi., adv.* قرعه qor'eh قسمت qesmat نصیب nasib

lot *n., vt., vi., adv.* قطعه زمین qat'eh zamin

lotion *n.* کرم kerem پماد pomâd

lottery *n.* بخت آزمایی bakht âzmâyi لاتاری lâtâri

lotus *n.* نیلوفرآبی nilufar-e' âbi

loud *adj., adv.* بلند boland پرسروصدا por sar-o sedâ

loud mouthed *n.* دادزن dâd-zan پرسروصدا por sar-o sedâ

loud-speaker *n.* بلندگو boland-gu

louden *vt., vi.* صدابلند کردن sedâ boland kardan

lounge *vi., vt., n.* لم دادن lam dâdan اطاق راحتی otâq-e' râhati
louse *n., vt.* شپش shepesh
louse *n., vt.* پست past
lousy *adj.* گند gand مزخرف mozakhraf
lout *n., vi., vt.* خرفت khereft
lovable *adj.* دوست داشتنی dust dâshtani
love *n.* عشق 'eshq مهر mehr محبت moheb~ât دوستی dusti
love *v.* دوست داشتن dust dâshtan عاشق بودن 'âsheq budan
love affair *np.* عشق و عاشقی 'eshq-o âsheqi
love match *np.* ازدواج عشقی ezdevâj-e' 'eshqi
love potion *np.* اکسیرعشق eksir-e' 'eshq مهردارو mehr daru
love seat *np.* مبل دونفره mobl-e' donafareh
love-making *n.* عشقبازی 'eshq-bâzi
loveless *adj.* بدون محبت bedun-e' moheb~ât
loveliness *n.* جذابی jaz~âbi دلربایی del-robâyi
lovelorn *adj.* دل شکسته del-shekasteh
lovely *adj., n., adv.* دوست داشتنی dust dâshtani
lover *n.* معشوقه ma'shuqeh
lover *n.* عاشق âsheq
lovesick *adj.* عشق زده 'eshq-zadeh مجنون majnun
loving *adj., v.* محبت آمیز moheb~at-âmiz
low *adj., vi., adv., n.* افسرده afsordeh
low *adj., vi., adv., n.* پست past بم bam
low *adj., vi., adv., n.* نازل nâzel کم بینی kam-bini
low *adj., vi., adv., n.* کوتاه kutâh پایین pâyin
low-brow *n.* بی تربیت bi-tarbiyat
low-class *n.* طبقه پایین tabaqeh pâyin فرومایه foru-mâyeh
low-cost *adj.* کم خرج kam-kharj
low-down *np., n., adj.* پست past فرومایه foru-mâyeh
low-frequency *adj.* بسامد کوتاه basâmad-e' kutâh
low-grade *adj.* نامرغوب nâ-marqub
low-minded *adj.* وقیح vaqih
low-pressure *adj.* کم فشاری kam feshâri
low-tide *n.* جزر jazr
lower *adj.* زیرین zirin پایین تر pâyin-tar
lower *v.* کم کردن kam kardan
lower *v.* پایین آوردن pâyin âvardan
lower *n.* تحتانی tahtâni سفلی soflâ

lower *v.* بم کردن bam kardan کلفت کردن koloft kardan
lowering *adj.* پایین آوری pâyin âvari تاریکی târiki
lowland *n., adj.* پستی زمین pasti zamin جلگه jolgeh
lowly *adj., adv.* پست past خوار khâr فرومایه foru-mâyeh
lox *n.* ماهی دودی mâhi dudi
loyal *adj.* باوفا bâ-vafâ وفادار vafâ-dâr
loyalist *n.* وفادار به دولت vafâ-dâr beh dolat
loyalty *n.* وفاداری vafâ-dâri
lozenge *n.* لوزی lozi لوزه lozeh قرص qors
lube *n.* گریس geris روغن roqan
lubricant *n., adj.* روغن roqan روان کن ravân-kon
lubricate *vt., vi.* روان کردن ravân kardan روغن زدن roqan zadan
lubricator *n.* روغن دان roqan-dân گریس geris
luck *n.* بخت bakht شانس shâns اقبال eqbâl طالع tâle'
luck out *n.* شانس آوردن shâns âvardan
luckily *adv.* خوشبختانه khosh-bakhtâneh
luckless *adj.* بدبخت bad-bakht
lucky *adj., n.* خوش بخت khosh-bakht خوش شانس khosh-shâns
lucrative *adj.* پردرآمد por-darâmad
lug *vt., vi., n.* میان حرف دویدن miân-e' harf davidan کشیدن keshidan
luggage *n.* چمدان chamedân باروبندیل bâr-o bandil
luggage rack *n.* باربند bâr-band
lugubrious *adj.* غم انگیز qam-angiz
lukewarm *adj.* ولرم velarm
lull *vt., vi., n.* آرامش ârâmesh سکوت sokut
lull *v.* آرام کردن ârâm kardan فرو نشاندن foru neshândan
lullaby *n., vt.* لالایی گفتن lâlâyi goftan
lumbago *n.* کمردرد kamar-dard
lumber *n., vi., vt.* الوار alvâr چوب chub
درخت بریدن derakht boridan
lumberjack *n.* چوب بر chub-bor درخت انداز derakht-andâz
lumberyard *n.* انبارالوار anbâr-e' alvâr
luminary *n., adj.* نوردهنده nur dahandeh
luminary *n., adj.* سرشناس sar-shenâs علامه al~âmeh
luminous *adj.* نورانی nurâni درخشان derakhshân شب نما shab namâ
lump *n., adj., vt., vi.* کلوخه kolukheh
یکجاجمع کردن yek jâ jam kardan غلنبگی qolonbegi
lumpy *adj.* تیکه تیکه tikeh tikeh غلنبه qolonbeh

lunacy *n.* دیوانگی divânegi
lunar *adj., n.* ماهانه mâhâneh قمری qamari
lunatic *n., adj.* دیوانه divâneh
lunch *n., vi., vt.* نهار nahâr
lunch room *n.* اطاق نهارخوری otâq-e' nahâr-khori
lunch(eon) *n.* نهار خوردن nahâr khordan
lung *n.* شش shosh ریه rieh
lunge *n., vi., vt.* یورش بردن yuresh bordan
حمله کردن hamleh kardan
lupine *adj., n.* گرگی gorgi
lupus *n.* پوست خوره pust-khoreh
lurch *vt., vi., n.* یکهو تلوتلوخوردن yek-ho telo-telo khordan
lure *v.* بدام انداختن be-dâm andâkhtan تطمیع کردن tatmi' kardan
lure *n.* دام dâm دانه dâneh اغفال eqfâl
lurid *adj.* ترسناک tars-nâk خوفناک khof-nâk
lurk *vi.* کمین کردن kamin kardan درنهان بودن dar nahân budan
luscious *adj.* خوشمزه khosh-mazeh خوشایند khosh-âyand
lush *adj., n., vi., vt.* آبدار âb-dâr سرسبز sar-sabz
lust *v.* شهوت داشتن shahvat dâshtan
luster *n., vt., vi.* تابش tâbesh درخشندگی derakh-shandegi
زرق و برق zarq-o barq
lustful *adj.* شهوتی shahvati حشری hashari
lustiness *n.* شهوانیت shahvâniyat
lute *n., vi., vt.* عود 'ud
luxe *n.* شیک shik لوکس luks
luxurious *adj.* پرتجمل por-tajam~ol خوش گذران khosh-gozarân
luxury *n., adj.* تجمل tajam~ol خوش گذرانی khosh-gozarâni
وفور vofur
lye *n.* آب قلیایی âb qalyâyi
lying *n., v., adj.* دروغگو doruq-gu
lymph *n.* لنف lenf خلط آبکی khelt-e' âbaki
lymphatic *adj., n.* لنفی lenfi
lynch *n., vt.* اعدام کردن e'dâm kardan
lynx *n.* گربۀ وحشی gorbeh-ye' vahshi
lyre *n.* بربط bar-bat چنگ chang
lyric(s) *n.* غزل qazal اشعار ash'âr
lyrical *n.* غزلی qazali غنایی qenâ'i
lyrist *n.* چنگ نواز chang-navâz غزلسرا qazal-sarâ

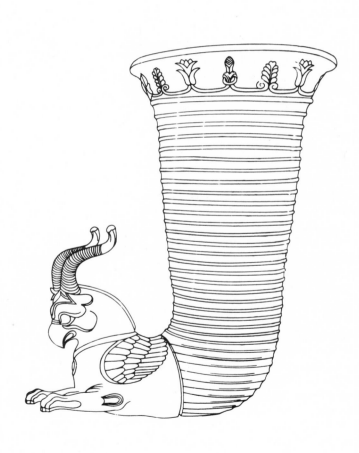

M M M

ma *n.* مادر mâdar مامان mâmân
macabre *n.* وحشتناک vah-shat nâk خوفناک khof-nâk
mace *n.* گرز gorz کوپال kupâl
machanic *n.* تعمیرکار ta'mir-kâr مکانیک mekânik
machete *n.* قداره qad~âreh
machination *n.* دسیسه dasiseh توطئه tote'eh
machine *n., vt.* دستگاه dast-gâh ماشین mâshin
machine gun *np.* مسلسل mosalsal
machine shop *np.* کارگاه kâr-gâh تعمیرگاه ta'mir-gâh
machine-made *n.* ماشینی mâshini
machinery *n.* دستگاه dast-gâh ماشین آلات mâshinâlât
machinist *n.* ماشینکار mâshin-kâr
mackle *n., v.* لکه انداختن lak~eh andâkhtan تارکردن târ kardan
macrame' *n.* گره بافی gereh bâfi
mad *n.* دیوانه divâneh عصبانی 'asabâni
madcap *adj., n.* بی پروا bi-parvâ
madden *vt., vi.* دیوانه کردن divâneh kardan
عصبانی کردن 'asabâni kardan
made *n., v.* ساخته شده sâkhteh shodeh
made-to-order *adj.* ساخت سفارشی sâkht-e' sefâreshi
made-up *adj.* ساختگی sâkhtegi
madhouse *n.* دارالمجانین dârol-majânin دیوانه خانه divâneh-khâneh
madly *n.* دیوانه وار divâneh-vâr
madman *n.* آدم دیوانه âdam-e' divâneh
madness *n.* دیوانگی divânegi جنون jonun
magazine *n.* مجله majal~eh وزین نامه vazin-nâmeh
magazine *n.* خشاب khashâb مخزن makhzan
maggot *n.* کرمک kermak
magic *n., adj.* سحر sehr جادو jâdu شعبده sho'badeh
magical *adj.* سحرآمیز sehr-âmiz جادویی jâduyi
magician *n.* جادوگر jâdu-gar شعبده باز sho'badeh-bâz
magistral *adj., n.* رهنمود rahnemud اصلی asli
magistrate *n.* قاضی شرع qâzi-e' shar'
magnanimity *n.* بزرگ طبعی bozorg-tab'i مناعت manâ'at
magnanimous *adj.* بزرگ طبع bozorg-tab' آقامنش âqâ-manesh
بلندنظر boland-nazar
magnate *n.* بانفوذ bâ-nofuz کله گنده kal~eh gondeh

magnesium *n.* منیزیم man-yaziom

magnet *n.* آهن ربا âhan-robâ مغناطیس meqnâtis

magnetic *adj.* آهن ربا âhan-robâ مغناطیسی meqnâtisi
کشنده keshandeh

magnetic field *np.* فضای مغناطیسی fazâ-ye' meqnâtisi

magnetic force *np.* قوهٔ جاذبه qov~eh-ye' jâzebeh

magnificent *adj.* باشکوه bâ-shokuh باعظمت bâ-'azemat

magnifier *n.* ذره بین zar~eh-bin بزرگ کن bozorg-kon

magnify *vt., vi.* بزرگ کردن bozorg kardan
درشت کردن dorosht kardan

magnifying glass *n.* ذره بین zar~eh-bin

magnitude *n.* بزرگی bozorgi اهمیت ahamiyat

magpie *n.* کلاغ جاره kalâq-jâreh تشقایی qashqa'i

mahogany *n., adj.* چوب ماهون chub-e' mâhun

maid *n.* کلفت kolfat خدمتکار khedmat-kâr

maiden *n.* دوشیزه dushizeh دوشیزگی dushizegi باکره bâ-kereh

mail *n., vt.* پست کردن post kardan نامه فرستادن nâmeh ferestâdan

mailbox *n.* صندوق پست sandoq-e' post

mailman *n.* پستچی postchi نامه بر nâmeh-bar

mailorder *n.* سفارش پستی sefâresh-e' posti

maim *vt.* پاره پاره کردن pâreh-pâreh kardan دریدن daridan

main *adj., n.* اصلی asli اساسی asâsi اصل کاری asl-e' kâri عمده 'omdeh

main course *np.* غذای اصلی qazây-e' asli

main drag *np.* خیابان مرکزی khiâbân-e' markazi

main in waiting *n.* ندیمه nadimeh

mainland *n.* سرزمین sar-zamin

mainly *adv.* اساساً asâsan عمدتاً 'om-datan

mainstay *n.* پشتوانه posht-vâneh پشتیبان poshtibân

maintain *v.* نگهداری کردن negah-dâri kardan

maintain *v.* اظهار کردن ez-hâr kardan

maintain *v.* ادامه دادن edâmeh dâdan

maintenance *n.* نگهداری negah-dâri

maitre d' *n.* شف گارسون shef gârson

maize *n.* ذرت zorat

majestic *adj.* شاهانه shâhâneh باعظمت bâ-'azemat

majesty *n.* عظمت 'azemat پادشاهی pâdeshâhi

major *n.* رشته reshteh

major *n.* سرگرد sar-gord

major

major *n.* بزرگتر bozorgtar اعظم a'-zam
major general *np.* سرلشگر sar-lashgar
majority *n.* اکثریت ak-sariyat
make *v.* واداركردن vâdâr kardan
make *v.* ساخت sâkht
make *v.* ساختن sâkhtan درست كردن dorost kardan
make believe *n.* خیال كردن khiâl kardan تصوركردن tasav~or kardan
make(for) *n.* عازم شدن 'âzem shodan
make(like) *n.* تقلید كردن taqlid kardan
make(money) *n.* پول درآوردن pul dar âvardan
make(off with) *n.* دزدیدن dozdidân
make(off) *n.* دررفتن dar raftan
make(or break) *n.* آمد نیامد âmad na-yâmad
make(out) *n.* موفق شدن movaf~aq shodan
make(out) *n.* تشخیص دادن tashkis dâdan
make(up to) *n.* ازدل درآوردن az del dar âvardan
make(up) *n.* ساختن sâkhtan جبران كردن jobrân kardan
make-up *n.* ساخت sâkht آرایش ârâyesh
maker *n.* سازنده sâzandeh خالق khâleq
makeshift *n., adj.* سرهمی sarhami موقتی movaq~ati
making *n., v.* ساختمان sâkhtemân شكل shekl تهیه tahiyeh
maladjusted *adj.* ناجور nâ-jur نامیزان nâ-mizân
malady *n.* ناخوشی nâ-khoshi
malaise *n.* احساس ناخوشی ehsâs-e' nâ-khoshi
malaria *n.* مالاریا mâlâriâ
malarkey *n.* چرت و پرت chart-o part
male *adj.* نر nar مردانه mardâneh مذكر mozak~ar
malefaction *n.* بدكاری bad-kâri تبهكاری tabah-kâri
maleficent *adj.* مضر mozer~ شیطانی sheytâni
malevolence *n.* بدخواهی bad-khâhi
malevolent *adj.* بدخواهانه bad-khâhâneh
malfeasance *n.* خلاف كاری khalâf-kâri رشوه گیری roshveh-giri
malformation *n.* بدشكلی bad-shekli نقص naqs
malice *n.* سوء نظر su'-e' nazar
malicious *adj.* باسوء نظر bâ su'-e' nazar بدخواهانه bad-khâhâneh
malign *n.* مضر mozer~ زیان آور ziân-âvar بدخیم bad-khim
malignant *adj.* مضر mozer~ مرگ آور marg âvar
malignment *n.* هتک hatk هتاكی hat~âki

mall *n., vt.* سرا sarâ بازارچه bâzârcheh
mallard *n.* اردک وحشی ordak vahshi
malleable *n.* له شدنی leh-shodani
mallet *n.* چکش چوبی chak~osh-e' chubi چوگان chogân
malnutrition *n.* کمبود تغذیه kambud-e' taqzieh
maltreat *vt.* بدرفتاری کردن bad-raftâri kardan
maltreatment *n.* بدرفتاری bad-raftâri
mammal *n.* پستاندار pestân-dâr
mammary *adj.* پستانی pestâni
mammoth *n., adj.* غول پیکر qul-peykar ماموت mâmut
mammy *n.* ننه naneh کاکا لله kâkâ laleh
man *v.* گماشتن gomâshtan سر کار گماشتن sar-e' kâr gomâshtan
man *n.* مرد mard آدم âdam انسان ensân بشر bashar
man hunt *n.* تعقیب فراری ta'qib-e' farâri
man-at-arms *n.* سرباز sarbâz
man-eater *n.* آدمخوار âdam-khâr
man-of-war *n.* کشتی جنگی kashti-e' jangi
manacle *n.* دستبند زدن dast-band zadan
manage *v.* ترتیب دادن tartib dâdan
manage *v.* مدیریت کردن modiriyat kardan گرداندن gardândan
manage *v.* اداره کردن edâreh kardan
manageable *n.* اداره کردنی edâreh kardani
management *n.* مدیریت modiriyat اداره edâreh
manager *n.* مدیر modir گرداننده gardânandeh
manager *n.* آخور âkhor
managerial *n.* مدیری modiri
mandate *n., vt., adj.* قیومیت qayumiyat رسالت resâlat
mandatory *adj.* دستوری dasturi اجباری ejbâri
mane *n.* یال yâl
maneuver *n., vi.* مانوردادن mânovr dâdan
mangle *n., vt.* ناقص کردن nâqes kardan
mangler *n.* ناقص کن nâqes kon اطوکش otu-kesh
mango *n.* عنبه 'anbeh
mangrove *n.* درخت باطلاقی derakht-e' bâtlâqi
manhandle *vt.* باخشونت رفتار کردن bâkhoshunat raftâr kardan
manhood *n.* مردی mardi بلوغ boluq
mania *n.* جنون jonun
maniac *n.* جنون دار jonun-dâr دیوانه divâneh

manicure *n.* مانیکور mânikur ناخن چینی کردن nâkhon chini kardan

manifest *adj., vt., n.* آشکار âsh-kâr ثابت کردن sâbet kardan بارنامه bârnâmeh

manifest destiny *n.* رسالت جهانی resâlat-e' jahâni

manifestation *n.* تبلور tabalvor پدید آمدگی padid-âmadegi مظهر maz-har

manifold *adj.* متعدد mote'ad~ed گوناگون gunâgun چندطرفه chand-tarafeh

manikin *n.* مانکن mânkan آدمک âdamak

manipulate *vt.* بازیچه دست کردن bâzicheh-ye' dast kardan

manipulation *n.* دستکاری dast-kâri

mankind *n.* آدمیت âdamiyat بشر bashar

manly *adj., adv.* مردانه mardâneh

mannequin *n.* مانکن mânkan آدمک âdamak

manner *n.* روش ravesh راه râh طریقه tariqeh سبک sabk

mannerless *adj.* بی ادب bi-adab بی تربیت bi-tarbiyat

mannerly *adj., adv.* مودبانه mo-ad~abâneh

manners *n.* رفتار raftâr اخلاق akhlâq

mannish *adj.* مرد خصلت mard kheslat

manor(house) *n.* خانهٔ اشرافی khâneh-ye' ashrâfi

manpower *n.* نیروی کار niruy-e' kâr

mansion *n.* خانهٔ اشرافی khâneh-ye' ashrâfi کاخ kâkh کوشک kushk ارگ arg

manslaughter *n.* آدمکشی âdam-koshi قتل غیرعمد qatl-e' qeyr-e' 'amd

mantel *n.* بخاری bokhâri طاقچه tâqcheh

mantle *n., vi.* شنل shenel

manual *adj.* دستی dasti دستورنامه dastur-nâmeh

manually *adv.* بادست bâ-dast دستی dasti

manufacture *n., vt.* ساختن sâkhtân تولید کردن tolid kardan

manure *n., vt.* تپاله tapâleh سرگین sergin

manuscript *n., adj.* دست نویس dast-nevis

many *pro., adj., n.* خیلی kheyli بسیار besyâr

many-sided *adj.* چندطرفه chand-tarafeh

map *v., n.* نقشه برداشتن naqsheh bardâshtan

maple *n.* افرا afrâ

mar *vt.* ناقص کردن nâqes kardan خراب کردن kharâb kardan

maraud *n.* حمله و غارت کردن hamleh va qârat kardan

marauder *n.* غارتگر qârat-gar
marble *n., adj., vt.* مرمر marmar تیله tileh
marc *n.* تفاله انگور tofâleh ângur
march *vt., n., vi.* رژه رفتن rezheh raftan مارش mârsh
margarine *n.* مارگارین mârgârin روغن نباتی roqan nabâti
margin *n.* حاشیه hâshieh لبه labeh تفاوت tafâvot
marginal *adj.* حاشیه ای hâshieh-i جزئی joz'i
marguerite *n.* گل داودی gol-e' dâvudi
marigold *n.* گل جعفری gol ja'fari
marijuana *n.* بتهٔ شاه دانه boteh-ye' shâh-dâneh
marinate *vt.* ترد کردن tord kardan
لای پیاز خواباندن lây-e' piâz khâbândan
marine *adj.* دریایی daryâyi
mariner *n.* ملوان malevân دریایی daryâyi
marionette *n.* عروسک خیمه شب بازی 'arusak-e' kheymeh shab-bâzi
mariposa *n.* زنبق وحشی zanbaq-e' vahshi
marital *n.* زن و شوهری zan-o shuhari ازدواج ezdevâj
maritime *n.* دریایی daryâyi دریاکناری daryâ kenâri
marjoram *n., vt., vi.* مرزنگوش marzan-gush گلپر golpar
mark *n.* نشان neshân علامت 'alâmat اثر asar مهر mohr
mark *v.* نشان کردن neshân kardan علامت گذاشتن 'alâmat gozâshtan
mark(down) *n.* نوشتن neveshtan قیمت کم کردن qeymat kam kardan
mark(out for) *n.* انتخاب کردن entekhâb kardan
mark(time) *n.* درجا زدن darjâ zadan وقت گذراندن vaqt gozarândan
mark(up) *n.* قیمت زیادکردن qeymat ziâd kardan
marked *adj.* علامتدار 'alâmat-dâr نشان شده neshân shodeh
مشخص moshakh~as
marker *n.* نشان کن neshân-kon سنگ قبر sang-e' qabr
market *v.* بازاریابی کردن bâzâr-yâbi kardan
market *n.* بازار bâzâr
market place *n.* بازار bâzâr
market price *np.* قیمت بازاری qeymat-e' bâzâri مظنه mazan~eh
market value *np.* ارزش بازاری arzesh-e' bâzâri
marketable *adj.* فروختنی forukhtani
marketing *n.* بازاریابی bâzâr-yâbi فروش forush
marksman *n.* تیرانداز ماهر tir andâz-e' mâher
marlin *n., pl.* نیزه ماهی neyzeh mâhi
marmalade *n.* مارمالاد mârmâlâd مربای پوست mor~abâ-ye' pust

marmoreal *adj.* مرمرى marmari
maroon *adj.* زرشكى zereshki بلوطى baluti
maroon *v.* تنها ول كردن tanhâ vel kardan
marooned *n.* گير كرده gir kardeh متروك matruk
marquee *n.* تابلوى سينما tâblo-ye' sinamâ چادر châdor
marriage *n.* ازدواج ezdevâj زناشويى zenâ-shuyi عروسى 'arusi
نكاح nekâh
marriage portion *np.* مهريه mehrieh كابين kâbin
married *v.* متاهل mote'ah~el زن دار zan-dâr شوهردار shuhar-dâr
marrow *n.* مغز استخوان maqz-e' ostekhân
marrowly *n.* بزور bezur بفاصلهٔ يك مو bâfâseleh-ye' yek mu
marry *vt., vi.* ازدواج كردن ezdevâj kardan عروسى كردن 'arusi kardan
Mars *n., adj.* مريخ merikh بهرام bahrâm
marsh *n.* مرداب mordâb باتلاق bâtlâq
marshal *n.* مارشال mârshâl كلانتر kalântar
marshal *v.* نظام دادن nezâm dâdan
marshmallow *n.* شل قندك shol qandak
mart *n.* بازارچه bâzâr-cheh
marten *n.* سمور samur
martial law *np.* حكومت نظامى hukumat nezâmi
martin *n.* پرستو parastu
martyr *n.* شهيد كردن shahid kardan
به شهادت رساندن be-shahâdat resândan
martyrdom *n.* شهادت shahâdat
marvel *n., vt.* درشگفت بودن dar shegeft budan شگفتى shegefti
marvelous *adj.* شگفت انگيز shegeft angiz عالى 'âli
mascara *n.* سرمه وسمه vasmeh سرمه sormeh
mascot *n.* مظهر maz hâr سمبل sambol
masculine *adj., n.* مذكر mozak~ar مردنما mard-namâ
ذكور zakur مردانه mardâneh
mash *n., vt.* له كردن leh kardan كوبيدن kubidan نواله navâleh
masher *n.* له كن leh-kon پر رو por-ru
mask *n., vi.* نقاب زدن neqâb zadan قايم كردن qâyem kardan
ماسك mâsk
masked *adj.* نقابدار neqâb-dâr مقنع moqana'
masking tape *np.* نوارچسب navâr chasb
masochism *n.* خودشكنجهايى khod-shekanjeh-yi
mason jar *n.* بطرى ترشى botri-e' torshi

mason(-ry) *n.* سنگ تراشی sang-tarâshi سنگ کاری sang-kâri
masquerade *n., vi.* هویت عوض کردن hoviyat 'avaz kardan
نقاب زدن neqâb zadan
mass *n., vi., vt.* انبوه anbuh توده کردن tudeh kardan جامع jâme'
massacre *n., vt.* قتل عام کردن qatl-e' 'âm kardan
massage *n., vt.* مشت و مال دادن mosht-o mâl dâdan ماساژ mâsâzh
masseuse *n.* ماساژیست mâsâzhist
massive *adj.* بزرگ جثه bozorg jos~eh پرحجم por-hajm
mast *n., vt.* دکل dakal تیرک tirak
mast head *n.* سردکل sar-dakal دیدبانگاه didebân-gâh
mastectomy *n.* جراحی پستان jar~âhi-e' pestân
master *vt.* استادشدن ostâd shodan ماهر شدن mâher shodan
master *n., adj.* ارباب arbâb صاحبکار sâheb-kâr استاد ostâd آقا âqâ
master key *np.* شاه کلید shâh kelid
master seargent *n.* گروهبان یک goruhbân yek
masterful *adj.* استادمنش ostâd-manesh بامهارت bâ-mahârat
masterly *adj., adv.* استادانه ostâdâneh ماهرانه mâherâneh
mastermind *n.* مغزمتفکر بودن maqz-e' motefak~er budan
masterpiece *n.* شاهکار shâh-kâr
mastery *n.* استادی ostâdi مهارت mahârat تسلط tasal~ot
masticate *vt., vi.* جویدن javidan خمیرکردن khamir kardan
mat *vt., vi.* بوریا buryâ قالی حصیری qâli-e' hasiri مات mât
matador *n.* ماتادور mâtâdor گاوباز gâv-bâz
match *n.* مسابقه mosâbeqeh
match *n.* لنگه lengeh مانند mânand
match *v.* باهم جورکردن bâ-ham jur kardan
بهم خوردن be-ham khordan
matchbox *n.* جعبه کبریت jâ'beh kebrit
matches *n.* کبریت kebrit
matchless *adj.* بیمانند bi-mânand بیهمتا bi-hamtâ
matchmaker *n.* جورکننده jur konandeh
mate *n.* همدم ham-dam همسر ham-sar
mate *v.* مات کردن mât kardan
mate *v.* جفت گیری کردن joft giri kardan
material *n., adj.* پارچه pârcheh مصالح masâleh
material *n., adj.* مواد mavâd مادیات mâd~iyât
materialist *n.* مادی گرا mâd~i-garâ مادی پرست mâd~i-parast
materialize *vt., vi.* شکل گرفتن shekl gereftan

مادی کردن .... mâd~i kardan

materially *adv.* عمدتاً 'omdatan مادهای mâd~eh-i

materiel *n.* مواد جنگی mavâd~-e' jangi تسلیحات taslihât

maternal *adj.* مادری mâdari مادرانه mâdarâneh

maternity *n., adj.* مادری mâdari

maternity ward *n.* زایشگاه zâyesh-gâh

mathematical *adj.* ریاضی riâzi دقیق daqiq

mathematician *n.* ریاضیدان riâzi-dân

mathematics *n.* ریاضیات riâziyât

mating *n., v.* جفتگیری joft-giri

matriarch *n.* مادر سالار mâdar sâlâr گیس سفید gis sefid

matriarchy *n.* مادر سالاری mâdar sâlâri گیس سفیدی gis sefidi

matricide *n.* مادرکشی mâdar koshi

matrimony *n.* ازدواج ezdevâj زندگی زناشویی zendegi-e' zenâ-shuyi
وصلت veslat

matrix *n.* بستر bastar قالب qâleb

matron *n.* کدبانو kad-bânu مدیره modireh خانم رئیس khânom ra'is

matronly *adj.* خانم khânom بانومنش bânu-manesh

matted *adj., v.* بهم پیچ خورده beham pich-khordeh

matter *n.* ماده mâd~eh مایه mâyeh

matter *n., vi.* بابت bâbat

matter *v.* اهمیت داشتن ahamiyat dâshtan

matter *n.* موضوع mozu' مطلب matlab مورد mored

mattock *n.* تیشه کلنگ tisheh kolang

mattress *n.* تشک toshak

maturation *n., vt., vi.* رسیدگی residegi بلوغ boluq

mature *v.* بالغ شدن bâleq shodan

mature *v.* سررسیدن sar-residan

maturity *n.* رسیدگی residegi بلوغ boluq سررسیدگی sar-residegi

maul *n.* کوبیدن kubidan پنجول زدن panjul zadan

mausoleum *n.* مقبره maqbareh آرامگاه ârâm-gâh بقعه boq'eh

maverick *n.* خودمختار khod-mokhtâr بی صاحب bi-sâheb

maxim *n.* کردار مشخص kerdâr-e' moshakh~as

maximize *vt.* بحداکثررساندن be-had~-e' aksar resândan

maximum *n., adj.* حداکثر had~-e' aksar

may *n., v., vi., vt.* ممکن بودن momken budan
امکان داشتن emkân dâshtan

maybe *n.* ممکن است momken ast

mayhem *n.* آشوب âshub ضرب و جرح zarb-o jarh
mayor *n.* شهردار shahr-dâr
maze *n., vt.* گیج کردن gij kardan پیچ واپیچ pich vâpich
mead *n.* شراب عسل sharâb-e' 'asal مرغزار morq-zâr
meadow *n.* چمن زار chaman-zâr مرغزار morq-zâr
meager *adj.* قلیل qalil کم kam اندک andak نازک nâzok
meal *n.* غذا qazâ آرد خرده ârd khordeh
mealy *adj.* آردی ârdi کمرنگ kamrang
mean *v.* قصدداشتن qasd dâshtan معنی دادن ma'ni dâdan
mean *n., adj., vt., vi.* میانگین miân-gin میانه miâneh
حد وسط had~-e' vasat
mean *adj.* شرور sharur خبیث khabis بدجنس bad-jens پست past
meander *vi., vt., n.* آوارگی âvâregi پیچ واپیچ رفتن pich vâpich raftan
meaning *n., v., adj.* مصداق mesdâq یعنی ya'ni معنی ma'ni
meaningful *adj.* پرمعنی por-ma'ni
meaningless *adj.* بی معنی bi-ma'ni
meanness *n.* خباثت khebâsat بدجنسی bad-jensi پستی pasti
means *n.* توانایی tavânâyi وسایل vasâyel وسیله vasileh
meantime *n.* دراین زمن dar in zemn ضمناً zemnan
meanwhile *n., adv.* دراین ضمن dar in zemn
measles *n.* سرخک sorkhak سرخچه sorkhcheh
measurable *adj.* قابل اندازه گیری qâbel-e' andâzeh-giri
measure *n.* اقدام eqdâm پیمانه peymâneh اندازه andâzeh
measure *v.* اندازه گرفتن andâzeh gereftan
measure out *v.* اندازه گیری کردن andâzeh-giri kardan
measure out *v.* اندازه گرفتن andâzeh gereftan
measure up to *n.* مطابق انتظار بودن motâbeq-e' entezâr budan
measured *adj.* شمرده shemordeh سنجیده sanjideh
measureless *n.* بی انتها bi-entehâ بی اندازه bi-andâzeh
measurement *n.* مساحت masâhat اندازه گیری andâzeh-giri
meat *n.* لحم lahm گوشت gusht
meat head *n.* دخو dakho کله پوک kal~eh puk
meaty *adj.* گوشتالو gushtâlu
mechanical *adj., n.* خودبخود khod be-khod ماشینی mâshini
mechanics *n.* فنون fonun ماشین شناسی mâshin shenâsi
mechanism *n.* دستگاه dastgâh اجزاء ماشینی ajzâ'-e' mâshini
mechanize *n.* ماشینی کردن mâshini kardan
مکانیزه کردن mekânizeh kardan

medal *n., vt.* نشان neshân مدال medâl
medallion *n.* مدال بزرگ bozorg medâl
meddle *vi.* دخالت کردن dekhâlat kardan
دستکاری کردن dast-kâri kardan
meddler *adj.* فضول fozul
meddlesome *adj.* مزاحم mozâhem فضول fozul
media *n.* خبرنگاریها khabar-negârihâ رسانه resâneh
medial *n.* میانی miâni وسطی vasati
median *adj., n.* میان miân وسط vasat
mediate *vt., vi., adj.* واسطه شدن vâseteh shodan
میانجیگری کردن miân-jigari kardan
mediation *n.* میانجیگری miân-jigari وساطت vesâtat
mediator *n.* میانجی miânji واسطه vâseteh
medic *n.* پزشکیار pezeshk-yâr پزشک ارتشی pezeshk-e' arteshi
medical *adj.* پزشکی pezeshki طبی teb~i
medicate *vt.* درمان کردن darmân kardan دارودادن dâru dâdan
medication *n.* دارو dâru درمانی darmâni دوا davâ
medicinal *n., vt.* دارویی dâruyi دوایی davâyi تجویزی tajvizi
medicine *n., v.* دارو dâru دوا davâ پزشکی pezeshki
medicine man *n.* جادوگر jâdugar
medieval *adj.* قرون وسطی qorun-e' vostâ
mediocre *adj.* متوسط motevas~et
mediocrity *n.* متوسطی motevas~eti
meditate *vt., vi.* تفکر کردن tafak~or kardan
ریاضت کشیدن riâzat keshidan
meditation *n.* تفکر tafak~or ریاضت riâzat
medium *n., adj.* متوسط motevas~et واسطه vâseteh محیط mohit
medlar *n.* ازگیل azgil
medley *adj., n.* مخلوط makhlut گلچین ترانه ها golchin-e' tarâneh-hâ
meek *adj.* صبور sabur بیرگ birag بره bareh
meet *v.* ملاقات کردن molâqât kardan برخوردکردن barkhord kardan
meet *adj.* مناسب monâseb شایسته shâyesteh
meeting *n.* ملاقات molâqât جلسه jaleseh تقاطع taqâto'
megalomaniac *n.* بزرگ پندار bozorg-pendâr
melancholy *n., adj.* مالیخولیا mâli-kholiâ پکر و دمغ pakar va damaq
mele'e *n.* زدوخورد zad-o khord دعوا da'vâ
mellow *vt., vi.* ملایم molâyem جاافتاده jâ-oftâdeh
melodic *adj.* آهنگی âhangi نغمه ای naqmeh-i

melodrama *n.* پرهیجان por-hayajân
melody *n.* آهنگ âhang نغمه naqmeh
melon *n.* گرمک garmak
melt *n.* ذوب کردن zob kardan آب کردن âb kardan
member *n.* عضو 'ozv عنصر 'onsor جزء joz'
membership *n.* عضویت 'ozviyat
membrane *n.* پرده pardeh غشاء qeshâ'
memento *n.* یادگاری yâd-gâri
memo(randum) *n.* یادداشت مختصر yâd dâsht-e' mokhtasar
memoir(e) *n.* یادداشت خاطرات khâterât yâd-dâsht
memorabilia *pl.* خاطرۀ ارزش دار khâtereh-ye' arzesh dâr
memorable *adj.* یادآوری yâd-âvardani
فراموش نشدنی farâmush nashodani
memorial *n., adj.* یادآورنده yâd-âvarândeh یادروز yâd-ruz
یادگاه yâd-gâh
memorization *n.* حفظ hefz یاد سپاری yâd-sepâri
memorize *vt.* حفظ کردن hefz kardan ازبرکردن az bar kardan
memory *n.* یاد yâd حافظه hâfezeh خاطره khâtereh یادبود yâd-bud
menace *n., vt.* تهدید کردن tahdid kardan شیطان sheytân
menagerie *n.* نمایشگاه حیوان namâyeshgâh-e' heyvân
mend *vt., vi., n.* درست dorost تعمیر ta'mir بهتر کردن behtar kardan
mendacious *n.* دروغ doruq کاذب kâzeb
mendacity *n.* دروغگویی doruq-quyi کذب kazb
menial *adj., n.* پست past نوکرانه nokarâneh
meningitis *n.* مننزیت menanzhit
menopause *n.* اتمام قاعدگی etmâm-e' qâ'edegi یائسه yâ'eseh
mensturate *n.* قاعده شدن qâ'edeh shodan رگل شدن regl shodan
mensturation *n.* قاعدگی qâ'edegi
mensural *adj.* اندازه‌ایی andâzeh-i قاعده‌ایی qâ'edeh-i
mental *adj.* فکری fekri ذهنی zehni عقلانی 'aqlâni روحی ruhi
mentality *n.* طرزفکر tarz-e' fekr نکری قوۀ qov~ eh-ye' fekri
mentally *adv.* روحی از لحاظ az lahâz-e' ruhi
mention *v.* نام بردن nâm bordan
mention *vt.* ذکر zekr
mention *v.* تذکردادن tazak~ or dâdan ذکرکردن zekr kardan
mentor *n.* مشاور moshâver آموزگار âmuzegâr مرشد morshed
menu *n.* صورت غذا surat qazâ
mercantile *adj.* تجارتی tejârat~ i بازرگانی bâzargâni

mercenary *adj., n.* مزدور mozdur سربازاجیر sarbâz-e' ajir
merchandise *n., vi., vt.* کالا kâlâ جنس jens مال التجاره mâlol tejareh
merchant *n.* تاجر tâjer بازرگان bâzargân کاسب kâseb
merciful *adj.* بخشنده bakhshandeh رحیمانه rahimâneh
merciless *adj.* بیرحمانه bi-rahmâneh
mercurial *n.* جیوهای jiveh-i ناثابت nâ-sâbet
Mercury *n.* عطارد 'atârod تیر tir
mercury *n.* جیوه jiveh سیماب simâb
mercy *n.* رحم rahm بخشش bakhshesh
mere *adj., n.* صرف serf محض mahz
merely *adv.* صرفاً serfan
merge *vt., vi.* توهم رفتن tu-ham raftan ادغام کردن edqâm kardan
merger *n.* ادغام edqâm ترکیب tarkib یکی شدگی yeki shodegi
meridian *n.* نصف النهار nesfonahâr
merit *v.* سزاواربودن sezâ-vâr budan
merit *n.* لیاقت liâqat شایستگی shâyestegi ارزش arzesh
merlin *n.* قرقی qerqi
mermaid *n.* زن ماهی zan-mâhi پری دریایی pari-e' daryâyi
merriness *n.* شادمانی shâdmâni
merry *adj.* شادمان shâdmân فرخنده farkhondeh خوش khosh
merry-go-round *n.* اسب گردونک asb gardunâk
mesh *n.* تور tur
mesmerize *vt.* خواب کردن khâb kardan
mess *n.* کثیف کاری kasif-kâri هچل hachal خوراک khorâk
mess *v.* کثیف کاری کردن kasif-kâri kardan
mess hall *np.* نهارخانهٔ ارتش nahâr khâneh-ye' artesh
mess(around) *n.* وررفتن var raftan سربسرگذاشتن sar besar gozâshtan
mess(up) *n.* خراب کردن kharâb kardan بهم زدن beham zadan
message *n.* پیغام peyqâm
messenger *n.* پیغام بر peyqâm-bar قاصد qâsed پیک peyk
Messiah *n.* مسیح masih مهدی mahdi
messy *adj.* کثیف kasif ریخت و پاشیده rikht-o pâshideh
metabolism *n.* سوخت غذایی sukht-e' qazâyi
metal *v., n.* فلز felez
metalic *n.* فلزی felez~i
metallurgy *n.* ذوب فلزات zob-e' felez~ât
metamorphosis *n.* مسخ maskh دگرگونی degar-guni
metaphor *n.* استعاره este'âreh تشبیه tashbih

metaphysics *n.* طبيعت ماوراى mâvarây-e' tabi'at معقولات ma'qulât
metathesis *n.* جا تعويض ta'viz-e'jâ
mete *vt.* كردن تقسيم taqsim kardan مرز marz
meteor(ite) *n.* شهاب shahâb
meteoric *adj.* شهابى shahâbi آسا برق barq-âsâ
meteorologist *n.* هواشناس havâ-shenâs
meteorology *n.* هواشناسى havâ-shenâsi
meter *n., vt.* متر metr گذاشتن كنتور kontor gozâshtan
method *n.* روش ravesh شيوه shiveh اسلوب oslub طريقه tariqeh
methodical *adj.* بانظم bâ-nazm بترتيب be-tartib
methodology *n.* شناسى طريقه tariqeh shenâsi
meticulous *adj.* وسواسى vas-vâsi زياددقيق ziâd daqiq
metropolis *n.* شهر بزرگ bozorg shahr
mettle *n.* شهامت shahâmat
mettlesome *adj.* باشهامت bâ-shahâmat دلير dalir
mezzanine *n.* بالكنى bâlkony
microbe *n.* ميكرب mikrob
microcosm *n.* كوچك دنياى donyâ-ye' kuchak
microphone *n.* ميكروفون mikrofon
microscope *n.* ميكروسكوپ mikroskop ريزبين rizbin
microscopic *adj.* ميكروسكوپى mikroskopi ريز خيلى kheyli riz
mid *adj., pre., n.* ميانى miâni نيمه nimeh وسطى vasati
midday *n., adj.* ظهر zohr روز نيم nim-ruz
middle *n.* ميانى miâni وسطى vasati
middle age *np.* مسن mosen سال ميان miân-sâl
Middle Ages *np.* وسطى قرون qorun-e' vostâ
middle class *np.* متوسط طبقة tabaqeh-ye' motevas~et
Middle East *np.* خاورميانه khâvar miâneh
middle-sized *n.* متوسط قد qad~-e' motevas~et
middleman *n.* واسطه vâseteh دلال dal~âl
middlemost *n.* وسط vasat-e' vasat
middleweight *n.* وزن ميان miân-vazn
midge(t) *n.* كوتوله kutuleh
midland *n.* زمين ميان miân zamin مملكت وسط vasat-e' mamlekat
midmost *adj., adv.* وسط vasat-e' vasat
midnight *n., adj.* شب نيمه nimeh-shab
midriff *n., adj.* تنه ميان miân-taneh
midst *pre.* ميان miân وسط vasat

midsummer n. چلهٔ تابستان chel~eh-ye' tâbestân
midterm n. امتحان میان ثلث emtehân-e' miân sols
midway n. میان راه miân-râh
midwife n. ماما قابله qâbeleh mâmâ
miff n. دلخورکردن del-khor kardan
might v., n. توانایی قدرت tavânâyi qodrat زور zur
mightily adv. باتوانایی خیلی bâ-tavânâyi kheyli
mightiness n. اقتدار توانایی tavânâyi eqtedâr
mighty adj., adv. توانا قادر tavânâ qâder عظیم 'azim بسیار besyâr
migraine n. سردردمزمن sar-dard-e' mozmen
migrant adj., n. مهاجر mohâjer
migrate vi. مهاجرت کردن mohâjerat kardan کوچ کردن kuch kardan
migration n. مهاجرت mohâjerat کوچ kuch
mild adj. ملایم molâyem نرم narm
mildew n. تارِچک کپک kapak qârchak
mildly adv. ملایمانه molâyemâneh
mile n. میل mil
mileage n. مصرف بنزین masraf-e' benzin
milestone n. واقعهٔ تاریخی vâqe'eh-ye' târikhi
militant adj., n. مبارز نبردی nabardi mobârez
militarily adv. ازلحاظ ارتشی az lahâz-e' arteshi
militarism n. روحیهٔ نظامی ruhieh-ye' nezâmi
militarization n. نظامیگری تجهیز tajhiz nezâmi-gari بسیج basij
militarize vt. تجهیز کردن tajhiz kardan بسیج کردن basij kardan
military adj., n. ارتش artesh نظامی nezâmi
military service n. خدمت سربازی khedmat-e' sar-bâzi
نظام وظیفه nezâm vazifeh
militria n. ارتش ملی artesh-e' mel~i
milk n. شیر shir شیره shireh
milk v. دوشیدن dushidan
milk tooth np. دندان شیری dandân-e' shiri
milkman n. شیرفروش shir-forush شیری shiri
milksop n. بچه ننه bach~eh-naneh
milky adj. شیری shiri شیردار shir-dâr
Milky Way np., vt., vi. کهکشان kahkeshân
mill n. آسیاب âsiâb خردکن khord-kon مشت بازی mosht-bâzi
mill v. آسیاب کردن âsiâb kardan خردکردن khord kardan
millennium n. هزاره hezâreh هزارسال hezâr sâl

miller *n.* آسیابان âsiâbân آسیابدار âsiâb-dâr
millet *n.* ارزن arzan
millionaire *n.* ملیونر mel-yuner
mimic *vt., n., adj.* تقلیدکردن taqlid kardan مقلد moqal~ed
mimicry *n.* تقلید taqlid ادادرآوردن adâ-dar âvardan
mince *v.* خردکردن khord kardan قیمه کردن qeymeh kardan
mince *v.* خرامیدن kharâmidan
mincing *adj.* نازدار nâz-dâr باطمانینه bâ-tomanineh
mind *n.* ذهن zehn نظر nazar مغز maqz مشاعر mashâ'er
mind *n.* خاطر khâter نکر fekr ذهن zehn
mind *v.* اهمیت دادن ahamiyat dâdan
mind *v.* اعتناکردن e'tenâ kardan توجه کردن tavaj~oh kardan
mind reader *n.* ذهن بین zehn-bin نکرخوان fekr-khân
mindful *adj.* ملتفت moltafet آگاه âgâh
mindless *adj.* بیفکر bifekr بی اعتنا bi-e'tenâ
mine *pro.* من mâl-e' man مال
mine *v.* استخراج کردن estekhrâj kardan مین گذاشتن min gozâshtan
mine *n.* معدن ma'dan کان kân مین min
miner *n., adj.* کارگرمعدن kârgar-e' ma'dan
mineral *n.* معدنی ma'dani
mineral oil *np.* روغن معدنی roqan-e' ma'dani
mineral spring *np.* چشمه معدنی cheshmeh ma'dani
mineral water *n.* آب معدنی âb ma'dani
mineralize *vt., vi.* مادۀ معدنی کردن mâd~eh-ye' ma'dani kardan
mineralogy *n.* معدن شناسی ma'dan shenâsi
mingle *vi., vt.* قاطی شدن qâti shodan آمیختن âmikhtan
miniature *n.* مینیاتور miny-âtor کوچک شده kuchek shodeh
minicam(era) *n.* دوربین کوچک durbin-e' kuchek
minimal *adj.* جزیی joz'i کمترین امکان kamtarin emkân
minimize *vt.* بحداقل رساندن be-hade aqal resândan
minimum *n., adj.* حداقل hade aqal
mining *n., v.* استخراج معدنی estekhrâj-e' ma'dani
مین گذاری min-gozâri
minion *n., adj.* ظریف châker چاکر zarif
minister *n., vt., vi.* وزیر vazir کشیش keshish
کمک کردن komak kardan
ministerial *adj.* وزارتی vaziri وزیری vezârati
ministry *n.* وزارتخانه vezârat khâneh

mink *n.* سمور samur

minor *adj., n., vi.* کوچکتر kuchek-tar صغیر saqir جزیی joz'i

minority *n., adj.* اقلیت aqaliyat خردسالی khord-sâli

minstrel *n.* آوازه خوان دوره گرد âvâzeh-khân-e' doreh-gard

mint *v.* سکه زدن sek~eh zadan

mint *n.* ضراب خانه zar~âb khâneh

mint *n.* نعنا na'nâ

minus *pre., adj., n.* منهای menhâ-ye' بدون bedun-e'

minuscule *n.* ریزنوشت riz nevesht

minute *adj.* ریز riz ناچیز nâchiz جزئی joz'i

minute *n.* دقیقه daqiqeh گزارش gozâresh

minute hand *np.* دقیقه شمار daqiqeh shemâr

minutely *adj., adv.* بطورناچیز betor-e' nâchiz

minuteness *n.* ناچیزی nâchizi دقت deq~at

miracle *n.* معجزه mo'jezeh

miraculous *n.* معجزه ای mo'jezeh-i اعجازآمیز e'jâz-âmiz معجزآسا mo'jez-asa

mirage *n.* سراب sarâb

mire *n., vt., vi.* گل آب gel âb توگل افتادن tu gel oftâdan

mirror *n., vt.* آئینه âyineh

mirth *n.* نشاط neshât

mirthful *adj.* بانشاط bâ-neshât

mirthless *adj.* بی نشاط bi-neshât

misadventure *n.* حادثهٔ ناگوار hâdeseh-ye' nâ-gavâr

misbehave *v.* بدرفتاری کردن bad-raftâri kardan

misbehave *v.* دست از پا خطا کردن dast az pâ khatâ kardan

misbehavior *n.* بدرفتاری bad-raftâri

miscalculate *vt., vi.* اشتباه محاسبه کردن eshtebâh mohâsebeh kardan

miscarriage *n.* بچه انداختن bach~eh andâkhtan

miscarry *v.* سقط جنین کردن saqt-e' janin kardan

miscarry *v.* کورتاژ کردن kurtâzh kardan

miscellaneous *adj.* متفرقه motefar~eqeh

mischief-maker *n.* فتنه انداز fetneh andâz آشوبگر âshub-gar

mischievous *adj.* آشوبگر âshub-gar شیطان sheytân آتش پاره âtash-pâreh

misconception *n.* سوء تفاهم su'-e' tafâh~om

misconduct *n., vt.* بدکاری bad-kâri خلاف کاری khalâf kari

misdemeanor *n.* جرم جزیی jorm-e' joz'i جنحه jonheh

misdirect *n.* گمراه کردن gomrâh kardan
miser *n.* خسیس khasis حریص haris
miserable *adj.* بدبخت bad-bakht اسفناک asaf-nâk
فلاکت بار felâkat-bâr
miserably *adv.* بابدبختی bâ-bad-bakhti بافلاکت bâ-felâkat
misery *n.* بدبختی bad-bakhti رنج ranj
misfit *adj.* ناجور nâ-jur نادرست nâ-dorost
misfortune *n.* بدبختی bad-bakhti بدشانسی bad-shânsi
misgive *vt., vi.* ترساندن tarsândan
misgiving *v.* ترس tars توهم tavah~om
misgovern *n.* بدحکومت کردن bad-hokumat kardan
misguide *n.* گمراه کردن gomrâh kardan
mishap *n.* بخت بد bakht-e' bad اتفاق بد et~efâq-e' bad
mishmash *n.* هردمبیل hardam-bil
misibform *n.* گمراه کردن gomrâh kardan
misinform *vt.* خبرنادرست دادن khabar-e' nâ-dorost dâdan
misinterpret *vt.* بدتفسیر bad-tafsir بدتعبیر bad-ta'bir
misjudge *n.* بدقضاوت کردن bad-qezâvat kardan
mislead *v.* به اشتباه انداختن beh-eshtebâh andâkhtan
mislead *v.* گمراه کردن gomrâh kardan
misled *adj.* گمراه gom-râh منحرف شده monharef shodeh
mismanage *v.* بد اداره کردن bad-edâreh kardan
mismanage *v.* بدترتیب دادن bad-tartib dâdan
mismatch *vt., n.* ناجور کردن nâjur kardan
misnomer *n.* اشتباه نام eshtebâh-nâm
اسم بی مسمی esm-e' bi-mosam~â
misplace *vt.* اشتباهاً یکجا گذاشتن eshtebâhan yekjâ gozâshtan
misplay *n., vt.* بدبازی کردن bad-bâzi kardan
misprint *n., vt.* اشتباه چاپ کردن eshtebâh châp kardan
mispronounce *n.* غلط تلفظ کردن qalat talaf~oz kardan
misread *vt.* غلط خواندن qalat khândan
misrepresent *vt.* بدجلوه دادن bad jelveh dâdan
miss *v.* خطا کردن khatâ kardan اصابت نکردن esâbat nakardan
miss *v.* دلتنگ بودن del-tang budan
miss *v.* ازدست دادن az dast dâdan نرسیدن naresidan
miss *vt., n.* دختر خانم dokhtar khânom
missile *n., adj.* موشک mushak پرتابی partâbi
missing *v.* مفقود mafqud گمشده gomshodeh

mission *n.* مأموریت ma'-muriyat هیئت اعزامی hey'at-e' e'zâmi
missionary *n., adj.* مبلغ دین mobal~eq-e' din کیش پاش kish-pâsh
misspell *vt., vi.* غلط هجی کردن qalat hej~i kardan
misstep *n.* غلط گام برداشتن qalat gâm bardâshtan
mist *n., vi., vt.* مه mah غبار qobâr نم nam
mistakable *n.* اشتباه شدنی eshtebâh shodani
mistake *n., vt., vi.* اشتباه کردن eshtebâh kardan
mistaken *v.* اشتباهی eshtebâhi
mistletoe *n.* گل بوسه gol-e' buseh
mistranslate *vt., vi.* غلط ترجمه کردن qalat tarjomeh kardan
mistreat *vt.* بدرفتاری کردن bad-raftâri kardan
mistress *n.* معشوقه ma'shuqeh نشمه nashmeh
mistrial *n.* محاکمهٔ غلط mohâkemeh-ye' qalat
mistrust *n., vt., vi.* بدگمان بودن bad-gamân budan
مشکوک بودن mashkuk budan
mistrustful *adj.* بدگمان bad-gamân مشکوک mashkuk
misty *adj.* مه آلود mah-âlud آلود اشگ ashg-âlud
misunderstand *v.* اشتباه فهمیدن eshtebâh fahmidan
misunderstand *v.* بدتعبیرکردن bad-ta'bir kardan
misunderstanding *vt., vi.* سوء تفاهم su'-e' tafâhom
misunderstood *vt., vi.* اشتباه فهمیده شده eshtebâh fahmideh shodeh
misuse *n., vt.* بدبکاربردن bad be-kâr bordan
mitigate *n.* ملایمتر کردن molâyem-tar kardan
تسکین دادن taskin dâdan
mitigation *n.* تسکین تخفیف taskin takhfif
mitt *n.* دستکش ورزشی dast-kesh-e' varzeshi
mitten *n.* دستکش dast-kesh
mix *v.* بهم زدن beham zadan آمیختن âmikhtan
mix *v.* قاطی کردن qâti kardan
mix-up *n.* قاطی شدگی qâti-shodegi
mixed *n.* قاطی پاتی qâti pâti آمیخته âmikhteh مخلوط makhlut
mixer *n.* بهم زن beham-zan
mixture *n.* ترکیب tarkib آمیختگی âmikhtegi
moan *n., vi., vt.* ناله کردن nâleh kardan
آخ و اوخ کردن âkh-o ukh kardan
moat *n., adj., vt.* خندق khandaq
mob *n., adj., v.* جمعیت jam'iyat دسته دزدها dasteh-ye' dozd-hâ
mobile *adj., n.* متحرک motehar~ek سیار say~âr موتوریزه motorizeh

mobility *n., vi.* تحرک tahar~ok روانى ravâni
mobilization *n.* بسيج basij تجهيز taj-hiz
mobilize *v.* بسيج دادن basij dâdan تجهيز كردن taj-hiz kardan
mobster *n.* گانگستر gângster تبهكار tabah-kâr
mock *vt., vi., n., adj.* ادا در آوردن adâ dar âvardan
مسخره كردن mas-khareh kardan
mock -up *n.* ماكت mâket ساختگى sâkhtegi
mockery *n.* ادا adâ تمسخر tamas-khor ريشخند rish-khand
modal(ity) *n.* وجهى vajhi
mode *n.* روش ravesh مد mod نسق nasq
model *v., n., adj.* نمونه nemuneh مدل model الگو olgu
modeling *n.* مدلى modeli قالب سازى qâleb-sâzi
moderate *v.* نظارت كردن nezârat kardan
moderate *adj.* ميانه رو miâneh-ro معتدل mo'tadel
moderation *n.* ميانه روى miâneh-ravi اعتدال e'-tedâl
moderator *n.* نظارت كننده nezârat-konandeh
modern *adj., n.* جديد jadid نو no موثر mo'âs~er مدرن modern
modernize *vt., vi.* مدرنيزه كردن modernizeh kardan
modest *adj.* فروتن forutan متواضع motevâze' محجوب mahjub
قانع qâne'
modesty *n.* فروتنى forutani تواضع tavâzo' قناعت qanâ'at حيا hayâ
modification *n.* تغييرجزيى taqyir-e' joz'i اصلاح eslâh
modifier *n.* تغييردهنده taqyir dahandeh وصفى vasfi قيدى qeydi
modify *vt., vi.* تغييرجزيى دادن taqyir-e' joz'i dâdan
وصف كردن vasf kardan
mohair *n.* پشم بز pashm-e' boz
moist *adj.* نمناك nam-nâk تر tar مرطوب martub
moisten *vt., vi.* خيس كردن khis kardan ترکردن tar kardan
moisture *n.* رطوبت rotubat نم nam
moke *n.* الاغ olâq
molar *n.* آسياب كننده âsiâb konandeh
molasses *n.* شيره قند shireh qand
mold *n.* طرح tarh قالب qâleb
mold *n.* كپك kapak
molder *n.* قالب ساز qâleb-sâz خاک شدن khâk shodan
molding *n.* قالب سازى qâleb sâzi گچبرى gach-bori
نوارچوب nâvâr chub
moldy *n.* كپک زده kapak-zadeh نم زده namzâdeh

mole

mole *n.* خال khâl
mole *n.* موش کور mush-e' kur
molecular *adj.* ذره ای zar~ehyi ملکولی molekuli
molecule *n.* ذره zar~ eh ملکول molekul
molest *vt.* دست درازی کردن dast derâzi kardan
دستمالی کردن dast-mâli kardan
تعرض کردن ta'ar~oz kardan
molestation *n.* دست درازی dast derâzi دستمالی dast-mâli
تعرض ta'ar~oz
molestor *adj.* متجاوز motejâvez متعرض mote'ar~ez
mollify *vt.* تسکین دادن taskin dâdan آرام کردن ârâm kardan
mom(my) *n.* مامان mâmân مادرجون mâdar jun مامک mâmak
moment *n.* لحظه lahzeh هنگام hengâm گشتاور gashtâvar
momentarily *adv.* برای یک لحظه barây-e' yek lahzeh
momentary *adj.* آنی âni زودگذر zud-gozar
momentous *adj.* مهم mohem~ خطیر khatir
momentum *n.* سرعت حرکت sor'at-e' harekat شتاب shetâb
mommy *n.* مامان mâmân مادرجون mâdar jun
monarch *n.* پادشاه pâdeshâh
monarchist *n., adj.* سلطنت طلب saltanat-talab
monarchy *n.* پادشاهی pâdeshâhi
monastery *n.* خانقاه khânqâh دیر dir صومعه some'eh
Monday *n.* دوشنبه do shanbeh
monetary *adj.* پولی puli
money *n., adj.* پول pul
money order *np.* حواله پولی havâleh-ye' puli
money-changer *n.* صراف sar~âf
money-lender *n.* رباخوار rebâ-khâr
money-maker *n.* پولساز pul-sâz
money-making *n.* پولسازی pul-sâzi پرسود por-sud
moneybag *n.* کیسه پول kiseh-ye' pul خرپول khar-pul
monitor *n.* مبصر mobser مراقب morâqeb
monitor *v.* پاییدن pâyidan مراقبت کردن morâqebat kardan
monitor *n.* گیرنده girandeh پرده pardeh
monitory *n.* گوشزد gush-zad اخطاری ekhtâri
monk *n.* راهب râheb رهبان rah-bân
monkey *n.* میمون meymun
monkey business *np.* میمون بازی meymun bâzi

مسخره بازی laskhareh bâzi کچلک بازی kachalak bâzi ....

monkey wrench *np.* آچارفرانسه âchâr farânseh

mono- *n.* تک tak تنها tanhâ

monocle *n.* عینک یک چشمی ’eynak-e’ yek cheshmi

monolith *n.* سنگ یک تکه sang-e’ yek tek~eh یک پارچه yek pârcheh

monolithic *adj.* یک تکه yek tek~eh یکپارچه yek pârcheh
یکدست yek dast

monologue *n.* تک سخنی tak-hsokhani
نطق یک نفره notq-e’ yek-nafareh

monopause *n.* یائسه yâ’eseh

monopolist *n.* انحصار کننده enhesâr konandeh

monopolize *n.* منحصرکردن monhaser kardan

monopoly *n.* انحصار enhesâr امتیازانحصاری emtiâz-e’ enhesâri

monotheist *n.* یکتاپرست yektâ parast موحد movah~ed

monotheistic *adj.* یکتاپرستی yektâ parasti

monotone *n.* یکنواختی yek-navâkhti

monotonous *adj.* یکنواخت yek-navâkht کسل کننده kesel konandeh

monotony *n.* یک نواختی yek navâkhti

monsoon *n.* باد موسمی bâd-e’ musemi فصل بارانی fasl-e’ bârâni

monster *n., adj.* غول qul هیولا hayulâ دیو div

monstrosity *n.* دیوصفتی div sefati

monstrous *adj.* غول پیکر qul peykar هیولا یی hayulâ-yi
دیوصفت div sefat

month *n.* ماه mâh برج borj

monthly *adj., n., adv.* ماهانه mâhâneh

monument *n.* یادبنا yâd-banâ یادگاه yâd-gâh

monumental *adj.* یادگاهی yâd-gâhi تاریخی târikhi شاهکار shâh-kâr

mooch *vi., vt., n.* دله دزدی کردن daleh-dozdi kardan
گدایی کردن gedâyi kardan

mood *n.* حال hâl خلق kholq وجه vajh

moodiness *n.* کج خلقی kaj-kholqi

moody *adj.* کج خلق kaj-kholq دمدمی مزاج damdami-mezâj

moon *n., vi., vt.* ماه mâh مه mah قمر qamar

moonlight *n., adj., vi.* شب کاری کردن shab-kâri kardan

moonlight *n., adj., vi.* مهتاب mahtâb

moonlit *adj.* مهتابی mahtâbi

moonshine *n.* مهتاب mahtâb

moonstruck *n.* ماه زده mâh zadeh

moor *vt., vi., n.* خلنگزار khalang-zâr
moot *n., vt.* بحث کردن bahs kardan
mop *n., vi.* جارو ابری jâru abri
mope *vi., vt., n.* کدربودن keder budan افسرده بودن afsordeh budan
moquette *n.* فرش ماشینی farsh-e' mâshini موکت moket
moral *adj., n.* اخلاقی akhlâqi معنوی ma'navi
moral *adj., n.* اخلاقی natijeh-ye' akhlâgi
morale *n.* روحیه ruhiyeh
moralist *n.* پیرواخلاق peyro-e' akhlâq
morality *n.* اصول اخلاقی osul-e' akhlâqi حیا hayâ
moralize *vi., vt.* اخلاقی کردن akhlâqi kardan
morally *n.* اخلاقاً akhlâqan
morass *n.* منجلاب manjelâb
moratorium *n.* تأخیریه ta'khiriyeh مهلت قانونی mohlat-e' qânuni
morbid *adj.* ناخوش nâkhosh ترسناک tars-nâk
more *adj., n.* بیشتر bish-tar زیادتر ziâd-tar دیگر digar
more or less *n.* کم یا بیش kam yâ bish
more(and more) *n.* هرچه بیشتر harcheh bishtar
بیشتر و بیشتر bishtar-o bishtar
morello *n.* آلبالو âlbâlu
moreover *adv.* بعلاوه be-'alâveh اضافه براین ezâfeh bar-in
افزون براین afzun bar-in
moribund *n.* مردنی mordani
morning *n., adj.* صبح sobh بامداد bâmdâd
moron *n.* ابله ablah احمق ahmaq سفیه safih
morose *adj.* دمغ damaq ترشرو torsh-ru
morpheme *n.* واژک vâzhak
morphology *n.* ساخت sâkht واژه بندی vâzheh-bandi
morque *n.* سرداب sardâb مرده خانه mordeh-khâneh
morrow *n.* صبح sobh روزبعد ruz-e' ba'd
morsel *n.* لقمه loqmeh غذای خوشمزه qazâ-ye' khoshmazeh
mortal *adj.* مردنی mordani فانی fâni کشنده koshandeh
mortality *n.* فنا پذیری fanâ paziri مرگ و میر marg-o mir
mortally *adv.* به طرز مرگ آور betarz-e' marg âvar
mortar *n.* ساروج sâruj سمنت sement
mortar *n.* خمپاره انداز khompâreh-andâz
mortar *n.* هاونگ hâvang
mortgage *n.* رهن rahn قرض رهنی qarz-e' rahni

mortgage v. گرو گذاشتن ger-o gozâshtan رهن گرفتن rahn gereftan
mortgage maturation n. نک رهن fak~-e' rahn
mortgagee n. رهن گیرنده rahn girandeh مرتهن mortahen
mortgagor n. رهن دهنده rahn dahandeh
mortician n. مرده شور mordeh-shur
mortification n. خفت khef~at خوف khof
mortified v. ترسیده tarsideh شرمنده sharmandeh
mortify vt., vi. وحشت انداختن vahshat andâkhtan
mortuary n., adj. مرده خانه mordeh-khâneh
mosaic n. موزائیک muzâ'ik
mosey vi. یواشکی رفتن yavâshaki raftan
Moslem adj., n. مسلمان mosalmân مسلم moslem
mosque n. مسجد masjed
mosquito n. پشه pasheh
mosquito net np. پشه بند pasheh-band
moss n., vt. خزه khazeh
most adj., adv. بیشترین bishtarin اکثر aksar
mostly n. اکثراً aksaran اساساً asâsan
mote n., v. ذره zar~eh خس khas
moth n. بید bid پروانه parvâneh
moth ball n. گوله نفتالین guleh naftâlin
mother n., adj., vt. مادر mâdar
mother superior np. مدیرهٔ صومعه modireh-ye' some'eh
mother tongue np. زبان مادری zabân-e' mâdari
mother-in-law n. مادرزن mâdar-zan مادرشوهر mâdar-shuhar
mother-of-pearl n., adj. صدف sadaf
motherhood n. مادری mâdari
motherland n. سرزمین مادری sarzamin-e' mâdari
motherly n. مادرانه mâdarâneh
motif n. موضوع mozu' موتیف motif
motion n., vt., vi. حرکت harekat جنبش jonbesh
motion n., vt., vi. اشاره eshâreh پیشنهاد pish-nahâd
motion-picture adj. فیلم سینمایی film-e' sinamâyi
motionless adj. بیحرکت bi-harekat فلج falaj
motivate vt. انگیختن angikhtan تحریک کردن tahrik kardan
motivation n. انگیزه angizeh
motive n. علت 'el~at انگیزه angizeh غرض qaraz منظور manzur
motor n. موتور motor

motor *v.* ماشین رانی کردن mâshin-râni kardan
motorboat *n., vi.* قایق موتوری qâyeq motori
motorcade *n.* اسکورت eskort ماشین کاروان kârvân-e' mâshin
motorcycle *n., vi.* موتورسیکلت motor-siklet
motorist *n.* ران ماشین mâshin-rân
motorize *vt.* موتوری کردن motori kardan
mott(e) *n.* واحه vâheh
motto *n.* شعار sho'âr
mound *n.* کپه kop~eh تپه tap~eh خاکریز khâk-riz
mount *n.* کوه kuh
mount *v.* سوارشدن savâr shodan بالارفتن bâlâ raftan
mountain *n., adj.* کوه kuh کوهستان kuhestân
mountain pass *n.* گذرگاه gozar-gâh گدوک gaduk
mountaineer *n.* کوه نورد kuh-navard
mountainous *adj.* کوهستانی kuhestâni
mounted *n.* سوار savâr نصب شده nasb shodeh
mounting سواری savâri نصب جای jây-e' nasb نگیندان negin-dân
mourn *v.* ماتم گرفتن mâtam gereftan عزاگرفتن azâ gereftan
سوگواری کردن sug-vâri kardan
mourner *n.* ماتم گرفته mâtam gerefteh عزادار azâ-dâr
mournful *n.* پرماتم por-mâtam غم انگیز qam-angiz
mourning *adj.* عزاداری 'azâ-dâri ماتم mâtam سوگواری sogavâri
mouse *n.* موش mush
mousetrap *n., vt.* تله موش taleh mush
mousy *adj.* موش مرده mush-mordeh
mouth *n., vt., vi.* دهان dahân دهنه dahaneh
mouthful *n.* یک دهان پر yek dahân-por
قلنبه سلنبه qolonbeh solonbeh
mouthpiece *n.* دهنه dahaneh سخنگو sokhan-gu
mouthy *adj.* پرحرف por-harf
movable *adj.* متحرک motehar~ek سیار say~âr منقول manqul
move *n.* تکان takân اسباب کشی asbâb keshi حرکت harekat
move *v.* تکان دادن takân dâdan
move *v.* حرکت دادن harekat dâdan اسباب کشیدن asbâb keshidan
move(along) *n.* ادامه برفتن دادن edâmeh beraftan dâdan
move(house) *n.* اسباب کشی کردن asbâb keshi kardn
move(in on) *n.* نفوذ کردن nofuz kardan
move(in) *n.* تو رفتن tu raftan رخنه کردن rekhneh kardan

move(on/over) n. حرکت کردن harekat kardan
آنورتررفتن ânvartar raftan
move(up) n. بالا رفتن bâlâ raftan ترقی کردن taraq~i kardan
movement n. حرکت harekat جنبش jonbesh تکان takân
mover n. تکان دهنده takân dahandeh حرکت دهنده harekat dahandeh
movie(s) n. سینما sinamâ
moving adj., v. متحرک motehar~ek تکان دهنده takân dahandeh
mow n., vi., vt. چمن زدن chaman zadan علف زدن 'alaf zadan
mower n. چمن زن chaman-zan
much adj., n., adv. زیاد ziâd خیلی kheyli بسیار besyâr
muck n., vt., vi. تپاله tapâleh
muckrake vi. افشاء کردن efshâ' kardan
پته روآب انداختن pateh ru-âb andâkhtan
mucous membrane np. پرده مخاطی pardeh-ye' mokhâti
mucus n. مخاط mokhât
mud n., vt., vi. گل gel
muddle n. قاطی پاتی کردن qâti pâti kardan گیج کردن gij kardan
muddy adj., vi. گلی geli
mudguard n., vi. گلگیر gel-gir
muff n., vt., vi. دست گرمکن dast-garm-kon
خراب کردن kharâb kârdan
muffin n. نرم کلوچه narm kolucheh
muffle v. صداخفه کردن sedâ khafeh kardan پیچاندن pichândan
muffler n. صداخفه کن sedâ khafeh-kon
muffler n. لوله اگزوس luleh egzos
muffler n. شال گردن shâl-gardan
mug v. مضروب کردن mazrub kardan
mug n. لیوان آبجو livân-e' âbejo صورت surat
mugger n. ضارب zâreb
muggy adj. مرطوب martub خفه khafeh
mulberry n. توت سفید tut sefid
mulch n., vt. خیس برگ khis-barg
mulct n. جریمه کردن jarimeh kardan باکلک گرفتن bâ-kalak gereftan
mule n. قاطر qâter استر astar
mule skinner np. قاطرچی qâter-chi
mulish adj. چموش kal~eh-shaq کله شق chamush
mull vi., vt. تفکر کردن tafak~or kardan شیرین الکلی shirin alkoli
multilingual adj., n. چند زبانه chand zabaneh

multiple *adj., n.* مضرب mazrab ضریب zarib چندتایی chand-tâyi
multiplication *n.* ضرب zarb تکثیر taksir
multiplier *n.* ضرب کننده zarb konandeh مضروب mazrub
multiply *v.* ضرب کردن zarb kardan
multiply *v.* زادوولدکردن zâd-o valad kardan
multitude *n.* کثرت kesrat بیشمار bi-shemâr مقدارزیاد meqdâr-e′ ziâd
mum *adj., n.* ساکت sâket هیس his
mum's the word *n.* هیچی نگو hichi nagu
mumble *v.* زیرلبی حرف زدن zir-labi harf zadan
mumble *v.* من ومن کردن men-o men kardan
mummify *vt., vi.* مومیایی کردن mumiâyi kardan
mummy *n., vt., vi.* مومیا mumiâ
mumps *n.* اریون orion گوشک gushak
munch *vt., vi.* نشخوارکردن nosh-khâr kardan
ته بندی کردن tah-bandi kardan
mundane *adj.* معمولی ma′muli دنیوی donyavi
municipal *adj.* شهرداری shahr-dâri شهری shahri
municipality *n.* شهرداری shahr-dâri
munificent *adj.* بخشنده bakh-shandeh
سخاوتمندانه sekhâvat-mandâneh
muniment *n.* دفاعی defâ′i قباله qabâleh
munition(s) *n.* مهمات دادن mohemât
mural *adj., n.* دیوارآویز divâr âviz دیواری divâri
murder *n., vt., vi.* جنایت کردن jenâyât kardan
بقتل رساندن be-qatl resândan
murderer *n.* جانی jâni آدمکش âdam-kosh قاتل qâtel
murderous *adj.* جنایت آمیز jenâyat-âmiz آدم کشنده âdam koshandeh
murk *n., adj.* تیرگی tiregi تاریکی târiki
murky *n.* تیره tireh تاریک târik
murmur *n., vi., vt.* زمزمه کردن zamzameh kardan
muscle *n., vt., vi.* عضله ′azoleh ماهیچه mâhicheh
muscle-bound *n.* عضله دار ′azoleh-dâr
muscular *adj.* عضلانی ′azolâni
muse *vi., vt.* تفکر کردن tafak~or kardan
museum *n.* موزه muzeh
mush *n.* خمیره khamireh
mushroom *n., adj., vi.* قارچ qârch
mushy *adj.* خمیری khamiri نرم دل narm-del

music *n.* موسیقی musiqi موزیک muzik
musical *adj., n.* موسیقیدار musiqi-dâr موزیکی muziki
musician *n.* موسیقیدان musiqi-dân
musk *n.* مشگ moshg
musk melon *n.* دستنبو dastanbu
musket *n.* شمخال sham-khâl تفنگ فتیله ای tofang fetileh-i
musketeer *n.* تفنگدار tofang-dâr
muskmelon *n.* طالبی tâlebi
muslin *n.* چیت موسلی chit-e' museli
muss *n., vt.* ژولیده zhulideh
muss *v.* درهم و برهم کردن darham-o barham
must *vt., n.* باید bâyad بایستی bâyasti
mustache *n.* سبیل sebil
mustang *n.* اسب وحشی asb-e' vahshi توسن tosan
mustard *n.* خردل khardal
muster *vt., vi., n.* جمع آوری کردن jam' âvari kardan
mutate *v.* عوض شدن' avaz shodan تحول یافتن tahav~ol yâftan
mutation *n.* تحول tahav~ol تغییر taqyir
mute *adj., n., vt.* لال lâl گنگ gong بیصدا bi-sedâ
زبان بسته zabân basteh
mutilate *vt.* پاره پاره کردن pâreh pâreh kardan
ناقص کردن nâqes kardan
mutineer *n.* شورشی shureshi یاغی yâqi
mutinous *n.* یاغی yâqi سرکش sarkesh
mutiny *n.* شورش shuresh یاغیگری yâqi-gari
mutiny *v.* شورش کردن shuresh kardan
mutt *n.* خرفت khereft
mutter *vi., vt., n.* زیرلبی گفتن zir labi goftan
mutton *n.* گوشت گوسفند gusht-e' gusfand
mutual *adj.* دوطرفه do-tarafeh متقابل moteqâbel
muzzle *v.* پوزه مالی کردن puzeh-mâli kardan
muzzle *v.* پوزه بند زدن puzeh-band zadan
muzzle *n.* دهنۀ تفنگ dahaneh-ye' tofang
myopia *n.* نزدیک بینی nazdik-bini
myriad *n., adj.* بیشمار bi-shemâr
myself *pro.* خودم khodam
mysterious *adj.* مرموز marmuz
mystery *n.* معما mo'am~â راز râz سر ser~

mystic *n.* صوفی sofi
mystical *adj.* صوفیانه sofiâneh
mysticism *n.* تصوف tasav~ of
mystify *vt.* گیج کردن gij kardan سردرگم کردن sar dargom kardan
myth *n.* افسانه afsâneh
mythical *adj.* افسانه‌ای afsâneh-i اساطیری asâtiri
mythology *n.* اسطوره ostureh اساطیر asâtir

N N n

nab *vt.* دستگیرکردن dastgir kardan گیراندا ختن gir andâkhtan
nadir *n.* عرش مقابل 'arsh-e' moqâbel سمت الرأس samt-ol ra's
nae *n., adv., adj.* نه nah
nag *n.* نق نقو neq nequ
nag *v.* نق زدن neq zadan غرغر کردن qor-qor kardan
ور زدن ver~ zadan
nail *n.* ناخن nâkhon
nail *n.* میخ mikh
nail *v.* میخکوب کردن mikh-kub kardan دستگیر کردن dast-gir kardan
nail clippers *n.* ناخنگیر nâkhon-gir
nail file *np.* سوهان ناخن suhân-e' nâkhon
nail polish *n.* لاک ناخن lâk-e' nâkhon
naive *adj.* ساده sâdeh
naivete *n.* سادگی sâdegi
naked *adj.* لخت lokht برهنه berahneh عریان 'oryân لوت lut
naked eye *n.* دید طبیعی did-e' tabi'i بدون دوربین bedun-e' durbin
namable *n.* نام گذاشتنی nâm gozâshtani
namby-pamby *n., adj.* شل و ول shol-o vel
name *v.* اسم گذاشتن esm gozâshtan نامیدن nâmidan نام nâm
name *v.* نامزد کردن nâmzad kardan اسم بردن esm bordan
nameless *adj.* بی نام bi-nâm ناشناس nâ-shenâs
namely *n.* یعنی yâ'ni صریحاً sarihan
namesake *n.* هم نام ham-nâm هم اسم ham-esm
nanny *n.* دایه dâyeh ننه naneh
nap *v.* چرت زدن chort zadan
nap *n.* کرک kork خواب پرز khâb porz
nape *n.* پشت گردن posht-e' gardan
napery *n.* دستمال سفره dastmâl sofreh
naphtha *n.* نفت naft
napper *n.* چرتی chorti
nappy *adj., n.* کرکدار kork-dâr خوابدار khâb-dâr
narcis(s)ism *n.* خودپرستی khod-parasti
narcissist *n.* خودپرست khod-parast
narcosis *n.* خمار بیهوشی khomâr-bihushi
narcotic(s) *n.* مخدرات mokhadarât افیونی ofyuni
narrate *v.* داستان گفتن dâstân goftan
narrate *v.* روایت کردن نقل کردن naql kardan ravâyat kardan

narration *n., adj.* شرح داستان sharh-e' dâstân نقل naql روایت ravâyat
narrative *n.* نقلی naqli حکایتی hekâyati
narrator *n.* داستانگو dâstân-gu نقل کننده naql konandeh راوی râvi
narrow *adj., vi., vt., n.* باریک bârik نازک nâzok
narrow-minded *adj.* باریک بین bârik-bin کوته فکر kutah-fekr
کوته نظر kutah-nazar
narrowness *n.* باریکی bâriki تنگی tangi
narrows *n.* تنگه‌ها tangeh-hâ راه باریک bârik-râh
nasal *adj., n.* تودماغی tu-damâqi انفی anfi
nasalization *n.* تودماغی کردن tu-damâqi kardan
nasalize *vt., vi.* تودماغی تلفظ کردن tu-damâqi talaf~oz kardan
nascent *v.* متولد شدن moteval~ed shodan نوظهور no-zohur
nascent *adj.* نوزاد nozâd تازه رس tâzeh-ras
nastily *adv.* بطرزبد betarz-e' bad
nastiness *n.* بی تربیتی bi-tarbiati کثیفی kasifi
nasturtium *n.* لادن lâdan نسترن nastaran
nasty *adj.* بی تربیت bi-tarbiat کثیف kasif بد bad
natal *n.* ولادتی veladati میلادی milâdi
nation *n.* ملت mel~at قوم qom
nation-wide *n.* درتمام کشور dar tamâm-e' keshvar
سرتاسری sar tâ sari
national *adj., n.* ملی mel~i قومی qomi
national *adj., n.* تبعه taba'eh
nationalism *n.* ملی گرایی mel~i garâyi
nationalist *n., adj.* ملی گرا mel~i garâ ملی پرست mel~i parast
nationality *n., vt., vi.* ملیت mel~iyat
nationalization *n.* ملی شدن mel~i-shodan
nationalize *n.* ملی کردن mel~i kardan
nationally *adv.* سراسر ملت sarâsar-e' mel~at
ازلحاظ ملی az lahâz-e' mel~i
native *adj., n.* بومی bumi محلی mahal~i اهل ahl
native-born *n.* بومی زاده bumi zâdeh
nativity *n.* تولد taval~od میلاد milâd
natural *adj., n.* طبیعی tabi'i عادی âd~i ذاتی zâti فطری fetri
natural science(s) *n.* علوم طبیعی 'olum-e' tabi'i
naturalist *n.* طبیعت گرا tabi'at-garâ طبیعت دان tabi'at-dân
naturally *n.* طبیعتاً tabi'atân البته albateh
nature *n.* طبیعت tabi'at ماهیت mâhiat سرشت seresht خوی khuy

naught *n.* هیچ چیز hich-chiz صفر sefr
naughtiness *n.* شیطنت sheytanat
naughty *adj.* شیطان sheytân آتشپاره âtesh-pâreh ناقلا nâ-qola
nausea *n., vt., vi.* حالت تهوع hâlat-e' tahavo'
nauseate *n.* حالت تهوع داشتن hâlat-e' tahavo' dâshtan
nauseating *adj.* تهوع آور tahavo'-âvar
nauseous *adj.* تهوع آور tahavo'-âvar
nautical mile *np.* گرهٔ دریایی gereh-ye' daryâyi
nautilus *n.* حلقه ماهی halqeh mâhi ناتیلوس nâtilus
naval *adj.* دریایی daryâyi
nave *n.* راهرو کلیسا râhro-e' kelisâ میان چرخ miân charkh
navel *n.* ناف nâf
navigable *adj.* کشتی گذر kashti-gozar قابل کشتیرانی qâbel-e' kashtirâni
navigate *v.* کشتی راندن kashti rândan
هواپیما راندن havâ-peymâ rândan
navigation *n.* کشتیرانی kashti-râni هواپیمابری hâvâ-peymâ-bari
navigator *n.* ناوبر nâv-bar رادارچی râdâr-chi
navvy *n.* عمله 'amaleh
navy *n.* نیروی دریایی niruy-e' daryâyi
navy bean *np.* لوبیاسفید lubiâ sefid
navy blue *n.* آبی سرمه ای âbi-e' sormeh-i
nay *adv.* نه nah آنهم نه ânham nah
ne'er-do-well *n., adj.* بیعرضه bi-'orzeh بدردنخور bedard-nakhor
neap *n.* جزرومدکم jazr-o mad-e' kam
near *adv., pre., vt., vi.* نزدیک nazdik شبیه shabih کوتاه kutâh
near miss *np.* نزدیک هدف nazdik-e' hadaf
ازبغل گوش az baqal-e' gush
near-sighted *n.* نزدیک بین nazdik-bin
nearby *adj., adv.* دم دست dam-e' dast
همین نزدیکی ها hamin nazdiki-hâ
nearly *adv.* تقریباً taqriban
neat *adj., n., pl.* تمیز tamiz خالص khâles مرتب morat~ab
نامخلوط nâ-makhlut
neatly *adv.* بانظافت bâ-nezâfat باترتیب bâ-tartib
nebula *n.* مه ستاره mah-setâreh
nebulous *adj.* ابری abri مبهم mobham کدر keder
necessarily *adv.* لزوماً lozuman
necessary *adj., n.* لازم lâzem ضروری zaruri واجب vâjeb

necessitate *vt.* ايجاب كردن ijâb kardan واجب كردن vâjeb kardan
necessity *n.* نيازمندى niâz mandi ضرورت zarurat احتياج ehtiâj
neck *n.* گردن gardan
neck *v.* ماچ و بوسه كردن mâch-o buseh kardan
neck and neck *n.* شانه بشانه shâneh be-shâneh
neckband *n.* بند گردن band-e' gardan
necking *n.* ماچ و بوسه mâch-o buseh معاشقه moâ'asheqeh
necklace *n.* گردنبند gardan-band طوق toq
necklet *n.* گردنبند gardan-band
neckpiece *n.* گردن پيچ gardan-pich
necktie *n.* كراوات kerâvât
necktie party *np.* اعدام e'dâm
nectar *n.* شهد shahd
nectarine *n.* شليل shalil
need *n.* احتياج ehtiâj حاجت hâjat نيازمندى niâzmandi
need *v.* احتياج داشتن ehtiâj dâshtan نياز داشتن niâz dâshtan
needful *adj.* محتاج mohtâj نيازمند niâz-mand لازم lâzem
needle *v.* سوزن زدن suzan zadan شيركردن shir kardan
needle *n.* سوزن برگ suzan-barg
needle-point *n.* سوزنكارى كردن suzan-kâri kardan
needless *n.* غيرضرورى qeyr-e' zaruri
needlessly *n.* بيخود و بيجهت bi-khod-o bi-jahat
needlework *n.* سوزنكارى suzan-kâri
needs *adv.* احتياجات لزوماً lozuman
needy *adj.* محتاج mohtâj نيازمند niâz-mand نقير faqir
nefarious *adj.* شرور sharur شنيع shani'
negate *n.* نفى كردن naf-y kardan انكاركردن enkâr kardan
negation *n.* نفى naf-y انكار enkâr
negative *v., adj., n.* منفى manfi نامثبت nâ-mosbat
فيلم منفى film-e' manfi
negative sign *n.* علامت منها 'alâmat-e' menhâ
negativism *n.* منفى انديشى manfi-andishi مخالفت mokhâlefat
negativity *n.* نامثبتى nâ-mosbati
negatory *n.* منفى manfi
neglect *v.* سهل انگارى كردن sahl engâri kardan
neglect *v.* غفلت كردن qeflat kardan
neglectful *adj.* سهل انگار sahl-engâr غفلت آميز qeflat-âmiz
neglector *n.* غافل qâfel غفلت كننده qeflat konandeh

neglige'(e) n. لباس خواب زنانه lebâs-e' khâb-e' zanâneh
negligence n. غفلت qeflat سهل انگاری sahl-engâri اهمال ehmâl
کوتاهی kutâhi
negligent n. غفلت کار qeflat-kâr اهمالگر ehmâl-gar
negligible adj. ناچیز nâchiz قابل اغماض qâbel-e' eqmâz
negotiable adj. قابل معامله qâbel-e' mo'âmeleh
مذاکره ای mozâkereh-i
negotiate n. مذاکره کردن mozâkereh kardan
negotiation n. مذاکره mozâkereh گفتگو goftegu
negotiator n. مذاکره کننده mozâkereh konandeh
negro n. سیاه پوست siâh-pust کاکا kâkâ
neigh n., adj., vt., vi. شیهه کشیدن shiheh keshidan
neighbor n. همسایه ham-sâyeh
neighborhood n. همسایگی ham-sâyegi محله mahal~eh حوالی havâli
جوار javâr
neighboring n. مجاور mojâver بغلی baqali
neighborly adj. همسایه وار hamsâyeh-vâr دوستانه dustâneh
neither con., adj., pro. هیچکدام hich-kodâm نه این nah in
هم نه ham nah
nemesis n. کیفردهنده keyfar dahandeh قصاص دهنده qesâs dahandeh
neo- n. نو no جدید jadid
neolithic n. آخر عصر حجر âkhar-e' 'asr-e' hajar
nepotism n. خویش التفاتی khish eltefâti هزارفامیلی hezâr fâmili
nervate n. رگه دار rageh-dâr عصبدار asab-dâr
nerve n., vt. عصب 'asab رگه rageh پی pey
nerve sl. قوت قلب qov~at-e' qalb رو ru دل del
nerve center n. تمرکز اعصاب tamarkoz-e' a'sâb مرکز markaz
nerve-wracking n. اعصاب خردکن a'sâb khord-kon
nerveless adj. بیرگ bi-rag بیحس bi-hes بی عصب bi-'asab
nervous adj. عصبی 'asabi بی تاب bi-tâb
nervous system np. سلسلة اعصاب selseleh-ye' a'sâb
nervy n. پردل و جرأت por del-o jor'at پررو por-ru
nescience n. جهل jahl نادانی nâdâni
nescient adj. جاهل jâhel نادان nâdân
nest v. لانه کردن lâneh kardan آشیانه کردن âshiâneh kardan
nest egg n. پس انداز pas-andâz
nestle n. درآغوش گرفتن dar âqush gereftan غنودن qonudan
nestling n. جوجه پرنده jujeh-ye' parandeh

net *adj.* خالص khâles دررفته dar-rafteh
net *n.* تور tur دام dâm
net *v.* بتور انداختن be-tur andâkhtan
nether(most) *n.* پایین ترین pâyintarin
netting *n., v.* تورسازی tursâzi
nettle(rash) *n.* گزنه gazaneh گزیدن gazidan کهیر kahir
network *n.* شبکه shabakeh
neuralgia *n.* درداعصاب dard-e' a'sâb
neuro- *n.* عصبی 'asabi
neurological *n.* مربوط به عصب شناسی marbut beh 'asab shenâsi
neurologist *n.* عصب شناس 'asab-shenâs
neurology *n.* عصب شناسی 'asab-shenâsi
neurolysis *n.* خرابی بافت عصب kharâbi-e' bâft-e' 'asab
neuter *v.* خنثی کردن khonsâ kardanedit اخته کردن akhteh kardan
neutral *n.* خلاص khalâs
neutral *n.* بیطرف bi-taraf خنثی khonsâ
neutrality *n.* بیطرفی bi-tarafi
never *adv.* هرگز hargez هیچوقت hichvaqt ابداً abadan
nevermore *adv.* دیگرنه digar-nah دوباره هرگز dobâreh hargez
nevertheless *n.* باوجوداین bâ-vojud-e' in معهذا ma'hâzâ
مع الوصف ma'al-vasf معذلک ma'zalek
nevus *n.* خال khâl
new *adj., adv., n.* نو no جدید jadid تازه کار tâzeh kâr
new year *n.* سال نو sâl-e' no
New Year's Eve *np.* شب ژانویه shab-e' zhânvieh
new-found *n.* تازه پیدا tâzeh peydâ
newborn *n., adj.* نوزاد no-zâd
newcomer *n.* نورسیده no-resideh
newel *n.* پله ستون pel~eh sotun
newlywed *n.* تازه عروس tâzeh-'arus تازه داماد tâzeh-dâmâd
news *n.* خبر khabar اخبار akhbâr
news room *np.* اطاق خبر otâq-e' khabar
newscast *n.* پخش اخبار pakhsh-e' akhbâr
newscaster *n.* گوینده اخبار guyandeh-ye' akhbâr
newsletter *n.* خبرنامه khabar-nâmeh
newsmonger *n.* خبرپخش کن khabar pakhsh-kon
newspaper *n., adj.* روزنامه ruz-nâmeh جریده jarideh
newsreel *n.* فیلم خبری film-e' khabari

newsworthy *adj.* خبر ارزش دار khabar-e' arzeshdâr
next *n., pre.* دیگر digar آینده âyandeh
next *n., pre.* بعدی ba'di پهلویی pahluyi
next of kin *np.* بستگان نزدیک bastegân-e' nazdik ورثه varaseh
next-door *adv., adj.* بغلی baqali همسایه ham-sâyeh
nexus *n.* ارتباط ertebât رابطه râbeteh
nib *n., vt.* منقار menqâr نوک nok
nibble *n., vi.* ناخنک زدن nâkhonak zadan دندان زدن dandân zadan
niblick *n.* چوگان گلف chogân-e' golf
nibs *n.* بانفوذ bâ-nofuz
nice *adj.* باصفا bâ-safâ خوب khub دلپسند del-pasand قشنگ qashang
nicely *adv.* بخوبی be-khubi مؤدبانه mo'ad~abâneh
nicety *n.* ظرافت zerâfat دقت deq~at
niche *n., vt.* طاقچه tâqcheh
nick *n.* خراش دادن kharâsh dâdan چوب خط کردن chub khat kardan
nickel *n., vt.* آب نیکل âb-nikel پنج سنتی panj-senti
nickelodeon *n.* شهرفرنگ shahr-e' farang
nicker *pl.* شیشه شکن shisheh-shekan پوزخند puz-khand
nickname *v.* اسم لقب گذاشتن esm-e' laqab gozâshtan
niece *n.* دختربرادر dokhtar-e' barâdar دختر خواهر dokhtar-e' khâhar
nifty *adj., n.* جالب jâleb باحال bâ-hâl
niggard *n., adj.* خسیس khasis کنس kenes
niggardly *adj., adv.* خسیسانه khasisâneh ناچیز nâ-chiz
چندرقاز chender qâz
night *n., adj.* شب shab
night clothes *np.* لباس خواب lebâs-e' khâb
night club *np.* کافه kâfeh کلوب kolub
night crawler *np.* شب خیز shab-khiz
night latch *np.* چفت در cheft-e' dar
night light *np.* شب چراغ shab cherâq
night owl *np.* مرغ حق morq-e' haq دیرخواب dir-khâb
night robe *np.* رب دوشامبر rob-doshâmbr لباس خواب lebâs-e' khâb
night school *n.* مدرسهٔ شبانه madreseh-ye' shabâneh
night stick *n.* باتون bâtun
night time *n.* شب shab تاریکی târiki
night watch *np.* شبگردی shab-gardi
night watchman *np.* شبگرد shab-gard نگهبان شب negahbân-e' shab
nightcap *n.* شب کلاه shab-kolâh

مشروب قبل از خواب mashrub qabl az khâb ....
nightdress *n.* لباس خواب lebâs-e′ khâb
nightfall *n.* شبانگاه shabân-gâh
nightgown *n.* لباس خواب lebâs-e′ khâb
nightingale *n.* andalib′ عندلیب hazâr(dastân) هزار(دستان) bolbol بلبل
nightlong *adj., adv.* تمام شب tamâm-e′ shab
nightly *adj.* شبانه shabâneh هرشب har-shab
nightmare *n.* کابوس kâbus خواب بد khâb-e′ bad بختک bakhtak
nightspot *n.* کلوب شب kolub-e′ shab
nightwalker *n.* شبرو shab-ro شبکار shab-kâr
nightwatch man *n.* پلیس شبگرد polis-e′ shab-gard
گشت شب gasht-e′ shab گزمه gazmeh
nightwear *n.* لباس شب lebâs-e′ shab پیژامه pizhâmeh
nighty *n.* پیژامه pizhâmeh لباس خواب lebâs-e′ khâb
nill *vt., vi.* هیچ hich
nimble *n.* نرم narm فرز ferz زیرک zirak
nimiety *n.* افراط efrât تکرار tekrâr
nincompoop *n.* احمق ahmaq کودن kodan
nine *n., adj.* نه noh
nineteen *n., adj.* نوزده nuz-dah
ninety *n., adj.* نود navad
ninny *n.* بچه ننه bach~eh naneh
nip *v.* سرمازدن sarmâ zadan
nip *v.* وشگون گرفتن veshgun gereftan چیدن chidan
nip(and tuck) *n.* نزدیک بهم nazdik-e′ behâm
nipper *n.* گازگیر gâz-gir سیم بر sim-bor دستبند dast-band
nipple *n.* نوک پستان nok-e′ pestân ممه mameh
nippy *n.* سوزدار suz-dâr گازگیر gâz-gir فرز ferz سرد sard
nitwit *n.* احمق ahmaq
nix *n., adv., int., vt.* هیچ hich به هیچ وجه be-hich vajh
no *adj., adv., n.* هیچ hich
no *adj., adv., n.* نه nah خیر kheyr نخیر na-kheyr
no one *n.* هیچکس hich-kas
nob *n.* سر گنده sar کله gondeh kal~eh
nobby *adj.* قلنبه qolonbeh درجه یک darejeh yek
nobility *n.* اشرافیت ashrâfiyat نجیب زادگی najib-zâdegi
noble *adj., n.* نجیب زاده najib-zâdeh اشرافی ashrâfi اصیل asil
nobleman *n.* نجیب زاده najib-zâdeh

nobody *pro., n.* هیچکس hich-kas هیچکاره hich-kâreh
nocturnal *adj., n.* شبانه‌ای shabâneh-i شب بیداری shab bidâri
nocturne *n.* شباهنگ shabâ-hang نقاشی شب naq~âshi-e' shab
nocuous *n.* مضر mozer سمی sam~i
nod *vi., vt., n.* سرتکان دادن sar takân dâdan
node *n.* گره gereh بند band مقطع maqta'
nodule *n.* گرهک gerehak
noise *n., vt., vi.* صدا sedâ سروصدا sar-o sedâ
noiseless *adj.* بیصدا bi-sedâ
noisemaker *n.* شلوغ کن sholuq-kon جغجغه jeq-jeqeh
noisily *adv.* باسروصدا bâ sar-o sedâ
noisiness *n.* شلوغی sholuq-i
noisome *adj.* مضر mozer بدبو bad-bu
noisy *adj.* پرسروصدا por sar-o sedâ
nom de guerre *np.* نام مستعار nâm-e' mosta'âr
nom de plume *n.* اسم قلم esm-e' qalam تخلص takhal~os
nomad *n., adj.* چادرنشین châdor neshin خانه بدوش khâneh-bedush
nomadic *adj.* چادرنشینی châdor neshini
nominal *adj.* اسمی esmi جزیی joz'i
nominally *n.* اسماً esman
nominate *vt., adj.* نامزد nâmzad کاندیدا کردن kândidâ kardan
nomination *n.* کاندیدایی kândidâyi
nominative *n.* فاعلی fâ'eli
non profit *n.* غیرانتفاعی qeyr-e' entefâ'i
nonage *n.* زیرسنی zir-e' sen~i صغر saqr
nonchalant *adj.* بی علاقه bi-'alâqeh لاقید lâqeyd
noncombat(ant) *n.* غیرنبردی qeyr-e' nabardi
noncommissioned *adj.* بدون درجه bedun-e' darejeh
noncommittal *n.* بی موضع bi-moze' مداخله نکن modâkheleh-nakon
noncompliance *n.* نافرمانی nâ-farmâni
nonconformity *n.* نامطابتی nâ-motâqebati
none *n.* هیچ کس hich-kas هیچ یک hich-yek
none *n.* هیچ hich هیچ کدام hich kodâm
nonentity *n.* عدم وجود 'adam-e' vojud نیستی nisti
nonessential *adj., n.* غیرضروری qeyr-e' zaruri
nonintervention *n.* عدم مداخله 'adam-e' modâkheleh
nonsense *n.* چرت و پرت chart-o part چرند charand جفنگ jafang
مزخرف mozakhraf

nonsensical *n.* مهملات mohmalât

nonstop *adj., adv.* بدون توقف bedun-e' tavaq~ of یکسره yek-sareh

noodle *n.* رشته reshteh

nook *n.* گوشه gusheh کنج konj

noon(time) *n.* ظهر zohr

noose *n., vt.* حلقه طناب halqeh tanâb

nope *adv.* نه nah

nor *con., n.* هم نه ham nah

norm *n.* رسم معمول rasm-e' ma'mul میزان mizân

normal *adj., n.* معمولی ma'muli طبیعی tabi'i عادی 'âd~i

normalcy *n.* حالت عادی hâlat-e' 'âd~i

normality *n.* حالت عادی hâlat-e' 'âd~i

normalize *v.* حسنه کردن hasaneh kardan

normalize *v.* عادی کردن 'âd~i kardan

normally *adv.* معمولاً ma'mulan

north *n., adj., adv.* شمال shomâl

North Pole *n.* قطب شمال qotb-e' shomâl

northeast *n.* شمال شرقی shomâl-e' sharqi

northerly *adj., adv., n.* شمالی shomâli

northern *n.* شمالی shomâli درشمال dar shomâl-e'

northward *adv., adj., n.* بطرف شمال betaraf-e' shomâl

northwest *n., adj., adv.* شمال غربی shomâl-e' qarbi

nose *n., vt., vi.* دماغ damâq بینی bini شامه shâm~eh

nose(around) *n.* فضولی کردن fozuli kardan

nose-dive *vi.* کله معلق شدن kal~eh mo'al~aq shodan

nosebleed *n.* خون دماغ khun-damâq

nosey(nosy) *n.* فضول fozul دماغ گنده damâq-gondeh

nosing *n., v.* لب پله lab-pel~eh

nostalgia *n.* یادگشتی yâd-gashti دلتنگی del-tangi

nostalgic *n.* یادگشت yâd-gasht دلتنگ del-tang

nostril *n.* سوراخ بینی surâkh-e' bini

nosy *adj.* فضول fozul

notability *n.* معروفیت ma'rufiyat

notable *adj., n.* معروف ma'ruf متشخص moteshakh~es

notable *adj., n.* قابل ملاحظه qâbel-e' molâhezeh

notarization *n.* تصدیق امضاء tasdiq-e' emzâ'

notarize *vt.* گواهی کردن gavâhi kardan تصدیق کردن tasdiq kardan

notary(public) *n.* سردفتر اسناد رسمی sar-daftar-e' asnâd-e' rasmi

notation *n.* يادداشت yâd-dâsht
notation *n.* اعداد نويسى 'adâd nevisi حروف نويسى horuf nevisi
notch *n., vt.* شكاف shekâf چوب خط chub-khat پله pel~eh
note *n.* يادداشت yâd-dâsht توضيح tozih
note *v.* يادداشت كردن yâd-dâsht kardan
note *n.* نت not
notebook *n.* دفترچه يادداشت daftar-cheh-ye' yâd-dâsht
noted *adj., v.* معروف ma'ruf بنام be-nâm
noteless *adj.* بى نام bi-nâm نت بى bi-not
noteworthy *adj.* قابل ملاحظه qâbel-e' molâhezeh
nothing *n.* هيچ چيز hich chiz صفر sefr
nothingness *n.* نيستى nisti عدم وجود 'adam-e' vojud
notice *v.* ملتفت شدن moltafet shodan
ملاحظه كردن molâhezeh kardan
notice *n.* اخطار ekhtâr تذكر tazâk~or
noticeable *adj.* قابل ملاحظه qâbel-e' molâhezeh
notification *n.* اخطار ekhtâr تذكر tazak~or
notifier *n.* تذكردهنده tazak~or dahandeh خبردهنده khabar dahandeh
notify *vt.* اطلاع دادن et~elâ' dâdan اخطاردادن ekhtâr dâdan
notion *n.* خيال khiâl تصور tasav~or هوس havas
notional *n.* خيالى khiâli تصورى tasav~ori
notoriety *n.* بدنامى bad-nâmi شهرت shohrat
notorious *adj.* بدنام bad-nâm بد شهرت bad-shohrat
notwithstanding *pre., con., adv.* بااينهمه bâ-inhameh
باوجود اين كه bâ vojud-e' in keh
nougat *n.* بادام شيرينى bâdâm shirini
noun *n.* اسم esm
nourish *vt.* تغذيه كردن taqzieh kardan پروردن parvardan
nourishing *n.* مقوى moqav~i پرقوت porqov~at
رشدپرور roshd-parvar
nourishment *n.* تغذيه taqzieh پرورش parvaresh قوت qut
nouveau riche *n.* تازه بدوران رسيده tâzeh bedorân resideh
nova *n.* ستاره نورانى setâreh-ye' nurâni
novel *adj., n.* جديد jadid
novel *adj., n.* رمان român
novelist *n.* رمان نويس român-nevis
novelty *n., adj.* تازگى jadidi جديدى tâzegi
novice *n.* تازه كار tâzeh-kâr مبتدى mobtadi ناشى nashi

now *adv., con., n.* حالا hâlâ الان alân اکنون aknun اینک inak

now(and then) *n.* گهگاهی gah-gâhi
هرچندوقت یکبار har-chand vaqt yek b

nowadays *adv., n.* اینروزها in ruz-hâ تازگی ها tâzegi-hâ

noway *adv.* بهیچ وجه be-hich vajh

nowhere *n.* هیچ جا hich-jâ

noxious *n.* مضر mozer زیان آور ziân-âvar

nozzle *n.* سرلوله sar-luleh دماغ damâq

nuance *n.* تنوع جزیی tanav o'-e' joz'i

nuclear *adj.* هستهای hasteh-i

nucleus *n.* هسته hasteh مرکز markaz مغز maqz

nude *n.* لخت lokht برهنه berahneh عریان 'oryân لوت lut

nudge *vt., vi., n.* با آرنج bâ-ârenj سقلمه زدن soqolmeh

nudism *n.* عریان مآبی 'oryân maâbi لختی گری lokhti-gari

nudist *n., adj.* عریان مآب 'oryân-maâb لخت دوست lokht-dust

nudity *n.* لختی lokhti برهنگی berahnegi عورت 'urat

nugget *n.* حبه hab~eh سنگ طلا sang-e' talâ

nuisance *n.* بلا balâ دردسر dard-e' sar

null *adj.* باطل bâtel صفر sefr

nullification *n.* القا elqâ' بطالت betâlat

nullify *v.* لغو laqv باطل bâtel کردن پوچ puch kardan

nullify *v.* باطل کردن bâtel kardan

nullify *v.* پوچ کردن puch kardan

nullity *n.* پوچی puchi باطلی bâteli

numb *adj., vt.* بیحس کردن bi-hes kardan

numb(ed) *adj.* بی حس bi-hes کرخت kerekht

numberless *adj.* بیشماره bi-shomâreh

numerable *n.* قابل شمردن qâbel-e' shemordan

numeral *n., adj.* عدد 'adâd رقم raqam

numerals *n.* اعداد a'dâd

numerate *vt.* شمردن shemordan عدد خواندن 'adad khândan

numerator *n.* صورت surat شمارنده shomârandeh

numeric(al) *n.* عددی 'adadi رقمی raqami

numerically *adv.* ازلحاظ تعداد az lahâz-e' te'dâd

numerous *n.* متعدد mote'ad~ed بسیار besyâr

numskull *n.* احمق ahmaq بی کله bi-kal~eh

nun *n.* راهبه râhebeh خواهر دینی khâhar-e' dini

nunnery *n.* راهبه خانه râhebeh khâneh

nupital *n.* نکاحی nekâhi ازدواجی ezdevâji
nurse *n.* پرستار parastâr دایه dâyeh
nurse *v.* شیردادن shir dâdan شیر خوردن shir khordân
nurse *v.* پرستاری کردن parastâri kardan
nurse *v.* پروردن parvardan
nursemaid *n.* دخترپرستار dokhtar-e' parastâr
nursery *n.* شیرخوارگاه shir-khâr-gâh پرورشگاه parvaresh-gâh
nursery *n.* درخت فروشی derakht forushi
nursery rhyme *np.* اشعارکودکان ash'âr-e' kudakân
nursery school *np.* کودکستان kudakestân
nursing home *n.* خانهٔ سالخوردگان khâneh-ye' sâl-khordegân
nurture *vt., n.* پرورش دادن parvaresh dâdan
nut *n., adj., vi.* بادام bâdâm مهره mohreh
nut *sl.* خل khol
nutcracker *n.* بادام شکن bâdâm-shekan فندق شکن fandoq-shekan
nutmeg *n.* جوز هندی joz hendi
nutrient *adj., n.* مقوی moqav~i
nutrition *n.* تغذیه taqzieh قوت qov~at
nutritional *n.* تغذیهای taqzieh-i قوتی qov~ati
nutritionist *n.* تغذیه شناس taqzieh shenâs
nutritious *adj.* قوت دهنده qov~at dahandeh
nuts! *n.* ! زکی zeki!
       ! زرشک zereshk!
nutshell *n.* پوست گردو pust-e' gerdu
nutty *n.* پربادام porbâdâm خل مسلک khol-maslak
nuzzle *n.* دماغ مالی کردن damâq-mâli kardan
nylon(s) *n.* نایلون nâylon جوراب نایلونی jurâb nâyloni
nymph *n.* زیبارو zibâ-ru پری pari
nymphomaniac *adj., n.* زن هوسباز zan-e' havas-bâz

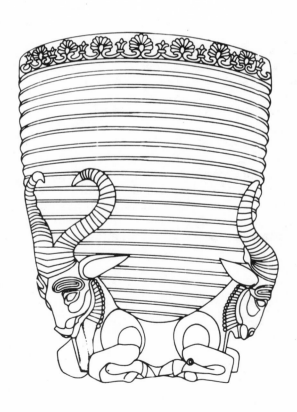

O o ο

o! *n.* ای ey آی ây یا - yâ ا - â
oaf *n.* بیدست و پا bi-dast-o pâ یبس yobs
oak *n.* بلوط balut
oar *n., vt., vi.* پارو زدن pâru zadan
oarless *adj.* بی پارو bi-pâru
oarsman *n.* پاروزن pâru-zan
oasis *n.* واحه vâheh
oat *n.* جووحشی jo-e' vahshi
oath *n.* سوگند sogand قسم qasam
oatmeal *n., adj.* بلغور جو وحشی balqur-e' jo-e' vahshi
obdurate *adj.* سنگدل sang-del سرسخت sar-sakht
obedience *n.* اطاعت etâ'at فرمانبری farmân-bari
obedient *adj.* مطیع moti' فرمانبر farmân-bar چاکر châker
obeisance *n.* مخلصی mokhlesi چاکری châkeri کرنش kornesh
obeisant *adj.* مخلص mokhles چاکر châker
obese *adj., vi.* خیکی khik~i فربه farbeh
obesity *n.* زیادچاقی ziâd châqi فربهی farbehi
obey *vt., vi.* اطاعت کردن etâ'at kardan گوش کردن gush kardan
obfuscate *vt.* تاریک کردن târik kardan گیج کردن gij kardan
obfuscation *n.* تاریکی târiki گیجی giji
obituary *n., adj.* آگهی درگذشت âgahi-e' dar-gozasht
object *n., vi., vt.* مفعول maf'ul
object *n.* چیز chiz شیء shey'
object *n.* مقصود maqsud هدف hadaf منظور manzur
object *v.* مخالفت کردن mokhâlefat kardan
object *v.* اعتراض کردن e'terâz kardan
objection *n.* اعتراض e'terâz ایراد irâd مخالفت mokhâlefat
objectionable *adj.* قابل اعتراض qâbel-e' e'terâz
objective *n.* بی غرض bi-qaraz هدف hadaf مفعولی maf'uli
objectively *adv.* بی غرضانه bi-qarazâneh
objectivism *n.* دور از اندیشه گری dur az andisheh-gari
objectivity *n.* بی غرضی bi-qarazi دور از اندیشه ای dur az andisheh-i
objectless *n.* بی هدف bi-hadaf بدون هیچ چیز bedun-e' hich chiz
objector *n.* اعتراض کننده e'terâz konandeh معترض mo'tarez
obligate *v.* توی رودروایسی گذاشتن tuy-e' rudarvâysi gozâshtan
obligate *v.* متعهد کردن mote'ah~ed kardan
obligated *n.* متعهد mote'ah~ed مرهون marhun مدیون madyun

obligation *n.* تعهد ta'ah~od اخلاقی وظیفهٔ vazifeh-ye' akhlâqi
obligatory *adj.* تعهدی ta'ah~odi
oblige *vt.* کردن مجبور majbur kardan گذاشتن منت men~at gozâshtan
obliged *v.* مدیون madyun گیر نمک namak-gir
obliger *n.* گذار منت men~at-gozâr
obliging *adj., v.* کمک به مایل mâyel beh-komak
oblique *adj., adv., vi., n.* مایل mâyel کج kaj مورب movar~ab
obliterate *vt.* بردن ازبین az beyn bordan کردن پاک pâk kardan
obliteration *n.* انهدام enhedâm نابودی nâ-budi
oblivion *n.* فراموشی farâmushi ورطه varteh
oblivious *adj.* توجه بی bi-tavaj~oh فراموشکار farâmush-kâr غافل qâfel
oblong *adj., n.* مستطیل دراز derâz mostatil
obnoxious *adj.* زننده zanandeh انزجارآور enzejâr âvar
obscene *adj.* وقیح vaqih بیشرمانه bi-sharmâneh رکیک rakik
قبیح qabih
obsceneties *n.* رکیک فحش fohsh-e' rakik مستهجنات mostah-janât
obscenity *n.* وقاحت veqâhat بیشرمی bisharmi رکیکی rakiki
obscurant *n., adj.* کننده پنهان penhân konandeh
obscure *adj., vt., n.* تیره tireh تار târ مبهم mobham
کردن گمنام gomnâm kardan
obscurity *n.* تیرگی tiregi تاریکی târiki گمنامی gomnâmi
observable *adj.* کردنی رعایت re'âyat kardani
ملاحظه قابل qâbel-e' molâhezeh
observance *n.* رعایت re'âyat ملاحظه molâhezeh مراعات morâ'ât
observant *n.* ملاحظه با bâ-molâhezeh بارعایت bâ-re'âyât
observation *n.* ملاحظه molâhezeh مشاهده moshâhedeh
عقیده 'aqideh
observation post *n.* دیدهبانگاه didebân-gâh
observational *n.* مشاهدهای moshâhedeh-i
observatory *n.* رصدخانه rasad khâneh دیدگاه did-gâh
observe *v.* کردن ملاحظه molâhezeh kardan
observe *v.* مشاهدهکردن moshâhedeh kardan
کردن رعایت re'âyat kardan
observer *n.* کننده مشاهده moshâhedeh konandeh بان دیده dideh-bân
obsess *vt.* عقده 'oqdeh دادن فکری آزار âzâr-e' fekri dâdan
obsession *n.* عقده 'oqdeh فکری مشغولیت mashquliyat-e' fekri
obsessive *adj.* ای عقده 'oqdeh-i آزارفکری âzâr-e' fekri
obsolescent *n.* بدردنخور bedard nakhor

obsolete *adj., vt.* اسقاط asqât بدردنخور bedard nakhor
obstacle *n.* مانع mâne' سد sad~
obstacle race *np.* دو بامانع do-e' bâ-mâne'
obstetrician *n.* پزشک زایمان pezeshk-e' zâyemân
obstetrics *n.* زایمان zâyemân قابلگی qâbelegi
obstinacy *n.* سرسختی sar-sakhti کله شقی kal~eh-shaqi سمجی semeji
لجاجت lejâjat
obstinate *adj.* سرسختی sar-sakhti کله شق kal~eh-shaq~ سمج semej
لجوج lajuj
obstruct *v.* سد کردن sad~ kardan مسدود کردن masdud kardan
مانع شدن mâne' shodan
کارشکنی کردن kâr-shekani kardan
obstruction *n.* ممانعت jelo-giri ممانعت momâne'at
کارشکنی kâr shekani مانع mâne'
obstructive *adj.* جلوگیر jelo-gir کارشکن kar-shekan
obtain *vt., vi.* بدست آوردن bedast âvardan
فراهم کردن farâham kardan
obtainable *n.* بدست آوردنی be-dast âvardani
obtainment *n.* بدست آوری be-dast âvari
obtrusion *n.* بیرونزدگی birun-zadegi فضولی fozuli دخالت dekhâlat
obtrusive *adj.* بیرون زن birun-zan فضول fozul
دخالت کننده dekhâlat konandeh مزاحم mozâhem
obturate *vt.* مسدود کردن masdud kardan
obturator *n.* مسدود کننده masdud konandeh
obtuse *adj.* باز bâz منفرجه monfarejeh
occasion *n.* موقعیت moqe'iyat فرصت forsat اکازیون okâzion
occasional(ly) *n.* گهگاهی gahgâhi بعضی مواقع ba'zi mavâqe'
occident(al) *n.* باختری bâkhtari
occlude *vt., vi.* مجرا بستن majrâ bastan مسدود کردن masdud kardan
occlusive *adj., n.* سوراخگیر surâkh-gir
occult *adj., n.* سحروجادو sehr-o jâdu خرافات khorâfâti
occultism *n.* سحروجادوگری sehr-o jâdu-gari
occupancy *n.* اشغال eshqâl سکونت sokunat ساکنین sâkenin
occupant *n.* اشغال کننده eshqâl konandeh ساکن sâken
occupation *n.* حرفه herfeh کار kâr شغل shoql
occupational *adj.* حرفهای herfeh-i کاری kâri شغلی shoqli
occupier *n.* اشغالگر eshqâl-gar متصرف شونده motesar~ef shavandeh
occupy *vt., vi.* اشغال کردن eshqâl kardan

تصرف کردن tasar~of kardan ....

occur *vi.* رخ دادن rokh dâdan اتفاق افتادن et~efâq oftâdan

occurrence *n.* رویداد ruydâd واقعه vâqe'eh اتفاق et~efâq

ocean *n.* اقیانوس oqiânus

oceanic *adj.* اقیانوسی oqiânusi

octagon *n.* هشت ضلعی hasht zel'i

octave *n.* اکتاو oktâv هشت گام hasht gâm

octogenarian *n.* هشتاد ساله hashtâd sâleh

octopus *n.* هشت پا hasht-pâ

odd *adj., n.* ناجور nâ-jur متفرقه motefar~eqeh

odd *adj., n.* عجیب 'ajib غریب qarib

odd *adj., n.* طاق tâq فرد fard تکی taki

oddish *n.* عجیب 'ajib غریب qarib عوضی 'avazi

oddity *n.* عجیبی 'ajibi غریبی qaribi

odds *n.* امتیاز emtiâz شانس shâns

odds *n.* آوانتاژ âvântâzh شانس shâns

odds *n.* نابرابری nâ-barâbari

odds and ends *np.* خرت و پرت khert-o pert خرده ریز khordeh riz

ode *n.* قصیده qasideh

odious *adj.* زننده zanandeh نفرت آمیز nefrat âmiz

odometer *n.* مسافت سنج masâfat-sanj

odor *n.* بو bu

odorless *adj.* بی بو bi-bu

odorous *adj.* بودار bu-dâr

odyssey *n.* سفرحماسه‌ای safar-e' hemâseh-i

of *n., pre.* از az

of course *n.* البته albat~eh

off *adv., pre., adj., n.* پرت part خل khol

off *adv., pre., adj., n.* خاموش khâmush

off *adv., pre., adj., n.* کسری kasri

off *adv., pre., adj., n.* تعطیل ta'til

off *adv., pre., adj., n.* از روی az ruy-e' دور از dur az

off and on *n.* گهگاهی gahgâhi

off with you! *n.* بزن بچاک bezan bechâk!

off-guard *n.* بی هوا bi-havâ

off-limit *n.* قدغن qadeqan ممنوع الورود mamnu'ol vorud

off-white *adj., n.* سفید خاکستری sefid-e' khâkestari

offcast *adj., n.* رهاشده rahâ-shodeh

offchance *n.* امکان جزیی emkân-e' joz'i
offcolor *n.* ناهنجار nâ-hanjâr نامناسب nâ-monâseb
offend *v.* دلخورکردن delkhor kardan رنجاندن ranjândan
offend *v.* بی احترامی کردن bi-ehterâmi kardan
offense *n.* حمله hamleh
offense *n.* بی احترامی bi-ehterâmi
offense *n.* تخلف takhal~of
offenseless *adj.* بی تخلف bi-takhal~of بدون رنجش bedun-e' ranjesh
offensive *adj., n.* حمله ای hamleh-i تهاجمی tahâjomi
offensive *adj., n.* اهانت آمیز ehânat-âmiz
offer *v.* پیشنهاد کردن pish-nahâd kardan
offer *v.* تعارف کردن ta'ârof kardan
offer *v.* اظهارکردن ez-hâr kardan
offer *n.* پیشنهاد pish-nahâd تعارف ta'ârof
offering *n.* هدیه hedyeh قربانی qorbâni
offhand *adv., adj.* همین جوری hamin-juri
بدون مطالعه bedun-e' motâle'eh
office *n.* اداره edâreh دفترخانه daftar khâneh مقام maqâm
منصب mansab
officeholder *n.* صاحب منصب sâheb mansab
officer *n., vt.* افسر afsar درجه دار darejeh-dâr
officer *n., vt.* مأمور ma'mur متصدی motesad~i
official *n., adj.* مأمور ma'mur صاحب منصب sâheb-mansab
official *n., adj.* رسمی rasmi قانونی qânuni اداری edâri
officially *adv.* رسما rasman
officiate *vi.* اداره کردن edâreh kardan داوری کردن dâvari kardan
offset *n., adj., vt., vi.* جبران کردن jobrân kardan
متعادل کردن mote'âdel kardan
offshoot *n.* شاخه shâkheh مشتق moshtaq شعبه sho'beh
offshore *adv., adj.* دریایی daryâyi ساحلی sâheli
offspring *pl.* فرزند farzand اخلاف akhlâf نسل nasl
often(times) *n.* اغلب aqlab بیشتر وقتها bishtar-e' vaqt-hâ بارها bârhâ
ogle *n.* باچشم خوردن bâ cheshm khordan
هیزچشمی کردن hiz-cheshmi kardan
نظربازی کردن nazar-bâzi kardan
ogler *n.* هیزچشم hiz-cheshm نظرباز nazar-bâz
oh brother! *n.* ای بابا ey bâbâ
oh! *n.* آه âh! ای وای ey vây!

.... آخ âkh!

oil *n.* روغن roqan گریس geris
oil *n.* نفت naft
oil *v.* روغن زدن roqan zadan چرب کردن charb kardan
oil *n.* روغن roqan
oil color *np.* رنگ روغن rang-roqan
oil well *n.* چاه نفت châh-e' naft
oilcan *n.* روغن دان roqan-dân
oilpaper *n.* کاغذ روغنی kâqaz roqani
oilskin *n.* مشمع mosham~a'
oily *n.* روغنی roqani چرب charb
ointment *n.* پماد pomâd
okay *adj., adv., vt., n.* باشه bâsheh!
okay *v.* تصویب کردن tasvib kardan
okra *n.* بامیه bâmieh
old *adj.* پیر pir کهنسال kohansâl مسن mosen فرتوت fartut
old *adj., n.* کهنه kohneh قدیمی qadimi
old *adj., n.* قدیم qadim گذشته gozashteh
old age *np.* سالخوردگی sâl-khordegi پیری piri
old hand *np.* کهنه کار kohneh-kâr باتجربه bâ-tajrobeh
old maid *np.* دخترترشیده dokhtar-e' torshideh
old man *sl.* پدر pedar شوهر shuhar رئیس ra'is پیرمرد pir-e' mard
old moon *n.* ماه کهنه mâh-e' kohneh
old school *np.* قدیمی مسلک qadimi maslak قدماً qodamâ
old wives' tale *n.* قصهٔ خاله زنک qes~eh-ye' khâleh zanak
old-fashioned *adj.* قدیمی مسلک qadimi maslak امل om~ol
old-line *adj.* محافظه کار mohâfezeh-kâr باسابقه bâ-sâbeqeh
old-timer *n.* سابقه دار sâbeqeh-dâr قدیمی مسلک qadimi maslak
oldish *n.* پیرنظر pir-nazar
oligarchy *n.* الیگارشی oligârshi
حکومت چندتایی hokumat-e' chand-tâyi
olive *n.* زیتون zeytun
olive *adj.* زیتونی zeytuni
olive branch *np.* پیشنهاد صلح pishnahâd-e' solh
olive drab *np.* سبززیتونی sabz-e' zeytuni لباس سربازی lebâs-e' sarbâzi
olive green *n.* سبززیتونی sabz-e' zeytuni
olive oil *n.* روغن زیتون roqan-e' zeytun
omelet(te) *n.* املت omlet

omen *n., vt.* فال fâl یمن yomn

ominous *n.* بد یمن bad-yomn

omissible *adj.* حذف شدنی hazf-shodani

omission *n.* حذف hazf

omit *vt.* حذف کردن hazf kardan

omni- *n.* همه hameh

omnipotent *adj., n.* قادر qâder توانا tavânâ قدرتمند qodrat-mand قهار qah~âr

omniscient *adj.* غیب دان qeyb-dân

on *pre., adv., adj., n.* دربر dar-bar سر sar-e' به پیش beh-pish

on *pre., adv., adj., n.* روشن roshan

on *pre., adv., adj., n.* روی ru-ye' بر bar

on(and off) *n.* گاهگذاری gâh-gozâr-i

on(and on) *n.* مدام modâm هی hey

on(the house) *n.* بحساب be-hesâb-e' میزبان mizbân مجانی maj~âni

on(time) *n.* سروقت sar-e' vaqt

on(to) *n.* باخبراز bâ-khabar az

onager *n.* خروحشی khar-e' vashshi منجنیق manjeniq

once *adv., adj., con., n.* یکبار yekbâr یکدفعه yekdaf'eh وقتیکه vaqtikeh

once(and again) *n.* پشت سرهم posht-e' sar-e' ham

once(and for all) *n.* بطور قطعی betor-e' qat'i

once(in a while) *n.* گهگاهی gah-gâhi
هرچندوقت یکبار har chand vaqt yek b

once(or twice) *n.* یکی دوبار yeki do bâr

once(upon a time) *n.* یکی بود یکی نبود yeki bud yeki na-bud

once-over *n.* نگاه اجمالی negâh-e' ejmâli

oncoming *adj., n.* نزدیک شونده nazdik shavandeh

one *adj., n., pro.* یکی yeki

one *adj., n., pro.* کس kas شخص shakhs آدم âdam

one *adj., n., pro.* یک yek تک tak یکتا yektâ یگانه yegâneh

one and all *n.* همه کس hameh-kas همه باهم hameh bâ-ham

one another *np.* یکدیگر yek-digar همدیگر ham-digar

one at a time *n.* نوبت بنوبت nobat be-nobat
دانه بدانه dâneh be-dâneh

one by one *n.* یکی بعد ازدیگری yeki ba'd az digari

one-night stand *np.* یک شبه yek shabeh

one-sided *adj.* یکطرفه yek tarafeh

one-step *n.* تک پا tak-pâ

one-time *adj.* یک زمانی yek zamâni
one-track *n.* یک خطی yek-khat~i باریک بین bârik-bin
one-way *adj.* یکطرفه yek tarafeh یکسره yek-sareh
oneness *n.* یکتایی yektâyi وحدت vahdat
onerous *adj.* پرمشقت por masheq~at کمرشکن kamar-shekan
بسیارسخت besyâr sakht
oneself *pro.* خودش khod-ash
ongoing *n.* درجریان dar jaryân
onion *n., adj.* پیاز piâz
onlooker *n., adj., con.* تماشاگر tamâshâ-gar ناظر nâzer
onlooking *n.* ناظر nâzer
only *adv., adj., con.* نقط faqat تنها tanhâ
only too *n.* خیلی kheyli
onrush *n.* حمله وری hamleh vari
onset *n.* شروع shoru' حمله hamleh
onshore *adv., adj.* ساحلی sâheli بطرف ساحل betaraf-e' sâhel
onside *n.* داخل dâkhel
onslaught *n.* هجوم سهمگین hojum-e' sahmgin
onto *pre.* بر روی bar ruy-e' به سوی beh suy-e'
onus(probandi) *n.* سنگینی اثبات sangini-e' esbât
onward(s) *n.* بجلو be-jelo بپیش be-pish
ooze *vi., vt., n.* تراوش کردن tarâvosh kardan
ooziness *n.* تراوشی tarâvoshi
oozy *adj.* تراوش کننده tarâvosh konandeh لجنی lajani
opacity *n.* ماتی mâti تاریکی târiki ابهام ebhâm
opal(ine) *n.* سنگ سیلیسی sang-e' silisi
opaque *adj., n., vt.* مات mât تار târ کدر keder مبهم mobham
open *n.* باز bâz روباز rubâz آزاد âzâd
open *v.* باز کردن bâz kardan افتتاح کردن eftetâh kardan
open air *n.* فضای باز fazâ-ye' bâz هوای آزاد havâ-ye' âzâd
open letter *n.* نامهٔ سرگشاده nâmeh-ye' sargoshâdeh
open season *n.* فصل شکار fasl-e' shekâr
open(out) *n.* توسعه دادن tose'eh dâdan آشکارکردن âshkâr kardan
open(to) *n.* حاضر hâzer پذیرا pazirâ مایل mâyel
open(up) *n.* باز کردن bâz kardan
توی دل بیرون ریختن tu-ye' del birun rikhtan
open-and-shut *adj.* واضح vâzeh آشکار âshkâr
open-door *adj.* درباز dar-bâz تجارت آزاد tejârat-e' âzâd

open-eyed *adj.* باچشم باز bâ-cheshm-e' bâz
open-faced *np.* روباز ru-bâz
open-handed *adj.* بخشنده bakhshandeh
open-minded *adj.* آزادفكر âzâd fekr بى تعصب bi-ta'as~ob
روشن بين roshan-bin بينا binâ
open-mouthed *adj.* بادهان باز bâ dahân-e' bâz
opener *n.* دربازكن dar bâz-kon گشايشى goshâyeshi
openhearted *n.* ركگو rok-gu خوش قلب khosh qalb
openhouse *n.* درباز dar-bâz بارعام bâ-re'âm
opening *n.* گشايش goshâyesh انتتاح eftetâh
opening *n.* روزنه rozaneh سوراخ surâkh
opening *n.* آغاز âqâz مقدمه moqad~ameh
openness *n.* رك گويى rok-quyi بى تعصبى bi-ta'as~ob
opera(house) *n.* تالار اپرا tâlâr-e' operâ
operable *adj.* كاركردنى kâr kardani قابل عمل qâbel-e' 'amal
operant *adj., n.* عمل كننده 'amal konandeh
operate *v.* بكارانداختن be-kâr andâkhtan
operate *v.* عمل كردن 'amal kardan جراحى كردن jar~âhi kardan
operation *n.* عملكرد 'amal kard اداره edâreh
operation *n.* عمل 'amal جراحى jar~âhi
operative *n., adj.* عملى 'amali كارگر kâr-gar كارگاه kâr-gâh
operator *n.* عامل 'âmel جراح jar~âh گرداننده gardânandeh
operator *n.* تلفنچى telefon-chi صفرهشت sefr-hasht
ophthalmologist *n.* پزشك چشم pezeshk-e' cheshm
opiate *n., adj., vt.* داروى مخدر dâru-ye' mokhad~ar
opiate *v.* تخديركردن takhdir kardan
opiate *adj.* تخديركننده takhdir konandeh
opinion *n.* عقيده 'aqideh نظر nazar رأى ray
opinionated *n.* خودراى khod ra'y
opium *n.* ترياك taryâk
opossum *n.* ساريگ sârig
opponent *n., adj.* حريف harif طرف مقابل taraf-e' moqâbel رقيب raqib
opportune *adj.* بجا bejâ بموقع bemoqe'
opportunism *n.* فرصت طلبى forsat-talabi
opportunist *n.* فرصت طلب forsat-talab
opportunistic *adj.* فرصت طلبانه forsat-talabâneh
opportunity *n.* فرصت forsat موقعيت moqe'iyat مجال majâl
oppose *vi.* مخالفت كردن mokhâlefat kardan

مقابله کردن .... moqâbeleh kardan
opposite *adj., n., pre., adv.* مخالف mokhâlef مقابل moqâbel
روبرو ru be-ru ضد zed~
opposite number *np.* طرف مقابل taraf-e' moqâbel
opposition *n.* مخالفت mokhâlefat ضدیت zediyat
oppress *v.* ستم کردن setam kardan ستمدیده setam-dideh ظلم zolm
oppress *v.* ستم کردن setam kardan
oppressed *n.* ستمدیده setam-dideh مظلوم mazlum
oppression *n.* جور jor ستم setam ظلم zolm
oppression *n.* ستم گری setam-gari
oppressive *n.* ستمگرانه setam-garâneh ظالمانه zâlemâneh
oppressor *n.* جبار jab~âr ستمگر setam-gar ظالم zâlem
optic *adj.* بصری basari چشمی cheshmi
optic nerves *n.* اعصاب بصری a'sâb-e' basari
optical *adj.* بینایی binâyi بصری basari
optical illusion *n.* خطای بصری khatâ-ye' basari
optician *n.* عینک ساز 'eynak-sâz
optics *n.* علم بینایی 'elm-e' binâyi
optimism *n.* خوش بینی khosh-bini
optimist *n.* خوشبین khosh-bin
optimistic *adj.* خوشبینانه khosh-binâneh
optimize *vi., vt.* خوشبین کردن khosh-bin kardan
optimum *n.* حد اعلا had~-e' a'lâ
option *n.* حق انتخاب haq~-e' entekhâb اختیار ekhtiâr
optional *adj.* دلبخواه del-bekhâh اختیاری ekhtiâri
optometrist *n.* چشم پزشک cheshm pezeshk
optometry *n.* چشم پزشکی cheshm pezeshki
opulence *n.* ونور vofur نعمت ne'mat تمول tamav~ol
opulent *adj.* متمول motemav~el فراوان farâvân
or *n., adj.* یا yâ
oracle *n.* معبد استخاره ma'bad-e' estekhâreh سروش sorush
oral *adj., n.* شفاهی shafâhi دهانی dahâni
oral *adj., n.* شفاهی shafâhi
orally *adv.* شفاهان shafâhan ازطریق دهان az tariq-e' dahân
orange *n.* نارنج nârenj پرتقال portoqâl
orange *adj.* نارنجی nârenji
orange juice *n.* آب پرتقال âb portoqâl
orate *vi., vt.* نطق کردن notq kardan سخنرائی کردن sokhan-râni kardan

oration *n.* نطق notq سخنرانى sokhan-râni
orator *n.* ناطق nâteq سخنران sokhan-rân
oratory *n.* مهارت سخنرانى mahârat-e' sokhanrâni
orb *n.* کره koreh
orbit *n., vi.* مدار madâri
orbit *n., vi.* چرخیدن charkhidan دورگشتن dor gashtan
orbital *adj., n.* مدارى madâri
orchard *n.* باغ میوه bâq-e' miveh
orchestra *n.* ارکستر orkester باند bând
orchestrate *vt., vi.* سرودن sorudan
 برنامه ریزى کردن barnâmeh-rizi kardan
orchid *n.* ثعلب sa'lab
ordain *vt., vi.* منسوب کردن mansub kardan پذیرفتن paziroftan
ordeal *n.* زجر zajr عذاب جسمى azâb-e' jesmi
order *v.* فرمان دادن farmân dâdan دستوردادن dastur dâdan
order *n.* فرمان farmân دستور dastur امر amr حکم hokm
order *n.* نظم nazm ترتیب tartib نظام nezâm
order *v.* حکم کردن hokm kardan
order *v.* سفارش دادن sefâresh dâdan
order *n.* نشان neshân
orderly *adv.* بانظم bâ-nazm باترتیب bâ-tartib منظم monaz~am
 مرتب morat~ab
orderly *n.* پرستارمرد parastâr-e' mard گماشته gomâshteh
ordinance *n.* حکم hokm مقرریه moqarariyeh
ordinarily *adv., n.* معمولاً ma'mulan
ordinary *adj., n.* معمولى ma'muli دستورنامه dastur-nâmeh عادى 'âd~i
ordnance *n.* آتشبار âtash-bâr مهمات mohem~ât
ordonnance *n.* تنظیم tanzim قانون qânun
ore *n.* سنگ معدن sang-e' ma'dan
oregano *n.* آویشن âvishan پونه وحشى puneh-ye' vahshi
organ *n.* آلت âlat عضو 'ozv
organ *n.* ارگ org
organ grinder *np.* ارگ زن سیار org-zan-e' say~âr
organic *adj., n.* آلى âli وجودى vojudi ساختمانى sâkhtemâni
organism *n.* موجود زنده mojud-e' zendeh
organist *n.* ارگ زن orgzan
organization *n.* سازمان sâzmân تشکیلات tashkilât ترتیب tartib
organize *vt., vi.* سازماندادن sâzmân dâdan تشکیل دادن tashkil dâdan

organized *adj.* سازمان یافته sazman-yafeth متشکل moteshak~el
organizer *n.* سازمان دهنده sâzmân dahandeh
orgasm *n.* اوج جماع oj-e' jamâ'
orient *n., adj., vt., vi.* خاور khâvar مشرق زمین mashreq zamin
oriental *adj., n.* خاوری khâvari مشرق زمینی mashreq zamini
oriental *adj., n.* شرقی شناس sharqi-shenâs
orientate *vt., vi.* آشنا کردن âshnâ kardan عادت دادن 'âdat dâdan
orientation *n.* آشنایی âshnâyi سمت یابی samt-yâbi توافق tavâfoq
orifice *n.* سوراخ surâkh مخرج makhraj
origan *n.* مرزنگوش marzan-gush
origin *n.* اصل asl نهاد nahâd سرچشمه sar-cheshmeh
original *adj., n.* اصلی asli ابتکاری ebtekâri اصیل asil
original sin *np.* گناه آدم و حوا gonâh-e' âdam va hav~â
originality *n.* اصالت esâlat ابتکار ebtekâr
originally *adv.* اصلاً aslan اساساً asâsan مبتکرانه mobtakerâneh
originate *v.* سرچشمه گرفتن sar-cheshmeh gereftan
ابتکار کردن ebtekâr kardan
origination *n.* مبداء mabda' سرچشمه sar-cheshmeh
ornament *n., vt.* تزیین کردن taz'in kardan زینت zinat
ornamental *adj., n.* تزیینی taz'ini زینتی zinati
ornate *adj.* زینت دار zinat-dâr مزین mozay~an
orphan *n.* یتیم yatim
orphan *v.* یتیم کردن yatim kardan
orphanage *n.* یتیم خانه yatim khâneh
orthodox *adj.* ارتدکس ortodoks
مطابق اصول دین motâbeq-e' osul-e' din
oscillate *v.* نوسان کردن navasân kardan
oscillate *v.* تاب خوردن tâb khordan
oscillate *v.* وسواس داشتن vasvâs dâshtan مرددبودن morad~ad budan
oscillator *n.* نوسان کن navasân kon
osmosis *n.* حلول holul تراوش tarâvosh
ostantatious *n.* خودنما khod-namâ جلوه گر jelveh-gar
ظاهرساز zâher-sâz
ostensible *n.* هویدا hoveydâ آشکار âshkâr ظاهری zâheri
ostensibly *adv.* ظاهراً zaheran بطور آشکار betor-e' âshkâr
ostensive *adj.* فاش کننده fâsh-konandeh
ostentation *n.* خودنمایی khod namâyi جلوه گری jelveh-gari
ظاهرسازی zâher-sâzi

osteology *n.* استخوان شناسی ostokhân shenâsi
ostracism *n.* تحریم tahrim تبعید tab'id
ostracize *n.* تحریم کردن tahrim kardan تبعید کردن tab'id kardan
ostrich *n.* شترمرغ shotor morq
other *adj., n., pro., adv.* دیگر digar غیر qeyr
otherwise *adv., adj.* وگرنه vagarnah جوردیگر jur-e' digar
otter *n.* سمور آبی samur-e' âbi
ouch *int., n., vt.* آخ âkh اخ okh اف of وای vây
ought *v., n., adv.* باید bâyad بایستی bâyasti
ounce *n.* انس ons
our(s) *n.* مال ما mâl-e'-mâ مان mân
ourselves *pro., pl.* خودمان khod-e' mân
oust *vt.* بیرون راندن birun rândan خلع ید کردن khal'-e' yad kardan
ouster *n.* بیرونرانی birun-râni اخراج ekhrâj
out *adv., adj., pre., int.* بیهوش bi-hush
out *adv., adj., pre., int.* بیرون birun خارج khârej
out *adv., adj., pre., int.* خاموش khâmush
out of order *n.* خراب kharâb شکسته shekasteh
out of order *n.* خارج ازنوبت khârej az nobat
out(and out) *n.* بکلی bekol~i
out(for) *n.* دنبال donbâl-e' درپی dar pey-e'
out(from under) *n.* دورازخطر dur az khatar
out(of) *n.* ازمیان az miân-e' ازروی az ruy-e' دوراز dur az
out(to) *n.* مصمم بودن mosam~am budan بیرون رفته birun rafteh
out-of-date *n.* قدیمی qadimi کهنه kohneh
out-of-the-way *n.* دور dur پرت part
outage *n.* خاموشی khâmushi برق رفتگی barq raftegi
outbalance *vt.* سنگین تر بودن sangin-tar budan
outbid *vt.* روی دست زدن ruy-e' dast zadan
outboard *adj., adv., n.* بیرون از قایق birun az qâyeq
outbound *n.* بیرون رفتنی birun raftani
outbreak *n.* بروز boruz شیوع shiu'
outburst *n., adj.* انفجار enfejâr طغیان toqyân
outcast *n., adj.* مردود mardud بیرون رانده birun-rândeh
outcome *n.* نتیجه natijeh دستاورد dast âvard
outcry *n.* اعتراض e'terâz فغان faqân
outdated *vt.* قدیمی qadimi دمده demodeh
outdo *vt.* بهترکارکردن behtar kâr kardan

outdoor *n., adj.* بیرونی biruni
outdoors *n.* درهوای آزاد dar havây-e' âzâd
outer *adj.* بیرونی biruni خارجی khâreji ظاهری zâheri
outer space *np.* فضای ماوراء fazâ-ye' mâvarâ'
outermost *adj.* بیرون ترین birun-tarin
outfit *n.* اسباب لباس lebâs âsbâb
outfit *n.* گروه goruh
outfit *v.* مجهز کردن mojah~az kardan
outflank *n.* محاصرهٔ جناحی mohâsereh-ye' jenâhi
outflow *n.* بیرون ریزی birun-rizi
outgoing *adj., n.* بیرون رفتنی birun raftani صادره sâdereh
outgrow *v.* بیشتر رشد کردن bishtar roshd kardan
outgrowth *n.* رشد بیرونی roshd-e' biruni شعبه sho'beh
outguess *vt.* زودتر حدس زدن zudtar hads zadan
outhouse *n.* مستراح بیرونی mostarâh-e' biruni
outing *n.* گردش gardesh
outland *n., adj.* زمین دوردست zamin-e' dur-dast
outlast *vt.* بیشتر دوام آوردن bishtar davâm âvardan
outlaw *n.* تبهکار tabah-kâr
outlaw *v.* غیرقانونی کردن qeyr-e' qânuni kardan
outlet *n.* مجرا majrâ در رو dar-ro جای فروش jâ-ye' forush
outline *v., n.* محیط مرئی mohit-e' mar'i خط شبح shabah khat~
outline *v., n.* مختصر مطالب mokhtasar-e' matâleb
outlive *vt.* بیشتر عمرکردن bi-shtar 'omr kardan
outlook *n.* چشم انداز cheshm andâz
نتیجهٔ احتمالی natijeh-ye' ehtemâli
outlying *adj.* بیرون پرت birun part
outmode *vt., vi.* دمده شدن de-modeh shodan
outnumber *vt.* نفرات بیشتر داشتن nafarât-e' bishtar dâshtan
outpatient *n.* بیمار سرپایی bimâr-e' sar pâyi
outplay *vt.* بهتر بازی کردن behtar bâzi kardan
outpoint *vt.* بیشترامتیاز آوردن bishtar emtiâz âvardan
outpost *n.* قراول گاه qarâvol-gâh پاسگاه pâs-gâh
output *n.* کارکرد kârkard راندمان rândemân محصول mahsul
outrage *n., vt.* خشمگین کردن khashmgin kardan
کلافه کردن kalâfeh kardan
outrageous *adj.* خشونت انگیز khoshunat-angiz
outrank *vt.* درجهٔ بالاترداشتن darejeh-ye' bâlâtar dâshtan

outreach *n.* بیشتر دسترسی داشتن bishtar dastresi dâshtan
outright *adj., adv.* صاف و پوست کنده sâf-o pust kandeh یکجا yek-jâ
outroot *vt.* ریشه کن کردن risheh-kan kardan
outrun *n.* تندتردویدن tondtar davidan
outsell *vt.* بیشترفروختن bishtar forukhtan
outset *n.* شروع shoru' آغاز âqâz
outside *n., adj., adv., pre.* بیرون birun خارج khârej ظاهر zâher
outside *n., adj., adv., pre.* بیرونی biruni خارجی khâreji
outsider *n.* خارجی khâreji بیگانه bi-gâneh
outsize *n., adj.* بزرگتر ازاندازه بودن bozorgtar az andâzeh budan
outskirt *n.* حوالی havâli بیرون birun
outspoken *v.* پربیان por-bayân رک rok سرراست sar-râst
outstanding *v.* برجسته bar-jesteh
outstrip *vt.* عقب گذاشتن 'aqab gozâshtan
outturn *n.* محصول mahsul کارکرد kâr-kard
outward(s) *n.* بیرونی biruni سطحی sat-hi
outwear *n.* بیشتر دوام آوردن bishtar davâm âvardan
outweigh *vt.* سنگینتر بودن sangintar budan
outwit *vt., n.* زرنگتربودن zerangtar budan
outwork *n.* بیشتر کارکردن bishtar kâr kardan
oval *adj.* بیضی مانند beyzi mânand
ovaritis *n.* ورم تخمدان varam-e' tokhm-dân
ovary *n.* تخمدان tokhm-dân
ovation *n.* کف زنی kafzani تشویق tashviq
oven *n.* اجاق ojâq کوره kureh تنور tanur فر fer
over *pre., adv., adj., n.* درضمن dar zemn-e' درطی dar te-ye'
over *pre., adv., adj., n.* بغلی baqali آنطرف ântaraf آنور ânvar
over *pre., adv., adj., n.* بالا be-bâlâ بالاتر bâlâtar
over *pre., adv., adj., n.* دوباره dobâreh ازاثر az-asar ازسر az sar
over *pre., adv., adj., n.* سر sar-e' بخاطر be-khâter-e'
over *pre., adv., adj., n.* روی ru-ye' بالای bâlâ-ye' ازروی az ru-ye'
over *pre., adv., adj., n.* تمام شده tamâm shodeh
over *pre., adv., adj., n.* زیادی ziâdi زیادتر ziâd-tar
over(and over) *n.* مدام modâm چندبار chand-bâr
over-the-counter *adj., vi., n.* مستقیم mostaqim بی واسطه bi-vâseteh
بی نسخه bi-noskheh
overabundance *n.* وفور بیش از حد vofur-e' bish az had~
overact *vt., vi.* بااغراق عمل کردن bâ eqrâq 'amal kardan

overage *adj., n.* مسن mosen سالمند sâl-mand
overall *adv., adj., n.* سرتاسری sar tâ sari
    روی همرفته ruy-e' ham rafteh
overalls *n.* لباس سرتاسری lebâs-e' sar-tâ sari
overbearing *v.* متکبر motekab~er تحمیلی tahmili
overblown *adj., v.* بیخودی بزرگ شده bikhodi bozorg shodeh
overboard *adv.* ازکشتی افتاده az kashti oftâdeh
overbuild *vt.* زیاد ساختن ziâd-sâkhtan
overcast *vt., vi., n.* ابر ناک mah مه abr nâk
    هوای گرفته havâ-ye' gerefteh
overcautious *adj.* خیلی محتاط kheyli mohtât
overcharge *n.* زیادی حساب کردن ziâdi hesâb kardan
overclothes *n.* رولباسی ru-lebâsi
overcoat *n.* پالتو pâlto
overcome *v.* مغلوب کردن maqlub kardan چیره شدن chireh shodan
overcome *v.* برطرف کردن bar-taraf kardân
overconfident *n.* زیادمطمئن ziâd motma'en
overdo *vt.* شورش را درآوردن shurash râ dar âvardan
overdress *vt., vi., n.* افراطی لباس پوشیدن efrâti lebâs pushidan
overdrive *vt., n.* دندهٔ سرعت dandeh-ye' sor'at
overdue *adj.* تاخیرشده ta'khir shodeh عقب افتاده 'aqab oftâdeh
overeat *vi., vt.* پرخوری کردن por-khori kardan
overestimate *n.* زیادتخمین زدن ziâd takhmin zadan
    بزرگ گرفتن bozorg gereftan
overexert *vt.* زیادبخودفشارآوردن ziâd be-khod feshâr âvardan
overflow *vt., n.* سرریزکردن sar-riz kardan لبریزشدن lab riz shodan
overgrow *vt.* زیادرشد کردن ziâd roshd kardan
overgrown *v.* زیادرشدکرده ziâd roshd kardeh
overhang *n., vt.* آویزان بودن âvizân budan پیشامدگی pishâmadegi
overhaul *vt., adj., n.* رموت کردن romut kardan
    بکلی تعمیرکردن bekol~i ta'mir kardan
overhead *n.* بالای سر bâlâ-ye' sar خرج kharj
overhear *vt.* تصادفاً شنیدن tasâdofan shenidan
overheat *vt., vi., n.* جوش آوردن jush âvardan
overindulgence *n.* افراط بیش ازحد efrât-e' bish az hâd~
overjoy *vt.* خیلی خوشحال کردن kheyli khoshhâl kardan
overland *adv., adj.* زمینی zamini ازتوخشکی az tu khoshki
overlap *v.* رویهم قرارگرفتن ru-ye' ham qarâr gereftan

overlap *v.* دربرگرفتن dar bar gereftan
overlay *vt., n.* روکش کردن rukesh kardan تحمیل کردن tahmil kardan
overload *vt., n.* زیادبارکردن ziâd bâr kardan
فشاربیش ازحد feshâr-e' bish az had~
overlook *vt., n.* نادیده گرفتن nadideh gereftan
چشم پوشی کردن cheshm-pushi kardan
overlord *n.* ارباب کل arbâb-e' kol
overly *adv.* بیش ازحد bish az had~
overnice *adj., n.* زیادی خوش رفتار ziâdi khosh raftâr
overnight *adv., adj.* شبانه shabâneh درطول شب dar tul-e' shab
overpass *n.* پل pol سبقت گرفتن sebqat gereftan
overpay *vt.* زیادی پرداختن ziâdi pardâkhtan
overpeopled *vt.* پرجمعیت por jam'iyat
overplay *vt., vi.* بدبازی کردن bad bâzi kardan
overpower *n.* غلبه کردن qalabeh kardan چیره شدن chireh shodan
overpowering *adj.* مقاومت ناپذیر moqâvemat nâ-pazir
overproduce *n.* بیش ازحد تولیدکردن bish az had tolid kardan
overproduction *n.* تولید اضافی tolid-e' ezâfi
overrate *vt.* زیاد ارزش گذاشتن ziâd arzesh gozâshtan
override *vt., n.* زیرپاگذاشتن zir-e' pâ gozâshtan
بی اعتنایی کردن bi-e'tenâyi kardan
overrun *v.* بزیرگرفتن bezir gereftan هجوم بردن hojum bordan
oversea(s) *n.* خارجه khârejeh
oversee *vt.* نظارت کردن nezârat kardan سرکشی کردن sarkeshi kardan
overseer *n.* مباشر mobâsher
oversell *vt., vi., n.* زیادفروختن ziâd forukhtan
overshadow *vt.* تاریک کردن târik kardan
تحت الشعاع قراردادن taht-olsho'â' qarâr
overshoe *n.* گالش gâlesh
overshot *n.* تورفته turafteh
oversight *n.* سهوانگاری sahv-engâri غفلت qeflat
چشم پوشی cheshm-pushi
oversize *adj.* زیادازحدبزرگ ziâd az had bozorg
oversleep *vi., vt.* زیادخوابیدن ziâd khâbidan
overspend *vi., vt.* زیادخرج کردن ziâd kharj kardan
overstate *n.* اغراق کردن eqrâq kardan
overstatement *n.* اغراق eqrâq
overstep *vt.* پاازخط فراگذاشتن pâ-az khat farâ gozâshtan

overt adj., vt., vi. آشكار âshkâr باز bâz
overtake vt., vi. بی هوا گرفتن bi-havâ gereftan
سبقت گرفتن sebqat gereftan
overthrow n. برانداختن bar andâkhtan براندازی bar andâzi
سقوط soqut
overthrown n. برافتاده bar oftâdeh مخلوع makhlu'
overtime adv., adj., v., n. اضافه کاری ezâfeh-kâri
وقت اضافه vaqt-e' ezâfeh
overture n., vt. پیش درآمد pish-dar âmad پیشنهادیه pish-nahâdieh
overturn v. چپ کردن chap kardan برگرداندن bar-gardândan
واژگون کردن vâzh-gun kardan
overweigh vt. زیادوزن داشتن ziâd vazn dâshtan
overweight n. وزن زیادی vazn-e' ziâdi چاق châq
overwhelm vt. دربرگرفتن dar bar gereftan چیره شدن chireh shodan
overwhelming adj. فراگیرنده farâ-girandeh خیلی زیاد kheyli ziâd
overwirte n. روی چیزی نوشتن ruy-e' chizi neveshtan
overwork vt., vi., n. بیش ازحدکارکردن bish az had kâr kardan
overwrought adj., v. خسته khasteh کوفته kufteh
ovine adj. گوسفندی gusfandi
ovular adj. تخمکی tokhmaki
ovulate n. تخمک تولید کردن tokhmak tolid kardan
ovulation n. خروج تخمک khoruj-e' tokhmak
ovule n. تخمک tokhmak اوول ovul
owe v. بدهکاربودن bedeh-kâr budan مقروض بودن maq-ruz budân
owe v. مدیون بودن madyun budan
owing adj., v. بدهکاری bedeh-kâri
owl n. جغد joqd بوف buf
own adj. خود khod خویش khish شخصی shakhsi
own v. مالک بودن mâlek budan صاحب بودن sâheb budan
owner n. صاحب sâheb مالک mâlek
ownerless n. بی صاحب bi-sâheb
ownership n. تصاحب tasâhob مالکیت mâlekiyat
ox(en) n. نره گاو nar~eh-gâv ورزو varzo
oxbow n. یوغ بند yoq band آهن پیچ âhan pich
oxtail n. دم گاو dom-e' gâv
oxygen n. اکسیژن oksizhen
oyes/yez! n. گوش کنید gush konid!
oyster n., vi. صدف sadaf

P P P

P.M. *n.* بعد ازظهر ba'd az zohr
P.T.A. *n.* انجمن مدرسه و والدین anjoman-e' madreseh vâ vâledeyn
pa *n.* بابا bâbâ
pace *n.* سرعت تندی sor'at tondi
pace *v.* یورغه رفتن yurqeh raftan
pace *v.* قدم زدن qadam zadan گام برداشتن gâm bardashtan
pace *pre., n., vt.* قدم qadam گام gâm
pacemaker *n.* تپش نما tapesh-namâ
pacer *n.* یورغه رو yurqeh-ro
pacifiable *n.* آرام شدنی ârâm shodani
pacific *adj.* آرام ârâm ساکن sâken صلح جو solh-ju
Pacific Ocean *np.* اقیانوس آرام oqiânus-e' ârâm
pacificate *vt.* آرام کردن ârâm kardan
pacification *n.* آرامش ârâmesh
pacificism *n.* صلح طلبی solh talabi آشتی خواهی âshti-khâhi
pacifier *n.* پستونک pestunak آرام کننده ârâm konandeh
pacifism *n.* صلح طلبی solh-talabi آشتی خواهی âshti-khâhi
pacifist *n., adj.* صلح طلب solh-talab آشتی خواه âshti-khâh
pacify *vt., adj.* آرام کردن ârâm kardan آرامش دادن ârâmesh dâdan
pack *n.* بسته basteh
pack *v.* فرستادن ferestâdan
pack *v.* پرکردن por kardan ازدحام کردن ezdehâm kardan
pack *n.* بقچه boqcheh کوله kuleh
pack *v.* بستن bastan
pack *n.* دسته dasteh گروه goruh
pack *v.* بسته بندی کردن basteh bandi kardan
pack animal *n.* قاطر qâter
pack horse *n.* یابو yâbu
package *n., vt.* بسته بندی کردن basteh-bandi kardan
package-deal *n.* همه چیزباهم hameh-chiz bâ-ham یکجا yek-jâ
packer *n.* بسته بند basteh-band
packet *n., vt.* پاکت pâkat
packing *n.* بسته بندی basteh-bandi
packman *n.* دست فروش dast-forush
pact *n.* پیمان peymân قرارداد qarâr-dâd میثاق misaq
pacydermous *n.* پوست کلفت pust koloft
pad *n.* خلوتگاه khalvat-gâh خانه khâneh

pad *n.* دسته یادداشت dasteh yâd dâsht
pad *v.* لایه گذاشتن lâyeh gozâshtan پرکردن por kardan
padding *n.* لایه بندی lâyeh-bandi آستر âstar
paddle *v.* پارو زدن pâru zadan
paddle *v.* درآب پازدن dar âb pâ zadan
paddle *n.* راکت râket
paddle wheel *n.* آب چرخ âb-charkh
paddock *n., vt.* علفزار 'alaf-zâr مرتع marta'
paddy *n.* شالیزار shâlizâr
padlock *n., vt.* قفل زدن qofl zadan
pagan *adj.* کافر kâfer خدانشناس khodâ-nashnâs ناسپاس nâ-sepâs
بیدین bi-din
page *n.* صفحه safheh
page *v.* صدازدن sedâ zadan
pageant *n.* نمایش namâyesh
paginal *n.* صفحه‌ای safhehi صفحه بصفحه safheh be-safheh
paginate *vt.* صفحه گذاری کردن safheh gozâri kardan
pagon *n.* بی دین bidin کافر kâfar
paid(-off) *n.* پرداخته‌شده pardâkhteh shodeh
pail *n.* سطل satl دلو dalv
pailful *n.* یک سطل پر yek satl por
pain *v.* رنج دادن ranj dâdan
pain *n.* درد dard رنج ranj
painful *adj.* دردناک dardnâk
painkiller *n.* مسکن mosak~en
painless *adj., n.* بی درد bi-dard
painstaking *n.* پرمشقت por masheq~at
paint *v.* رنگ زدن rang zadan رنگ کردن rang kardan
paint *v.* نقاشی کردن naq~âshi kardan
paint *v.* عکس کشیدن aks keshidan تصویرکشیدن tasvir keshidan
paintbrush *n.* قلم مو qalam-mu
painted *adj.* رنگ شده rang shodeh
painter *n.* نقاش naq~âsh
painter *n.* رنگرز rang-raz
painting *n.* نقاشی naq~âshi تصویر tasvir تابلو tâblo
pair *n.* لنگه lengeh
pair *v.* جور کردن jur kardan
pair *v.* جفت کردن joft kardan

pair off n. دوبدوکردن do-be-do kardan
pajamas n. پیژامه pizhâmeh
pal n., vi. رفیق rafiq دوست dust
palace n. کاخ kâkh قصر qasr
palate n. سقف دهن saqf-e' dahân
palatial adj. کاخ مانند kâkh mânand
pale adj. رنگ پریده rang-parideh مثل گچ mesl-e' gach
pale n. میخ چوبی mikh chubi
pale n. مرز marz
paleface n. رنگ پریده rang-parideh
paleontology n. فسیل شناسی fosil-shenâsi دیرین شناسی dirin-shenâsi
pall-bearer n. تابوت کش tâbut-kesh
palm n. کف دست kaf-e' dast
palm n. نخل nakhl درخت خرما derakht-e' khormâ
palm off n. قالب کردن qâleb kardan انداختن andâkhtan
palmist n. کف بین kafbin
palpable adj. لمس شدنی lams shodani محسوس mahsus
palpate vt. لمس کردن lams kardan
paltry adj. کوچک kuchek محقر mohaq~ar
pamper vt. درنازپروراندن dar nâz parvarândan
لوس وننرکردن lus-o nonor kardan
pampered n. نازپرورده nâz-parvardeh
pamphlet n. جزوه jozveh
pan n., vt., vi. ماهی تابه mâhi-tâbeh
pan(out) n. دور گشتن dor gashtan
panacea n. نوشدارو nush-dâru
pancreas n. لوزالمعده lozolme'deh
pandering n. جاکشی jâ-keshi
pane n. قطعه qat'eh لبه labeh
panel v. تخته کوب کردن takhteh-kub kardan
panel n. هیئت hey'at
panel discussion n. بحث گروهی bahs-e' goruhi
paneling n. تخته کوبی takhteh kubi دیوارپوش divârpush
panelist n. عضوهیئت ozv-e' hey'at
panhandle vi., vt. دسته کتری dasteh ketri
panic n. وحشت کردن vahshat kardan هراس harâs
panic-stricken adj. وحشت زده vahshat-zadeh
panic-struck n. وحشت زده vahshat-zadeh

panicky *adj.* وحشتى vahshati پرهراس porharâs
panorama *n.* پانوراما pâ-norâmâ تمام ديد tamâm did
panoramic *adj.* تمام ديدى tamâm-didi تمام منظره tamâm manzareh
pansy *n.* ديوس day~us قرمساق qorom-sâq
pansy *n.* بنفشه banafsheh
pant *vi., vt., n.* نفس نفس زدن nafas-nafas zadan
pantaloon *n.* دلقک dalqak شلوار shalvâr
pantheism *n.* همه خدايى hameh-khodâyi چند خدايى chand-khodâyi
panther *n.* پلنگ palang
pantheress *n.* ماده پلنگ mad~eh palang
panties *pl.* تنکه tonekeh خشتک kheshtak
pantomime *v., n.* لال بازى کردن lâl-bâzi kardan
تياترصامت te'âtr-e' sâmet
pantry *n.* آبدارخانه âbdâr khâneh خوراک خانه khorâk khâneh
pants *pl.* شلوار shalvâr پاجامه pâ jâmeh
papa *n.* بابا bâbâ
papacy *n.* پاپى pâpi
papal *adj.* مربوط به پاپ marbut beh pâp
paper *n.* کاغذ kâqaz
paper *n.* نوشته neveshteh مقاله maqâleh
paper money *n.* اسکناس eskenâs
paper work *np.* کاغذکارى kâqaz-kâri
paperback *n., adj.* جلد کاغذى jeld kâqazi
paperback-bag *n.* پاکت کاغذى pâkat kaqazi
papillon *n.* پروانه parvâneh
papoose *n.* تنداق ghondâgh
pappy *n.* بابا bâbâ
paprika *n., adj.* فلفل سرخ felfel sorkh پاپريک pâprik
par *n.* برابرى barâbari عادى 'âd~i
parable *n.* مثل masal
parabola *n.* پارابل pârâbol قطع مخروط qat' makhrut
parabolic *adj.* پارابلى pârâboli سهمى sahmi
parachute *n., vt., vi.* چترنجات chatr-e' nejât
parachutist *n.* چترباز chatr-bâz
parade *n., vt., vi.* رژه rezheh مارش mârsh
parade *v.* رژه دادن rezheh dâdan
parade *v.* رژه رفتن rezheh raftan
paradigm *n.* نمونه nemuneh مثال mesâl

paradigmatic *adj.* نمونه‌ای nemuneh-i
paradise *n.* بهشت behesht پردیس pardis فردوس ferdos
paradox *n.* نقض حقیقت naqz-e' haqiqat خلاف باوری khalâf-e' bâvari
paradoxical *adj.* حقیقت‌نقض haqiqat-e' naqz نقیض naqiz
paragon *n., vt.* نمونه nemuneh بی‌عیب bi-'eyb
paragraph *n.* بند band پاراگراف pârâgrâf
parakeet *n.* طوطی کوچک tuti kuchek
parallax *n.* زاویۀ دید zâvieh-ye' did
parallel *v.* مقایسه کردن moqâyeseh kardan
parallel *v.* موازی بودن movâzi budan
parallel *adj.* نظیر nazir
parallelogram *n.* متوازی الاضلاع motevâziol azlâ'
paralysis *n.* فلجی falaji رکود rokud
paralytic *n., adj.* فلج falaj
paralyze *vt.* فلج کردن falaj kardan
parameter *n.* محدوده mahdudeh شرط متغیر shart-e' moteqay~er
paramount *adj., n.* باعظمت bâ-'azemat پرقدرت por-qodrat
برترین bar-tarin اصلح as-lah
paranoia *n.* ترس دایمی tars-e' dâ'emi
وحشت بیهوده vahshat-e' bihudeh
paranoid *adj., n.* دایم الترسو dâ'emol tarsu
paraphernalia *n., vt., vi.* خرت و پرت khert-o pert دارایی dârâyi
paraphrase *n., vt., vi.* تفسیر کردن tafsir kardan
تأویل کردن ta'vil kardan
paraplegia *n.* سکته ناقص sekteh-ye' nâqes
paraplegic *adj., n.* فلج falaj مفلوج mâflooj
parasite *n.* انگل angal طفیلی tofeyli مفت خور moft-khor
جرثومه jorsumeh
parasitic *adj.* انگلی angali مفت خوری moft-khori
paratrooper *n.* چترباز chatr-bâz
paratroops *n.* چتربازان chatr-bâzân
parboil *vt.* جوش آوردن jush âvardan نیم جوش nim-jush
parcel *n.* قسمت qesmat پارچه pârcheh
parcel *n.* بسته basteh
parch *vt.* سوزاندن suzân-dan برشته کردن bereshteh kardan
parched *n.* سوخته sukhteh برشته bereshteh
parchment *n.* پوست نوشت pust nevesht
pardon *n.* بخشیدن bakhshidan عفوکردن 'afv kardan

pardonable *adj.* بخشیدنی bakhshidani
pare *vt.* تراشیدن tarâshidan پوست کندن pust kandan
parent *v.* پدرشدن pedar shodan مادرشدن mâdar shodan
parent *n.* پدر pedar مادر mâdar
parentage *n.* نسب nasab
parental *adj.* پدرمادری pedar mâdari
parenthesis *n.* پرانتز pârântez
parenthood *n.* پدرمادری pedar-mâdari
parents *n.* والدین vâledeyn پدرو مادر pedar-o mâdar
pariah *n.* طردشده tard shodeh مردود mardud
parish *n.* بخش مذهبی bakhsh-e' mazhabi
parity *n.* برابری barâbari هم ارزشی ham arzeshi
park *v.* پارک کردن pârk kardan
park *n.* گردشگاه gardesh-gâh شکارگاه shekâr-gâh پارک pârk
park ranger *n.* جنگلبان jangal-bân
parkway *n.* جنگل راه jangal-râh
parlance *n.* بحث bahs صحبت sohbat
parley *n., vi.* مذاکره کردن mozâkereh kardan
parliament *n.* مجلس majles پارلمان pârlemân
parliamentary *adj.* مجلسی majlesi
parlor *n.* اطاق نشیمن otâq-e' neshiman سالن sâlon
parochial *adj.* بخشی bakhshi مذهبی maz-hâbi
parodist *n.* نکاهی نویس fokâhi-nevis طنزنویس tanz-nevis
parody *n., vt.* نکاهی نویسی fokâhi-nevisi طنز tanz
parole *n., vt., adj.* اززندان آزاد کردن az zendân âzâd kardan
parolee *n.* آزادشده âzâd shodeh
parquet *n., vt.* چوب فرش chub-farsh
parrot *n.* طوطی tuti
parsley *n., adj.* جعفری ja'fari
parsnip *n.* زردک zardak
parson *n.* کشیش keshish
part *n.* فرق farq
part *n.* سهم sahm
part *n.* نقش naqsh رل rol
part *n.* قسمت qesmat
part *v.* فرق بازکردن farq bâz kardan
part *v.* ازهم جداشدن az ham jodâ shodan راه افتادن râh oftâdan
part *v.* جداکردن jodâ kardan

part *n.* منطقه mantaqeh بخش bakhsh
part *n.* لوازم یدکی lavâzem yadaki
part(from) *n.* ترک کردن tark kardan
part(with) *n.* ول کردن vel kardan صرفنظرکردن sarfenazar kardan
part-time *n.* نصف وقت nesf-e' vaqt
partake *vi., vt.* شرکت کردن sherkat kardan
شریک شدن sharik shodan
parted *adj.* قسمت شده qesmat-shodeh باز شده bâz-shodeh
partial *adj., n.* طرفدار taraf-dâr جانبدار jâneb-dâr جزیی joz'i
partiality *n.* طرفداری taraf-dâri جانبداری jâneb-dâri
partially *n.* طرفدارانه taraf-dârâneh یک قسمت yek qesmat
participal *n.* دارای وجه وصفی dârâ-ye' vajh-e' vasfi
participance *n.* شرکت sherkat
participant *n., adj.* شرکت کننده sherkat konandeh شریک sharik
participate *vi., vt.* شرکت کردن sherkat kardan
شریک بودن sharik budan
participation *n.* شرکت sherkat شریکی shariki
participator *n.* شرکت کننده sherkat konandeh
participle *n.* وجه وصفی vajeh vasfi
particle *n.* ذره zar~eh خرده khordeh
particular *adj.* ویژه vizheh بخصوص be-khosus
particularism *n.* اختصاص مفرد ekhtesâs-e' mofrad
particularity *n.* موشکافی mu-shekâfi
particularly *adv.* بخصوص be-khosus
parting *n., adj.* جدایی jodâ'i تقسیم taqsim
partisan *n.* حزبی hezbi طرفدارحزب tarafdâr-e' hezb
partisan *n.* چریک cherik پارتیزان pârtizân
partition *n., vt.* تقسیم کردن taqsim kardan دیوار divâr
partly *n.* تایک اندازه tâ yek-andâzeh
partner *n., vt.* شریک sharik سهیم sahim
partnership *n.* شراکت sherâkat
partridge *n.* کبک kabk
party *n.* حزب hezb
party *n.* مهمانی mehmâni پارتی pârti محفل mahfel
party *n., vi.* طرف taraf متعامل mote'âmel
party line *n.* خط حزب khat~-e' hezb خط مشی khat~-e' mash-y
party man *np.* وفاداربه حزب vafâ-dâr be-hezb
parvis *n.* حیاط کلیسا hayât-e' kelisâ

pass *v.* رد کردن rad kardan
pass *n.* پارول pârol
pass *v.* قبول شدن qabul shodan
pass *v.* قالب کردن qâleb kardan
pass *v.* اتفاق افتادن etef~âq oftâdan
pass *n.* جواز javâz عبور اجازهٔ ejâzeh-ye' 'obur
pass *v.* گذاشتن gozâshtan ردشدن rad shodan
pass *v.* پاس دادن pâs dâdan
pass *n.* گردنه gardaneh گذرگاه gozar-gâh
pass *v.* عبورکردن' obur kardan گذشتن gozashtan
pass *v.* تصویب کردن tasvib kardan
pass(away) *n.* مردن mordan فوت کردن fot kardan
pass(for) *n.* پذیرفته شدن pazirofteh shodan جاکردن jâ kardan
pass(on) *n.* ردکردن rad kardan جازدن jâ zadan
pass(out) *n.* غش کردن qash kardan
pass(over) *n.* اعتنانکردن e'tenâ na-kardan
pass(through) *n.* طی کردن tey kardan
       ازوسط ردکردن az vasat rad kardan
pass(time) *n.* وقت گذراندن vaqt gozarândan
pass(up) *n.* غنیمت شمردن qanimat shemordan
passable *adj.* قابل عبور qâbel-e' 'obur ردشدنی rad shodani
passage *n., v., vi.* نقل قول naql-e' qol عبارت' ebârat
passage *n., v., vi.* تبدیل tabdil تحول tahav~ol
passage *n., v., vi.* تصویب tasvib
passage *n., v., vi.* گذرگاه gozar-gâh پاساژ pâsâzh
passage *n., v., vi.* عبور' obur گذشت gozasht
passage *n., v., vi.* نقل قول naql-e' qol عبارت ebârat
passage(way) *n.* گذرگاه gozar-gâh سرا sarâ پاساژ pâsâzh
passbook *n.* کتابچهٔ بانکی ketâbcheh-ye' bânki
passe' *n.* کهنه شده kohneh-shodeh گذشته gozashteh دمده demodeh
passed *adj.* قبول شده qabul-shodeh
passenger *n.* مسافر mosâfer
passer-by *n.* رهگذر rah-gozar عابر' âber
passible *n.* حساس has~âs
passing *adj., adv., n.* گذرنده gozarandeh قبولی qabuli
passion *n.* شور shor هیجان hayajân احساس شدید ehsâs-e' shadid
passion flower *n.* گل ساعت gol-e' sâ'at
passion play *np.* تعزیه ta'zieh

passionate adj. پرشور por-shor پراحساس por-ehsâs شهوانی shahvâni
passionless adj. بی احساس bi-ehsâs
passive adj. متعدی mote'ad~i
passive adj. بی مقاومت bi-moqâvemat بی تفاوت bi-tafâvot
passivity n. بی مقاومتی bi-moqâvemati بی حرکتی bi-harekati
passkey n. شاه کلید shâh kelid
passport n. گذرنامه gozar-nâmeh
password n. اسم شب esm-e' shab
past adj., n., pre. گذشته gozashteh ماضی mâzi
past participle np. ماضی وصفی mâzi-e' vasfi
past perfect np. ماضی بعید mâzi-e' ba'id
paste n., vt. خمیر khamir چسباندن chasbândan
pastel n. مداد رنگی medâd rangi
pasteurize n. پاستوریزه کردن pâstorizeh kardan
pastime n. سرگرمی sargarmi
pastor n. کشیش keshish
pastoral adj., n. چوپانی chupâni روستایی rustâyi
pastoral adj., n. کشیشی keshishi
pastry n. شیرینی shirini کیک keyk
pasture n., vt., vi. چراگاه charâ-gâh مرتع marta'
pasty adj. خمیری khamiri کیک keyk
pat v. آرام دست زدن ârâm dast zadan
pat n. تکه tek~eh قالب qâleb
pat-a-cake n. دس دسی das-dasi
patch n., vt. وصله زدن vasleh zadan تکه tek~eh زمین zamin
patch up n. بهبوددادن beh-bud dâdan
patchwork n. وصله کاری vasleh-kâri چهل تیکه chehel-tikeh
patchy adj. وصله وصله vasleh vasleh تکه تکه tek~eh tek~eh
pate' n. خمیره khamireh پاته pâteh
patent n., vt. ثبت اختراع sabt-e' ekhterâ'
patentee n. صاحب اختراع sâheb-e' ekhterâ'
paternal adj. پدری pedari
paternalism n., adj. پدر مآبی pedar ma-âbi
paternalistic n. پدرمآب pedar ma-âb
paternity n. پدری pedari اصلیت asliyat
path n. راه râh مسیر masir طریقه tariqeh سبیل sabil
pathetic n. رقت انگیز req~at-angiz
pathfinder n. راه یاب râh-yâb

pathologist *n.* آسیب شناس âsib shenâs
pathology *n.* آسیب شناسی âsib shenâsi
pathos *n.* دلرحمی delrahmi
pathway *n.* راه râh مسیر masir
patience *n.* صبر sabr حوصله hoseleh
patient *n.* مریض mariz بیمار bimâr
patient *ad.* صبور sabur پرحوصله por-hoseleh بردبار bordbâr
شکیبا shakibâ
patio *n.* حیاط خلوت hayât khalvat
patriarch *n.* ریش سفید rish-sefid
patriarchy *n.* پدرشاهی pedar-shâhi
patrician *n.* اشرافی ashrâfi
patricide *n.* پدرکشی pedar-koshi
patriot *adj.* میهن پرست mihan parast وطن پرست vatan parast
patriotism *n.* میهن پرستی mihan parasti وطن پرستی vatan parasti
patrol *vi., vt., n.* گشت زدن gasht zadan پاس دادن pâs dâdan
patrol(man) *n.* پاسبان pâs-bân پاسدار pâs-dâr
patron *n.* خیرخواه kheyr-khâh حامی hâmi مشوق moshav~eq
patron *n.* ارباب arbâb
patron *n.* مشتری دائمی moshtari-e' dâ'emi
patron saint *n.* ولینعمت vali ne'mat امامزاده emâmzâdeh
patronage *n.* حمایت hemâyat پشتیبانی poshtibâni خرید kharid
patronize *vt.* حمایت کردن hemâyat kardan خریدکردن khârid kardan
patten *vt., n.* کفش چوبی kafsh-e' chubi
patter *n., vi., vt.* بلغورکردن balqur kardan زبان ویژه zabân-e' vizheh
pattern *v.* سرمشق قراردادن sar-mashq qarâr dâdan
pattern *n.* طرح tarh الگو olgu نمونه nemuneh
paunch *n.* شکم گنده shekam-e' gondeh
paunchy *adj.* شکم گنده shekam gondeh
pauper *n.* صدقه گیر sadaqeh-gir گدا gedâ
pause *v.* تأمل کردن ta'am~ol kardan درنگ کردن derang kardan
pause *v.* مکث کردن maks kardan
pause *n.* مکث maks تأمل ta'am~ol درنگ derang وقفه vaqfeh
pave *vt.* صاف کردن sâf kardan آسفالت کردن âsfâlt kardan
pavement *n.* جاده آسفالتی jâd~eh âsfâlti پیاده رو piâdeh-ro
paver *n.* صاف کن sâf-kon
paving *n., vt.* جاده آسفالتی jâd~eh âsfâlti پیاده رو piâdeh-ro
paw *v.* پنجه زدن panjeh zadan چنگول زدن changul zadan

paw *n.* پنجه panjeh چنگول changul
pawky *n.* آب زیرکاه âb zir-e′ kâh
pawn *n.* گرویی geroyi
pawn *v.* گرو گذاشتن gero gozâshtan
pawn *n.* پیاده piâdeh آلت دست âlat-e′ dast
pawnbroker *n.* سمسار semsâr
pawnshop *n.* سمساری semsâri
pay *n.* پولی puli غنی qani
pay *v.* ارزش داشتن arzesh dâshtan
pay *n.* پول pul حقوق hoquq مزد mozd
pay *v.* پرداختن pardâkhtan پول دادن pul dâdan
pay load bare *n.* بار درآمددار bâr-e′ darâmâd-dâr
pay roll *n.* حقوق کارکنان hoquq-e′ kârkonân
pay(as you go) *n.* خرج برداشتن kharj bar-dâshtan
pay(back) *n.* پس دادن pas dâdan جورکشیدن jor keshidan
pay(back) *n.* تاوان دادن tâvân dâdan
pay(for) *n.* جزا دادن jazâ dâdan
pay(off) *n.* تصفیه حساب کردن tasfieh hesâb kardan
pay(one's way) *n.* خرج خود دادن kharj-e′ khod dâdan
pay(out) *n.* خرج کردن kharj kardan بیرون دادن birun dâdan
pay(up) *n.* حساب پرداختن hesâb pardâkhtan
pay-off *n.* تصفیه حساب tasfieh hesâb
payable *adj.* پرداختنی pardâkhtani قابل پرداخت qâbel-e′ pardakht
payday *n.* روز پرداخت ruz-e′ pardâkht روزحقوق ruz-e′ hoquq
paydirt *n.* خاک پرارزش khâk-e′ por-arzesh
payee *n.* گیرندهٔ حقوق girandeh-ye′ hoquq
payer *n.* پرداخت کننده pardâkht konandeh
paymaster *n.* حقوق پرداز hoquq-pardâz
payment *n.* قسط qest
payments *n.* اقساط aqsât
pea *n., adj.* نخود nokhod
peace *v., int., n.* صلح solh آشتی âshti آرامش ârâmesh
peace offering *np.* قربانی qorbâni
peace offering *np.* پیشنهاد صلح pishnahâd-e′ solh
peace officer *np.* پاسبان pâsebân پلیس polis
peaceful *adj.* صلح جو solh-ju آرام ârâm
peacefully *adv.* صلح جویانه solh-ju yâneh آرام ârâm
peacemaker *n.* آشتی دهنده âshti dahandeh

peacetime *n., adj.* دوران صلح dorân-e' solh
peach *n., vi., vt.* هلو holu
peachy *adj.* هلویی holuyi راحت râhat
peacock *n., vi.* طاووس tâvus
peafowl *n.* طاووس tâvus
peak *v.* بیالاترین درجه رسیدن be-bâlâ-tarin darajeh residan
peak *n.* نوک nok قله qol~eh منتهادرجه montahâ darajeh
peaked *adj., vi.* لاغر نوک تیز nok-tiz
peanut *n.* بادام کوهی bâdâm kuhi پسته شام pesteh shâm
peanut butter *np.* خمیربادام کوهی khamir-e' bâdâm kuhi
pear *n.* گلابی golâbi
pearl *n., vt., vi., adj.* مروارید morvârid در dor~ لؤلؤ lo'-lo'
pearl diver *n.* غواص مروارید qav~âs-e' morvârid
pearly *adj.* مرواریدی morvâridi
peasant *adj.* دهقان dehqân دهاتی dehâti
peasantry *n.* روستایی rustâyi دهقانان dehqânân
pebble *n., vt.* ریگ rig
pecan *n.* فندق fandoq
peck *vt., vi., n.* نوک زدن nok zadan بوس bus
peck(at) *n.* کم خوردن kam khordan ایرادگرفتن irâd gereftan
pecker *n.* نوک زن nok zan روحیه ruhieh
pectoral *adj., n.* سینهای sineh-i
peculiar *adj., n.* بخصوص be-khosus ویژه vizheh
peculiarity *n.* خصوصیت khosusiyat
pecuniary *adj.* مربوط به پول marbut beh pul نقدی naqdi
pedagogic(al) *n.* تدریسی tadrisi مکتبی maktabi
pedagogue *n.* معلم mo'al~em سختگیر sakht-gir
pedal *n., vi., vt., adj.* پایی pâyi پا زدن pâ zadan پدال pedâl
pedant *n.* ایرادگیر irâd-gir خرده گیر khordeh-gir
pedantic *adj.* خرده گیر khordeh-gir ایرادگیر irâd-gir ملا کتابی mol~â-ketabi
pedantry *n.* ایرادگیری irâd-giri مکتبی maktabi
peddle *vt., vi.* دستفروشی کردن dast-forushi kardan
pedestal *n., vt.* زیرستون zer sotun پایه pâyeh
pedestrian *n.* عابر 'âber پیاده‌رو piâdehro
pediatrician *n.* پزشک کودکان pezeshk-e' kudakân
pediatrics *n.* پزشکی کودکان pezeshki-e' kudakân
peek *vi., n.* دزدکی نگاه کردن dozdaki negâh kardan

peekaboo! *n.* دالی dâl~i !
peel *n.* پوست کندن pust kandân ورآمدن var âmadan خلال khalâl
peel(off) *n.* درآوردن dar âvardan جداشدن jodâ shodan
peeling *n.* پوست pust خلال khalâl
peep *v.* دزدکی نگاه کردن dozdaki negâh kardan
peep *v.* جیک جیک کردن jik jik kardan
peephole *n.* سوراخ نگاه surâkh-e' negâh
peer *v.* بادقت نگاه کردن bâ-deq~at negâh kardan
peer *n.* همتا hamtâ نظیر nazir
peerage *n.* اشراف ashrâf
peerless *adj.* بی نظیر bi-nazir بی مانند bi-mânand
peevish *adj.* بدخو bad-khu بداخلاق bad-akhlâq
peewee *adj., n.* فسقلی fesqeli یک وجبی yek-vajabi
peg *n.* میخ چوبی mikh-e' chubi گیره gireh
peg *v.* میخ کردن mikh kardan کارکردن پیوسته peyvasteh kâr kardan
peg leg *np.* پای چوبی pây-e' chubi
pejorative *n.* بدتر bad-tar
pellet *n.* ساچمه sâchmeh
pelt *v.* پرتاب کردن partâb kardan سخت باریدن sakht bâridan
pelt *n.* پوست پشم pust-e' pashm
peltry *n.* پوست آلات pust-âlât
pelvis *n.* لگن خاصره lagan khâsereh باسن bâsan
pen *n.* قلم خودنویس qalam khodnevis کلک kelk
pen *n., vt.* آغل âqol
pen *n., vt.* هلفدونی holof-duni
pen name *n.* اسم قلم esm-e' qalam نام مستعار nâm-e' mosta'âr
penal *adj.* کیفری key-fari بامجازات bâ-mojâzât
penal code *n.* قوانین کیفری qavânin-e' keyfari
penalize *vt.* جریمه کردن jarimeh kardan
penalty *n.* جریمه jarimeh مجازات mojâzât
penalty *n.* جریمه jarimeh پنالتی penâlti
penance *n.* توبه tobeh
penchant *n.* تمایل tamâyol علاقهٔ شدید 'alâqeh-ye' shadid
pencil *v., n.* مداد medâd
pendant *n., adj.* آویز âvizân زینت آویز zinat âviz
pendent *adj., n.* آویزان âvizân معلق mo'al~aq
pending *pre., adj.* درجریان dar jâriân موکول به mokul beh
penetrable *n.* قابل نفوذ qâbel-e' nofuz

penetrant *n., adj.* تيز tiz نفوذكننده nofuz konandeh
penetrate *vi.* نفوذ كردن nofuz kardan رخنه كردن rekhneh kardan
penetrating *adj.* تيز tiz اثربخش asar-bakhsh نافذ nâfez
penetration *n.* نفوذ nofuz رخنه rekhneh دخول dokhul
penholder *n.* قلمدان qalam-dân
peninsula *n.* شبه جزيره shebh-e' jazireh
peninsular *adj.* شبه جزيره اى shebh-e' jazireh-i
penis *n.* آلت مرد âlat-e' mard
penitence *n.* پشيمانى pashimâni
penitent *adj.* پشيمان pashimân توبه كار tobeh-kâr
penitentiary *adj., n.* زندان zendân
penknife *n.* چاقو جيبى châqu jibi
penman *n.* نويسنده nevisandeh
penmanship *n.* نويسندگى nevisandegi دست خط dast khat
pennant *n.* پرچم سه گوش parcham-e' seh gush
penniless *adj.* بى پول bi-pul
penny *n.* پنى peni دهشاهى dah shâhi
penny royal *n.* پونه puneh
penny-wise *n.* حسابگر hesâb-gar
pension *n., vt.* حقوق بازنشستگى hoquq-e' bâz-neshastegi
pensionary *n., adj.* حقوق بگير hoquq be-gir
pensioner *n.* حقوق بگير hoquq be-gir
pensive *adj.* متفكر motefak~er پكر pakar
pentagon *n., adj.* پنج گوش panj gush پنج ضلعى panj zel'i
penthouse *n.* اطاق روى سقف otâq-e' ruy-e' saqf
penultimate *adj., n.* ماقبل آخر mâqabl-e' âkhar
penumbra *n.* نيم سايه nim-sâyeh
peon *n.* عمله 'amaleh
peony *n.* شقايق shaqâyeq
people *n., vt.* مردم آوردن mardom âvardan قوم qom
pep *n., vt., vi.* انرژى enerzhi دلگرمى del garmi
pep-talk *n.* صحبت تشويقى sohbat-e' tashviqi
pepper *n.* فلفل felfel
pepper *v.* پاشيدن pâ shidan پشت سرهم زدن posht-e' sar-e' ham
pepper-and-salt *adj., n.* نمك و فلفل namak-o felfel
peppermint *n.* نعناى وحشى na'nâ-ye' vahshi
peppery *adj.* فلفلى felfeli آتشين âtashin
peppin apple *n.* سيب گلاب sib golâb

peppy *adj.* پرانرژی por-enerzhi
per *pre.* مطابق motâbeq-e' طبق tebq-e'
per *pre.* بوسیله‌ی bevasileh-ye
per *pre.* در dar با bâ
per annum *n.* سالیانه sâliâneh
per capital *n.* سرانه sarâneh
per cent *n.* درصد darsad
per chance *n.* احتمالاً ehtemâlan شانسی shânsi
perceivable *adj.* درک شدنی dark shodani
perceive *vt.* درک کردن dark kardan
percentage *n., adj.* درصد darsad پورسانتاژ pursântâzh
percept *n.* درک dark
perceptible *adj.* قابل درک qâbel-e' dark محسوس mâhsus
perception *n.* درک dark شناخت shenâkht ادراک edrâk
perceptional *adj.* ادراکی edrâki
perceptive *adj.* زودفهم zud fahm باشناخت bâ-shenâkht
perceptual *adj.* درکی darki ادراکی edrâki
perch *v.* نشستن neshastan
perch *n.* میله mileh تیر tir
percolate *v.* نفوذ کردن nofuz kardan
percolate *v.* جوشاندن jushândan قل قل کردن qol-qol kardan
percolator *n.* قهوه جوش qahveh jush
percussion *n.* تصادم tasâdom ارتعاش erte'âsh
perdition *n.* انهدام enhedâm فنا fanâ
perfect *v.* کامل کردن kâmel kardan تکمیل کردن takmil kardan
perfect *n.* کامل kâmel
perfectible *adj.* کامل شدنی kâmel shodani
perfection *n.* کمال kamâl تکمیل takmil
perfectionist *n., adj.* کمال طلب kamâl-talab
perfectly *n.* کاملاً kâmelan
perforated *adj.* سوراخ سوراخ surâkh surâkh مشبک moshab~ak
perform *vt.* انجام دادن anjâm dâdan اجراکردن ejrâ kardan
performance *n.* انجام اجرا anjâm ejrâ نمایش namâyesh
performer *n.* اجرا کننده ejrâ konandeh
perfume *n., vt.* عطر 'atr
perfunctory *adj.* سرسری sar-sari الکی alaki بی مبالات bi-mobâlât
perhaps *n.* شاید shâyad
peril *n., vt.* خطر khatar مخاطره mokhâtereh

perilous *n.* خطرناک khatar-nâk

perimeter *n.* محیط mohit پیرامون pirâmun حریم harim
گرداگرد gerdâ gerd

period *n., adj.* مدّت mod~at دوره doreh نقطه noqteh

period *n., adj.* رگل regl قاعده qâ'edeh عادت ماهانه 'âdat-e' mâhâneh
حیض heyz

periodic *adj., n.* نوبتی nobati متناوب motenâveb

periodical *adj.* نشریه nashrieh دوره نامه doreh-nâmeh

periodically *adv.* درفواصل معین dar favâsel-e' mo'ây~an

peripheral *adj.* محیطی mohiti پیرامونی pirâmuni
همه جهتی hameh jahati

periphery *n.* محیط mohit پیرامون pirâmun اطراف atrâf

periscope *n.* دوربین زیردریایی durbin-e' zir-daryâyi

perish *vi.* هلاک کردن halâk kardan

perishable *adj., n.* ازبین رفتنی az-beyn raftani
خراب شدنی kharâb shodani

perished *n.* ازبین رفته az-beyn rafteh خراب شده kharâb shodeh

periwinkle *n.* گل تلگرافی gol-e' telegrâfi

perjure *vt.* قسم دروغ خوردن qasam-e' doruq khordan

perjury *n., vt., adj.* قسم دروغ qasam-e' doruq
شهادت دروغ shahâdat-e' doruq نقض قسم naqz-e' qasam

perk *n., vi., vt.* سربلند کردن sar boland kardan
سینه جلو دادن sineh jelo dâdan

perky *adj.* جسور jasur بزن برو bezan-boro

permanence *n.* دوام davâm بقا baqâ

permanency *n.* دوام davâm

permanent *adj., n.* دائمی dâ'emi همیشگی hamishegi ثابت sâbet

permeable *adj.* ردشدنی rad shodani نفوذپذیر nofuz-pazir

permeant *adj.* نفوذپذیر nofuz-pazir

permeate *vt.* نفوذکردن nofuz kardan رخنه کردن rekhneh kardan

permissible *adj.* مجاز majâz جایز jâyez روا ravâ

permission *n.* اجازه ejâzeh

permissive *adj.* اجازه دهنده ejâzeh dahandeh اجازه آزاد ejâzeh âzâd

permit *v.* اجازه دادن ejâzeh dâdan

permit *n.* اجازه ejâzeh پروانه parvâneh جواز javâz

permutation *n.* تغییر taqyir دگرگونی degârguni

permute *vt.* تغییردادن taqyir dâdan دگرگون کردن degargun kardan

pernicious *adj.* زیان آور ziân-âvar شریر sharir

perpendicular *n.* عمودى 'amudi قائم qâ'em
perpetrate *vt.* مرتكب شدن mortakeb shodan
perpetrator *n.* مرتكب mortakeb
perpetual *adj., n.* همیشگى hamishegi دائمى dâ'emi ابدى abadi
perpetually *adv.* براى همیشه barây-e' hamisheh دائماً dâ'eman
perpetuate *vt.* ابدى كردن abadi kardan جاودانى كردن jâvdâni kardan
perpetuity *n.* ابدیت abadiyat
perplex *vt.* گیج كردن gij kardan مغشوش كردن maqshush kardan
perplexed *adj.* گیج gij متحیر motehay~er مبهوت mabhut
perplexing *n.* گیج كننده gij konandeh پیچیده pichideh
perplexity *n.* گیجى giji پیچیدگى pichidegi
persecute *vt.* آزاردائمى رساندن âzâr-e' dâ'emi resândan
persecution *n.* آزاردائمى âzâr-e' dâ'emi اختناق ekhtenâq
Persepolis *n.* تخت جمشید takht-e' jamshid
perseverance *n., vt.* پشتكار poshtekâr
persevere *vi., vt.* پشتكارداشتن poshtekâr dâshtan
persevering *adj.* پشتكاردار poshtekâr-dâr
Persian Gulf *np.* خلیج فارس khalij-e' fârs
persimmons *n.* خرمالو khormâlu
persist *vi.* پافشارى كردن pâ-feshâri kardan اصراركردن esrâr kardan
persistence *n.* پافشارى pâ-feshâri اصرار esrâr ابرام ebrâm
persistent *adj.* بااصرار bâ-esrâr سمج semej مصر moser~ مقر moqor~
person *n.* شخص shakhs كس kas تن tan
persona non grata *np.* شخص نامطلوب shakhs-e' nâ-matlub
personable *adj.* خوش قیافه khosh qiâfeh
personage *n.* شخصیت دار shakhsiyat-dâr باشخصیت bâ-shakhsiyat
personal *adj., n.* شخصى shakhsi خصوصى khosusi
personal effects *np.* دارایى شخصى dârâyi-e' shakhsi
personal pronoun *np.* ضمیرشخصى zamir-e' shakhsi
personal property *np.* ملک شخصى melk-e' shakhsi
personality *n.* شخصیت shakhsiyat خوى khuy طینت tinat نطرت fetrat
personalize *n.* شخصى shakhsi خصوصى كردن khosusi kardan
personification *n.* جانبخشى jân-bakhshi مظهر maz-har
personify *vt.* جان بخشیدن jân bakhshidan
شخصیت دادن shakhsiyat dâdan
personnel *n.* كاركنان kâr-konân ادارى edâri
perspective *n.* چند جانبه chand jânebeh همه طرفه hameh tarafeh
perspiration *n.* عرق 'araq

perspiratory *adj.* عرق آور 'araq âvar
perspire *vi., vt.* عرق کردن 'araq kardan
persuadable *adj.* وادارشدنی vâdâr shodani
persuade *vt.* وادارکردن vâdâr kardan متقاعد کردن moteqâ'ed kardan
persuasible *n.* وادارشدنی vâdâr shodani
persuasion *n.* دین din مذهب maz-hab
persuasion *n.* وادارى vâdâri اغوا eqvâ
persuasive *adj., n.* وادارکننده vâdâr konandeh
اغواکننده eqvâ konandeh
pert *adj.* گستاخ gostâkh جسور jasur
pertain *vi.* مربوط بودن marbut budan مناسب بودن monâseb budan
pertinacious *adj.* لجباز laj-bâz یک دنده yek-dandeh لجوج lajuj
pertinacity *n.* لجبازى laj-bâzi یک دندگی yek-dandegi لجاجت lejâ-jat
pertinence *n.* ربط rabt مناسبت monâsebat دخل dakhl اقتضا eqteza
pertinent *adj.* مربوط marbut مناسب monâseb مقتضى moqtazi
pertly *adv.* گستاخانه gostâkhâneh جسورانه jasurâneh
perturb *v.* آشفته کردن âshofteh kardan
مضطرب کردن moztareb kardan
perturbation *n.* اغتشاش eqteshâsh آشفتگی ashoftegi تشویش tashvish
perturbative *n.* اغتشاشى eqteshâshi مشوش moshav~ash
pervasion *n.* سرایت کننده sarâyat konandeh فراگیر farâ-gir
pervasion *n.* سرایت sarâyat فراگیرى farâ-giri
perverse *adj.* گمراه gomrâh خیره سر khireh-sar منحرف monhâref
perversion *n.* گمراهى gomrâhi خیره سرى khireh-sari انحراف enherâf
perversity *n.* انحراف enherâf هرزگى harzegi
perversive *n.* منحرف کننده monharef konandeh
pervert *adj.* آدم هرزه âdam-e' harzeh منحرف monharef کجراه kaj-râh
pervert *v.* منحرف کردن monharef kardan
ازراه بدرکردن az râh bedar kardan
perverted *adj.* منحرف monharef
pervious *adj.* نفوذ پذیر nofuz pazir بازفکر bâz fekr
pesky *adj.* مزاحم mozâhem
pessimism *n.* بدبینی bad-bini
pessimist *n.* بدبین bad-bin
pessimistic *n.* بدبینانه bad-binâneh
pest *n.* حشره hashareh بلا balâ مردم آزار mardom-âzâr
pester *vt.* مردم آزارى کردن mardom âzâri kardan
اذیت کردن azyat kardan

pesticide *n.* حشره کش hashâreh-kosh
pestilence *n.* بلا balâ طاعون tâ'un فتنه fetneh
pestilent *adj.* مرگ آور marg âvar مضر mozer
pestle *n., vt., vi.* دسته هاون dasteh hâvan
pet *n.* حیوان همدم heyvân-e' hamdam موردعلاقه mored-e' 'alâqeh
pet *v.* نازکردن nâz kardan نوازش کردن navâzesh kardan
petal *n.* گلبرگ gol-barg
petcock *n.* شیرک shirak سرفنتیل sar fentil
petit(te) *n.* کوچولو kuchulu نقلی noqli
petition *n.* دادخواست dâd-khâst عرضحال 'arz-e' hâl
petition *v.* درخواست کردن dar-khâst kardan
petitionary *adj.* درخواستی dar-khâsti
petitioner *n.* عارض 'ârez دادخواه dâd-khâh خواهان khâhân
متظلم motezal~em
petrify *vt., vi.* بسنگ تبدیل کردن besang tabdil kardan
ازترس خشک شد az tars khoshk shod
petrol *n., vt.* نفت naft بنزین benzin
petroleum *n.* نفت خام naft-e' khâm
petticoat *n., adj.* زیردامنی zir dâman-i
petty *adj.* ناچیز nâ-chiz بی اهمیت bi-ahamiyat جزئی joz'i
petty cash *np.* تنخواه گردان tankhâh-e' gardân پول دخل pul-e' dakhl
petty larceny *np.* دزدی جزئی dozdi-e' joz'i
petty officer *n.* مهناو mahnâv
petty theft *n.* دزدی جزئی dozdi-e' joz'i خرده دزدی khordeh dozdi
petulance *n.* تندخویی tond-khuyi بی حیایی bi-hayâyi
petulant *adj.* تندخو tond-khu بی حیا bi-hayâ
petunia *n.* گل اطلسی gol-e' atlasi
pewit *n.* زیاک ziâk
Ph.D. *n.* دکترا doktorâ
phalanx *n., vi.* صف فشرده saf-e' feshordeh
phallic *adj.* آلتی âlati
phallus *n.* آلت مرد âlat-e' mard
phantasm *n.* تخیل takhay~ol تجسم tajas~om
phantom *n., adj.* لولو lulu خیالی khiâl-i
pharmaceutical *adj., n.* داروخانهای dâru-khâneh-i
pharmaceutist *n.* داروساز dâru-sâz
pharmacist *n.* داروساز dâru-sâz
pharmacology *n.* داروشناسی dâru-shenâsi

pharmacy *n.* داروخانه dâru-khâneh
pharoah *n.* فرعون fer'on
pharyngeal *n.* حلقومی holqumi
pharyngitis *n.* ورم گلو varam-e' galu
pharynx *n., vt.* حلقوم holqum حلق halq
phase *n., vt.* مرحله marhaleh ناز fâz
phase(out) *n.* کنارگذاشتن kenâr gozâshtan
pheasant *n.* ترقاول qarqâvol
phenomena *n.* پدیده pâdideh
phenomenal *adj.* پدیده ای pâdideh-i خارق العاده khâr-e' qol'âdeh
phenomenon *n.* پدیده padideh
phew! *n.* پیف pif! به bah!
phial *n.* بطری کوچک botri-e' kuchek
philanderer *n.* عشقباز 'eshq-bâz
philanthropist *n.* مردم دوست mardom-dust خیرخواه kheyr-khâh
philanthropy *n.* مردم دوستی mardom dusti
philosopher *n.* فیلسوف filsuf حکیم hakim
philosophic(al) *n.* فلسفهای falsafeh-i
philosophize *vi.* فلسفه ای کردن falsafeh-i kardan
philosophy *n.* فلسفه falsafeh حکمت hekmat
phlebitis *n.* ورم رگ varam-e' rag
phlebotomy *n.* هجومت hojumat
phlegm *n.* خلط khelt بلغم balqam
phobia *n.* وحشت vahshat ترس tars
phoenix *n.* مرغ آتش morq-e' âtash سیمرغ simorq
phone *n.* صدا sedâ تلفن telefon
phone *v.* تلفن زدن telefon zadan تلفن کردن telefon kardan
phoneme *n.* واج vâj
phonemic(s) *n.* واجی vâji
phonetic(ally) *n.* صوتی soti آوایی âvâyi
phonetics *n.* آواشناسی âvâ-shenâsi
phonetist *n.* آواشناس âvâ-shenâs
phonic(s) *n.* صوت شناسی sot shenâsi
phonograph *n.* صداسنج sedâ sanj فونوگراف fonogrâf
گرامافون gerâmâfon
phonography *n.* آوانویسی âvâ nevisi
phony *adj., n.* تقلبی taqal~obi قلابی qol~âbi متقلب moteqal~eb
phosphor *n., adj.* گوگرد gugerd فسفر fosfor

photo *n.* عکس 'aks
photogenic *adj.* فتوژنیک foto-zhenik خوش عکس khosh-'aks
photograph *n.* عکس 'aks
photograph *v.* عکس برداشتن 'aks bar dâshtan
photographer *n.* عکاس 'ak~âs
photographic *adj.* عکسی 'aksi
photography *n.* عکس برداری 'aks-bardâri عکاسی ak~âsi
photostat *n.* کپی kopi
phrase *n., vt.* عبارت 'ebârat گروه goruh
phrasing *n., v.* عبارت سازی 'ebârat-sâzi
physical *adj., n.* بدنی badani جسمی jesmi طبیعتی tabi'ati
physical education *np.* تربیت بدنی tarbiat-e' badani
physical fitness *n.* تناسب بدنی tanâsob-e' badani
physically *adv.* بدنی badani جسمی jesmi شخصاً shakhsan
physician *n.* پزشک pezeshk طبیب tabib دکتر doktor
physicist *n.* فیزیک شناس fizik shenâs
physics *n.* فیزیک fizik
physiotherapy *n.* تن درمانی tan-darmâni
physiotherapy *n.* کار درمانی kâr darmâni
physique *n.* بدن badan اندام andâm
pi *n., vt.* پی pi
pianist *n.* پیانوزن piâno zan
piano *n., adj., adv.* پیانو piâno
pick *v.* انتخاب کردن entekhâb kardan جداکردن jodâ kardan
pick *v.* کندن kandan
pick *v.* جیب بریدن jib boridan
pick *n.* میخ mikh
pick *v.* بهانه جویی کردن bahâneh-juyi kardan
pick *n.* مضراب mezrâb زخمه zakhmeh
pick *v.* قفل بازکردن qofl bâz kardan
pick *v.* خلال کردن khalâl kardan انگشت کردن angosht kardan
pick *v.* سوراخ کردن surâkh kardan
pick *n.* منتخب montakhab گل چین golchin
pick *v.* کلنگ زدن kolang zadan
pick *v.* چیدن chidan
pick(a fight) *n.* دعوا راه انداختن da'vâ râh andâkhtan
pick(and choose) *n.* بادقت انتخاب کردن bâ-deq~at entekhâb kardan
pick(at) *n.* ناخنک زدن nâ-khonak zadan نوک زدن nok zadan

pick(on) *n.* اذیت کردن azyat kardan
سربسرگذاشتن sar besar gozâshtan
pick(one's way) *n.* بادقت پیشروی کردن bâdeq~at pish-ravi kardan
pick(out) *n.* انتخاب کردن entekhâb kardan جدا jodâ
pick(over) *n.* بادقت معاینه کردن bâdeq~at mo'âyeneh kardan
pick(up) *n.* بهبودیافتن behbud yâftan
pick(up) *n.* سوارکردن savâr kardan
pick(up) *n.* پیشرفت کردن pish-raft kardan
pick(up) *n.* بلندکردن boland kardan گرفتن gereftan
pickaninny *n.* بچه سیاه bach~eh siâh
pickax(e) *n.* تیشه کلنگ tisheh-kolang
picked *adj.* برگزیده bargozideh
picket *v.* اعتراض e'terâz اعتصاب کردن e'tesâb kardan
picket *n.* چوب میخ chub mikh
picket fence *np.* چوب پرچین chub parchin چوب نرده chub nardeh
picket line *np.* صف معترضین saf-e' mo'tarezin
picking *n.* ناخنک زنی nâkhonak-zani ته مانده tahmândeh
pickle *n., vt.* ترشی انداختن torshi andâkhtan
خیارشور کردن khiâr-shur
نمک سودکردن namak-sud kardan
picklock *n.* قفل شکن qofl shekan
pickpocket *n.* جیب بر jib-bor
pickup *n.* وانت vânet
pickup *n.* گیرندگی girandegi
pickup *n.* بهبود behbud رونق ronaq
pickup *n.* وانت vânet
picky *adj.* وسواسی vasvâsi خرده گیر khordeh-gir
picnic *n., vi.* پیک نیک piknik
pictorial *adj., n.* مصور mosav~ar
picture *n.* عکس 'aks تصویر tasvir
picture *v.* مجسم کردن mojas~am kardan
picture show *np.* سینما sinamâ
picturesque *adj.* منظرهایی manzareh-i
picturize *vt.* مصورکردن mosav~ar kardan
piddle *vi., vt.* جیش کردن jish kardan
piddle(away) *n.* تلف کردن talaf kardan
pidgin *n.* زبان قرقاطی zabân-e' qareqâti
دست و پاشکسته dast-o pâ shekasteh

pie *vt., n.* کیک میوه keyk-e′ miveh
piece *n., vt., vi.* تکه tek~eh قطعه qat′eh
piecemeal *adv., adj.* ذره ذره zar~eh zar~eh
خرده خرده khordeh khordeh
piecework *n.* قطعه کاری qat′eh kâri
pier *n., vi.* اسکله eskeleh
pierce *n.* سوراخ کردن surâkh kardan
piercing *adj.* گوش خراش gush-kharâsh
piety *n.* دینداری din-dâri مومنی mo′meni
pig *n., vi., vt.* خوک khuk
pig iron *np.* آهن پاره âhan pâreh
pigeon *n.* کبوتر kabutar
pigeon hawk *np.* قرقی qerqi
pigeonhearted *n.* ترسو tarsu
piggish *n.* خوک صفت khuk-sefat
piggy *n., adj.* خوک صفت khuk-sefat شکمو shekamu
piggy bank *np.* قلک qol~ak
piggyback *adv., adj., vt., vi.* قلندوش qalan-dush کولی kuli
pigheaded *n.* کله شق kal~eh-shaq
piglet *n.* خوکچه khuk-cheh
pigment *n., vt., vi.* رنگ rang یاخته رنگ yâkhteh rang
pigpen *n.* خوک دان khuk-dân
pigskin *n.* چرم خوک charm-e′ khuk توپ tup
pigsty *n.* خوک دان khuk-dân
pigtail *n.* گیس بافت gis bâft
pike *n.* زوبین zubin
pike *v.* نیزه زدن neyzeh zadan
pile *n.* کپه kop~eh پل ستون pol sotun پرز porz
pile *v.* کپه کردن kopeh kardan
pile *n.* پیل pil
pile *v.* دسته کردن dasteh kardan
piles *n.* بواسیر bavâsir
pilfer *n.* دزدیدن dozdidan دله دزدی کردن daleh-dozdi kardan
ناخنک زدن nâkhonak zadan
pilferage *n.* دله دزدی daleh-dozdi ناخنک nâkhonak
pilgrim *n.* زوار zavâr حاجی hâji
pilgrimage *n.* زیارت ziârat حج haj
pill *n.* قرص qors حب hab~

pill *v.* پوست کندن pust kandan
pillage *v.* غارت کردن qârat kardan
pillage *v.* چپاول کردن chapâvol kardan
pillar *n.* ستون sotun پایه pâyeh عماد 'emâd
pillbox *n.* سنگر بتون آرمه sangar-e' boton-ârmeh
pillow *n., vt., vi.* متکا motak~â بالش bâlesh
pillowcase *n.* روبالشی ru-bâleshi
pilot *v.* خلبانی کردن khalebâni kardan
راهنمایی کردن râhnamâyi kardan
pilot *n.* خلبان khalebân
pilot *n.* استارتر estârter
pimp *n., vi.* جاکش jâkesh
pimple *n.* جوش jush
pin *n., vt.* سنجاق sanjâq سوزن suzan
pin stripe *np.* راه راه نازک râh râh-e' nâzok
pin(down) *n.* ضربه کردن zarbeh kardan
pin(on) *n.* بگردن انداختن begardan andâkhtan
مقصرشناختن moqas~er shenâkhtan
pin-up *n.* عکس دیواری 'aks-e' divâri
pincers *vi., n.* گازانبر gâz-anbor
pinch *v.* دزدیدن dozdidan
pinch *v.* دستگیرکردن dast gir kardan
pinch *v.* نیشگان گرفتن nishgân gereftan
وشگون گرفتن veshgun gereftan
pine *n.* کاج سرو sarv
pine *v.* غصه خوردن qos~eh khordan درحسرت بودن dar hasrat budan
pineal *adj.* کاج مانند kâj mânand
pinhead *n.* نوک سوزن noksuzan جزئی joz'i
pinhole *n.* سوراخ سوزن surâkh suzan
pink *n.* صورتی surati
pinky *n.* انگشت کوچک angosht kuchekeh
pinnacle *n., vt.* قله qol~eh
pinnacle *n., vt.* سرلوله sar luleh
pinnacle *n., vt.* نوک nok
pinprick *n.* سوراخ ریز surâkh-e' riz
pins and needles *np.* خواب رفتگی khâb-raftegi
pinto bean *n.* لوبیا چیتی lubiâ chiti
pinwheel *n.* فرفره fer-fereh

pioneer *adj.* پیشرو pish-ro پیش قدم pish-qadam
pioneer *n., vi., vt.* پیش قدمی کردن pish-qadami kardan
pioneer *v.* پیشروی کردن pish-ravi kardan
pious *adj.* بادین bâ-din مومن momen
pip *n.* سالار sâlâr
pip *v.* جیک جیک کردن jik-jik kardan
pipe *n.* چپق chopoq پیپ pip
pipe *n.* لوله luleh نی ney
pipe *v.* لوله کشیدن luleh keshidan
pipe dream *n.* خواب خیالی khâb-e' khiâli
pipe(down) *n.* آرامترشدن ârâmtar shodan
pipe(up) *n.* شروع به خواندن کردن shoru' beh khândan kardan
pipe-line *n.* خط لوله کشی khat~-e' luleh keshi
شبکۀ خبری shabakeh-ye' khabari
piper *n.* نی انبان زن ney anbân-zan
pirate *n.* دزددریایی dozd-e' daryâyi
pirate *v.* دزدی کردن dozdi kardan کش رفتن kesh raftan
piss *n., vi.* شاشیدن shâshidan شاش کردن shâsh kardan
pistachio *n.* پسته pesteh
pistil *n.* تخمدان tokhm-dân
pistol *n., vt.* هفت تیر haft-tir تپانچه tapâncheh
piston *n.* پیستون piston سنبه sonbeh
pit *n.* گودال godâl چاله châleh زیربغل zir-baqal
pit *v.* خال خال کردن khâl-khâl kardan
pit *n.* هسته hasteh
pit-stop *n.* توقف کوتاه tavaq~of-e' kutâh
pitch *v.* پرتاب کردن partâb kardan
pitch *v.* قیراندودکردن qir andud kardan
pitch *n.* تن ton کوک kuk
pitch *v.* زدن zadan برپاکردن bar pâ kardan
pitch *n.* زیروبم zir-o bam
pitch(in) *n.* سهم خودددادن sahm-e' khod dâdan
pitch(into) *n.* حمله ورشدن hamleh var shodan
pitch(on) *n.* انتخاب کردن entekhâb kardan
pitch-black *adj.* سیاه siâh قیرگون qirgun
pitch-dark *adj.* سیاه siâh قیرگون qirgun
pitched-battle *n.* جنگ مغلوبه jang maqlubeh
pitcher *n.* پارچ pârch کوزه kuzeh سبو sabu

pitcher *n.* توب انداز tup andâz
pitchfork *n., vt.* کاه انداز kâh-andâz سه شاخه seh shâkheh
pitchy *adj.* قیری qiri سیاه siâh
pitfall *n.* گودالی t:ۂ tleh-ye' godâli دام dâm
pith *n., vt.* میان ساقه miân sâqeh مغزحرام maqz harâm
pitiful *adj.* رقت انگیز req~at angiz پست past
pitiless *adj.* بیرحمانه birahmâneh
pittance *n.* پول جزئی pul-e' joz'i
pity *adj.* ترحم tarah~om رحم rahm دلسوزی delsuzi رقت req~at
pity *n.* جای تأسف jâ-ye' ta'as~of
pity *v.* ترحم کردن tarah~om kardan متأسف بودن mote'as~ef budân
pivot *n., vi., vt.* محور mehvar پاشنه گردی pâshneh gardi
pivotal *adj.* محوری mehvari چرخشی charkheshi قطبی qotbi
plac *n.* جا jâ مکان makân محل mahal
placard *n., vt.* آگهی دیواری âgahi divâri پلاکارد pelâ kârd
placate *n.* تسکین دادن taskin dâdan فرونشاندن foru neshândan
place *v.* گذاشتن gozâshtan گماشتن gomâshtan
place *v.* قراردادن qarâr dâdan
place *v.* بیادآوردن be-yâd âvardan
placement *n.* ورودیه vorudiyeh کارگزاری kâr-gozâri
placer *n.* گذارنده gozârandeh
placid *adj.* آرام ârâm ساکت sâket متین matin
plagiarism *n.* نوشته دزدی neveshteh-dozdi
plagiarist *n.* نوشته دزد neveshteh-dozd
plagiarize *vt.* نوشته دزدی کردن neveshteh-dozdi kardan
plague *n.* طاعون tâ'un
plague *v.* طاعون زدن tâ'un zadan بستوه آوردن besotuh âvardan
plaid *n., adj.* چهارخانه chahâr-khâneh
plain *adj., vi., adv., n.* ساده sâdeh معمولی ma'muli
plain *adj., vi., adv., n.* دشت dasht
plain *adj., vi., adv., n.* صاف sâf
plain-clothes *n.* لباس عادی lebâs-e' 'âd~i
plain-spoken *adj.* رک گویی rok guyi
plainsman *n.* دشت زیست dasht zist
plaintiff *n.* شاکی shâki مدعی mod~a'i
plan *v.* نقشه کشیدن naqsheh keshidan درصددبودن dar-sadad budan
plan *n.* نقش naqsheh طرح tarh برنامه barnâmeh
plane *n., adj., vi., vt.* هواپیما havâ-peymâ

plane *n., adj., vi., vt.* سطح صاف sat-h-e' sâf مسطح mosat~ah
planet *n.* کره koreh سیاره say~âreh
planetarium *n.* نجوم خانه nojum-khâneh
planetary *adj., n.* کروی koravi زمینی zamini
plank *n., vt.* الوار alvâr تیرچوب tirchub
plant *n.* کارخانه kâr-khâneh
plant *v.* کاشتن kâshtan ثبت کردن sabt kardan
plant *n.* گیاه giâh نبات nabât
plaster *n., vt., vi.* گچ gach
plate *n.* بشقاب boshqâb ظرف zarf
plate *v.* آب دادن âb dâdan روکش کردن rukesh kardan
plate *n.* کلیشه kelisheh
plateau *n.* فلات falât جلگه jolgeh
plated *adj., v.* روکشدار rukeshdâr آب داده âb dâdeh
platform *n.* سکو saku خط مشی khât~-e' mâshy
platinum *n.* پلاتین pelâtin طلای سفید talây-e' sefid
platoon *n.* دسته dasteh گروه goruh
platter *n.* سینی sini دوری dori
plaudit *n.* کف زنی kaf zani تحسین tahsin
plausible *adj.* قابل قبول qâbel-e' qabul خوش ظاهر khosh zâher
play *n.* بازی bâzi
play *v.* بازی کردن bâzi kardan
play *v.* نواختن navâkhtan زدن zadan
play hooky *n.* ازمدرسه دررفتن az madreseh dar raftan
play on words *np.* بازی باکلمه bâzi bâ kalameh تجنیس tajnis
play(out) *n.* تاآخربازی کردن tâ-âkhar bâzi kardan
play-off *n.* بازی تعیین کننده bâzi-e' ta'yin konandeh
playback *n.* بازگرد bâz-gard بازگشت baz-gasht
playboy *n.* دخترباز dokhtar-bâz
player *n.* بازیکن bâzi-kon
playful *adj.* بازیگوش bâzi-gush خوش مشرب khosh-mashrab
playground *n.* زمین بازی zamin-e' bâzi
playhouse *n.* نمایش خانه namâyesh-khâneh
تماشاخانه tamâshâ-khâneh
playmate *n.* همبازی ham-bâzi
playroom *n.* اطاق بازی otâq-e' bâzi
plaything *n.* بازیچه bâzicheh
playtime *n.* وقت بازی vaqt-e' bâzi

playwright *n.* نمایش نامه نویس namâyesh-nâmeh nevis
plea *n.* درخواست dar-khâst مدافعه modâfe'eh
plead *vi.* درخواست کردن dar-khâst kardan
التماس کردن eltemâs kardan
pleasant *adv.* باصفا bâ-safâ خوش مشرب khosh-mashrab
pleasantry *n.* شوخی shukhi خوش مشربی khosh-mashrabi
please *vt., vi.* خوشنود کردن khoshnud kardan راضی کردن râzi kardan
please! *n.* خواهش میکنم khâhesh mikonam!
لطفاً lotfan!
pleasing *adj.* خوش آیند khosh âyand دلپذیر del-pazir
pleasurable *adj.* لذت بخش lez~at-bakhsh کیف دار keyf-dâr
pleasure *n., vt., vi.* لذت lez~at خوشی khoshi مسرت maser~at
کیف keyf
pleat *n., vt.* تاچین کردن tâ-chin kardan
plebiscite *n.* آراء عمومی ârâ-e' 'omumi
pledge *n., vt., vi.* قسم خوردن qasam khordan
pledge *v.* ضمانت کردن zemânat kardan
متعهدشدن mote'ah~ed shodan
pledge *v.* سوگند خوردن sogand khordan
Pleiades *pl.* پروین parvin ثریا soray~â
plenipotentiary *n., adj.* تام الاختیار tâmol-ekhtiâr
plenish *vt.* پرکردن por kardan انبار کردن anbâr kardan
plenitude *n.* پری pori ونور vofur
plenty *n., adj., adv.* فراوانی farâvâni بحدکافی be-hâd~-e' kâfi
plethora *n.* کثرت kesrat زیاده ازحد ziâdeh az had
pliers *n.* انبردستی anbor dasti
plight *n.* قسم خوردن qasam khordan
plight *n.* موقعیت بد moqe'iyat-e' bad پیسی pisi
plod *vi., vt., n.* بسختی کارکردن besakhti kâr kardan
راه رفتن râh raftan
plodder *n.* کند کار kond kâr
plot *n.* قطعه زمین qat'eh zamin پارچه pârcheh
plot *v.* توطئه چیدن tote'eh chidan
plot *adj., vt., vi.* قبر qabr
plotter *n.* توطئه چین tote'eh-chin
plowshare *n.* خیش khish تیغه tiqeh
pluck *vt., vi.* پر کندن par kandan
plucky *adj.* باشهامت bâ-shahâmat

plug *v.* سوراخ گرفتن surâkh gereftan توپی گذاشتن tupi gozâshtan
plug *v.* آگهی کردن âgahi kardan
plug *n.* پریز periz
plug(in) *n.* توی برق کردن tu-ye' barq kardan
plug(up) *n.* مسدود کردن mas-dud kardan جلو گرفتن jelo gereftan
plum *adj., adv., n.* گوجه gojeh
plumage *n.* پروبال par-o bâl
plumb *n., vt.* سرب sorb بکلی be-kol~i
plumb-line *n.* شاقول shâqul
plumbago *n.* گرافیت gerâfit مداد سربی medâd-e' sorbi
plumber *n.* لوله کش luleh-kesh
plumbing *n.* لوله کشی luleh-keshi
plume *n., vt.* پر آرایی par ârâyi
plummet *n., vi.* شاقول shâqul پایین افتادن pâyin oftâdan
plump *n.* چاق و چله châq-o cheleh تپل topol
plump *v.* تلپی افتادن tolopi oftâdan
plumy *adj.* پردار par dâr
plunder *vt., vi., n.* تاراج کردن târâj kardan غارت کردن qârat
چاپیدن châpidan بیغمابردن be-yaqmâ bordan
plunderage *n.* چاول chapâvol غارت qârat
plunge *vt., vi., n.* فرو بردن foru bordan فرو رفتن foru raftan
غوطه ورشدن qoteh-var shodan
plunger *n.* تلمبه tolombeh
plunk *vt., vi., n., adv.* چنگ زدن chang zadan
پرتاب کردن partâb kardan
pluperfect *n.* ماضی بعید mâzi-e' ba'id
plural *adj., n.* جمع jam'
pluralism *n.* چند منصبی chand-mansabi
pluralist *n.* چندمنصب chand-mansab
plurality *n.* مجموعه majmu'eh اکثریت aksariyat
pluralize *vt., vi.* جمع کردن jam' kardan
plus *pre., adj., n.* بعلاوهٔ be-'alâveh-ye' باضافهٔ be-ezâfeh-ye'
مثبت mosbat
plush *n., adj.* تجملی tajamol~i لوکس luks
ply *n., vt., vi.* لا tâ تا lâ
plywood *n.* تخته سه لا takhteh sheh lâ
pneumonia *n.* سینه پهلو sineh pahlu
poach *v.* آب پز کردن âb-paz kardan

poach v. شکارکردن دزدی dozdi shekâr kardan
pock n. جای آبله jâ-ye' âbeleh
pocket n. پاکت pâkat کیسه kiseh
pocket n. جیب jib
pocket n. چاه châh
pocket v. بجیب زدن bejib zadan پنهان کردن penhân kardan
pocket money n. پول جیبی pul jibi
pocketbook n. کتاب جیبی ketâb jibi کیف جیبی kif jibi
pocketful n. جیب پر jib-e' por
pocketknife n. چاقو جیبی châqu jibi
pockmark(ed) n. آبله دار âbeleh-dâr
pod n. غلاف qalâf تخمدان tokhm-dân
pod v. پیله کردن pileh kardan گله کردن geleh kardan
podium n. سکو saku تریبون teribun میزخطابه miz-e' khatâbeh
poem n. شعر she'r چکامه chakâmeh
poet n. شاعر shâ'er جامه سرا chameh-sara
poet laureate np. ملک الشعراء malekol sho'arâ
شاه چامه سرا shâh chameh-sarâ
poetess n. شاعره shâ'ereh
poetic(al) n. شاعرانه shâ'erâneh
poetics vi., vt. شعروشاعری she'r-o shâ'eri
poetry n. شعر نویسی she'r nevisi
pogo stick n. چوب فنری chub-fanari فنرورجه fanar-varjeh
pogrom n. اقلیت کشی aqâliyât-koshi
poignancy n. تندی tizi تندی tondi
poignant adj. تیز tiz تند tond نیشدار nish-dâr
poind n. مزایده کردن mozâyedeh kardan
point n., vt., vi. لحظه lahzeh حد had~ شرف shorof دم dam
point v. نقطه گذاشتن noqteh gozâshtan
point v. قراول رفتن qarâvol raftan نشان گرفتن neshân gereftan
point n. مقصود maqsud نکته nokteh موضوع mozu'
point n. ممیز momay~ez
point n. امتیاز emtiâz
point n. حقیقت haqiqat
point v. روکردن ru kardan
point v. متوجه ساختن motevaj~eh sâkhtan
point n. نوک nok تیزی tizi
point n. قله qol~eh

point v. اشاره کردن eshâreh kardan
point of view np. نقطهٔ نظر noqteh-ye' nazar
point(out) n. نشان دادن neshân dâdan اشاره کردن eshâreh kardan
point(the way) n. راهنمایی کردن râhnamâyi kardan
point(up) n. تأکید کردن ta'kid kardan
point-blank adj., adv. ازنزدیک az nazdik
رک و پوست کنده rok va pust kandeh
point-by-point n. نکته به نکته nokteh be-nokteh
pointed adj. تیز tiz نشان گرفته neshân gerefteh
pointer n. تازی tâzi نشانگیر neshân-gir خط کش khat-kesh
pointless n. بی نتیجه bi-natijeh بیخود bi-khod
poise n. موازنه movâzeneh متانت metânat
poison n. سم sam~ زهر zahr
poison v. مسموم کردن masmum kardan
poison ivy np. گزنه gazaneh
poisonous n. سمی sam~i زهرآلود zahr âlud
poke vt., vi., n. سیخ زدن sikh zadan مشت زدن mosht zadan
سقلمه soqolmeh
poke fun(at) n. مسخره کردن mas-khareh kardan
poker n. سیخ sikh میله هیزم mileh hizom
poker n. پوکر poker
polar adj. قطبی qotbi متقارن moteqâren
polar bear np. خرس قطبی khers-e' qotbi
Polaris n. ستارهٔ قطبی setâreh-ye' qotbi جدی jadi
polarity n. جاذبه دوقطبی jâzebeh doqotbi
polarization n. تقارن taqâron تناقض tanâqoz
polarize vt. متقارن کردن moteqâren kardan
pole n., vt., vi. تیر tir دیرک dirak
pole vault np. پرش بانیزه paresh bâ neyzeh
poleax n. تبرزین tabar zin
police v. حفاظت کردن hefâzat kardan تمیزکردن tamiz kardan
police n. پلیس polis پاسبان pâsbân شهربانی shahrbâni
police dog np. سگ پلیس sag-e' polis
police station n. کلانتری kalântari
policeman n. پاسبان pâsbân آژدان âzhdân
policewoman n. پلیس زن polis-e' zan
policy n. رویه raviyeh سیاست siâsat
policy n. بیمه نامه bimeh-nâmeh

policyholder *n.* بیمه نامه دار bimeh nâmeh-dâr
polio *n.* فلجی اطفال falaji-e' atfâl
polish *v.* واکس زدن vâks zadan براق کردن bar~âq kardan
polish *v.* جلا دادن jalâ dâdan
polish(off) *n.* کلک کندن kalak kandan
polished *n.* مودب mo'ad~ab براق bar~âq
polite *adj.* باادب bâ-adab مودب moad~ab
politeness *n.* باادبی bâ-adabi ادب adab
politic *adj.* بااحتیاط bâ-ehtiât
political *adj.* سیاسی siâsi
political science *np.* حقوق سیاسی hoqug-e' siâsi
politically *n.* ازلحاظ سیاسی az lahâz-e' siâsi
politician *n.* سیاستمدار siâsat-madâr
politics *n.* سیاست siâsat
polka dot *n.* خال خالی khâl-khâli
poll *n.* سر sar نظرخواهی nazar-khâhi
poll *v.* رأی گرفتن ra'y gereftan
poll-tax *n.* مالیات سرانه mâliyât-e' sarâneh
pollard *n., vt.* شاخ بریده shâkh borideh بی شاخ bi-shâkh
polled *n., vt.* بی شاخ bi-shâkh
pollen *n.* گرده گل gardeh-ye' gol
pollinate *vt.* گرده پاشیدن gardeh pâshidan
pollination *n.* گرده پاشی gardeh-pâshi
pollster *n.* آمارگیر âmâr-gir رأی گیر ra'y-gir
pollute *vt.* آلوده کردن âludeh kardan
pollution *n.* آلودگی âludegi
polo *n.* چوگان chogân
polygamist *n.* چندزنه chand-zaneh
polygamy *n.* چندزنی chand-zani
polyglot *adj., n.* چند زبانه chand-zabaneh
polytechnic *adj., n.* دارالفنون dârolfonun پلی تکنیک politeknik
pomegranate *n.* انار anâr
pommel *n., vt.* قاچ زین qâch-e' zin قپه qop~eh
pomp *n.* طمطراق tomtorâq کبکبه kab-kabeh جاه و جلال jâh-o jalâl
دنگ و فنگ dang-o fang
pomposity *n.* تکبر takab~or تشخص tashakh~os
فروشکوه far~-o shokuh
pompous *n.* پر آب و تاب por âb-o tâb متشخص moteshakh~es

pond *n.* حوض hoz
ponder *vi., vt.* عميق فكر كردن 'amiq fekr kardan
پندار كردن pendâr kardan تعقل كردن ta'aq~ol kardan
ponderous *adj.* ثقيل saqil سنگين sangin
pontiff *n.* پاپ pâp اسقف osqof
pontificate *n., vi.* سفت و سخت گرفتن seft-o sakht gereftan
pontoon *n.* پل شناور pol-e' shenâvar
pony *n.* اسب كوتوله asb-e' kutuleh
pony express *np.* پست سوار post savâr چاپار châpâr
pooch *n.* سگ sag
pooh *vt.* اه ah
pooh-pooh *vt., vi.* اخ akh اهى ahi
pool *n.* بيليارد bil-yârd
pool *v.* روى هم گذاشتن ruy-e' ham gozâshtan
pool *n.* استخر estakhr حوض hoz
pool table *np.* ميز بيليارد miz-e' bil-yârd
poolroom *n.* سالن بيليارد sâlon-e' bil-yârd
pooped *n.* خسته khasteh بى نفس bi-nafas
poor *adj., n.* فقير faqir گدا gedâ بى نوا bi-navâ مستمند mostamand
poor-spirited *adj.* بزدل boz-del
poorhouse *n.* نوان خانه navân khâneh
poorly *adv., adj.* بد bad
pop *n.* تپ tap بابا bâbâ گازدار gâz dâr
pop *v.* تركيدن târekidan
popcorn *n.* ذرت بوداده zorat-e' bu dâdeh چسفيل chos-fil
pope *n.* پاپ pâp
popeyed *adj.* چشم باباقورى cheshm-e' bâbâ-quri
popgun *n.* تفنگ چوب پنبهاى tofang-e' chub-panbeh-i
poplar *n.* تبريزى tabrizi
poppy *n.* خشخاش khash khâsh
poppy flower *n.* شقايق shaqâyeq
poppy seed *np.* خشخاش khash khâsh
poppycock *n.* چرند charand
populace *n.* جمعيت jam'iyat توده tudeh سكنه sakaneh
popular *adj.* محبوب mahbub مردمى mardomi
popularity *n.* محبوبيت mahbubiyat وجهه vej-heh
popularize *n.* محبوب كردن mahbub kardan
populate *n.* پرجمعيت كردن por jam'iyat kardan

population n. جمعیت jam'iyat
porcelain n. پورسلین porselin چینی chini
porch n. هشتی hashti جلوخانه jelo-khâneh
porcupine n. جوجه تیغی jujeh tiqi خارپشت khâr-posht
pore n. پرز porz
pore v. بادقت نگاه کردن bâ-deq~at negâh kardan
pork n. گوشت خوک gusht-e' khuk
porky adj. خوک مانند khuk mânand چاق châq
pornography adv. مستهجنات mostah-janât
فیلمهای لختی film-hâ-ye' lokhti
porosity n. پرسوراخی por surâkhi
porous adj. پرسوراخ por surâkh
porpoise n. دلفین dolfin
port vt., n. سمت چپ samt-e' chap
port vt., n. بندر bandar
port vt., n. شراب شیرین sharâb-e' shirin
port of call n. بندرتوقف bandar-e' tavaq~of
port of entry n. بندر ورودی bandar-e' vorudi
portable adj., n., vi., vt. قابل حمل qâbel-e' haml دستی dasti
portage n. حمل haml هزینه hazineh
portal adj., n. دروازه dar vâzeh
portend n. پیش خبر pish-khabar
portent n. پیش خبری pish-khabari
porter n. باربر bârbar حمال ham~âl
porterage n. باربری bârbari حمالی ham~âli
portfolio n. کیف دستی kif-dasti منصب mansab
porthole n. دریچه daricheh پنجره کشتی panjereh-ye' kashti
portion n. قسمت qesmat بخش bakhsh تقسیم کردن taqsim kardan
portliness n. گندگی gondegi
portly adj. گنده gondeh
portrait n. تصویر tasvir تمثال temsâl
portray vt. منعکس کردن mon'akes kardan جلوه دادن jelveh dâdan
portrayal n. انعکاس en'ekâs نمایش namâyesh
pose n. ژست zhest پز poz
pose v. ژست گرفتن zhest gereftan مدلی کردن modeli kardan
pose v. مطرح کردن matrah kardan
posh adj. مجلل mojal~al
position n. مقام maqâm موقعیت moqe'iyat موضع moze'

منزلت .... manzelat

position *n.* وضع vâz'

position *v.* قراردادن qarâr dâdan

position *n.* سمت semat

positive *adj., n.* مثبت mosbat مطمئن motma'en

posse *n.* گروه دزدگیر goruh-e' dozd-gir

possess *n.* دارا بودن dârâ budan صاحب بودن sâheb budan

possessed *adj.* جن زده jen zadeh

possession *n.* دارایی dârâyi تصاحب tasâhob حصه hes~eh
مایملک mâ-yamlak

possessive *adj.* ملکی melki

possessor *n.* مالک mâlek صاحب sâheb متصرف motesar~ef

possibility *n.* امکان emkân

possible *adj.* ممکن momken امکان پذیر emkân-pazir مقدور maqdur

possibly *adv.* امکاناً emkânan احتمالاً ehtemâlan

possum *n.* ساریگ sârig موش مردگی mush mordegi

post *v.* گماشتن gomâshtan قراردادن qarâr dâdan

post *n.* پست post سمت semat منصب mansab

post *v.* اعلان کردن e'lân kardan چسباندن chasbândan

post *n.* تیر tir

post *v.* پست کردن post kardan نامه فرستادن nâmeh ferestâdan

post office *np.* پست خانه post-khâneh ادارهٔ پست edâreh-ye' post

post(al)card *n.* کارت پستال kârt postâl

post- *n.* بعد از ba'd az

post-bellum *adj.* بعدازجنگ ba'd az jang

post-mortem *adj., n.* بعدازمرگ ba'd-az-marg

postage *n.* تمبر tambr

postal *adj., n.* پستی posti

postbox *n.* صندوق پست sandoq-e' post

postdate *vt.* دیرترتاریخ گذاشتن dirtar târikh gozâshtan

poster *n.* عکس بزرگ 'aks-e' bozorg

posterior *adj., n.* کپل kapal پشت سر posht-e' sar

posterity *n.* نسل آینده nasl-e' âyandeh

posthumous *adj.* بعدازمرگ ba'd-az-marg

postiche *adj., n.* تقلبی taqal~obi مصنوعی masnu'i

postman *n.* پستچی post-chi نامه بر nâmeh-bar

postmark *n., vt.* مهرزدن mohr zadan

postmaster *n.* رئیس پست خانه ra'is-e' post khâneh

postpone *vt.* موكول كردن mokul kardan
بتاخيرانداختن be-ta'-khir andâkhtan
postponement *n.* تعويق ta'viq
postscript *n.* پس نوشت pas-nevesht تبصره tabsereh
postulate *vt., n.* فرض كردن farz kardan ادعاكردن ed~e'â kardan
postulation *n.* فرض ادعا farz ed~e'â
posture *n., vt., vi.* وضعیت vaz'iyat شكل shekl
postwar *n.* بعد ازجنگ ba'd az jang
posy *n.* دسته گل dasteh gol
pot *n., vt.* گلدان goldân
pot *n., vt.* ديگ dig
pot *n., vt.* كاسه پول kâseh pul
pot iron *n.* چدن chodan
pot metal *n.* چدن chodan
pot roast *np.* ديگ پخت dig pokht
potage *n.* آش âsh
potash *n.* پتاس potâs
potato *n.* سيب زمينی sib zamini
potato chip *np.* چيپس سيب زمينی chips-e' sib zamini
potbelly *n.* شكم گنده shekam gondeh
potency *n.* توانایی tavânâyi قوت qov~at
potent *n., adj.* توانا tavânâ قوی qavi مردانكن mard-afkan
potential *adj., n.* استعداد este'-dâd امكان emkân
potentially *n.* امكانی emkâni
potluck *n.* غذاهای مختلف qazâ-hâ-ye' mokhtalef
potpouri *n.* هردمبيل har-dambil
pottage *n.* سبزی خورشت sabzi khoresht شوربا shurbâ
potter *n., vi.* كوزه گر kuzeh-gar
pottery *n.* كوزه گری kuzeh-gari
potty *adj., n.* جيش jish جزیی joz'i
pouch *n., vt., vi.* كيسه kiseh
poultry *n.* مرغ و جوجه morq-o jujeh ماكيان mâkiân
pounce *n., vi., vt.* ناگهانی جستن nâgahâni jestan
pound *n.* حيوان خانه heyvân khâneh سگ دانی sag-dâni
pound *n.* پوند pond
pound *v.* مشت زدن kubidan كوبيدن mosht zadan
pour *n.* ريختن rikhtan پاشيدن pâshidan
pour-boire *n.* پول چایی pul châyi

pout *pl., vi., vt., n.* قهرکردن qahr kardan تولب رفتن tu-lab raftan
pouter *n.* قهرکن qahr-kon
poverty *n.* فقر faqr تنگ دستی tang dasti
poverty-stricken *adj.* فقیر faqir مفلس mofles
POW *n.* زندانی جنگی zendâni-e' jangi
pow-wow *n.* مشورت کردن mashverat kardan
powder *n.* پودرزدن pudr zadan گردپاشیدن gard pâshidan
powder blue *np.* آبی کمرنگ âbi-e' kam-rang
powder room *np.* دستشویی زنانه dastshuyi zanâneh
power *n., vt.* برق barq
power *n., vt.* نیرو niru قدرت qodrat توانایی tavânâ-yi مکنت moknat
power of attorney *np.* وکالت نامه vekâlat-nâmeh
power plant *np.* کارخانهٔ برق kâr-khâneh-ye' barq
power-play *n.* زورآزمایی zur-âzmâyi
powerful *adj.* پرقدرت por qodrat نیرومند nirumand
powerhouse *n.* موتورخانه motor khâneh پرانرژی por-enerzhi
powerless *adj.* بی قدرت bi-qodrat بی زور bi-zur
prospect *n.* جستجوکردن josteju kardan
practical *adj.* عملی 'amali قابل استفاده qâbel-e' estefâdeh
practically *adv.* عملاً 'amalan ... میشودگفت mishavad goft...
practice *n.* شغل shoql تجربه tajrobeh
practice *v.* تمرین کردن tamrin kardan
practitioner *n.* مجرب mojreb مشغول به کار mashqul bekâr
pragmatic *adj.* عملی 'amali معقول ma'qul
pragmatism *n.* عملی گرایی 'amali garâyi
pragmatist *n., adj.* عملی گرا 'amali garâ واقع گرا vâqe' garâ
prairie *n.* علفزار 'alaf-zâr
praise *v.* ستایش کردن setâyesh kardan تحسین کردن tahsin kardan
تمجید کردن tamjid kardan
praiseworthy *adj.* قابل تحسین qâbel-e' tahsin
prance *v., n.* جفت زدن joft zadan خیزبرداشتن khiz bardâshtan
prank *v.* آراستن ârâstan
prank *n.* شوخی shukhi
prankish *n.* شوخ shukh زبل zebel
prankster *n.* شوخی کننده shukhi-konandeh
prat *n.* کپل kapal
prate *vi., vt., n.* وراجی کردن ver~âji kardan
pratfall *n.* زمین خوری zamin khori

prattle *vi., vt., n.* حرف زدن بچگانه bach~egâneh harf zadan
prawn *n., vt.* میگو meygu
pray *vt., vi.* دعاکردن do'â kardan نمازخواندن namâz khândan
prayer *n.* دعا do'â نماز namâz
prayer rug *np.* سجاده saj~âdeh
praying mantis *n.* آخوندک âkhundak
pre- *n.* ماتبل mâ-qabl پیش pish
pre-eminent *n.* برتر bar-tar سرور sarvar
pre-empt *n.* پیش دستی کردن pish-dasti kardan
پیش خالی کردن pish-khâli kardan
pre-emptive *n.* پیش دستانه pish-dastâneh
pre-shrunk *n.* پیش آب رفته pish-âb rafteh
preach *vt., vi.* وعظ کردن va'z kardan
preacher *n.* واعظ vâ'ez
preaching *n.* وعظ va'z
preamble *n.* مقدمه moqad~ameh پیش گفتار pish-goftâr
prearrange *vt.* پیش تنظیم کردن pish tanzim kardan
precarious *adj.* بی پایه bi-pâyeh خطیر khatir
precaution *vt.* پیش احتیاط pish-ehtiât
precautionary *adj.* پیش احتیاطی pish-ehtiâti
precede *vt., vi., n.* تقدم داشتن taqad~om dâshtan
جلوترآمدن jelotar âmadan
precedence *n.* تقدم taqad~om بدعت bed'at
precedent *adj., n.* سابقه sâbeqeh
preceding *adj.* قبلی qabli جلویی jeloyi پیشی pishi
precept *n.* فرمان farmân حکم hokm
preceptive *adj.* دستوردهنده dastur dahandeh
preceptor *adj.* آموزگار âmuz-gâr
precinct *n.* حوزه hozeh صحن sahn
precious *adj., n., adv.* پرارزش por-arzesh گرانبها gerân-bahâ
گرانمایه gerân-mâyeh نفیس nafis
precious stone *np.* جواهر javâher
precipice *n.* پرتگاه part-gâh صخره sakhreh سرازیری sarâziri
precipitant *n., vi., adj.* رسوبگر rosub-gar کله معلق kal~eh mo'al~âq
precipitate *n.* ته نشین کردن tah-neshin kardan رسوب rosub
precipitation *n.* رسوب rosub ته نشینی tah-neshini بارندگی bâ-randegi
precipitous *adj.* پرتگاهی part-gâhi سرازیری sarâziri
صخره ای sakhreh-i

precise *adj.* دقیق daqiq
precisely *adv.* دقیقاً daqigan
precisian *n.* دیندار din-dâr
precision *n., adj.* دقت deq~at
precisionist *n.* دقیق مآب daqiq mâ'âb
preclude *vt.* جلوگیری کردن jelo-giri kardan
ممانعت کردن momâne'at kardan
preclusion *n.* جلوگیری jelo-giri ممانعت momâne'at
preclusive *n.* جلوگیر jelo-gir مانع mâne'
preconception *n.* پیش تصوری pish-tasavori
precondition *vt., n.* پیش شرط pish-shart
precursory *adj.* پیشقدمی pish-qadami معرفی mo'arefi
predacious *n.* شکاری shekâri
predate *n.* پیش تاریخ گذاشتن pish-târikh gozâshtan
predator *n.* شکارگر shekâr-gar غارتگر qârat-gar
predatory *adj.* شکارگری shekâr-gari غارتگری qârat-gari
predecessor *n.* شخص قبلی shâkhs-e' qabli
predesignate *vt.* ازپیش تعیین کردن az pish ta'yin kardan
predestination *n.* سرنوشت sar-nevesht تقدیر taqdir
predestined *vt.* سرنوشتی sar-neveshti مقدر moqad~ar
predetermine *n.* ازپیش معلوم کردن az pish ma'lum kardan
predicament *n.* گرفتاری gereftâri بدبیاری bad-biâri
predicate *adj., n., vt.* اسناد کردن esnâd kardan مسند mosnad
predict *vt., vi.* پیشگویی کردن pish-guyi kardan
prediction *n.* پیشگویی pish-guyi
predictor *n.* پیشگو pish-gu
predispose *n.* مستعد کردن mosta'ed kardan
predominant *n.* مسلط mosal~at حکمفرما hokm-farmâ بیشتر bishtar
مستولی mostoli
predominate *vi., vt.* مسلط بودن mosal~ât budan
preen *n.* تمیزکردن tamiz kardan آراستن ârâstan
prefabricate *n.* پیش ساخت کردن pish-sâkht kardan
preface *n., vt.* دیباچه dibâcheh پیش گفتار pish-goftâr
prefect *n.* رئیس ra'is
prefecture *n.* حوزه hozeh ناحیه nâhiyeh
prefer *vt.* ترجیح دادن tarjih dâdan
preferable *adj.* ترجیح دادنی tarjih dâdani
preferably *adv.* ترجیحاً tarjihan

preference *n.* ميل meyl تقدم taqad~om
preference *n.* برترى bartari ارجحيت arjahiyat
preferential *n.* استثنايى estesnâ'i
prefix *n., vt.* پيشوند گذاشتن pish-vand gozâshtan
pregnable *adj.* نفوذ پذير nofuz pazir
pregnancy *n.* آبستنى âbestani حاملگى hâmelegi باردارى bâr-dâri
pregnant *adj.* آبستن âbestan حامله hâmeleh باردار bâr-dâr
preheat *vt.* ازپيش گرم كردن az pish garm kardan
prehensile *adj.* گيرپيچ gir-pich گيركننده gir-konandeh
prehension *n.* گيرايى girâyi فهم fahm
prehistoric *adj.* ماقبل تاريخ mâ-qabl-e' târikh
prehistorical *n.* ماقبل تاريخ mâ-qabl-e' târikh
prejudge *n.* پيش قضاوتى كردن pish-qezâvati kardan
prejudgement *n.* پيش قضاوتى pish-qezâvati
prejudice *n.* تعصب ta'as~ob غرض qaraz
prejudice *v.* تعصب داشتن ta'as~ob dâshtan لطمه زدن latmeh zadan
prejudicial *n.* تعصب آميز ta'as~ob-âmiz لطمه زننده latmeh-zanandeh
prelate *n.* اسقف osqof
preliminary *adj., n.* مقدماتى moqadâmâti
prelude *n., vt., vi.* پيش درآمد pish-darâmad
پيش مقدمه pish-moqadameh
premature *adj.* زودرس zud-res بى موقع bi-moqe'
prematurely *adv.* زودترازموعد zud-tar az mo'ed
premedical *n.* پيراپزشكى pirâ-pezeshki
premeditate *vi.* ازپيش نقشه كشيدن az pish naqsheh keshidan
premier *n.* نخستين nakhostin
premier *n.* نخست وزير nakhost vazir
premiere *n., vt., vi., adj.* نمايش افتتاحى namâyesh-e' eftetâhi
premise *n., vt., vi.* مبنى mabnâ اظهار ez-hâr ملك melk
محوطه mohavateh
premium *n.* مزايا mazâyâ ممتاز momtâz
premium *n.* قسط بيمه qest-e' bimeh
premonition *n.* پيش آگاهى pish-âgâhi بدل براتى be-del barâti
preoccupation *n.* گرفتارى فكرى gereftâri-e' fekri
preoccupied *vt.* مشغول gereftâr مشغول mashqul
preoccupied *adj.* گرفتار gereftâr مشغول mashqul
preoccupy *vt.* مشغول كردن mashqul kardan
سرشلوغ كردن sar-sholuq kardan

prep *n.* مقدماتى moqad~amâti
prepaid *n.* پیش پرداخته pish-pardâkhteh
preparation *n.* تهیه tahiyeh آمادگى âmâdegi
preparatory *adj.* مقدماتى moqad~amâti
prepare *vt.* تهیه کردن tahiyeh kardan آماده کردن âmâdeh kardan
prepared(ly) *n.* آماده âmâdeh مهیا mohay~â روبراه ru be-râh
preparedness *n.* آمادگى âmâdegi
prepay *n.* ازپیش پرداختن az pish pardâkhtan
prepayment *n.* پیش پرداخت pish pardâkh
prepense *adj.* پیش فکرشده pish-fekr shodeh
prepoderance *n.* سنگینى sangini وزن vazn
prepoderant *n.* سنگین sangin وزین vazin
preposition *n.* حرف اضافه harf-e' ezâfeh
prepositional *adj.* اضافه اى ezâfeh-i
preposterous *adj.* مزخرف mozakhraf چرند charand
prerecorded *n.* قبلاً ضبط شده qablan zabt-shodeh
prerequisite *adj., n.* پیش نیاز pish-niâz
prerogative *n., adj.* حق haq اختیار ekhtiâr
prescience *n.* علم غیب 'elm-e' qeyb پیش دانى pish-dâni
prescient *adj.* پیش دان pish-dân غیب دان qeyb-dân
prescribe *vt., vi.* تجویزکردن tajviz kardan
نسخه نوشتن noskheh neveshtan
prescription *n.* نسخه noskheh
prescriptive *adj.* تجویزى tajvizi دستورى dasturi
presence *n.* حضور hozur وجود vojud
presence of mind *n.* حضورذهن hozur-e' zehn
present *adj.* حاضر hâzer کنونى konuni حال hâl
present *v.* معرفى کردن mo'arefi kardan تقدیم کردن taqdim kardan
present *n.* هدیه hadyeh پیشکش pish-kesh سوغات soqât
ارمغان armaqân
present arms *np.* پیش فنگ pish-fang
present perfect *np.* گذشتۀ نقلى gozashteh-ye' naqli
present tense *n.* زمان حال zamân-e' hâl
present-day *n.* امروزى emruzi
presentable *adj.* قابل دار qâbel dâr عرضه شدنى arzeh shodani
presentation *n.* معرفى mo'arefi عرضه 'arzeh
presenter *n.* اهداکننده ehdâ-konandeh
presently *adv.* همین الان hâmin al-ân

presentment *n.* نمایش namâyesh ارایه erâ'eh
preservation *n.* نگهداری negah-dâri حفاظت hefâzat ابقاء ebqâ'
preservative *n., adj.* نگهدارنده negah-dârandeh
preserve *v.* مرباکردن mor~abâ kardan
preserve *v.* نگهداری کردن negah-dâri kardan حفظ کردن hefz kardan
preside *n.* ریاست کردن riâsat kardan
presidency *n.* ریاست جمهوری riâsat-e' jomhuri
president *n.* رئیس جمهور ra'is jomhur پرزیدنت perezident
president *n.* رئیس ra'is
president-elect *n.* رئیس جمهور منتخب ra'is jomhur-e' montakhab
presidential *n.* رئیس جمهوری ra'is jomhuri
presidio *n.* قلعه qal'eh
press *v.* اتو کردن otu kardan
press, the *n.* مطبوعات matbu'ât ها روزنامه ruz-nâmeh-hâ
مجلات جرائد jarâ'ed majal~ât
press *v.* فشاردادن feshâr dâdan له کردن leh kardan نشردن feshordan
press(charges) *n.* متهم کردن mot~aham kardan
pressing *n.* فوری fori سمج semej
pressure *v., n.* فشار feshâr بار bâr
pressure cooker *np.* دیگ زودپز dig-e' zud-paz
pressure guage *n.* فشارسنج feshâr-sanj
pressurize *vt.* فشرده کردن feshordeh kardan
پرفشارکردن por-feshâr kardan
prestige *n., adj.* حیثیت heysiyat آبرو âberu
prestigeous *n.* حیثیت دار heysiyat-dâr آبرومندانه âberu-mandâneh
presto *adv., adj., n.* زود zud
presumable *adj.* فرض شدنی farz-shodani محتمل mohtamal
presumably *adv.* محتملاً mohtamalan یقیناً yaginan
presume *v.* گمان کردن gamân kardan
presume *v.* فرض کردن farz kardan
presumption *n.* فرض گمان farz gamân یقین yaqin
presumptive *adj.* احتمالی ehtemâli یقینی yaqini
presumptuous *adj.* گستاخ gostâkh پررو por-ru
presuppose *v.* ازپیش فرض کردن az pish farz kardan
presuppose *v.* مستلزم بودن mostalzam budan
presupposition *n.* پیش فرض pish-farz
pretence *n.* بهانه bahâneh وانمود vânemud
pretend *vt.* وانمود کردن vânemud kardan مدعی شدن mod~a'i shodan

pretended *adj.* دروغین doruqin
pretender *n.* مدعی mod~a'i
pretense *n.* ادعا ed~e'â
pretentious *n.* پرمدعا por-mod~e'â خودنما khod-namâ
pretext *n.* بهانه bahâneh عذر 'ozr
prettify *vt.* خوشگل کردن khoshgel kardan
prettiness *n.* خوشگلی khoshgeli تشنگی qashangi
pretty *adj., n., adv.* خوشگل khoshgel تشنگ qashang
pretzel *n.* چوب شور chub-shur
prevail *vi.* غلبه کردن qalabeh kardan موفق شدن movaf~aq shodan
prevailing *adj.* غالب qâleb متداول motedâvel
prevalent *adj.* متداول motedâvel مستولی mostoli
prevent *vt., vi.* ممانعت کردن momâne'at kardan
 جلوگیری کردن jelo-giri kardan
preventing *n.* جلوگیری jelo-giri
prevention *n.* جلوگیری jelo-giri ممانعت momâne'at
preventive *adj.* جلوگیر jelogir
preview *n., vt.* پیش نگر pish-negar برنامه آینده barnâmeh âyandeh
previous *adj.* پیشین pishin قبلی qabli
previously *n.* سابقاً sâbeqan قبلاً qablan
prevision *n.* پیش خبری pish-khabari
prewar *adj.* قبل ازجنگ qabl az jang
prey *n.* شکار shekâr صید seyd
prey *v.* شکارکردن shekâr kardan سرکیسه کردن sar-kiseh kardan
price *n., vt.* قیمت گذاشتن qeymat gozâshtan نرخ nerkh بها bahâ
priceless *adj.* بی قیمت bi-qeymat گرانبها gerânbahâ
prick *n.* سوراخ کردن surâkh kardan سوزنی suzan suzani
prickle *n., vt., vi.* خار khâr سوزنی سوزن شدن suzan suzani shodan
prickly *adj.* خاردار khâr-dâr سوزدار suz-dâr
pride *n., vt.* غرور qorur دسته dasteh
priest *n., vt.* کشیش keshish مغ moq
priesthood *n.* کشیشی keshishi کهانت kehânat
prig *v.* دزدیدن dozdidan
prig *adj.* خرده گیر khordeh gir
prim *n., adj., vi., vt.* باوقارکردن bâ-vaqâr kardan
 قیافه گرفتن qiâfeh gereftan
primacy *n.* اولیت av~aliyat سروری sarvari
primal *adj.* اولین av~alin اصلی asli

primarily *adv.* اصلاً aslan اساساً asâsan
primary *n., adj.* اولیه av~aliyeh ابتدایی ebtedâ'i اصلی asli
primary school *np.* دبستان dabestân
primate *n.* سرور sarvar سراسقف sar-osqof
prime *v.* آماده کردن âmâdeh kardan
prime *n.* عنفوان 'onfavân آغاز âqâz
prime *adj.* درجه یک darejeh yek ناب nâb مرغوب marqub
prime *v.* آستر زدن âstar zadan
prime *adj.* اولین av~alin نخست nakhost
prime *n.* پریم perim
prime minister *n.* نخست وزیر nakhost vazir
prime mover *np.* محرک اصلی mohar~ek-e' asli
prime ribs *n.* بیفتک دنده biftak-e' dandeh
primecost *n.* خرج اصلی kharj-e' asli
primely *n.* بنحوعالی benahv-e' 'âli
primer *n.* آماده کن âmâdeh-kon
priming *n.* آماده کنی âmâdeh-koni
primitive *n.* اولیه av~aliyeh بدوی badavi
primp *vt., vi.* شیک پوشیدن shik pushidan
primrose *n., adj.* پامچال pâmchâl
prince *n.* شاهزاده shâhzâdeh شاهپور shâhpur
princely *adj.* شاهزاده وار shâh-zâdeh-vâr
princess *n., adj.* شاهدخت shâh-dokht
principal *adj., n.* اصلی asli عمده 'omdeh مدیر modir
principal parts *np.* مشتقات افعال moshtaq~ât-e' af'âl
principality *n.* قلمرو شاهزاده qalam-ro-e' shâhzâdeh
principally *adv.* اصلاً aslan عمدتاً 'omdatan
principle *n.* مرام marâm مسلک maslak
principle *n.* اساس asâs
principle *n.* اصلی asl اساسی asâs
principled *adj.* بامرام bâ-marâm باادب bâ-adab
print *v.* چاپ کردن châp kardan
print *n.* چاپی châpi
print shop *np.* چاپخانه châp-khâneh
printable *adj.* چاپ شدنی châp shodani
printer *n.* چاپ کن châp-kon چاپگر châp-gar
printing *n.* چاپ châp طبع tab'
prior *n.* قبلی qabli پیشین pishin

priority *n.* اولویت oloviyat تقدم taqad~om
prism *n.* منشور manshur
prismatic *n.* منشوری manshuri
prison *n.* زندان zendân
prisoner *n.* زندانی zendâni اسیر asir
prissy *n.* وسواسی vasvâsi
pristine *adj.* پیشین pishin بکر bekr
privacy *n.* خلوت khâlvat سکوت sokut
private *n.* خصوصی khosusi دنج denj خلوت khalvat
private *n.* خصوصی khosusi غیردولتی qeyr-e' dolati
private *n.* سربازصفر sarbâz-e' sefr تابین tâbin
privateer *n.* ناخدای مزدور nâkhodâ-ye' mozdur
privation *n.* فقدان feqdân نبود nabud
privilege *n., vt.* امتیاز emtiâz مزیت maziyat
privileged *v.* بااامتیاز bâ-emtiâz بامزیت bâ-maziyat
privy *adj., n.* محرمانه mahramâneh خصوصی khosusi باخبر bâ-khabar
prize *v.* گرامی داشتن gerâmi dâshtan
prize *n.* جایزه jâyezeh
prize *adj.* گل سربسد gol-e' sarsabad
pro *adv., n.* حرفهای herfeh-i کارکشته kâr koshteh
pro and con *n.* برله و برعلیه barlah va bar-'aleyh
pro rata *np.* به نسبت beh-nesbat
probability *n.* احتمال ehtemâl امکان emkân
probable *adj.* احتمالی ehtemâli امکانی emkâni محتمل mohtamal
probable cause *np.* دلیل احتمالی dalil-e' ehtemâli
probably *adv.* احتمالاً ehtemâlan
probate *n., adj., vt.* انحصاروراثت enhesâr-e' verâsat تصدیقی tasdiq-i
probation *n.* التزام eltezâm شرط shart
probation *n.* التزامی eltezâmi شرطی sharti
probationary *n.* التزامی eltezâmi
probe *vt., vi., n.* وارسی کردن vâresi kardan تحقیق کردن tahqiq kardan
problem *n., adj.* اشکال eshkâl
problem *n., adj.* مسئله mas'aleh
problematic *adj.* پرمسئله por-mas'aleh
procedural *n.* روشی raveshi متدی metodi
procedure *n.* روش ravesh متد metod رویه raviyeh
proceed *vi., n.* بجلورفتن be-jelo raftan ادامه دادن edâmeh dâdan
proceeding *n.* جلوروی jeloravi ادامه دهندگی edâmeh dahandegi

proceedings *n.* جلسه نامه jaleseh nâmeh
proceeds *n.* درآمد dar-âmad عایدات 'âyedât
process *n.* جریان jaryân مرحله marhaleh عمل 'amal
process *v.* بجریان انداختن bejaryân andâkhtan
چاپ کردن châp kardan
process server *np.* ابلاغ کننده eblâq konandeh
procession *n., vi.* رژه دست جمعی rezheh dast-jam'i
proclaim *vt., vi.* رسماً اعلام کردن rasman e'lâm kardan
proclamation *n.* اعلامیه e'lâmiyeh
proclivity *n.* گرایش gerâyesh تمایل tamâyol
procrastinate *vi., vt.* موکول کردن mokul kardan
امروز فردا کردن emruz fardâ kardan
procrastination *n.* معطلی mo'at~ali عقب اندازی 'aqab-andâzi
proctologist *n.* مقعدشناس maq'ad-shenâs
proctology *n.* مقعدشناسی maq'ad-shenâsi
proctor *n.* ناظم nâzem مسئول mas'ul
proctorship *n.* ناظمی nâzemi
procurable *adj.* بدست آوردنی be-dast âvardani
procurator *n.* مسئول مالی mas'ul-e' mâli
procure *vt., vi.* فراهم کردن farâham kardan
بدست آوردن be-dast âvardan
procurer *n.* فراهم کننده farâham-konandeh کارچاق کن kâr châq kon
prod *vt., n.* سیخونک زدن sikhunak zadan
prodder *n.* سیخونک زن sikhunak-zan
prodigal *adj., n.* تلف کننده talaf-konandeh پشیمان pashimân
prodigality *n.* اتلاف etlâf ولخرجی vel-kharji
prodigious *adj.* شگفت انگیز shegeft-angiz
prodigy *n.* نبوغ nobuq
prodigy *n.* نابغه nâbeqeh اعجوبه o'jubeh نادره nâdereh
produce *v.* محصول دادن mahsul dâdan تولیدکردن tolid kardan
produce *n.* محصولات mahsulât سبزیجات sabzijât
producer *n.* تهیه کننده tahayeh-konandeh سازنده sâzandeh
product *n.* محصول mahsul حاصل ضرب hâsel-e' zarb
production *n.* تولید tolid تهیه tahayeh
productive *n.* سودمند sudmand
productive *n.* حاصل خیز hâsel-khiz
productivity *n.* حاصل خیزی hâsel-khizi تولید قدرت تولید qodrat-e' tolid
profanatory *adj.* رکیکانه rakikâneh

profane *adj., vt.* بی حرمتی کردن bi-hormati kardan رکیک rakik
profanity *n.* سخن رکیک sokhan-e' rakik
profess *v.* ایمان آوردن imân âvardan
profess *v.* اظهارکردن ez-hâr kardan اقرارکردن eqrâr kardan
professed *adj.* معترف mo'taref اعلان شده e'lân-shodeh
profession *n.* حرفه herfeh شغل shoql پیشه pisheh
professional *adj.* حرفه ای herfeh-i
professor *n.* پروفسور porofosor استاد ostâd
professorial *n.* استادوار ostâd vâr
professorship *n.* استادی ostâdi
proficiency *n.* استادی ostâdi تسلط tasal~ot
proficient *n.* استاد ostâd مسلط mosal~at
profile *n.* پرونده parvandeh سابقه sâbeqeh
profile *n.* سیما simâ نیمرخ nimrokh چهره chehreh رخسار rokh-sâr
profile *v.* چهره ساختن chehreh sâkhtan
profit *n.* سود sud منفعت manfa'at نفع naf'
profit *v.* سودبردن sud bordan منفعت کردن manfa'at kardan
profit sharing *np.* سهام شرکتی sahâm-e' sherkati
profitable *adj.* پرمنفعت por manfa'at
profiteer *n., vi.* منفعت چی manfa'at-chi کلاش kal~âsh
profound *adj.* عمیق 'amiq ازته قلب az-tah-e' qalb
profuse *adj.* بیش ازحد bish-az-had فائض fâ'ez
profusely *adv.* باشدت bâ-shed~at زیاد ziâd
profusion *n.* افراط efrât وفور vofur
progeny *n.* اولاد olâd فرزندان farzandân
prognose *n.* تشخیص دادن tashkhis dâdan
prognosis *n.* تشخیص tashkis
prognostic *adj., n.* نشانه ای neshâneh-i
program(me) *n.* برنامه barnâmeh
برنامه ریزی کردن barnâmeh-rizi kardan
programer *n.* برنامه ریز barnâmeh-riz
progress *n.* پیشرفت کردن pishraft kardan ترقی کردن taraq~i kardan
progression *n.* پیشرفت pishraft سلسله selseleh فرایاز farâyâz
progressive *n.* پیشرفته pishrafteh ترقی خواه taraq~i-khâh
فرایازی farâyâzi
prohibit *vt.* قدغن کردن qadeqan kardan ممنوع کردن mamnu' kardan
prohibition *n.* منع man' قدغنی qadeqani
project *v.* تصویر انداختن tasvir andâkhtan تصورکردن tasav~or kardan

project *n.* طرح tarh پروژه perozheh
projectile *n., adj.* پرتابی partâbi گلوله goluleh موشک mushak
projection *n.* تصویر tasvir تصور tasav~ or برآمدگی bar-âmadegi
projectionist *n.* آپارات چی âpârât-chi
projector *n.* آپارات âpârât
prolate *adj.* کشیده keshideh
proletarian *adj., n.* کارگر kârgar
proletariat *n.* کارگری kârgari پرولتاریا peroletâriâ
proliferate *n.* بسرعت زیادشدن be-sor'at ziâd shodan
proliferation *n.* ازدیاد سریع ezdiâd-e' sari'
prolific *adj.* بارور bâr-var پراثر por-asar
prologue *n., vt.* پیش درآمد pish-darâmad مقدمه moqad~ameh
prolong *vt.* طول دادن tul dâdan کش دادن kesh dâdan
prolongate *vt.* طولانی کردن tulâni kardan
prolongation *n.* طولانی گری tulâni-gari
prolonged *n.* طولانی tulâni طویل tavil
promendade *n.* پیاده رو piâdeh ravi پیاده روی piâdeh-ro
prominence *n.* معروفی ma'rufi برجستگی barjestegi
prominent *adj.* معروف ma'ruf برجسته barjesteh
promiscuity *n.* باهمه خوابی bâ-hameh-khâbi
promiscuous *adj.* باهمه خواب bâ-hameh-khâb
promise *n., vi.* وعده دادن va'deh dâdan قول دادن qol dâdan
Promised Land *np.* سرزمین موعود sarzamin-e' mo'ud
promising *v.* امیدبخش omid-bakhsh خوش آتیه khosh-âtieh
promisor *n.* قول دهنده qol dahandeh
promissory *n.* متضمن motezam~en قولی qoli
promissory note *np.* سفته safteh
promote *v.* ارتقاء رتبه دادن erteqâ'-e' rotbeh dâdan
promote *v.* ترویج دادن tarvij dâdan کارسازی کردن kâr-sâzi kardan
promoter *adj.* ترویج دهنده tarjiv dahandeh مبلغ mobal~eq کارساز kâr-sâz
promotion *n.* ترویج tarvij تبلیغ tabliq
promotion *n.* ارتقاء erteqâ' درجه گیری darejeh-giri ترفیع tarfi'
promotional *adj.* ترویجی tarviji تبلیغی tabliqi
prompt *n.* فوری fori بی معطلی bi-mo'at~ali
prompt *v.* مجبوربحرکت کردن majbur be-harekat kardan
prompt-up *adj.* ساختگی sakhtegi من درآوردی man dar âvardi
promptly *adv.* نوراً foran بدون معطلی bedun-e' mo'at~ali

promulgate *n.* انتشار دادن enteshâr dâdan ترویج دادن tarvij dâdan
promulgation *n.* انتشار enteshâr ترویج tarvij اعلام e'lâm
prone *adj., n.* دمرو damaru متمایل motemâyel
proned *n.* مایل mâyel متمایل motemâyel
prong *n., vt.* سرچنگال sar-changâl
pronominal *adj.* ضمیری zamiri
pronoun *n.* ضمیر zamir
pronounce *vt., vi.* تلفظ کردن talaf~oz kardan
اعلان کردن e'lân kardan
pronounced *v.* مشخص moshakh~as
pronouncement *n.* تلفظ talaf~oz بیان bayân
pronto *adv.* فوری fori
pronunciation *n.* تلفظ talaf~oz
proof *n., adj., vt.* فیلم منفی film-e' manfi
proof *n., adj., vt.* مدرک madrak اثبات esbât دلیل dalil
proofread *vt., vi.* غلط گیری کردن qalat-giri kardan
prop *n.* پایه pâyeh حائل hâ'el ساختگی sâkhtegi
prop *v.* حائل شدن hâ'el shodan پشتیبانی کردن poshtibâni kardan
propaganda *n.* تبلیغات tabliqât
propagandist *n., adj.* تبلیغ کننده tabliq konandeh مبلغ mobal~eq
propagandize *vt., vi.* تبلیغ کردن tabliq kardan
propagate ziad *n.* زیادکردن ziâd kardan
تولیدمثل کردن tolid-e' mesl kardan
زیاد شدن ziâd shodan
propagation *n.* ازدیاد نسل ezdiâd-e' nasl تکثیر taksir
propagator *n.* ترویج کننده tarvij konandeh
propane *n.* گاز متان gâz-e' metân
propel *vt., n.* بجلوراندن bejelo rândan سوق دادن soq dâdan
propellent *n.* سوق دهنده soq dahandeh برون افکن borun-afkan
propeller *n.* پروانه parvâneh ملخ malakh
propensity *n.* تمایل tamâyol
proper *adj., n.* درست dorost شایسته shâyesteh صحیح sahih روا ravâ
properly *adv.* بدرستی be-dorosti بنحوشایسته be-nahv-e' shâyesteh
property *n.* دارایی dârâyi مال mâl ملک melk خاصیت khâsiyat
prophecy *n., vi.* پیش گویی pish-guyi نبوت nabov~at
prophet *n.* پیغمبر peyqambâr رسول rasul نبی nabi
prophetic *adj.* الهامی elhâmi پیامبری peyâmbari
proponent *n.* طرفدار taraf-dâr پشتیبان poshtibân

proportion *n., vt.* تناسب tanâsob بعد bo'd نسبت nesbat
proportional *adj.* متناسب motenâseb نسبی nesbi
proportionally *n.* به نسبت beh nesbat
proportionate *adj., vt.* متناسب کردن motenâseb kardan
proportioned *adj.* باتناسب bâ-tanâsob
proposal *n.* پیشنهاد pishnahâd
propose *v.* پیشنهاد ازدواج کردن pishnahâd-e' ezdevâj kardan
propose *v.* پیشنهاد کردن pishnahâd kardan
proposition *n.* پیشنهاد pish-nahâd
proposition *v.* پیشنهاد وقیحانه کردن pishnahâd-e' vaqihâneh dâdan
propositional *adj.* پیشنهادی pishnahâdi
propound *n.* پیشنهاد pishnahâd مطرح کردن matrah kardan
proprietary *adj., n.* مالکانه mâlekâneh
proprietor *n.* مالک mâlek ملک صاحب sâheb melk
proprietorship *n.* مالکیت mâlekiyat
propriety *n.* شایستگی shâyestegi رعایت ادب re'âyat-e' adab
propulsion *n.* سوق soq جلوپرتابی jelo-partâbi
propulsive *n.* جلو برنده jelo-barandeh
prorate *vi.* به نسبت حساب کردن beh-nesbat hesâb kardan
prorogation *n.* خاتمه khâtemeh
pros and cons *n.* موافق و مخالف movâfeq-o mokhâlef
prosaic *adj.* نثری nasri کسل کننده kesel konandeh
proscribe *v.* تحریم کردن tahrim kardan
proscribe *v.* تبعید کردن tab'id kardan
proscription *adj.* تحریم tahrim تبعید tab'id
prose *n., adj., vt., vi.* نثر nasr
prosector *n.* کالبدشکاف kâlbod-shekâf
prosecute *vt., vi.* تعقیب کردن ta'qib kardan
دادستانی کردن dâdsetâni kardan
prosecutor *n., vi., vt.* دادستان dâdsetân
proselytize *vt., vi.* اشاعهٔ دینی کردن esha'eh-ye' dini kardan
proser *n.* نثرنویس nasr-nevis
prospect *n., vt., vi.* دورنما durnamâ شانس shâns
prospective *n.* احتمالی ehtemâli آینده ای âyandeh-i
prospector *n.* معدن جو ma'dan-ju جستجوکن josteju-kon
prosper *vi., vt.* خوب رشد کردن khub roshd kardan
موفق شدن movaf~aq shodan
prosperity *n.* پیشرفت pishraft ترقی taraq~i نیک بختی nik bakhti

prosperous *adv.* پیشرو pishro مونق movaf~aq نیک بخت nik-bakht
prostate *n.* پروستات porostât
prosthesis *n.* عضومصنوعی 'ozv-e' masnu'i
prostitute *n.* فاحشه fâhesheh جنده jendeh روسپی ruspi
prostitution *n.* فاحشگی fâheshegi نحشاء fahshâ'
prostrate *v.* سجده کردن sajdeh kardan
روی زمین افتادن ruy-e' zamin oftâdan
prostration *n.* سجود sojud بخاک افتادگی be-khâk oftâdegi
protagonist *n.* قهرمان داستان qahremân-e' dâstân
protect *v.* حمایت کردن hemâyat kardan
protect *v.* محافظت کردن mohâfezat kardan
protectable *n.* حمایت شدنی hemâyat shodani
protection *n.* حمایت hemâyat محافظت mohâfezat
protective *adj.* حفاظتی hefâzati
protector *n.* محافظ mohâfez حامی hâmi نگهدار negahdâr
protectorate *n.* قیومت qoyumat تحت الحمایه tahtol-hemâyeh
protege *n.* تحت الحمایه tahtol-hemâyeh نورچشمی nur-e' cheshmi
دست پرورده dast-parvardeh
protest *n., vi.* اعتراض کردن e'terâz kardan
protestant *n.* معترض mo'tarez پروتستان porotestân
protestation *n.* اعتراض e'terâz
protestor *n.* اعتراض کننده e'terâz konandeh
protocal *n.* عهدنامه 'ahd-nâmeh رسوم تشریفاتی rosum-e' tashrifâti
عرف تشریفاتی 'orf-e' tashrifâti
prototype *n.* ریشهٔ اصلی risheh-ye' asli اولین مدل av~alin model
protract *vt.* طول tul ادامه دادن edâmeh dâdan
protracted *adj.* طویل tavil طولانی tulani متمادی motemâdi
protractor *n.* نقاله naqâleh
protrude *vi., vt.* بیرون آمدن birun âmadan
protrusion *n.* بیرون آمدگی birun-âmadegi
protrusive *adj.* بیرون آمده birun-âmadeh فضول fozul
proud *adj., adv.* مغرور maqrur مفتخر moftakhar باشکوه bâ-shokuh
prove *v.* ثابت کردن sâbet kardan
prove *v.* اثبات کردن esbât kardan
proved *n.* ثابت شده sâbet-shodeh مبرهن mobarhan
provenance *n.* ریشه risheh
proverb *n., vt.* ضرب المثل zarbol-masal
proverbial *n.* ضرب المثلی zarbol-masali معروف ma'ruf

provide *vt., vi.* فراهم farâham تدارک دیدن tadârok didan
تهیه دیدن tahayeh didan
provided *con.* فراهم داده شده farâham dâdeh-shodeh
providence *n.* مآل اندیشی ma-'âl andishi نعمت خدا ne'mat-e' khodâ
عاقبت اندیشی 'âqebat andishi
provident *adj.* مآل اندیش ma-'âl andish محتاط mohtât
provider *n.* فراهم کننده farâham konandeh
نعمت دهنده ne'mat-dahandeh
providing *v.* بشرط اینکه beshart-e' inkeh
province *n.* استان ostân
provincial *adj., n.* استانی ostâni شهرستانی shahrestâni ولایتی velâyati
provision *n.* تهیه tahay~eh آمادگی âmâdegi
provision *v.* آذوقه دادن âzuqeh dâdan
provisional *adj., n.* موتی movaq~ati
provisions *n.* مقررات moqar~arât
proviso *n.* شرط shart قید qeyd
provisory *n.* شرطی sharti
provocation *n.* تحریک tahrik
provocative *adj., n.* تحریک کننده tahrik konandeh محرک mohar~ek
provoke *vt.* تحریک کردن tahrik kardan
provoking *vt.* تحریک کننده tahrik konandeh
prowess *n.* دلاوری delâvari زبردستی zebardasti
prowl *vi.* پرسه زدن parseh zadan
proximal *adj.* بغلی baqali نزدیکترین nazdiktarin
proximate *adj.* بعدی bâ'di تقریبی taqribi
proximity *n.* نزدیکی nazdiki جوار javâr
proxy *n.* نماینده namâyandeh وکالت vekâlat
prude *n.* محتاط mohtât مواظب movâzeb
prudence *n.* احتیاط ehtiât تدبیر tadbir
prudent *adj.* بااحتیاط bâ-ehtiât باتدبیر bâ-tadbir
prudential *adj.* احتیاطی ehtiâti
prudish *adj.* محتاط mohtât
prune *n.* آلو âlu
prune *v.* حرث کردن haras kardan شاخه زدن shâkheh zadan
pry *v.* اهرم زدن ahrom zadan میله انداختن mileh andâkhtan
pry *v.* فضولی کردن fozuli kardan
prying *adj., v.* فضول fozul
psalm *n., vt.* سرودمذهبی sorud-e' mazhabi مزمور mazmur

psalmbook *n.* سرودنامه sorud-nâmeh
psaltery *n.* قانون qânun
pseudo *adj.* مصنوعی masnu'i کاذب kâzeb
pseudonym *n.* اسم مستعار esm-e' mosta'âr
pshaw *int., n., vi., vt.* اه ah
psyche *n.* روان ravân
psychiatrist *n.* روان پزشک ravân-pezeshk
psychiatry *n.* روان پزشکی ravân-pezeshki
psychic *adj., n.* روانی ravâni روح شناس ruh-shenâs
psychoanalysis *n.* روان کاوی ravân-kâvi
psychoanalyst *n.* روان کاو ravân-kâv
psychological *adj.* روانی ravâni روحی ruhi
psychologist *n., adj.* روانشناس ravân-shenâs
psychology *n.* روانشناسی ravân-shenâsi
psychopath *n.* روانی ravâni
psychosis *n.* اختلال روحی ekhtelâl-e' ruhi
psychosomatic *adj.* نشارنفکری feshâr-e' fekri فکروخیالی fekr-o khiâli
psychotherapy *n.* درمان روانی darmân-e' ravâni
psychotic *adj., n.* دارای اختلال روانی dârâ-ye' ekhtelâl-e' ravâni
pub *n.* کافه kâfeh میخانه mey-khâneh
puberty *n.* بلوغ boluq
pubescent *adj.* بالغ شده bâleq shodeh تکلیف شده taklif shodeh
pubic *n.* عورتی 'orati زیرشکمی zir-shekami
public *adj., n.* عمومی 'omumi مردم mârdom تسخیری taskhiri
عامه 'âm~eh
public address *n.* بلندگو boland-gu
public defender *np.* وکیل تسخیری vakil-e' taskhiri
public domain *np.* مال عمومی mâle 'omumi
دردسترس عام dar dastres-e' 'âm
public enemy *np.* دشمن جامعه doshman-e' jâme'eh
public relations *np.* روابط عمومی ravâbet-e' 'omumi
public works *np.* خدمات اجتماعی khadamât-e' ejtemâ'i
public-school *adj.* مدرسهٔ دولتی madreseh-ye' dolati
publication *n.* انتشار enteshâr چاپ châp
publicist *n.* مبلغ انتشارات mobaleq-e' enteshârât
publicity *n.* تبلیغ tabliq معروفیت ma'rufiyat
publicize *n.* تبلیغ کردن tabliq kardan انتشار دادن enteshâr dâdan
publicly *adv.* عموماً 'omuman آشکارا âshkâra

publish *vt., vi.* منتشر کردن montasher kardan
انتشاردادن enteshâr dâdan
publisher *n.* منتشرکننده montasher konandeh ناشر nâsher
puce *adj., n.* آلبالویی âlbâluyi
pucheon *n.* تیر چوب tir-chub بشکه boshkeh
puck *n.* توپ مهره ای tup mohreh-i
pucker *vt., vi., n.* هم آوردن ham âvardan
چین و چروک دادن chin-o choruk dâdan
puckish *n.* شیطان sheytân
pudding *n.* شله sholeh
puddle *n., vi.* چاله آب châleh-âb
pudgy *n.* خپل khepel
puff *n., vi., vt.* پک زدن pok zadan پف کردن pof kardan پفک pofak
puffy *adj.* پف کرده pofkardeh نفس تنگ nafas-tang
pugatorial *n.* پاک کننده pâk-konandeh کیفری keyfari
pugnacious *adj.* جنگجو jang-ju
puissance *n.* قدرت qodrat توانایی tavânâyi
puissant *adj.* باقدرت bâ-qodrat قوی qavi
puke *n.* استفراغ کردن estefrâq kardan بالا آوردن bâlâ âvardan
pull *n.* نفوذ nofuz زور zur
pull *v.* کشیدن keshidan
pull(apart) *n.* پاره کردن pâreh kardan جردادن jer dâdan
pull(down) *n.* خراب کردن kharâb kardan
پایین کشیدن pâyin keshidan
pull(for) *n.* هواخواه بودن havâ-khâh budan
pull(off) *n.* موفق شدن movaf~aq shodan انجام دادن anjâm dâdan
pull(over) *n.* کنارکشیدن kenâr keshidan
pull(through) *n.* جان بدربردن jân bedar bordan
بهبودیافتن behbud yâftan
pull(together) *n.* بخودآمدن bekhod âmadan
pull(up) *n.* نگاه داشتن negâh dâshtan جلوکشیدن jelo keshidan
pull-over *n.* ژاکت zhâkat
pullback *n.* عقب نشینی 'aqab-neshini
pulley *n.* قرقره qerqereh
pulmonary *adj.* ششی shoshi شش دار shosh-dâr
pulp *n., vt., vi.* خمیر khamir تفاله tofâleh
pulpit *n.* منبر manbar
pulpiteer *n.* بالامنبری bâlâ manbari روضه خوان rozeh-khân

pulpwood n. چوب کاغذسازی chub-e' kâqaz-sâzi
pulsate vi. تپیدن tapidan زدن zadan
pulse n. نبض nabz ضربان قلب zarabân-e' qalb
pulse v. بنشن bonshan
pulverize vt., vi. خردکردن khord kardan داغان کردن dâqân kardan
pumice n. سنگ پا sang-e' pâ
pump N. تلمبه tolombeh پمپ pomp
pump V. پمپ کردن pomp kârdan
pump V. تلمبه زدن tolombeh zadan
pumpernickel n. نان سیاه nân siâh
pumpkin n. کدو تنبل kadu tanbal
pumpkin seed n. تخمه کدو tokhmeh kadu
pun n., vi. شوخی بالغات shukhi bâ-loqât تجنیس tajnis
punch v. مشت زدن mosht zadan
punch n. آبمیوه âbmiveh
punch v. سوراخ کردن surâkh kardan منگنه کردن mangeneh kardan
punctual adj. وقت شناس vaqt-shenâs سروقت sar-e' vaqt
punctuality n. وقت شناسی vaqt-shenâsi
punctuate n. نقطه گذاری کردن noqteh-gozâri kardan
punctuation n. نقطه گذاری noqteh-gozâri
puncture v. سوراخ کردن surâkh kardan
puncture v. پنچرکردن panchar kardan
pungent adj. تند tond زننده zanandeh
punish v. مجازات کردن mojâzât kardan تنبیه کردن tanbih kardan
گوشمالی دادن gush-mâli dâdan
punishable n. لازم به تنبیه lâzem beh-tanbih
punishment n. مجازات mojâzât کیفر keyfar تنبیه tanbih
گوشمالی gush-mâli
punitive adj. مجازاتی mojâzâti کیفری keyfari
punk n., adj. بچه مزلف bach~eh-ye' mozalef قرتی qerti
punster n. طنز نویس tanz-nevis
punt vi., n. شوت کردن shut kardan شرط بستن shart bastan
punty n. میله mileh
puny adj. فسقلی fesqeli لاغر lâqar
pup n., vi. توله سگ tuleh sag
pupil n. مردمک mardomak
pupil n. شاگرد shâgerd
pupilary n. شاگردی shâgeri

puppet *n., vi.* عروسک 'arusak دست نشانده dast neshândeh
puppeteer *n.* خیمه شب باز kheimeh-shab-bâz
puppetry *n.* خیمه شب بازی kheymeh-shab bâzi
puppy *n.* سگ توله sag tuleh
purchasable *n.* قابل خریداری qâbel-e' kharidâri
purchase *vt., n.* خرید کردن kharid kardan ابتیاع کردن ebtiâ' kardan
pure *adj.* خالص khâles پاک pâk منزه monaz~ah سره sareh
purebred *n.* نژادخالص nezhâd-e' khâles اصیل asil
خوش نژاد khosh-nezhâd نیکوتبار niku-tabâr
puree *n.* پوره pureh
purely *adv., vt., n.* صرفاً serfan
purgatory *n.* جزاگاه jazâ-gâh اعراف a'râf
purge *v.* پاکسازی کردن pâk-sâzi kardan
purge *n.* پاکسازی pâk-sâzi تطهیر tat-hir
purification *n.* تصفیه tasfieh پاکسازی pâksâzi
purified *adj.* تصفیه شده tasfieh-shodeh خالص khâles پیراسته pirâsteh
purify *v.* تصفیه کردن tasfieh kardan صاف کردن sâf kardan
خالص کردن khâles kardan پیراستن pirâstan
purist *n.* اصالت طلب esâlat-talab
puritan *n.* خالص طلب khâles-talab
puritanic(al) *n.* خالص طلبی khâles-talabi
purity *n.* پاکی pâki اصالت esâlat خالصی khâlesi
purl *vi., n.* رده رده radeh-radeh شر شر shor-shor
purloin *n.* دزدیدن dozdidan
purple *adj., n., vt., vi.* ارغوانی arqavâni
purport *vt.* مفهوم رساندن mafhum resândan مبنی بودن mabnâ budan
purpose *n., vt., vi.* مقصود maqsud منظور manzur
purposeful *adj.* مصمم mosam~am پرمعنی por-ma'nâ
purposely *n.* ازقصد az qasd
purr *vi., vt., n.* خرخرکردن khor-khor kardan
purse *n., vt.* کیف زنانه kif zanâneh
purse *n., vt.* جایزه jâyezeh جمع پول jam'-e' pul
purser *n.* بلیط گیر belit-gir مسافربان mosâferbân
pursuant(to) *n.* مطابق با motâbeq-bâ متعاقب mote'âqeb
pursue *vt., vi.* تعقیب کردن ta'qib kardan دنبال کردن donbâl kardan
pursuit *n.* تعقیب ta'qib دنبال donbâl
purulent *n.* چرکین cherkin
purvey *vt.* آذوقه دادن âzuqeh dâdan

purveyor *n.* آذوقه دهنده âzuqeh dahandeh
pus *n.* چرک cherk
push *vt., vi., n.* هل دادن hol dâdan نشاردادن feshâr dâdan
push button *np.* دگمه نشاری dogmeh feshâri
push(off) *n.* حرکت کردن harekat kardan
push(on) *n.* بجلورفتن be-jelo raftan
push-over *n.* زودگول خور zud gul-khor آسان âsân
push-up *n.* شناروزمین shenâ-ye' ru zamin
pushcart *n.* گاری دستی gâri dasti
pusher *n.* فروشنده forushandeh دلال dal~âl
pushing *adj.* بزن برو bezan-boro
puss *n.* صورت surat لب lab
pussycat *n.* پیشی pishi گربه gorbeh
pussyfoot *n.* اجتناب کردن ejtenâb kardan
     این پاآن پاکردن inpâ-ânpâ kardan
pussywillow *n.* بیدمشگ bid-meshg
pustule *n.* تاول tâval جوش jush
put *vt., vi., n.* گذاشتن gozâshtan قراردادن qarâr dâdan
put away *n.* خوردن khordan کشتن koshtan
put(about) *n.* تغییرجهت دادن taqyir-e' jahat dâan
put(across) *n.* شیرفهم کردن shir-fahm kardadn
put(aside) *n.* کنارگذاشتن kenâr gozâshtan
     ذخیره کردن zakhireh kardan
put(at ease) *n.* خیال راحت کردن khiâl râhat kardan
put(down) *n.* تحقیرکردن tah-qir kardan
put(down) *n.* نوشتن neveshtan
put(down) *n.* سرکوب کردن sarkub kardan
put(forward) *n.* مطرح کردن matrah kardan
put(off) *n.* بتأخیرانداختن be-ta'khir andâkhtan
put(on) *n.* پوشیدن pushidan دست انداختن dast andâkhtan
     تظاهر tazâhor
put(out) *n.* خاموش کردن khâmush kardan
put(out) *n.* بیرون دادن birun dâdan بیرون گذاشتن birun gozâshtan
put(over) *n.* موکول کردن mokul kardan انجام دادن anjâm dâdan
put(to) *n.* رک گفتن rok goftan
put(up to) *n.* تحریک کردن tahrik kardan اغفال کردن eqfâl kardan
put(up with) *n.* تحمل کردن taham~ol kardan ساختن با sâkhtan bâ
put(up) *n.* عرضه کردن 'arzeh kardan ساختن sâkhtan

put(upon) *n.* تحمیل کردن tahmil kardan
putrefy *vt., vi.* گندیده کردن gandideh kardan
putrescent *adj.* گندیده gandideh فاسد fâsed
putrid *adj.* فاسد fâsed متعفن mote'af~en
putrified *adj.* گند gand بدبو bad-bu فاسد fâsed متعفن mote'af~en
putsch *n.* شورش shuresh
putt *vt., vi., n.* چوگانک chogânak
putter *v.* نس نس کاری کردن fes-fes kâri kardan
putter *n.* میله چوگان mileh-chogân
putty *n.* بتونه batâneh
puzzle *n.* معما mo'am~â جدول jad-val
puzzle *v.* گیج کردن gij kardan متحیرکردن motehay~er kardan
puzzlement *n.* گیجی giji حیرت heyrat
pygmy *n.* کوتوله kutuleh
pylon *n.* دروازه darvâzeh برج ستون borj-sotun
pyorrhea *n.* چرک لثه cherk-e' laseh پیوره piureh
pyramid *n., vt.* هرم heram
pyre *n.* آتش âtash آتش پشته âtash-poshteh
python *n.* اژدرمار azhdar-mâr

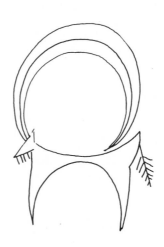

Q Q q

quack *adj.* دکترقلابی doktor-e' qol~âbi
quack *v.* صدای اردک درآوردن sedâye ordak dar âvardan
quackery *n.* چاچول بازی châ-chul bâzi
quad *n., vt.* چهاردیواری chahâr-divâri
quadruplet *n.* چهارقلو chahâr qolu
quagmire *n.* باتلاق bâtlâq مهلکه mahlakeh مخمصه makhmaseh
quail *n.* بلدرچین baldar-chin
quail *v.* جا زدن jâ zadan
quaint *adj.* عجیب 'ajib
quake *vi., n.* لرزیدن larzidan
qualification *n.* صلاحیت salâhiyat شرط لازم shart-e' lâzem
qualified *adj.* صلاحیت دار salâhiyat-dâr واجدشرایط vâjed-e' sharâyet
qualifier *n.* صلاحیت دهنده salâhiyat dahandeh
qualify *v.* صلاحیت دادن salâhiyat dâdan
qualify *v.* صلاحیت داشتن salâhiyat dâshtan
qualitative *adj.* کیفی keyfi
quality *n., adj.* کیفیت keyfiyat جنس jens
qualm *n.* تردید tardid ناراحتی nârâhati شک shak~
quandary *n.* مخمصه makh-maseh
quantitative *adj.* مقداری meqdâri
quantity *n.* مقدار meqdâr کمیت kamiyat
quantum *n.* مقدار meqdâr
quarantine *n.* قرنطینه کردن qarantineh kardan
quareller *n.* دعوایی da'vâyi
quarrel *v.* دعوا کردن da'vâ نزاع کردن nezâ' kardan
quarrel *n.* دعوا da'vâ نزاع nezâ'
quarrelsome *n.* دعوایی da'vâyi متنازع motenâze'
quarry *n.* شکار shekâr صید seyd
quarry *n.* معدن سنگ ma'dan-e' sang
quart *n.* چارک chârak
quarter *n., vt., vi., adj.* بیست پنج سنتی bist-panj senti
quarter *n., vt., vi., adj.* یک چهارم yek-chahâr~om ربع rob'
quarter *n., vt., vi., adj.* محله mahal~eh مرکز markaz
quarterly *adj., n., adv.* سه ماهه seh-mâheh هرسه ماه har-seh-mâh
quartermaster *n.* کارپرداز kâr-pardâz مسئول جا mas'ul-e' jâ
quartet *n.* چهارنفره chahâr nafareh
quash *n., vt., adv.* سرکوب کردن sar-kub kardan

quasi *n.* نیمه nimeh
quatrain *n.* رباعیات robâ'iyât
quay *n.* اسکله eskeleh
queasy *adj.* تهوع آور tahavo'-âvar ناراحت nârâhat
queen *n.* ملکه malakeh
queen *n.* بی بی bibi
queen *n.* وزیر vazir فرزین farzin
queenly *adj., adv.* ملکه وار malakeh-vâr
queer *adj.* غریب qarib عوضی 'avazi کونی kuni
quell *vt.* سرکوب کردن sar-kub kardan آرام کردن ârâm kardan
quench *vt.* فرونشاندن foru neshândan رفع کردن raf' kardan
query *n., vt.* پرسش porsesh شک shak
quest *n.* جستجو josteju
quest *n.* طلب talab
question *n., vt.* سؤال کردن so'âl kardan پرسش porsesh
question mark *n.* علامت سؤال 'alâmat-e' so'âl
questionable *adj.* قابل سؤال qâbel-e' so'âl مشکوک mashkuk
questionary *n.* سؤالی so'âli پرسشی porseshi
questionless *n.* بدون سؤال bedun-e' so'âl
questionnaire *n.* پرسشنامه porsesh-nâmeh
queue *n., vi., vt.* صف saf ردیف radif
quibble *n.* طفره رفتن tafreh raftan
quick *adj., n., adv.* زود zud تند tond سریع sari'
quick-tempered *adj.* تندخو tond-khu
quick-witted *n.* تیزهوش tiz-hush
quicken *vt., vi.* تند کردن tond kardan
quickie *n.* زودکی zudaki
quickly *adv.* بسرعت besor'at تند tond
quicksand *n.* باتلاق شن bâtlâq-e' shen
quicksilver *n., vt.* جیوه jiveh سیماب simâb
quickstep *n.* تندقدم tond qadam
quid pro quo *np.* این عوض آن in 'avaz-e' on
quiet *adj., n.* ساکت sâket آرام ârâm
quill *n., vt.* شاه‌پر shâh-par تیغ tiq
quilt *n., vt., vi.* پتو چهل تکه patu chehel tek~eh
quilting *n.* تکه دوزی tek~eh-duzi
quince *n.* به beh
quinine *n.* گنه گنه ganeh ganeh

quip *n., vi.* شوخی shukhi لطیفه latifeh
quirk *n.* پیچ pich چرخش charkhesh
quiscence *n.* سکون sokun بیحرکتی bi-harekati
quiscent *n.* ساکن sâken بیحرکت bi-harekat
quit *vi., adj.* استعفادادن este'fâ dâdan دست کشیدن dast keshidan
quitclaim *n., vt.* سلب مالکیت کردن salb-e' mâlekiyat kardan
quite *adv.* کاملاً kâmelan نسبتاً nesbatan
quits *adj.* یربیر yer be-yer مساوی mosâvi
quittance *n.* خلاصی khalâsi رسید خلاصی resid-e' khalâsi
quitter *n.* زود جا بزن zud jâ bezan
quiver *n.* ترکش tarkesh
quiver *v.* لرزیدن larzidan لرزش larzesh
quixotic *n.* لجوج lajuj غد qod
quiz *vt., n.* امتحان کردن emtehân kardan
quizzical *n.* آب زیرکاه âb zir-e' kâh پرسوأل por-so'âl
quorum *n.* حد نصاب had~-e' nesâb
quota *n.* سهمیه sahmiyeh تعداد معین te'dâd-e' mo'ay~an
quotable *adj.* نقل کردنی naql-kardani
quotation *n.* نقل naql ذکر zekr مظنه mazan~eh
quotation mark *np.* نشان نقل قول neshân-e' naql-e' qol
quote *vt., vi., n.* نقل قول کردن naql-e' gol kardan

R R r

R.P.M. *n.* دوردردقیقه dor dar daqiqeh
R.S.V.P. *n.* لطفاً جواب بدهید lotfan javâb bedahid
rabbi *n.* خاخام khâkhâm
rabbinate *n.* خاخامی khâkhâmi
rabbit *n.* خرگوش khargush
rabble *v.* شلوغ بازی درآوردن sholuq-bâzi dar âvardan
rabble *vi., n., vt.* شلوغی sholughi ازدحام ezdehâm
rabble rouser *n.* شلوغ کن sholuq-kon
rabid *adj.* هار hâr
rabies *n.* هاری hâri
raccoon *n.* نقاب موش neqâb-mush
race *v.* مسابقه دادن mosâbeqeh dâdan
race *n.* نژاد nezhâd
race *v.* مسابقه گذاشتن mosâbeqeh gozâshtan
race track *np.* میدان اسب دوانی meydân-e' asb-davâni
racer *n.* مسابقه دهنده mosâbeqeh-dahandeh
raceway *n.* آبراه âbrâh
racial *n.* نژادی nezhâdi
racism *n.* نژادپرستی nezhâd-parasti تعصب نژادی ta'as~ob-e' nezhâdi
racist *n., adj.* نژاد پرست nezhâd-parast
rack *n., vi., vt.* جاکلاهی jâ-kolâhi قفسه qafaseh
rack *n., vi., vt.* خراب kharâb
rack *n., vi., vt.* قدم رو qadam-ro
rack *n., vi., vt.* تودهٔ ابر tudeh-ye' abr
racket *n.* باند bând
racket *n.* راکت râket
racket *n.* سروصدا sar-o sedâ هیاهو hayâhu
racketeer *n., vi.* باج گیر bâj-gir گانگستر gângester
racy *adj.* شیک shik ژیگول zhigul
radar *n.* رادار râdâr
radial *adj.* شعاعی sho'â'i
radian *n.* قوس qos
radiance *n.* پرنوری pornuri تابش tâbesh
radiant *adj.* پرنور por-nur تابان tâbân
radiate *adj., vi., vt.* منور بودن monav~ar budan
از خود برون دادن az khod borun dâdan
radiation *n.* پرتوافکنی parto-afkani تابش tâbesh

radiator *n.* رادیاتور râdiâtor
radical *adj., n.* رادیکال râdikâl تندرو tond-ro
radically *n.* رادیکالی râdikâli اساسی asâsi
radilogy *n.* رادیولوژی râdiolozhi
radio *v.* مخابره کردن mokhâbereh kardan
radio *n.* رادیو râdio
radish *n.* تربچه torobcheh
raff *n.* اُشغال âshqâl
raffish *adj.* بی آبرو bi-âberu
raffle *n., v.* بخت آزمایی bakht-âzmâyi لاتاری lâtâri
raft *n., vi.* تخته قایق takhteh-qâyeq
rafter *n., vt.* تیرچوب tir-chub
rag *v.* سربسرگذاشتن sar be-sar gozâshtan
rag *n.* کهنه kohneh
ragamuffin *n.* ژنده پوش zhendeh-push
rage *n., vi.* خشم khashm
ragged *adj., v., vt.* پاره پاره pâreh-pâreh ناهموار nâ-hamvâr
ragman *n.* کهنه فروش kohneh-forush
ragtag *n.* اراذل arâzel
ragtime *n.* موسیقی جاز musiqi-e' jâz
ragweed *n.* علف هرزه 'alaf harzeh
raid *n., vt., vi.* حمله کردن hamleh kardan هجوم آوردن hojum âvardan
raider *n.* مهاجم mohâjem
rail *n.* خط آهن khat~-e' âhan ریل reyl نرده nardeh
rail *v.* انتقادشدیدکردن enteqâd-e' shadid kardan
railing *n.* نرده nardeh
railroad *n.* راه آهن râh âhan
railroad *v.* پاپوش ساختن pâ-push sâkhtan
rain *n., vi., vt.* باران آمدن bârân âmadan
rain check *np.* یک دفعه دیگر yek daf'eh digar
rainbow *n.* رنگین کمان rangin-kamân قوس قزح qos-e' qazah
raincoat *n.* بارانی bârâni
raindrop *n.* قطرهٔ باران qatreh-ye' bârân
rainfall *n.* بارندگی bârandegi
rainproof *n.* ضد باران zed~-e' bârân
rainy day *np.* روزبارانی ruz-e' bârâni روزمبادا ruz-e' mabâdâ
raise *v.* بمیان آوردن be-miân âvardan
raise *v.* بزرگ کردن bozorg kardan پرورش دادن parvaresh dâdan

raise

raise *v.* اضافه حقوق دادن ezâfeh hoquq dâdan
raise *v.* بالا بردن bâlâ bordan بلند کردن boland kardan
raised *adj., v.* برآمده bar-âmadeh بزرگ شده bozorg shodeh
raisin *n.* کشمش keshmesh
raj(ah) *n.* مهاراجه mohârâjeh
rake *v.* جستجو کردن josteju kardan جمع کردن jam' kardan
rake *n.* شنکش shen-kesh
rake-off *n.* حق حساب haq~-e' hesâb
rakehell *n., adj.* فاسق fâseq هرزه harzeh
rally *v.* مسخره کردن mas-khareh kardan
rally *v.* دورهم جمع کردن dor-e' ham jam' kardan
rally *n.* رالی râli اجتماع ejtemâ'
ram *n.* قوچ quch
ram *v.* چپاندن chapândan فروکردن foru kardan
ramble *v., n.* الاف گشتن al~âf gashtan
rambler *n.* الاف al~âf ولگرد velgard
rambunctious *n.* چموش chamush جنجالی janjâli
ramification *n.* انشعاب enshe'âb اثر asar
ramiform *adj.* شاخه ای shâkheh-i
ramify *vt., vi.* شاخه شاخه شدن shâkheh-shâkheh shodan
rammer *n.* فروکننده foru-konandeh
ramp *v.* روی دوپا ایستادن ruy-e' dopâ istâdan
ramp *n.* ورود راه vorud-râh خروج راه khoruj-râh
rampage *n., vi.* الم شنگه alam-shangeh وحشیگری vahshi-gari
rampageous *adj.* چموش chamush
rampant *n.* گسترده gostardeh
rampart *n., vt.* سپر بلا separ-e' balâ بارو bâru
ramrod *n.* سنبه sonbeh
ramshackle *adj.* نکسنی fakasâni
ranch *n., vi.* مزرعه mazra'eh
rancher(o) *n.* مزرعه دار mazra'eh-dâr گاودار gâv-dâr
rancid *adj.* ترشیده torshideh
rancor *n.* کینه kineh
rancorous *adj.* کینه ای kineh-i
random(ly) *n.* همین جوری hamin-juri خارج ازترتیب khârej az tartib
randy *adj., n.* پتیاره patiâreh حشری hashari
range *v.* ردیف کردن radif kardan
range *v.* تغییرکردن taqyir kardan فرق کردن farq kardan

range *n.* سلسله selseleh
range *v.* دور و برگشتن dor-o bar gashtan
range *n.* برد bord تیررس tir-res
range *n.* فر fer
ranger *n.* جنگل بان jangal-bân
rank *adj., n., vt.* پریشت porposht نامطلوب nâ-matlub
rank *adj., n., vt.* درجه darejeh رتبه rotbeh
rank and file *np.* معمولی ma'muli عامه 'âm~eh
rankle *vi.* دردناک بودن dârd-nâk budan
ransack *n.* غارت کردن qârat kardan
ransom *n., vt.* جانبها خواستن jân-bahâ khâstan فدیه fedyeh
  تن بها tan-bahâ
rant *n.* دادوبیدادکردن dâd-o bidâd kardan
rap *v.* تق زدن taq zadan ضربه زدن zarbeh zadan
rap *v.* گپ زدن gap zadan
rap *vt., vi., n.* جرم jorm گناه gonâh
rapacious *n.* غارتگر qârat-gar حریصانه harisâneh
rapacity *n.* غارتگری qârat-gari حرص hers
rape *n.* تجاوز tajâvoz
rape *v.* تجاوزکردن tajâvoz kardan
rapid *adj., n.* تند tond سریع sari'
rapids *n.* تندآب tond-âb
rapier *n.* سخمه sokhmeh شمشیردودم shamshir-e' dodam
rapist *n.* متجاوز motejâvez تجاوزگر tajâvoz-gar
rapport *n.* تماس tamâs میانه miâneh
rapprochement *n.* تجدیدروابط tajdid-e' ravâbet
rapture *n., vt.* شعف sha'f وجد vajd
rare *adj.* کمیاب kamyâb نادر nâder
rare *adj.* نیم پخته nim-pokhteh
rarely *adv.* بندرت be-nodrat
rarity *n.* کمیاب kamyâb ندرت nodrat
rasberry *n.* شیشکی shishaki
rascal *n., adj.* دغل daqal تخم جن tokhm-e' jen
  آب زیرکاه âb zir-e' kâh
rash *n.* جوش jush
rash *adj.* عجول 'ajul نسنجیده nasanjideh
rasp *vt., vi., n.* سوهان درشت suhân dorosht
raspberry *n.* تمشک tameshk

raspy *adj.* گرفته gerefteh خشن khashen
rat *adj.* موذی muzi
rat *n.* موش mush
rat race *n.* سگدوی زندگی sagdo-ye' zendegi
rat trap *n.* تله موش taleh mush مخمصه makhmaseh
rat(on) *n.* خبرچینی کردن khabar-chini kardan لودادن lo dâdan
ratchet *n.* چرخ دندۀ ضامن دار charkh daneh-ye' zâmendâr
rate *n.* نسبت nesbat درجه dareieh
rate *v.* نرخ گذاشتن nerkh gozâshtan شماردن shemârdan
rate *n.* نرخ nerkh
rather *n., int.* ترجیح دادن tarjih dâdan نسبتاً nesbatan بلکه balkeh
ratification *n.* تصویب tasvib تصدیق tasdiq
ratify *vt.* تصویب کردن tasvib kardan تصدیق کردن tasdiq kardan
rating *n., v.* درجه بندی darejeh-bandi نرخ بندی nerkh-bandi
ratio *n.* نسبت nesbat
ration *n., vt.* جیره بندی کردن jireh-bandi kardan کوپن kopon
rational *adj.* منطقی manteqi معقول ma'qul
rationale *n.* دلیل اصلی dalil-e' asâsi منطق manteq
rationalism *n.* استدلال مآبی estedlâl ma'âbi خرد بینی kherad-bini
rationalist *n.* استدلال مآب estedlâl ma'âb منطقی manteqi
rationality *n.* دلیل dalil منطق manteq
rationalization *n.* استدلال estedlâl
rationalize *vt., vi.* استدلال کردن estedlâl kardan
rats! *n.* اه ah!
rattle *v.* تلق تلق کردن teleq-teleq kardan
rattle *n.* جغجغه jeq-jeqeh
rattlesnake *n.* مارزنگی mâr-e' zangi
raucous *adj.* خشن khashen دورگه do-rageh
ravage *n., vt., vi.* ویران کردن virân kardan خراب کردن kharâb kardan
rave *vi., vt., n.* هذیان گفتن hazyân goftan یاوه گفتن yâveh goftan
ravel *n.* گره خوردن gereh khordan نخ نخ شدن nakh-nakh shodan
raven *vt., n.* کلاغ سیاه kalâq siâh زاغ zâq غراب qorâb
ravenous *adj.* حریص haris گرسنه gorosneh
ravine *n.* خشک رود khoshk-rud مسیل masil
raving *adj., v., n.* دیوانه کننده divâneh konandeh
دیوانه وار divâneh-vâr
ravish *vt.* دل ربودن del robudan تجاوزکردن tajâvoz kardan
ravishing *adj.* دلربا del-robâ

raw *adj.* لخت lokht
raw *adj.* خام khâm ناشی nâshi
raw material *np.* موادخام mavâd~-e' khâm
rawhide *n.* شلاق چرمی shal~âq charmi
ray *n.* پرتو parto اشعه asha'eh
rayon *n., adj.* ابریشم مصنوعی abrishâm masnu'i
raze *vt.* ازجاکندن az jâ kandan پاک کردن pâk kardan
razor *n., vt.* تیغ tiq
razor blade *n.* تیغ ریش تراشی tiq-e' rish-tarashi
razz *vt., n.* مسخره کردن maskhareh kardan
re-educate *n.* بازآموزشی کردن bâz-âmuzeshi kardan
re-enactment *n.* بازتصویبی bâz-tasvibi
re-enter *n.* بازواردشدن bâz-vâred shodan
re-entry *n.* بازورودی bâz-vorudi
re-examination *n.* بازآزمایشی bâz-âzmâyeshi
re-examine *n.* بازآزمایش کردن bâz-âzmâyesh kardan
reach *n.* دسترس dastres
reach *v.* دسترسی پیداکردن dastresi peydâ kardan
reach *n.* دسترسی dastresi استطاعت estetâ'at
reach *v.* رسیدن residan
react *vi.* عکس العمل نشان دادن 'aksol 'amal neshân dâdan
reaction *n.* عکس العمل 'aksol 'amal واکنش vâkonesh
reactionary *n.* ارتجاعی ertejâ'i واپسگرا vâ-pasgarâ مرتجع mortaje'
reactive *adj.* واکنشی vâkoneshi رآکتیو re-âktiv
reactor *n.* رآکتور re-âktor واکنش کننده vâkonesh-konandeh
read *adj., vt.* خواندن khândan قرائت کردن qarâ'at kardan
readable *n.* قابل خواندن qâbel-e' khândan خوانا khânâ
reader *n.* خواننده khânandeh
readily *adv.* به آسانی beh-âsâni فوری fori
readiness *n.* آمادگی âmâdegi
reading *n., vt., adj.* خواندن khândan قرائت qarâ'at
reading room *n.* قرائت خانه qarâ'at khâneh
readjust *vt.* دوباره تنظیم کردن dobâreh tanzim kârdan
readmission *n.* بازپذیری bâz-paziri
readmit *v.* دوباره قبول کردن dobâreh qabul kardan
ready *n., adj., int.* آماده âmâdeh حاضر hâzer
ready-made *adj., n.* ساخته آماده sâkhteh âmâdeh
reaffirm *vt.* بازاثبات کردن bâz-esbât kardan

real *adj., adv., n.* ملک melk مستغل mostaqel
real *adj., adv., n.* حقیقی haqiqi واقعی vâqe'i
real estate *np.* ملک واملاک melk va amlâk مستغلات mostaqelât
realism *n.* حقیقت بینی haqiqat-bini واقع بینی vâqe'-bini
realist *n.* حقیقت بین haqiqat-bin واقع بین vâqe'-bin
realistic *adj.* واقعی vâqe'i
reality *n.* حقیقت haqiqat واقعیت vâqe'iyat
realization *n.* درک dark تحقق tahâq~oq
realize *vt., vi.* درک کردن dark kardan تحقق یافتن tahaq~oq yâftan
really *adv.* حقیقتاً haqiqatan واقعاً vâqe'an جدی jed~i
realm *n.* سرزمین sar-zamin قلمرو qalam-ro خطه khet~eh ملک molk
realtor *n.* دلال معاملات ملکی dal~âl-e' mo'âmelât-e' melki
realty *n.* بنگاه معاملات ملکی bongâh-e' mo'âmelât-e' melki
ream *n., vt.* گشاد کردن goshâd kardan
reamer *n.* سوراخ گشادکن surâkh goshâd-kon
reap *vt., vi.* جمع کردن jam' kardan درو کردن dero kardan
reaper *n.* دروکن dero-kon درو گر dero-gar
rear *n.* پشت posht عقب 'aqab
rear *v.* بزرگ کردن bozorg kardan پرورش دادن parvaresh dâdan
rear admiral *np.* دریادار daryâ-dâr
rear guard *np.* پس قراول pas-qarâvol
rearm *n.* دوباره مسلح کردن dobâreh mosal~ah kardan
rearmament *n.* بازتسلیحات bâz-taslihat
rearrange *v.* بازتنظیم کردن bâz-tanzim kardan
rearward *adj., adv., n.* بطرف عقب be-taraf-e' 'aqab
reason *n.* دلیل dalil سبب sabab علت 'el~at
reason *v.* دلیل آوردن dalil âvardan
 بامنطق حرف زدن bâ manteq harf zadan
reasonable *adj.* منطقی manteqi معقول ma'qul مناسب monâseb
reasonably *adv.* انصافاً ensâfan
reasoning *n.* استدلال estedlâl
reasonless *vt.* بی دلیل bi-dalil
reassurance *n.* بازاطمینانی bâz-etminâni
reassure *n.* بازاطمینان دادن bâz-etminân dâdan
reave *vt.* بزورگرفتن bezur gereftan
rebald *n.* رکیک rakik بیچاک دهن bi-châk dahan وقیح vaqih
rebate *n., vt., vi.* تخفیف برگشتی takhfif-e' bargashti
rebel *v.* شورش کردن shuresh kardan سرپیچی کردن sar-pichi kardan

rebel *n.* یاغی yâqi شورشی shureshi گردنکش gardan-kesh
متمرد motemar~ed
rebellion *n.* شورش shuresh عصیان 'osyân ستیزه جویی setizeh-juyi
عناد 'enâd
rebellious *adj., n.* شورشی shureshi سرکش sar-kesh
عصیانگر 'osyân-gar
rebirth *n.* باززایی bâz-zâyi
reborn *adj.* باززاده bâz-zâdeh
rebound *n.* برگشت bar-gasht
rebound *v.* برگشتن bar-gashtan
rebuff *n., vt.* ردکردن rad kardan محل نگذاشتن mahal nagozâshtan
rebuild *vt., vi.* بازسازی کردن bâz-sâzi kardan
rebuilt *n.* دوباره ساخته‌شده dobâreh sâkhteh-shodeh
rebuke *vt., n.* توبیخ tobikh سرزنش کردن sar-zanesh kardan
rebut *vt., vi.* جواب اعتراضی دادن javâb-e' e'terâzi dâdan
rebuttal *n.* جواب اعتراضی javâb-e' e'terâzi تکذیب takzib
recalcitrant *n.* سرپیچ sar-pich متمرد motemar~ed
recall *v.* فراخواندن farâ khândan احضارکردن ehzâr kardan
recall بیادآوردن beyâd âvardan
recant *v.* حرف پس گرفتن harf pas gereftan انکارکردن enkâr kardan
recap *n., vt.* روکش کشیدن rukesh keshidan
خلاصه کردن kholâseh kardan
recapture *vt., n.* بازتسخیرکردن bâz-taskhir kardan
recede *vt., vi.* عقب رفتن 'aqab raftan
receding *vi.* عقب رفته 'aqab rafteh کم پشت kam-posht
receipt *n., vt., vi.* رسید resid
receiptor *n.* رسیدگیر resid-gir
receivable *adj., n.* دریافتی daryâfti وصولی vosuli
receive *vt., vi.* دریافت کردن daryâft kardan
تحویل گرفتن tahvil gereftan
receiver *n.* گیرنده girandeh
receiver *n.* گوشی gushi
recent *adj., n.* تازه tâzeh اخیر akhir پسین pasin
recently *adv.* بتازگی be-tâzegi اخیراً akhiran
recepient *n.* گیرنده girandeh
receptible *n.* دریافت شدنی daryâft shodani
reception *n.* گیرندگی girandegi موج گیری moj-giri
reception *n.* پذیرایی pazirâyi مهمانی mehmâni

reception room *np.* اطاق پذيرايی otâq-e' pazirâyi
receptionist *n.* منشی monshi مسئول اطلاعات mas'ul-e' et~elâ'ât
receptive *adj.* پذيرا mâyel مايل pazirâ
recess *n., vt., vi.* تورفتگی tu-raftegi تعطيل موقتی ta'til-e' movaq~ati
recession *n.* پس رفتگی pasraftegi
recession *n.* رکوداقتصادی rokud-e' eqtesâdi
recessive *adj., n.* پسرو pasro پس نشين pas-neshin
recharge *v.* دوباره شارژ کردن dobâreh shârzh kardan
recipe *n.* دستورعمل dastur-e' 'amal دستورپخت dastur-e' pokht
reciprocal *adj., n.* دوجانبه dojânebeh برعکس bar'aks متقابل moteqâbel
reciprocate *v.* متقابلاً عمل کردن moteqâbelan 'amâl kardan
reciprocity *n.* دوجانبه ای do-jânebeh-i تقابل taqâbol
recital *n.* بازگويی bâz-guyi تکنوازی tak-navâzi
recitation *n.* نقل naql ازبرخوانی az-bar-khâni
recite *vt., vi.* ازبرخواندن az-bar khândan
دکلمه کردن deklameh kardan
reckless *adj.* بی پروا biparvâ لاابالی lâ-ebâli
reckon *vt., vi.* گمان کردن gamân kardan حساب کردن hesâb kardan
reckoning *vi., n.* تصفيه حساب tasfieh hesâb قيامت qiâmat
reclaim *n.* پس گرفتن pas gereftan احيا کردن ehyâ kardan
reclamation *n.* پس گيری pas-giri احيا ehyâ
recline *vi., vt.* تکيه دادن takyeh dâdan
recluse *n., adj.* گوشه گير gusheh-gir منزوی monzavi
reclusion *n.* گوشه گيری gusheh-giri انزوا enzevâ عزلت 'ozlat
reclusive *adj.* گوشه گير gusheh-gir
recognition *n.* شناسايی shenâsâyi شناخت shenâkht
recognizable *adj.* قابل شناسايی qâbel-e' shenâsâyi نمايان namâyân
recognize *vt.* شناختن shenâkhtan بجاآوردن be-jâ âvardan
recoil *v.* عقب زدن 'aqab zadan جا خوردن jâ khordan
recoil *v.* لگدزدن lagad zadan
recollect *vt., vi.* بخاطرآوردن bekhâter âvardan
recollection *n.* بيادآوری beyâd-âvari
recommend *vt.* سفارش کردن sefâresh kardan
توصيه کردن tosiyeh kardan
recommendation *n.* توصيه tosiyeh تمجيد tamjid
recompense *vt., vi., n.* جبران مالی کردن jobrân-e' mâli kardan
reconcilable *adj.* آشتی دادنی âshti dâdani
reconcile *vt.* آشتی دادن âshti dâdan رفع کردن raf' kardan

reconciliation *n.* آشتی âshti اختلاف رفع raf'-e' ekhtelâf
recondition *vt.* بازتعمیرکردن bâz-ta'mir kardan
reconnaissance *n.* تجسسی tajas~osi اطلاعاتی et~elâ'âti
reconnoiter *vt., vi.* تجسس کردن tajas~os kârdan
بازدید کردن bâzdid kardan
reconsider *vt., vi.* دوباره ملاحظه کردن dobâreh molâhezeh kardan
reconstruct *vt.* بازسازی کردن bâz-sâzi kardan
record *v.* ضبط کردن zabt kardan
record *n.* صفحه safheh آلبوم âlbom
record *v.* ثبت کردن sabt kardan واردکردن vâred kardan
record *n.* رکورد rekord
record *n.* یادداشت yâd dâsht
record *n.* سابقه sâbeqeh پرونده parvandeh
recorder *n.* ثبت کننده sabt konandeh فلوت folut
recording *n.* ثبت sabt ضبط zabt
recount *vt.* کلمه به کلمه گفتن kalameh be-kalameh goftan
recoup *vt.* جبران کردن jobrân kardan تلافی کردن talâfi kardan
recourse *n.* چاره châreh توسل tavas~ol
recover *vt.* بازپس گرفتن bâz-pas gereftan بهبود یافتن behbud yâftan
recovery *n.* بازپس گیری bâzpas-giri بهبود behbud
recreate *vt., vi.* دوباره خلق کردن dobâreh khalq kardan
recreation *n.* تفریح tafrih سرگرمی sargarmi
recreation room *np.* اطاق تفریحات otâq-e' tafrihât
recreational *adj.* تفریحی tafrihi
recrement *n.* زائده zâ'edeh
recruit *adj.* سرباز تازه sarbâz-e' tâzeh
recruit *v.* استخدام کردن estekhdâm kardan
سرباز گرفتن sarbâz gereftan
recruitment *n.* سربازگیری sarbâz-giri استخدام estekhdâm
rectangle *n.* مستطیل mostatil راست گوش râst-gush
rectangular *adj.* مستطیلی mostatili
rectifiable *n.* اصلاح شدنی eslâh shodani
rectification *n.* اصلاح eslâh تصحیح taslih تصفیه tasfiyeh
rectifier *n.* تصحیح کننده tas-hih konandeh
rectify *v.* تصفیه کردن tasfiyeh kardan
rectify *v.* اصلاح کردن eslâh kardan تصحیح کردن tas-ih kardan
rector *n.* ناظم nâzem
rectum *n.* مقعد maq'ad

recumbent *adj., n., vt.* خوابیده khâbideh خمیده khamideh
recuperate *n.* بهبود یافتن behbud yâftan جبران کردن jobrân kardan
recuperation *n.* بهبودی behbudi جبران jobrân
recur *n.* برگشتن bargashtan عودکردن 'od kardan
recurrence *n.* برگشت bargasht عود 'od تکرار tekrâr
recurrent *adj.* عودکننده 'od konandeh مزمن mozmen
recurvate *adj.* خمیده khamideh
red *vt., adj., n.* قرمز qermez سرخ sorkh
red blood cell *np.* گلبول سرخ golobul-e' sorkh
red cent *n.* پشیز pashiz پول سیاه pul-e' siâh پاپاسی pâpâsi
Red Crescent *np.* هلال احمر helâl-e' ahmar
Red Cross *n.* صلیب سرخ Salib-e' sorkh
red herring *np.* نخودسیاه nokhod siâh ایزگم کن iz-gom kon
red light *np.* چراغ خطر cherâq khatar
red-blooded *adj.* متعصب mote'as~eb دوآتشه do-âtesheh
red-handed *adj., adv.* مچ باز moch-e' bâz دست خونین dast-e' khunin
red-hot *n.* داغ داغ dâq-e' dâq
red-neck *n.* متعصب mote'as~eb
redden *vt., vi.* سرخ کردن sorkh kardan
redeem *n.* پس گرفتن pas gereftan
گناه شویی کردن gonâh-shuyi kardan
رهایی بخشیدن rahâ-yi bakhshidan
redeemable *adj.* پس دادنی pasdâdani بازخریدنی bâz-kharidani
redeemer *n.* ناجی nâji مسیح masih رهایی بخش rahâ-yi bakhsh
redemption *n.* بازخرید bâz-kharid رهایی rahâyi ندیه fedyeh فک fak~
redeposit *v., n.* بازواریزکردن bâz-vâriz kardan
redicule *n.* مسخره کردن maskhâreh kardan
استهزاء کردن estehzâ' kardan
ریشخند کردن rish-khand kardan
rediculous *n.* مسخره آمیز maskhareh-âmiz مضحک moz-hek
redirect *vt., adj.* بازجلب کردن bâz-jalb kardan
redo *vt.* دوباره انجام دادن dobâreh anjâm dâdan
redress *n., vt.* تصحیح tas-hih جبران کردن jobrân kardan
reduce *vt.* کم کردن kam kardan کاهش دادن kâhesh dâdan
reduction *n.* کاهش kâhesh تقلیل taqlil
redundancy *n.* زیادی ziâdi اضافی ezâfi
redundant *adj.* زاید zâ'ed اضافه ezâfeh
redwood *adj., n.* سرخ چوب sorkh-chub

reed *n.* نی ney خوز khuz
reef *n.* ساحل lab sâhel
reefer *n.* کت دوجیب kot-e' do-jib-e'
reek *n., vi., vt.* بو دود دادن bu dud dâdan
reeky *adj.* بودار bu-dâr
reel *v.* گیج رفتن gij raftan تلوتلوخوردن telo-telo khordan
reel *n.* قرقره qer-qereh نخ پیچ nakh-pich حلقه halqeh
reeve *n., vt.* کدخدا kad-khodâ کلانتر kalântar
refectory *n.* نهارخانه nahâr-khâneh
refer *v.* رجوع کردن roju' kardan مراجعه کردن morâje'eh kardan
refer *v.* ارجاء کردن erjâ' kardan اشاره کردن eshâreh kardan
referable *n.* رجوعی roju'i
referee *n., vt., vi.* داور dâvar رفری referee
reference *n., vt.* معرف mo'aref سابقه sâbeqeh
reference *n., vt.* رجوع roju' مراجعه morâje'eh
referendum *n.* همه پرسی hameh-porsi رفراندوم referândom
referent *n.* مرجوع marju'
referential *n.* مراجعه ای morâje'eh-i
referral *n.* توصیه tosiyeh معرفی mo'arefi
refill *vt., n.* بازپرکردن bâz-por kardan
refine *vt., vi.* تصفیه کردن tasfiyeh kardan اصلاح کردن eslâh kardan
پالودن pâludan
refinement *n.* تصفیه tasfiyeh اصلاح eslâh پالایش pâlâyesh
تهذیب tah-zib
refinery *n.* پالایشگاه pâlâyesh-gâh
refit *n.* بازآماده کردن bâz-âmâdeh kardan
reflect *vt., vi.* منعکس کردن mon'akes kardan فکرکردن fekr kardan
reflecting *n.* انعکاسی en'ekâsi
reflection *n.* انعکاس en'ekâs تصویر tasvir بازتاب bâz-tâb
reflective *adj.* انعکاسی en'ekâsi تفکری tafak~ori متفکر motefak~er
reflector *n.* منعکس کننده mon'akes konandeh براق bar~âq
reflex *adj., n.* عکس العمل 'aksol 'amal
reflexive *adj., n.* عکس العملی 'aksol 'amali
reform *n., vt., vi.* اصلاح کردن eslâh kardan
سربراه کردن sar-berâh kardan
reformatory *adj., n.* دارالتأدیب dârol-ta'dib
reformed *adj.* اصلاح شده eslâh-shodeh سربراه sar-berâh
reformer *n.* اصلاح کننده eslâh-konandeh

reformist *n.* اصلاح طلب eslâh-talab مصلح mosleh
refract *vt.* کج کردن kaj kardan شکستن shekastan
refracting *n.* کجی kaji انکساری enkesâri
refraction *n.* انکسار enkesâr شکست shekast
refractor *n.* نورشکن nur-shekan
refractory *adj., n.* سمج semej سرسخت sarsakht
refrain *n., vi., vt.* خودداری کردن khod-dâri kardan
refresh *vt., vi.* تازه کردن tâzeh kardan
    دل نشاطی دادن del-neshâti dâdan
refresher *n.* مروری moruri تازه کننده tâzeh konandeh
refreshing *adj.* روحبخش ruh-bakhsh نفس تازه کن nafas tâzeh-kon
    مفرح mofar~ah
refreshment(s) *n.* آلات نوشیدنی nushidani âlât
refrigerate *vt.* سردکردن sard kardan نگه داشتن negah dâshtan
refrigerator *n.* یخچال yakhchâl
refuel *vt., vi.* دوباره بنزین گیری کردن dobâreh benzin-giri kardan
refuge *n., vt., vi.* پناه‌گاه panâh-gâh گریزگاه goriz-gâh
refugee *n.* پناهنده panâhandeh
refund *vt., vi., n.* بازپس دادن bâz-pas dâdan
    پول پس دادن pul pas dâdan
    مسترد کردن mostared kardan
refurbish *n.* ترمیم کردن tarmim kardan
    سروصورت دادن sar-o surat dâdan
refusal *n.* امتناع emtenâ' اباء ebâ' استنکاف estenkâf
refuse *v.* رد کردن rad kardan امتناع کردن emtenâ' kardan
refuse *n.* آشغال âshqâl فضله fazleh
refuse *v.* قبول نکردن qabul nakardan
refutable *adj.* تکذیب شدنی takzib-shodani
refutation *n.* تکذیب takzib
refute *vt.* تکذیب takzib ردکردن rad kardan
regain *vt.* دوباره بدست آوردن dobâreh be-dast âvardan
regal *adj., n.* شاهانه shâhâneh
regale *vt., vi., n.* پذیرایی شاهانه pazirâyi-e' shâhâneh
regalia *n.* نشانه های شاهانه neshâneh-hâ-ye' shâhâneh
regard *v.* درنظرگرفتن dar nazar gereftan قبول داشتن qabul dâshtan
regard *n.* مورد mored ملاحظه molâhezeh
regardful *adj.* باملاحظه bâ-molâhezeh
regarding *pre.* راجع به râje' beh مربوط به marbut beh

regardless *adj.* بی ملاحظه bi-molâhezeh
بدون توجه bedun-e' tavaj~oh
regards *n.* سلام salâm پیغام peyqâm احترام ehterâm
regency *adj., n.* نیابت niâbat
regenerate *adj., vt.* بازتولیدکردن bâz-tolid kardan
regenerative *adj.* بازتولیدی bâz-tolidi
regent *n., adj.* نایب سلطنه nâyeb saltaneh
regicide *n.* شاه کشی shâh-koshi
regime *n.* رژیم rezhim حکومت hokumat
regimen *n.* رژیم rezhim
regiment *n., vt.* هنگ hang
reginal *n.* ملکه ای malakeh-i
region *n.* ناحیه nâhiyeh منطقه mantaqeh
regional *n.* ناحیه ای nâhiyeh-i
register *n.* دفتر ثبت daftar-e' sabt
register *v.* ثبت کردن sabt kardan نام نویسی کردن nâm-nevisi kardan
registered *adj.* ثبت شده sabt-shodeh سفارشی sefâreshi
registrant *n.* نام نویس nâm-nevis
registrar *n.* دفترنام نویسی daftar-e' nâm-nevis
registration *n.* نام نویسی nâm-nevisi ثبت sabt
registry *n.* دفتر ثبت daftar-e' sabt محضر mahzar
regress *n.* به عقب beh-'aqab به قهقرا رفتن beh qah-qarâ raftan
regression *n.* برگشت bargasht
regressive *adj.* قهقرایی qah-qarâyi عقب رو aqab-ro
regressor *n.* عقب بر 'aqab-bar
regret *v.* متأسف بودن mote-'as~ef budan
افسوس خوردن afsus khordan
regretful *adj.* متأسف mote'as~ef
regrettable *adj.* باعث تأسف bâ'es-e' ta'as~of
regroup *v.* دوباره جمع کردن dobâreh jam' kardan
regular *adj., n.* مرتّب morat~ab منظم monaz~am معمولی ma'muli
regularity *n.* ترتیب tartib نظم nazm
regularly *adv.* سروقت bâ-nazm بانظم sar-e' vaqt
regulate *vt., adj.* ترتیب دادن tartib dâdan
منظم کردن monaz~am kardan
regulation *n.* ترتیب tartib تنظیم tanzim
regulations *n.* مقررات moqar~ârât قوانین qavânin
آئین نامه â'in-nâmeh

regulator n. تنظیم کننده tanzim konandeh
regurgitate vi. نشخوار کردن noshkhâr kardan
rehabilitate vt. اصلاح اخلاقی کردن eslâh-e' akhlâqi kardan
rehabilitation n. بازتربیتی bâz-tarbiati
rehearsal n. تمرین tamrin
rehearse vt., vi. تمرین کردن tamrin kardan
reign n., vi. سلطنت کردن saltanat kardan
reimburse vt. بازپرداخت کردن bâz-pardâkht kardan
پول پس دادن pul pas dâdan
reimbursement n. بازپرداخت bâz-pardâkht
rein n. افسار afsâr لگام legâm دهنه dahaneh عنان 'anân
rein v. افسارزدن afsâr zadan دهنه کردن dahaneh kardan
reincarnate n. کالبد نو دادن kâlbod-e' no dâdan
تجسم یافتن tajas~om yâftan
reincarnation n. تناسخ tanâsokh بازگشت روح bâz-gasht-e' ruh
reindeer pl. گوزن gavazn
reinforce vt. تقویت کردن taqviyat kardan
reinforcement n. تقویت taqviyat نیروی امدادی niruy-e' emdâdi
reins n. قلوه golveh
reinstate vt. بازگماشتن bâz-gomâshtan
reinstatement n. بازگماری bâz-gomâri
reiterate n. تکرار کردن tekrâr kardan بازگوکردن bâz-gu kardan
reject adj. ردشده rad-shodeh پس مانده pas-mândeh
reject v. ردکردن rad kardan قبول نکردن qabul nakardan
rejected adj. ردشده rad-shodeh
پس فرستاده شده pas ferestâdeh shodeh
واخورده vâ-khordeh
rejection n. رد rad ناقبولی nâ-qabuli
rejoice vi., vt. خوش حالی کردن khosh-hâli kardan
rejoicing v. خوش حالی khosh-hâli شادمانی shâdmâni
rejoin v. جواب دادن javâb dâdan
rejoin v. بازملحق شدن bâz-molhaq shodan
rejoinder n. جواب javâb
rejuvenate vt. بازجوان کردن bâz-javân kardan
rejuvenation n. بازجوانی bâz-javâni
rejuvenescent n. بازجوان bâz-javân
relapse n., vi. عود 'od برگشت bargasht
relate vt., vi. نسبت دادن nesbat dâdan نقل کردن naql kardan

related v. مربوط marbut قوم و خویش qom-o khish
relation n. نسبت nesbat ربط rabt خویش khish
relationship n. نسبت nesbat بستگی bastegi ارتباط ertebât
relative n., adj. نسبی nesbi
relative n., adj. خویشاوند khishâvand فامیل fâmil
relativist n. نسبی گرا nesbi-garâ
relativity n. نسبیت nesbiyat نسبیه nesbieh
relax vt., vi. شل کردن shol kardan راحت بودن râhat budan
relaxation n. استراحت esterâhat راحتی râhati
relaxed n. راحت râhat خستگی درکرده khastegi dar-kardeh
relay v. رساندن resândan
relay v. تازه نفس دادن tâzeh nafas dâdan عوض کردن avaz kardan
relay vt., n., vi. امدادی emdâdi
relay vt., n., vi. بازپخش bâz-pakhsh مخابره ای mokhâbereh-i
relay vt., n., vi. ذخیره zakhireh تازه نفس tâzeh nafas
release v. آزاد کردن âzâd kardan ول کردن vel kardan
release v. ترخیص کردن tar-khis kardan
release v. صرف نظرکردن sarf-e' nazar kardan
release v. انتشاردادن enteshâr dâdan
relegate vt. محول کردن mohav~al kardan
بپایین ردکردن be-pâyin rad kardan
relegation n. تحویل tahvil ارجاع erjâ'
relent vi., vt. ول کردن vel kardan کوتاه آمدن kutâh âmadan
relentless adj. سفت و سخت seft-o sakht سمج semej
relevance n. ارتباط ertebât ربط rabt
relevant adj. مربوط marbut
reliability n. اطمینان etminân
reliable adj. قابل اعتماد qâbel-e' e'temâd موثق movas~aq
reliance n. وابستگی vâbastegi وثوق اعتماد e'temâd vosuq
reliant adj. وابسته vâbasteh مطمئن motma'em
relic n. اثر asar باقیمانده bâqimândeh
relict n. جان بدربرده jân bedar bordeh
relief n. اعانه e'âneh
relief n. تسکین taskin آرامش ârâmesh تعویض ta'viz
relieve vt., vi. تسکین دادن taskin dâdan خلاص کردن khalâs kardan
religion n. دین din کیش kish مذهب maz-hab
religious adj., n. دیندار din-dâr مذهبی maz-habi
relinquish vt. ول کردن vel kardan سلب کردن salb kardan

relish *v.* لذت بردن lez~at bordan
relish *n.* مزه mazeh چاشنی châshni
reluctance *n.* بی میلی bi-meyli اکراه ekrâh
reluctant *adj.* بی میل bi-meyl
rely *v.* تکیه کردن tak-yeh kardan حساب کردن hesâb kardan
rely *v.* اعتماد کردن e'temâd kardan
remain *vi., n.* ماندن mândan باقی ماندن bâqi mândan
remainder *adj., vt., n.* باقی مانده bâqi-mândeh
remains *n.* بقایا baqâyâ
remake *n.* دوباره ساختن dobâreh sâkhtan
remand *vt., n.* پس فرستادن pas ferestâdan تحویل دادن tahvil dâdan
remanent *n.* باقیمانده bâqimândeh
remark *vt., vi., n.* اظهار کردن ez-hâr kardan نظردادن nazar dâdan
remarkable *adj.* فوق العاده foqol-'âdeh قابل تحسین qâbel-e' tahsin
remarkably *n.* بطورفوق العاده betor-e' foqol-'âdeh
remedial *n.* درمان بخش darmân-bakhsh علاج بخش 'alâj-bakhsh
remediless *adj.* علاج ناپذیر 'alâj-nâ-pazir
درمان ناپذیر darmân-nâpazir
remedy *n.* درمان darmân علاج 'alâj
remedy *v.* علاج کردن 'alâj kardan اصلاح کردن eslâh kardan
remember *n.* بیادآوردن be-yâd âvardan یادآمدن yâd âmadan
بخاطرآوردن be-khâter âvardan
remembrance *n.* یادآوری yâd-âvari یادگاری yâd-gâri ذکر zekr
remind *vt.* یادآوری کردن yâd-âvari kardan تذکردادن tazak~or dâdan
reminder *n.* یادآور yâd-âvar تذکر tazak~or
remindful *n.* یادآورنده yâd-âvarandeh
reminisce *n.* یادگذشته کردن yâd-e' gozashteh kardan
reminiscence *n.* یادآوری yâd-âvari خاطره khâtereh
reminiscent *adj.* یادآور yâd-âvar حاکی hâki
remiss *adj.* بی احتیاط bi-ehtiât لاابالی lâ-ebâli
remission *n.* بخشایش bakhshâyesh پایین آمدگی pâyin âmadegi
remit *vt., vi., n.* بخشیدن bakhshidan پایین آوردن pâyin âvardan
remittance *n.* وجه ارسالی vajh-e' ersâli پرداختی pardâkhti
عودت،تأدیه ta'dieh،'odat
remittent *adj., n.* بالا و پایینی bâlâ-o pâyini
remnant *n.* باقیمانده bâqimândeh
remodel *vt.* بازسازی کردن bâz-sâzi kardan
remodeling *vt.* دکوراسیون dekorâsion

remorse *n.* پشیمانی pashimâni ندامت nedâmat
remorsefull *n.* پشیمان pashimân متأسف mote'as~ef
remorseless *adj.* بیرحم birahm
remote *n., adj.* دورافتاده dur oftâdeh پرت part جزئی joz'i
remote control *np.* کنترل بی سیم kontorol-e' bi-sim
removable *adj.* برداشتنی bar-dâshtani
removal *n.* برداشت bar-dâsht برکناری bar-kenâri
remove *v.* برکنارکردن bar-kenâr kardan
remove *v.* برداشتن bar-dâshtan درآوردن dar âvardan
removed *adj.* دور dur برکنار bar-kenâr
renal *n.* قلوهای qolveh-i
render *vt., vi., n.* دادن dâdan انجام دادن anjâm dâdan
ارائه دادن erâ'eh dâdan
rendezvous *n.* راندوو rândevu قرار ملاقات qarâr-e' molâqât
rendition *n.* انجام anjâm ارایه erâ'eh
renegade *adj., vt., n.* یاغی yâqi
renege *n.* جازدن jâ zadan زیرقول زدن zir-e' qol zadan
عدول کردن 'odul kardan
renew *vt.* تجدید کردن tajdid kardan تازه کردن tâzeh kardan
renewal *n.* تجدید tajdid
renounce *v.* دست کشیدن dast keshidan کنارگذاشتن kenâr gozâshtan
منکرشدن monker shodan
renounce *v.* انکارکردن enkâr kardan عاق کردن 'âq kardan
renovate *v., adj.* بازسازی کردن bâz-sâzi kardan
renovation *n.* بازسازی bâz-sâzi
renovator *n.* بازساز bâz-sâz
renowned *adj.* مشهور mash-hur معروف ma'ruf
rent *n.* شکاف shekâf سوراخ surâkh
rent *v.* اجاره کردن ejâreh kardan
rental *n., adj.* اجاره ای ejâreh-i
renter *n.* مستأجر mosta'jer
renunciation *n.* چشم پوشی cheshm-pushi انکار enkâr
renunciatory *adj.* چشم پوشانه cheshm-pushâneh
reopen *vt., vi.* دوباره بازکردن dobâreh bâz kardan
reorder *vt., n.* دوباره سفارش دادن dobâreh sefâresh dadan
بازنظمی bâz-nazmi
reorganization *n.* بازسازمانی bâz-sâzmâni
reorganize *vt., vi.* بازسازمان دادن bâz-sâzmân dâdan

reorientation *n.* بازآشنایی bâz-âshnâyi

repaint *vt., n.* دوباره رنگ زدن dobâreh rang zadan

repair *vi., vt., n.* تعمیر کردن ta'mir kardan

repairable *adj.* تعمیرشدنی ta'mir shodani

repairman *n.* تعمیرکن ta'mir-kon

reparation *n.* جبران مالی jobrân-e' mâli غرامت qarâmat تقاص taqâs تاوان tâvân

repatriate *vt., n., vi.* به میهن برگرداندن beh-mihan bar-gardândan

repay *vt., vi.* بازپرداختن bâz-pardâkhtan

repayment *n.* بازپرداخت bâz-pârdâkht

repeal *vt., n.* لغوکردن laqv kardan

repeat *v.* تکرارکردن tekrâr kardan

repeat *n.* تکراری tekrâri

repeated *adj.* تکراری tekrâri مکرر mokar~ar

repeatedly *adv.* مکرراً mokar~âran کراراً kar~âran بکرات be-kar~ât

repeater *v.* تکرارکننده tekrâr konandeh

repeater *n.* خودکار khod-kâr اتوماتیک otomâtik

repel *vt.* دفع کردن daf' kardan

repellent *adj., n.* دفع کننده daf' konandeh

repeller *n.* دافع dâfe'

repent *vi., vt.* توبه کردن tobeh kardan

repentance *n.* توبه tobeh

repentant *adj.* توبه کار tobeh-kâr نادم nâdem

repercussion *n.* عکس العمل 'aksol-'amal انعکاس en'ekâs

repercussive *n.* انعکاسی en'ekâsi

repertoire *n.* مجموعهٔ هنری majmu'e-ye' honari

repetition *n., vt.* تکرار tekrâr

repetitious *n.* تکراری tekrâri

repetitive *adj.* تکراری tekrâri

rephrase *vt.* به عبارت دیگر گفتن beh-'ebârat-e' digar goftan

replace *vt.* جانشین شدن jâ-neshin shodan عوض کردن avaz kardan

replacement *n.* جانشینی jâ-neshini تعویض ta'viz

replenish *vt., n.* بازپرکردن bâz-por kardan بازآذوقه دادن bâz-âzuqeh dâdan

replete *adj.* پرپر por-e' por تاخرخره tâ-kher-khereh سرشار sar-shâr لبالب labâ lab

replica *n.* کپیه kopieh

reply *n.* جواب javâb پاسخ دادن pâsokh dâdan

report *n., vi.* گزارش gozâresh خبردادن khabar dâdan
report card *np.* کارنامه kârnâmeh
reportable *adj.* قابل گزارش qâbel-e' gozâresh
reporter *n.* خبرنگار khabar-negâr مخبر mokhber
repose *vt., n., vi.* آرامیدن ârâmidan آسودن âsudan
reposit *vt.* ذخیره کردن zakhireh kardan
reposit *n.* سپرده sepordeh ودیعه vadi'eh
reposition *n.* تعویض ta'viz
repository *n.* مخزن makhzan انبار anbâr
repossess *vt.* بازپس گرفتن bâz-pas gereftan
repossession *n.* بازپسگیری bâz-pasgiri
reprehend *vt.* سرزنش کردن sarzanesh kardan توبیخ tobikh
reprehensible *adj.* سزاوار سرزنش sezâvâr-e' sarzanesh
reprehension *n.* سرزنش sarzanesh توبیخ tobikh
reprehensive *n.* سرزنش آمیز sarzanesh-âmiz
represent *vt.* نشان دادن neshân dâdan
نماینده بودن namâyandeh budan
representation *n.* نمایندگی namâyandegi
representative *n., adj.* نماینده namâyandeh
repress *n.* سرکوب کردن sarkub kardan خواباندن khâbândan
repressed *n.* سرکوب شده sarkub-shodeh
repression *n.* سرکوبی sarkubi اختناق ekhtenâq
repressive *adj.* سرکوب گر sarkub-gar
reprieve *vt., n.* مهلت موقت mohlat-e' movaq~at نفس کش nafas-kesh
reprimand *v.* توبیخ کردن tobikh kardan
گوشمالی دادن gush-mâli dâdan
reprint *vt., n.* بازچاپ کردن bâz-châp kardan
reprisal *n.* تلافی talâfi
reprise *n.* تکرار tekrâr
reproach *vt., n.* مقصرشناختن moqas~er shenâkhtan
سرزنش کردن sar-zanesh kardan
نکوهش کردن nekuhesh kardan
reproachment *n.* سرزنش sar-zanesh نکوهش nekuhesh
بدگویی bad-guyi مذمت mazam~at
reprobate *n., adj., vt.* تقبیح کردن taqbih kardan مطرود matrud
reprobation *n.* تقبیح taqbih طرد tard
reprobative *adj.* تقبیحی taqbihi
reproduce *vt.* بازتولیدکردن bâz-tolid kardan

reproduction *n.* بازتولید bâz-tolid تناسل tanâsol

reproductive *adj., n.* تناسلی tanâsoli

reptile *n., adj.* خزنده khazandeh

reptiles *n.* خزنده‌گان khazandeh-gân

reptilian *adj., n.* خزنده khazandeh

republic *n.* جمهوری jomhuri

republican *adj., n.* جمهوری خواه jomhuri-khâh

repudiate *vt.* ازخود ندانستن az-khod nadânestan

باطل شناختن bâtel shenâkhtan منکرشدن monker shodan

repugn *vt., vi.* مخالفت کردن mokhâlefat kardan

repugnance *n.* انزجار enzejâr تنفر tanaf~or

repugnant *n.* متنفر motenaf~er ضد و نقیض zed~-o naqiz

repulse *vt., n.* دفع کردن daf' kardan تحویل نگرفتن tahvil na-gereftan

repulsion *n.* دفع daf' انزجار enzejâr

repulsive *adj.* دفع کننده daf'-konandeh زننده zanandeh

reputable *n.* معتبر mo'tabar خوش آیند khosh-âyand

آبرومند âberu-mand

reputation *n.* شهرت shohrat آبرو âberu

repute *n., v.* شهرت shohrat

reputed *adj.* شناخته شده shenâkhteh shodeh

reputedly *adv.* ازقرارمعلوم az qarâr-e' ma'lum

request *n., vt.* خواهش کردن khâhesh kardan

درخواست کردن dar-khâst kardan

request *n.* خواهش khahesh درخواست dar-khâast تمنا taman~â

مسئلت mas'alat

requiem *n.* فاتحه fâteheh موزیک عزا muzik-e' 'azâ

نمازوحشت namâz-e' vah-shat مرثیه marsieh

require *v.* لازم داشتن lâzem dâshtan خواستار شدن khâstâr shodan

requirement *n.* لازمه lâzemeh شرط shart

requisite *adj., n.* لازمه lâzemeh احتیاجی ehtiâji

requisition *n., vt.* درخواست کردن dar-khâst kardan

مصادره کردن mosâdereh kardan

requisition *n., vt.* استیفاء estifâ'

requital *n.* جبران jobrân جزا jazâ

reroute *v.* مسیرعوض کردن masir 'avaz kardan

resalable *adj.* بازفروختنی bâz-forukhtani

rescind *vt.* لغو laqv باطل کردن bâtel kardan

rescue *vt., n.* نجات دادن nejât dâdan

research n. تحقیق tahqiq پژوهش pazhuhesh
research v. تحقیق کردن tahqiq kardan
پژوهش کردن pazhuhesh kardan
researcher np. محقق mohaq~eq پژوهنده pazhu-handeh
resemblance n. شباهت shebâhat
resemble vt. شباهت داشتن shebâhat dâshtân
مانندبودن mânand budan
resend vt. بازفرستادن bâz ferestâdan
resent vt. رنجیدن ranjidan دلخوربودن del-khor budan
resentful n. دلخور del-khor رنجیده ranjideh
resentment n. دلخوری del-khori رنجش ranjesh
reservation n. قرارگاه qarâr-gâh
reservation n. رزرو جا rezerv-e' jâ جاگیری jâ-giri
reserve n. ذخیره zakhireh رزرو rezerv
reserve v. رزرو کردن rezerv kardan اختصاص دادن ekhtesâs dâdan
reserved v. اندوخته andukhteh ساکت sâket موقر movaq~ar
reservoir n. مخزن makh-zan سد sad~
reset vt., n. بازمیزان کردن bâz-mizân kardan
reside vi. سکونت داشتن sokunat dâshtan
اقامت داشتن eqâmat dâshtan
residence n. مسکن maskan محل اقامت mahal~-e' eqâmat
مقر maqar~
residency n. اقامت eqâmat
resident n., adj. مقیم moqim ساکن sâken
residential adj., n. مسکونی maskuni
residual adj., n. رسوبی rosubi باقی مانده bâqi-mândeh تتمه tatam~eh
residue n. ته نشین tah-neshin باقی مانده bâqi-mândeh
resign vi., vt. استعفا دادن este'fâ dâdan تسلیم شدن taslim shodan
resignation n. استعفا este'fâ تسلیم taslim
resigned n. تسلیم شده taslim shodeh
resilience n. جهندگی jahandegi پایداری pâydâri
resiliency n. پایداری pâydâri
resilient adj. پایدار pâydâr جهنده jahandeh
resin n., vt. صمغ samq
resinate n. صمغ مالیدن samq mâlidan
resist vt. مقاومت کردن moqâvemat kardan
ایستادگی کردن istâdegi kardan
resistance n. مقاومت moqâvemat ایستادگی istâdegi تاب tâb

resistant *n.* مقاوم moqâvem کننده مقاومت moqâvemat konandeh
resistible *adj.* قابل جلوگیری qâbel-e' jelo-giri
resistive *adj.* مقاوم moqâvem پایدار pâydâr
resistless *n.* غیرقابل مقاومت qeyr-e' qâbel-e' moqâvemat
resolute *adj.* پابرجا pâ-barjâ راسخ râsekh استوار ostovâr
resolution *n.* حل hal رفع raf'
resolution *n.* قطعنامه qat'-nâmeh
resolution *n.* ثبات sabât عزم 'azm استواری ostovâri
resolution *n.* آرزو ârezu عزم 'azm نیت niyat
resolve *vt., vi., n.* حل کردن hal kardan برطرف کردن bar-taraf kardan
resolved *adj.* پابرجا pâ-barjâ
resolvent *n.* حل کننده hal konandeh
resonance *n.* پیچش صدا pichesh-e' sedâ
resonate *vi., vt.* طنین داشتن tanin dâshtan
resonator *n.* طنین انداز tanin-andâz
resonent *n.* پیچنده pichandeh
resort *v.* متوسل شدن motevas~el shodan
مراجعه کردن morâje'eh kardân
متشبث شدن moteshab~es shodan
متمسک شدن motemas~ek shodan
resort *n.* استراحتگاه esterâhat-gâh گردشگاه gardesh-gâh
resound *vi., vt.* صداپیچ شدن sedâpich shodan
تشویق کردن tashviq kardan
resounding *n.* طنین انگیز tanin-angiz پرحرارت por-harârat
resource *n.* منبع manba'
resource *n.* تدبیر tad-bir چاره châreh
resourceful *n.* باتدبیر bâ-tadbir کاردان kâr-dân
respect *n., vt.* احترام گذاشتن ehterâm gozâshtan
ارج گذاشتن arj gozâshtan
respectability *n.* احترام ehterâm
respectable *adj.* محترم mohtaram آبرومند âberu-mand
respectably *n.* آبرومندانه âberu-mandâneh
respectful *adj.* احترام گذار ehterâm-gozâr مؤدب mo'adab
respectfully *adv.* محترماً mohtaraman
respecting *pre.* دربارهٔ dar bâreh-ye' درخصوص dar-khosus-e'
respective *adj.* مخصوص بخود makhsus be-khod
respectively *adv.* بترتیب betartib
respects *n.* سلام salâm

respirable *n.* قابل تنفس qâbel-e' tanaf~os
respiration *n.* نفس کشی nafas-keshi تنفس tanaf~os
respirator *n.* نفس کش nafas-kesh دستگاه اکسیژن dastgâh-e' oksyzhen
respiratory *n., vi., vt.* تنفسی tanaf~osi
respire *vi., vt.* نفس کشیدن nafas keshidan
respite *n., vt.* نفس کش nafas-kesh مهلت mohlat فرجه forjeh
resplendent *n.* درخشان derakhshân
respond *vi., vt., n.* جواب دادن javâb dâdan پاسخ دادن pâsokh dâdan
respondent *adj., n.* جوابگو javâb-gu
response *n.* جواب javâb پاسخ pâsokh عکس العمل aksol-'amal
responsibility *n.* مسئولیت mas'uliyat عهده داری 'ohdeh-dâri
responsible *adj., n.* مسئول mas'ul معتمد mo'tamed
عهده دار 'ohdeh-dâr
responsibly *adv.* مسئولانه mas'ulâneh بامسئولیت bâ-mas'uliyat
responsive *n.* جوابگو javâb-gu حساس has~âs
rest *n.* استراحت esterâhat سکون sokun
rest *v.* خواباندن khâbândan آسوده کردن âsudeh kardan
rest *n., vi.* دیگران digarân سایرین sâyerin
rest *n.* بقیه baqiyeh دیگر digar
rest *v.* استراحت کردن esterâhat kardan
rest-room *n.* دستشویی dast-shuyi مستراح mostarâh
restate *vt.* بازبیان کردن bâz-bayân kardan
restatement *n.* بازبیان bâz-bayân
restaurant *n.* رستوران resturân
restauranteur *n.* رستوران چی resturân-chi
restful *adj.* آرام بخش ârâm-bakhsh
restitution *n.* پرداخت غرامت pardâkht-e' qarâmat استرداد esterdâd
تأدیه ta'dieh
restive *adj.* ناآرام nâ-ârâm سرکش sar-kesh
restless *n.* ناآرام nâ-ârâm بیقرار bi-qarâr
restock *vt., vi.* بازاندوختن bâz-andukhtan
restoration *n.* بازپس گیری bâz-pasgiri احیاء ehyâ'
restorative *n.* نیروبخش niru-bakhsh بهوش آور be-hush-âvar
restore *v.* تعمیرکردن ta'mir kardan
تجدید بنا کردن tajdid-e' banâ kardan
restore *v.* بازپس گرفتن bâz-pas gereftan احیاء کردن ehyâ' kardan
restrain *vt.* جلوگرفتن jelo gereftan کنترل کردن kontorol kardan
restrained *n.* مسلط بخود mosal~at be-khod باکنترل bâ-kontorol

restraining *n.* جلوگیر jelo-gir منع تماس man'-e' tamâs
restraint *n.* خودداری khod-dâri جلوگیری jelo-giri
restrict *vt.* محدودکردن mahdud kardan
منحصر کردن monhaser kardan
restricted *adj.* محدود mahdud ممنوع mamnu' اختصاصی ekhtesâsi
restriction *n.* منع man' محدودیت mahdudiyat تحدید tahdid
restrictive *adj.* محدودکننده mahdud konandeh مختص mokhtas
result *n.* نتیجه natijeh دست آورد dast-âvard ماحصل mâ-hasal
result *v.* منتج شدن montaj shodan منتهی شدن montahi shodan
resultant *adj., n.* نتیجه natijeh برآیند bâr-âyand
resulting *n.* نتیجه ای natijeh-i ناشی nâshi
resumable *adj.* پس گرفتنی pas-gereftani
resume *v.* ازسرگرفتن az-sar gereftan
دوباره ادامه دادن dobâreh edâmeh dâdan
resume *n.* خلاصه kholâseh کارنامه kâr-nâmeh
resumption *n.* ازسرگیری az-sar giri ادامه edâmeh
resupinate *adj.* آویزان âvizân
resurface *vt.* دوباره سردرآوردن dobâreh-sar dar âvardan
resurge *vi.* دوباره برخواستن dobâreh bar-khâstan
resurgence *n.* رستاخیزی rastâkhizi بازخیزش bâz-khizesh
resurgent *adj.* رستاخیز rastâkhiz بازخیز bâz-khiz
resurrect *vt., vi.* زنده کردن zendeh kardan احیاء کردن ehyâ' kardan
resurrection *n.* قیامت qiâmat احیاء ehyâ' رستاخیز rastâkhiz
معاد ma'âd
resuscitate *vt.* بهوش آوردن behush âvardan
زنده کردن zendeh kardan
resuscitation *n.* بهوش آوری be-hush-âvari
retail *n., adj., adv., vt.* خرده فروشی khordeh forushi
retailer *n.* خرده فروش khordeh forush
retain *vt.* نگه داشتن negah dâshtan
retainer *n.* استخدامی estekhdâmi پیش پرداختی pish-pardâkhti
retaining wall *np.* دیوار حائل divâr-e' hâ'el
retake *n.* بازگرفتن bâz gereftan
retaliate *vi., vt.* تلافی کردن talâfi kardan
retaliatory *adj.* تلافی آمیز talâfi-âmiz انتقامی enteqâmi
retard *vi., n., vt., adj.* آهسته کردن âhesteh kardan
عقب افتادن 'aqab oftâdan
retardation *n.* عقب افتادگی 'aqab-oftâdegi

retarded *adj.* عقب افتاده 'aqab-oftâdeh
retch *vi.* غ ا ق زدن oq zadan
retched *n.* تهوع آور tahavo'-âvar
retention *n.* نگهداری negah-dâri حافظه hâfezeh
reticence *n.* کم حرفی kam-harfi
reticent *adj.* کم حرف kam-harf دهن سفت dahan-seft خوددار khod-dâr
تولب tu-lab
retinue *n.* اسکورت eskort ملتزمین moltazemin
retire *vi., vt., n.* بازنشسته کردن bâz-neshasteh kardan
استراحت کردن esterâhat kardan
retired *v.* بازنشسته bâz-neshasteh
retirement *n., adj.* بازنشستگی bâz-neshastegi
retiring *adj., vi.* کناره گیر kenâreh-gir
retort *vt., n.* جواب مشابه دادن javâb-e' moshâbeh dâdan
retortion *n.* دور خود پیچی dor-e' khod-pichi بدرفتاری bad-raftâri
retouch *vt., n.* رتوش کردن rotush kardan
retrace *v.* دوباره دنبال کردن dobâreh donbâl kardan
retract *v.* تو رفتن tu raftan پس گرفتن pas gereftan
retraction *n.* عقب کشی 'aqab-keshi پس گیری pas-giri
retractor *n.* عقب زن 'aqab-zan
retread *vt., n.* بازبافت کردن bâz-bâft kardan
روکش کردن rukesh kardan
retreat *n.* خلوتگاه khalvat-gâh
retreat *v.* عقب نشینی کردن 'aqab- neshini kardan
retrench *vt., vi.* حذف کردن hazf kardan کم کردن kam kardan
retrenchment *n.* کاهش kâhesh سنگرگاه sangar-gâh
retribution *n.* جزا jazâ کیفر keyfar مکافات mokâfât
retrievable *adj.* بازبدست آوردنی bâz bedast-âvardani
retrieval *n.* بازبدست آوری bâz bedast-âvari
retrieve *vt., vi., n.* بازبدست آوردن bâz be-dast âvardan
retriever *n.* شکارگیر shekâr-gir
retroact *vi.* ارجاع بگذشته کردن erjâ' be-gozashteh kardan
retroaction *n.* پیش شاملی pish-shâmeli
retroactive *n.* پیش شامل pish-shâmel
عطف به ماسبق 'atf beh mâ-sabaq
retrograde *adj., vt.* عقب رونده 'aqab-ravandeh پسرو pas-o
retrogress *vi.* پائین آمدن pâyin âmadan عقب رفتن 'aqab raftan
retrogression *n.* تنزل tanaz~ol برگشت bar-gasht

retrogressive *adj.* برگشت کننده bar-gasht-konandeh

retrospect *n., vi., vt.* بازنگر bâz-negar نظریگذشته nazar be-gozashteh

retrospection *n.* بازنگری bâz-negari پس نگری pas-negari

retrospective *adj., n.* بازنگرانه bâz-negar-âneh
پس نگرانه pas-negar-âneh

return *n.* بازگشت bar-gashtan رجعت rej'at

return *v.* برگرداندن bar gardân-dan پس دادن pas dâdan
برگشتن bar gashtan رجوع کردن roju' kardan

return ticket *np.* بلیط برگشت belit-e' bar-gasht

returnable *adj.* پس دادنی pas-dâdani

retuse *adj.* لب گرد lab-gerd

reunion *n.* بازپیوست bâz-peyvast

reunite *vt., vi.* بازمتحدکردن bâz-mot~ahed kardan

revamp *vt.* دوباره سروسامان دادن dobâreh sar-o sâmân dâdan

reveal *vt., n.* آشکارکردن âshkâr kardan
نمایان ساختن namâyân sâkhtan

reveille *n.* بیدارباش bi-dâr bâsh

revel *vi., n.* شادی کردن shâdi kardan لذت بردن lez~at bordan

revelation *n.* الهام elhâm آشکاری âshkâri تجلی tajal~i وحی vah-y

revelry *n.* شادی shâdi

revenge *vt., vi., n.* انتقام گرفتن enteqâm gereftan

revengeful *adj.* انتقام جو enteqâm-ju

revenue *n.* درآمد dar-âmad

reverberate *vi., vt., adj.* منعکس کردن mon'akes kardan
طنین انداختن tanin andâkhtan

reverberation *n.* انعکاس en'ekâs برگشت bargasht

revere *n., vt.* محترم شمردن mohtaram shemordan

reverence *n., vt.* احترام ehterâm حرمت hormat

reverend *adj., n.* کشیش keshish

reverent *adj.* حرمت گذار hormat-gozâr

reverential *n.* محترمانه mohtaramâneh

reversal *n.* برگشت bargasht نقض naqz

reverse *n.* پشت و رو posht-o ru وارونه vâruneh

reverse *v.* ازآنوری کردن az-ânvari kardan
برعکس کردن bar'aks kardan

reversely *adv.* برعکس bar'aks

reversible *adj., n.* پشت و روشدنی posht-o ru-shodani

reversion *n.* برگشت bargasht

revert *n., vi.* برگشتن bargashtan
review *v.* سان دیدن sân didan
review *v.* انتقادکردن enteqâd kardan
review *v.* مرورکردن morur kardan تجدیدنظرکردن tajdid-e' nazar kard
reviewer *n.* تجدیدنظرکننده tajdid-e' nazar konandeh
revile *vt., vi.* ناسزاگفتن nâ-sezâ goftan
رکیک حرف زدن rakik harf zadan
revise *vt., n.* اصلاح کردن eslâh kardan تکمیل کردن takmil kardan
revision *n.* اصلاح eslâh بازنگری bâznegari
revisionist *n., adj.* رویزیونیست revisionist
تجدیدنظرطلب tajdid-e' nazar-talab
revival *n.* احیاء ehyâ' بازگرد bâz-gard تجدیدحیات tajdid-e' hayât
revive *vt.* احیاء کردن ehyâ' kardan بهوش آوردن be-hush âvardan
revocable *n.* لغو شدنی laqv shodani
revocation *n.* لغو laqv نسخ faskh
revoice *vt.* بازصدادادن bâz-sedâ dâdan
revoke *vt., vi., n.* لغو کردن laqv kardan نسخ کردن faskh kardan
revolt *n.* شورش shuresh طغیان toqyân
revolt *v.* شورش کردن shuresh kardan طغیان کردن toqyân kardan
revolting *adj.* زننده zanandeh متهوع motehave'
مشمئزکننده moshma'ez-konandeh
revolution *n.* انقلاب enqelâb شورش shuresh
revolution *n.* گردش gardesh چرخش charkhesh
revolutionalize *n.* تغییراساسی دادن taqyir-e' asâsi dâdan
revolutionary *adj., n.* انقلابی enqelâbi
revolve *vi., vt.* چرخیدن charkhidan دور گشتن dor gâshtan
revolver *n.* ششلول sheshlul
revolving *adj.* گردان gardân
revue *n.* نمایش نامه namâyesh-nâmeh
revulsion *n.* چندش chendesh
revulsive *adj., n.* چندش آور chendesh-âvar
reward *n.* پاداش pâdâsh اجر ajr ثواب savâb
reward *v.* پاداش دادن pâdâsh dâdan جایزه دادن jâyezeh dâdan
rewire *vt.* بازسیم پیچی کردن bâz-sim-pichi kardan
rewrite *v.* بازنویسی کردن bâz-nevisi kardan
rhetoric *n.* علم بیان 'elm-e' bayân غلنبه گویی qolonbeh-guyi
rhetorical *n.* علم بیانی 'elm-e' bayâni غلنبه گو qolonbeh-gu
rhetorician *n.* عالم بیان 'âlem-e' bayân غلنبه گو qolonbeh-gu

rheum *n.* ریزش زکامی rizesh-e′ zokâmi
rheumatic *adj., n.* رماتیسمی româtismi
rheumatism *n.* رماتیسم româtism بادمفاصل bâd-e′ mafâsel
rhinestone *n.* الماس شیشه ای almâs-e′ shisheh-i
rhinoceros *n.* کرگدن kar-gadan
rhombus *n.* لوزی lozi
rhubarb *n.* ریواس rivâs
rhyme *n., vt., vi.* قافیه داشتن qâfieh dâshtan
rhythm *n.* ریتم ritm توازن tavâzon
rhythmic(al) *adj.* باتناسب bâ-tanâsob موزون mozun
rib *v.* دست انداختن dast andâkhtan
rib *n.* دنده dandeh میله mileh
ribbon *n., vt., vi.* نوار navâr روبان rubân
rice *n., adj., vt.* برنج berenj
rich *adj., n.* غنی qani پرچربی por-charbi
rich *adj., n.* پولدار pul-dâr ثروتمند servat-mand توانگر tavân-gar
دارا dârâ
riches *n.* مال mâl ثروت servat
richly *adv.* بطورغنی betor-e′ qani
rickets *n.* راشیتیسم râshitism استخوان نرمی ostokhân narmi
rickety *adj.* ضعیف za′if نکسنی fakasani
ricochet *n., vi.* کمانه کردن kamâneh kardan
rid *v.* خلاص کردن khalâs kardan
riddance *n.* شرخلاصی shar khalâsi
riddle *n., vt.* معما mo′am~â
ride *n., vi., vt.* سوارشدن savâr shodan سواری savâri
ride(down) *n.* زدن و انداختن zadan va andâkhtan
ride(out) *n.* تحمل taham~ol کردن سپری separi kardan
rider *n.* سوار savâr
ridge *n., vt., vi.* لبه labeh تیغه tiqeh گرده gordeh
ridicule *n., vt.* مسخره maskhareh استهزاء کردن estehzâ′ kardan
riding *n., adj.* سواری savâri
rife *adj.* متداول motedâvel فراوان farâvân
riff-raff *n.* خرت و پرت khert-o pert آشغال âshqâl
riffle *n.* ورق برزدن varaq bor zadan
rifle *n.* تفنگ tofang
rifle *v.* جستجووغارت کردن josteju va qârat kardan
rifle range *np.* تیررس tir-res میدان تیراندازی meydân-e′ tirandâzi

rifleman *n.* تفنگدار tofang-dâr

rift *n., vt., vi.* شكاف دادن shekâf dâdan چاك châk

rig *n.* لوازم lavâzem

rig *v.* مجهز كردن mojah~az kardan دستكارى كردن dast-kâri kardan

rig *n.* كشتى kashti

rig *n.* كاميون kâmion

rigger *n.* نصب كننده nasb konandeh داربست dârbast

right *adj., n., adv., vi.* راست râst

right *adj., n., adv., vi.* حق haq~

right *adj., n., adv., vi.* درست dorost صحيح sahih

right angle *n.* زاوية نود درجه zâviyeh-ye' navad darajeh

right wing *n.* دست راستى dast-e' râsti

right-handed *adj., adv.* راست دست râst-dast

right-minded *adj.* راست بين râst-bin درست نكر dorost-fekr

right-of-way *n.* حق تقدم haq~-e' taqad~om

rightabout *n., adv.* براست راست be-râst râst

righteous *adj., n.* راست-كار râst-kâr پارسا pârsâ

righteousness *n.* راستكارى râst-kâri پارسايى pârsâyi

rightful *adj.* حقدار haq-dâr ذيحق zihaq~ محق moheq~

rightfully *adv.* حقاً haq~an درحق dar haq

rightly *adv.* انصافاً ensâfan درست dorost

righto! *n.* باشه bâsheh!

rigid *adj.* سفت seft سخت sakht

rigidity *n.* سفتى sefti سختى sakhti

rigor *n.* سختى sakhti سختگيرى sakht-giri پشتكار poshtekâr

rigorous *adj.* سختگير sakht-gir باپشتكار bâ-poshtekâr

rile *vt.* غليظ كردن qaliz kardan عصبانى كردن 'asabâni kardan

rill *n.* جويبار juy-bâr

rim *v., n.* لبه labeh طوقه toqeh

rime *vi., n., vt.* برفك barfak

rimose *n.* چاك چاك châk châk

rind *n.* پوست pust

ring *n.* حلقه halqeh انگشتر angoshtar گود god

ring *v.* زنگ زدن zang zadan

ring(in) *n.* باكلك آوردن bâ kalak âvardan

ring(up) *n.* حساب كردن hesâb kardan

ringed *adj., v.* حلقه دار halqeh-dâr

ringer *n.* شبيه shabih قلابى qol~âbi

ringleader *n.* سردسته sar-dasteh
ringmaster *n.* رهبرسیرک rahbar-e' sirk
ringside *n.* کنار گود kenâr-e' god
ringworm *n.* پوست خوره pust-khoreh
rink *n.* میدان یخ meydân-e' yakh
rinse *vt., n.* آب کشیدن âb keshidan شستن shostan
riot *v.* آشوب بپاکردن âshub be-pâ kardan غوغاکردن qoqâ kardan
riot *n.* آشوب âshub غوغا qoqâ بلوا balvâ
riotous *n.* آشوب گر âshub-gar فتنه جو fetneh-ju
rip *v.* پاره کردن pâreh kardan جردادن jer dâdan
rip *n.* پاره گی pâreh-gi
rip *n.* امواج amvâj
rip(into) *n.* حمله کردن hamleh kardan
rip(off) *n.* دزدی کردن dozdi kardan
کلاه برداری کردن kolâh-bardâri kardan
rip-off *n.* دزدی dozdi کلاه برداری kolâh bardâri
ripe *vt.* رسیده resideh مستعد mosta'ed
ripen *vt., vi.* رسیدن residan
ripper *n.* جردهنده jer dahandeh
ripping *adj., v.* عالی 'âli
ripple *vi., vt., n.* موج کوچک moj-e' kuchek تشنج tashan~oj
ripsaw *n.* اره مویی ar~eh muyi
riptide *n.* جزر مخالف jazr-e' mokhâlef
rise *v.* بلند شدن boland shodan بالارفتن bâlâ raftan
rise *v.* قیام کردن qiâm kardan
rise *n., vi., vt.* پف کردن pof kardan ور آمدن var âmadan
riser *n.* برخیزنده bar-khiz-andeh
risible *adj., n.* خنده آور khandeh-âvar خندیدنی khandidani
rising *v.* صعودی so'udi طلوع tolu'
risk *n., vt.* بخطرانداختن be-khatar andâkhtan ریسک کردن risk kardan
risky *adj.* خطرناک khatar-nâk ریسک دار risk-dâr
risque' *n.* خارج ازادب khârej az adab دورازنزاکت dur az nezâkat
rite(s) *n.* آیین âyin مراسم marâsem
ritual *n., adj.* رسم rasm تشریفات tashrifât
ritualist *n.* تشریفاتی tashrifâti
ritually *adv.* مطابق رسم motâbeq-e' rasm
ritzy *adj.* مجلل mojal~al
rival *n.* رقیب raqib

rival *v.* رقابت کردن reqâbat kardan
rival *n.* حریف harif
rivalry *n.* رقابت reqâbat
rive *vt., vi.* پاره کردن pâreh kardan شکستن shekastan
riven *v., adj.* پاره شده pâreh-shodeh
river *n.* رود rud رودخانه rud-khâneh
riverside *n.* کنار رودخانه kenâr-e' rud-khâneh
rivet *n., vt.* میخ پرچ mikh-parch
roach *n.* سوسک susk
roach *n.* ماهی قنات mâhi-e' qanât
road *n.* راه râh جاده jâd~eh طریق tariq سبیل sabil
roadblock *n.* راه بند râh-band جاده بست jâd~eh-bast
roadside *n.* کنارجاده kenâr-e' jâd~eh
roam *vi., vt., n.* گشتن gashtan آواره بودن âvâreh budan
roan *adj., n.* قزل qezel
roar *vi.* غرش کردن qor~esh kardan
roaring *n., adj., adv.* غرش qoresh پررونق por ronaq
roast *vt., n., adj.* کباب kabâb سرخ کردن sorkh kardan
roaster *n.* کباب کن kabâb-kon
rob *vt.* دزدیدن dozdidan
robber *n.* دزد dozd سارق sâreq
robbery *n.* دزدی dozdi سرقت serqat
robe *n., vt., vi.* جامه jâmeh ردا radâ خرقه kherqeh
robin *n.* سینه سرخ sineh sorkh
robot *n.* آدم مکانیکی âdam mekâniki
robust *adj.* گردن کلفت gardan koloft ترگل ورگل targol vargol
roc *n.* رخ rokh
rock *n.* سنگ sang صخره sakhreh تکان takân
rock *v.* تکان دادن takân dâdan جنباندن jonbândan
rock bottom *np.* نازلترین nâzel-tarin
rock candy *n.* نبات nabât
rock-bound *adj.* صخره دار sakhreh-dâr
rocker *n.* روروئه roro'eh گهواره gah-vâreh
rockery *n.* سنگ فروشی sang-forushi
rocket *n., vt., vi.* موشک mushak سفینه safineh
rocket launcher *np.* موشک انداز mushak-andâz
rocking chair *np.* صندلی گهواره ای sandali-e' gahvâreh-i
rocky *adj.* سنگی sangi صخره ای sakhreh-i

rod *n., vt.* ميله mileh
rodent *adj.* جونده javandeh
rogue *n., vi., vt.* الاف alâf شياد shayâd
roil *vt.* گل آلود gel-âlud عصبانى كردن 'asabâni kardan
roiled *adj.* تيره tireh تار târ كدر keder
roily *adj.* گل آلود gel-âlud عصبانى 'asabâni
role *n.* نقش naqsh رل rol
roll *v.* لخت كردن lokht kardan
roll *n.* قرص qors گرده gordeh
roll *v.* غلتاندن qaltândan گرداندن gardândan
roll *n.* ليست list طومار tumâr
roll call *n.* حاضرغايبى hâzer qâyebi
rollaway *adj.* چرخ دار charkh-dâr
rollback *n.* برگشت به سابق bargasht beh-sâbeq
roller *n.* غلتك qaltak بوم غلتون bum-qaltun
roller-skate *vi.* اسكيت eskeyt
rollick *vi.* خوشى كردن khoshi kardan
rollicking *adj.* خوش گذران khosh-gozarân
rolling *n.* گردان gardân
rolling pin *np.* غلتك آرد qaltak-e' ârd
roly-poly *n.* خپل khepel
romance *n.* عشق و عاشقى 'eshq-o 'âsheqi
romantic *adj., n.* عاشق مآب 'âsheq-maâb عشقى 'eshqi
romantically *adv.* عاشقانه 'âsheqâneh
romanticize *vt., vi.* عشق بافى كردن 'eshq-bâfi kardan
romp *vi., n.* شلوغ بازى sholuq-bâzi
rompish *adj.* شلوغ كن sholuq-kon
roof *v., n.* بام bâm طاق tâq سقف saqf
roofer *n.* سقف گذار saqf-gozâr
roofing *n.* سقف گذارى saqf-gozâri
roofless *adj.* بى سقف bi-saqf
rook *n.* رخ rokh
rook *n.* كلاغ kalâq
rook *n.* كلاش kal~âsh
room *v.* جادادن jâ dâdan اطاق دادن otâq dâdan
room *n.* اطاق otâq جا jâ فضا fazâ
room and board *np.* پانسيون pânsion
roomful *n.* يک اطاق پر yek otâq por

roominess *n.* جادارى jâ-dâri
roommate *n.* هم اطاق ham-otâq
roomy *adj., n.* جادار jâ-dâr
roost *n.* کرچ کردن korch kardan نشستن neshastan
rooster *n.* خروس khorus
root *n., vi., vt.* ریشه گرفتن risheh gereftan
root *n.* ریشه risheh بیخ و بن bikh-o bon عرق erq
root(and branch) *n.* بکلى be-kol~i
root(out) *n.* ریشه کن کردن risheh-kan kardan
rooty *n., vt.* پرریشه por risheh
rope *n., vt., vi.* طناب tanâb ریسمان rismân بند band
ropery *n.* طناب سازى tanâb-sâzi
rosary *n.* تسبیح tasbih گلستان golestân
rose *adj., n., vt.* گل سرخ gol-e' sorkh
rose water *n.* گلاب golâb
rosebud *n.* غنچهٔ گل سرخ qoncheh-ye' gol-e' sorkh
rosebush *n.* گلبن gol-bon
roster *n.* لیست اسم list-e' esm
rostrum *n.* منبر menbar تریبون teribun میزخطابه miz-e' khatâbeh
rosy *adj.* گلگون gol-gun درخشان derakhshân
rot *vi., vt., n.* پوسیدن pusidan گندیدن gandidan
      فاسد شدن fâsed shodan
rotary *n., adj.* گرداننده gardandeh بل برنگى bol-berengi
rotate *adj.* چرخیدن charkhidan چرخاندن charkhândan
rotation *n.* چرخش charkhesh گردش gardesh
rotator *n.* گرداننده gardâ-nandeh
rote *n.* حافظهاى hâfezeh-i عادتى 'âdati
rotgut *n.* عرق سگى 'araq sagi
rotisserie *n.* کباب کن kabâb-kon
rotor *n.* چکش برق chakosh barq
rotten *adj.* گندیده gandideh فاسد fâsed
rotund *adj.* گرد gerd غلنبه qolonbeh
rotunda *n.* سالن گرد sâlon-e' gerd
rouge *adj., n., vt., vi.* روژ ruzh ماتیک mâtik
rough *adj., n., adv., vt.* خشن khashen زبر zebr ناملایم nâ-molayem
rough peach *n.* شفتالو shaf-tâlu
roughly *adv.* تقریباً taqriban همین جورى hamin-juri
roughneck *adj.* لمپن lompan لات lât گردن کلفت gardan-koloft

round *adj., n., adv., pre.* گرد gerd مدور modav~ar
round *adj., n., adv., pre.* روند rond دوره doreh
round *adj., n., adv., pre.* کامل kâmel بی کسر bi-kasr
round *adj., n., adv., pre.* شلیک shelik نشنگ feshang
round robin *np.* دوره ای doreh-i همه بازی hameh-bâzi
round(about) *n.* همه طرف hameh taraf
round(off) *n.* گردکردن gerd kardan تمام کردن tamâm kardan
round(up) *n.* جمع کردن jam' kardan
round-table *adj.* میزگرد miz-e' gerd
round-trip *adj.* سفر دوطرفه safar-e' do-tarâfeh
  رفت و برگشت raft-o bargasht
roundabout *adj., n.* غیرمستقیم qeyr-e' mostaqim
rounded *adj.* گرد gerd
rounder *n.* گشتی gashti
rounds *n.* گشت gasht
roundup *n.* جمع آوری jam'-âvari گردآوری gerd-âvari
rouse *n.* بیدارکردن bidâr kardan انگولک کردن angulak kardan
rousing *adj.* پرهیجان por-hayajân
roust *n.* تکان دادن takân dâdan بیرون کردن birun kardan
rout *vi., vt., n.* تاروماركردن târ-o mâr kardan
route *v., n.* جاده jâd~eh راه râh
routine *n., adj.* معمولی ma'muli هرروزی har-ruzi
rove *n., v.* آواره گشتن âvâreh gashtan
rover *n.* آواره âvâreh ولگرد velgard
row *n.* ردیف radif صف saf
row *v.* پاروزدن pâru zadan
rowdy *n., adj.* جنجالی janjâli پرهیاهو por hayâ-hu
royal *adj., n.* سلطنتی saltanati پادشاهی pâdeshâhi شاهانه shâhâneh
  ملوکانه molukaneh
royalist *n.* سلطنت طلب saltanat-talab
royalty *n.* خانوادهٔ سلطنتی khânvâdeh-ye' saltanati
royalty *n.* حق الامتیاز haq~ol-emtiâz
rub *n., vt., vi.* مالش mâlesh ماساژ mâsâzh
rub(down) *n.* مالش دادن mâlesh dâdan ماساژ دادن mâsâzh dâdan
  مالیدن mâlidan
rub(off) *n.* ماسیدن mâsidan
rub(out) *n.* پاک کردن pâk kardan کلک کندن kalak kandan
rub(the wrong way) *n.* باعث ناراحتی شدن bâ'es-e' nârâhati shodan

rubber *n., vi., adj.* لاستیک lâstik

rubber-stamp *vt.* بدون فکرتصدیق کردن bedun-e' fekr tasdiq kardan

rubberneck *n.* گردن کشی کردن gardan-keshi kardan

rubbers *n.* کاپوت kâput

rubbers *n.* گالش gâlesh

rubbish *n.* آشغال âshqâl چرند charand مزبله mazbaleh

rubble *n.* خرابه kharâbeh آوار âvâr

rubella *n.* سرخک sorkhak

rubescent *adj.* سرخ شده sorkh shodeh

ruby *adj., n.* یاقوت yâqut یاقوتی yâquti

ruck *n.* دسته dasteh چین خوردن chin khordan

rucksack *n.* کوله بار kuleh-bâr

ruckus *n.* شلوغی sholuqi هیاهو hayâhu

rudder *n.* سکان sok~ân

ruddle *n., vt.* سرخ کردن sorkh kardan

ruddy *adj., adv.* سرخ چهره sorkh chehreh گلگون golgun

rude *adj.* بی تربیت bi-tarbiyat بی نزاکت bi-nezâkat

rudiment(s) *n.* اصل asl ابتدا ebtedâ

rudimentary *adj.* اصلی asli ابتدایی ebtedâyi

rueful *n.* متأسف mote'as~ef تأسف آور ta'as~of-âvar

ruff *n., vt., vi.* یخه چین چین yakheh chin-chin

ruffian *n.* لمپن lompan جاهل jâhel لات lât چاقوکش châqu-kesh

ruffle *vt., vi., n.* چین چین کردن chin chin kardan
چروک دادن choruk dâdan

rug *n.* قالیچه qâlicheh

rugged *adj.* ناهموار nâ-hamvâr زمخت zomokht

ruin *v.* خراب کردن kharâb kardan ویران کردن virân kardan

ruin *n.* خرابه kharâbeh خرابی kharabi

ruinous *adj.* خراب کننده kharâb-konandeh مخرب mokhar~eb

rule *n.* قانون qânun قاعده qâ'edeh ضابطه zâbeteh دستور dastur

rule *v.* حکومت کردن hokumat kardan

rule *n.* حکومت hokumat سلطه solteh

rule(of thumb) *n.* قانون تجربهای qânun-e' tajrobeh-i

rule(out) *n.* ردکردن rad kardan

ruler *n.* حاکم hâkem فرمانروا farmân-ravâ

ruler *n.* خط کش khat-kesh

ruling *n., v., adj.* حکم hokm

rum *adj., n.* عرق نیشکر 'araq-e' ney-shekar

rumble *vi., vt., n.* غرش کردن qor~esh kardan
غرنب صدا دادن qoronb sedâ dâdan
ruminant *n., adj.* نشخوارکننده nosh-khâr konandeh
ruminate *vi., vt.* نشخوارکردن nosh-khâr kardan
rummage *n.* خرت و پرت khert-o pert
rummage *v.* زیرورو کردن zir-o ru kardan
بدقت گشتن be-deq~at gashtan
rumor *vt.* شایعه shâye'eh
rump *n.* کفل kafal بالای ران bâlâ-ye' rân
rumple *vt., vi., n.* چروک دادن choruk dâdan
run *v.* جاری بودن jâri budan
run *v.* گرداندن gardândan
run *v.* دویدن davidan فرارکردن farâr kardan
run *v.* شرکت کردن sherkat kardan
run(across) *n.* برخورد کردن barkhord kardan
run(away with) *n.* راحت بردن râhat bordan
run(down) *n.* زدن و انداختن zadan va andâkhtan
run(for it) *n.* دررفتن dar raftan
run(in) *n.* اضافه کردن ezâfeh kardan دستگیر کردن dastgir kardan
run(into) *n.* برخوردن bar khordan تصادف کردن tasâdof kardan
run(on) *n.* ادامه دادن edâmeh dâdan
run(out of) *n.* تمام کردن tamâm kardan
run(out) *n.* تمام کردن tamâm kardan بیرون کردن birun kardan
run(over) *n.* زیرگرفتن zir gereftan
run(through) *n.* بباد دادن bebâd dâdan
سرسری نگاه کردن sarsari negâh kardan
run-around *n., adj.* دست بسری dast be-sari سردرگمی sar dar gomi
run-down *adj.* ازکارافتاده az kâr oftâdeh خراب شده kharâb shodeh
run-in *n., adj.* برخورد bar-khord
run-of-the-mill *adj.* معمولی ma'muli
run-off *n.* سرریز sar-riz مساوی شکن mosâvi-shekan
runabout *n.* ولگرد vel-gard
runaway *n.* فراری farâri سرسام آور sar-sâm-âvar
rung *n., v.* پله نردبان pel~eh nardebân میل mil
runner *n.* دونده davandeh
runner-up *n.* نفردوم nafar-e' dov~om
running *n., vi., vt., adj.* دوندگی davandegi جاری jâri روان ravân
runt *n.* نسقلی fesqeli

runty *adj.* كوتوله kutuleh

runway *n.* نشین‌گاه neshin-gâh باند bând

rupee *n.* روپیه rupieh

rupture *n., vt., vi.* قطع کردن qat' kardan ترکیدن tarekidan

rural *adj.* روستایی rustâyi

ruse *vt., n., adj.* کلک kalak حیله hileh

rush *v.* عجله کردن 'ajaleh kardan هل کردن hol kardan

rush *n.* یورش yuresh هجوم hojum

rush *v.* یورش بردن yuresh bordan هجوم آوردن hojum âvardan

rush hour *np.* شلوغی ترافیک sholuqi-e' terâfik

russet *n., adj.* حنایی hanâyi

Russia *n.* روسیه rusiyeh

rust *n., vi., vt., adj.* زنگ زدن zang zadan

rustic *adj., n.* ناموزن nâ-mozun دهاتی dehâti

rustle *vi., vt., n.* خش و خش khesh-o khesh

rustle up *n.* جمع آوری کردن jam' âvari kardan

rustler *n.* دزد dozd گاو دزد gâv-dozd

rusty *adj.* زنگ زده zang-zadeh خشک khoshk آجری رنگ âjori-rang

rut *n., vi.* شیاردادن shiyâr dâdan

ruthless *adj.* بیرحم bi-rahm قصی القلب qasyol qalb

rutilant *n.* درخشان derakh-shân

rye *n.* چاودار châvdâr دیوک diuk

S s s

S.O.S. *n.* کمک komak
sabbatical *n.* مرخصی morkhasi
saber *n., vt.* شمشیر shamshir
saber rattling *n.* شمشیرکشی shamshir-keshi
saber-toothed *n.* تیزدندان tiz-dandân
sable *n., adj.* سمور samur سیاه پوش siâh-push
sabotage *n., vt.* خرابکاری کردن kharâb-kâri kardan
کارشکنی کردن kâr-shekani kardan
saboteur *n.* خرابکار kharâb-kâr
sac *n.* کیسه kiseh
sachet *n.* کیسه کوچک kiseh kuchek عنبرچه 'anbar-cheh
sack *n.* کیسه kiseh ساک sâk
sack *n.* رختخواب rakhte-khâb
sack *v.* بیرون کردن birun kardan
sack *v.* غارت کردن qârat kardan
sack *v.* تاراج کردن târâj kardan
sackful *n.* یک کیسه پر yek kiseh por
sacrament *n.* آئین مقدس â'in-e' moqad~as
sacramental *adj.* آئین مقدسی â'in-e' moqad~asi
sacred *adj.* مقدس moqad~as
sacrifice *n., vt., vi.* قربانی qorbâni فداکردن fadâ kardan
sacrificial *n.* قربانی qorbâni فدایی fadâyi
sacrilegious *adj.* توهین به مقدسات tohin beh moqad~asât
sad *n.* غمگین qamgin متأسف mote'as~ef
sadden *vt., vi.* غمگین کردن qamgin kardan
saddle *n., vt.* زین کردن zin kardan
saddle strap *n.* فتراک fetrâk
saddlebag *n.* خورجین khorjin
saddler *n.* زین ساز zin-sâz
saddlery *n.* زین سازی zin-sâzi
sadism *n.* جنون sâdism جنون jonun
sadist *n., adj.* سادیست sâdist
sadistic *adj.* سادیستی sâdisti دیوانه وار divâneh-vâr
safari *n.* سفرشکاری safar-e' shekâri
safe *adj., n.* مطمئن motma'en سالم sâlem امن amn
safe *adj., n.* گاوصندوق gâv-sandoq
safe deposit box *n.* صندوق امانتی sandoq-e' amânati

safebreaker *n.* گاوصندوق شکن gâv-sandoq-shekan
safeconduct *n.* عبورسالم 'obur-e' sâlem
safecracker *n.* گاوصندوق شکن gâv-sandoq-shekan
safeguard *n., vt.* مواظبت کردن movâzebat kardan
محافظت کردن mohâfezat kardan
safekeeping *n.* امانت amânat
safety *n.* سلامت salâmat ایمنی imani ضامن zâmen
safety pin *np.* سنجاق قفلی sanjâq qofli
saffron *n.* زعفران za'ferân
sag *vi., vt., n.* شل شدن shol shodan افت کردن oft kardan
saga *n.* داستان پهلوانی dâstân-e' pahlevâni حماسه hemâseh
sagacity *n.* تیزهوشی tiz-hushi زیرکی ziraki
sage *n., adj.* یوشن yoshan درمنه deramneh
sage *n., adj.* دانا dânâ خردمند kherad-mand
Sagittarius *n.* قوس qos آذر âzar
sail *n.* بادبان bâd-bân
sail *v.* کشتی راندن kashti rândan
sail(into) *n.* حمله ورشدن hamleh-var shodan
sailboat *n.* قایق بادبانی qâyeq-e' bâd-bâni
sailer *n.* بادبان رو bâd-bân-ro
sailing *n.* کشتیرانی kashti-râni
sailor *n.* ملوان malevân
saint *n., vt.* مقدس moqad~as
sainthood *n.* تقدس tagad~os
saintly *adj.* مقدسانه moqad~asâneh
sake *n.* خاطر khâter محض mahz
salable *adj.* فروش رفتنی forush-raftani
salad *n.* سالاد sâlâd
salad dressing *np.* سس سالاد sos-e' sâlâd
salamander *n.* سمندر samandar
salary *n.* مزد mozd حقوق hoquq مواجب mavâjeb
sale *n.* فروش forush
sale *n.* حراج harâj
sales *n., adj.* فروش forush
sales tax *n.* مالیات فروش mâliât-e' forush
salesgirl *n.* فروشندۀ زن forushandeh-ye' zan
saleslady *n.* خانم فروشنده khânom-e' forushandeh
salesman *n.* فروشنده forushandeh

salient *n.* برجسته barjesteh جهنده jahandeh
saline *adj., n.* نمکی namaki نمکدار namak-dâr
saliva *n.* آب دهان âb-dahân بزاق bozâq
salon *n.* سالن آرایش sâlon-e' ârâyesh
saloon *n.* کافه kâfeh میخانه meykhâneh
saloon keeper *np.* کافه چی kâfeh-chi
salt *adj., vt.* نمک namak
salt of the earth *n.* بی نظیر bi-nazir ممتاز momtâz
salt shaker *np.* نمکدان namak-dân
salt water *np.* آب نمک âb namak آب شور âb-e' shur
salted *adj.* نمک زده namak-zadeh
saltiness *n.* شوری shuri
saltpeter *n.* شوره shureh
salty *n.* نمکی namaki شور shur زیرک zirak
salutary *adj.* سلامت آور salâmat-âvar سودمند sud-mand
salutation *n.* سلام salâm تهنیت tahniyat
salute *adj., v., vt., vi.* سلام دادن salâm dâdan
درود فرستادن dorud ferestâdan
salute! *n.* بسلامتی be-salâmati!
salvage *n., vt.* نجات دادن nejât dâdan بازیابی کردن bâzyâbi kardan
salvation *n.* نجات nejât رستگاری rastegâri
salve *n., v., vi., vt.* داروزدن dâru zadan تسکین دادن taskin dâdan
salvo *n.* شلیک shelik
same *adj., pro.* یک جور yekjur همان hamân
sameness *n.* یک جوری yekjuri یکسانی yeksâni
samll *n.* کم kam جزئی joz'i
sample *n., adj., vt.* نمونه گرفتن nemuneh gereftan
امتحان کردن emtehân kardan
sample *n., adj., vt.* نمونه nemuneh
sampling *n., v.* نمونه گیری nemuneh-giri
sanatorium *n.* نوانخانه navânkhâneh آسایشگاه âsâyeshgâh
sanatory *adj.* سلامت آور salâmat-âvar
sanctification *n.* تقدیس taqdis تطهیر tat-hir
sanctified *adj.* مقدس moqad~as مطهر motah~ar
sanctify *n.* تقدیس taqdis تطهیر کردن tat-hir kardan
sanctimonious *adj.* زاهدانه zâhedâneh روحانی نما rohâni-namâ
sanctimony *n.* شبه روحانی shebhe ruhâni
sanction *v.* تصویب کردن tasvib kardan تصدیق کردن tasdiq kardan

sanction *n.* تحریم tahrim جریمه jarimeh
sanctity *n.* تقدس taqad~os روحانیت ruhâniyat
sanctuary *n.* پناهگاه panâhgâh حرم haram
sand *n., vt.* شن shen ریگ rig ماسه mâseh
sand trap *np.* چاله شن châleh-ye shen
sand-blind *adj.* نیم کور nimkur
sand-cast *n.* شن قالبی کردن shen-qâlebi kardân
sandal(s) *n.* کفش صندل kafshe sandal
sandalwood *n.* چوب صندل chube sandal
sandbag *n.* کیسه شن kiseh-shen
sandbag *v.* دون پاچیدن dun pâchidan
sandblast *n., vt., vi.* شن پاشی shen-pâshi
sandbox *n.* جعبه شن ja'beh shen
sander *n.* سنباده زن sonbâdeh-zan
sandglass *n.* ساعت شنی sâ'ate sheni
sandpaper *n., vt.* سنباده sonbâdeh
sandpiper *n.* یلوه yalveh
sandstone *n.* سنگ شنی sange sheni
sandstorm *n.* شن باد shenbâd
sandwich *vt.* ساندویچ sândevich
sandy *adj.* شنی sheni زردکمرنگ zarde kamrang
sane *adj.* عاقل 'âqel سالم sâlem
sane *adj.* عاقلانه 'âqelâneh معقولانه ma'qulâneh
sang-froid *n.* خونسردی khun sardi
sanguinary *adj.* خونین khunin
sanguine *n.* خونی khuni دلگرم delgarm
sanitarian *adj., n.* بهداشت behdâsht
sanitarium *n.* آسایشگاه âsâyeshgâh
sanitary *n.* بهداشتی behdâshti تمیز tamiz
sanitation *n.* بهداشت behdâsht تمیزکاری tamiz-kâri
sanity *n.* سلامت عقل salâmate 'aql
sans *pre.* بدون bedun-e' بی bi
Santa Claus *np.* پاپانویل pâpâ no'el
sap *adj.* خرفت khereft ببو babu پخمه pakhmeh
sap *n.* شیره shireh عصاره 'osâreh
sap *v.* ازپایه کندن az pâyeh kandan
sapid *n.* خوش طعم khosh-ta'm
sapience *n.* عقل 'aql خرد kherad

sapient *adj.* عاقل 'âqel خردمند kherad-mand
sapless *n.* بی شیره bishireh بی جان bijân
sapling *n.* نهال nahâl
sapphire *n., adj.* یاقوت کبود yâqute kabud
sappy *adj.* پرشیره porshireh ابله ablah
sarcasm *n.* طعنه ta'neh کنایه kenâyeh
sarcastic *adj.* کنایه دار kenâyeh-dâr
sarcophagus *n.* مقبره maqbareh
sardonic *adj.* کنایه دار kenâyeh-dâr
sash *n.* کمربند kamar-band
sashay *vi.* سرخوردن sor khordan
sass *n., vt.* حاضرجوابی کردن hâzer-javâbi kar
گستاخی کردن gostâkhi kardan
sassy *adj., n.* حاضرجواب hâzer-javâb گستاخ gostâkh
Satan *n.* شیطان sheytân
satanic(al) *n.* شیطانی sheytâni
satchel *n.* کیف رکابی kif-e'rekâbi
satellite *n., adj.* قمرمصنوعی qamar masnu'i ماهواره mâhvâreh
satiable *adj.* راضی شدنی râzi-shodani سیرشدنی sir-shodani
satiate *vt., adj.* راضی râzi سیرکردن sir kardan
satiation *n.* اقناع eqnâ' ارضاء erzâ'
satin *n., adj.* ساتن sâtan
satire *n.* طنز tanz هجو hajv
satirical *adj.* طنزآمیز tanz-âmiz
satirist *n.* طنزنویس tanz-nevis
satirize *vt.* طنزنویسی کردن tanz-nevisi kard
بمسخره گرفتن be-maskhareh gereftân
satisfaction *n.* رضایت rezâyat خشنودی khoshnoudi
رضامندی rezâ-mandi
satisfaction *n.* جبران jobrân ایفا ifâ
satisfactory *adj.* رضایت بخش rezâyat-bakhsh
satisfied *adj., vi.* راضی râzi متقاعد moteqâ'ed خشنود khoshnoud
satisfy *vt., vi.* راضی کردن râzi kardan سیرکردن sir kardan
satrap *n.* ساتراپ sâtrâp استاندار ostândâr
satrapy *n.* استانداری estândâri
saturate *n., adj.* اشباع کردن eshbâ' kardan
saturated *adj.* اشباع شده eshbâ'-shodeh
saturation *n.* اشباع eshbâ'

Saturday *n.* شنبه shanbeh
Saturn *n.* زحل zohal کیوان keyvân
sauce *n., vt.* سس sos رب rob
saucepan *n.* کماجدان komâj-dân
saucer *n.* نعلبکی na'lbeki
saucy *adj.* پررو por-ru گستاخ gostâkh
sauna *n.* حمام بخار hamâme bokhâr
saunter *vi.* ول گشتن vel gashtan الاف گشتن alâf gashtan
sausage *n.* سوسیس sosis سوسیسون sosison
saute' *n.* تفت دادن tâfte dâdân
savage *adj.* درنده darandeh وحشی vahshi
savagery *n.* وحشی گری vahshigari بیرحمی birahmi
savanna *n.* علف زار 'alafzâr
savant *n.* دانا dânâ
save *v.* پس انداز کردن pasandâz kardan اندوختن andukhtan
save *v.* نجات دادن nejât dâdan
save -prep. *n.* جز joz بجز bejoz
saver *n.* صرفه جو sarfeh-ju ناجی nâji
saving *v.* پس انداز pas-andâz
saving *v.* نجات nejât
saving *v.* پس اندازی pas-andâzi صرفه جویی sarfeh-juyi
savings *n.* پس انداز pasandâz اندوخته andukhteh
savings account *np.* حساب پس انداز hesâb-e' pasandâ
savior *n.* ناجی nâji نجات دهنده nejât-dahandeh
savor *n., vi., vt.* مزه دادن mazeh dâdan لذت بردن lez~at bordan
savory *adj., n.* خوش مزه khosh-mazeh
savvy *n.* نهمیدن fahmidan شیرفهم شدن shir-fahm shodan
saw *n., vt., vi.* اره کردن ar~eh kardan
sawdust *n.* خاک اره khâk-ar~eh
sawmill *n.* چوب بری کارخانۀ kârk-hâneh-ye' chu
sawyer *n.* اره کش ar~eh-kesh
say *n.* حرف harf نظر nazar
say *v.* گفتن goftan
say-so *n.* حق حرف زدن haq~-e' harf-zadan
saying *n., v.* گفته gofteh سخن sokhan
scab *n.* چرک پوست cherk-pust
scab *n.* اعتصاب شکن e'tesâb
scabbard *n., vt.* غلاف qalâf

scabby *adj.* زخم و زیلی zakhmo zili

scads *n.* خیلی زیاد kheyli ziâd یک خروار yek kharvâr

scaffold *n., vt.* داربست dârbast

scald *adj., n., vt.* آب جوش کردن âbjush kardan سوزاندن suzândan

scale *v.* بالا رفتن bâlâ raftan

scale *n.* طبقه بندی tabaqeh-bandi مقام maqâm

scale *n.* ترازو tarâzu

scale *v.* پوست کندن pust kandan

scale *n.* ردیف radif

scale *n.* گام gâm

scale *n.* درجه darejeh

scale *n.* فلس fels پولک pulak

scale *v.* پوسته پوسته شدن pusteh-pusteh shod

scale *n.* میزان mizân مقیاس meqyâs

scalp *v.* پوست سرکندن pust-e' sar kand

scalp *v.* بازارسیاهی کردن bâzâr siâhi kardân

scalp *n.* پوست سر pust-e' sar

scalpel *n.* نیشتر جراحی nishtar jar~âhi

scalper *n.* بلیت فروش بازار سیاه belit-forush-e' bâzâr siâh

scaly *adj.* پوسته پوسته pusteh-pusteh پولک دار pulak-dâr

scamp *adj.* موذی muzi

scamp *v.* شل کارکردن shold kâr kardan

scamper *vi., n.* بچاک زدن be-châk zadan

scan *vt., vi., n.* بررسی کردن bar-resi kardan
تمام دیدکردن tamâm-did kardan

scandal *n., vt.* افتضاح eftezâh رسوایی rosvâyi

scandalous *n.* افتضاح آمیز eftezâh-âmiz رسواخیز rosvâ-khiz

scanner *n.* تمام بین tamâm-bin

scant *adj., vt., adv.* مختصر mokhtasar کم kam

scanty *adj.* مقدارکم meqdâr-e'kam

scar *n., vi.* جای زخم jâye zakhm داغ dâq

scarce *adj., adv.* کمیاب kamyâb نادر nâder

scarcely *n.* بندرت benodrat

scarcity *n.* کمیابی kamyâbi

scare *vt., vi., n.* ترساندن tarsândan

scarecrow *n.* مترسک matarsak لولوسرخرمن lulu sar-kharman

scared *v.* ترسیده tarsideh

scaremonger *n.* مردم ترسان mardom-tarsân

scarf *n., vt.* شال گردن shâl-gardan روسری rusari
scarify *vt.* نیشترزدن tiq تیغ nishtar zadan
scarlet *n., adj.* سرخ sorkh
scarlet fever *n.* سرخک sorkhak مخملک makhmalak
scarp *n., vt.* پرتگاه partgâh
scary *adj.* ترسو tarsnâk ترسناک tarsu
scary *adj.* ترسناک tars-nâk وحشتناک vahshat-nâk
scat *n., vi.* بچاک زدن bechâk zadan
scathe *vt., n.* صدمه رساندن sadameh resândan
تویبخ کردن tobikh kardan
scathing *adj., v.* صدمه رسان sadameh-resân شدیداللحن shadiol lahn
scatter *v.* پخش و پلا کردن pakhsh-o palâ kardân
scatter *v.* پراکنده کردن parakandeh kardân
scatterbrain(ed) *n.* بی مخ bimokh
scattered *n.* پراکنده parâkandeh
scattering *adj., n.* پراکنده parâkandeh
scavenge *n.* آشغال جمع کردن âshqâl jam' kardân
scavenger *n.* سپور sopur رفتگر roftegar
scavenger *v.* آشغال جمع کن âshqâl jam'kon لاشخور lâsh-khor
scene *n.* صحنه sahneh منظره manzareh دکور dekor
scenery *n.* منظره manzareh چشم انداز cheshm-andâz
scenic *adj.* بامنظره bâ-manzareh
scent *n., vt., vi.* بوکشیدن bu keshidan
scepter *n.* عصای سلطنت 'asâye saltanat
schedule *n., vt.* برنامه barnâmeh
schema *n.* برنامه barnâmeh
scheme *v.* نقشه کشی کردن naqsheh-keshi kardân
توطئه چیدن tote'eh chidan
scheming *adj.* توطئه چین tote'eh-chin
schism *n.* جدایی jodâyi شیعه shi'eh فرقه ferqeh
schismatic *adj., n.* شیعه گرا shi'eh-garâ
scholar *n.* اندیشمند andish-mand عالم 'âlem علامه 'al~âmeh
scholarly *n.* اندیشمندانه andishmand-âneh
scholarship *n.* بورس تحصیلی burs-e' tahsili
scholastic *adj., n.* مدرسه ای madreseh-i اسکولاستیک eskolâstik
school *n., vi.* مدرسه madreseh
school *n., vi.* مکتب maktab
school *n., vi.* گروه goruh دسته dasteh

schooling *n.* (تحصیل(ات tahsil(ât)
schoolmaster *n.* مدیر modir ناظم nâzem
schoolmate *n.* هم شاگردی ham-shâgerdi
schooner *n.* کشتی چنددکله kashti chand dakaleh
science *n.* علم 'elm
scientific *adj.* علمی 'elmi
scientist *n.* دانشمند dânesh-mand
scimitar *n.* شمشیراسلامی shamshire eslâmi
scion *n.* شاخه shâkheh بازمانده bâzmândeh
scissors *n.* قیچی qeychi مقراض meqraz
scissure *n.* شکاف shekâf برش boresh
scoff *v.* استهزاء کردن estehzâ' kardan بریش خندیدن berish khandidan
scoff *n.* تمسخر tamaskhor استهزاء estehzâ'
scold *n.* سرزنش کردن sarzanesh kardân
سرکوفت زدن sar-zanesh kardan
ملامت کردن malâmat kardan
scoop *n.* خبر khabar
scoop *n.* چمچه قاشق qâshoq cham-cheh
scoop *v.* بیل زدن bil zadan
scooter *n., vi.* روروئک roro'ak
scope *n.* برد bord بعد bo'd وسع vos'
scorch *vt., vi., n.* سطحی سوزاندن sat-hi suzandan
scorcher *n.* روزداغ ruz-e' dâq زخم زبان (ی) zakhme zabân(i)
score *n.* خرده حساب khordeh hesâb
score *n.* پوئن po'an
score *n.* موضوع mozu' جریان jaryân
score *n.* تنظیم آهنگ tanzim-e' âhang
score *n.* خط khat~
score *v.* شیارانداختن shiâr andâkhtan
scorn *v.* خوار کردن khâr kardan حقیرشماردن haqir shemârdan
scorn *n.* خواری khâri حقارت heqârat استنکاف estenkâf
scornful *adj.* خوارکننده khâr-konandeh حقارت آمیز heqârat-âmiz
Scorpio *n.* عقرب 'aqrab آبان âbân
scorpion *n.* عقرب 'aqrab کژدم kazhdom
scot-free *n.* مجانی maj~âni قصردررفته qeser dar-rafteh
scotch-tape *vt.* نوارچسب navâr-chasb
scoundrel *n.* رذل razl شیاد shay~âd
scour *vt., vi., n.* حسابی پاک کردن hesâbi pâk kardan

کف سابیدن .... kaf sâbidan

scourge *n., vt.* شلاق زدن shalâq zadan

scout *n.* راه شناس râh-shenâs دیده‌ور dideh-var

scout *n.* پیشاهنگ pishâ-hang

scout *v.* پیشیابی کردن pish-yâbi kardan تجسس کردن tajasos kardan

scoutmaster *n.* سرپیشاهنگ sar-pishâhang

scowl *vi., vt., n.* اخم کردن akhm kardan
ترشرویی کردن torshroyi kardan

scraggly *n.* نامرتب nâ-morat‿ab

scram! *n.* بزن بچاک bezan bechâk!

scramble *vi., vt., n.* بهم زدن beham zadan
چهارچنگولی رفتن chahâr chânguli raftan

scrap *adj.* تیکه tikeh پاره pâreh قراضه qorâzeh

scrap *v.* اسقاط کردن esqât kardan اوراق کردن orâq kardan

scrap iron *np.* آهن پاره âhan-pâreh

scrape *vt., n.* خراش دادن kharâsh dâdan
بزمین کشیدن bezamin keshidan

scraper *n.* کف تراش kaf-tarâsh

scrappy *adj.* پاره پاره pâreh pâreh

scratch *v.* خاراندن khârândan

scratch *v.* خراش دادن kharâsh dâdan چنگول زدن changul zadan

scratchy *adj.* خط خطی khat-khati خط انداز khat-andâz

scrawl *vt., n.* خرچنگ قورباغه نوشتن kharchang qurbâq nâvâshtân

scrawly *adj.* خرچنگ قورباغه kharchang qurbâq

scrawny *adj.* لاغر lâqar

scream *vi.* فریادزدن faryâd zadan جیغ کشیدن jiq keshidan
هوارکشیدن dâd zadan داد زدن havâr keshidan

screamer *n.* جیغو jiqu داد و بیدادی dâdo bidâdi

screaming *n.* فریادی faryâdi

screech *vi., vt., n.* جیغ کشیدن jiq keshidan
زوزه کشیدن zuzeh keshidan

screen *n.* توری turi پرده pardeh

screen *v.* پیش دیدکردن pishdid kardan

screw *v.* اجحاف کردن ejhâf kardan چپاندن chapândan

screw *v.* پیچ کردن pich kardan

screw *n.* پیچ pich

screw(up) *n.* خراب کردن kharâb kardan گاف زدن gâf zadan

screwball *n.* قاطی پاطی qâti-pâti

screwdriver *n.* پیچ گوشتی pich-gushti
scrimmage *n., vt., vi.* دعوا da'vâ دست گرمی dast-garmi
scrimpy *adj., vi., vt.* کم kam کنس kenes
script *n.* دست نوشت dast-nevesht داستان dâstân
scripture *n.* نوشته neveshteh
scrivener *n.* دست نویس dast-nevis
scroll *n., vt.* طومار tumâr
Scrooge *n.* کنس kenes
scrotum *n.* خایه khâyeh
scrub *vt., vi., n.* مالاندن mâlândan سایدن sâ'idan سابیدن sâbidan
scrubber *n.* کف ساب kaf-sâb
scrubby *adj.* کوتوله kutuleh
scruff *n.* پس گردن pas-gardan
scrumptious *adj.* خیلی خوب kheyli khub باشکوه bâshokuh
scrunch *vt., vi., n.* قرچ قروچ کردن qerech qoruch kardân
scruple *n., vi., vt.* تردید tardid وجدان vejdân
scrupulous *n.* وسواسی vasvâsi باوجدان bâ-vejdân
scrutinize *n.* بدقت نگاه کردن bedeq~at negâh kardân
scrutiny *n.* نگاه دقیق negâhe daqiq
scuff *vi., vt., n.* بزمین کشیدن bezamin keshidan
scuffle *v.* دست بیقه شدن dast beyaqeh shodân
scuffle *n.* دعوا da'vâ درگیری dargiri
sculptor *n.* مجسمه ساز mojasameh-sâz
sculpture *n., vt., vi.* مجسمه سازی mojasameh-sâzi
scum *n., vt., vi.* پست past
scum *n., vt., vi.* کف kaf پس مانده pas-mândeh
scurry *vi., vt., n., adj.* جیم شدن jim shodan
scurvy *n.* لثه چرکی laseh-cherki
scuttle *n., vt., vi.* گریختن gorikhtan سبد sabad
scuttlebutt *n.* شایعه shâye'eh شرور shero-ver
scythe *n., vt.* داس dâs
sea *n., adj.* دریا daryâ
sea breeze *np.* نسیم دریایی nasime daryâyi
sea food *n.* خوراک دریایی khorâk-e' daryâyi
sea front *np.* کناردریا kenâr daryâ
sea shell(s) *n.* گوش ماهی gush-mâhi
sea-born *n.* دریازاد daryâ-zâd
seaboard *n., adj.* دریاکنار daryâ kenâr

seacost *n.* ساحل دریا sâhele daryâ
seafaring *n.* دریارو daryâro
seagoing *adj.* دریارونده daryâ-ravandeh
seal *n.* مهر mohr
seal *v.* درزگیری کردن darz-giri kardan
seal *v.* مهرزدن mohr zadan مهروموم کردن mohro mum kardan
seal *n.* فک fok
sealed *n.* مهرشده mohr-shodeh درزگرفته darz-gerefteh
sealing *n.* درزگیری darz-giri
seam *n., vt., vi.* درز darz چاک châk
seaman *n.* ملوان malevân
seamstress *n.* خیاط khay~ât
seamy *adj.* درزدار darz-dâr
seaplane *n.* هواپیمای دریایی havâ-peymâye daryâi
seaport *n.* بندرشهر bandar shahr
sear *v.* خشکاندن khoshkândan تنوری کردن tanuri kardan
sear *adj.* خشک khoshk تنوری tanuri سوخته sukhteh
search *vt.* جستجو کردن josteju kardan گشتن gashtan
search warrant *np.* حکم تفتیش hokm-e'taftish
search(out) *n.* دنبال گشتن donbâl gashtan
searching *adj.* تفتیشی taftishi
seashore *n.* ساحل sâhel کرانه karâneh
seasick *n.* دریاناخوش daryâ nâkhosh دریازده daryâ-zadeh
seasickness *n.* ناخوشی دریا nâkhoshi-e daryâ
دریاگرفتگی daryâ gereftegi
seaside *n., adj.* دریاکنار daryâ-kenâr
season *v.* ادویه زدن advieh zadan خشک کردن khoshk kardan
season *n.* فصل fasl موسم mosem
seasonal *adj.* فصلی fasli موسمی mosemi
seasoning *n.* ادویه advieh چاشنی châshni
seat *n.* صندلی sandali نشیمن neshiman مسند masnad کرسی korsi
seat *v.* نشاندن neshândan
seat *n.* مسند masnad کرسی korsi مقام maqâm
seating *n.* نشاندن neshândan جادادن jâ dâdan
seaward *adv., adj., n.* بسوی دریا besu-ye' daryâ
secant *n., adj.* خط قاطع khat~-e qâte'
secede *n., vi.* رسماًجدا شدن rasman jodâ shodân
secession *n.* جدایی jodâyi تجزیه tajzieh

secessionist *n., adj.* تجزیه طلب tajzieh-talab
seclude *n.* جداکردن jodâ kardan
مجزانگه داشتن mojazâ negah-dâshtân
secluded *adj.* جدا jodâ مجزا mojazâ امن amn
seclusion *n.* انزوا enzevâ خلوت khalvat
second *n.* ثانیه sânieh
second *v.* تائید کردن ta'yid kardan
second *adj.* دوم dov~om ثانی sâni
second class *np.* درجه دو darejeh do
second fiddle *np.* نقش دوم naqsh-e' dov~om
second floor *np.* طبقهٔ دوم tabaqeh-ye' dov~om
second lieutenant *np.* ستوان دو sotvân do
second-guess *vt.* پیش گمانی کردن pish-gamâni kardân
secondary *adj., n.* ثانوی sânavi متوسطه motevas~et(eh)
secondary school *n.* دبیرستان dabirestân
secondhand *n.* دست دوم dast dov~om
secondly *adv.* ثانیاً sânian دوماً dov~oman
secrecy *n.* پنهانی penhâni سرپوشی sarpushi مرموزی marmuzi
secret *adj., n.* راز râz سر ser~
secret *adj., n.* محرمانه mahramâneh سری ser~i
secret agent *np.* مأمورمخفی ma'mur-e' makhfi
secret service *np.* سرویس مخفی servise makhfi
secretarial *adj.* دبیری dabiri
secretariat *n.* دبیرخانه dabir-khâneh
secretary *n.* وزیر vazir
secretary *n.* منشی monshi ماشین نویس mâshin-nevis
secretary *n.* دبیر dabir
secretary general *n.* دبیرکل dabir kol
secretary of state *np.* وزیرامورخارجه vazir-e' omur-e' khârejeh
secrete *n.* ترشح کردن tarashoh kardan تراوش کردن tarâvosh kardan
secretion *n.* ترشح tarashoh تراوش tarâvosh
secretive *adj., n.* مرموز marmuz
sect *n.* فرقه ferqeh تیره tireh
sectarian *adj., n.* فرقه ای ferqeh-i
sectarianism *n.* فرقه گرایی ferqeh-garâyi
section *v.* قسمت کردن qesmat kardan
section *n.* بخش bakhsh قسمت qesmat
section *n.* برش boresh مقطع maqta'

sectional *adj., n.* بخشی bakhshi
sector *n., vt.* قطاع qatâ' بخش bakhsh
sectorial *adj., n.* قطع کننده qat'-konandeh
secular *adj., n.* جدا ازدین jodâ az din لائیک lâ'ik
secularism *n.* جدایی دین ازسیاست jodâyi-e din az siâsat
secularist *n.* جداخواه jodâ-khâh
secularize *n.* دین از سیاست جداکردن din az siâsat jodâ kardân
securable *adj.* قابل حفاظت qâbele hefâzat
secure *n.* محفوظ mahfuz امن amn
secure *v.* محفوظ کردن mahfuz kardan تأمین کردن tamin kardan
security *n., adj.* وثیقه vasiqeh ضمانت zemânat
security *n., adj.* امنیت amniyat تأمین ta'min حراست herâsat
Security Council *n.* شورای امنیت shorâye amniyat
sedan *n.* سواری savâri
sedate *adj., vt.* آرام کردن ârâm kardan
آمپول تسکین زدن âmpule taskin zadân
sedation *n.* آرامش تسکین ârâmesh آمپول تسکین âmpule taskin
sedative *adj., n.* مسکن mosaken
sedentary *adj.* نشسته neshasteh ثابت sâbet
sedge *n.* سعد so'd
sediment *n.* رسوب rosub درد dord
sedimentary *adj.* رسوبی rosubi
sedition *n.* فتنه گری fetneh gari آشوب گری âshub gari
seditious *adj.* آشوبگر âshub-gar
seditious *adj.* فتنه جو fetneh-ju آشوبگر âshub-gar
فتنه آمیز fetmeh-âmiz
seduce *vt.* ازراه بدرکردن az râh bedar kardan
تجاوز کردن tajâvoz kardan
seducer *n.* متجاوز motejâvez فریب دهنده farib-dahandeh
seduction *n.* گمراهی gomrâhi فریب farib
seductive *adj.* فریبا faribâ
see *n.* دیدن didan
see you later! *n.* بعداً می بینمت ba'dan mibinamet
see(about) *n.* دنبال گشتن donbâl gashtan
see(after) *n.* مواظبت کردن movâzebat kardan
see(double) *n.* دوتایی دیدن dotâyi didan
see(into) *n.* پیگیری کردن peygiri kardan
see(off) *n.* مشایعت کردن moshâye'at kardân

see(out)

see(out) n. تاآخرصبرکردن tâ-âkhar sabr kârdân
see(through) n. تاآخررفتن tâ-âkhar raftan
see(to) n. مواظبت کردن movâzebat kardan
seed n. تخم tokhm بذر bazr دانه dâneh
seeder n. بذرافشان bazr-afshân
seediness n. پرتخمی por-tokhmi
seedling n. نشاء neshâ'
seedsman n. بذرافشان bazr-afshân
seedy adj. پرتخم por-tokhm بدنما badnamâ
seeing n. بینش binesh باشناخت bâshenâkht
seeing dog n. سگ راهنما sage râhnamâ
seek vt., vi. دنبال گشتن donbâl gashtan جستجوکردن josteju kardan
seeker n. جویا juyâ طالب tâleb جوینده juyandeh خواهان khâhân
seel vt. بهم دوختن beham dukhtan
seem vi. بنظررسیدن benazar residan
seeming n. ظاهری zâheri
seemingly n. ظاهراً zâheran
seemingly n. ظاهراً zâheran
seemly adj., adv. شایسته shâyesteh
seep vi., n. تراوش کردن tarâvosh kardan نشت کردن nasht kardan
seepage n. برون ریز borun-riz
seer n. بیننده binandeh پیغمبر peyqambar
seersucker n. پارچه نخی pârcheh nakhi
seesaw adj., vi., vt., n. الاکلنگ alâ-kolang
seethe n. آبجوش کردن âbjush kardan
segment n., vt., vi. قسمت qesmat قطعه qat'eh
segmental adj. قطعه ای qat'eh-i
segmentation n. قطعه قطعه کردن qat'eh-qat'eh kârdân
segregate vt., vi., n. جداکردن jodâ kardan
مجزاکردن mojaz~â kardan
segregation n. جدایی نژادی jodâyi-e nezhâdi
seismic adj. زلزله ای zelzelh-i
seismograph n. زلزله سنج zelzeleh-sanj
seize v. گرفتن gereftan تصرف کردن tasar~ of kardan
seize v. دستگیرکردن dast-gir kardan
seize on/upon n. بزورگرفتن bezur gereftan
seizing n., v. گرفتگی gereftegi
seizure n. تصرف tasar~ of قبض qabz حمله hamleh

seldom *adj.* بندرت benodrat
select *n.* برگزیده bargozideh منتخب montakhab
select *v.* برگزیدن bargozidan انتخاب کردن entekhâb kardan
selected *n.* برگزیده bargozideh
selection *n.* انتخاب entekhâb مجموعه majmu'eh گلچین golchin
selective *adj.* انتخابی entekhâbi
selective service *np.* نظام وظیفه nezâm vazifeh
selectivity *n.* برگزینش bargozinesh موج گیری moj-giri
selector *adj.* انتخاب کننده entekhâb konandeh گزیننده gozinandeh
self *n., adj., pro.* خود khod خویشتن khishtan نفس nafs
self-abuse *n.* خودزیانی khod-ziâni
self-addressed *adj.* نشانی دار neshâni-dâr آدرس دار âdres-dâr
self-appointed *adj.* خودمنتخب khod-montakhab
self-assertion *n.* ادعا بخود ede'â bekhod
self-assurance *n.* اطمینان بخود etminân bekhod
self-assured *adj.* مطمئن بخود motma'en bekhod
self-centered *adj.* خودمرکز khod-markaz خودخواه khod-khâh
self-complacent *n.* ازخودراضی az khod-râzi
self-composed *adj.* خونسرد khun-sard
self-conceited *adj.* مغروربخود maqrur-bekhod
self-confidence *n.* اتکاء بنفس etekâ'-benafs
self-confident *adj.* متکی بنفس mot~aki-benafs
self-conscious *n.* خجالتی khejâlati حساس has~âs
self-consistent *n.* خوداستوار khod-ostovâr
self-contained *adj.* خوددار khod-dâr همه چیزدار hamechiz-dâr
self-content *n., adj.* خودقانع khodqâne'
self-contradiction *adj.* خودنقضی khod-naqzi
self-control *n.* خودداری khod-dâri مسک نفس mask-e' nafs
self-defense *n.* دفاع ازخود defâ' az khod
self-defensive *adj.* خودمدافع khod-modâfe'
self-destruction *n.* خودنابودی khod-nâbudi
self-determination *n.* خودمختاری khod-mokhtâri
self-discipline *n.* خودانظباطی khod-enzebâti
self-driven *adj.* خودرو khod-ro
self-esteem *n.* اعتماد بنفس ehterâm-bekhod مناعت menâ'at
self-evident *n.* خودآشکار khod-âshkâr بدیهی badihi
self-examination *n.* خودآزمایی khod-âzmâyi
self-existent *adj.* موجودبخود mojud bekhod

واجب الوجود .... vâjebol-vojud
self-expression *n.* خودبیانی khod-bayâni
self-governed *n.* خودحاکم khod-hâkem
self-imposed *n.* خودخواسته khod-khâsteh
self-induced *adj.* خودانگیخته khod-angikhteh
self-indulgent *n.* تن پرور tan-parvar
self-inflicted *adj.* خودوارد khod-vâred
self-interest *n.* نفع شخصی naf'e shakhsi
self-knowledge *n.* خودآگاهی khod-âgâhi
self-loading *adj.* خودپر khod-por
self-made *n.* خودساخته khod-sâkhteh
self-moving *adj.* خودران khod-rân
self-opinionated *n.* معتقدبخود mo'taqed bekhod
self-ordained *adj.* خودگماشته khod-gomâshteh
self-possessed *n.* خوددار khod-dâr متین matin
self-possession *n.* خودداری khod-dâri متانت metânat
self-preservation *n.* خوددوامی khod-davâmi بقای نفس baqâye nafs
self-respect *n.* طبع tab' مناعت manâ'at عزت نفس ez~at-e' nafs
self-restraint *n.* خودداری khod-dâri خویشتن داری khishtan-dâri
self-righteous *adj.* ازخودراضی az khod râzi
self-satisfaction *n.* ارضاء erzâ' خودخوشنودی khod-khoshnudi
self-satisfied *adj.* خوشنودازخود khoshnud az khod
self-service *n.* خود سرو khod-serv
self-sufficient *adj.* خودکفا khod-kafâ
self-taught *adj.* خودآموخته khod-âmukhteh
selfish *adj.* خودخواه khod-khâh
selfless *adj.* فاقد خودخواهی fâqed-e' khod-khâh
sell *adj., pro., vt., vi.* فروختن forukhtan فروش کردن forush kardan
sell(off) *n.* کم فروختن kam forukhtan آب کردن âb kardan
sell(on) *n.* معتقد کردن mo'taqed kardan
sell(oneself) *n.* خودفروشی کردن khod-forushi kardân
sell(out) *n.* خیانت کردن khiânat kardan
sell(out) *n.* تمام فروش کردن tamâm-forush kardân
sell(up) *n.* همه چیزرافروختن hamehchiz râ forukhtân
sell-out *n.* تمام فروخته tamâm-forukhteh
seller *n.* فروشنده forushandeh
selling *v.* فروش forush
semantic *n.* معنی ma'nâ

semantical *n.* معنائى ma'nâ'i
semantics *n.* معنى شناسى ma'nâ-shenâsi
semaphore *n., vt., vi.* مخابره باپرچم mokhâbereh bâ-parchâm
sematic *adj.* علامت خطر 'alamate khatâr
semblance *n.* شباهت shebâhat صورت ظاهر surate zâher
semen *n.* آب منى âb-mani
semester *n.* ترم term دوره doreh
semi- *n.* نيم nim نيمه nimeh
semi-annual *n.* شش ماهه shesh-mâheh
semi-circle *n.* نيم دايره nim-dâyereh
semi-final *n.* نيمه نهايى nimeh-nahâyi
seminal *adj.* نطفه اى notfeh-i
seminar *n.* جلسۀ آموزشى jaleseh-ye âmuzeshi سمينار seminâr
seminary *n.* مدرسۀ مذهبى madreseh-ye maz-hâbi
semination *n.* تخم پاشى tokhm-pâshi
senate *n.* سنا senâ
senator *n.* سناتور senâtor
send *n., vt., vi.* فرستادن ferestâdan ارسال داشتن ersâl dâshtan
send-off *n.* مشايعت moshâye'at
sender *n.* فرستنده ferestandeh
senile *adj., n.* پير pir فرتوت fartut خرف kheref
senility *n.* پيرى za'fe piri ضعف كهولت kohulât كبرسن kebar-e' sen
senior *adj., n.* پيرتر pirtar بزرگتر bozorg-tar
senior *adj., n.* ارشد arshad بالارتبه bâlâ-rotbeh
senior *adj., n.* سال آخر sâl-e' âkhar
seniority *n.* ارشديت arshadiyat قدمت qedmat
sensation *n.* احساس ehsâs شور shor
sensational *adj.* شورانگيز shor-angiz
sensationalism *n.* شورانگيزى shor-angizi
sense *n., vt.* معنى ma'ni مصداق mesdâq
sense *n., vt.* حس كردن hes kardan احساس كردن ehsâs kardan
senseless *n.* بى حس bihes بى معنى bima'ni
senses *n.* مشاعر mashâ'er
sensibility *n.* حساسيت hasâsiyat
sensible *adj.* محسوس mahsus باادراک bâ-edrâk
sensitive *adj.* حساس has~âs
sensitivity *n.* حساسيت hasâsiyat
sensorium *n.* سيستم حسى sistem-e' hes~i

sensory *adj.* حسى hes~i
sensual *adj.* شهوانى shahvâni نفسانى nafsâni
sensuous *n.* احساساتى ehsâsâti
sentence *n.* جمله jomleh
sentence *n.* حکم hokm
sentence *v.* محکوم کردن mahkum kardan
sentiment *n.* احساس ehsâs عاطفه 'âtefeh سانتیمان sântimân
sentimental *adj.* پرعاطفه por-'âtefeh سانتیمانتال sântimântâl
sentimentalist *n.* احساساتى ehsâsâti
sentimentality *n.* پرعاطفه اى por-'âtefeh-i
sentinel *n., vt.* نگهبان negahbân کشیک کشیدن keshik keshidan
sentry *n.* کشیک keshik نگهبان negahbân
separable *adj.* جداشدنى jodâ-shodani
separate *adj.* جدا jodâ سوا savâ مجزا mojaz~â
separate *v.* جداکردن jodâ kardan مجزاکردن mojaz~â kardan
separated *v.* جداشده jodâ-shodeh علیحده alâhedeh
separation *n.* جدایى jodâyi تفکیک tafkik فراق farâq
separatist *n.* تجزیه طلب tajzieh-talab
separator *n.* جداکن jodâ-kon خامه گیر khâmeh-gir
septic *adj., n.* مستراحى mostarâhi عفونى ofuni
septic tank *n.* چاه مستراح châhe mostarâh
septuagenarian *adj., n.* هفتادساله haftâd-sâleh
septum *n.* جداره jedâreh دیوار divâr
sepulcher *n., vt.* مقبره maqbareh مرقد marqad
sequacious *adj.* دنباله رو donbâleh-ro
sequel *n.* دنباله donbâleh
sequence *n.* پشت سرهمى poshte sarhami یک ردیفى yekradifi
sequent *adj., n.* پس آمد pas-âmad
sequester *vt.* جداکردن jodâ kardan قبض کردن qâbz kardan
sequestered *adj.* مجزا mojaz~â
seraglio *n.* حرم haram اندرون andarun
serenade *n., vt., vi.* آوازعشقى âvâz-e' 'eshqi تصنیف tasnif
serene *n.* آرام ârâm باصفا bâsafâ
serenity *n.* آرامش ârâmesh صفا safâ
serf *n.* رعیت ra'yat
serfdom *n.* رعیتى ra'yati
sergeant *n.* گروهبان goruhbân
sergeant major *np.* گروهبان یک goruhbân-yek

sergeant-at-arms *n.* مامور انتظامات mamure entezâmât
serial *n., adj.* سریال seriâl پشت سرهم posht sare-ham
serial number *np.* شمارهٔ مسلسل shomâreh-ye mosalsal
series *pl.* سری seri ردیف radif
series *pl.* مجموعه majmu'eh دسته dasteh
serious *adj., n.* جدی jed~i وخیم vakhim
serious-minded *n.* جدی jed~i
seriously *adv.* جداً jed~an
seriousness *n.* اهمیت ahamiyat وخامت vekhâmat
sermon *n.* موعظه mo'ezeh خطبه khotbeh وعظ va'z
sermonize *vi., vt.* موعظه خواندن mo'ezeh khândan
خطبه خواندن khotbeh khândan
serology *n.* سرم شناسی serom-shenâsi
serpent *n.* افعی af'i مار mâr
serpentine *adj., n.* مارمانند mâr-mânand
serrate(d) *n.* دندانه دار dandâneh dandâne dâr
serration *n.* دندانه دندانگی dandâneh dandânegi
serum *n.* سرم serom
servant *n.* خدمتکار khedmatkâr پیشخدمت pish-khedmat
servant *n.* کلفت kolfat
servant *n.* نوکر nokaâr
serve *v.* سرو زدن serv zadan
serve *v.* ارزش داشتن arzesh dâshtan سزاواربودن sezâvâr budan
serve *v.* خدمت کردن khedmat kardan
serve *v.* کشیدن keshidan سرو کردن serv kardan
serve *v.* بسربردن gozarândan گذراندن besar bordan
serve *v.* خدمت کردن khedmat kardan بندگی کردن bandegi kardan
service *v.* سرویس کردن servis kardan تعمیرکردن ta'mir kardan
service *n.* مراسم marâsem عبادت ebâdat
service *n.* خدمت khedmat استخدام estekhdâm
service *n.* سنجد senjed
service station *np.* پمپ بنزین pomp-e' benzin
serviceable *n.* قابل استفاده qâbel-e' estefâdeh
serviceman *n.* سرباز sarbâz
servile *adj.* برده وار bardeh vâr پست past
servitude *n.* بندگی bandegi بردگی bardegi
sesame *n.* کنجد konjed
session *n.* نشست neshast جلسه jaleseh

set *v.* درست شده dorost-shodeh ثابت sâbet
set *v.* سوارکردن savâr kardan
set *n.* دست dast دور dor
set *n.* دستگاه dastgâh
set *n.* دسته dasteh مجموعه majmu'eh
set *v.* خشک کردن khoshk kardan
set *v.* میزان کردن mizân kardan
set *v.* گذاشتن gozâshtan قراردادن qarâr dâdan
set *v.* مقررداشتن moqar~ar dâshtan قرارگذاشتن qarâr gozâshtan
set *n.* دست dast سری seri
set *v.* مرتب کردن morat~ab kardan چیدن chidan
set *v.* خواباندن khâbândan
set *n.* صحنه sahneh زمینه zamineh
set *n.* حاضر hâzer آماده âmâdeh
set *v.* جاانداختن jâ andâkhtan
set *v.* صحنه سازی کردن sahneh-sâzi kardân
set *v.* زمینه ساختن zamineh sâkhtan
set *v.* تعیین کردن ta'in kardan معین کردن mo'ay~an kardan
set(about) *n.* شروع کردن shoru' kardan
مبادرت کردن mobâderat kardan
set(an example) *n.* سرمشق گذاشتن sar-mashq gozâshtân
set(apart) *n.* کنارگذاشتن kenâr gozâshtan
set(aside) *n.* کنارگذاشتن kenâr gozâshtan
set(back) *n.* به عقب بردن be'aqab bordan
set(down) *n.* پیاده کردن piâdeh kardan وضع کردن vaz' kardan
set(forth) *n.* منتشرکردن montasher kardan بیان کردن bayân kardan
set(in) *n.* شروع کردن shoru' kardan
set(off) *n.* راه انداختن râh andâkhtan ترکاندن tarekândan
set(on fire) *n.* به آتش کشیدن be-âtash keshidan
set(on) *n.* ترغیب کردن tarqib kardan
set(out) *n.* حد گذاشتن had gozâshtan نقشه کشیدن nâqsheh keshidan
set(sail) *n.* بادبان افراشتن bâdbân afrâshtan راه افتادن râh oftâdan
set(to) *n.* ازاول شروع کردن az aval shoru'kârdân
set(up) *n.* برپاکردن bârpâ kardan دائرکردن dâ'er kardan
set(up) *n.* آماده کردن âmâdeh kardan
set(upon) *n.* حمله ورشدن hamleh-var shodân
set-back *n.* رکود rokud توقف tavaqof
setoff *n.* درعوض dar-'avaz تصفیه حساب tasfieh-hesâb

settee *n.* مبل mobl کاناپه kânâpeh
setter *n.* گذارنده gozârandeh
setting *n., v.* صحنه sahneh دکور dekor نصب nasb
settle *v.* تسویه کردن tasvieh kardan سازش کردن sâzesh kardan
settle *v.* ساکن شدن sâken shodan مستقرشدن mostaqar shodan
settle *v.* ته نشین کردن tah-neshin kardân رسوب کردن rosub kardan
settle *v.* اسکان دادن oskân dâdan
settle(a score) *n.* تسویه حساب کردن tasvieh hesâb kardân
settle(down) *n.* سر و سامان گرفتن saro sâmân gereftan
آرام گرفتن ârâm gereftan
settle(upon/on) *n.* توافق کردن tavâfoq kardan
settlement *n.* سازش sâzesh استقرار esteqrâr قرارگاه qarâr-gâh
settler *n.* کوچ نشین kuch-neshin
setup *n.* ساختگی sâkhtegi نقشه naqsheh
seven *n., adj.* هفت haft
seventeen) *n.* هفده hefdah
seventy *n., adj.* هفتاد haftâd
sever *vt.* بریدن boridan جداشدن jodâ shodan
severable *adj.* تفکیکی tafkiki
several *adj., n.* چند(تن) chand(in) چندتن chandtan
severance *n.* تفکیک tafkik قطع qat'
severe *adj.* سخت sakht شدید shadid
severely *adv.* سخت sakht شدیداً shadidan
severity *n.* سختی sakhti شدت shed~at
sew *vt., vi., n.* دوختن dukhtan
sewage *n.* فاضلاب fâzel-âb گنداب رو gandâb-ro
sewer *n.* فاضلاب مجرای majrâye fâzel-âb
sewing *v.* دوخت و دوز dukhto duz دوزندگی duzandegi
sewing machine *np.* چرخ خیاطی charkh khay~âti
sewn *v.* دوخته dukhteh
sex *adj., n.* جنس jens سکس seks
sex appeal *np.* سکس آپیل seks-âpil جاذبهٔ جنسی jâzebeh-ye jensi
sexagenarian *adj., n.* شصت ساله shast-sâleh
sexless *n.* ناجنس nâ-jens یخ yakh
sexology *n.* جنس شناسی jens-shenâsi
sexual *adj.* جنسی jensi تناسلی tanâsoli
sexuality *n.* جنسیت jensiyat
sexually *n.* جنساً jensan

sexy *adj.* سکسی seksi

shabbiness *n.* ژنده گی zhendegi ژولیدگی zhulidegi

shabby *adj.* ژولیده zhulideh ژنده پوش zhendeh-push

shack *n., vt., vi.* اطاقک otâqak کلبه kolbeh

shack(up) *n.* هم بستر شدن ham-bastar shodân

shackle *v., n.* پابندزدن pâ-band zadan

shackles *n.* پابند pâ-band زنجیر zanjir

shade *n., vt., vi.* سایه sâyeh سایبان sâybân

shade *n., vt., vi.* آباژور âbâzhur

shading *n., v.* سایه sâyeh تفاوت جزیی tafâvote joz'i

shadow *v.* تعقیب کردن ta'gib kardan

shadow *n.* سایه sâyeh

shadowy *n.* سایه دار sâyeh-dâr مشکوک mashkuk مرموز marmuz

shady *n.* پر سایه por-sâyeh مشکوک mashkuk

shaft *n.* میله mileh چوبه chubeh ساقه sâqeh

shaft *v.* چپاندن chapândan

shag *n., v., vt.* پرمو por-mu

shaggy *adj.* پشمالو pashmâlu ژولیده zhulideh

shake *vi., vt., n.* تکان دادن takân dâdan لرزاندن larzândan

shake(down) *n.* باج گرفتن bâj gereftan

shake(hands) *n.* دست دادن dast dâdan

shake(off) *n.* دورانداختن dur andâkhtan

shake(up) *n.* ترساندن tarsândan شوکه کردن shokeh kardan

shake-up *n.* ترمیم tarmim باز سازی bâz-sâzi

shakedown *vi.* باج گیری bâj-giri

shaken *v.* ترسان tarsân لرزان larzân تکان خورده takân-khordeh

shaker *n.* تکان دهنده takân-dahandeh

shakily *n.* لرزان larzân

shaking *n., v.* تکان takân لرزش larzesh

shaky *adj.* متزلزل motezalzel بی ثبات bisabât

shale *n.* سنگ رستی sange rosti

shallot *n.* موسیر musir

shallow *adj., vt., vi.* سطحی sat-hi کم عمق kam-'omq کم مایه kam-mâyeh

sham *adj.* کلک kalak ساختگی sâkhtegi کشکی kalak

shamble *vi., n.* شلخته وار shelakhteh-vâr

shambles *n.* بهم ریخته beham-rikhteh ریخته و پاشیده rikhto pâshideh

shame *n.* شرم sharm ننگ nang خجالت khejâlat آزرم âzarm

shame *v.* بی آبرو کردن bi-âberu kardan
shame on you! *n.* خجالت بکش khejâlat bekesh!
shameful *n.* شرم آور sharm-âvar ننگین nangin
shameless *n.* بی شرم bi-sharm بی حیا bi-hayâ
shampoo *vt., n.* شامپو shâmpu مو شور mu-shur
shank *n.* ساق پا sâqe-pâ ماهیچه mâhicheh
shanty *n., adj., vi., vt.* آلونک âlunak
shanty town *n.* حلبی آباد halabi-âbâd آلونک âlunak
shape *n., vt., vi.* شکل (دادن) shekl(dâdan) ترکیب tarkib
shape(up) *n.* اصلاح (کردن) eslâh(kardan)
shapless *n.* بی ترکیب bi-shekl بی ترکیب bi-tarkib
shard *n.* خرده سفال khordeh-sofâl
share *n.* خیش khish گاوآهن gâv-âhan
share *n.* سهم sahm قسمت qesmat حصه has~ah
share *v.* شریک کردن sharik kardan قسمت کردن qesmat kardan
sharecrop *vt., vi.* شریک محصولی sharik-mahsuli
shareholder *n.* سهام دار sahâm-dâr
shark *n., vt., vi.* کوسه kuseh کلاه بردار kolâh-bardâr
sharp *adj., vt., vi., adv.* دیز diez
sharp *adj., vt., vi., adv.* متمایز motemâyez شیک shik
sharp *adj., vt., vi., adv.* تیز tiz
sharp *adj., vt., vi., adv.* تیزهوش tiz-hush هوشیار hush-yâr
sharp *adj., vt., vi., adv.* زننده zanandeh تند tond
sharp-edged *adj.* تیز لب lab-tiz
sharp-eyed *n.* تیزچشم tiz-cheshm
sharp-tongued *n.* زبان دراز zabân-derâz
sharp-witted *n.* تیزهوش tiz-hush باذکاوت bâ-zekâvat
sharpen *vt., vi.* تیز کردن tiz kardan
sharper *n.* تیز کن tiz-kon تیزتر tiz-tar
sharpshooter *n.* تیرانداز ماهر tir-andâze mâher
shatter *vt., vi., n.* خرد کردن khord kardan بهم زدن be-ham zadan
shatter-proof *n.* ضدضربه zed~-e' zarbeh
shave *n., vi., vt.* تراشیدن tarâshidan زدن zadan
shaven *v., adj.* ریش تراشیده rish-tarâshideh
shaver *n.* ریش تراش rish-tarâsh
shaving *n., v.* ریش تراشی rish-tarâshi تراش tarâsh
shaving brush *np.* فرچه fercheh
shaving cream *np.* خمیر ریش تراشی khamir-e' rish-tarâshi

shawl *n.* روسری rusari رودوشی rudushi
she *nom., pro.* او u
sheaf *n., vt.* دسته dasteh
shear *n., vt., vi.* پشم‌زدن pashm zadan قیچی کردن qeychi kard/ân
shearing *n.* پشم زنی pashm-zani
shears *n.* قیچی باغبانی qeychi bâqbâni
sheath *v., n.* غلاف qalâf پوشش pushesh نیام niâm
sheathe *vt.* غلاف کردن qalâf kardan
sheathing *n., vt.* پوشش pushesh
shed *v.* ریختن rikhtan
shed *v.* انداختن andâkhtan درآوردن dar âvardan
sheen *n.* نورانی nurâni برق bargh
sheep *n., pl.* گوسفند gusfand
sheep dog *n.* سگ گله sag-e' galeh
sheepherder *n.* شبان shabân چوپان chupân
sheepish *adj.* گوسفندوار gusfand-vâr
sheepman *n.* گوسفنددار gusfand-dâr
sheer *adj., vi., adv., n.* نازک nâzok حریری hariri
sheer *adj., vi., adv., n.* نقط fagat محض mahz
sheer(off) *n.* منحرف شدن monharef shodan
sheet *n., vt.* ورقه varageh صفحه safheh
sheet *n., vt.* شمد shamâd ملحفه malhafeh
sheet metal *np.* ورقه آهن varageh-ye âhan
sheeting *n.* پارچه شمد pârcheh shamad پوشش pushesh
shelf *v.* کنار گذاشتن kenâr gozâshtan
shelf *n.* طاقچه tâqcheh
shelfish *n.* صدف ماهی sadaf-mâhi
shell *v.* خمپاره انداختن khompâreh andâkht
shell *v.* پوست کندن pust kandan
shell *n.* گلوله goluleh پوکه pukeh
shell *n.* بدنه badaneh پوسته pusteh قشر qeshr
shell *n.* پوست pust صدف sadaf
shell game *np.* حقه بازی hoq~eh-bâzi
shell-shocked *adj.* از جنگ ترسیده az jang-tarsideh
shelter *v.* پناه دادن panâh dâdan
shelter *n.* پناهگاه panâhgâh
shelve *vi., vt.* موکول کردن mokul kardan
shenanigan *n.* کلک kalak حقه hoq~eh

shephered *n.* چوپان chupân شبان shabân
sherbet *n.* بستنی میوه bastani-e' miveh
sheriff *n.* کلانتر kalântar
shield *n.* سپر separ
shield *v.* حمایت کردن hemâyat kardan
shift *v.* عوض کردن 'avaz kardan
shift *n.* نوبت کار nobate kâr
shift *v.* تغییرمکان دادن tagyir-e' makân dâdân
shifty *adj.* مرموز marmuz موذی muzi
Shiite *n.* شیعه shi'eh
shill *adj., n.* گاوبندی در قمار gâv-bandi dar qomâr
shimmer *vi., n.* برق زدن barg zadan
shimmy *n.* لق لق زدن laq-laq zadan
shin *n., vt., vi.* ساق پا sâq-e' pâ
shin guard *n.* ساق بند sâg-band
shinbone *n.* قلم پا qalam-e' pâ
shine *v.* برق‌انداختن barq andâkhtan واکس زدن vâks zadan
shine *v.* درخشیدن derakhshidan تاباندن tâbândan
shingle *n.* توفال tufâl تخته پوش takhteh-push
shingles *n.* زوستر zoster
shining *n.* درخشان derakhshân تابش tâbesh
shinny(up) *n.* بالارفتن bâlâ raftan
shiny *adj.* براق bar~âg درخشان derakhshân
ship *v.* فرستادن ferestâdan
ship *n.* کشتی kashti سفینه safineh
ship(out) *n.* بیرون رفتن birun raftan
ship-wrecked *n.* کشتی شکسته kashti shekasteh
shipload *n.* بارکشتی bâr-e' kashti
shipment *n.* حمل haml محموله mahmuleh
shipper *n.* فرستنده ferestandeh
shipping *v.* کشتیرانی kashti-râni باربری bârbari
shipshape *adj., adv.* مرتب morat~ab منظم monaz~am
shipyard *n.* کشتی گاه kashti-gâh
shirk *vt., vi., n.* از زیرش (دررفتن) az ziresh(dar râftân)
shirt *n.* پیراهن pirâhan
shive *n.* قاش qâsh براده borâdeh
shiver *n.* ریزه rizeh تکه tek~eh
shiver *v.* لرزیدن larzidan

shivery *adj.* لرزان larzân

shock *v.* وحشت زده کردن vahshat-zadeh kardân

shock *n.* تکان takân شوک shok ضربت zarbat هول hol

shock *n.* دسته dasteh توده tudeh

shock absorber *np.* کمک فنر komak-fanar

shocker *n.* تکان دهنده takân-dahandeh

shocking *n.* وحشت آور vahshat-âvar

shoddy *n.* بنجل bonjol مصنوعی masnu'i

shoe *n., vt.* کفش kafsh نعل na'l

shoe-in *n.* راحت râhat مثل آب خوردن mesle âb-khordan

shoehorn *n.* پاشنه کش pâshneh-kesh

shoelace *n.* بندکفش band-e' kafsh

shoemaker *n.* کفاش kaf~âsh

shoemaking *n.* کفاشی kaf~âshi

shoeshine *n.* واکس vâks

shoeshine boy *n.* واکسی vâksi

shoestring *n.* بندکفش band-e' kafsh

shoestring *n.* مرتاضی mortâzi بودجهٔ کم bud-jeh-ye' kam

shoing *n.* پایه گذاری pâyeh-gozâri

shoo! *n.* چخه chekheh! پیشده pishdeh!

shook *n.~ v., adj.* تکه چوب tek~eh-chub

shoot *v.* تیراندازی کردن tir-andâzi kardân باتیرزدن bâ-tir zadan

shoot *v.* تیرکشیدن tir keshidan

shoot *v.* برداشتن bar dâshtan

shoot *n.* جوانه javâneh نهال nahâl

shop *n.* دکان dok~ân مغازه maqâzeh

shop *v.* خریدکردن kharid kardan

shop *n.* کارگاه kâr-gâh

shopkeeper *n.* مغازه دار maqâzeh-dâr

shoplifter *n.* جنس دزد jens-dozd

shoplifting *n.* دزدی از مغازه dozdi az maqâzeh

shopper *n.* خریدار kharidâr مشتری moshtari

shopping *n., v., adj.* خرید kharid

shopping center *np.* مرکز خرید markaze kharid بازار bâzâr

shore *adj., vt.* ساحل sâhel کرانه karâneh

shore(up) *n.* پایه گذاشتن pâyeh gozâshtan تقویت کردن tagviat kardan

short *adj., adv., n., vt.* کوتاه kutâh قد کوتاه qad kutâh

short *adj., adv., n., vt.* مختصر mokhtasar

short cut n. ميان برزدن miân-bor zadan
short-circuit np., vt., vi. اتصال برقى et~es~ âl-e' barqi
short-handed n. دست تنها dast-tanhâ
short-lived adj. مدت كم عمر kam-'omr كوتاه kutâh-mod~at
short-order adj. زودحاضرى zud-hâzeri
short-range n. كم برد kam-bord فاصله كوتاه fâseleh-ye kutâh
short-sighted adj. نزديک بين nazdik-bin
short-sighted adj. كوته بين kutah-bin كوته فكر kutah-fekr
short-tempered adj. كم حوصله kam hoseleh
short-term adj. كوتاه مدت kutâh mod~at
short-winded adj. تنگ نفس tang-nafas
shortage n. كمبود kambud
shortchange n. كم دادن kam dâdan كلاه گذاشتن kolâh gozâshtan
shortcomming n. كوتاهى kutâhi قصور qosur
shorten vt., vi. كوتاه كردن kutâh kardan
shortening n. كوتاهى kutâhi روغن roqan
shorthand n., adj. تندنويسى tond-nevisi
shortly adv. بطورمختصر betore mokhtasar بزودى bezudi
shorts n. شلوارکوتاه shalvâr kutâh زيرشلوارى zirshalvâri
shortstop n. توقف كوتاه tavaqofe kutâh
shorty n., adj. كوتوله kutuleh
shot n., vt., adj. عكس 'aks
shot n., vt., adj. چتول chatval جرعه jor'eh
shot n., vt., adj. احتمال ehtemâl شانس shâns
shot n., vt., adj. تير tir گلوله goluleh ساچمه sâchmeh
shot-put n. پرتاب توپ patâbe tup
shotgun v., n., adj. تفنگ دولول tofange dolul
shotten adj. بدردنخور bedard-nakhor
should v. بايد bâyad بايستى bâyasti
shoulder n. كنار kenâr
shoulder n. شانه shâneh دوش dush كتف ketf سفت soft
shoulder v. متحمل شدن moteham~el shodan
shoulder v. بدوش كشيدن bedush keshidan
shoulder arms n. دوش فنگ dush-fâng
shoulder blade np. كتف ketf
shoulder strap np. ركاب rekâb
shout vi., vt., n. فريادزدن faryâd zadan دادزدن dâd zadan
shout n. فرياد faryâd داد dâd هوار havâr

shove *vt., vi., n.* هل دادن hol dâdan شاف کردن shâf kardan
shovel *n., vt., vi.* بیل زدن bil zadan
show *n.* نمایش نامه nâmâyesh nâmeh شو sho
show *v.* نشان دادن neshân dâdan هدایت کردن hedâyat kardan
show *v.* نمایش دادن namâyesh dâdan
بنمایش گذاردن benamâyesh gozârd
show bill *np.* آگهی نمایش âgahi-e namâyesh
show place *n.* نمایشگاه namâyesh-gâh
show(in) *n.* بداخل هدایت کردن bedâkhel hedâyat kardân
show(off) *n.* پزدادن poz dâdan خودنمایی کردن khod-namâyi kardân
show(up) *n.* ظاهرشدن zâher shodan
show-off *n.* خودنما khod-namâ متظاهر motezâher
showboat *n.* کشتی تیاتری kashti-e te-âtri
shower *n.* رگبار ragbâr ریزباران riz-bârân
shower *v.* روی سرریختن ruy-e' sar rikhtân
shower *v.* دوش گرفتن dush gereftan
showing *n., v.* ارائه erâ'eh
showman *n.* مجری mojri گرداننده gardânandeh
showroom *n.* سالن نمایش sâlone namâyesh
showy *adj.* متظاهر motezâher زرق و برق دار zarqo barq-dâr
shrapnel *n.* ترکش tarkesh
shred *n., vt., vi.* پاره pâreh ذره zar~eh ریزه rizeh
shredder *n.* ریزریزکن riz-riz kon
shrewd *adj.* زیرک zirak ناتو nâ-to
shrewish *adj.* غرغرو qorqoru سلیته saliteh
shriek *n., vi.* جیغ زدن jiq zadan
shrill *adj., vt., vi., n.* صدای زیر sedâye zir گوش خراش gush-kharâsh
shrimp *n., vi., adj.* میگو meygu
shrine *n., vt.* زیارتگاه ziârat-gâh امام زاده emâm-zâdeh
shrink *v.* آب رفتن âb raftan کوچک شدن kuchek shodan
shrink *n.* روانشناس ravân-shenâs
shrinkage *n.* آب رفتگی âb-raftegi کاهش kâhesh
shrivel *v.* پلاسیدن palâsidan پژمرده شدن pazhmordeh shodan
shroud *v.* پوشاندن pushândan کفن کردن kafan kardan
shroud *n.* کفن kafan پوشش pushesh لفافه lafâfeh
shrub *n.* بته boteh
shrubbery *n.* بته زار boteh-zâr
shrubby *adj.* پربته por-boteh

shrunk(en) *n.* آب رفته âb-rafteh

shuck *n., vt., int.* پوسته pusteh درآوردن dar âvardan

shucks! *n.* اه ah! تف tof!

shudder *vi., n.* لرزیدن larzidan چندش شدن chendesh shodan

shuffle *v.* بر زدن bor zadan

shuffle *v.* اطفاری راه رفتن atfâri râh raftân

shun *vt., n., adj.* دوری کردن duri kardan اجتناب کردن ejtenâb kardan

shush! *n.* هیس his!

shut *v.* بستن bastan

shut *n.* بسته basteh

shut(down) *n.* تعطیل کردن ta'til kardan

shut(in) *n.* محاصره کردن mohâsereh kardan

shut(off) *n.* خاموش کردن khâmush kardan

shut(out) *n.* بهیچ گذاشتن be-hich gozâshtan

shut(up) *n.* حبس کردن habs kardân ساکت کردن sâket kardan

shut(up)! *n.* خفه شو khafeh sho!

shut-eye *n.* چرت chort

shut-in *adj., n.* زمین گیر zamin-gir

shutdown *n.* تعطیلی ta'tili

shutoff *n.* قطع qat'

shutter *n., vt.* کرکره ker-kereh دریچهٔ عدسی daricheh-ye 'adâ

shuttle *n.* مسافری mosâferi

shuttle *n.* ماکو mâku

shuttle *v.* مسافربری کردن mosâfer-bari kardân

shy *adj.* خجالتی khejâlati کمرو kam-ru خجول khajul

shy *v.* پرتاب کردن partâb kardan

shy *adj.* کم دار kam-dâr

shy *v.* خجالت کشیدن khejâlat keshidan

shylock *n.* حاج جبار hâj-jabâr

shyster *n.* کلاش kal~âsh حقه باز hoq~eh-bâz

sibling(s) *n.* خواهربرادر khâhar barâdar اولاد olâd

sic *n., vt.* اینجوری injuri

sick *adj., n.* مریض mariz بیمار bimâr بیزار bizâr

sick bay *n.* بیمارستان کشتی bimârestân-e' kashti

sick bed *n.* بستر بیماری bastar-e' bimâri

sick(on) *n.* برانگیختن bar angikhtan

sicken *vt., vi.* ناخوش کردن nâ-khosh kardan بیزار کردن bizâr kardan

sickening *adj.* متهوع motehav~e' حال بهم زن hâl beham-zan

sickle *n.* داس dâs
sickly *adj., adv., vt.* نحیف nahif آور تهوع tahav~o'-âvar
sickness *n.* بیماری bimâri مرض maraz ناخوشی nâkhoshi سقم soqm
side *n.* طرف taraf سو su کنار kenâr جانب jâneb
side *v.* کردن داری طرف taraf-dâri kardan
side *n.* پهلو pahlu شقه shaq~eh
side *n.* ضلع zel'
side *n.* کناری kenâri بغلی baqali
side splitting *n.* دار خنده khandeh-dâr
side(by side) *n.* پهلو به پهلو pahlu be-pahlu
side(with) *n.* گرفتن طرف taraf gereftan
side-kick *n.* وردست var-dast دوست dust
side-line *n.* خط کنار kenâr-e' khat
side-step *vi., vt.* کردن اجتناب ejtenâb kardan
گرفتن ندیده nadideh gereftan
sidearm *n.* کمری اسلحهٔ aslaheh-ye' kamari
sidedish *n.* اضافی غذای qazây-e' ezâfi
sidelong *adj., adv.* بگوشه begusheh بری یک yek-bari
sidewalk *n.* رو پیاده piâdeh-ro
sideway *n., adj., adv.* راه کناره kenâreh-râh
sideways *adv., adj.* ازبغل az baqal بری یک yek-bari
siding *n., v.* جدار jedâr دیوارپوشی divâr pushi
siege *n., vt.* محاصره mohâsereh دوران dorân
sierra *n.* تیز نوک کوه kuh-e' nok-tiz
sieve *n., vt., vi.* کردن الک alak kardan
sieve *n.* الک alak غربیل qarbil
sift *vt., vi.* کردن وارسی vâresi kardan
sifter *n.* الک alak
sigh *vi., vt., n.* کشیدن آه âh keshidan
sight *n., vt., vi.* بینایی binâyi دید did منظره manzareh
sight unseen *n.* ندیده nadideh همینجوری hamin-juri
sight-seeing *n.* منظره تماشای tamâshâ-ye' manzareh
sight-seer *n.* تماشاگرمنظره tamâshâ-gar-e' manzareh
sightless *adj.* نابینا nâ-binâ
sign *n.* نشان neshân تابلو tâblo
sign *n.* نشانه neshâneh علامت 'alâmat
sign *n.* منزله manzaleh آیت âyat
sign *n.* برج borj

sign *v.* امضاء کردن emzâ' kardan
sign language *np.* زبان کر و لال zabân-e' kar-o lâl
sign(off) *n.* پایان دادن pâyân dâdan خاتمه دادن khâtemeh dâdan
sign(on) *n.* استخدام کردن estekhdâm kardan
sign(over) *n.* به اسم کردن be-esm kardan
sign(up) *n.* نام نویسی کردن nâm-nevisi kardan
signal *n., adj., vt.* علامت دادن 'alâmat dâdan راهنما râhnamâ
signalman *n.* مخابر علامت mokhâber-e' 'alâma
signatory *n.* امضاء کننده emzâ'-konandeh
signature *n.* امضاء emzâ'
signet *n.* مهرکردن mohr kardan خاتم khâtam
significance *n.* اهمیت ahamiyat مفهوم mafhum
significant *adj.* مهم mohem پرمعنی por-ma'nâ
signify *vt., vi.* نشان دادن neshân dâdan نموداربودن nemudâr budan
silence *n.* سکوت sokut خاموشی khâmushi
silence *v.* ساکت کردن sâket kardan خاموش کردن khâmush kardan
silencer *n.* صداخفه کن sedâ khafeh-kon
silent *adj.* ساکت sâket بیصدا bi-sedâ خاموش khâmush
silent partner *np.* شریک کناری sharik-e' kenâri
silently *adv.* بیصدا bi-sedâ آهسته âhesteh
silex *n.* پارچ قهوه pârch-e' qahveh
silhouette *n., vt.* سایه sâyeh شبح shabah
silk *n., adj., vi.* ابریشم abrisham پرند parand حریر harir
silk-stocking *np.* جوراب ابریشمی jurâb-e' abrishami
silken *adj.* ابریشمی abrishami
silkworm *n.* کرم ابریشم kerm-e' abrisham
silky *adj.* ابریشمی abrishami نرم narm
sill *n.* لبه labeh آستانه âstâneh
silly *n.* خل khol مسخره mas-khareh
silo *n., vt.* انبار غله anbâr-e' qal~eh انبارموشک anbâr-e' mushak
silt *n., vi., vt.* لای lây درده dordeh
silver *n., adj., vt., vi.* نقره noqreh سیم sim
silver *n., adj., vt., vi.* نقره ای noqreh-i سیمین simin
silver lining *np.* روزنۀ امید rozaneh-ye' omid
silver screen *np.* پردۀ سینما pardeh-ye' sinamâ
silverware *n.* قاشق چنگال qâshoq changâl
simian *adj., n.* میمونی meymuni
similar *adj.* مانند mânand شبیه shabih همتا ham-tâ مشابه moshâbeh

similarity *n.* شباهت shebâhat
similarly *adv.* متشابهاً moteshâ-behan همينطور hamintor
simmer *vi.* آهسته جوشاندن âhesteh jushândan
simmer(down) *n.* خنک شدن khonak shodan
آرام گرفتن ârâm gereftan
simper *vi., vt., n., adj.* ابلهانه خنديدن ablahâneh khandidan
simple *adj., n.* ساده sâdeh
simple-hearted *adj.* ساده دل sâdeh-del
simple-minded *adj.* ساده لوح sâdeh loh
simplicity *n.* سادگی sâdegi
simplification *n.* ساده سازی sâdeh-sâzi تسهيل tas-hil
simplify *n.* ساده ترکردن sâdeh-tar kardan
simply *adv.* مختصراً mokhtasaran بسادگی be-sâdegi
simulation *n.* وانمودی vânemudi
simultaneous *adj.* هم زمان ham zaman چندمجهوله chand-majhuleh
simultaneously *adv.* باهم bâ-ham هم زمان hamzamân
sin *n.* گناه gonâh بزه bazah معصيت ma'siyat
sin *v.* گناه کردن gonâh kardan
since *adv., pre., con.* تا ازآنوقت az ânvaqt tâ از az
since *adv., pre., con.* چونکه chonkeh نظربااينکه nazar be-inkeh
sincere *adj.* صادق sâdeg مخلص mokhles
sincerely *adv.* صادقانه sâdeqâneh مخلصانه mokhlesâneh
sincerity *n.* صداقت sedâqat خلوص نيت kholus-e' niyat
sine *n.* سينوس sinus
sinewy *adj.* 'عضلانی 'azolâni
sinful *adj.* گناهکار gonâh-kâr
sing *n., vi., vt.* آواز خواندن âvâz khândan
singe *n., v., vt.* کزدادن kez dâdan سوزاندن suzândan
singer *n.* آوازه خوان âvâzeh-khân نغمه سرا naqmeh-sarâ
single *adv., adj., vt., vi.* تک tak تنها tanhâ
single *adv., adj., vt., vi.* يکنفره yek-nafareh
single *adv., adj., vt., vi.* مجرد mojar~ad عزب 'azab يالغوز yal-quz
single(out) *n.* جداکردن jodâ kardan نشان کردن neshân kardan
single-handed(ly) *adj., adv.* دست تنها dast-tanhâ يکنفره yek-nafareh
يک تنه yek-taneh
singular *adj., n.* مفرد mofrad
sinister *adj.* پليد palid شيطانی sheytâni منحوس manhus
sinistral *adj.* چپی chapi

sink *v.* غرق کردن qarq kardan
sink *n.* چاهک châhak ظرف شویی zarf-shuyi
sink *v.* تنزل کردن tanaz~ol kardan افت کردن oft kardan
sinless *n.* بیگناه bi-gonâh مظلوم mazlum
sinner *n.* گناهکار gonâh-kâr بزه کار bazah-kâr
sinus *n.* سینوس sinus
sinusitis *n.* سینوزیت sinozit
sip *vt., vi., n.* یک قلپ خوردن yek qolop khordan لب زدن lab zadan
siphon *n.* سیفون زدن sifon zadan
siphon(off) *n.* خالی کردن khâli kardan
sir *n.* آقا âqâ قربان qorbân
sire *v.* توله انداختن tuleh andâkhtan
sire *n.* قربان qorbân
siren *n., adj., vi., vt.* آژیر âzhir
sirloin *n.* راسته râsteh
sissy *n., adj., vt.* نی نی ni-ni فوفول fu-ful
sister *n., adj., vt.* خواهر khâhar آبجی âbji همشیره ham-shireh
sister-in-law *n.* خواهرزن khâhar zan
sister-in-law *n.* خواهرشوهر khâhar shuhar
sister-in-law *n.* زن برادر zan barâdar
sisterhood *n.* خواهری khâhari
sisterly *n.* خواهرانه khâhar-âneh
sit *vi., vt.* نشستن neshastan
sit down! *n.* بشین beshin! بنشینید beneshinid
sit(in) *n.* شرکت کردن sherkat kardan
sit(out) *n.* تاتهنشستن tâ-tah neshastan
sit(out) *n.* کنارنشستن kenâr neshastan
sit(up) *n.* راست نشستن râst neshastân
sit-down *n.* بست bast
site *n., vt.* محل mahal صحنه sahneh
sitter *n.* بچه نگهدار bach~eh negah-dâr
sitting *n., v.* نشست neshast جلسه jaleseh
sitting room *n.* اطاق نشیمن otâq-e' neshiman
situate *v., adj.* قراردادن qarâr dâdan
situated *v.* واقع vâqe'
situation *n.* وضعیت vaz'iyat
situation *n.* موقعیت moqe'iyat
situation *n.* وضع vaz'

six(th) *n.* ششم sheshom
six-shooter *n.* ششلول shesh-lul شش تیر shesh-tir
sixteen(th) *n.* شانزدهم shânz-dahom
sixth sense *np.* حس ششم hes~-e' sheshom
sixtieth *adj.* شصتم shastom
sixty *n., adj.* شصت shast
sizable *n.* نسبتاً بزرگ nesbatan bozorg
size *n., vt.* اندازه andâzeh مقدار meqdâr
size(up) *n.* براندازکردن bar-andâz kardan
size(up) *n.* اندازه‌گرفتن andâzeh gereftan
sizing *n., v.* اندازه گیری andâzeh-giri آهار âhâr
sizzle *vi., n.* جلز و ولز کردن jelez-o velez kardan
sizzling *v.* سوزان suzân داغ dâq
skate *n., pl., v.* اسکیت eskeyt
skeet *n.* هدف گلی hadaf-e' geli
skeleton *n., adj.* اسکلت eskelet استخوان بندی ostokhân-bandi
skeleton key *np.OS* شاه کلید shâh-kelid
skeptic *n., adj.* اهل شک ahl-e' shak شکاک shak~âk
بدگمان bad-gamân
skeptical *adj.* شک کننده shak-konandeh
skepticism *n.* شک shak خلاف یقینی khalâf-e' yaqin-i
sketch *n., vt., vi.* طراحی کردن tar~âhi kardan
sketchbook *n.* کتاب نقاشی ketâb-e' naq~âshi
sketchy *n.* ناکامل nâ-kâmel ناواضح nâ-vâzeh
skew *vi., vt., adj., n.* کج کردن kaj kardan مایل کردن mâyel kardan
skewer *n., vt.* سیخ کباب sikh kabâb بسیخ کشیدن be-sikh keshidan
ski *n.* اسکی کردن eski kardan
skid *n., vt., vi.* لیز خوردن liz khordan سرخوردن sor khordan
skid row *np.* محله گداها mahal~eh-ye' gedâhâ
skiing *n.* اسکی بازی eski-bâzi
skill *n., vi.* مهارت mahârat استادی ostâdi کاردانی kâr-dâni
تبحر tabah~ or
skilled *adj.* ماهر mâher استاد ostâd کارآمد kâr-âmad نخبه nokhbeh
skillet *n.* ماهیتابه mâhi-tâbeh
skillful *adj.* با مهارت bâ-mahârat
skillfull *adj.* کاردان kâr-dân ماهر mâher استاد ostâd
متبحر motebah~ er
skim *vt., vi., n.* کف گرفتن kaf gereftan خامه‌گرفتن khâmeh gereftan

skim milk *np.* شیر بی خامه shir-e' bi-khâmeh
skim(off) *n.* از رو برداشتن az ru bar dâshtan
سرشیر گرفتن sar- shir gereftan
skimmer *n.* کف گیر kaf-gir خامه گیر khâmeh-gir
skimp *n.* خسیس بودن khasis budan
skimpy *n.* کم kam ناقابل nâ-qâbel
skin *n., vt., vi.* پوست کندن pust kandan جلد jeld
skin diving *np.* غواصی qav~âsi
skin grafting *np.* پیوندپوستی pey-vand-e' pusti
skin(alive) *n.* زنده پوست کندن zendeh pust kandan
skin-deep *adj., adv.* سطحی sat-hi
skinned *v.* پوست کنده pust-kandeh
skinner *n.* پوست کن pust-kan
skinny *adj.* لاغر lâqar نحیف nahif
skinny-dip *vi.* لخت شناکردن lokht shenâ kardan
skip *v.* پریدن paridan
skip *v.* از زیرش در رفتن az-ziresh dar raftan
skipper *n.* ناخدا nâ-khodâ
skirmish *n., vi.* زد و خورد zad-o-khord کشمکش kesh-makesh
skirt *n.* دامن dâman دامنه dâmaneh
skirt *v.* دورزدن dor zadan
skitter *vi.* پراندن parândan
skivvy *n.* زیر شلواری zir-shalvâri زیر لباسی zir-lebâsi
skulduggery *n.* دوز و کلک duz-o kalak
skulk *vi., n.* از زیرکاردررفتن az zir-e' kâr dar raftan
skull *n.* جمجمه jomjomeh
skullcap *n.* عرق چین 'araq-chin
skunk *n.* راسوی بدبو râsu-ye' bad-bu
sky *n.* آسمان âsemân سپهر sepehr فلک falak
sky-blue *adj.* آبی آسمانی âbi-e' âsemâni
sky-high *adv., adj.* تاآسمان tâ-âsemân به عرش be-'arsh
skylark *n., vi.* چکاوک chakâvak
skylight *n.* پنجرهٔ سقفی panjereh-ye' saqfi
skyline *v., n.* افق ofogh خط افق khat~-e' ofoq
skyrocket *n., vi., vt.* سرسام آور بالارفتن sarsâm-âvar bâlâ raftan
skyscraper *n.* آسمان خراش âsemân-kharâsh
skyward *adv., adj.* بطرف آسمان betaraf-e' âsemân
slab *adj.* تکه tek~eh پاره سنگ pâreh-sang

slab-sided *adj.* لخت lakht پت وپهن pat-o pahn

slack *adj., n., vt., vi.* شل کردن shol kardan آهسته کردن âhesteh kardan

slack(off) *n.* فرونشین کردن foru-neshin kardan

slack(up) *n.* آهسته تررفتن âhesteh-tar raftan

slacken *n.* آهسته کردن âhesteh-târ kardan

slacks *n.* شلوار shalvâr

slag *n., v.* سوخته جوش sukhteh-jush

slain *v.* بقتل رساندن be-qatl resândan

slain *v.* مقتول maqtul

slake *vt., vi.* فرو نشاندن foru neshândan

slalom *n.* زیگ زاگ zig-zâg

slam *n.* شلم shelem

slam *v.* قایم بستن qâyem bastan

slam-bang *adv.* زود zud سرپایی sarpâyi

slammer *n.* هلفدونی holof-duni

slander *v.* افترازدن efterâ zadan

slander *n.* افترا efterâ نسبت دروغ nesbat-e' doruq
هتک شرف hatk-e' sharaf

slanderer *n.* افترازننده eftera zanandeh مفتری moftari

slanderous *n.* افترا آمیز efterâ-âmiz

slang *n., vi., vt.* اصطلاحی estelâhi مصطلح mostalah

slant *vi., adj.* کج کردن kaj kardan مایل کردن mâyel kardan

slanted *n.* مورب movar~ab بادامی bâdâmi کج kaj

slap *n.* چک chak سیلی sili تودهنی tu-dahani

slap *v.* چک زدن chak zadân سیلی زدن sili zadan

slash *vt., vi., n.* چاقو زدن châqu zadan بریدن boridan

slashing *n., adj.* خارق العاده khâreqol-'âdeh

slat *n., vi.* تونال tofâl

slate *n.* لیست اسامی list-e' asâmi پرونده parvandeh

slate *v.* سرزنش کردن sarzanesh kardan

slaughter *n.* کشتار koshtâr قتل عام qatl-e' 'âm

slaughter *v.* ذبح کردن zebh kardan

slaughter *v.* کشتار کردن koshtâr kardan
قتل عام کردن qatl-e' 'âm kardan

slaughterhouse *n.* کشتارگاه koshtâr-gâh سلاخ خانه salâkh-khâneh
مسلخ maslakh

slave *n.* برده bardeh غلام qolâm بنده bandeh

slave *v.* سخت کارکردن sakht kâr kardan بردگی کردن bardegi kardan

slave woman *adj.* کنیز kaniz
slavery *n.* بردگی bardegi
slaw *n.* کلم ریز kalam-riz
slay *n., vt.* کشتن koshtan بقتل رساندن be-qatl resândan
sleave *vt., n.* نخ پیچ nakh-pich
sleaze *n.* کثافت kesâfat بی محتوی bi-mohtavâ
sleaze-bag *n.* کثیف kasif شیشو shepeshu
sleazy *adj.* کثیف kasif لجن lajân درب و داغون darb-o dâqun
sled *n., vi., vt.* درشکه برفی doroshkeh barfi لوژ luzh
sledge *n., vt., vi.* پتک زدن potk zadan
sledge-hammer *vt., vi., adj.* پتک potk
sleep *vi., vt., n.* خوابیدن khâbidan خواب رفتن khâb raftan
sleep(away) *n.* درخواب گذراندن dar khâb gozarândan
sleep(off) *n.* باخواب فراموش کردن bâ-khâb farâmush kardan
sleep-head *n.* خوابالو khâbâlu
sleeper *n.* با تختخواب bâ takhte-khâb
sleeping bag *np.* کیسۀ خواب kiseh-ye' khâb
sleepless *adj.* بی خواب bi-khâb
sleet *n., vi.* تگرگ باریدن tagarg bâridan
sleety *adj.* تگرگی tagargi
sleeve *n., vt.* آستین âstin
sleeveless *adj.* بی آستین bi-âstin
sleigh *n., vt., vi.* درشکه برفی doroshkeh barfi لوژ luzh
sleight *n.* تردستی tar-dasti چشمه cheshmeh
slender *adj.* باریک bârik قلمی qalami
sleuth *n., vt., vi.* کارآگاه kâr-âgâh
slew *n., v., vt., vi.* چرخاندن charkhândan
slice *n., vt., vi.* قاچ دادن qâch dâdan برش دادن boresh dâdan
slicer *n.* قاچ کن qâch-kon
slick *vt., n.* لیز liz
slick *vt., n.* ماهر mâher تردست tar-dast
slick *vt., n.* چرب charb
slide *vi., vt., n.* سرسره sor-soreh
slide *vi., vt., n.* سرخوردن sor khordan
slide rule *np.* خط کش محاسبهای khat-kesh-e' mohâsebeh-i
slight *adj., vt., n.* جزئی joz'i کم kam
slightly *n.* یک کمی yek-kami جزئی joz'i
slim *adj., vt., vi.* باریک bârik لاغر lâqar

slime

slime *n., vt.* لجن lajan
slimy *adj., vt.* لجنی lajani
sling *n.* گردن آویز gardan-âviz
sling *v.* سنگ قلاب انداختن sang-qol~âb andâkhtan
sling *n.* فلاخن falâkhon
slingshot *n.* تیرکمان tir-kamân
slip *n.* زیرپوش zir-push
slip *v.* لیزخوردن liz khordan لغزیدن laqzidan
slip(up) *n.* اشتباه کردن eshtebâh kardan خراب کردن kharâb kardan
slip-up *n.* خطا khatâ خراب کاری kharâb-kâri
slippage *n.* لغزش laqzesh
slipper(s) *n.* دم پایی dam-pâyi ارسی orsi
slippery *adj.* لیز liz
slipshod *n.* شلخته shelakhteh پاشنه سابیده pâshneh-sâbideh
slipslop *n.* شر و ور sher-o ver سگی sagi
slit *vt., n.* چاک دادن châk dâdan برش دادن boresh dâdan
slither *n.* لیزخوردن liz khordan مارپیچ رفتن mâr-pich raftan
slithery *adj.* لیز liz کج و کوله kaj-o koleh
sliver *n., vt., vi.* تراشه tarâsheh
slob *n.* کثیف kasif شلخته shelakhteh
slobber *vi., vt., n.* آب لب و لوچه ریختن âb-e' lab-o lucheh rikhtan
sloe *n.* آلوچه âlucheh
slogan *n.* شعار sho'âr
slop *n.* شلخته shelakhteh
slope *vi., vt., n.* شیب دادن shib dâdan سرازیری sarâ-ziri
sloping *v.* شیب دار shib-dâr
sloppy *adj.* کثیف کاری kasif-kâri
slosh *n.* شلپ راه رفتن sholop-sholop râh raftan
slot *n., vt.* جای پول jây-e' pul سوراخ surâkh
slot machine *np.* جک پات jak pât
slouch *sln.* دست ازپا درازتر dast az pâ derâz-tar
slouch *v.* دولادولا راه رفتن dolâ-dolâ râh raftan
slouchy *adj.* شانه افتاده shâneh oftâdeh
slough *n.* لجن زار lajan-zâr
slough *v.* پوست انداختن pust andâkhtan
sloven *n., adj.* لاابالی وار lâ-ebâli-vâr شلختگی shelakhtegi
slovenly *adj., adv.* لاابالی lâ-ebâli شلخته shelakhteh
slow *v.* آهسته کردن âhesteh kardan یواش کردن yavâsh kardan

slow *adj.* آهسته âhesteh کند kond
slow(down) *n.* کمترکردن kam-tar kardan
slow-motion *adj.* حرکت آهسته harekat-e' âhesteh
slow-moving *adj.* کند kond کم سرعت kam-sor'at
slow-witted *adj.* کند kond
slowdown *n.* کاهش kâhesh کم کاری kam-kâri
slowly *adv.* به آهستگی be-âhestegi یواش یواش yavâsh-yavâsh
slowness *n.* کندی kondi آهستگی âhestegi
sludge *n.* لای lây گل gel لجن lajan
slue *n.* چرخیدن charkhidan
slug *n.* گلوله goluleh
slug *n.* حلزون بی صدف halazun-e' bi-sadaf
slug *v.* با مشت زدن bâ mosht zadan
sluggard *n., adj.* تنبل tanbal
slugger *n.* بکسور boksor
sluggish *adj.* کند kond تنبل tanbal
sluice *n., vi.* آبگیره âb-gireh کانال آب kânâl-e' âb
slum *n., vi.* محلهٔ فقرا mahal~eh-ye' foqarâ
slumber *vi., vt.* خوابیدن khâbidan خواب فراموشی khâb-e' farâmushi
slumberous *adj.* خواب آور khâb-âvar خوابالو khâb-âlu
slump *vi., n.* پایین افتادن pâyin oftâdan تنزل کردن tanaz~ol kardan
slur *n., vt.* افترا زدن efterâ zadan لکه دار کردن lakeh-dâr kardan
slur(over) *n.* ماست مالی کردن mâst-mâli kardan لوث کردن los kardan
slurred *v.* من و من men-o men
slurry *n., vt., adj.* گلاب gelâb
slush *n., vt.* برف گلی barf-e' geli
slush fund *np.* پول رشوه pul-e' reshveh
slut *n.* جنده jendeh پتیاره patiâreh سلیطه saliteh
sly *n.* آب زیرکاه âb zir-e' kâh موذی muzi
slyly *adv.* موذیانه muziâneh
smack *n.* ملچ ملچ moloch moloch ماچ باصدا mâch-e' bâ-sedâ
smack -*v.* باصداماچ کردن bâ-sedâ mâch kardan
smack *v.* مزه دادن mazeh dâdan بو دادن bu dâdan
smack *v.* چک زدن chak zadan
smacking *adj., adv., n.* پرنشاط por-neshât
small *adj., adv., n.* کوچک kucheck
small arms *n.* اسلحهٔ سبک aslaheh-ye' sabok
small change *np.* پول خرد pul khord

small intestine *np.* روده کوچک rudeh kuchek
small of the back *n.* حفرهٔ کمر hofreh-ye' kamar
small potatoes *np.* کم ارزش kam-arzesh
small talk *np.* گپ gap
small time *np.* درجه دو darejeh do
smallpox *n.* آبله âbeleh
smart *vi., vt., adj., n.* شیک shik تشنگ qashang
smart *vi., vt., adj., n.* زرنگ zerang زیرک zirak باهوش bâ-hush
          نخاله nokhâleh
smart aleck *np.* بچه پررو bach~eh-por-ru مردرند mard-e' rend
smartmouth *n.* حاضرجوابی کردن hâzer-javâbi kardan
smartmouth *n.* حاضرجواب hâzer-javâb گستاخ gostâkh
smash *vt., vi., n., adj.* خرد کردن khord kardan
          درهم شکستن dar ham shekastan
smash-up *n.* تصادف tasâdof درهم شکنی dar ham-shekani
smashing *n.* خیلی عالی kheyli 'âli محشر mah-shar
smattering *n., adj.* علم ظاهری 'elm-e' zâheri
smear *v.* بی آبرو کردن bi-âberu kardan
smear *v.* مالیدن mâlidan آلودن âludan
smell *vt., vi., n.* بوکشیدن bu keshidan بو کردن bu kardân
smeller *n.* بوکن bu-kon بینی bini
smelly *adj.* بدبو bad-bu
smelt *v., vt.* تصفیه فلزی tasfieh felez~i آهن گدازی âhan godâzi
smelte *n.* فلز تصفیه کن felez tasfieh-kon آهن گداز âhan-godâz
smile *v.* لبخند زدن labkhand zadan تبسم کردن tabas~om kardan
smile *n.* لبخند labkhand تبسم tabas~om
smiling *adj.* متبسم motebas~em
smirch *vt., n.* کثیف کردن kasif kardan لکه دارکردن lakeh-dâr kardan
smirk *vi., vt., n.* پوزخند زدن puz-khand zadan
          تسخرزدن tas-khar zadan?
smite *vi.* زدن zadan خوردن khordan
smith *n.* آهنگر âhan-gar
smitten *adj., v.* مبتلا mobtalâ
smock *n., vt.* روپوش rupush
smog *n.* دود ماشین dud mâshin
smoke *v.* سیگار کشیدن sigâr keshidan دود کردن dud kardan
smoke *n.* دود dud
smokehouse *n.* دودخانه dud-khâneh

smoker *n.* سیگاری sigâri دودی dudi
smoking *n., v.* سیگار کشی sigâr-keshi
smokless *n.* بی دود bi-dud
smoky *adj.* دودی dudi دودآلود dud-âlud پر دود por-dud
smolder *vi., n.* آهسته دودکردن âhesteh dud kardan
smoldering *n.* کم دود kam-dud
smooch *n.* بوس کردن bus kardan ماچ کردن mâch kardan
smooth *adj.* نرم narm صاف sâf
smooth *v.* صاف وصوف کردن sâf-o suf kardan نرم کردن narm kardan
smooth(away) *n.* برطرف کردن bar-taraf kardan
smooth(down) *n.* آرام کردن ârâm kardan
smooth-tongued *n.* چرب زبان charb-zabân
smoothen *n.* نرم کردن narm kardan صاف کردن sâf kardan
smorgasbord *n.* بوفه bufeh
smother *vt.* خفه کردن khafeh kardan
smudge *n., vt., vi.* لک انداختن lak andâkhtan
لکه دار کردن lakeh-dâr kardan
smudgy *n.* لکه دار lakeh-dâr
smug *adj.* از خود راضی az khod-râzi
smuggle *vt., vi.* قاچاق کردن qâchâq kardan
قاچاقی ردکردن qâchâqi rad kardan
smuggler *n.* قاچاقچی qâchâq-chi
smuggling *v.* قاچاق qâchâq
smut *n., vt.* رکیک rakik مستهجن mostahjan
smutch *n.* لکه lakeh دود dud
smutty *adj.* کثیف kasif رکیک rakik
snack *n./adj.* مختصرغذا mokh-tasar qazâ ته بندی tah-bandi
snack *v.* ته بندی کردن tah-bandi kardan
snafu *n.* اغتشاش eqteshâsh خرابکاری kharâb-kâri
snag *n., vt., vi.* گرفتاری gereftâri اشکال eshkâl
snag *n., vt., vi.* پارگی pâregi شکاف shekâf جر jer
snaggy *adj.* پر از شاخه por az shâkheh
snail *n.* حلزون halazun
snail-paced *adj.* حلزون وار halazun-vâr
snake *n.* مار mâr
snake *v.* کشیدن keshidan
snake charmer *np.* مرتاض مارگیر mortâz-e' mâr-gir
snaky *adj.* مارمانند mâr-mânand پرازمار por az mâr

snap *v.* شکستن shekastan
snap *v.* زود عمل کردن zud 'amal kardan
snap *v.* بشکن زدن beshkan zadan
snap *adj.* زود zud برقی barqi
snap *v.* بستن bastan
snap *adj.* راحت râhat آب خوردن âb-khordan
snap *v.* قاپ زدن qâp zadan بردن bordan
snap(at) *n.* تشرزدن tashar zadan پریدن paridan
snapdragon *n.* گل میمون gol-e' mymun
snappy *adj.* تند tond زود zud
snapshot *n., vt., vi.* عکس 'aks
snare *n., vt.* بدام انداختن be-dâm andâkhtan
تله گذاشتن taleh gozâshtan
snarl *vt., n., vi.* خرناس کشیدن khornâs keshidan
snarly *adj.* اخمو akhmu قاطی پاطی qâti pâti
snatch *n.* قاپ زدن qâp zadan دزدیدن dozdidan
snatch(at) *n.* چنگ انداختن chang andâkhtan
sneak *vi., vt., n.* یواشکی بردن yavâshaki bordan
sneak(out) *n.* دزدکی دررفتن dozdaki dar raftan
sneaker(s) *n.* کفش کتانی kafsh-e' katâni
sneaking *n.* موذی muzi آب زیرکاه âb-zir-e' kâh
sneaky *adj.* آب زیرکاه âb-zir-e' kâh
sneer *vi., vt., n.* ریشخند زدن rish-khand zadan
استهزاء کردن estehzâ' kardan
sneeze *vi., n.* عطسه کردن 'atseh kardan
snicker *vi.* هرهر خندیدن her-her khandidan
snide(ly) *n.* خبیث khabis پست past
sniff *vi., vt., n.* بوکردن bu kardan فین فین کردن fin-fin kardan
sniffles *n.* سرماخوردگی sarmâ-khordegi
snip *vt., vi., n.* بریدن boridan چیدن chidan
snipe *n., vi.* از کمینگاه تیراندازی کردن az kamingâh tirandâzi kardan
sniper *n.* تیرانداز مخفی tirandâz-e' makhfi
snitch *v.* جاسوسی کردن jâsusi kardan
snitch *adj.* جاسوس jâsus خبرچین khabar-chin
snival *n.* فین کردن fin kardan ادا درآوردن adâ dar âvardan
snob *n.* متکبر motekab~er دماغ بالا damâq bâlâ
snobbery *n.* تکبر takab~or
snobish *n.* دماغ بالا damâq bâlâ

snoop *adj.* فضول fozul فضول باشی fozul-bâshi
snoop *v.* فضولی کردن fozuli kardan
snoot *n.* بینی bini صورت surat
snooze *vi., n.* چرت زدن chort zadan
snore *vi., vt., n.* خروپف کردن khor-o pof kardan
خرناس کشیدن khornâs keshidan
snot *n.* اندماغ an-damâq سنده sendeh
snotty *n.* زننده zanandeh
snout *n.* پوزه puzeh
snow *n.* برف barf
snow *v.* چاپلوسی کردن châplusi kardan
snow job *np.* چاپلوسی châplusi تملق تملق tamal~oq
snow-capped *n.* پوشیده از برف pushideh az barf
snow-white *adj.* سفید برفی sefid barfi
snowball *n., vt., vi.* گوله برف guleh-barf
تندحرکت کردن tond harekat kardan
snowbird *n.* کبک برفی kabk-e' barfi
snowfall *n.* ریزش برف rizesh-e' barf
snowflake *n.* ذره برف zar~eh bârf
snowshoe *n., vi.* کفش برفی kafsh-e' barfi
snowstorm *n.* کولاک برف kulâk-e' barf
snub *vt., n., adj.* خوارشماردن khâr shemârdan
تحقیر کردن tahqir kardan
snub-nosed *adj.* دماغ بالا damâq bâlâ
snubby *adj.* سربالا sar bâlâ
snuff *n., vi., vt.* انفیه anfieh
snuff(out) *n.* خاموش کردن khâmush kardan
ازبین بردن az beyn bordan
snuffbox *n.* انفیه دان anfieh-dân
snuffle *vt., n.* تودماغی حرف زدن tu damâqi harf zadan
snuffles *n.* سرما خوردگی sarmâ khordegi
snug *adj., adv., n.* تنگ tang دنج denj
snuggle *vi., vt., n.* بغل کردن baqal kardan چسباندن chasbândan
so *adv., n., pro., int.* که اینطور keh in-tor
so *adv., n., pro., int.* که چی keh chi
so *adv., n., pro., int.* پس pas بنابراین banâ bar-in
so far *n.* تا اینجا tâ injâ تاکنون tâ-konun
so long *np.* بامید دیدار be-omid-e' didâr خداحافظ khodâ hâfez

so much *n.* اینقدر inqadr بقدری be-qadri
so-and-so *n.* فلانی felâni
so-called *adj.* کذائی kazâ'i ملقب به molaq~ab beh
so-so *n.* ای ey بی تعریف bi-ta'rif
soak *vi., vt., n.* خیساندن khisândan خیس کردن khis kardan
soap *vt.* صابون زدن sâbun zadan
soap bubble *np.* کف صابون kaf-sâbun
soap opera *n.* تئاترتلویزیونی te'âtr-e' televizyoni
soapy *adj.* صابونی sâbuni
soar *vi., n.* اوج گرفتن oj gereftan روی هوا رفتن ruy-e' havâ raftan
sob *n., vi.* هق هق گریه کردن heq-heq geryeh kardan
sobeit *n.* چنین باشد chenin bâshad
sober *adj.* هوشیار hushyâr مستی ازسرپریده masti az sar parideh
sober(up) *n.* هوشیارکردن hushyâr kardan
مستی ازسرپریدن masti az sar pâridân
sobriety *n.* هوشیاری hushyâri اعتدال e'tedâl
soccer *n.* فوتبال futbâl
sociable *adj.* معاشرتی mo'âsherati
social *adj., n.* اجتماعی ejtemâ'i
social science(s) *n.* علوم اجتماعی 'olum-e' ejtemâ'i
social service *np.* خدمات اجتماعی khadamât-e' ejtemâ'i
social work *np.* خدمات اجتماعی khadamât-e' ejtemâ'i
social worker *np.* کارمنداموراجتماعی kârmand-e' omur-e' ejtemâ'i
socialism *n.* سوسیالیسم sosiâlism جامعه گرایی jâme'eh-garâyi
socialist *n.* سوسیالیست sosiâlist جامعه گرا jâme'eh-garâ
socialite *n.* سرشناس sar-shenâs
socialization *n.* جامعه گری jâme'eh-gari معاشرت mo'âsherat
socialize *vt.* معاشرت کردن mo'âsherat kardan
society *n., adj.* جامعه jâme'eh
society *n., adj.* انجمن anjoman کانون kânun
sociologist *n.* جامعه شناس jâme'eh-shenâs
sociology *n.* جامعه شناسی jâme'eh-shenâsi
sock *v.* زدن zadan
sock *n.* جوراب jurâb
socket *n., vt.* مفصل mafas~al
socket *n., vt.* پریز periz
socket *n., vt.* کاسه kâseh حدقه hâdaqeh
soda jerk *n.* پپسی فروش pepsi forush

soda lime *n.* آهک âhak
soda water *np.* آب گاز دار âb-e′ gâz-dâr
sodden *n.* خیس خیس khis-e′ khis
sodomy *n.* لواط lavât
soever *adv.* بهرنوع be-har no′
sofa *n.* مبل mobl
soft drink *n.* نوشابه nushâbeh
soft head *n.* نفهم nafahm ببو babu
soft shoulder *np.* کنارجاده kenâr-e′ jâd~eh
soft-boiled *adj.* نیم پز nim pâz عسلی ′asali
soft-hearted *adj.* دل رحم del-rahm
soft-shell(ed) *n.* نرم پوست narm-pust
soft-soap *n.* چاپلوسی châp-lusi
soft-spoken *adj.* نرم زبان narm-zabân
نحوهٔ ملایم nahveh-ye′ molâyem
soften *vt., vi.* نرم کردن narm kardan
softie *n.* نرم دل narm-del
softy *n.* نرم دل narm-del
soggy *n.* خیس khis وارفته vârafteh
soil *vt., n.* خاک khâk زمین zamin چرک cherk
soilage *n.* علیق ′aliq
soire'e *n.* شب نشینی shab-neshini
sojourn *vi.* دیدار موقتی didâr-e′ movaq~ati
solace *v., n.* تسکین‌دادن taskin dâdan آرامش دادن ârâmesh dâdan
solar *n.* خورشیدی khorshidi
solar plexus *np.* شکم shekam اعصاب شکم a′sâb-e′ shekam
solar system *n.* منظومهٔ شمسی manzumeh-ye′ shamsi
Solar System *n.* منظومهٔ شمسی manzumeh-ye′ shamsi
solar year *np.* سال شمسی sâl-e′ shamsi
solarium *n.* آفتاب خانه âftâb-khâneh
solarize *vt., vi.* خورشیدی کردن khorshidi kardan
sold *v.* فروخته شده forukhteh shodeh
solder *n., vt., vi.* لحیم کردن lahim kardan
soldering iron *n.* دستگاه لحیم کنی dastgâh-e′ lahim-koni
soldier *n., vi.* سرباز sarbâz سپاهی sepâhi عسکر ′askar
soldier of fortune *n.* ماجراجو mâjerâ-ju مزدور mozdur
soldierly *n.* شجاعانه shojâ′âneh
soldiery *n.* سربازی sarbâzi

sole *n., vt.* كف پا kaf-e' pâ
sole *n., vt.* تخت كفش takht-e' kafsh
sole *n., vt.* انحصارى enhesâri تنها tanhâ
sole *n., vt.* حلوا ماهى halvâ-mâhi
solely *adv.* منحصراً mon-haseran نقط faqat
solemn *adj.* جدى jed~i رسمى rasmi
solemnity *n.* جديت jed~iyat وقار vaqâr
solemnize *vt., vi.* رسمى كردن rasmi kardan
solicit *vt., vi.* تقاضا كردن taqâzâ kardan خواستار شدن khâstâr shodan
solicitation *n.* تقاضا taqâzâ درخواست dar-khâst
solicitor *n.* متقاضى moteqâzi نماينده namâyandeh
solicitous *adj.* علاقمند 'alâqe-mand دلواپس del-vâpas
solicitude *n.* علاقمندى 'alâqe-mandi دلواپسى del-vâpasi
solid *adj., n.* سفت seft توپر tu-por يك پارچه yek-pârcheh
solid *adj., n.* جامد jâmed
solid *adj., n.* استوار ostovâr محكم mohkam پابرجا pâ-bar jâ
solidarity *n.* اتحاد et~ehâd يك پارچه گى yek-pârchegi
solidary *adj.* متحد mot~ahed يگانه yegâneh
solidify *vt., vi.* محكم mohkam تثبيت كردن tasbit kardan
solidity *n.* استحكام estehkâm سفتى sefti
soliloquy *n.* باخودصحبتى bâ-khod-sohbati
solitaire *n.* تنها tanhâ فال ورق fâl-e' varaq
solitary *adj., n.* انفرادى enferâdi تنها tanhâ
solitude *n.* تنهايى tanhâyi خلوت khalvat
solo *adv., v., n., adj.* تنها tanhâ تكى taki
solo *adv., v., n., adj.* تك نواز tak-navâz
soloist *n.* تك نواز tak-navâz
solstice *n.* تحويل خورشيدى tahvil-e' khorshidi
soluble *adj., n.* حل شدنى hal-shodani
solution *n.* محلول mahlul
solution *n.* حل hal
solve *vt.* حل كردن hal kardan
solvency *n.* تحليل tahlil
solvency *n.* توانائى پرداخت tavânâ'i-e' pardâkht
solvent *adj.* محلل mohal~el حل كننده hâl-konandeh
somatic *adj.* جسمانى jesmâni بدنى badani
somber *adj.* غمناك qam-nâk تيره tireh
some *adj., pro., adv.* يك مقدار yek meqdâr كمى kami

some *adj., pro., adv.* بعضی از ba'zi az برخی از barkhi az
somebody *pro., n.* یکنفر yek-nafar یک کسی yek-kasi
someday *adv.* یک روز (ی) yek-ruz(i)
somehow *adv.* یک جوری yek-juri بدلیلی be-dalili
someone *n.* یکنفر yek-nafar یک کسی yek-kasi
somersault *n.* پشتک واروزدن poshtak-vâru zadan
معلق زدن mo'al~aq zadan
something *pro., n., adv.* یک چیزی yek-chizi
sometime *adv., adj.* یک وقتی yek-vaqti
sometimes *adv.* بعضی وقتها ba'zi-vaqt-hâ گاهی gâhi
someway(s) *n.* به یک طریق beh-yek tariq
somewhat *adv., n.* تااندازه ای tâ-andâzeh-i قدری qadri
somewhere *pro., n., adv.* یکجایی yek-jâyi
son *n.* پسر pesar فرزند farzand
son of a bitch *n.* مادرجنده mâdar jendeh
son of a gun *np* ناقلا nâqolâ ناکس nâ-kes
son-in-law *n.* داماد dâmâd
sonance *n.* صدا sedâ آوا âvâ
sonant *adj., n.* صدادار sedâ-dâr آوایی âvâyi
sonar *n.* موج صدا moj-e' sedâ
song *n.* آواز âvâz ترانه tarâneh
sonic *adj.* صدایی sedâyi
sonnet *n., vi., vt.* غزل qazal
sonny *n.* آقاپسر âqâ pesar پسرجان pesar jân
sonorant *n.* صدادار sedâ-dâr
sonorous *adj.* باصدا bâ-sedâ
sonship *n.* فرزندی farzandi
soon *adj.* بزودی bezudi زود zud
sooner *n.* زودتر zud-tar
sooner or later *n.* دیریازود dir yâ zud
soot *n., vt.* دوده dudeh
sooth *n.* حقیقی haqiqi
soothe *vt., vi.* تسکین دادن taskin dâdan
soothfast *adj.* راست گو râst-gu
soothing *v.* تسکین دهنده taskin-dâhandeh آرام ده ârâm-deh
آرامش بخش ârâmesh-bakhsh
soothsayer *n.* غیبگو qeyb-gu فالگیر fâl-gir
sooty *n.* دوده ای dudeh-i

sop *n., v.* خیس کردن khis kardan تیلیت کردن tilit kardan
sophism *n.* سفسطه گرایی saf-sateh-garâyi
sophist *n.* سفسطه گرا saf-sateh-garâ
sophistical *n.* سفسطه آمیز saf-sateh-âmiz
sophisticated *adj.* پیش رفته pish-rafteh
sophomore *n.* محصل سال دوم mohas~el-e' sâl-e' dov~om
sopping *adj., v.* خیس khis
soppy *adj.* خیس khis بارانی bârâni
soprano *n., adj.* صدای زیر sedâ-ye' zir
sorcerer *n.* ساحر sâher افسونگر afsun-gar سحرکننده sehr-konandeh
sorcerer *n.* جادوگر jâdugar ساحر sâher
sorcerous *adj.* جادوگرانه jâdu-garâneh
sorcery *n.* جادوگری jâdu-gari
sordid *adj.* کثیف kasif پست past
sore *adj., n., adv.* زخم zakhm درد dard
sore *adj., n., adv.* دلخور del-khor رنجیده ranjideh آزرده âzordeh
مکدر mokad~ar
sorehead *n.* اوقات تلخ oqât-talkh
sororicide *n.* خواهرکشی khâhar-koshi
sorority *n.* انجمن دختران anjoman-e' dokhtarân
sorosis *n.* توت tut
sorrel *n., adj.* ترشک torshak
sorrow *n.* غم qam غصه qos~eh اندوه anduh الم elam
sorrowful *n.* غمگین qamgin غصه دار qos~eh-dâr
sorry *adj., vt., vi.* متأسف mote'as~ef پشیمان pashimân نادم nâdem
sorry excuse *n.* عذر ناموجه 'ozr-e' nâ-movajah
sort *v.* جورکردن jur kardan دسته کردن dasteh kardan
sort *n.* جور jur قسم qesm نوع no'
sort of *n.* همچین ham-chin
sortie *n., vi.* یورش yuresh حمله hamleh
sough *n., vt.* خش خش khesh-khesh
soul *n.* روان ravân روح ruh جان jân نفس nafs
soulful *adj.* پراحساس por-ehsâs
sound *adj.* سالم sâlem تخت takht
sound *n.* تنگه tangeh
sound *n.* صدا sedâ صوت sot
sound *v.* بصدادرآمدن be-sedâ dar âmadan
sound effects *n.* صداسازی sedâ-sâzi

sound track *n.* موزیک فیلم muzik-e' film
sound(off) *n.* بترتیب صدا کردن betar-tib sedâ kardan
sounder *n.* صداکن sedâ-kon
sounding *adj.* عمق پیمایی 'omq-peymâyi
soundless *adj.* بیصدا bi-sedâ
soundly *adv.* کاملاً kâmelan درست dorost
soundman *n.* صدابردار sedâ-bardâr
soundproof *adj., vt.* صداگیر sedâ-gir ضدصدا zed~-e' sedâ
soup *n., vt.* آش âsh سوپ sup
soup kitchen *np.* غذاخوری مجانی qazâ-khori-e' maj~âni
soup(up) *n.* سریعترکردن sari'-tar kardan
sour *adj., n., vi., vt.* ترش شدن torsh shodan ترش رو torsh-ru
source *n.* منشاء mansha' سرچشمه sar-cheshmeh مأخذ ma'khaz
مرجع marja'
sourdough *n.* خمیر ترش khamir torsh
sourpuss *n.* اخمو akhmu
souse *n.* ترشی torshi مست mast
souse *v.* ترشی انداختن torshi andâkhtan
soused *v.* مست mast پاتیل pâtil
south *n.* جنوب jonub
South Pole *np.* قطب جنوب qotb-e' jonub
southbound *adj.* بطرف جنوب be-taraf-e' jonub
southeast *n.* جنوب شرقی jonub-e' sharqi
southerly *adj., adv., n.* جنوبی jonubi ازطرف جنوب az taraf-e' jonub
southern *adj., n.* جنوبی jonubi
southerner *n.* اهل جنوب ahl-e' jonub
southpaw *n., adj.* چپول chapul
southward *adj.* بطرف جنوب be-taraf-e' jonub
southwest *n.* جنوب غربی jonub-e' qarbi
souvenir *n.* یادگاری yâdgâri سوغاتی soqâti
sovereign *n., adj.* مستقل mostaqel
sovereign *n., adj.* پادشاه pâdeshâh
sovereign *n., adj.* سکه sek~eh
sovereignty *n.* استقلال esteqlâl تمامیت tamâmiyat
soviet *n., adj.* شوروی shoravi شورایی shorâyi
sow *n.* خوک ماده khuk-e' mâd~eh
sow *v.* تخم کاشتن tokhm kâshtan بذرافشاندن bazr afshândan
spa *n.* ورزشگاه varzesh-gâh

space *v.* فاصله دادن fâseleh dâdan
space *n.* فضا fazâ
space *n.* جا jâ فاصله fâseleh
space fiction *n.* داستان فضانوردی dâstân-e' fazâ-navardi
spaced-out *n.* هپروتی haparuti گیج gij
spaceless *adj.* بدون فضا bedun-e' fazâ
spaceman *n.* فضا نورد fazâ-navard
spacer *n.* فاصله دهنده fâseleh-dahandeh
spaceship *n.* سفینه safineh
spacing *n.* فاصله‌گیری fâseleh giri
spacious *adj.* جادار jâ-dâr وسیع vasi'
spade *n.* بیل bil
spade(s) *n.* پیک pik
spaghetti *n.* اسپاگتی espâgeti ماکارونی mâkâroni
Spain *n.* اسپانیا espânyâ
spall *n., vt., vi.* خرده سنگ khordeh sang
span *v.* در بر گرفتن dar-bar geraftan طول داشتن tul dâshtan
span *n.* فاصله fâseleh وجب vajab طول tul
spank *vi., vt., n.* کتک زدن kotak zadan
spanking *adj., adv.* کتک kotak
spanking *adj., adv.* تند tond سریع sari'
spar *v.* بوکس بازی کردن boks-bâzi kardan
spar *n.* میله mileh دکل dakal
spare *v.* گذشتن gozashtan نجات دادن nejât dâdan
spare *adj.* اضافی ezâfi زیادی ziâdi
spare *adj.* یدکی yadaki زیادی ziâdi
spare *adj.* کم kam
spare time *n.* اوقات فراغت oqât-e' farâqat
spare-rib *n.* گوشت دنده gusht-e' dandeh
sparg *n.* ستون sotun
spark *n.* جرقه jeraq~eh اخگر akh-gar
spark plug *np.* شمع sham'
sparkle *n., vt., vi.* برق زدن barq zadan درخشیدن derakh-shidan
sparkler *n.* براق barâq درخشان derakhshân bar~âq
sparkling *vi.* پرجوش por-jush پرگاز por-gâz
sparring partner *n.* حریف تمرینی harif-e' tamrini
sparrow *n.* گنجشگ gonjeshk
sparrow-hawk *n.* ترقی qerqi

sparse *adj.* پراكنده parâkandeh متفرق motefar~eq

sparsely *adv.* كم kam متفرقاً motefar~eqan

spasm *n.* گرفتگى عضله gereftegi-e' 'azoleh

spat *n., v.* درگيرى dar-giri قوزك پوش quzak-push

spate *n.* سيل seyl

spatter *n.* پاشيدن pâshidan پت پت كردن pet-pet kardan

spatula *n.* كفگير kaf-gir

spawn *n.* تخم ريختن tokhm rikhtan

spay *n., vt.* عقيم كردن 'aqim kardan

speak *vi.* صحبت كردن soh-bat kardan

speak(up) *n.* بلند صحبت كردن boland soh-bât kardan

speaker *n.* سخنگو sokhan-gu سخنران sokhan-rân ناطق nâteq

speaking *v., n.* نمايان namâyân گفتگو goftegu

spear *adj., vt., vi., n.* نيزه زدن neyzeh zadan

spearhead *n., vt.* پيشتاز بودن pish-tâz budan

spearman *n.* نيزه دار neyzeh-dâr

spearmint *n.* نعنا na'nâ

special *adj.* ويژه vizheh مخصوص makhsus استثنايى estesnâ'i

special delivery *np.* پست مخصوص post-e' makhsus

specialist *n.* متخصص motekhas~es كارشناس kâr-shenâs

speciality *n.* رشته اختصاصى reshteh-ye' ekhtesâsi

specialization *n.* تخصص takhas~os كارشناسى kâr-shenâsi

specialize *vi., vt.* تخصص داشتن takhas~os dâshtan
پيداكردن peydâ kardan

specially *adv.* مخصوصى makhsusi بطور ويژه betor-e' vizheh

specialty *adj., n.* تخصص takhas~os

specie *n.* نوع no' موجود mojud

species *n.* موجود ات mojudât

specific *adj., n.* ويژه vizheh معين mo'ay~an خاص khâs

specifically *n.* بويژه be-vizheh صريحاً sarihan

specification *n.* تشخيص tashkhis تعيين ta'yin

specifications *n.* مشخصات moshakhas~ât

specify *vt., vi.* تائين كردن ta'in kardan
مشخص كردن moshakhas kardan

specimen *n.* نمونه nemuneh

speck *n., vt.* ذره zar~eh خال khâl

speckle *n.* لكه دار كردن lakeh-dâr kardan

spectacle *n.* تماشا tamâshâ منظره manzareh

spectacles *n.* عینک 'eynak
spectacular *adj., n.* تماشایی tamâshâyi فوق العاده fogol-'âdeh
spectator *n.* تماشاگر tamâshâ-gar تماشاچی tamâshâ-chi
spectral *adj.* روح مانند ruh-mânand
spectrum *n.* طیف teyf وسعت vos'at پهنای رنگ pahnâ-ye' rang
speculate *vi.* حدس زدن hads zadan
بورس بازی کردن burs-bâzi kardan
speculation *n.* حدس hads گمان gamân زعم za'm
speculative *adj.* حدسی hadsi فرضی farzi ریسک دار risk-dâr
speech *n.* صحبت sohbat نطق notq سخن sokhan گفتار goftâr
speech-maker *n.* ناطق nâteq متکلم motekal~em
speechless *adj.* زبان بسته zabân-basteh
زبان بندآمده zabân band-âmadeh
speed *v.* سرعت گرفتن sor'at gereftan
speed *n.* سرعت sor'at شتاب shetâb
speed(up) *n.* سرعت دادن sor'at dâdan سریعتر کردن sari'-tar kardan
speed-up *n.* تسریع tasri'
speeding *v.* سرعت sor'at
speedometer *n.* سرعت نما sor'at-namâ
speedy *adj., vi., vt.* فوری zud فوری fori
spell *v.* طلسم کردن telesm kardan
spell *v.* هجی کردن heji kardan
spell *v.* نمودار بودن nemudâr budan
spell *n.* نوبت nobat وهله vahleh
spellbind *vt.* طلسم کردن telesm kardan مفتون maftun
spellbound *adj.* طلسم شده telesm shodeh مفتون maftun
spelling *n.* هجی heji املاء emlâ'
spend *v.* مصرف کردن masraf kardan بسر بردن be-sar bordan
spend *v.* خرج کردن kharj kardan
spending money *n.* پول خرجی pul kharji
spent *v., adj.* خرج شده kharj-shodeh خسته khasteh
sperm *n.* اسپرم esperm نطفه notfeh
spew *vi., vt., n.* بالا آوردن bâlâ âvardan
استفراغ کردن estefrâq kardan
sphere *n., vt.* قلمرو qalam-ro حوزه hozeh
spice *v.* ادویه زدن advieh zadan
spice *n.* ادویه advieh چاشنی châshni مزه mazeh
spick-and-span *adj., adv.* تر و تمیز tar-o tamiz

spicy *adj.* تند tond چاشنی دار châshni-dâr
spider *n.* عنکبوت 'ankabut
spider web *n.* تار عنکبوت tar-e' 'ankabut
spiffy *adj.* شیک shik تر و تمیز tar-o tamiz
spigot *n., vt.* توپی tupi سوراخ گیر surâkh-gir
spike *n.* پل pol
spike *v.* آبشار زدن âbshâr zadan
spike *n.* میخ mikh
spill *n.* ریختن rikhtan پاشیدن pâshidan
spin *vi., n.* ریستن ristan چرخاندن charkhândan
spinach *n.* اسفناج esfenâj
spinal *n.* نقراتی faqarâti نخائی nokha'i
spinal column *np.* ستون نقرات sotun-e' faqarât
spinal cord *np.* مغز تیره maqz-e' tireh نخاع nokhâ'
spindle *n., adj., vt., vi.* میله mileh دوک duk
spine *n.* ستون نقرات sotun-e' faqarât تیغ tiq نخاع nokhâ'
spineless *adj.* بدون استخوان پشت bedun-e' ostokhân-e' posht
     بزدل bozdel
spinner *n.* نخ ریس nakh-ris
spinning *n.* نخ ریسی nakh-risi ریسندگی risandegi
spinning wheel *n.* چرخ نخ ریسی charkh-e' nakh-risi
spinster *n.* دختر ترشیده dokhtar-e' torshideh
spiny *adj.* تیغ دار tiq-dâr سخت sakht
spiral *n., adj., vi., vt.* مارپیچ mâr-pich فنر پیچ fanar-pich
spirit *n., adj., vt.* دل del جرأت jor-'at
spirit *n., adj., vt.* روح ruh روان ravân
spirit(away) *n.* یواشکی بردن yavâshaki bordan
spirited *adj.* پرنشاط por-neshât سرزنده sar-zendeh
spiritless *adj.* بی نشاط bi-neshât بیروح bi-ruh
spirits *n.* ارواح arvâh اجنه ajan~eh
spiritual *adj.* روحانی ruhâni معنوی ma'navi
spiritualist *n.* روان گرا ravân-garâ
spit *vi., vt., n.* تف کردن tof kardan
spite *n., vt.* کینه داشتن kineh dâshtan غرض داشتن qaraz dâshtan
spiteful *adj.* کینه دار kineh-dâr
spittle *n.* آب دهان âb-dahân تف tof
splash *vt., vi., n.* پاشیدن pâshidan
     شلپ شلپ کردن sholop-sholop kardan

splashy n. پاشیدنی pâshidani
splatter vt., vi. پهن کردن pahn kardan پخش کردن pakhsh kardan
spleen n. طحال tahâl
splendid n. باشکوه bâ-shokuh
splendor n. شکوه shokuh جلال jalâl جبروت jabarut
splice n., vt. بهم چسباندن beham chasbândan
splint n. استخوان بند ostokhân-band تخته takhteh
splinter v. شکستن shekastan خرد کردن khord kardan
splinter n. تراشه tarâsheh
split v. نصف کردن nesf kardan شکافتن shekâftan
split v. ترک کردن tark kardan بچاک زدن be-châk zadan
splotch vt., vi., n. لکه lakeh
splurge n. ولخرجی vel-kharji
splurge v. تظاهر کردن tazâhor kardan
spoil v. لوس کردن lus kardan بد عادت کردن bad-'âdat kardan
spoil v. خراب کردن kharâb kardan فاسد کردن fâsed kardan
spoilage n. فاسد شدگی fâsed-shodegi
spoils n. غنایم qanâ'em
spoke n., vt. پره pareh
spokesman n. سخنگو sokhan-gu
sponge v. تمیز کردن tamiz kardan
sponge n. ابر abr اسفنج esfanj
sponger n. طفیلی tofeyli انگل angal کاسه لیس kâseh-lis
spongy adj. اسفنجی esfanji
sponsor n., vt. ضامن zâmen قیم qay~em خرج دهنده kharj-dahandeh
sponsorship n. ضمانت zemânat خرج دهندگی kharj-dahandegi
spontaneity n. خود بخودی khod-be-khodi بی اختیاری bi-ekhtiâri
spontaneous adj. خود بخود khod-be-khod بی اختیار bi-ekhtiâr
spoof n., vt., vi. کلک زدن kalak zadan شکلک shaklak
spook n., vt. روح ruh جن jen~
spooky adj. جنی jen~i
spool n. قرقره qer-qereh ماسوره mâsureh
spoon n., vi. قاشق qâshoq
spoonful n. یک قاشق پر yek qâshoq por
sporadic adj. نامرتب nâ-morat~ab تک و توک tak-o tuk
sporadical n. جدا جدا jodâ-jodâ
spore n., vi. تخم tokhm هاگ hâg
sport n., adj., vi., vt. ورزش varzesh تفریح tafrih اسپورت esport

sporting *adj.* ورزشی varzeshi ورزشکاری varzesh-kâri
sporting goods *n.* اجناس ورزشی ajnâs-e′ varzeshi
sportive *adj.* تفریحی tafrihi
sports car *np.* ماشین شکاری mâshin-e′ shekâri
sportsman *n.* ورزشکار varzesh-kâr اهل تفریح ahl-e′ tafrih
sportsmanship *n.* ورزشکاری varzesh-kâri
روحیۀ ورزشی ruhiyeh-ye′ varzeshi
sportswear *n.* لباس ورزشی lebâs-e′ varzeshi
sporty *adj.* ورزشی varzeshi شیک shik
spot *v.* تشخیص دادن tash-khis dâdan پیدا کردن peydâ kardan
spot *n.* لکه lak لکه lak~eh
spot *n.* محل mahal مکان makân
spot *n.* خال khâl نقطه noqteh
spotless *n.* بی لکه bi-lakeh تمیز tamiz
spotlight *n., vt.* نورافکن nur-afkan
spotted *adj., n., v.* لکه دار lakeh-dâr نقطه نقطه noqteh-noqteh
spotter *n.* دیده بان dideh-bân ناظر nâzer
spotty *n.* خال خال khâl-khâl نامنظم nâ-monazam
spouse *n., vt.* همسر hamsar زوجه zojeh
spout *n.* لوله luleh دهنه dahaneh
sprain *vt.* پیچیدن pichidan رگ برگ کردن rag be-rag kardan
sprawl *vt., n., vi.* پت و پهن شدن pat-o pahn shodan
پهن کردن pahn kardan
spray *n.* پاشیدن pâshidan گردپاش gard-pâsh
spread *n.* پخش pakhsh شیوع shiu′ پهنا pahnâ
spread *v.* پهن کردن pahn kardan پخش کردن pakhsh kardan
پاشیدن pâshidan
spread-eagle *adj., vt., vi.* طاق باز tâq-bâz
spree *n.* خوشی khoshi خوش گذرانی khosh gozarâni
sprig *n.* ترکه tarkeh
spring *n.* بهار bahâr
spring *v.* فرار دادن farâr dâdan
spring *n.* چشمه cheshmeh
spring *n.* فنر fanar
spring *v.* جستن jestan پریدن paridan جهیدن jahidan
spring chicken *n.* بی تجربه bi-tajrobeh
spring fever *n.* احساس تنبلی ehsâs-e′ tanbali
springboard *n.* تختۀ شیرجه takhteh-ye′ shirjeh

springer *n.* جهنده jahandeh
springtime *n.* فصل بهار fasl-e' bahâr
springy *adj.* فنری fanari
sprinkle *vt., vi., n.* پاشیدن pâshidan ریختن rikhtan
sprinkler *n., vt.* آب پاش âb-pâsh فواره fav~âreh
sprinkling *v.* خرده پاشی khordeh pâshi
sprint *vi., vt.* سریع دویدن sari' davidan
sprit *n.* زه بادبان zeh-e' bâd-bân
sprocket *n.* چرخ دندانه charkh dandâneh
sprout *vi., vt., n.* جوانه زدن javâneh zadan سبز شدن sabz shodan
spruce *n.* صنوبر sanobar
spruce *v.* تر و تمیزکردن tar-o tamiz kardan
spunk *n.* دل del شهامت shahâmat
spur *n.* مهمیز mehmiz
spur *v.* مهمیززدن mehmiz zadan تحریک کردن tahrik kardan
spurge *n.* شیره گیاه shireh giâh
spurn *vt., vi., n.* ناچیز شماردن nâchiz shemârdan
پشت کردن posht kardan
spurt *vi., vt.* فوران کردن favarân kardan پراندن parândan
sputter *vi., vt.* تف پرانی کردن tof-parâni kardan
بیرون ریختن birun rikhtan
spy *n.* جاسوس jâsus خبرچین khabar-chin
spy *v.* جاسوسی کردن jâsusi kardan مراقب بودن morâqeb budan
spyglass *n.* دوربین durbin
squabble *n.* جر و بحث کردن jar~-o bahs kardan
squad *n., vt.* دسته dasteh جوخه jukheh
squad car *np.* ماشین پلیس mâshin-e' polis
squadron *n.* اسکادران eskâd-rân
squalid *adj.* کثیف kasif چرک cherk
squalor *n.* کثافت kesâfat
squander *n., vt., vi., adj.* برباددادن bar-bâd dâdan
بهدردادن be-hadar dâdan
square *n., vt., vi., adj.* میدان meydân فلکه falakeh
square *n., vt., vi., adj.* چهار گوش chahâr-gush مربع morab~a'
square *n., vt., vi., adj.* مجذور majzur به توان دو beh tavân-e' do
square deal *np.* معامله عادلانه mo'âmeleh-ye' 'âdelâneh
square root *n.* جذر jazr ریشۀ دوم risheh-ye' dov~om
square(off) *n.* تسویه حساب کردن tasvieh hesâb kardan

square(up) *n.* سازش کردن sâzesh kardan
squash *n.* کدو زرد kadu zard
squash *v.* له کردن leh kardan
squashy *adj.* نرم narm له شدنی leh-shodani
squat *v.* چنباته زدن chan-bâteh zadan
squat *v.* بی اجازه ساکن شدن bi-ejâzeh sâken shodan
squatter *n.* زمین نشین غیر قانونی zamin-neshin-e' qeyr-e' qânuni
squaw *n.* زن سرخ پوست zan-e' sorkh-pust
squawk *vi., vt., n.* جیغ کشیدن jiq keshidan
قر قر کردن qor-qor kardan
squeak *n., vi., vt.* جیغ زدن jiq zadan
squeaky *adj., vt.* جیغو jiqu
squeal *n., vi., vt.* جیغ زدن jiq zadan
squeal(on) *n.* لو دادن lo dâdan
squeamish *adj.* بادلشوره bâ del-shureh
squeegee *n., vt., vi.* آبشور لاستیکی âbshur lâstiki
squeezable *n.* فشردنی feshordani
squeeze *v.* آب گرفتن âb gereftan
squeeze *v.* فشردن feshordan فشاردادن feshâr dâdan
squelch *v.* له کردن leh kardan
squelch *v.* شلپ شلپ راه رفتن sholop sholop râh raftan
squib *v.* انتقاد کردن enteqâd kardan
squib *v.* ترقه درکردن taraq~eh dar kardan
squint *v.* چشم غره رفتن cheshm-qor~eh raftan
squint *n.* چشم غره cheshm-qor~eh تنگ چشمی tang-cheshmi
squirm *vi., n.* لولیدن lulidan وول زدن vul zadan
squirmy *adj.* وول زن vul-zan
squirrel *n., adj., vt.* سنجاب sanjâb
squirt *vi., vt.* پاشیدن pâshidan نواره زدن fav~âreh zadan
stab *vt., vi., n.* چاقو زدن châqu zadan
stability *n.* ثبات sabât استواری ostovâri
stabilization *n.* تثبیت tasbit موازنه movâzeneh تعادل ta'âdol
stabilize *v.* تثبیت کردن tasbit kardan
stabilize *v.* موازنه کردن movâzeneh kardan
stabilizer *n.* متعادل کننده mote'âdel-konandeh
stable *n., vt., vi.* ثابت sâbet استوار ostovâr باثبات bâ-sabât
stable *n., vt., vi.* طویله tavileh اسطبل establ
stack *v.* دسته کردن dasteh kardan

روپهم گذاشتن .... ruy-e' ham gozâshtan

stack *n.* دسته dasteh توده tudeh

stack *v.* چیندن chindan

stadium *n.* ورزشگاه varzesh-gâh استادیوم estâdiom

staff *v.* کارمند گرفتن kâr-mand gereftan

staff *n.* عصا 'asâ چوب دستی chub dasti

staff *n.* کارکنان kâr-konân هیئت hey'at

stag *n.* مردانه mardâneh

stag *n.* گوزن نر gavazn-e' nar

stag party *n.* مهمانی مردانه mehmâni-e' mardâneh

stage *n.* مرحله marhaleh

stage *v.* بصحنه آوردن be-sahneh âvardan بپا کردن be-pâ kardan

stage *n.* صحنه sahneh سن sen

stagecoach *n.* دلیجان delijân کالسکه kâleskeh

stagger *vi., n.* تلو تلو خوردن telo-telo khordan گیج کردن gij kardan

staggering *n.* گیج کننده gij-konandeh سرسام آور sar-sâm-âvar

stagnant *adj.* راکد râked گندیده gandideh

stagnate *vi.* راکد ماندن râked mândan گندیدن gandidan

stagnation *n.* رکود rokud ایستادگی istâdegi گندیدگی gandidegi

staid *adj., v., vt., vi.* هوشدار hush-dâr متین matin

stain *n., vt., vi.* لکه انداختن lakeh andâkhtan
لکه دار کردن lakeh-dâr kardan

stained glass *np.* شیشه رنگی shisheh rangi

stainless *n.* ضد زنگ zed~-e' zang زنگ نزن zang nazan

stainless steel *np.* فولاد ضد زنگ fulâd-e' zed~-e' zang

stair *n.* پله pel~eh سکو saku

staircase *n.* پلکان pel~ekân

staith *n.* بارانداز bâr-andâz

stake *n., vt.* میخ چوبی mikh-e' chubi تیرک tirak

stake *n., vt.* درمیان dar miân گرو gero

stakes *n.* جایزه jâyezeh شرط shart

stale *vi.* کهنه kohneh مانده mândeh

stalemate *v.* پات کردن pât kardan

stalemate *n.* بن بست bon-bast پات pât

stalk *v.* تعقیب کردن ta'qib kardan

stalk *n.* ساقه sâqeh تنه taneh

stalking-horse *n.* رد گم کن rad gom-kon

stalky *vt., vi., n.* ساقه دار sâqeh-dâr

stall *n.* اطاقک طویله otâqak-e' tavileh
stall *n.* غرفه اطاقچه qorfeh otâq-cheh
stall *v.* خاموش شدن khâmush shodan خفه کردن khafeh kardan
stall *v.* وقت تلف کردن vaqt talaf kardan
stallion *adj., n.* اسب نر asb-e' nar نریان nariyân
stalwart *adj., n.* مصمم قوی qavi mosam~am
stamina *n.* بنیه bonyeh طاقت tâqat نا nâ
stammer *vi.* تته پته کردن teteh peteh kardan
stamp *v.* تمبر زدن tambr zadan
stamp *v.* کوبیدن kubidan
stamp *v.* مهر زدن mohr zadan
stamp(out) *n.* فرو نشاندن foru neshândan ازبین بردن az beyn bordan
stampede *n.* رم ram هجوم hojum
stampede *v.* رم دادن ram dâdan
stamper *n.* تمبر زن tambr-zan
stance *n.* موضع moze' طرز ایستادن tarz-e' istâdan
stanch *adj., vt., vi., n.* جلوگیری کردن jelo-giri kardan
stanchion *n.* تیر پایه tir pâyeh
stand *v.* واقع شدن vâqe' shodan
stand *v.* طاقت آوردن tâqat âvardan تحمل آوردن taham~ol âvardan
stand *n.* جا ایست ist jâ سکو saku
stand *n.* عقیده موضع moze' 'aqideh
stand *n.* میزکوچک miz-e' kuchek دکانچه dok~ân-cheh
stand *v.* ایستادن istâdan
stand(a chance) *n.* یک ذره شانس داشتن yek-zar~eh shâns dashtan
stand(by) *n.* صبرکردن sabr kardan پشتیبانی کردن poshtibâni kardan
stand(down) *n.* ایستاده نگه داشتن istâdeh negah dâshtan
stand(for) *n.* نشانه بودن neshâneh budan طاقت آوردن tâqat âvardan
stand(in) *n.* رابطه داشتن râbeteh dâshtan
stand(off) *n.* دورنگه داشتن dur-negah dâshtan
حذر کردن hazar kardan
stand(on) *n.* استوار بودن ostovâr budan
stand(one's ground) *n.* سرجا ایستادن sar-e' jâ istâdan
stand(out) *n.* یک سروگردن بلندتربودن yek saro gardan bolând-tar budan
برجسته بودن barjesteh budan
stand(over) *n.* موکول کردن mokul kardan
stand(trial) *n.* محاکمه شدن mohâkemeh shodan
stand(up for) *n.* پشتیبانی کردن poshtibâni kardan دفاع defâ'

stand(up) *n.* قال گذاشتن qâl gozâshtan
بملاقات نیامدن be-molâqât nayâmadan
stand(up) *n.* بلندشدن boland shodan
stand-by *n., adj.* ایستاده istâdeh مطمئن motma'en
stand-in *n.* جای کسی ایستادن jây-e' kasi istâdan
stand-off *adj.* ایستادگی istâdegi ول معطلی vel mo'atali
stand-up *np.* ایستاده istâdeh ایستادنی istâdani
standard *n., adj.* یکجور yek-jur استاندارد estândârd میزان mizân
معیار me'yar
standard of living *np.* سطح زندگی sat-h-e' zendegi
standardize *n.* یکجور کردن yek-jur kardan
standfast *n.* ایستادگی کردن istâdegi kardan
standing *n., v., adj.* وضع vaz' شهرت shohrat
standing *n., v., adj.* ایستاده istâdeh دائمی dâ'emi
standpoint *n.* نقطۀ نظر noqteh-ye' nazar لحاظ lahâz
standstill *n.* ایستادگی istâdegi توقف tavaq~of
stanza *n.* بند band
stapl *n.* اساسی asâsi عمده 'omdeh
staple *n., vt., adj.* منگنه mangeneh مفتول maftul
stapler *n.* ماشین منگنه mâshin-e' mangeneh
star *v.* شرکت کردن sherkat kardan
star *n.* ستاره setâreh کوکب kokab اختر akhtar
star dust *np.* دور ستاره dur-setâreh رویایی royâyi
starboard *n.* سمت راست samt-e' râst
starch *n.* نشاسته neshâsteh
starch *v.* آهار زدن âhâr zadan
stardom *n.* معروفیت ma'rufiyat
stare *n., vi.* خیره شدن khireh shodan نگاه کردن negâh kardan
stare(down) *n.* با نگاه از رو بردن bâ-negâh az-ru bordan
starfish *n.* ستارۀ دریایی setâreh-ye' daryâyi
stargazer *n.* ستاره بین setâreh-bin خیالی khiâli
stark *adj., adv.* بکلی be-kol~i سخت sakht
stark-naked *adj.* لخت مادر زاد lokht-e' mâdar-zâd
starless *adj.* بی ستاره bi-setâreh
starlight *n., adj.* نور ستاره nur-e' setâreh
start *vi., vt.* شروع کردن shoru' kardan روشن کردن roshan kardan
start(in) *n.* شروع بکار کردن shoru' be-kâr kardan
start(out) *n.* شروع شدن shoru' shodan قصد کردن qasd kardan

start(up) *n.* روشن کردن roshan kardan جهیدن jahidan
starter *n.* شروع کننده shoru'-konandeh استارتر estâr-ter
startle *vt., vi., n., adj.* ترساندن tarsân-dan شوکه کردن shokeh kardan
startling *v.* تکان دهنده takân-dahandeh
starvation *n.* گرسنگی gorosnegi
starve *vi., vt.* گرسنگی کشیدن gorosnegi keshidan
گرسنه نگه داشتن gorosneh negah dâshtan
stash *vt., n.* قایم کردن qâyem kardan پنهان کردن penhân kardan
state *n.* وضعیت vaz'iyat حالت hâlat
state *v.* بیان کردن bayân kardan اظهار داشتن ez-hâr dâshtan
state *n.* ایالت ayâlat کشور keshvar
State Department *n.* وزارت امور خارجه vezârat-e' omur-e' khârejeh
state of mind *n.* حضوریقین hozur-e' yaqin
وضعیت ذهنی vaz'iyat-e' zehni
state university *np.* دانشگاه ایالتی dânesh-gâh-e' ayâlati
state-wide *n.* سرتاسری sar-tâ-sari تمام ایالتی tamâm-ayâlati
stated *adj., v.* بیان شده bayân-shodeh معین شده mo'ay~an-shodeh
statehood *n.* ایالت شدگی ayâlat-shodegi
stately *adj., adv.* باوقار bâ-vaqâr متین matin
statement *n.* بیانیه bayâniyeh اظهاریه ez-hâriyeh
statesman *n.* سیاست مرد siâsat-mard
statesmanlike *adj.* سیاست مردانه siâsat-mardâneh
statesmanship *n.* سیاست مردی siâsat-mardi
static *adj., n.* استکاکی estekâki ایستاده istâdeh پارازیت pârâzit
station *n.* جایگاه jây-gâh ایستگاه ist-gâh جا jâ
station *v.* مستقر کردن mostaqar kardan قرار دادن qarâr dâdan
stationary *adj., n.* ایستاده istâdeh ساکن sâken
stationery *n.* لوازم التحریر lavâzem tahrir نوشت افزار nevesht-afzâr
statistical *adj.* آماری âmâri
statistics *n.* آمار âmâr
statuary *n., adj.* مجسمه سازی mojasameh-sâzi
statue *n.* مجسمه mojasameh پیکر pey-kar تندیس tandis
statuesque *adj.* مجسمه ای mojas~ameh-i
خوش قد و بالا khosh qad-o bâlâ
stature *n.* قامت qâmat مقام maqâm قوام qavâm
status *n.* وضع vaz' موقعیت moqe'iyat
status quo *np.* وضع فعلی vaz'-e' fe'li
statute *n.* قانون qânun

statute law *np.* قانون مقننه qânun-e' moqananeh
statutory *adj.* مجازاتى قانونى qânuni mojâzâti
staunch *adj.* پر و پا قرص par-o-pâ qors
stave *n., vt., vi.* تخته بشکه takhteh boshkeh
stave(off) *n.* دفع کردن daf' kardan جلوگیری jelo-giri kardan
stay *n.* تعویق ta'viq
stay *v.* ماندن mândan توقف کردن tavaqof kardan
stead *n.* جا jâ عوض 'avaz
steadfast *adj.* ثابت قدم sâbet qadam استوار ostovâr
steadily *adv.* یکنواخت yek-navâkht پیوسته peyvasteh
steady *adj., int., n., vt.* یکنواخت کردن yek-navâkht kardan
ثابت رفتن sâbet raftan
steak *n.* بیفتک biftak
steal *vt., n.* دزدیدن doz-didan دزدی کردن dozdi kardan
ربودن robudan
stealing *n., v.* دزدی dozdi دزدانه dozdâneh
stealth *n.* سری ser~i مرموزی marmuzi
stealthy *adj.* مرموز marmuz موش مرده mush-mordeh
steam *n.* بخار bokhâr
steam *v.* بخار کردن bokhâr kardan با بخار پختن bâ bokhâr pokhtan
steam engine *np.* ماشین بخار mâshin-e' bokhâr
steam roller *np.* غلطک qaltak جاده صاف کن jâd~eh sâf-kon
steamboat *n.* کشتی بخار kashti-e' bokhâr
steamer *n.* کشتی بخار kashti-e' bokhâr بخار کن bokhâr-kon
steamy *adj.* بخار دار bokhâr-dâr بخار مانند bokhâr mânand
steed *n.* اسب سواری asb-e' savâri
steel *n., adj., vt.* فولادی fulâdi
steel *n., adj., vt.* فولاد fulâd پولاد pulâd
steel mill *np.* کارخانهٔ ذوب آهن kârkhâneh-ye' zob-e' âhan
steel worker *n.* فولاد کار fulâd-kâr
steelhead *n.* پولاد سر pulâd-sar
steely *n.* فولادی fulâdi
steep *adj.* شیب دار shib-dâr سربالا sarbâlâ
steep *adj.* گزاف gazâf
steep *v.* دم کردن dam kardan خیساندن khisândan
steeple *n.* برج کلیسا borj-e' kelisâ
steer *n.* گاو اخته gâv-e' akhteh
steer *v.* راندن rândan هدایت کردن hedâyat kardan

steering wheel *np.* رل rol فرمان farmân
stellar *adj.* ستاره ای setâreh-i
stem *v.* ناشی شدن nâshi shodan سد کردن sad kardan
stem *n.* ریشه risheh ساقه sâqeh
stenographer *n.* تند نویس tond-nevis
step *n.* پله pel~eh
step *n.* مرحله marhaleh پایه pâyeh
step *n.* گام gâm قدم qadam
step *v.* قدم گذاشتن qadam gozâshtan لگد گذاشتن lagad gozâshtan
step on it! *n.* بجنب be-jonb! سریعتر برو sari'-tar boro
step(by step) *n.* قدم بقدم qadam be-qadam پله پله pel~eh-pel~eh
step(down) *n.* استعفاء دادن este'fâ dâdan
step(in) *n.* میانجی گری کردن miânji-gari kardan
step(out) *n.* بیرون رفتن birun raftan
step(up) *n.* سریعتر کردن sari'-tar kardan
پیشرفت کردن pish-raft kardan
stepbrother *n.* برادر ناتنی barâdar-e' nâ-tani
stepchild *n.* فرزند ناتنی farzand-e' nâ-tani
stepdaughter *n.* دختر ناتنی dokhtar-e' nâ-tani
stepfather *n.* ناپدری nâ-pedari
stepmother *n.* زن پدر zan pedar نامادری nâ-mâdari
steppe(s) *n.* دشت dasht جلگه زار jolgeh-zâr
steppingstone *n.* سنگ زیر پا sang zir-e' pâ
stepsister *n.* خواهر ناتنی khâhar-e' nâ-tani
stepson *n.* ناپسری nâ-pesâri
stereo *n.* استریو esterio دوطرفه do-tarafeh
stereoptype *n.* بایک چوب زدن bâ yek-chub zadan
stereotype *v.* یک قماش حساب کردن yek-qomâsh hesâb kardan
stereotype *n.* یک قماشی yek-qomâshi
stereotype *n.* یک قماشی yek-qomâshi
sterephonic *n.* صدای دوطرفه sedây-e' do-tarafeh
sterile *n.* استرلیزه ester-lizeh تمیز tamiz
sterile *n.* نازا nâzâ عقیم 'aqim سترون satarvan
sterilization *n.* استرلیزهای ester-lizeh-i عقیمی 'aqimi
sterilize *vt., n.* استرلیزه کردن ester-lizeh kardan
خنثی کردن khonsâ kardan
sterling *n.* استرلینگ ester-ling عیار تمام 'ayâr tamâm 'ayâr
stern *adj., n.* عقب کشتی 'aqab-e' kashti

stern *adj., n.* سخت sakht سختگیر sakht-gir جدی jed~i عنق 'onoq
sternum *n.* استخوان وسط سینه ostokhân-e' vasat sineh
stethoscope *n.* گوشی معاینه gushi-e' mo'âyeneh
stew *n.* خورش khoresh
stew *v.* جوش خوردن jush khordan
steward *n., vt., vi.* پیشکار pish-kâr مهماندار mehmân-dâr
stewardess *n.* مهماندار mehmân-dâr
stewed *adj.* مست mast
stick *v.* چسباندن chas-bândan چسبیدن chas-bidan
فرو کردن foru kardan
stick *n.* چوب chub عصا 'asâ قلم qalam
stick(around) *n.* همین اطراف بودن hamin atrâf budan
پلکیدن palekidan
stick(by) *n.* وفاکردن vafâ kardan پشتیبانی poshtibâni
stick(up for) *n.* حمایت کردن hemâyat kardan
stick(up) *n.* دزدی کردن dozdi kardan سرقت کردن serqat kardan
stick-in the-mud *n.* بی ابتکار bi-ebtekâr خشک khoshk عوضی 'avazi
stick-up *n.* سرقت با اسلحه serqat bâ aslaheh
sticker *n.* برچسب bar-chasb
stickiness *n.* چسبندگی chas-bandegi نوچی nuchi
stickle *vi.* ایراد گرفتن irâd gereftan
stickler *n.* ایرادگیر irâd-gir
sticky *adj.* چسبناک chasb-nâk نوچ nuch
stiff *adj., n., adv., vt.* سفت seft شق shaq خشک khoshk جسد jasad
stiff-necked *adj.* کله شق kal~eh-shaq
stiffen *n.* سفت کردن seft kardan سفت شدن seft shodan
stifle *n., vt., vi.* خفه کردن khafeh kardan خفه شدن khafeh shodan
stifling *n.* خفه کننده khafeh-konandeh
stigma *n.* داغ dâq نشانه neshâneh
stiletto *n.* دشنه deshneh
still *n.* دستگاه تقطیر dast-gâh-e' taqtir
دستگاه عرق سازی dast-gâh-e' 'araq-sâ
still *v.* ساکت کردن sâket kardan بیحرکت کردن bi-harekat kardan
still *n., vt., vi.* هنوز hanuz
still *adj.* بیصدا bi-sedâ بیگاز bi-gâz آرام ârâm بیحرکت bi-harekat
stilt *n.* پاچوب pâ-chub
stilted *n.* پایه بلند pâyeh boland دبدبه dab-dabeh
stimulant *n., adj.* محرک mohar~ek انگیزه angizeh

stimulate *vt., vi.* تحریک کردن tahrik kardan انگیختن angikhtan
stimulation *n.* تحریک tahrik تهیج tahâyoj
stimulus *n.* انگیزه angizeh
sting *vt., vi., n.* نیش زدن nish zadan گزیدن gazidan
stinger *n.* نیش زن nish-zan نیش دار nish-dâr
stingray *n.* پهن ماهی pahn-mâhi
stingy *adj.* خسیس khasis کنس kenes
stink *n., v., vi.* بوی بد دادن buy-e' bad dadan
بوی گند دادن buy-e' gand dâdan
stinking *adj.* بدبو bad-bu متعفن mote'afen
stint *vt., vi., n.* کار kâr محدود کردن mahdud kardan
stipel *n.* گوش وارک gush-vârak
stipend *n.* حقوق hoquq مقرری moqar~ari
stipendiary *adj., n.* حقوق بگیر hoquq be-gir
stipulate *adj., vi., vt.* شرط کردن shart kardan
صریحاً خواستن sarihan khâstan
قرارگذاشتن qarar gozâshtan
stipulation *n.* شرط shart قرار qarâr
stir *vt., vi., n.* بهم زدن beham zadan تکان خوردن takân khordan
حرکت harekat
stirrup *n.* رکاب rekâb پابند pâ-band
stitch *n.* بخیه bakhiy~eh تکه tek~eh دوخت dukht کوک kuk
stitch *v.* بخیه زدن bakhiyeh zadan وصله کردن vasleh kardan
stithy *n., vt.* سندان sandân
stoat *n.* قاقم qâqom
stock *n., adj., vi.* ذخیره کردن zakhireh kardan موجودی mojudi
stock *n., adj., vi.* قنداق qondâq قبضه qabzeh
stock *n., adj., vi.* سهم sahm سهام sahâm بورس burs
stock *n., adj., vi.* نژاد nezhâd سرسله sar sel-seleh
stock *n., adj., vi.* ماده mâd~eh مواد خام mavâd~-e' khâm
stock *n., adj., vi.* ساقه sâqeh تنه taneh
stock car *np.* ماشین مسابقه mâshin-e' mosâbeqeh
stock certificate *np.* سهام نامه sahâm-nâmeh
stock company *np.* شرکت سهامی sherkat sahâmi
stock exchange *np.* بورس burs
stock in trade *np.* ابزار کار abzâr-e' kâr مایه mâyeh
stock market *np.* شرکت سهامی sherkat sahâmi
stockade *n., vt.* سنگر چوب sangar-chub زندان zendân

stockbroker *n.* دلال سهام dal~âl-e' sahâm
stockbrokerage *n.* سهام فروشی sahâm forushi
stockholder *n.* سهام دار sahâm-dâr
stocking *n.* جوراب jurâb
stockman *n.* انبار دار anbâr-dâr
stockpile *n., vt., vi.* ذخیره کردن zakhireh kardan
stocky *adj.* قطور qatur کت و کلفت kat-o koloft
stockyard *n.* چهارپاگاه chahâr-â-gâh
stogy *n.* سیگار ارزان sigâr arzân
stoic *n.* صبور sabur رواقی ravâqi
stoke *n.* آتش کردن âtash kardan تابیدن tâbidan
stole *n., v.* روسری ru-sari
stolen goods *n.* اموال مسروقه amvâl-e' mas-uqeh
stolid *adj.* بی احساس bi-ehsâs
stomach *v.* طاقت آوردن tâqat âvardan
حالش را داشتن hâlash-râ dâshtan
stomach *n.* شکم shekam معده me'deh حال hâl
stomach-ache *n.* شکم درد shekam-dard
stomp *n.* لگد زدن lagad zadan
stoncutter *n.* سنگ تراش sang-tarâsh حجار hajâr
stone *v.* سنگ انداختن sang andâkhtan سنگسار کردن sang-âr kardan
حجر hajar
stone *n.* سنگ sang حجر hajar
stoned *adj.* مست مست mast-e' mast لول lul
stonewall *vi.* سخت ایستادگی کردن sakht istâdegi kardan
stoneware *n.* ظروف سنگی zoruf-e' sangi
stooge *n., vt., vi.* ملیجک malijak
stool *vi., vt., n.* چارپایه châr-âyeh سه پایه seh-âyeh
stool pigeon *n.* جاسوس jâsus خبرچین khabar-chin
stoop *v.* پست کردن past kardan زبون کردن zabun kardan
stoop *v.* دولا شدن dolâ shodan
stop *v.* مکث کردن maks kardan قطع کردن qat' kardan
stop *v.* نگه داشتن negah dâshtan توقف کردن tavaq~of kardan
stop *v.* جلوگیری کردن jelo-giri kardan بند آوردن band âvardan
stop light *n.* چراغ خطر cherâq-e' khatar
stop payment *n.* جلوگیری از پرداخت jelo-giri az pardâkht
stop watch *n.* کورنومتر korno-metr
stop! *n.* نگه دار ایست! ist! negah-dâr

stop(off) *n.* سر راه ایستادن sar-e' râh istâdan
stop(over) *n.* توقف کردن tavaq~ of kardan
stopcock *n.* سوپاپ supâp
stopover *n.* توقف گاه tavaq~ of-gâh
stoppage *n.* جلوگیری jelo-giri انسداد ense-dâd
stopper *n., vt.* جلوگیر jelo-gir توپی tupi
storage *n.* انبار کردن anbâr kardan انباری anbâri
store *n.* مغازه maqâzeh فروشگاه forush-gâh
store *v.* انبار کردن anbâr kardan ذخیره کردن zakhireh kardan
store(away) *n.* ذخیره کردن zakhireh kardan
storehous *n.* انبار anbâr
storekeeper *n.* مغازه دار maqâzeh-dâr انبار دار anbâr-dâr
storeroom *n.* انباری anbâri
stork *n.* لکلک lak-lak
storm *v.* حمله ور شدن hamleh-var shodan
storm *n.* طوفان tufân غوغا qoqâ
stormy *adj.* طوفانی tufâni
story *n.* طبقه tabaqeh
story *n.* داستان dâstân قصه qes~ eh حکایت hekâyat
storyteller *n.* داستان گو dâstân-gu نقال naq~ âl
stout *adj.* کت و کلفت kat-o koloft قوی qavi یقر yoqor
stove *v., n.* اجاق ojâq خوراک پز khorâk-paz
stover *n.* یونجه yonjeh
stow away *n.* قایم کردن qâyem kardan پنهان کردن penhân kardan
stowaway *n.* مسافر قاچاقی mosâfer-e' qâchâqi
straddle *vi., vt., n.* سوار شدن savâr shodan
       پا باز ایستادن pâ-bâz istâdan
straggle *vi.* پرت شدن part shodan منحرف شدن mon-haref shodan
straight *adj., adv., n.* مستقیم mostaqim راست râst صاف sâf
straight *adj., adv., n.* رک rok بی پرده bi-pardeh
straight angle *np.* زاویه قائمه zâvieh-ye' qâ'emeh
straight-faced *n.* خونسرد khun-sard
straight-laced *adj.* سختگیر sakht-gir انضباطی enzebâti
straight-line *n.* خط مستقیم khat~ -e' mostaqim
straighten *vt., vi.* صاف کردن sâf kardan
strain *n.* فشار feshâr کشش keshesh نسل nasl رگه rageh
strain *v.* فشار آوردن feshâr âvardan کشیدن keshidan
       صاف کردن sâf kardan

strain(at) *n.* زیاد فشار آوردن ziâd feshâr âvardan
strainer *n.* صافی sâfi آبکش âbkesh
strait *adj.* تنگه tangeh بغاز boqâz
straiten *vt.* تنگ کردن tang kardan سخت کردن sakht kardan
strand *v.* گیر کردن gir kardan
strand *n.* رشته reshteh ریشه risheh
stranded *n.* گیرکرده gir kardeh
strange *adv., adj.* عجیب 'ajib غریب qarib
stranger *adj.* بیگانه bi-gâneh غریبه qaribeh اجنبی ajnabi
strangle *vt.* خفه کردن khafeh kardan
strangulation *n.* خفگی khafegi اختناق ekhtenâq
strap *n.* تسمه tasmeh بند band نوار navâr
strap *v.* بابند بستن bâ-band bastan
strapping *adj., n.* بلند بالا boland bâlâ
stratagem *n.* حیله hileh
strategic *adj.* سوق الجیشی soqol-jeyshi
strategically *n.* بطور سوق الجیشی be-tor-e' soqol-jeyshi
strategist *n.* نقشه ریز naqsheh-riz طراح tar~âh
strategy *n.* استراتژی esterâtezhi
stratify *vt., vi.* طبقه طبقه کردن tabaqeh tabaqeh kardan
straw *n.* کاه kâh حصیر hasir پوشال pushâl
straw *adj.* پوشالی pushâli حصیری hasiri کاهی kâhi
straw *n.* نی ney کلک kelk
straw hat *n.* کلاه حصیری kolâh-e' hasiri
straw man *np.* مترسک matarsak
strawberry *n.* توت فرنگی tut farangi
stray *v.* گم شدن gom shodan منحرف شدن monharef shodan
stray *n.* گم شده gom-shodeh ولگرد vel-gard
streak *v.* لخت کردن lokht kardan
streak *n.* دوره doreh مدت mod~at
streak *n.* خط khat~ رگ rag
streaky *adj.* خط خطی khat-khati رگه دار rageh-dâr
stream *n., vt.* جویبار juybâr جریان یافتن jariân yâftan سری seri
streamer *n.* نوار navâr ریبون ribon
streamline *n., vt.* کشیده keshideh باریک کردن bârik kardan
سرتاسری sartâ-sari
street *n.* خیابان khiâbân برزن barzan
streetcar *n.* تراموا terâmvâ

streetwalker *n.* جنده jendeh ناحشه fâhesheh
strenght *n.* قدرت qodrat توانایی tavânâyi نیرو niru
strenghten *n.* قوی کردن qavi kardan تقویت کردن taqviyat kardan
strength *n.* توانایی tavânâ-yi قدرت qodrat نا nâ قوت qut
strenuous *adj.* پر مشقت por-masheq~at با حرارت bâ-harârat
stress *n.* نشار feshâr تأکید ta'kid تکیه takiyeh
stretch *v.* دراز کشیدن derâz keshidan دراز کردن derâz kardan
stretch *v.* کش دادن kesh dâdan کش آمدن kesh âmadan
امتداد دادن emtedâd dâdan
stretch *n.* پهنا pahnâ امتداد emtedâd دراز کشی derâz-keshi
stretcher *n.* برانکار berânkâr
stretchy *adj.* کشی keshi
strew *vt.* پاشیدن pâshidan
stricken *n.* زده zadeh دچار dochâr
strict *adj.* سختگیر sakht-gir اکید akid
stride *vi., vt., n.* شلنگ برداشتن shelang bar-dâshtan
stridence *n.* خشنی khasheni
strident *adj.* خشن khashen
strife *n.* درگیری dar-giri ستیزه setizeh
strike *n., vt., vi.* زدن zadan ضربه زدن zarbeh zadan خوردن khordân
strike(..workers) *n.* اعتصاب کردن e'tesâb kardan
strike(camp) *n.* اردو بستن ordu bastan
strike(down) *n.* بزمین زدن be-zamin zadan
بیماری شدید داشتن bi-mâri-e' shadid dâshtan
striker *n.* اعتصاب گر e'tesâb-gar
striking *adj.* چشمگیر cheshm-gir قابل توجه qâbel-e' tavâj~oh
string *v.* به نخ کشیدن be-nakh keshidan
string *n.* نخ nakh رشته reshteh ریسمان rismân تار târ
string bean *np.* لوبیا سبز lubiâ sabz
string(up) *n.* به دار کشیدن be-dâr keshidan
stringency *n.* سختی sakhti کساد kesâd
stringent *adj.* سخت sakht وخیم vakhim
stringer *n.* نخ کش nakh-kesh
strip *n.* نوار navâr باند bând
strip *v.* لخت کردن lokht kardan لخت شدن lokht shodan
سلب مقام کردن salb-e' maqâm kardan
strip mining *np.* معدن روباز ma'dan-e' ru-bâz
strip(..screw) *n.* هرز شدن harz shodan

stripe *n., vt.* خط khat نوار navâr يراق yarâq
striped *adj., v.* راه راه râh-râh
striper *n.* نوار دار navâr-dâr يراق دار yarâq-dâr
stripling *n.* مرد جوان mard-e' javân
strive *vi.* كوشش كردن kushesh kardan تقلا كردن taqal~â kardan
stroke *-v.* نوازش كردن navâzesh kardan
stroke *-n.* ضربه zarbeh ضربت zarbat حركت harekat
stroke(..brain) *n.* سكته مغزى sekteh-ye' maqzi
stroll *vi., vt., n.* تفريحى راه رفتن tafrihi râh raftan
stroller *n.* كالسكهٔ بچه kâleskeh-ye' bach~eh
strong *adj., adv.* قوى qavi نيرومند niru-mand محكم mohkam
strong-arm *np.* زورگويى كردن zur-guyi kardan
strong-minded *adj.* مصمم mosam~am
strongbox *n.* گاو صندوق gâv-sandoq
stronghold *n.* قلعه qal'eh نيروگاه niru-gâh
structural *adj.* ساختمانى sâkhtemâni
structure *v., n.* ساختمان sâkhtemân ساختار sâkhtâr
struggle *v.* سخت كوشيدن sakht kushidan
　　　　كش مكش كردن kesh-makesh kardan زور زدن zur dadan
struggle *n.* كشمكش kesh-makesh كشاكش keshâ-kesh
strut *vi., vt., n.* سيخ راه رفتن sikh râh raftan
stub *adj., n., vt.* ته چك tah chek كنده kondeh
stubbed *n., v.* كلفت و كوتاه koloft va kutâh
stubble *n.* ته ريش tah rish
stubborn *adj.* سرسخت sar-sakht كله شق kal~eh-shaq
stubby *n.* خپل khepel
stuck-up *n.* متكبر motekab~er دماغ بالا damâq-bâlâ
stud(..horse) *n.* اسب جفت گيرى asb-e' joft-giri
stud(..metal) *n.* ميخ mikh گل ميخ gol-mikh قپه qopeh
student *n.* دانش آموز dânesh-âmuz شاگرد shâgerd محصل mohas~el
studied *adj.* مطالعه شده motâle'eh-shodeh عمدى 'amdi
studio *n.* استوديو estudio
studious *adj.* درس خوان ساعى sâ'i dars-khân
study *-n.* مطالعه motâle'eh اطاق مطالعه otâq-e' motâle'eh
study *-v.* مطالعه كردن motâle'eh kardan درس خواندن dars khândan
study hal *n.* سالن مطالعه sâlon-e' motâle'eh
study room *n.* اطاق مطالعه otâq-e' motâle'eh
stuff *-n.* چيز chiz ماده mâd~eh

stuff -v. پرکردن por kardan تپاندن tapân-dan
stuffed shirt np. پرافاده por-efâdeh
stuffing n. تودلی tu-deli
stuffy n. خفه khafeh گرنته gerefteh
stultify vt. بی ارزش bi-arzesh کردن مسخره maskhareh kardan
stumble vi., vt., n. سکندری رفتن sekandari raftân
بر خوردن bar khordan
stumbling block n. سنگ جلوی راه sang-e' jelo-ye' râh
stumpt n. کنده kondeh ته tah
stumpy adj. غلنبه qolonbeh
stun vt., n. گیج gij بیحس bi-hes خشک کردن khoshk kardan
stunned v. گیج gij متحیر motehay~er
stunning v. گیج کننده gij-konandeh بهت انگیز boht-angiz
stunt n., vi., vt. جلوگیری ازرشد jelo-giri az roshd
stunt man np. بدل هنرپیشه badal-e' honar-pisheh
stupefaction n. بهت boht حیرت heyrat
stupefy vt. متحیر motehay~er مبهوت کردن mabhut kardan
stupendous adj. عظیم 'azim خارق العاده khâreqol-'âdeh
stupid adj., n. نفهم nafahm خر khar نادان nâdân احمق ahmaq
stupidity n. نفهمی nafahmi خریت khariyat حماقت hemâqat
stupor n. نشئه nash'eh خلسه khalseh خماری khomâri
sturdy adj., n. محکم mohkam قرص qors
sturgeon pl. ماهی خاویار mâhi-e' khâviâr
stutter vt., vi., n. لکنت زبان داشتن lok-nat-e' zabân dâshtan
زبان گرفتن zabân gereftan
sty(..pig) n. خوکدانی khuk-dâni
sty(e) n. گلمژه gol-mozheh
style -n. سبک sabk شیوه shiveh لقب laqab سیاق siâq
style v. آرایش دادن ârâyesh dâdan
style (..fashion) n. مد mod استیل estil اسلوب oslub
stylish adj. شیک shik مطابق مد motâbeq-e' mod
stylist n. آرایش دهنده ârâyesh-dahandeh طراح tar~âh
stymie/stymy n. سدراه کردن sad~-e' râh kardan
suave adj. باادب bâ-adab متین matin
sub n., vi., vt. زیر zir
subconscious adj., n. ناخودآگاهی nâ-khod-âgâhi
ضمیر ناخودآگاه zamir-e' nâ-khod-âgâh
subconsciousness n. بیهوشی bi-hushi ناخودآگاهی nâ-khod-âgâhi

subcontinent *n.* شبه قاره shebh-e' qâreh
subcontractor *n.* مقاطعه کارجزء moqâte'eh-kâr-e' joz'
subdivide *vt.* قسمت قسمت کردن qesmat qesmat kardan
subdivision *n.* قسمت جزء qesmat-e' joz' مفروز mafruz
subdue *v.* چیره شدن chireh shodan غلبه شدن qalabeh shodan
subdue *v.* فرونشاندن foru neshândan
subject *n.* موضوع mozu' مطلب matlab سوژه suzheh
subject *v.* مورد قراردادن mored qarâr dâdan
subject *n.* تابع tâbe' رعیت ra'iy~at پیرو pey-ro
مسندالیه mosnad elayh
subject *n.* مبحث reshteh رشته mab-has
subject *n.* مسند الیه fâ'el ناعل mosnad elayh
subject matter *n.* موضوع بحث mozu'-e' bahs
subject(to) *n.* مشروط بر mashrut bar موکول به mokul beh
subjection *n.* تابعیت tâbe'iyat انقیاد enqiâd
subjective *adj.* ناعلی fâ'eli باغرض bâ-qaraz شخصی shakhsi
subjectivity *n.* اغراض eqrâz غرض نگری qaraz-negâri
subjugate *vt.* قلع و قمع کردن qal'o qam' kardan
تحت سلطه قراردادن tahte' salteh qarâr
subjugation *n.* قلع و قمع qal'-o qam' انقیاد enqiâd
subjunctive *n.* التزامی sharti شرطی eltezâmi
sublease/sublet *n.* نصفه اجاره دادن nesfeh ejâreh dâdan
sublimate *vi., n., adj.* تصفیه کردن tasfieh kardan
sublime *adj., n., vt.* عالی 'âli والا vâlâ
subliminal *adj.* ناخودآگاه nâ-khod-âgâh
submachine gun *np.* مسلسل دستی mosal-sal-e' dasti
submarine *n., vi.* زیردریایی zir-daryâyi
submerge *vt., vi.* زیرآب کردن zir-e' âb kardan فروبردن foru bordan
submission *n.* تقدیم taqdim ارائه erâ'eh
submission *n.* تسلیم taslim اطاعت etâ'at
submissive *adj.* مطیع moti' حرف گوش کن harf gush-kon
submit *v.* ارائه دادن erâ'eh dâdan تسلیم کردن taslim kardan
submit *v.* دادن dâdan تسلیم شدن taslim shodan
submittal *n.* ارائه erâ'eh تسلیم taslim
subordinate *n.* زیردست zir-e' dast تابع tâbe'
subordinate *v.* زیردست قراردادن zir-e' dast qarâr dâdan
تابع قراردادن tâbe' qarâr dâdan
subordination *n.* فرمان برداری farmân-bardâri تبعیت taba'iyat

subpoena *n.* احضار کردن ehzâr kardan احضاریه ehzâriyeh
subrogate *vt.* عوض و بدل کردن 'avaz-o badal kardan
subrogation *n.* عوض بدلی 'avaz badali تعویض ta'viz
subscribe *v.* تصدیق tas-diq کردن پشتیبانی poshtibâni kardan
subscribe *v.* مشترک شدن moshtarek shodan
آبونه شدن âbuneh shodan
subscriber *n.* مشترک moshtarek
subscription *n.* اشتراک eshterâk آبونمان âbunemân
subsequent *adj.* بعدی ba'di متعاقب mote'âqeb
subside *vi.* فرونشستن foru neshastan فرو نشاندن foru neshândan
subsidiary *adj., n.* فرعی far'i اضافی ezâfi شعبه sho'-beh
subsidize *n.* کمک هزینه دادن komak hazineh dâdan
subsidy *n.* کمک هزینه دولتی komak hazineh dolati سوبسید sub-sid
subsist *vi., vt.* بخورو نمیر زندگی کردن bekhor-o namir zendegi kardan

subsistence *n.* زندگانی zendegâni معاش ma'âsh
subsistent *adj.* وجود vojud
substance *n.* ماده mâd~eh مفاد mofâd ذات zât
substandard *n.* سطح پایین sat-h-e' pâyin
substantial *adj., n.* اساسی asâsi معتنابه mo'tenâbeh
قابل ملاحظه qâbel-e' molâhezeh
substantially *adv.* بطور اساسی betor-e' asâsi حقیقتاً haqiqatan
substantiate *n.* اثبات کردن esbât kardan
substantive *n., adj.* ذاتی zâti اساسی asâsi مستقل mostaqel
substitute *n., vt., vi.* عوض 'avaz جانشین کردن jâ-neshin kardan
substitution *n.* تعویض ta'viz جانشینی jâ-neshini
substructure *n.* زیربنا zir-banâ
subterranean *n.* زیرزمینی zir-zamini
subtitle *n.* زیرنویس zir-nevis
subtle *adj.* دقیق daqiq زیرکانه zirakâneh
subtlety *n.* دقت deq~at
subtract *n.* کم kam تفریق کردن tafriq kardan
subtraction *n.* تفریق tafriq
subulate *adj.* باریک bârik
suburb *n.* حومه homeh بیرون شهر birun-e' shahr
suburban(ite) *n.* حومه نشین homeh-neshin
subversion *n.* حکومت براندازی hokumat bar-andâzi
subversive *adj., n.* حکومت برانداز hokumat bar-andâz منافق monâfeq

subvert *vt.* ساقط کردن sâqet kardan واژگون کردن vâzh-gun kardan
subway *n., vi.* مترو metro
succeed *v.* جانشین شدن jâneshin shodan
succeed *v.* موفق شدن movaf~aq shodan
کامیاب شدن kâm-yâb shodan
succeeding *n.* جانشین jâ-neshin بعدی ba'di
success *n.* موفقیت movaf~aqiyat کامیابی kâm-yâbi
successful *adj.* موفق movaf~aq کامیاب kâm-yâb کامروا kâm-ravâ
کامران kâm-rân
succession *n.* پی درپی pey dar pey سری seri
succession *n.* جانشینی jâ-neshini توالی tavâli
successive *adj.* متوالی motevâli پشت سرهم posht-e' sar-e' ham
متواتر motevâter
successor *n.* جانشین jâ-neshin
succinct *adj.* مختصر و واضح mokhtasar va vâzeh
succulent *n.* آبدار âb-dâr
succumb *vi.* ازپادرآمدن az pâ dar âmadan تسلیم شدن taslim shodan
such *adj., pro.* این چنین in chenin این قبیل in-qabil
such and such *np.* فلان felân
such(as) *n.* ازقبیل az qabil-e' مثلاً masalan
suchlike *n.* این نوع in-no'
suck *vi., n., vt.* مکیدن mekidan مک زدن mek zadan
sucker *n.* گول خور gul-khor خر khar
suckle *vt., vi.* شیرخوردن shir khordan
suckling *n.* شیرخواره shir-khoreh
suction *n.* مک mek هواکشی havâ-keshi
sudden *n.* ناگهانی nâgahâni
sudden death *n.* مرگ ناگهانی marg-e' nagahâni
اجل معلق ajal-e' mo'al~aq گل برنده gol-e' barandeh
suddenly *adv.* ناگهان nâgahân یکهو yek-ho یک دفعه yek-daf'eh
suddenness *n.* بی انتظاری bi-entezâri
suds *n.* کف صابون kaf sâbun
sudsy *n.* کف صابونی kaf-sâbuni
sue *v.* اقامه دعواکردن eqâmeh-ye' da'vâ kardan
sue *v.* عرضحال دادن 'arz-e' hâl dâdan
suede *n., vt., vi.* جیر jir
suffer *vi., vt.* رنج کشیدن ranj keshidan زجربردن zajr bordan
sufferance *n.* بالاجبار bel ejbâr تحمل taham~ol

suffering *n.* رنج ranj عذاب 'azâb محنت mehnat آلام âlâm
suffice *vi., vt.* کفایت کردن kefâyat kardan کافی بودن kâfi budan
بسنده کردن basandeh kardan
sufficiency *n.* کفایت kefâyat
sufficient *adj.* کافی kâfi بس bas بسنده basandeh مکفی mokfi
sufficiently *n.* بقدرکافی be-qadr-e' kâfi
sufficiently *adv.* بقدرکافی be-qadr-e' kâfi
suffix *n., vt., vi.* پسوندزدن pas-vand zadan
suffocate *vt., vi.* خفه کردن khafeh kardan
suffrage *n.* حق رأی haq~-e' ra'y
sugar *n., vt., vi.* شکر shekar
sugar beet *n.* چغندرقند choqondar-e' qand
sugar bowl *np.* شکردان shekar-dân قنددان qand-dân
sugar cane *np.* نیشکر ney-shekar
sugar crystal *n.* نبات nabât
sugar-cube *n.* قند qand
sugary *adj.* شکری shekari شیرین shirin
suggest *vt.* پیشنهادکردن pish-nahâd kardan
suggestible *adj.* پیشنهادی pish-nahâdi
suggestion *n.* پیشنهاد pish-nahâd اظهارعقیده ez-hâr-e' 'aqideh
suggestive *adj.* دال dâl حاکی hâki بامنظور bâ-manzur
suicidal *adj.* انتحاری entehâri کشنده koshandeh
suicide *n.* خودکشی khod-koshi انتحار entehâr
suicide *v.* خودکشی کردن khod-koshi kardan
suit *v.* مناسب بودن monâseb budan درخوربودن dar-khor budan
suit *n.* دادخواست dâd-khâst دعوی da'vi
suit *n.* کت و شلوار kot-o shalvâr
suit *n.* خواستگاری khâst-gâri
suit *v.* خوش آمدن khosh âmadan
suit *n.* خال khâl
suitability *n.* تناسب tanâsob
suitable *adj.* مناسب monâseb شایسته shâyesteh فراخور farâkhor
suitcase *n.* چمدان chamedân جامه دان jâmeh-dân
suite *n.* اداره edâreh
suite *n.* اطاق لوکس otâq-e' luks
suitor *n.* دادخواه dâd-khâh خواستگار khâst-gâr
sulcate *adj.* شیارشیار shiâr shiâr
sulfate *n., vt., vi.* سولفات sulfât

sulk *vi., n.* قهر کردن qahr kardan
اخم و تخم کردن akhm-o takhm kardan
sulky *adj., n., vt.* قهرکن qahr-kon اخمو akhmu
sullen *adj.* عبوس 'abus گرفته gerefteh
sulphur *n.* گوگرد gugerd
sultry *adj.* داغ dâq سوزان suzân
sum *n., vt., vi.* مبلغ mablaq مجموع majmu'
sum(to) *n.* جمع کردن jam' kardan
sum(up) *n.* خلاصه کردن kholâseh kardan
sumac(h) *n.* سماق somâq
summarily *adv.* بطورخلاصه be-tor-e' kholâseh زود zud
بلافاصله belâ-fâseleh
summarization *n.* اختصار ekhtesâr کوتاهی kutâhi
summarize *vt.* خلاصه کردن kholâseh kardan
مختصرکردن mokhtasar kardan
summary *n., adj.* خلاصه kholâseh مختصر mokhtasar مجمل mojmal
summation *n.* جمع بندی jam'-bandi
summer *n., adj., vi., vt.* تابستان tâbestân
summer solstice *np.* اول تابستان av~al-e' tâbestân
summerhouse *n.* خانۀ ییلاقی khâneh-ye' yey-lâqi
summertime *n.* فصل تابستان fasl-e' tâbestân
summit *n., adj.* ملاقات صلح جویانه molâqât-e' solh-juyâneh
summit *n., adj.* قله qol~eh اوج oj
summon *vt.* احضار کردن ehzâr kardan فراخواندن farâ khândan
summoner *n.* احضارکننده ehzâr-konandeh
summons *n., vt.* احضاریه ehzâriyeh فراخوان farâ-khân
sump *n.* چاهک châhak
sumptuous *adj.* پرخرج por-kharj مجلل mojal~al
sun *v.* آفتاب دادن âftâb dâdan
sun *n.* خورشید khorshid آفتاب âftâb شمس shams
sun bath *np.* حمام آفتاب hamâm-e' âftâb
sun bathe *n.* حمام آفتاب گرفتن hamâm-e' âftâb gereftan
sun deck *np.* بالکن آفتابی bâl-kon-e' âftâbi
sun tan *np.* برنزه boronzeh
sunbeam *n.* پرتوآفتاب parto-e' âftâb
sunburn *n., vt., vi.* آفتاب سوختگی âftâb sukhtegi
sunburst *n., adj.* نورآفتاب nur-e' âftâb
sundae *n.* بستنی مخلوط bastani makh-lut

Sunday *n., adj.* يكشنبه yek-shanbeh
sunder *n.* جدا jodâ مجزا كردن mojaz~â kardan
sundial *n.* ساعت آفتابى sâ'at-e' âftâbi
sundown *n.* غروب qorub
sundries *pl.* مخلفات فروشى mokhalafât forushi
sundry *adj.* گوناگون gunâ-gun
sunflower *n.* گل آفتابگردان gol-e' âftâb-gardân
sunflower seeds *n.* تخمه آفتابگردان tokhmeh âftâb-gardan
sunglass(es) *n.* عينک آفتابى 'eynak-e' âftâbi
sunken *v., adj.* غرق شده qarq-shodeh گود god
sunlight *n.* نورخورشيد nur-e' khorshid آفتاب âftâb
sunlit *adj.* روشن ازآفتاب roshan az âftâb
sunny *adj.* آفتابى âftâbi
sunny side *np.* جنبۀ خوب janbeh-ye' khub
sunny side up *n.* نيمرو nim-ru
sunrise *n.* طلوع آفتاب tolu'-e' âftâb سحر sahar بامداد bâm-dâd
sunset *n.* غروب qorub شامگاه shâm-gâh
sunshine *n.* آفتاب âftâb
sunspot *n.* لكۀ خورشيد lakeh-ye' khorshid
sunstroke *n.* آفتاب زدگى âftâb-zadegi
sunstruck *n.* آفتاب زده âftâb-zadeh
super *n., adj.* عالى 'âli مافوق mâfoq ابر abar
superficial *adj.* سطحى sat-hi قشرى qeshri
superficially *adv.* بطورسطحى be-tor-e' sât-hi
superfluous *n.* اضافى ezâfi زيادى ziâdi زائد zâ'ed
superhuman *adj.* مافوق بشرى mâfoq-e' bashari
superimpose *vt.* روى هم انداختن ruy-e' ham andâkhtan
superintendent *n.* مدير modir سرپرست sar-parast
superior *adj.* برتر bartar عالى 'âli اعلى a'lâ مافوق mâ-foq
superior *n.* بالادست bâlâ-dast رئيس ra'is
superiority *n.* برترى bartari بالاترى bâlâ-tari فضيلت fazilat
superlative *adj.* عالى 'âli بالاترين bâlâ-tarin
superman *n.* سوپرمن super-man ابرمرد abar-mard
supermarket *n.* سوپر super
supernatural *adj., n.* ماوراءالطبيعه mâvar'ol tabi'eh
ازما بهتران az mâ behtarân
superpower *n.* ابرقدرت abar-qodrat
superscript *n.* آدرس âdres عنوان 'onvân

supersede *vt.* کنارگذاشتن kenâr gozâshtan
جانشین شدن jâ-neshin shodan
supersession *n.* برکناری bar-kenâri الغاء elqâ'
supersonic *adj.* مافوق صوتی mâfoq-e' soti
superstition *n.* خرافات khorâfât
superstitious *adj.* خرافاتی khorâfâti
superstructure *n.* روبنا ru-banâ
supervene *vi.* متعاقب شدن mote'âqeb shodan
supervise *vt.* نظارت nezârat سرپرستی کردن sar-parasti kardan
supervision *n.* نظارت nezârat سرپرستی sar-parasti
مباشرت mobâsherat
supervisor *n.* سرپرست sar-parast ناظر nâzer
supine *adj.* روپشت خوابیده ru-posht khâbideh بی بخار bi-bokhâr
supository *n.* شاف shâf
supper *n., adj.* شام shâm عصرانه 'asrâneh
suppertime *n.* شامگاه shâm-gâh
supplant *vt.* جانشین شدن jâ-neshin shodan جاگرفتن jâ gereftan
supple *adj., vt., vi.* نرم narm باانعطاف bâ-en'etâf
supplement *n.* کامل کننده kâmel-konandeh
تکمیل کردن takmil kardan
supplementary *adj., n.* مکمل mokam~el اضافی ezâfi
متمم motam~am ضمیمه zamimeh
suppletion *n.* اتمام etmâm
supplier *n.* تدارک دهنده tadârok-dahandeh
عرضه کننده 'arzeh-konandeh
supply *n.* موجودی mojudi ذخیره zakhireh تدارکات tadârokât
supply *v.* تهیه کردن tahiyeh kardan عرضه کردن 'arzeh kardan
رساندن resândan
support *v.* خرجی دادن kharji dâdan مخارج دادن makhârej dâdan
support *n.* تکیه گاه takyeh-gâh پایه pâyeh
support *n.* حمایت hemâyat پشتیبانی poshti-bâni
support *v.* نگهداری کردن negah-dâri kardan
پشتیبانی کردن poshti-bâni kardan
supporter *n.* پشتیبان poshtibân حامی hâmi
supporting *n.* حامیانه hâmiâneh دومی dov~omi
suppose *vt.* فرض کردن farz kardan گمان کردن gamân kardan
supposed *v.* فرضی farzi خیالی khiâli
supposedly *adv.* فرضاً farzan برحسب گمان bar hasb-e' gamân

supposition *n.* فرض farz گمان gomân حدس hads ظن zan~
suppress *vt.* جلو گرفتن jelo gereftan سرکوب کردن sar-kub kardan
suppression *n.* سرکوب sar-kub اختناق ekhtenâq
قلع و قمع qal'-o qam'
suppressive *n.* سرکوب گر sarkub-gar جلوگیر jelo-gir
supra *n.* بالا bâlâ مافوق mâfoq
supremacy *n.* برتری bartari بالایی bâlâyi
supreme *n.* عالی 'âli اعلا a'lâ
surcharge *n., vt.* عوارض اضافی 'avârez-e' ezâfi
sure *adj., adv.* مطمئن motma'en خاطرجمع khâter-jam' واثق vâseq
sure enough *n.* مسلماً mosalaman
sure-fire *n.* موفق movaf~aq حتمی hatmi
sure-footed *n.* ثابت قدم sâbet-qadam
surely *adv., int.* مطمئناً motma'enan بطوریقین be-tor-e' yaqin
surety *n.* اطمینان etminân ضامن zâmen
surf *n., vi.* موج ساحلی moj-e' sâheli
surface *v., n., adj.* سطح sat-h رویه ruyeh بیرون birun
surfeit *n., vt., vi.* افراط efrât زیاده روی ziâdeh-ravi
surfer *n.* موج سوار moj-savâr
surfy *adj.* پرموج por-moj
surge *n., vi., vt.* خروشیدن khorushidan جریان jaryân یورش yuresh
surgeon *n.* جراح jar~âh
surgery *n.* جراحی jar~âhi
surly *adj.* بداخلاق bad-akhlâq
surmise *vt., vi., n.* حدس زدن hads zadan گمان کردن gamân kardan
surmount *vt.* فایق آمدن fâ'eq âmadan پوشاندن pushândan
surname *n., vt.* نام خانوادگی nâm-e' khânevâdegi
surpass *vt.* برتربودن bartar budan جلوزدن jelo zadan
surpassing *n.* برتر bartar بالاتر bâlâ-tar
surplus *n., adj.* مازاد mâzâd اضافی ezâfi
surprise *n.* بیخبر bi-khabar بیهوا bi-havâ سورپریز sur-periz
surprise *v.* متعجب کردن mote'aj~eb kardan
غافلگیرکردن qâfel-gir kardan
surprising *v.* تعجب آور ta'aj~ob-âvar
surrender *vt., vi., n.* تسلیم شدن taslim shodan
surreptitious *adj.* پنهانی penhâni مخفی makhfi
surrey *n.* کالسکه kâleskeh
surrogate *n., vt.* نماینده namâyandeh اجیر ajir

surround *vt., n.* محاصره mohâsereh احاطه کردن ehâteh kardan
surrounding(s) *n.* اطراف atrâf دوروبر dor-o bar
surtax *n.* مالیات اضافی mâliât-e' ezâfi
surveillance *n.* نظارت nezârat مراقبت morâqebat
surveillant *adj., n., vi.* تحت نظر taht-e' nazar
survey *v.* نقشه برداری کردن naqsheh-bardâri kardan
survey *v.* تحقیق کردن tahqiq kardan
survey(ing) *n.* نقشه برداری naqsheh-bardâri تحقیق tah-qiq
surveyor *n.* نقشه بردار naqsheh-bardâr بازرس bâz-res
survival *n., adj.* بازماندگی bâz-mândegi بقا baqâ
survive *vi., vt.* جان بدربردن jân bedar bordan
زنده ماندن zendeh mândan
surviver *n.* بازمانده bâz-mândeh نجات یافته nejât-yâfteh
susceptibility *n.* آمادگی âmâdegi استعداد este'dâd
susceptible(of) *n.* قابل اثر qâbel-e' asar واجز vâjez
susceptible(to) *n.* آماده âmâdeh مستعد mosta'ed
susceptive *n.* آماده âmâdeh مستعد mosta'ed
suspect *n.* مظنون maznun موردظن mored-e' zan~
suspect *v.* مظنون بودن maznun budan
سوء ظن داشتن su'-e' zan dâshtan
suspected *n.* مظنون maznun موردسوء ظن mored-e' su'-e' zan
suspend *vt.* معلق کردن mo'al~aq kardan تعطیل کردن ta'til kardan
suspended *n.* معلق mo'al~aq تعلیقی ta'liqi
suspended bridge *n.* پل معلق pol-e' mo'al~aq
suspenders *n.* رکاب شلوار rekâb-e' shalvâr
suspense *n.* هیجان hayajân دلهره del-horeh بی تکلیفی bi-tak-lifi
suspension *n.* تعلیق ta'liq کنارگذاری kenâr-gozâri شاه فنر shâh-fanar
suspicion *n., vt.* سوء ظن su'-e' zan شک shak بدگمانی bad-gamâni
suspicious *adj.* مشکوک mashkuk مظنون maznun
sustain *vt.* نگاه داشتن negâh dâshtan تحمل کردن taham~ol kardan
sustenance *n.* نگهداری negah-dâri بقا baqâ' تغذیه taqzieh
suture *n., vt.* بخیه زدن bakhieh zadan
suzerain *n., adj.* حاکم hâkem خان khân
suzerainty *n.* حکومت hokumat تسلط tasal~ot
swab *v.* گوش پاک کن gush pâk-kon لوله پاک کن luleh pâk-kon
swab *adj.* شل و ول shol-o vel
swallow *n.* چلچله chel-cheleh
swallow *v.* قورت دادن qurt dâdan باورکردن bâvar kardan

swamp v. روی سرریختن ruy-e' sar rikhtan
swamp n. منجلاب باتلاق bâtlâq manjelâb
swampy adj. باتلاقی bâtlâqi
swan n. قو qu
swan's-donwn n. پرقو pâr-e' qu
swank adj., vi. افاده‌ای efâdeh-i
swanky adj. پرافاده por-efâdeh
swap n. معامله mo'âmeleh
swap v. باهم عوض کردن bâ ham 'avaz kardan
swarm n., vi., vt. ازدحام کردن ezdehâm kardan
گله شدن gal‿eh shodan
swarthy adj. گندم گون gandom-gun
swash vi., adj. پاشیدن pâshidan
swashbuckler n. ماجراجو mâjerâ-ju
swashbuckling adj., n. ماجراجویانه mâjerâ-juyâneh
swatter n. مگس کش magas-kosh
sway v. نوسان کردن navasân kardan تاب خوردن tâb khordan
sway v. قردادن qer dâdan
swear v. قسم خوردن qasam khordan سوگند خوردن sogand khordan
swear v. فحش دادن fohsh dâdan ناسزادادن nâ-sezâ dâdan
دشنام دادن doshnâm dâdan
swear to God! n. بخدا قسم be-khodâ qasam!
swear(in) n. قسم دادن qasam dâdan
swear(off) n. توبه کردن tobeh kardan غلط کردن qalat kardan
swearword n. فحش fohsh
sweat v. عرق ریختن 'araq rikhtan
sweat v. عرق کردن 'araq kardan
sweat shirt np. گرمکن ورزشی garm-kon-e' varzeshi
sweat(blood) n. مثل سگ کارکردن mesl-e' saq kâr kardan
sweat(out) n. باسختی گذراندن bâ sakhti gozarândan
sweatband n. پیشانی بند pishâni-band
sweater n. بلوز boluz
sweatshop n. بیگارخانه bi-gâr-khâneh
sweep v. سریع گذشتن sari' gozashtan
sweep v. جاروکردن jâru kardan
sweeper n. جاروکش jâru-kesh
sweeping v., n. سریع sari' فراگیر farâgir
sweet adj. شیرین shirin خوش khosh

sweet and sour *adj.* ترش و شیرین torsh-o shirin ملس malas
sweet pea *n.* نخودسبز nokhod sabz
sweet tooth *np.* علاقه به شیرینی 'alâqeh beh shiri
sweet-scented *adj.* خوش بو ḵhosh-bu معطر mo'at~ar
sweetbread *n.* خوش گوشت khosh-gusht دنبلان don-balân
sweetbrier *n.* نسترن nastaran
sweetening *n.* شیرین کننده shirin-konandeh
sweetheart *n.* دلبر del-bar معشوق ma'shuq
sweetie *n.* عزیزجون 'aziz-jun
sweets *n.* شیرینی‌جات shirini-jât
swell *n.* خوب khub عالی 'âli
swell *v.* ورم کردن varam kardan بادکردن bâd kardan
swelling *v.* ورم varam آماس âmâs
swelter *n.* عرق کردن 'araq kardan
     خیس عرق شدن khis-e' 'araq shodan
sweltering *adj.* خفه کننده ḵhâfeh konandeh هوای دم havâ-ye' dam
swerve *n.* ویراژ دادن virâzh dâdan
swift *adj., adv., n.* سریع sari' چابک châbok
swiftly *adv.* بسرعت be-sor'at
swig *n., vt., vi.* جرعه jor'eh قلپ qolop
swill *n.* سرکشیدن sar keshidan آشغال کله âshqâl kaleh
swim *vi., vt., n.* شناکردن shenâ kardan
swim suit *n.* مایو mâyo
swimmer *n.* شناگر shenâ-gar
swimming *n., v., adj.* شنا shenâ آب تنی âb-tani
swimming pool *vt., vi., n.* استخرشنا estakhr-e' shenâ
swindle *vt., vi., n.* گول زدن gul zadan کلاشی کردن kal~âshi kardan
swindler *adj.* کلاش kal~âsh کلاه بردار kolâh-bardâr
     گوش بر gush-bor
swindling *n.* کلاهبرداری kolâh-bardâri غبن qabn
swine *n., pl.* خوک khuk
swing *n.* تاب tâb
swing *v.* عیاشی کردن 'ayâshi kardan
swing *v.* تاب خوردن tâb khordan تاب دادن tâb dâdan
swing-shift *n.* بعدازظهر kâr-e' ba'd az zohr
swinger *n.* عیاش 'ayâsh پارتی رو pârti-ro
swinging door *np.* در چرخان dar-e' charkhân
swipe *n., vt.* بلندکردن zadan boland kardan

swipes *n.* آبجو âbe-jo
swirl *vi., vt., n.* چرخ زدن charkh zadan گیج رفتن gij raftan
swish *vi., vt.* نز qezh غمزه qamzeh
switch *n.* سوئیچ su'ich کلید kelid
switch *n.* ترکه tarkeh
switch *v.* عوض کردن 'avaz kardan
switchblade *n.* چاقوی ضامن دار châqu-ye' zâmen-dâr
switchboard *n.* مرکزتلفن markaz-e' telefon
swivel *v.* گرداندن gardân-dan چرخاندن charkhândan
swivel *n.* چرخدار charkh-dâr گردان gardân
swollen *v., adj.* متورم motevarem ورم کرده varam-kardeh
swoop *vi., vt., n.* فرودآمدن forud âmadan نازل شدن nâzel shodan
sword *n.* شمشیر sham-shir سیف seyf
swordsman *n.* شمشیرزن sham-shir-zan
sworn *v., adj.* قسم خورده qasam khordeh خونی khuni
sycophant *n.* چاپلوس châplus طفیلی tofeyli خایه مال khâyeh-mâl
sycophant *adj.* کاسه لیس kâseh-lis خایه مال khâyeh-mâl
syllabic *n.* سیلابی sylâbi هجایی hejâ'i
syllable *n., v.* سیلاب sylâb هجاء hejâ'
syllogism *n.* قیاس qiâs شکل shekl
symbiotic *adj.* هم زیستی ham-zisti
symbol *n., vt.* نشان neshân سمبل sambol
symbolic *adj.* نمایان گر namâyân-gar حاکی hâki
symbolism *n., adj.* سمبولیسم sambolism نشان گرایی neshân-garâyi
symbolize *vt., vi.* نمایان گر namâyân-gar حاکی بودن hâki budan
symmetry *n.* تقارن taqâron قرینه qarineh
sympathetic *adj.* همدرد hamdard دلسوزانه del-suz-âneh
sympathize *n.* همدردی کردن ham-dardi دلسوزی کردن del-suzi kardan
sympathy *n.* همدردی ham-dardi دلسوزی del-suzi
symphonic *adj.* هماهنگ ham-âhang
symptom(s) *n.* نشانه neshâneh علامت 'alâmat آثار âsâr
symptomatic *adj.* باعلائم bâ-'alâ'em
synagogue *n.* کنیسا kanisâ کنشت kenesht
synchronic *n.* همزمان ham-zamân هم تاریخ ham-târikh
synchronize *vi.* هم زمان کردن ham-zamân kardan
تطبیق دادن tat-biq dâdan
syndicate *n., vt.* شبکه کردن shabakeh kardan سندیکا sandikâ
syndicated *v.* شبکه‌ای shabakeh-i جمعی jam'i

syndication *n.* شبکه گری shabakeh-gari
syndrome *n.* پدیده padideh
synonym *n.* همنام ham-nâm مترادف moterâdef
synonymous *adj.* همنام ham-nâm هم معنی ham-ma'ni
مترادف moterâdef
synonymy *n.* همنامی ham-nâmi
synoptic *adj.* خلاصه kholâseh چکیده chekideh
syntactic *adj.* نحوی nahvi
syntax *n.* نحو nahv ترتیب کلمات tartib-e' kalamât
synthesis *n.* ترکیب tarkib توحید tohid
synthesize *vt.* ترکیب کردن tarkib kardan یکی کردن yeki kardan
synthetic *adj., n.* مصنوعی masnu'i ترکیبی tarkibi
syphilis *n.* سفلیس sef-lis کونت kuft
syringe *n., vi.* آمپول âmpul
syrup *n., vt.* شیره shireh شربت قند sharbat-e' qand
system *n.* دستگاه dast-gâh سیستم sistem
systematic *adj.* منظم monaz~am بترتیب be-tartib
systematically *n.* مرتباً morat~aban
باروش معین bâ ravesh-e' mo'ay~ân
systematize *vt.* منظم monaz~am مرتب کردن morat~ab kardan
systole *n.* انقباض قلب enqebâz-e' qalb
syzygy *n.* نقطهٔ مخالف noqteh-ye' mokhâlef

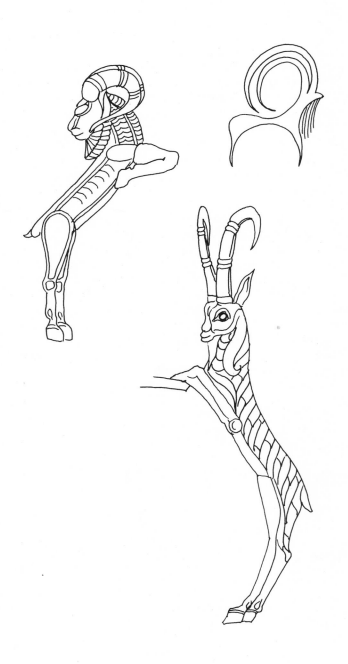

T T ت

T-shirt *n.* عرق گیر 'araq-gir
tab *n., vt.* لبه labeh برگه bargeh
tab *n., vt.* صورت حساب surat hesâb
table *n., vt.* جدول jad-val فهرست fehrest
table *n., vt.* میز miz
tablecloth *n.* رومیزی ru-mizi سفره sofreh
tablespoon *n.* قاشق نهارخوری qâshoq-e' nahâr-khori
tablet *n., vt.* لوحه loheh قرص qors
tabloid *n.* روزنامه ruz-nâmeh
taboo *adj., n., vt.* حرام harâm ممنوع mamnu'
tabulate *vt., vi., adj.* جدول بندی کردن jadval-bandi kardan
tabulation *n.* جدول بندی jadval-bandi
tachometer *n.* دوران سنج davarân-sanj
tacit *adj.* ضمنی zemni بااشاره bâ-eshâreh
tack *n.* میخ mikh پونز punez
tack *n.* رویه ravieh خط مشی khat~-e' mashi
tack(on) *n.* اضافه کردن ezâfeh kardan
tackle *n.* نخ و قرقره nakh-o qer-gereh
tackle *v.* گلاویزشدن galâviz shodan
tacky *adj.* مبهم mobham پیچیده pichideh
tacky *adj.* چسبناک chasb-nâk
tactful *adj.* باشناخت bâ-shenâkht
tactic *n.* رویه raviyeh تاکتیک tâktik
tactical *adj.* تدبیری tad-biri تاکتیکی tâktiki موضعی moze'i
tactician *n.* باتدبیر bâ-tadbir تاکتیسین tâktisian
tactics *n.* تدابیر جنگی tadâbir-e' jangi
tadpole *n.* بچه وزغ bach~eh vazaq
tag *n.* برچسب bar-chasb
tag *v.* برچسب زدن bar-chasb zadan
tag *v.* بادست زدن bâ-dast zadan
tag game *n.* گرگم بهوا gor-gam be-havâ
tag(along) *n.* همراه رفتن hamrâh raftan تعقیب کردن ta'qib kardan
tail *n.* دم dom دنباله donbâleh ته tah
tail *v.* تعقیب کردن ta'qib kardan
tailgate *n., vi., vt.* سپر به سپر رفتن separ be-separ raftan
tailight *n.* چراغ عقب cherâq-e' 'aqab
tailor *n., vi., vt.* خیاط khay~ât

tails *n.* خط khat~

taint *v.* آلودن âludan لکه‌دارکردن lakeh-dâr kardan

taint *n.* آلودگی âludegi لکه lak~eh

take *v.* گرفتن gereftan برداشتن bar-dâshtan

take *v.* بردن bordan

take down *n.* از هم جدایی az-ham jodâyi

take five! *n.* پنج دقیقه استراحت panj daqiqeh esterâhat

take(after) *n.* شبیه بودن shabih budan

take(apart) *n.* جداکردن jodâ kardan پیاده کردن piâdeh kardan

take(back) *n.* پس گرفتن pas gereftan

take(care) *n.* مواظبت کردن movâzebat kardan

take(down) *n.* پایین آوردن pâyin âvardan خراب کردن kharâb kardan

take(for) *n.* خیال کردن khiâl kardan حساب کردن hesâb kardan

take(in) *n.* تو بردن tu bordan تو دادن tu dâdan پذیرفتن paziroftân

take(it out of) *n.* برداشتن bardâshtan خالی کردن khâli kardan

take(it out on) *n.* تلافی درآوردن talâfi dar âvardan

take(it) *n.* تصور کردن tasav~or kardan تحمل کردن taham~ol kardan

take(notes) *n.* یادداشت کردن yâd-dâsht kardan

take(off) *n.* درآوردن dar âvardan کندن kandan برداشتن bar dâshtan

take(off) *n.* بلند شدن boland shodan

از جا کنده شدن az jâ kandeh shodan

take(on) *n.* طرف شدن taraf shodan گرفتن gereftan

take(out) *n.* درآوردن dar âvardan بیرون بردن birun bordan

take(over) *n.* تحویل گرفتن tahvil gereftan

به عهده گرفتن beh-'ohdeh gereftan

take(time) *n.* طول دادن tul dâdan عجله نکردن 'ajaleh nakardan

take(to) *n.* علاقه پیدا کردن 'alâqeh peydâ kardan

take(up with) *n.* معاشرت کردن mo'âsherat kardan

take(up) *n.* بالا بردن bâlâ bordan قبول کردن qabul kardan

take-home pay *np.* حقوق خالص hoquq-e' khâles

take-in *n.* درآمد dar âmad باج bâj

take-off *n.* پرواز parvâz حرکت harekat طیران tayarân

taken aback *n.* جا خورده jâ-khordeh

taker *n.* گیرنده girandeh خواستار khâstâr بگیر be-gir

taking *n., v.* گیرا girâ تسخیر tas-khir

tale *n.* داستان dâstân قصه qes~eh

talebearing *adj., n.* غیبت گویی qeybat-guyi

talemonger *n.* غیبت گو qeybat-gu

talent *n.* قنطار qantâr تالانت tâlânt
talent *n.* استعداد este'-dâd ذوق zoq
talented *n.* با استعداد bâ-este'dâd باذوق bâ-zoq
talisman *n.* طلسم telesm
talk *v.* حرف زدن harf zadan صحبت کردن sohbat kardan
مذاکره کردن mozâkereh kardan
talk(around) *n.* متقاعد کردن moteqâ'ed kardan
talk(at) *n.* غیر مستقیم گفتن qeyr-e' mostaqim goftan
talk(away) *n.* وراجی کردن ver~âji kardan
talk(back) *n.* حاضر جوابی کردن hâzer-javâbi kardan
talk(down) *n.* صدا خواباندن sedâ khâbândan
talk(out) *n.* باحرف راضی کردن bâ-harf râzi kardan
talk(over) *n.* باهم صحبت کردن bâ-ham sohbat kardan
talk(up) *n.* باحرف نرم کردن bâ-harf narm kardan
talk(with) *n.* مذاکره کردن mozâkereh kardan
talkative *adj.* پرحرف por-harf وراج ver~âj
talking *n.* حرف harf صحبت sohbat
tall *adj.* بلندقد boland-qad دراز derâz
tally *n., vt.* حساب کردن hesâb kardan چوب خط chub-khat
tamarind *n.* تمبر هندی tambr-e' hendi
tambourine *n.* دایره dâr-yeh دایره زنگی dâyereh zangi
tame *adj., vt.* اهلی کردن ahli kardan رام کردن râm kardan
tan *n.* خرمایی khormâyi برنزه boronzeh
tan *v.* برنزه کردن boronzeh kardan دباغی کردن dab~âqi kardan
tanbark *n.* جفت jaft
tandem *adv., adj., n.* دوتایی do-tâyi دونفره do-nafareh
tangelo *n.* نارنگی فرنگی nârengi farangi
tangential *adj.* تقریباً مماس taqriban momâs
tangerine *n., adj.* نارنگی nârengi
tanget *n.* مماس momâs تانژانت tân-zhânt
tangibility *n.* لمس پذیری lams paziri احساس ehsâs
tangible *adj., n.* لمس پذیر lams-pazir قابل احساس qâbel-e' ehsâs
tangle *vt., vi., n.* گیر کردن gir kardan درگیر شدن dar-gir shodan
tank *n., vt.* مخزن makhzan بشکه boshkeh
tank *n., vt.* تانک tânk
tank *n., vt.* باک bâk
tanker *n.* تانکر tân-ker نفتکش naft-kesh
tanner *adj., n.* دباغ dab~âq

tanning *n.* دباغی dab~âqi
tantalize *n.* تهییج کردن tahyij kardan
tantalizing *adj.* تهییج کننده tahyij-konandeh هیجان آور hayajân-âvar
tantamount *n.* مساوی mosâvi معادل mo'âdel
tantrum *n.* ادا adâ
tap *n., vt., vi.* لوله کشی luleh-keshi شیر shir
tap *n., vt., vi.* یواش زدن yavâsh zadan سوراخ کردن surâkh kardan
وصل کردن vasl kardan
tap *n., vt., vi.* ضربه zarbeh دق دق daq-daq
tap *n., vt., vi.* استراق سمع esterâq-e' sam'
tape *n., vt.* نوار بستن navâr bastan ضبط کردن zabt kardan
tape *n., vt.* نوار navâr
tape measure *np.* متر metr
tape recorder *np.* ضبط صوت zabt-e' sot
taper *n., vi., vt.* نازک شدن nâzok باریک شدن bârik shodan
tapered *n.* نازک nâzok باریک bârik
tapestry *n.* قالی پارچه‌ای qâli-e' pârcheh-i
tapeworm *n.* کرم روده kerm-e' rudeh
taps *n.* شیپور خواب shey-pur-e' khâb
tar *v., adj., n.* قیر qir
tarantula *n.* رطیل roteyl
tardiness *n.* کندی kondi دیری diri
tardy *adj.* کند kond دیر dir
target *n., vt.* نشان neshân هدف hadaf آماج âmâj
target *n., vt.* نشان گرفتن neshân gereftan هدف گرفتن hadaf gereftan
tariff *n.* تعرفه ta'refeh عوارض 'avârez
tarnation *int., n., adv.* لعنتی la'nati
tarnish *vt.* تیره کردن tireh kardan اکسیده کردن oksideh kardan
tarp(ulin) *n.* روکش برزنت rukesh-e' berezent
tart *adj., n.* ترش کیک torsh-keyk
tart *adj., n.* لگوری laguri تاشی lâshi
task *n., vt.* کار kâr زحمت zahmat
task force *np.* گروه ضربتی goruh-e' zarbati
taskwork *n.* کار سخت kâr-e' sakht
tassel *v., n.* منگوله manguleh
taste *vt., n.* مزه کردن mazeh kardan چشیدن cheshidan
taste *vt., n.* طعم ta'm مزه mazeh سلیقه saliqeh ذائقه zâ'eqeh
tasteful *adj.* با سلیقه bâ-saliqeh باذوق bâ-zoq

tasteless *adj.* بی سلیقه bi-saliqeh بی مزه bi-mazeh
taster *n.* غذا چش qazâ-chesh
tasty *n.* خوش مزه khosh-mazeh
tatter(s) *n.* پاره پاره pâreh-pâreh ژنده zhendeh
tattered *n.* ژنده پوش zhendeh-push
tattle *vi., vt., n.* دری وری گفتن dari-vari goftan
غیبتگویی کردن qeybat-guyi kardan
tattletale *n., adj.* دری وری dari-vari
tattoo *n., vt.* خال کوبی khâl-kubi
taunt *adj., vt., n.* سر بسر گذاشتن sar be-sar gozâshtan
taupe *n.* خاکستری khâkestari
Taurus *n.* ثور sor اردیبهشت ordi-behesht
taut *adj.* سفت seft
tavern *n.* کافه kâfeh میخانه mey-khâneh
taverner *n.* کافه چی kâfeh-chi می فروش mey-forush
tax *vt., n.* مالیات گرفتن mâliât gereftan
tax-exemp *n.* معاف از مالیات mo'âf az mâliât
tax-payer *n.* مالیات دهنده mâliât-dahandeh
taxable *n.* مشمول مالیات mash-mul-e' mâliât
taxation *n.* مالیات گیری mâliât-giri
taxi(cab) *n.* تاکسی tâksi
taxidermy *n.* حیوانات خشک پوست heyvânât-e' khoshk-pust
te-hee *int., n., vi.* هه هه heh heh کر کر ker ker
tea *n.* چای chây چایی châyi
tea tray *np.* سینی چای sini-e' chây
teach *vt., vi., n.* درس دادن dars dâdan آموختن âmukhtan
یاد دادن yâd dâdan
teachable *n.* درس دادنی dars dâdani تعلیمی ta'limi
teacher *n.* آموزگار âmuzegâr معلم mo'al~em دبیر dabir
مرشد morshed
teaching *n., v.* تعلیم ta'lim تدریس tad-ris
teacup *n.* فنجان چای fenjân-e' chây
teahouse *n.* چای خانه chây-khâneh قهوه خانه qahveh-khâneh
teak(wood) *n.* چوب ساج chub-e' sâj
team *n., vt.* دسته dasteh تیم tim اسبها asb-hâ
teammate *n.* همبازی ham-bâzi
teamster *n.* قاطرچی qâter-chi بارکش bâr-kesh
teamwork *n.* همکاری دسته جمعی ham-kâri-e' dasteh jâm'i

teapot *n., vi.* توری qori
tear *n.* اشک ashk
tear *n.* جر jer پاره گی pârehgi
tear *v.* پاره کردن pâreh kardan جر دادن jer dâdan
tear gaz *n.* گازاشک آور gâz-e' ashk-âvar
tear(at) *n.* بزور کشیدن be-zur keshidan کندن kandan
tear(down) *n.* خراب کردن kharâb kardan
tear(into) *n.* حمله ور شدن hamleh-var shodan
tear-jerker *n.* غم انگیز qam-angiz
نمایش گریه دار namâyesh-e' geryeh-d
teardrop *n.* قطرهٔ اشک qatreh-ye' ashk
tearful *n.* اشک آلود ashk-âlud
tearless *adj.* بدون اشک bedun-e' ashk
teary *adj.* اشک آلود ashk-âlud
tease *v.* سر بسر گذاشتن sar be-sar gozâshtan
tease *v.* شانه کردن shâneh kardan
teaser *n.* لاس زن lâs-zan لاس زدن lâs zadan
teaspoon *n.* قاشق چای خوری qâshoq-e' chây-khori
teat *n.* ممه mameh
technic *n., adj.* فن fan تکنیک teknik
technical *n.* فنی fan~i تکنیکی tekniki
technicality *n.* نکتهٔ فنی nokteh-ye' fan~i
technically *adv.* بطور فنی betor-e' fan~i
technician *n., adj.* متخصص فنی motekhases-e' fan~i
تکنیسین teknisian
technology *n.* تکنولوژی teknolozhi فن شناسی fan-shenâsi
techy *adj.* حساس has~âs
tedious *n.* خسته کننده khasteh-konandeh کسل کننده kesel-kokandeh
tedium *n.* یکنواختی yek-navâkhti
tee *adj., n., v.* سه راهی seh-râhi
tee(off) *n.* شروع کردن shoru' kardan
teem *vi., vt.* مملو بودن mamlo budan
teeming *adj.* مملو mamlo پر por
teen *adj., n.* خرد khord سیزده تا نوزده sizdah-tâ-nuzdah
teen-age *n.* خردسال khord-sâl
teen-ager *n.* نوجوان no-javân
teeny *adj.* ریز riz فسقلی fes-qeli
teeter *n.* لرزیدن larzidan

teeter-totter *n.* الاكلنگ alâ-kolang
teeth *n., pl.* دندان ها dandân-hâ
teethe/teething *n.* دندان در آوردن dandân dar âvardan
teetotal *n.* كامل kâmel
teetotaler *n.* شخص مشروب نخور shakhs-e' mashrub-nakhor
telecast *n.* پخش تلویزیونی كردن pakhsh-e' televizioni kardan
telegram *n.* تلگرام telegrâm
telegraph *n.* تلگراف telegrâf
telepathy *n.* ارتباط مغزی ertebât-e' maqzi
telephone *n., vt.* تلفن زدن telefon zadan تلفن كردن telefon kardan
telephonic *adj.* تلفنی telefoni
telescope *n., adj., vt., vi.* تلسكوپ teleskop
دوربین نجومی durbin-e' nojumi
telescopic *n.* تلسكوپی teleskopi
television *n.* تلویزیون televizion
tell *n., vt., vi.* گفتن goftan
tell(off) *n.* توبیخ كردن tobikh kardan گوشمالی دادن gush-mâli dâdan
tell(on) *n.* چغلی كردن choqoli kardan خبر دادن khabar dâdan
tellable *n.* گفتنی goftani
teller *n.* گوینده guyandeh
teller *n.* متصدی motes~adi تحویل دار tahvil-dâr
telling *adj., v.* مؤثر mo'aser گفتار goftâr
telltale *n., adj.* نشان گر neshân-gar
temper *n.* اخلاق akhlâq خوی khuy درست كردن dorost kardan
temperament *n.* اخلاق akhlâq مزاج mezâj خوی khuy
temperamental *adv.* دمدمی مزاج dam-dami mezâj
temperance *n.* اعتدال e'tedâl خودداری khod-dâri
temperate *adj.* معتدل mo'tadel خوددار khod-dâr پرهیزگار parhiz-gâr
temperature *n.* درجهٔ حرارت darejeh-ye' harârat
tempered *adj.* آب داده âb-dâdeh خلق kholq
tempest *n.* طوفان tufân خشم khashm
template *n.* تیرک tirak
temple *n.* معبد ma'bad بتكده bot-kadeh
temple *n.* شقیقه shaqiqeh گیج گاه gij-gâh
tempo *n.* میزان سرعت mizân-e' sor'at
temporal *adj., n.* موقتی movaq~ati دنیوی donyavi
temporary *adj., n.* موقتی movaq~ati
tempt *vt.* وسوسه كردن vas-vaseh kardan اغوا كردن eqvâ kardan

temptation *n.* اغوا وسوسه eqvâ vas-vaseh
tempter *n.* اغوا کننده eqvâ konandeh
tempting *adj.* وسوسه انگیز vas-vaseh-angiz
ten *n.* ده dah
tenable *adj.* قابل نگهداری qâbel-e' negah-dâri
tenacious *adj.* محکم mohkam قرص qors
tenacity *n.* استحکام esteh-kâm سفتی sefti
tenancy *n., vt., vi., adj.* مستاجری mosta'jeri
مدت اجاره mod~at-e' ejâreh
tenant *n., vt., vi.* مستاجر mosta'jer
tend *v.* نگهداری کردن negah-dâri kardan
مواظبت کردن movâzebat kardan
tend *v.* متمایل بودن motemâyel budan تمایل داشتن tamâyol dâshtan
tendency *n.* تمایل tamâyol
tender *v.* ارائه کردن erâ'eh kardan تقدیم کردن taq-dim kardan
tender *n.* پول pul
tender *adj.* نرم narm دلسوز del-suz ملایم molâyem ترد tord
tender-hearted *adj.* نرم دل narm-del
tenderfoot *n.* تازه کار tâzeh-kâr
tenderize *vt.* ترد کردن tord kardan
tenderizer *n.* ترد کن tord-kon نرم کن narm-kon
tenderloin *n.* ژامبون zhâmbon
tendon *n.* پی pey وتر vatar
tenement *n.* خانهٔ مسکونی khâneh-ye' maskuni
tenet *n.* عقیده 'aqideh مسلک maslak مرام marâm
tenfold *adj., adv.* ده برابر dah-barâbar
tennis shoe *n.* کفش کتانی kafsh-e' katâni
tenor *n., adj.* رویه ravieh زیر zir
tense *n., adj., vt., vi.* زمان zamân
tense *n., adj., vt., vi.* سفت seft کشیده keshideh گرفته gerefteh
tension *vt.* کشش keshesh گرفتگی gereftegi تیرگی tiregi
tent *n., vt., vi.* چادر châdor خیمه kheymeh
tentacle *n.* شاخک shâkhak دست dast
tentative *adj.* آزمایشی âzmâyeshi همین جوری hamin-juri
tenuous *n.* باریک bârik رقیق raqiq
tepee *n.* چادر مخروطی châdor-e' makhruti
tepid *adj.* ولرم velarm
tercel *adj., n.* قرقی نر qerqi-e' nar

term *n., vt.* اصطلاح estelâh
term *n., vt.* شرط shart شرایط sharâyet
term *n., vt.* نامیدن nâmidan
term *n., vt.* دوره doreh ثلث sols
terminable *adj.* تمام شدنی tamâm-shodani
terminal *adj., n.* کشنده koshandeh بدخیم bad-khim
terminal *adj., n.* ایستگاه ist-gâh سالن فرودگاه sâlon-e' forud-gâh
terminally *adv.* درآخر dar âkhar بطور بدخیم betor-e' bad-khim
terminate *vt., vi.* پایان دادن pâyân dâdan
خاتمه دادن khâtemeh dâdan
termination *n.* پایان pâyân خاتمه khâtemeh نسخ faskh
terminator *n.* تمام کننده tamâm-konandeh
terminology *adj.* اصطلاح ویژه estelâh-e' vizheh
termite *n.* موریانه mury-âneh لبنگ labang
terrace *v., n.* تراس terâs بالکن bâlkon مهتابی mahtâbi
terrain *n.* راه râh زمین zamin
terrestrial *n.* زمینی zamini دنیوی donyavi خاکی khâki
terrible *adj.* وحشتناک vah-shat-nâk مخوف makhof
terribly *adv.* خیلی kheyli بطور وحشتناک be-tor-e' vah-shat-nâk
terrific *adj.* هولناک hol-nâk عالی 'âli
terrified *vt.* وحشت زده vah-shat-zadeh
terrify *vt.* ترساندن tarsân-dan وحشت انداختن vah-shat ândâkhtan
territorial *adj.* زمینی zamini کشوری keshvari
داخل مرزی dâkhel marzi
territory *n.* زمین zamin خاک khâk خطه khot~eh بوم bum
terror *n.* وحشت vahshat رعب ro'b خوف khof
terrorism *n.* وحشت اندازی vahshat-andâzi
terrorist *n.* تروریست terorist
terrorization *n.* وحشت اندازی vahshat-andâzi ارعاب er'âb
terrorize *vt., adj.* وحشت انداختن vah-shat ândâkhtan
ایجاد وحشت کردن ijâd-e' vah-shat kardan
terse *adj.* مختصر mokhtasar دقیق daqiq
tertiary *adj., n.* سومی sev~omi
test *v.* امتحان کردن emtehân kardan آزمایش کردن âzemâyesh kardan
test tube *n.* آزمایش luleh-ye' âzmâyesh
testament *n.* پیمان peymân عهد 'ahd وصیت نامه vasiyat-nâmeh
testate *adj.* وصیت کرده vasiyat-kardeh
tester *n.* ممتحن momtahen

testicle *n.* بيضه beyzeh تخم tokhm
testifier *n.* گواهی دهنده gavâhi-dahandeh
testify *vi., vt.* گواهی دادن gavâhi dâdan شهادت دادن shahâdat dâdan
testily *n.* بطور آزمایشی be-tor-e' âzmâyeshi
testimonial *n.* استشهاد estesh-hâd گواهینامه gavâhi-nâmeh
testimony *n.* شهادت shahâdat گواهی gavâhi
testy *n.* حساس has~âs زودرنج zud-ranj
tetanus *n.* کزاز kozâz
tether *n., vt.* افسار زدن afsâr zadan
text *n.* متن matn نوشته neveshteh نامه nâmeh مکتوب maktub
textbook *n.* کتاب درسی ketâb-e' darsi
textile *n., adj.* نساجی nas~âji بافته bâfteh
texture *v., n.* بافت bâft ساخت sâkht
than *con., pre.* از az
thank *vt.* تشکر کردن tashakor kardan شکر کردن shokr kardan
thank you! *n.* متشکرم moteshakeram!
    ممنونم mam-nunam!
    مرسی mersi!
thank-worthy *n.* قابل تشکر qâbel-e' tashakor
thankful *adj.* متشکر moteshaker ممنون mam-nun
    شاکر shâker سپاسگزار sepâs-gozâr
thankless *adj.* بدون تشکر bedun-e' tashakor
thanks *n.* سپاس گذاری sepâs-gozâri
thanks! *n.* متشکرم moteshakeram!
    ممنونم mam-nunam!
    مرسی mersi!
thanks(to) *n.* بخاطر be-khâter-e' به لطف beh-lotf-e'
thanksgiving *n.* شکر گذاری shokr-gozâri
that *pro., adv., con.* آن ân که آن ân-keh
that-conj. *n.* که keh
thaw *vi., vt., n.* آشتی âshti
thaw *vi., vt., n.* آب شدن âb shodan
theater *n.* تئاتر te'âtr
theatrics *n.* تئاتر بازی te'âtr-bâzi
thee *pro.* تو را to-râ بتو be-to
theft *n.* دزدی dozdi سرقت serqat
theirs *n.* مال آنها mâl-e' ânhâ مالشان mâleshân
theism *n.* خدا پرستی khodâ-parasti

them *pro., adj.* را آنها ânhâ râ را ایشان ishân râ
theme *n.* موضوع mozu' مطلب mat-lab
theme song *np.* موسیقی فیلم musiqi-e' film
themselves *pro., pl.* را خودشان khodeshân râ
then *adv., adj., n.* سپس sepas بعد ازآن ba'd az ân پس pas
thence(forth) *n.* از آن بعد az ân be-ba'd پس از آن از az ân pas
theocentric *adj.* خدا مرکزی khodâ-markazi
theocracy *n.* حکومت مذهبی hokomat-e' maz-habi
theologian *n.* فقیه faqih روحانی ruhâni
theological *adj.* فقهی feq-hi الهی elâhi
theology *n.* فقه feq-h الهیات elâhiyât
theomachy *n.* محاربه با خدا mohârebeh bâ-khodâ
theorem *n.* قضیه qazieh برهان borhân
theoretical *n.* فرضی farzi وابسته به تئوری vâ-basteh beh te'ori
theoretically *n.* بطور فرضی be-tor-e' farzi
theoretician *n.* فرضیه دان farzieh-dân تیوریسین te'oresian
theoretics *n.* علم فرضیه 'elm-e' farzieh
theorize *n.* فرض کردن farz kardan فرضیه دادن farzieh dâdan
theory *n.* فرضیه farzieh تئوری te'ori
therapeutic *n.* معالجه‌ای mo'âlejeh-i درمانی darmâni
therapeutics *n.* درمان شناسی darmân-shenâsi
therapist *n.* درمان شناس darmân-shenâs
therapy *n.* درمان darmân معالجه mo'âlejeh
there *adv., pro., n., adj.* آنجا ânjâ
there you go! *n.* بارک اله bârikalâ!
there! *n.* بیا biâ! دیدی گفتم didi goftam?
there, there! *n.* ناراحت نباش nârâhat na-bâsh
thereabouts *n.* همان اطراف hamân atrâf
thereafter *adv.* از آن پس az ân pas پس از آن pas az ân
thereby *adv.* بدان وسیله bedân-vasileh
therefore *adv.* بنابراین banâ-bar-in لاجرم lâ-jeram
therein *adv.* در آن dar-ân
thereinafter *adv.* در قسمت بعدی dar qesmat-e' ba'di
thereinto *adv.* درآنجا dar ânjâ
thereof *adv.* از آن az ân بخاطرآن be-khâter-e' ân
thereon *adv.* از آنرو az-ânru
thereto *n.* به آن جا beh-ân jâ
theretofore *adv.* تا آن زمان tâ-ân-zamân

thereunder *adv.* در زیر آن dar zir-e' ân
thereupon *adv.* از آنرو az-ânru
thermal *adj., n.* گرم garm داغ dâq
thermometer *n.* درجه dârejeh گرماسنج garmâ-sanj
thermonuclear *adj.* حرارت اتمی harârat-e' atomi
thermos *n.* ترموس termos آب داغ قمقمه qom-qomeh âb-dâq
thermostat *n.* کنترل حرارت درجهٔ darejeh-ye' kontrol-e' harârat
thershold *n.* آستانه âstâneh در حجله dar-e' hejleh
thesaurus *n.* فرهنگ لغات مترادف farhang-e' loqât-e' moterâdef
these *pl., pro., adj.* اینها in-hâ
thesis *n.* تز tez رساله resâleh اصل asl نهاده nahâdeh
they *nom.* آنها ânhâ ایشان ishân
thick *adj., adv., n.* غلیظ qaliz
thick *adj., adv., n.* کلفت koloft ضخیم zakhim قطور qatur
thick-headed *n.* کله شق kal~eh shaq سرسخت sar-sakht
thick-skinned *n.* پوست کلفت pust-koloft
thicken *vt., vi.* کلفت کردن koloft kardan
thickness *n., vt.* کلفتی kolofti ضخامت zekhâmat غلظت qel-zat
thief *n.* دزد dozd سارق sâreq
thievery *n.* دزدی dozdi سرقت serqat
thigh *n.* ران rân
thighbone *n.* استخوان ران ostokhân-e' rân
thill *n.* یوغ بند yoq-band
thimble *n.* انگشتانه angosh-tâneh
thin *v.* کم پشت کردن kam-posht kardan
thin *adj.* لاغر lâqar
thin *adj.* رقیق raqiq
thin *adj.* نازک nâzok
thin-skinned *adj.* پوست نازک pust-nâzok زود رنج zud-ranj
thine *n.* مال تو mâl-e' to
thing *n.* چیز chiz شیئی shey'
think *vt., adj.* فکر کردن fekr kardan اندیشیدن andishidan
think(nothing of) *n.* اهمیت ندادن ahamiyat nadâdan
thinkable *adj.* قابل تصور qâbel-e' tasav~or
thinking *v., adj.* فکر fekr اندیشه andisheh
thinner *adj., n.* مایع رقیق کننده mâye'-e' raqiq-konandeh
third *n.* یک سوم yek-sev~om ثلث sols
third *n.* سوم sev~om

third person *n.* شخص سوم shakhs-e' sev~om
third-class *n.* درجه سه darejeh seh
thirdly *adv.* سوماً sev~oman
thirst *n., vi.* عطش 'atesh تشنگی tesh-negi
thirsty *adj.* تشنه teshneh
thirteen *n., adj.* سیزده siz-dah
thirteenth *adj., n.* سیزدهم siz-dahom
thirtieth *adj., n.* سیم siom
thirty *adj., n.* سی si
this *pro., adj., adv.* این in
this year *n.* امسال emsâl
thistle *n.* بتهٔ خار boteh-ye' khâr
thither *adv., adj.* آنطرفی ân-tarafi به آنجا beh ânjâ
thorax *n.* قفسهٔ سینه qafaseh-ye' sineh
thorn *n., vt.* خار khâr تیغ tiq
thorny *adj.* خاردار khâr-dâr پر درد سر por-dardesar
thorough *adj., adv., pre., n.* کامل kâmel دقیق daqiq مطلق motlaq
thorough-bred *n.* اصیل asil
thoroughfare *n.* خیابان khiâbân جاده jâd~eh
thoroughgoing *adj.* دقیق daqiq
those *pro., adj.* آنها ân-hâ
thou *pro., vt., vi.* تو to
though *con., adv.* اگرچه agar-cheh هرچند har-chand با اینکه bâ-inkeh
thought *n., v.* فکر fekr اندیشه andisheh عقیده 'aqideh
thoughtful *adj.* بافکر bâ-fekr باملاحظه bâ-molâhezeh
thoughtless *adj.* بی فکر bi-fekr بی ملاحظه bi-molâhezeh
thousand *adj., n.* هزار hezâr
thrash *vt., vi., n.* کتک زدن kotak zadan خرد کردن khord kardan
thread *n.* نخ nakh رشته reshteh
threadbare *adj.* ساییده sâbideh نخ نما nakh-namâ
threat *n.* تهدید tahdid
threaten *vt., vi.* تهدید کردن tahdid kardan
threatening *n.* تهدید کننده tahdid konandeh
three *n., adj.* سه seh
three-piece *adj., n.* سه تکه seh-tek~eh
three-ply *adj.* سه برابر seh-barâbar سه لا seh-l~â
three-quarter *adj.* سه چهارم seh-chahârom
threefold-ply *n.* سه برابر seh-barâbar سه لا seh-l~â

threesome *adj., n.* سه نفری seh-nafari
thresh *n.* کوبیدن kubidan گندم کوبی gandom-kubi
thrice *n.* سه بار seh-bâr
thrift *n.* صرفه جویی sarfeh-juyi
thrifty *adj., vi., n.* صرفه جو sarfeh-ju
thrill *n.* لرزش larzesh شعف sha'f
thrill *v.* لرزاندن larzândan
thriller *n.* تکان دهنده takân-dahandeh
thrive *vi.* رو آمدن ru âmadan رشد کردن roshd kardan
throat *n., vt.* گلو galu حلقوم holqum دهانه dahâneh
throaty *adj.* صدای گرفته sedâ-ye' gerefteh
throb *n., vi.* طپیدن tapidân زدن zadan
throne *n.* تخت takht اریکه arikeh سریر sarir اورنگ orang
throng *n.* جمعیت jam'iyat
throng *v.* ازدحام کردن ezdehâm kardan
throttle *v., n.* گاز دستی gâz-e' dasti
through *pre., adj.* تاآخر tâ-âkhar تا ته tâ-tah سر تا پا sar-tâ-pâ
through *conj.* از میان az miân از وسط az vasat
through *pre., adj.* بدون توقف bedun-e' tavaq~ of راه باز râh-e' bâz
through *pre., adj.* تمام شده tamâm-shodeh
through *pre., adj.* بوسیلهٔ be-vasileh-ye'
throughout *pre., adv.* در تمام مدت dar tamâm-e' mod~ at
throw *vt., vi., n.* انداختن andâkhtan پرتاب کردن partâb kardan
throw(away) *n.* دور انداختن dur andâkhtan
throw(in) *n.* اضافه دادن ezâfeh dâdan
throw(off) *n.* رد گم کردن rad gom kardan
throw(open) *n.* آزاد کردن âzâd kardan باز کردن bâz kardan
throw(out) *n.* دور انداختن dur andâkhtan رد کردن rad kardan
throw(over) *n.* دست کشیدن dast keshidan
throw(up) *n.* بالا آوردن bâlâ âvardan استفراغ کردن estefrâq kardan
قی کردن qey kardan
throwaway *n.* دور انداختنی dur-andâkhtani
throwback *n.* پس رفت pas-raft سیر به عقب seyr-e' beh 'aqab
thrown *v.* زمین افتاده zamin-oftâdeh
thrush *n.* برفک barfak
thrush *n.* باسترک bâstarak
thrust *n., vt., vi.* فرو کردن foru kardan چپاندن chapândan
thud *n., vt., vi.* صدای خفه sedâ-ye' khafeh

thug *n.* اوباش obâsh لات lât لمپ lompan

thumb *n.* شست shast

thumb(through) *n.* ورق زدن varaq zadan

thumbnail *n., adj.* ناخن شست nâkhon-e' shast

thumbs(up) *n.* علامت موافقت 'alâmat-e' movâfeqat

thumbscrew *n.* پیچ انگشتی pich-e' angoshti

thumbtack *n., vt.* پونز punez

thump *n., vt., vi.* صدای خفه sedâ-ye' khafeh

thumping *n.* بزرگ bozorg

thunder *n., vi., vt.* رعد ra'd تندر tondar غرش qor~esh

thunderbird *n.* سیمرغ si-morq

thunderbolt *n.* صاعقه sâ'eqeh

thunderclap *n.* رعد ra'd تندر tondar

thunderous *n.* رعد آسا ra'd-âsâ

thunderstorm *n.* رعد وبرق ra'd-o barq

thunderstruck *adj.* برق گرفته barq-gerefteh مبهوت mabhut

Thursday *n.* پنج شنبه panj-shanbeh

thus *n.* بنابراین banâ bar-in بدین قرار bedin-qarâr اینچنین in-chenin

thwack *vt., n.* محکم mohkam با صدا زدن bâ-sedâ zadan

thwart *vt., pre., adv.* خنثی کردن khonsâ kardan
نقش برآب کردن naqsh bar-âb kardan

thyroid *adj.* تیروئید tiro'id

thyself *pro.* خودت khodat

tiara *n.* تاج tâj

tick *v.* تیک تیک کردن tik-tik kardan

tick *n.* کنه kaneh

tick-tack-toe *n.* دوز بازی duz-bâzi

ticket *n., vt.* جریمه jarimeh

ticket *n., vt.* بلیط belit برچسب bar-chasb لیست list

ticket office *n.* باجه bâjeh گیشه gisheh

tickle *n., vt.* قلقلک دادن qel-qelak dâdan
خوشنود کردن khosh-nud kardan

tickler *n.* یادآورنده yâd-âvarandeh مزاحم mozâhem

ticklish *adj.* قلقلکی qel-qelaki

tidal *adj.* جزر و مدی jazr-o mad~i

tidal wave *np.* موج طوفانی moj-e' tufâni

tidbit *n.* هله هوله haleh huleh دری وری dari vari

tide *v., vi., n.* جزر و مد jazr-o mad سیر seyr

tidy *adj., v.* منظم monaz~am پاکیزه pâkizeh معتنابه mo'tenâbeh
tie *n.* کراوات kerâvât
tie *v.* گره زدن gereh zadan
tie(down) *n.* دست و پا گرفتن dast-o pâ gereftan
tie(up) *n.* دست وپا بستن dast-o pâ bastan
     معطل کردن mo'at~al kardan
tie-up *n.* توقف tavaq~of رابطه râbeteh
tier *n., vt., vi.* ردیف کردن radif kardan
tiger *n.* ببر babr
tight *adj., adv.* خسیس khasis کنس kenes
tight *adj., adv.* سفت seft کشیده keshideh
tight *adj., adv.* کساد kesâd
tight *adj.* تنگ tang سفت seft کیپ kip
tight-fisted *adj.* کنس kenes
tight-lipped *adj.* راز دار râz-dâr دهن سفت dahan seft
tighten *vt., vi.* تنگ کردن tang kardan سفت کردن seft kardan
tights *n.* شلوار تنگ shalvâr tang
tigress *n.* ببر ماده babr-e' mâd~eh
tile *n., vt.* کاشی kâshi
tiling *n., v.* کاشی کاری kâshi-kâri
till *n.* دخل dakhl تا tâ
till *v.* شخم زدن shokhm zadan
tillage *n.* شخم shokhm کشت kesht
tiller *n.* کشت کار kesht-kâr اهرم سکان ahrom-e' sok~ân
tilt *vt., vi., n.* کج شدن kaj shodan یک وری شدن yek-vari shodan
timber *n.* چوب chub الوار alvâr
timberland *n.* زمین پر درخت zamin-e' por-derakht
time *n., adj., vi.* زمان zamân موقع moqe' مدت mod~at
time *n., adj., vi.* دفعه daf'eh بار bâr
time *n., adj., vi.* دوره doreh عهد 'ahd روزگار ruzegâr
time *n., adj., vi.* وقت گرفتن vaqt gereftan ساعت گرفتن sâ'at gereftan
time *n., adj., vi.* وقت vaqt ساعت sâ'at موقع moqe'
time limit *n.* مدت زمان mod~at-e' zamân
time lock *np.* قفل ساعتی qofl-e' sâ'ati
time out *n.* وقت vaqt تایم tâym
time(after time) *n.* چندین بار chan-din bâr هی hey
time(s) *n.* ضربدر zarb-dar
timecard *n.* برگ ساعت کار barg-e' sâ'at kâr

timekeeper *n.* وقت گیر vaqt-gir
متصدى ساعت كار motesad~i-e' sâ'at-e' kâ
timeless *n.* زمان نا معلوم zamân-e' nâ-ma'lum
timely *adj., adv.* بموقع be-moqe' بجا be-jâ
timer *n.* تنظيم كنندهٔ وقت tanzim konandeh-ye' vaqt
timesaving *n.* صرفه جويى در وقت sarfeh-juyi dar vaqt
timeserver *n.* ابن الوقت ebnol vaqt
timetable *n.* برنامهٔ ساعت barnâmeh-ye' sâ'at
timework *n.* كاركرد kâr-kard
timid *adj.* خجول khajul ترسو tarsu
timidity *n.* كمرويى kam-ruyi ترس tars
timing *n., v.* تنظيم وقت tanzim-e' vaqt
tin *n., adj., vt.* قلع qal' حلبى halabi
tin foil *np.* ورقهٔ آلومينيوم varaqeh-ye' âluminiyum
tincture *v., n.* رنگ rang تنتور tantur
tinder *n.* چوب زود سوز chub-e' zud-suz
tinderbox *n.* هيزم دان hizom-dân زود آتشگير zud âtash-gir
tinge *vt., n.* طعم ta'm بو bu لكه lak~eh
tingle *vi., n.* زنگ zang سوزش suzesh
tinker *n., vi., vt.* مسگر mes-gar بازى بازى كردن bâzi-bâzi kardan
tinkle *vi., vt., n.* جلينگ جلينگ jeling-jeling جيش كردن jish kardan
tinned *adj., v.* حلبى halabi
tinsel *n., adj., vt.* زرق وبرق zarq-o barq
tint *n., vt.* رنگ rang سايه sâyeh
tiny *adj.* كوچولو kuchulu ريزه rizeh فسقلى fesqeli
tip *v.* چپ كردن yek-vari kardan يكورى كردن chap kardan
tip *n.* نصيحت nasihat ندا nedâ
tip *v.* انعام دادن an'âm dâdan پول چايى pul châyi
tip *n.* نوک nok سر sar
tip-off *n.* اطلاع دادن et~elâ' dâdan خبر دادن khabar dâdan
tipsy *adj.* شنگول shan-gul يک كم مست yek kam mast ملنگ malang
tiptoe *v., adj., adv., n.* نوک پنجه راه رفتن nok-e' panjeh râh raftan
پاورچين رفتن pâ-varchin raftan
tiptop *n., adj., adv.* بالاى بالا bâlâ-ye' bâlâ
tirade *n.* نطق شديدالحن notq-e' shadidol-lâhn
tire *n.* تاير lâstik لاستيک tâyer
tire *v.* خسته كردن khasteh kardan خسته شدن khasteh shodan
tired *adj., v.* خسته khasteh

tireless *adj.* خستگی ناپذیر khastegi nâ-pazir
tiresome *adj.* خسته کننده khasteh konandeh
tissue *n., vt.* بافته bâfteh
tissue *n., vt.* بافت bâft لایه lâyeh
tissue paper *n.* دستمال کاغذی dast-mâl kâqazi
tit *n.* ممه mameh
tit(for tat) *n.* این در عوض آن in dar 'avaz-e' ân
tithe *n., vi.* مالیات ده در صد mâliât-e' dah dar-sad
title *n., vt.* عنوان 'onvân لقب laqab سمت semat رتبه rotbeh
title deed *n.* سند مالکیت sanad mâlekiyat
title role *np.* نقش اول naqsh-e' av~al
titter *vi.* پوزخند زدن puz-khand zadan
titular *adj., n.* اسمی esmi لقب دار laqab-dâr
to *pre., adv.* به beh تا tâ پیش pish-e'
to (and fro) *n.* برو بیا boro biâ
toad *n.* وزغ vazaq
toast *n.* نان برشته nân-e' bereshteh سخاری sokhâri
toast *v.* برشته کردن bereshteh kardan
toast *v.* بسلامتی نوشیدن be-salâmati nushidan
toaster *n.* نان برشته کن nân bereshteh-kon
toastmaster *n.* میزبان مهمانی misbân-e' meh-mâni
tobacco *n.* توتون tutun تنباکو tan-bâku
toboggan *n.* لژ lozh
today *n., adv.* امروز emruz
toddler *n.* بچۀ یکی دوساله bach~eh-ye' yeki-do sâleh
toe *v.* بانوک پا زدن bâ nok-e' pâ zadan
toe *n., vt., vi.* انگشت پا angosht-e' pâ پنجۀ کفش panjeh-ye' kafsh
toenail *n., vt.* ناخن انگشت پا nâkhon-e' angosht-e' pâ
together *adv.* باهم bâ-ham بهم be-ham توأم to'am
toggle *n.* ضامن قفل zâmen-e' qofl
toil *n., vi.* زحمت کشیدن zahmat keshidan کار سخت kâr-e' sakht
toilet *n.* مستراح mostarâh
toilette *n.* آرایش ârâyesh توالت to-âlet
toilsome *adj.* پر زحمت por-zahmat
token *n.* نمونهای nemuneh-i نخودی nokhodi
token *n.* نشان neshân ژتون zheton
tolerable *adj.* قابل تحمل qâbel-e' taham~ol
tolerance *n.* تحمل taham~ol حوصله hoseleh اغماض eqmâz

tolerant *adj.* باتحمل bâ-taham~ol باحوصله bâ-hoseleh
tolerate *vt.* تحمل کردن taham~ol kardan ساختن sâkhtan
toleration *n.* تحمل taham~ol سازگاری sâze-gâri بردباری bord-bâri
toll *n.* تلفات 'oburieh عبوریه talafât
toll *v.* زنگ زدن zang zadan
toll bridge *np.* پل پولی pol-e' puli
toll call *np.* تلفن راه دور telefon-e' râh-e' dur
tollbooth *n.* بودجۀ سرپل bâjeh-ye' sar-e' pol
tom *n.* نر nar
tomato *n.* گوجه فرنگی gojeh farangi
tomb *n.* گور gur قبر qabr آرامگاه ârâm-gâh
tomboy *n.* دختر پسر نما dokhtar-e' pesar-namâ
tomcat *n., vi.* گربۀ نر gorbeh-ye' nar
tomorrow *n., adv.* فردا fardâ
tomstone *n.* سنگ قبر sang-e' qabr
ton *n.* تن ton
tonality *n.* کیفیت آهنگ keyfiyat-e' âhang
tone *n., vt., vi.* لحن lahn آهنگ âhang سایه sâyeh رنگ rang
tone(down) *n.* نرمتر شدن narmtar shodan
tone(in with) *n.* هم آهنگی کردن ham-âhangi kardan
tone(up) *n.* بلندتر شدن boland-tar shodan قویتر شدن qavi-tar shodan
tongs *n.* انبر anbor
tongue *n., vt.* زبان zabân زبانه zabâneh
tongue twister *np.* زبان پیچ zabân-pich زبان گیر zabân-gir
tongue-in-cheeck *n.* شوخی shukhi قاسم کاری qâsem-kâri
tongue-tied *n.* زبان بسته zabân-basteh
tongued *v.* زبان دار zabân-dâr
tonic *n., adj.* لحنی lahni مقوی moqav~i
tonic water *n.* آب معدنی âb-ma'dani
tonight *n., adv.* امشب emshâb
tonnage *n.* ظرفیت تنی zarfiyat-e' toni
tonsil *n.* لوزه lozeh بادامک bâ-dâmak
tonsils *n.* لوزتین lozateyn
too *adv.* خیلی kheyli زیاد ziâd
too *adv.* هم چنین ham chenin همین جور hamin-jur نیز niz
tool *n., vt.* آلت âlat ابزار abzâr
toolmaker *n.* ابزار ساز abzâr-sâz
tools *n.* اسباب asbâb لوازم lavâzem

toot *n.* سوت زدن sut zadan بوق زدن buq zadan
tooth *n., vt., vi.* دندان dandân دندانه dandâneh
tooth(and nail) *n.* با چنگ و ناخن bâ chang-o nâkhon
toothache *n.* دندان درد dandân dard
toothbrush *n.* مسواک mesvâk
toothed *v.* دندانه دار dandâneh-dâr
toothpaste *n.* خمیر دندان khamir dandân
toothpick *n.* خلال دندان khalâl dandân
toots *n.* جگر jegar عزیز 'aziz
tootsy *n.* پا کوچولو pâ-kuchulu عزیز جون 'aziz jun
top *v.* رو دست زدن ru dast zadan
top *n.* سر sar نوک nok بالا bâlâ رو ru
top secret *n.* خیلی محرمانه kheyli mah-ramâneh
top-flight *n.* بهترین beh-tarin
top-heavy *np.* سر سنگین sar-sangin
top-notch *n.* درجه یک darejeh yek
topaz *n.* یاقوت زرد yâqut-e' zard
topic *n.* موضوع mozu' مطلب matlab
topical *adj.* مطلبی matlabi موضعی moze'i
topmost *adj.* بالای بالا bâlâ-ye' bâlâ
topping *n., v.* لایهٔ رو lâyeh-ye' ru عالی 'âli
topple *vi., vt.* سرنگون کردن sar-negun kardan
topsail *n.* بادبان بالایی bâd-bân-e' bâlâyi
topsy-turvy *adv., adj., n.* وارونه vâruneh مغشوش maqshush
Torah *n.* تورات torât
torch *vt.* مشعل mash'al چراغ قوه cherâq qov~eh
torment *vt., n.* زجر دادن zajr dâdan عذاب دادن 'azâb dâdan
tormented *n.* عذاب دیده 'azâb dideh معذب mo'az~ab
tormenting *n.* زجر کش zajr-kosh عذاب دار 'azâb-dâr
tormentor *n.* عذاب دهنده 'azâb-dahandeh
tornado *n.* گردباد تند gerd-bâd-e' tond
torpedo *n., vt., vi.* اژدر azhdar
torque *n.* چرخش char-khesh
torrent *n., adj.* سیلاب seylâb
torrential *adj.* سیلابی seylâbi
torrid *adj.* خشک khoshk سوزان suzân
torso *n.* بالا تنه bâlâ taneh نیم تنه nim-taneh
tort *n.* جرم جزئی jorm-e' joz'i

tortoise *n.* لاک پشت lâk-posht
torture *n., vt.* شکنجه دادن shekanjeh dâdan
شکنجه کردن shekânjeh kardan
torturous *n.* زجر آور zajr-âvar
toss *n.* غلتاندن qaltândan قل دادن qel dâdan پرت کردن part kardan
toss up *n.* مساوی mosâvi شیر یا خط shir yâ khat
toss(off) *n.* ماست مالی کردن mâst-mâli kardan
بالا انداختن bâlâ andâkhtan
toss(up) *n.* بالا انداختن bâlâ ândâkhtan
tot *vt., vi., n.* کودک kudak
total *n.* جمع jam' مجموع majmu' کل kol~ کامل kâmel
total *v.* جمع زدن jam zadan
totalitarian *adj., n.* تام روا tâm-ravâ مطلق گرا motlaq-garâ
totalitarian(ism) *n.* تام روایی tâm-ravâyi مطلق گرایی motlaq-garâyi
totally *adv.* بکلی be-kol~i کاملاً kâmelan جمعاً jam'an
tote *n.* حمل کردن haml kardan
totter *vi., n.* تلو تلو خوردن telo-telo khordan
touch *v.* متأثر کردن mote-'as~er kardan
touch *n.* ذره zar~eh خرده khordeh
touch *v.* دست زدن dast zadan لمس کردن lams kardan
touch *n.* هنر honar مایه mâyeh
touch(off) *n.* در رفتن dar raftan در کردن dar kardan
touch(on) *n.* اشاره کردن eshâreh kardan
touch(up) *n.* دستکاری کردن dast-kâri kardan
touch-and-go *adj.* ریسکی riski باعجله bâ-'ajaleh
touchdown *n.* گل gol زمین نشینی zamin neshini
touche' *n.* آ بارک اله â bâr-k-alâh!
touched *adj.* تحت تاثیر taht-e' ta'sir
touching *n.* تأثر انگیز ta'as~or-angiz
touchstone *n.* محک mehak~
touchy *adj.* حساس has~âs خطرناک khatar-nâk
tough *adj., n.* گردن کلفت gardan koloft قلچماق qol-chomâq
tough *adj., n.* سخت sakht کلفت koloft
toughen *vt., vi.* سفت کردن seft kardan سخت کردن sakht kardan
toupee *n.* کلاه گیس kolâh-gis
tour *vi., vt., n.* گردش کردن gardesh kardan دور زدن dor zadan
tourism *n.* سیاحت siâhat جهانگردی jahân-gardi
tourism *n.* سیاح say~âh جهانگرد jahân-gard

tournament *n.* مسابقهٔ دوره ای mosâ-beqeh-ye' doreh-i
tourniquet *n.* شریان بند sharyân-band
tow *n., adj.* بدنبال کشیدن be-donbâl keshidan
toward(s) *n.* بطرف be-taraf-e' رو به ru-beh اطراف atrâf-e'
towel *n., vt.* حوله holeh
tower *n., vi.* برج borj
towering *adj.* بلند boland مرتفع mortafa'
towline *n.* طناب عقب کش tanâb-e' 'aqab-kesh
town *n.* شهر shahr شهرک shah-rak
town hall *n.* مرکزشهرداری markaz-e' shahr-dâri
town house *np.* آپارتمان âpârtemân
township *n.* شهرستان shahrestân
townsman *n.* ساکن شهر sâken-e' shahr
townspeople *pl.* مردم شهر mardom-e' shahr اهالی شهر ahâli-e' shahr شهروندان shahr-vandân
toxic *adj.* سمی sam~i
toxin *n.* زهر zahr
toy *n.* اسباب بازی asbâb bâzi بازیچه bâzi-cheh
toy *v.* بازی کردن bâzi kardan
trace *n.* ردپا rad~-e' pâ جاپا jâ-pâ پی pey
trace *n.* نشان neshân اثر asar
trace *v.* تعقیب کردن ta'-qib kardan پیگیری کردن pey-giri kardan
tracer *n.* پی گرد pey-gard دنباله رو donbâleh-ro
trachea *n.* نای nây خرخره kher-khereh
tracheotomy *n.* جراحی نای jar~âhi-e' nây
trachoma *n.* تراخم tarâkhom
tracing *n., v.* اثر asar کپی kopi
track *n., vt., vi.* ورزش دو و میدانی varzesh-e' do va meydâni
track *n., vt., vi.* خط khat مسیر masir ریل reyl
track *n., vt., vi.* ردپا rad~-e' pâ جاپا jâ-pâ پی pey
track(down) *n.* تعقیب کردن ta'-qib kardan
    ردپاگرفتن rad~-e' pâ gereftan
tract *n.* قطعه زمین qat'eh zamin رساله resâleh
traction *n.* کشش keshesh اصطکاک estekâk
tractor *n.* تراکتور terâk-tor
trade *v.* معامله کردن mo'âmeleh kardan
    مبادله کردن mobâdeleh kardan
trade *n.* پیشه pisheh حرفه herfeh

trade *v.* تجارت کردن tejârat kardan بازرگانی کردن bâzar-gâni kardan

trade name *np.* اسم تجارتی esm-e' tejârati

trade union *np.* اتحادیهٔ اصناف et~ehâdieh-ye' asnâf

trade wind *np.* بادشرقی bâd-e' sharqi

trade(off) *n.* ردکردن rad kardan معاوضه کردن mo'âvezeh kardan

trademark *n., vt.* مارک تجارتی mârk-e' tejârati

trader *n.* تاجر tâjer بازرگان bâzargân

tradesman *n.* کاسب kâseb بازرگان bâzargân

trading *n.* تجارت tejârat

tradition *n.* رسم rasm آئین â'in سنت son~at حدیث hadis

traditional *adj.* سنتی son~ati

traditionally *n.* بطور سنتی be-tor-e' son~ati
بطورمرسوم be-tor-e' marsum

traditionist *n.* سنت گرا son~at-garâ

traduce *vt.* بی آبرو کردن bi-âberu kardan

traffic *n.* ترافیک terâfik عبور و مرور 'obor-o morur
نقل و انتقال naql-o enteqâl

traffic light *n.* چراغ راهنمایی cherâq-e' râh-namâyi

trafficker *n.* تاجر tâjer قاچاقچی qâchâq-chi

tragedy *n.* مصیبت mosibat تراژدی terâzhedi

tragic *adj.* مصیبت آمیز mosibat-âmiz نجیح fajih ناگوار nâ-govar

trail *n.* رد پا rad~-e' pâ اثر asar

trail *n.* جاده jâd~eh راه کوهستانی râh-e' kuhestâni

trail *v.* بدنبال کشیدن be-donbâl keshidan
پشت سرکشیدن posht-e' sar keshidan

trail *v.* رد پاگرفتن rad~-e' pâ gereftan اثر asar

trail blazer *n.* پیشتاز pish-tâz

trailer *n.* تریلی tereyli

train *n.* قطار qatâr ترن teran دنباله don-bâleh

train *v.* تعلیم دادن ta'-lim dâdan تربیت کردن tarbiyat kardan

train *v.* نشان گرفتن neshân gereftan

trainee *n., adj.* کارآموز kâr-âmuz

trainer *n.* مربی morab~i پرورش دهنده par-varesh dahandeh

training *n.* کارآموزی kâr-âmuzi تعلیم ta'lim

trait *n.* خصلت kheslat طینت tinat جنس jens

traitor *n.* خائن khâ'en

traitorous *adj.* خائنانه khâ'enâneh

trajectory *n.* مسیرتیر masir-e' tir مسیرموشک masir-e' mushak

tram(car) *n.* تراموا terâm-vâ

tramp *vt., n., vi.* ولگرد velgard خانه بدوش khâneh be-dush

tramp *vt., n., vi.* سفت راه رفتن seft râh raftan

tramp *vt., n., vi.* جنده jendeh

trample *vi., vt., n.* لگدمال lagad-mâl پایمال کردن pây-mâl kardan

trance *n., vi., vt.* حالت بهت hâlat-e' boht عالم دیگر 'âlam-e' digar

tranquil *adj.* آرام ârâm آسوده âsudeh

tranquility *n.* آرامش ârâmesh آسودگی âsudegi طمأنینه toma'nineh

tranquilize *vt., vi.* آرام کردن ârâm kardan تسکین دادن taskin dâdan

tranquilizer *n.* مسکن mosak~en بیحس کننده bi-hes konandeh

trans- *n.* ماوراء mâvarâ' سرتاسری sar-tâ-sari

transaction *n.* معامله mo'âmeleh گزارش gozâresh

transactor *n.* معامله گر mo'âmeleh-gar

transcend *vt., vi.* مافوق بودن mâfoq budan فراسورفتن farâsu raftan

transcendent *adj., n.* برتر bartar فراسوی دانش farâsu-ye' dânesh

transcendentalism *n.* اندیشه گری andisheh-gari
فراسوگرایی farâsu-garâyi

transcribe *vt.* نوشتن neveshtan تنظیم کردن tanzim kardan

transcript *n.* نوشته neveshteh رونوشت ru-nevesht

transcription *n.* رونویسی ru-nevisi تنظیم tanzim
نسخه برداری nos-kheh bardâri

transfer *n.* انتقال enteqâl واگذاری vâgozâri

transfer *v.* انتقال دادن enteqâl dâdan واگذارکردن vâgozâr kardan

transferable *adj.* قابل انتقال qâbel-e' enteqâl

transference *n.* انتقال enteqâl

transferer *n.* انتقال دهنده enteqâl dahandeh

transfiguration *n.* تغییرشکل taqyir-e' shekl

transfigure *n.* تغییرشکل دادن taqyir-e' shekl dâdan

transfix *vt.* درجاخشک شدن dar jâ khoshk shodan

transform *vt.* تغییرشکل دادن taqyir-e' shekl dâdan
قیافه عوض کردن qiâfeh 'avaz kardan

transformation *n.* تغییرشکل taqyir-e' shekl استحاله este-hâleh

transformer *n.* مبدل mobad~el ترانسفورمر terânsformer

transgress *vt., vi.* تخطی کردن takhat~i kardan
تجاوزکردن tajâvoz kardan تعدی کردن ta'ad~i kardan

transgression *n.* تخطی takhat~i تجاوز tajâvoz تعدی ta'ad~i

transgressor *n.* متخطی motekhat~i تجاوزکار tajâvoz-kâr
متعدی mote'ad~i

---

transient *adj.* زودگذر zud-gozar ولگرد vel-gard گذران gozarân
transistor *n., adj.* ترانزیستور terânzistor
transit *n., vt., vi.* عبور 'obur ترانزیت terânzit
transition *n.* انتقال enteqâl تحول tahav~ol تغییر taqyir
transitional *adj.* انتقالی enteqâli موقتی movaq~ati
transitive *adj., n.* متعدی mote'ad~i
transitory *adj.* ناپایدار nâ-pâydâr زودگذر zud-gozar
translate *vi.* ترجمه کردن tarjomeh kardan
translation *n.* ترجمه tarjomeh
translator *n.* مترجم motar-jem دیلماج dil-mâj
translucent *adj.* نیمه شفاف nimeh-shafâf
transmission *n.* ارسال ersâl پخش pakhsh جعبه دنده ja'beh dandeh
transmit *vt., vi.* فرستادن ferestâdan پخش کردن pakhsh kardan
transmitter *n.* فرستنده ferestandeh
transparency *n.* شفافی shafâfi
transparent *n.* شفاف shafâf
transpire *vi., vt.* گذشتن gozashtan پس دادن pas dâdan
transplant *vt.* جای دیگر کاشتن jâ-ye' digar kâshtan
جابجاکردن jâ be-jâ kardan
transport *vt., n.* حمل کردن haml kardan بردن bordan
transportation *n.* حمل و نقل haml-o naql بارکشی bâr-keshi
transpose *vt., n.* جابجاکردن jâ be-jâ kardan
transposition *n.* جابجایی jâ be-jâyi
trap *n., vi.* دام dâm تله taleh بدام انداختن be-dâm andâkhtan
trap door *np.* دریچه daricheh
trapeze *n.* تاب tâb بندبازی band-bâzi
trapezoid *n., adj.* ذوزنقه zuzanaqeh
trapper *n.* شکارچی پوست shekârchi-e' pust
trappings *n.* تجملات tajam~olât دنگ و فنگ dang-o fang
سورسات sur-sât
trash *n.* آشغال âshqâl بنجل bonjol
trash *v.* افسار زدن afsâr zadan
trashy *n.* آشغال âshqâl چرند charand
trauma *n.* صدمهٔ روحی sadameh-ye' ruhi
تجربهٔ تلخ tajrobeh-ye' talkh
traumatic *adj.* پرعذاب por-'azâb
traumatize *vt.* صدمه زدن sadameh zadan عذاب دادن 'azâb dâdan
travel *vi., vt., n.* سفر safar مسافرت کردن mosâferat kardan

traveler *n.* مسافر mosâfer
traverse *n., vt., vi., adj.* عبور 'obur پرده pardeh تراورس terâvers
travesty *n., vt.* مسخره mas-khareh
trawler *n.* قایق ماهیگیری توردار qâyeq-e' mâhigiri-e' turdâr
tray *n.* سینی sini
treacherous *adj.* خائنانه khâ'enâneh
treachery *n.* خیانت khiânat
tread *n.* کف kaf-e' pâ پا پایه pâyeh
tread *v.* پا زدن pâ zadan لگدگذاشتن lagad gozâshtan
tread(water) *n.* توی آب دست و پازدن tuy-e' âb dast-o pâ zadan
treadmill *n.* خرکاری khar-kâri آسیاب حمالی âsiâb-e' hamâl~i
treason *n.* خیانت khiânat
treasure *v., n.* گنج ganj خزانه khazâneh ارزش دادن arzesh dâdan
دفینه dafineh
treasure-trove *n.* گنج ganj دفینه dafineh گنجینه ganjineh
treasurer *adj.* خزانه دار khazâneh-dâr گنجور ganj-var
treasury *n.* خزانه داری khazâneh dâri
treasury note *n.* اسکناس eskenâs
treat *v.* معالجه کردن mo'âlejeh kardan درمان کردن darmân kardan
treat *v.* مهمان کردن meh-mân kardan سوردادن sur dâdan
treat *v.* رفتار کردن raftâr kardan
treat(as) *n.* تلقی کردن talaq~i kardan پنداشتن pen-dâshtan
treat(with) *n.* زدن zadan مالیدن mâlidan
treating physician *n.* پزشک معالج pezeshk-e' mo'âlej
treatise *n.* رساله resâleh
treatment *n.* رفتار raftâr درمان darmân معالجه mo'âlejeh
treaty *n.* قرارداد qarâr-dâd معاهده mo'âhedeh میثاق misaq
treble *adj., n.* سه برابرکردن seh-barâbar kardan صدای ریز sedâ-ye' riz
tree *n., vt.* درخت derakht شجر shajar
tree surgeon *n.* درخت شناس derakht-shenâs
trek *vi., vt., n.* راه دشوار râh-e' dosh-vâr
trellis *n., vt.* داربست dâr-bast تاک بست tâk-bast
tremble *vi., n.* لرزیدن larzidân
tremble *n.* لرزش larzesh رعشه ra'sheh
trembling *v.* لرزان larzân
tremendous *adj.* خیلی بزرگ kheyli bozorg فوق العاده foqol-'âdeh
tremor *n.* لرزش larzesh تکان takân
trench *n., vt., vi.* چاله کندن châleh kandan سنگر sangar گودال godâl

trench coat *n.* بارانی bârâni
trenchant *adj.* برنده bor~andeh قاطع qâte'
trencher *n.* چاله کن châleh-kan
trend *n., vi.* روند ravand تمایل tamâyol سیاق siâq
trespass *n.* عبورغیرقانونی کردن 'obur-e' qeyr-e' qânuni kardan
trespasser *n.* متخلف motekhal~ef تجاوزکار tajâvoz-kâr
trestle *n.* پایه pâyeh خرک kharak
trey *n.* سه خال seh-khâl
tri- *n.* سه تایی seh-tâyi
triad *n.* گروه سه نفره goruh-e' seh-nafareh
trial *n.* دادگاه dâd-gâh محاکمه mohâkemeh امتحان emtehân
trial and error *np.* آزمایش âzmâyesh امتحان emtehân
trial baloon *n.* زمینه سنج zamineh-sanj
trial jury *n.* هیئت ژوری hey'at-e' zhuri
triangle *n.* مثلث mosalas سه گوشه seh-gusheh
triangular *adj.* مثلثی mosalasi سه گوش seh-gush
tribe *n.* قبیله qabileh طایفه tâyefeh
tribesman *n.* اهل قبیله ahl-e' qabileh
tribulation *n.* اندوه anduh محنت mehnat
tribunal *n.* کرسی قضاوت korsi-e' qezâvat
tribune *n.* تریبون teribun هیئت دادخواهی hey'at-e' dâd-khâhi
tributary *n., adj.* شاخه فرعی shâkheh-ye' far'i
خراج دهنده kharâj-dahandeh
tribute *n.* اهدایی ehdâyi تقدیمی taqdimi خراج kharâj
trice *n., vt.* لحظه lahzeh دم dam
triceps *n.* ماهیچه سه سر mâhicheh-ye' seh-sar
trick *v.* کلک زدن kalak zadan گول زدن gul zadan
trick *n.* کلک kalak حقه hoq~eh حیله hileh نیرنگ nirang
trickery *n.* حقه بازی hoq~eh-bâzi
trickle *vi., vt., n.* چکیدن chekidan
قطره قطره ریختن qatreh-qatreh rikhtan
trickster *n.* حقه باز hoq~eh-bâz شیاد shay~âd
tricksy *adj.* ذبل zebel
tricky *adj.* کلک زن kalâk-zan پیچیده pichideh
tricolor *adj., n.* سه رنگ seh-rang
tricycle *n.* سه چرخه seh-charkheh
trident *n.* نیزه سه سر neyzeh-ye' seh-sar
tried *v.* آزموده âzmudeh

trifle *n., vi., vt.* جزیی joz'i پشیز pashiz
trifling *adj.* ناچیز nâchiz
trigger *n.* ماشه mâsheh
trigonometry *n.* مثلثات mosal~âsât
trill *vt., vi., n.* چرخاندن charkhândan لرزاندن larzândan
trilogy *n.* سه نمایشی seh-namâyeshi
trim *v.* کوتاه کردن kutâh kardan
trim *n.* باریک bârik تمیز tamiz صاف و صوف sâf-o suf
trim(away/off) *n.* کوتاه کردن kutâh kardan بریدن boridan
trim(away/off) *n.* کوتاه کردن kutâh kardan
trim(down) *n.* کم کردن kam kardan وزن کم کردن vazn kam kardan
trim(up) *n.* آراستن ârâstan تمیزکردن tamiz kardan
trimester *n.* ثلث sols
trimmer *adj., n., v.* کوتاه کن kutâh-kon حزب بادی hezb-e' bâdi
trimming(s) *n.* مخلفات mokhal~afât آرایش ârâyesh تزئین taz'in
trinity *n.* تثلیث taslis
trinket *n., vi.* کم ارزش kam-arzesh
trio *n.* سه نفره seh-nafareh
trip *v.* پشت پا زدن posht-e' pâ zadan
trip *n.* سفر safar مسافرت mosâferat
trip *n., vi., vt.* راه انداختن râh andâkhtan
trip wire *n.* سیم خطر sim-e' khatar
tripe *n.* شکمبه shekambeh سیرابی sirâbi
triple *adj., n., vt., vi.* سه برابر کردن seh-barâbar kardan
         سه ضربی seh-zarbi
triplet *n.* سه قلو seh-qolu
tripod *n.* سه پایه seh-pâyeh
tripper *n.* سوزن suzan مسافر mosâfer
triumph *n., vi., vt.* پیروزی piruzi شادی shâdi
triumphant *adj.* پیروز piruz موفق movaf~aq
trivia *pl.* جزئیات joz'iât
trivial *n.* جزئی joz'i
troika *n.* سه نفری seh-nafari
trolley bus *n.* اتوبوس برقی otubus-e' barqi تراموابرقی terâmvâ barqi
troop(s) *n.* گروه goruh سربازان sarbâzân
trooper *n.* سواره savâreh پلیس سوار polis-e' savâr
trophy *n.* جایزه jâyezeh غنیمت qanimat
tropic *n., adj.* مدار madâr

tropical *adj.* مداری madâri گرم سیری garm-siri
trot *n., vi., vt.* یورتمه رفتن yurtmeh raftan
troubadour *n.* غزل خوان qazal-khân
trouble *v.* ناراحت کردن nârâhat kardan
trouble *n.* زحمت zahmat دردسر dard-e' sar
trouble *v.* زحمت دادن zah-mat dadan دردسردادن dard-e' sar dâdan
troublemaker *n.* مزاحم mozâhem مردم آزار mardom-âzâr
troubleshooter *n.* حلال مشکلات hal~âl-e' mosh-kelât
troublesome *adj.* پردردسر por-dard-e' sar
trough *n.* آبخور âb-khor جوی juy
trounce *vt.* زدن zadan
troupe *n., vi.* باند bând دستۀ بازیگران dasteh-ye' bâzi-garâ
trouper *n.* بازیگر bâzi-gar
trousers *n.* شلوار shalvâr
trout *pl.* قزل آلا qezel-âlâ
trowel *n., vt.* ماله mâleh بیلچه bil-cheh
truancy *n.* گریز goriz گریزاز مدرسه goriz az madreseh
truant *adj.* گریزپا gori-pâ ازمدرسه دررفته az madreseh dar-raf
مکتب گریز maktab-goriz
truce *n.* متارکه motârekeh صلح موقتی solh-e' movaq~ati
truck *v.* باکامیون فرستادن bâ kâmion ferestâdan
truck *n.* کامیون kâmion تریلی tereyli
truck-driver *n.* رانندۀ کامیون rânandeh-ye' kâmion
trudge *n., v., vi.* سگ دو زدن sag-do zadan
true *adj., vt.* اصلی asli حقیقی haqiqi
true *adj., vt.* باوفا bâ-vafâ خوش قول khosh-qol
true *adj., vt.* راست râst حقیقت haqiqat
true-hearted *n.* باوفا bâ-vafâ شریف sharif
trueborn *adj.* اصیل asil حلال زاده halâl-zâdeh
truebred *n.* اصیل asil بهزاد behzâd
truelove *n.* عشق حقیقی 'eshq-e' haqiqi
truffle *n.* دنبلان don-balân
truism *n.* سخن بدیهی sokhan-e' badihi
truly *adv.* حقیقتا haqiqatan صمیمانه samimâneh
trump *n., vi., vt.* حکم hokm آتو âto
trump(up) *n.* جعل کردن ja'l kardan
trumpet *n., vi., vt.* شیپور shey-pur کرنا kornâ
trumpeter *n.* شیپور زن shey-pur-zan

truncate *n.* بریدن boridan کوتاه کردن kutâh kardan
truncheon *vt., vi., n.* باتون bâtun چماق chomâq
trunk *n., adj.* خرطوم khortum
trunk *n., adj.* صندوق عقب sandoq-e' 'aqab
trunk *n., adj.* صندوق sandoq چمدان chamedân
trunk *n., adj.* تنه taneh بدنه badaneh
trunks *n.* شلوارکوتاه shalvâr-e' kutâh مایو mâyo
truss *v.* حائل شدن hâ'el shodan
truss *n.* فتق بند fatq-band کپه کاه kop~eh kâh
trust *v.* امانت گذاشتن amânat gozâshtan
trust *n.* اعتماد e'temâd اطمینان etminân عهده 'ohdeh
trust *n.* امانت amânat
trust *n.* کارتل kârtel
trust *v.* اطمینان داشتن etminân dâshtan اعتمادداشتن e'temâd dâshtan
trust *n.* حساب سپرده hesâb-e' sepordeh
trust fund *np.* پول سپرده pul-e' sepordeh
trustee *n., vt.* امین amin مورداطمینان mored-e' etminân
trusteeship *n.* قیومت qoyumat
trustful *n.* مطمئن motma'en بااعتماد bâ-e'temâd
trustless *adj.* بی اعتماد bi-e'temâd
trustworthy *adj.* قابل اعتماد qâbel-e' e'temâd معتمد mo'tamed
trusty *n.* معتمد mo'tamed امین amin
truth *n.* راستی râsti حقیقت haqiqat
truthful *adj.* حقیقی haqiqi راستگو râst-gu
try *v.* محاکمه کردن mohâkemeh kardan
try *v.* سعی کردن sa'y kardan کوشش کردن kushesh kardan
try(on) *n.* پوشیدن pushidan
try(out) *n.* امتحان کردن emtehân kardan آزمودن âzmudan
trying *adj., v.* سخت sakht دشوار doshvâr
tryout *n.* آزمایش ورزشی âzmâyesh-e' varzeshi
tryst *n., vt., vi.* قرارملاقات qarâr-e' molâqât راندوو rânde-vu
tub *n., vt., vi.* تشت tasht وان vân
tubal *n.* لوله ای luleh-i
tubby *adj.* بشکه ای boshkeh-i خیکی khik~i
tube *v., n.* لاستیک تویی lâstik-e' tuyi
tube *v., n.* لوله luleh
tube *v., n.* لامپ lâmp
tuck *vt., vi., n.* تادادن tâ dâdan

tuck *vt., vi., n.* چین chin دست کاری dast-kâri
tuck(away) *n.* لمباندن lombân-dan
tuck(in) *n.* توگذاشتن tu-gozâshtan زیرپتوکردن zir-e' patu kardan
Tuesday *n.* سه شنبه seh-shanbeh
tuft *n., vt., vi.* دسته dasteh انبوه anbuh
tufted *adj.* دسته شده dasteh shodeh
tug *vt., vi., n.* کشیدن keshidan تقلا کردن taqal~â kardan
tug of war *np.* مسابقة طناب کشی mosâbeqeh-ye' tanâb-keshi
tugboat *n.* کشتی یدک کش kashti-e' yadak-kesh
tuition *n.* شهریه shah-rieh
tulip *n.* لاله lâleh
tumble *vi., n.* افتادن oftâdan معلق خوردن mo'al~aq khordan
tumbler *n.* آکروبات âkrobât لیوان livân
tumbleweed *n.* بته غلتان boteh qaltân
tummy *n.* شکم shekam
tumor *n.* ورم varam غده qod~eh
tumorous *n.* غده دار qod~eh-dâr
tumult *n.* هیاهو hayâhu هلهله hel-heleh همهمه ham-hameh
tumultuous *adj.* پرسروصدا por sar-o sedâ
tundra *n., vt.* یخ زار yakh-zâr
tune *n.* آهنگ âhang تن ton
tune *v.* کوک کردن kuk kardan
tune(in) *n.* گوش دادن gush dâdan موج گرفتن moj gereftan
tune(out) *n.* درعالم دیگری بودن dar 'âlam-e' digari budan
tune(up) *n.* تنظیم کردن tanzim kardan
  هم کوک کردن ham-kuk kardan
tune-up *n.* تنظیم موتور tanzim-e' motor
tuner *n.* کوک کن kuk-kon
tunic *n.* کت kot
tunnel *n., vt.* تونل زدن tunel zadan
turban *n.* عمامه 'amâmeh
turbid *adj.* تیره tireh تار târ کدر keder
turbine *n.* توربین turbin
turbulent *adj.* آشفته âshofteh مغشوش maq-shush
turf *v., n.* چمن chaman زمین zamin
turkey *n.* بوقلمون buqalamun پخمه pakhmeh
turmeric *n.* زردچوبه zard-chubeh
turmoil *n.* آشوب âshub اغتشاش eqteshâsh

turn *v.* پیچ pich گردش gardesh تغییر taq-yir
turn *v.* گرداندن gardândan پیچاندن pichândan
turn into *n.* تبدیل شدن tabdil shodan
turn(about) *n.* عقب گردکردن 'aqab-gard kardan
turn(against) *n.* برضدشدن bar zed shodan
مخالف شدن mokhâlef shodan
turn(around) *n.* برگرداندن bar gardândan برگشتن bar gashtan
turn(away) *n.* دک کردن dak kardan روگرداندن ru gardândan
turn(down) *n.* ردکردن rad kardan برگرداندن bar gardândan
turn(in) *n.* خوابیدن khâbidan
turn(in) *n.* وارد شدن vâred shodan تحویل دادن tahvil dâdan
turn(off) *n.* کنارزدن kenâr zadan منشعب شدن monsha'eb shodan
turn(off) *n.* خاموش کردن khâmush kardan بستن bastan
turn(off) *n.* حال گرفتن hâl gereftan زده کردن zadeh kardan
turn(on) *n.* حمله کردن hamleh kardan
turn(on) *n.* حالی بحالی کردن hâli be-hâli kardan
turn(on) *n.* روشن کردن roshan kardan بازکردن bâz kardan
turn(out) *n.* خاموش کردن khâmush kardan
turn(out) *n.* درآمدن dar âmadan
turn(out) *n.* شدن shodan
turn(out) *n.* دک کردن dak kardan اخراج کردن ekhrâj kardan
turn(out) *n.* بوجودآوردن bevojud âvardan ساختن sâkhtan
turn(over) *n.* روشن کردن roshan kardan استارت زدن estârt zadan
turn(over) *n.* تحویل دادن tahvil dâdan
turn(over) *n.* غلط زدن qalt zadan
turn(the corner) *n.* بحران را گذراندن bohrân râ gozarândan
turn(to) *n.* متوسل شدن motevas~el shodan
دست بدامن شدن dast be-damân shodan
turn(up) *n.* سردرآوردن sar dar âvardan حاضرشدن hâzer shodan
turn(up) *n.* بلندکردن boland kardan
turn(up) *n.* تاکردن tâ kardan
turn(up) *n.* برگرداندن bar gardândan
turn(up) *n.* پیچیدن pichidan
turn(up) *n.* رخ دادن rokh dâdan اتفاق افتادن et~efâq oftâdan
turn(upon) *n.* برضدشدن bar zed-shodan
turn-about-face *n.* عقب گرد 'aqab-gard
turn-out *n.* جمعیت jam'iyat
turnabout *n.* عقب گرد 'aqab-gard

turncoat *n.* خاین khâ'en
turndown *adj.* رد دست dast-e' rad برگشته bar-gashteh
turning point *np.* عطف نقطهٔ noqteh-ye' 'atf
turnip *n.* شلغم shalqam
turnover *n., adj.* برگشت bar-gasht آمدورفت âmado raft
turnpike *n.* شاهراه shâhrâh
turntable *n.* انون گرام gerâm-âfon
turnup *n., adj.* برگشته bar-gashteh
turpitude *n.* نساد fesâd رسوایی rosvâyi
turquoise *n.* فیروزه firuzeh
turret *n.* برج borj دودکش dud-kesh
turreted *adj.* برجی borji
turtle *n., vi.* پشت لاک lâk-posht
turtle neck *n.* کیپ یخه yakheh-kip
tusk *n., vt., vi.* دندان dandân نیش dandân nish-dandân
tussle *vi., n.* کردن دعوامرافعه da'vâ morâfe'eh kardan
tutelage *n.* قیومت qoyumat
tutor *n., vt., vi.* خصوصی معلم mo'al~em-e' khosusi لله laleh
tutorial *adj., n.* معلمی mo'al~emi للگی lalegi
tuxedo *n.* نراک ferâk اسموکینگ esmoking
twaddle *n.* نوشتن وری دری dari vari neveshtan
twain *adj., n.* دو do
twang *vt., n.* دهاتی لهجه lahjeh-e' dehâti تودماغی tu-damâqi
tweak *vt., n.* گرفتن وشگون veshgun gereftan نیشگان nishgân
tweed *n.* پشمی پارچه pârcheh pashmi
tweedle *n.* کردن بازی بازی bâzi-bâzi kardan
tweet *n.* کردن جیک جیک jik-jik kardan
tweezer(s) *n.* موچین mu-chin منقاش menqâsh
twelfth *adj., n.* دوازدهم davâz-dahom
twelve *n., adj.* دوازده davâzdah
twentieth *n., adj.* بیستم bistom
twenty *n., adj.* بیست bist
twice *adv.* دوبار do-bâr دومرتبه do-martabeh
twice-told *adj.* شده گفته gofteh -shodeh
twiddle *vt., vi., n.* کردن بازی هاابازی باانگشت bâ-angosht-hâ bâzi kardan
twig *v.* نهمیدن fahmidan
twig *n.* ترکه tarkeh
twiggy *adj.* باریک ای شاخه bârik shâkheh-i

twilight *n.* دم دم صبح dam-dam-e' sobh گرگ و میش gorg-o mish
twilight of life *n.* آخرهای عمر âkhar-hâ-ye' 'omr
twin *adj., n., vt., vi.* دوقلو do-qolu جفت joft
twine *vt., vi.* ریسمان rismân نخ قند nakh-e' qand
twinge *n.* تیرکشیدن tir keshidan درد dard
twinkle *vi., vt., n.* چشمک زدن cheshmak zadan
twinkling *n.* چشم برهم زدن cheshm bar-ham-zadan
twirl *vt., vi., n.* چرخاندن charkhândan پیچ pich چرخش charkhesh
twist *n.* پیچ pich تاب tâb
twist *v.* پیچ دادن pich dâdan تابیدن tâbidan
twist(off) *n.* کندن kandan
twist-top *n.* سرپیچ sar-pich
twitch *vi., n., vt.* کشش keshesh انقباض enqebâz
two *n., adj.* دو do
two bits *np.* بیست پنج سنت bist panj sent
two-bit *adj.* بی ارزش bi-arzesh آشغال âshqâl
two-edged *adj.* دولبه do-labeh دوطرفه do-tarafeh
two-faced *adj.* دورو do-ru
two-fisted *adj.* دومشتی do-moshti قادر qâder
two-handed *adj.* دودستی do-dasti
two-legged *n.* دوپا do-pâ
two-piece *adj., n.* دوتکه do-tek~eh دوپیس do-pies
two-ply *n.* دولا do-lâ
two-sided *adj.* دوطرفه do-tarafeh
two-way *n.* دوطرفه do-tarafeh
twofold *n.* دوبرابر do-barâbar دولا do-lâ
twosome *adj., n.* دوتایی do-tâyi دونفری do-nafari
tycoon *n.* ثروتمندبزرگ servat-mand-e' bozorg
type *v.* ماشین کردن mâshin kardan
type *n.* تیپ tip رقم raqam قماش qomâsh
type *n.* نوع no' قسم qesm جور jur گونه guneh
typesetting *n., adj.* حروف چینی horuf-chini
typewriter *n.* ماشین تحریر mâshin-e' tahrir
typewritten *vt., vi.* ماشین شده mâshin-shodeh
typhoid *n., adj.* تیفویید tifo'id
typhoon *n.* طوفان tufân
typhus *n.* تیفوس tifus
typical *n.* نمونه‌ای nemuneh-yi سمبلی samboli

typify *vt.* نمونه بودن nemuneh budan سمبل بودن sambol budan
typist *n.* ماشین نویس mâshin-nevis
typographical *n.* چاپی châpi
typography *n.* چاپ châp
tyrannic(al) *n.* ستمگرانه setam-garâneh دیکتاتوری diktâtori
tyrannize *n.* ظالمانه حکومت کردن zâlemâneh hokumat kardan
tyranny *n.* ستمگری setam-gari ظلم zolm استبداد esteb-dâd
tyrant *n.* دیکتاتور diktâtor مستبد mostabed ستمگر setam-gâr

U U u

U.H.F. *n.* فرکانس خیلی بالا ferekâns-e' kheyli bâlâ
ubiquitous *adj.* حاضردرهمه جا hâzer dar hameh-jâ
ubiquity *n.* حضوردرهمه جا hozur dar hameh-jâ
ubsequently *n.* بعداً متعاقباً ba'dan mote'âqeban
udder *n.* پستان گاو pestân-e' gâv
ugh! *n.* اه ah!
ugliness *n.* زشتی zeshti
ugly *adj.* زشت zesht بیریخت birikht کریه karih
ulcer *n.* زخم معده zakhm-e' ma'deh
ulceration *n.* زخم شدن zakhm shodan
ulterior *n.* ماوراء mâvarâ' نامعلوم nâ-ma'lum
ultimate *adj., n., v.* نهائی nahâ'i آجل âjel غائی qâ'i
ultimately *adv.* نهایتاً nahâyatan سرانجام sar-anjâm
ultimatum *n.* اتمام حجت etmâm-e' hoj~at التیماتوم oltimâtom
ultra *adj., n.* ماوراء mâvarâ' افراطی efrâti
ultraconservative *n.* محافظه کار افراطی mohâfezeh-kâr efrâti
ultraviolet *adj.* ماوراء بنفش mâvarâ'-e' banafsh
ululate *vi.* لیلی لیلی کردن lili-lili kardan
umber *n.* گل اخرى gel-e' okhrâ
umbilical cord *np.* بند جفت band-e' joft
umbra *n.* سایه sâyeh نیم سایه nim-sâyeh
umbrella *n., adj.* چتر chatr
ump(s)teen *n.* یک عالم yek-'âlam
umpire *n., vt., vi.* داور dâvar
unabashed *adj.* بی شرم bi-sharm وقیح vaqih
unabated *adj.* بدون کاهش bedun-e' kâhesh
unabetted *adj.* تقویت نشده taq-viyat na-shodeh
unable *adj.* ناتوان nâ-tavân عاجز 'âjez
unabridged *adj., n.* خلاصه نشده kholâseh na-shodeh
unacceptable *adj.* غیر قابل قبول qeyr-e' qâbel-e' qabul
unaccepted *adj.* قبول نشده qabul nashodeh
unaccountable *adj.* ناواضح nâ-vâzeh نامسئول nâ-mas'ul
unaccounted-for *np.* حساب نشده hesâb na-shodeh
unaccustomed *n.* نا آشنا nâ-âshnâ
unacquainted *adj.* آشنا نشده âshnâ -nashodeh
unadvisable *adj.* نا مقتضى nâ-moqtazi
unadvised *adj.* بدون مشورت bedun-e' mashverat

unanimity *n.* اتفاق آراء et~efâq-e' ârâ'
unanimous *adj.* یک صدا هم رأی ham-ra'y yek-sedâ
unanimously *n.* متفق الرأی mot~afeqol ra'y
unannounced *adj.* بی خبر bi-khabar
unanswered *n.* بلا جواب belâ javâb
unarmed *adj.* نا مسلح nâ-mosal~ah
unashamed *adj.* بی خجالت bi-khejâlat
unassailable *n.* حمله ناپذیر hamleh-nâ-pazir
unauthorized *adj.* بی اجازه bi-ejâzeh ناموجه nâ-movajah
unavoidable *adj.* اجتناب ناپذیر ejtenâb-nâpazir
unaware *adj., adv.* نا آگاه nâ-âgâh غافل qâfel
unbeaten *adj.* شکست نخورده shekast-nakhordeh
unbecoming *adj.* خلاف شأن khalâf-e' sha'n
unbefitting *adj.* ناشایسته nâ-shâyesteh
unbeknown(st) *n.* نامعلوم nâ-ma'lum
unbeknown(to) *n.* بدون اطلا ع bedun-e' et~elâ'-e'
unbelief *n.* ناباوری nâ-bâvari
unbelievable *n.* غیر قابل قبول qeyr-e' qâbel-e' qabul
unbeliever *adj.* بی اعتقاد bi-e'teqâd بیدین bi-din کافر kâfer
unbelieving *adj.* ناباور nâ-bâvar
unbending *adj.* نرم نشو narm-nasho سخت sakht
unbiased *adj.* بدون غرض bedun-e' qaraz
unbind *vt.* باز کردن bâz kardan
unborn *adj.* زاییده نشده zâyideh-nashodeh
unbreakable *adj.* نشکستنی nash-kastani
unbutton *vt.* دگمه باز کردن dogmeh bâz kardan
uncalled-for *n.* نالازم nâ-lâzem
uncanny *adj.* ناجور nâjur مرموز marmuz
uncapable *adj.* ناتوان nâ-tavân عاجز 'âjez
uncensored *adj.* سانسور نشده sânsor-nashodeh
uncertain *adj.* نامطمئن nâ-motma'en
uncertainty *n.* بی اطمینانی bi-etminâni
unchain *vt.* زنجیرباز کردن zanjir bâz kardan
unchallenged *adj.* بدون حریف bedun-e' harif بلا منازع belâ-monâze'
unchangeable *adj.* عوض نشدنی 'avaz-nashodani
unchanged *adj.* عوض نشده 'avaz-nashodeh
uncharted *adj.* بی نقشه bi-naqsheh
uncircumcised *adj.* ختنه نشده khatneh-nashodeh

uncivil *adj.* بی ادب bi-adab
uncivilized *n.* نامتمدن nâ-motemad~en
unclad *adj.* لخت lokht
unclaimed *adj.* بدون مدعی bedun-e' mod~a'i
unclassified *adj.* غیر محرمانه qeyr-e' mahramâneh
uncle *n.* عمو 'amu
uncle *n.* شوهر عمه shuhar 'âm~eh
uncle *n.* شوهر خاله shuhar khâleh
uncle *n.* دائی dâ'i
unclean *adj.* ناپاک nâ-pâk نجس najes
uncleaned *adj.* پاک نشده pâk-nashodeh
unclear *adj.* ناصاف nâ-sâf نامعلوم nâ-ma'lum
uncleared *adj.* معلوم نشده ma'lum-nashodeh
uncloak *vt., vi.* پرده برداشتن pardeh bar-dâshtan
uncollectible *adj.* وصول نشدنی vosul-nashodani
uncomfortable *adj.* ناراحت nâ-râhat
uncommitted *adj.* مرتکب نشده mortakeb na-shodeh
ناگرفتار nâ-gereftâr
uncommon *adj.* نامعمول nâ-ma'mul
uncommonly *n.* غیرمعمولی qeyr-e' ma'muli
uncomplicated *adj.* آسان âsân
uncompromising *adj.* ناساز nâ-sâz
unconcerned *adj.* بیخیال bi-khiâl
unconditional *n.* بلا شرط belâ shart
unconscionable *adj.* بی وجدان bi-vejdân نامعقول nâ-ma'qul
خلاف عقل khalâf-e' 'aql
unconscious *adj., n.* غافل qâfel
unconscious *adj., n.* ناخودآگاه nâkhod-âgâh بیخبر bi-khabar
unconscious *adj., n.* بیهوش bi-hush
unconsciousness *n.* بیهوشی bi-hushi ناخودآگاهی nâ-khod-âgâhi
unconstitutional *adj.* خلاف قانون اساسی khalâf-e' qânun-e' asâsi
unconstrained *adj.* بدون فشار bedun-e' feshâr
unconstricted *adj.* نامنقبض nâ-monqabez
uncontaminated *adj.* آلوده نشده âludeh na-shodeh
uncontested *adj.* نامعترض nâ-mo'tarez
uncontrollable *adj.* خارج از اراده khârej az erâdeh
uncontrolled *adj.* کنترل نشده kontorol-nashodeh
غیراِرادی qeyr-e' erâdi

unconvenience *n.* ناراحتی nârâhati
unconventional *n.* غیرمعمولی qeyr-e' ma'muli
uncooked *adj.* نپخته na-pokhteh
uncorrected *adj.* صحیح نشده sahih-nashodeh
uncorruptable *n.* سالم رشوه نگیر sâlem roshveh-nagir
uncounted *adj.* ناشمرده nâ-shemordeh
uncouple *adj.* ازهم بازکردن az-ham bâz kardan
uncouth *adj.* ناجور nâjur خشن khashen
uncover *vt.* پرده برداشتن pardeh bar dâshtan
uncovered *n.* فاش شده fâsh-shodeh
uncrowded *adj.* خلوت khalvat
uncultivated *adj.* کشت نشده kesht-nashodeh
تربیت نشده tarbiyat-nashodeh
uncultured *adj.* بی فرهنگ bi-farhang بیتربیت bi-tarbiyat
uncut *adj.* نبریده naborideh
undamaged *adj.* صدمه ندیده sadameh-nadideh
undated *adj.* بدون تاریخ bedun-e' târikh
undaunted *n.* نترسیده natarsideh
undecided *adj.* نامصمم nâ-mosam~am
undeclared *adj.* اعلان نشده e'lân-nashodeh
undefeatable *adj.* شکست ناپذیر shekast nâ-pazir
undefeated *adj.* نامغلوب nâ-maqlub
undefended *adj.* بیدفاع bi-defâ'
undefensible *adj.* غیرقابل دفاع qeyr-e' qâbel-e' defâ'
undefined *adj.* نامعلوم nâ-ma'lum
undemocratic *adj.* خلاف دمکراسی khalâf-e' demokrâsi
undeniable *adj.* غیرقابل انکار qeyr-e' qâbel-e' enkâr
undeniably *adv.* بدون شک bedun-e' shak
under *pre., adv., adj.* زیر zir-e' تحت taht-e'
under-developed *n.* عقب افتاده 'aqab-oftâdeh
under-handed *n.* دست تنها dast tanhâ
underage *adj., n.* زیرسن zir-e' sen صغیر saqir
underbid *vt.* کمتر پیشنهادکردن kamtar pish-nahâd kardan
underbrush *n.* بتۀ زیردرختی boteh-ye' zir-derakhti
underbuy *n.* کمترخریدن kamtar kharidan
undercarriage *n.* شاسی shâsi
undercharge *n., vt.* کمترحساب کردن kamtar hesâb kardan
underclothes *n., pl.* زیرپوش zir-push

undercoat *n., vt.* کت زیر kot-e′ zir لایه زیری lâyeh-ye′ ziri
undercover *n.* مخفی makhfi
undercurrent *n.* موج زیری moj-e′ ziri
undercut *adj., vt., vi., n.* دست زدن روی ruy-e′ dast zadan
underdog *n.* طرف ضعیفتر taraf-e′ za′if-tar
underestimate *v.* کم گرفتن دست dast-e′ kam gereftan
کم بهادادن kam-bahâ dâdan
underexpose *n.* نورکم دادن nur-e′ kam dâdan
undergarment *n.* لباس زیر lebâs-e′ zir
undergo *vt.* طی کردن tey kardan گذراندن gozarândan
undergraduate *n., adj.* دوره لیسانس doreh-ye′ lisâns
underground *n.* زیرزمین zir-e′ zamin زیرزمینی zir-zamini
underhand *n.* دست پایین dast-e′ pâyin
underlay *vt., n.* پوشش زیری pushesh-e′ ziri
underlie *n.* اساس بودن پایه pâyeh asâs budan
underlying *n.* اساس پایه pâyeh asâs
undermine *vt.* تیشه بریشه زدن tisheh be-risheh zadan
خراب کردن kharâb kardan
undermost *adj., adv.* پایین ترین pâying-tarin
underneath *pre.* زیر zir-e′ درزیر dar zir-e′
undernourished *n.* کم تغذیه داده شده kam taqzieh-dâdeh shodeh
underpass *n.* زیرپل zir-e′ pol
underpay *n.* کم حقوق دادن kam hoquq dâdan
underprivileged *adj.* محروم ازمزایا mahrum az mazâyâ
underproduction *n.* تحت تهیه taht-e′ tahiyeh
underquote *vt.* کمترقیمت دادن kamtar qeymat dâdan
underscore *vt., n.* تاکید کردن ta′kid kardan
زیرش خط کشیدن ziresh khat keshidan
undersecretary *n.* معاون mo′âven
undersell *vt.* کمترنروختن kamtar forukhtan
undershirt *n.* پیرهن زیر pir-han zir
underside *n.* سطح زیری sat-h-e′ ziri
undersigned *n.* امضاء کنندهٔ زیر emzâ′ konandeh-ye′ zir
undersized *adj.* کوچک kuchek
understand *vt., vi.* فهمیدن fahmidan ملتفت شدن moltafet shodan
understandable *adj.* فهمیدنی fahmidani قابل فهم qâbel-e′ fahm
understanding *n.* فهم fahm تفاهم tafâhom قرار qarâr
understanding *adj.* فهمیده fahmideh بانهم bâ-fahm فهیم fahim

understatement *n.* کم گفتار kam-goftâr
understood *v.* فهمیده شده fahmideh shodeh
understudy *vt., n.* هنرپیشه رزرو honar-pisheh-ye' rezerv
undertake *vt., vi.* تعهد کردن ta'ah~od kardan
بعهده گرفتن be-'ohdeh gereftan
undertaker *n.* مرده شور mordeh-shur مسئول دفن mas'ul-e' dafn
underwater *n.* زیرآبی zir-âbi
underwear *n.* زیرپوش zir-push زیرجامه zir-jâmeh
underweight *n., adj.* کم وزن kam-vazn
underworld *n.* دنیای تبهکاران donyâ-ye' tabah-kârân
underwrite *vt., vi.* قبول کردن qabul kardan
متعهدشدن mote'ah~ed shodan
underwriter *n.* تعهدکننده ta'ah~od-konandeh
undeserving *adj.* ناسزاوار nâ-sezâvâr ناقابل nâ-qabel
undesignated *adj.* تعیین نشده ta'yin-nashodeh
undesirable *adj., n.* نامطلوب nâ-matlub
undesired *adj.* ناخواسته nâ-khâsteh
undeveloped *n.* توسعه نیانته tose'eh nayâfteh
undies *n.* لباس زیر lebâs-e' zir
undigestible *adj.* هضم نشدنی hazm-nashodani
undignified *adj.* بیو قار bi-vaqâr
undiplomatic *adj.* خلاف دیپلماتی khalâf-e' diplomâti
undiscernible *adj.* غیرقابل تشخیص qeyr-e' qâbel-e' tashkhis
undisciplined *adj.* بی انظباط bi-enzebât
undisclosed *adj.* افشانشده efshâ-nashodeh
undiscovered *adj.* کشف نشده kashf-nashodeh
undisputable *adj.* بحث نشدنی bahs-nashodani
undisputed *adj.* بلا منازع belâ monâze'
undivided *adj.* تقسیم نشده taqsim-nashodeh مشاع moshâ'
undo *vt.* باز کردن bâz kardan مضمحل کردن mozmahel kardan
undoing *vt.* اضمحلال ezmehlâl نابودی nâ-budi
undone *vt.* بازشده bâz-shodeh تمام شده tamâm-shodeh
undoubted *adj.* مسلم mosal~am
undoubtedly *adv.* بی شک bi-shak مسلماً mosal~aman
undress *adj., vt., vi., n.* لباس درآوردن lebâs dar âvardân
لخت شدن lokht shodan
undressed *adj.* لخت lokht
undrinkable *adj.* غیرقابل نوشیدن qeyr-e' qâbel-e' nushidan

undue *adj.* اضافی ezâfi بیجهت bi-jahat
unduly *adv.* غیرعادلانه qeyr-e' 'âdelâneh بیجهت bi-jahat
undying *adj.* ابدی abadi لا یزال lâyazâl
unearned *adj.* نشده تحصیل tahsil-nashodeh
unearth *vt.* درآوردن dar âvardan کشف کردن kashf kardan
unearthly *adj.* غیرطبیعی qeyr-e' tabi'i
uneasiness *n.* ناراحتی nârâhati تشویش tashvish
uneasy *n.* ناراحت nârâhât مضطرب moz-tareb
unedible *adj.* غیرقابل خوردن qeyr-e' qâbel-e' khordan
uneducated *adj.* نکرده تحصیل tahsil-nakardeh
unemotional *adj.* احساسات بدون bedun-e' ehsâsât
unemployed *adj.* بیکار bi-kâr
unemployment *n.* بیکاری bi-kâri
unequal *adj., n.* نامساوی nâ-mosâvi همتا بی bi-hamtâ
unequipped *adj.* نامجهز nâ-mojah~az
unequivocal *adj.* ابهام بدون bedun-e' ebhâm
unerring *adj.* اشتباه بدون bedun-e' eshtebâh
unessential *adj.* غیراساسی qeyr-e' asâsi
unethical *adj.* اخلاق خلاف khalâf-e' akhlâq
uneven *adj.* نامساوی nâ-mosâvi ناصاف nâ-sâf ناهموار nâ-hamvâr
uneventful *adj.* اتفاق بدون bedun-e' et~efâq
unexceptionable *adj.* استثناء بدون bedun-e' estesnâ'
unexceptional *adj.* استثنایی بی bi-estesnâ'i
unexpected *adj.* غیرمنتظره qeyr-e' montazereh
unexploded *adj.* نشده منفجر monfajer-nashodeh
unexploited *adj.* نشده برداری بهره bahreh-bardâri nashodeh
unexplored *adj.* نشده کشف kashf-nashodeh
unexposed *adj.* نوردیده nur-nadideh نشده عیان 'ayân-nashodeh
unfailing *adj.* پایدار pây-dâr ناپذیر خستگی khastegi nâ-pazir
unfair *adj.* ناعادلانه nâ-'âdelâneh
unfaithful *adj.* بیوفا bi-vafâ زناکار zenâ-kâr
unfamiliar *adj.* ناآشنا nâ-âshnâ ناوارد nâ-vâred
unfamiliarity *n.* ناآشنایی nâ-âshnâyi ناواردی nâ-vâredi
unfashionable *adj.* نامتداول nâ-motedâvel
unfasten *n.* بازکردن bâz kardan
unfathomed *adj.* ناپیموده nâ-peymudeh
unfavorable *adj.* نامساعد nâ-mosâ'ed
unfeeling *adj.* احساس بی bi-ehsâs

unfeigned *n.* حقیقی haqiqi بی کلک bi-kalak
unfinished *adj.* ناتمام nâ-tamâm رنگ نخورده rang-nakhordeh
unfit *adj., vt.* نامناسب nâ-monâseb ناقابل nâ-qâbel
unfledged *n.* بی پروبال bi par-o bâl بچه bach~eh
unflinching *adj.* جدی jed~i
unfold *vt., vi.* باز bâz آشکار کردن âshkâr kardan
unforeseen *adj.* پیش بینی نشده pish-bini nashodeh
unforgettable *adj.* فراموش نشدنی farâmush-nashodani
unforgetting *adj.* بی بخشش bi-bakhshesh
unforgivable *adj.* غیرقابل بخشش qeyr-e' qâbel-e' bakhshesh
unforgiven *adj.* نابخشوده nâ-bakhshudeh
unforgiving *adj.* بدون بخشش bedun-e' bakhshesh
unforgotten *adj.* فراموش نشده farâmush-nashodeh
unfortunate *adj., n.* بدبخت bad-bakht
مایهٔ تأسف mâyeh-ye' ta'âs~of فلک زده falak-zadeh
unfortunately *adv.* بدبختانه bad-bakhtâneh
unfounded *adj.* بی پایه bi-pâyeh بی اساس bi-asâs واهی vâ-hi
فروهشته foru-heshteh
unfriendly *adj., adv.* نارفیقانه nâ-rafiqâneh
unfruitful *adj.* بی ثمر bi-samar
unfurnished *adj.* مبله نشده mobleh-nashodeh
ungainly *adj., adv.* ناجور nâ-jur زشت zesht
unglue *vt.* ازهم بازکردن az-ham bâz kardan
unglued *vt.* بازشده bâz-shodeh ازهم پاشیده az-ham pâshideh
ungodly *adj.* خدانشناس khodâ-nash-nâs خیلی kheyli
ungovernable *adj.* غیرقابل حکومت qeyr-e' qâbel-e' hokumat
ungracious *n.* نامطلوب nâ-matlub بی تربیت bi-tarbiyat
ungrammatical *adj.* خلاف دستوری khalâf-e' dasturi
ungrateful *adj.* نمک نشناس namak nash-nâs ناشکر nâ-shokr
unguarded *n.* بلامحافظ belâ-mohâfez
unhappiness *n.* بی سعادتی bi-sa'âdati نارضایت nâ-rezâyat
unhappy *adj.* بی سعادت bi-sa'âdat ناراضی nâ-râzi
unhealthy *adj.* ناسالم nâ-sâlem ناخوش nâ-khosh
unheard *adj.* نشنیده نشده nashenideh-shodeh
unheard-of *n.* بیسابقه bi-sâbeqeh
unhelpful *adj.* بیفایده bi-fâyedeh
unholy *adj.* نامقدس nâ-moqad~as شریر sharir
unhook *vt., vi.* قلاب بازکردن qol~âb bâz kardan

unicorn *n.* اسب شاخ دار asb-e' shâkh-dâr
unicycle *n.* یک چرخه yek-charkheh
unidentified *adj.* ناشناس nâ-shenâs بی هویت bi-hoviyat
unification *n.* وحدت vah-dat توحید tohid
unifier *n.* متحدکننده motah~ed-konandeh موحد movah~ed
uniform *adj., n.* یک شکل yek-shekl یکنواخت yek-navâkht
متحدالشکل motehad~ol shekl یکسان yek-sân
uniform *adj., n.* اونیفورم Oniform
uniformed *adj.* بااونیفورم bâ-oniform
uniformity *n.* یک شکلی yek-shekli
unify *vt.* یک شکل کردن yek-shekl kardan
متحدکردن motah~ed kardan
unilateral *n.* یک طرفه yek-tarafeh یک جانبه yek-jânebeh
unimaginable *adj.* غیرقابل تصور qeyr-e' qâbel-e' tasav~or
unimpassioned *n.* سرد sard بی احساس bi-ehsâs
unimpeachable *adj.* بدون سؤأل bedun-e' so'âl
unimportant *adj.* بی اهمیت bi-ahamiyat
unimpressed *adj.* بی تأثیر bi-ta'-sir
unimpressive *adj.* ناموثر nâ-mo-aser
unimproved *adj.* بهتر نشده behtar-nashodeh
تعمیرنشده ta'mir-nashodeh
unimproving *n.* بدون اصلاح bedun-e' eslâh
uninformed *adj.* نامطلع nâ-motal~e'
uninhabitable *adj.* غیرقابل زندگی qeyr-e' qâbel-e' zendegi
uninhabited *adj.* نامسکونی nâ-mas-kuni بی سکنه bi-sakaneh
uninhibited *adj.* بلامنع belâ man' بدون عقده bedun-e' 'oqdeh
uninjured *adj.* بدون زخم bedun-e' zakhm
صدمه ندیده sadameh-nadideh
uninspiring *adj.* بی نشاط bi-neshât
uninsured *adj.* بدون بیمه bedun-e' bimeh
unintelligent *adj.* بدون فهم bedun-e' fahm
unintelligible *n.* غیرقابل فهم qeyr-e' qâbel-e' fahm
unintended *adj.* بی منظور bi-manzur
unintentional *adj.* بدون منظور bedun-e' manzur همینجوری hamin-juri
uninterested *adj.* بی علاقه bi-'alâqeh
uninterrupted *adj.* بی دخالت bi-dekhâlat
پشت سرهم posht-e' sar-e' ham
uninvited *adj.* ناخوانده nâ-khândeh

union *n.* اتحاد et~e-hâd همبستگی ham-bastegi
union *n.* اتحادیه et~ehâdiyeh
unique *adj.* بیمانند bi-mânand یکتا yektâ بخصوص be-khosus
    فرید farid
unisexual *adj.* یک جنس yek-jens
unison *n.* هماهنگی hamâ-hangi
unit *n.* یگان yegân واحد vâhed دستگاه dast-gâh
unite *vt., vi.* متحد mot~ahed یکی کردن yeki kardan
united *adj., v.* متحد mot~ahed یک صدا yek-sedâ
United States of America *n.* ایالات متحده ayâlât-e' mot~ahedeh
unity *n.* اتحاد et~ehâd یگانگی yegânegi توحید tohid وحدت vahdat
univalent *adj.* تکی taki
univalve *adj., n.* تک صدف tak-sadaf
universal *adj., n.* جهانی jahâni کلی kol~i جامع jâme'
    عالمگیر 'âlam-gir
universally *adv.* بطورهمگانی be-tor-e' hamegâni عموماً 'omuman
universe *n.* جهان jahân عالم 'âlam فلک falak کائنات kâ'enât
university *n.* دانشگاه dânesh-gâh
unjoined *n.* وصل نشده vasl-nashodeh
unjudged *adj.* قضاوت نشده qezâvat-nashodeh
unjust *adj.* ناعادلانه nâ-'âdelâneh ناروا nâ-ravâ
unjustifiable *adj.* غیرقابل توجیه qeyr-e' qâbel-e' tojih
unjustified *adj.* ناحق nâ-haq توجیه نشده tojih-nashodeh
unjustly *adv.* بطورناحق be-tor-e' nâhaq
unkeep *n.* نگهداری کردن negah-dâri kardan
unkempt *adj.* شانه نکرده shâneh-nakardeh
unkept *adj.* مواظبت نکرده movâzebat-nakardan
unkind *adj.* نامهربان nâ-mehrabân
unknowable *adj., n.* ندانستنی na-dânestani
unknowing *adj.* ناآگاه nâ-âgâh
unknown *adj., n.* ناشناس nâ-shenâs مجهول maj-hul
    شناخته نشده nâ-shenakhteh نامعروف nâ-ma'ruf
unlash *vt.* زخم زبان زدن zakhm-e' zabân zadan
unlawful *adj.* غیرقانونی qeyr-e' qânuni
unlawful detainer *n.* تصرف عدوانی tasar~of-e' 'odvâni
unleaded *n.* بدون سرب bedun-e' sorb
unleash *vt.* ول کردن vel kardan روی سرریختن ruy-e' sar rikhtan

unleavened *adj.* فطیر fatir ورنیامده var-nayâmadeh
unless *con., pre.* مگراینکه magar-inkeh
unlicensed *adj.* بدون پروانه bedun-e' parvâneh
unlike *adj., pre., n.* برخلاف bar-khalâf-e' برعکس bar-'aks
unlikeable *adj.* دوست نداشتنی dust na-dâshtani
unlikelihood *n.* غیراحتمال qeyr-e' ehtemâl
unlikely *adj., n.* بعید ba'id غیرمحتمل qeyr-e' mohtamal
unlimited *adj.* نامحدود nâ-mahdud
unlisted *adj.* لیست نشده list-nashodeh
unlit *adj.* تاریک târik بی چراغ bi-cherâq
unload *vt., vi.* بارخالی کردن bâr khâli kardan
unlock *vt., vi.* قفل بازکردن qofl bâz kardan
unloving *adj.* بی محبت bi-moheb~at
unlucky *adj.* بدشانس bâd-shâns نحس nahs
unmake *vt.* خراب کردن kharâb kardan
unmanageable *adj.* اداره نشدنی edâreh-nashodani
unmanly *n.* نامردانه nâ-mardâneh
unmanned *adj.* بدون آدم bedun-e' âdam بی سرنشین bi-sar-neshin
unmannerly *adj., adv.* بدرفتارانه bad-raftârâneh
unmarked *adj.* بی نشان bi-neshân مخفی makhfi
unmarried *adj.* مجرد mojar~ad عزب 'azab
unmask *adj.* نمایان namâyân فاش کردن fâsh kârdân
unmatched *adj.* بیمانند bi-mânand
unmentionable *n.* غیرقابل تذکر qeyr-e' qâbel-e' tazâk~or
نگفتنی na-goftani
unmerciful *adj.* بی شفقت bi-shafeqat
unmistakable *n.* غیرقابل اشتباه qeyr-e' qâbel-e' eshtebâh
unmistakably *adv.* بدون اشتباه bedun-e' eshtebâh
unmitigated *adj.* مطلق motlaq بتمام معنی be-tamâm-e' ma'ni
unmoved *adj.* تکان نخورده takân-nakhordeh
unnamed *n.* بی اسم bi-esm ناشناس nâ-shenâs
unnatural *adj.* غیرطبیعی qeyr-e' tabi'i
unnecessary *adj., n.* نالازم nâ-lâzem بیخود bikhod
unnoticeable *adj.* بدون جلب توجه bedun-e' jalb-e' tav~ajoh
unnoticed *adj.* بدون توجه bedun-e' tav~ajoh
unnumbered *n.* بدون شماره bedun-e' shomâreh
unobjectionable *adj.* غیرقابل اعتراض qeyr-e' qâbel-e' e'terâz
unobliging *adj.* نامایل بکمک nâ-mâyel be-komak

unobserved *adj.* دیده نشده dideh-nashodeh
unobstructed *adj.* نامسدود nâ-masdud
unobtainable *adj.* بدست نیامدنی bedast nayâmadân
unoccupied *adj.* اشغال نشده eshqâl-nashodeh
unofficial *adj.* غیررسمی qeyr-e' rasmi
unopened *adj.* بازنشده bâz-nashodeh
unorthodox *adj.* نامعمولی nâ-ma'muli
unpack *n.* بسته بازکردن basteh bâz kardan
unpaid *adj.* نپرداخته na-par-dâkhteh
unpaid-for *adj.* تمام پرداخت نشده tamâm-pardâkht nashodeh
unpaved *adj.* آسفالت نشده âsfâlt-nashodeh
unperturbed *adj.* نامضطرب nâ-moztareb
unpleasant *adj.* ناموافق nâ-movâfeq نامطبوع nâ-matbu'
تاخوش آیند nâ-khosh âyand ناگوار nâ-govar
unplug *vt.* ازپریز درآوردن az periz dar âvardan
unpopular *adj.* نامحبوب nâ-mahbub
unpracticed *adj.* بی تمرین bi-tamrin بی تجربه bi-tajrobeh
unprecedented *adj., n.* بیسابقه bi-sâbeqeh
unpredictable *n.* غیرقابل پیش بینی qeyr-e' qâbel-e' pish-bini
unprepared *adj.* ناآماده nâ-âmâdeh
unpretending *n.* بی تظاهر bi-tazâhor
unpretentious *adj.* بی ادعا bi-ed~e'â بی تظاهر bi-tazâhor
unprevileged *n.* بی مزایا bi-mazâyâ
unprincipled *adj.* بی پرنسیب bi-peransip بی شخصیت bi-shakhsiyat
لا کردار lâ-kerdâr
unprofessional *adj., n.* غیرحرفه ای qeyr-e' herfeh-i
unprofitable *adj.* بی منفعت bi-manfa'at
unproved *adj.* ثابت نشده sâbet-nashodeh
unproven *adj.* ثابت نشده sâbet-nashodeh
unprovided *adj.* تهیه ندیده tahiyeh-nadideh
unpublished *adj.* چاپ نشده châp-nashodeh
unqualified *n.* فاقد صلاحیت fâqed-e' salâhiyat
unquestionable *adj.* غیرقابل تردید qeyr-e' qâbel-e' tardid
unquestionably *adv.* مسلماً mosalaman
unravel *vt., vi.* ازهم بازکردن az-ham bâz kardan
unreadable *adj.* ناخوانا nâ-khânâ
unready *adj.* ناآماده nâ-âmâdeh
unreal *adj.* غیرواقعی qeyr-e' vâqe'i

unreality *n.* غیرواقعیت qeyr-e' vâqe'iyat
unreasonable *adj.* نامعقول nâ-ma'qul ناعادلانه nâ-'âdelâneh
unregistered *adj.* ثبت نشده sabt-nashodeh
unrehearsed *adj.* تمرین نشده tamrin-nashodeh
unrelated *adj.* نامربوط nâ-marbut بدون نسبت bedun-e' nesbat
unrelenting *n.* سخت sakht دست برندار dast bar-nadâr
unreliable *adj.* غیرقابل اعتماد qeyr-e' qâbel-e' e'temâd
unremorseful *adj.* ناپشیمان nâ-pashimân
unrepentant *adj.* بدون توبه bedun-e' tobeh
unrepresented *adj.* بی نماینده bi-namâyandeh
unresistant *adj.* بی دفاع bi-defâ'
unrest *n.* آشوب âshub اغتشاش eqteshâsh
unrestricted *adj.* نامحدوده nâ-mahdudeh آزاد âzâd
unripe *adj.* کال kâl نارس nâres
unrivaled *adj.* بی رقیب bi-raqib یکه تاز yek~eh-taz
unruffled *v.* بدون چروک bedun-e' choruk
unruly *n.* بی انظباط bi-enzebât بی نظم bi-nazm
unsafe *adj.* ناامن nâ-amn
unsaid *adj.* ناگفته nâ-gofteh
unsalted *adj.* بی نمک bi-namak
unscrew *vt., vi.* پیچ بازکردن pich bâz kardan
unscrupulous *adj.* بی وجدان bi-vejdân ناصادق nâ-sâdeq
unseat *vt.* ازمقام انداختن az maqâm andâkhtan
خلع کردن khal' kardan
unseemly *adj.* ناجور nâ-jur ناشایسته nâ-shâyesteh
unselfish *adj.* متواضع motevâze'
unsettled *adj.* تصفیه نشده tasfieh-nashodeh
unshaven *n.* ریش نزده rish-nazadeh
unsight *adj.* ندیده nadideh
unskilled *adj.* ناماهر nâ-mâher بی تخصص bi-takhas~os
unsociable *adj.* غیرقابل معاشرت qeyr-e' qâbel-e' mo'âsherat
ناسازگار nâ-sâzgâr
unspeakable *adj.* ناگفتنی nâ-goftani
unspent *adj.* خرج نشده kharj-nashodeh
مصرف نشده masraf-nashodeh
unstable *n.* ناثابت nâ-sâbet نااستوار nâ-ostovâr متزلزل motezal-zel
unsteady *v., adj.* ناپیوسته nâ-peyvasteh
unsubstantial *adj.* ناقابل nâ-qâbel

unsuccessful *adj.* نا موفق nâ-movaf~aq ناكام nâkâm
unsuitable *adj.* نامناسب nâ-monâseb
unsuspected *adj.* نامظنون nâ-maznun
untamable *adj.* رام نشدنی râm-nashodani
untamed *adj.* رام نشده râm-nashodeh
untangle *vt.* گره بازکردن gereh bâz kardan
unthinkable *n.* غیرقابل تصور qeyr-e' qâbel-e' tasav~or
untidy *adj., vt.* شلخته shelakhteh نامرتب nâ-morat~ab
untie *vt., vi.* گره بازکردن gereh bâz kardan
until *con., pre.* تا tâ تااینکه tâ-inkeh الی elâ
untimely *adj., adv.* بیجا bi-jâ بیموقع be-moqe' نابهنگام na-behengâm
untitled *adj.* بدون عنوان bedun-e' 'onvân
unto *pre.* به beh
untold *adj.* ناگفته nâgofteh بیحد bi-had
untouchable *adj., n.* دست نیافتنی dast-nayâftani
untraceable *adj.* بدون ردپا bedun-e' rad~-e' pâ
untrained *adj.* تعلیم ندیده ta'lim-nadideh
untroubled *adj.* بیخیال bi-khiâl
untrue *adj.* دروغ doruq غیر حقیقت qeyr-e' haqiqat
untruthful *adj.* دروغین doruqin دروغگو doruq-gu كاذب kâzeb
untruthfully *adv.* كاذبانه kâzebâneh بدروغ bedoruq
unusable *adj.* غیرقابل استفاده qeyr-e' qâbel-e' estefâdeh
unused *adj.* استفاده نشده estefâdeh nashodeh
unusual *adj.* غیرمعمولی qeyr-e' ma'muli بعید ba'id
unusually *adv.* بطورخارق العاده be-tor-e' khâreqol'âdeh
unveil *n.* پرده برداشتن pardeh bardâshtan
unwanted *adj.* ناخواسته nâ-khâsteh
unwashed *adj., n.* نشسته nashosteh
unwed(ed) *n.* بی شوهر bi-shuhar
unwilling *adj., vi.* نامایل nâ-mâyel بیمیل bi-meyl
unwind *n.* بازکردن bâz kardan خستگی درکردن khastegi dar kardan
unwise *adj.* ناعاقلانه nâ-'âqelâneh لا یعقل lâ-ya'qal
unwordly *n.* غیردنیوی qeyr-e' donyavi
unworthy *n., adj.* نالایق nâlâyeq ناسزاوار nâ-sezâvâr ناقابل nâ-qabel
unwrap *vt., vi.* بسته بازکردن basteh bâz kardân
unwritten *adj.* ننوشته na-neveshteh
up *v., adv., pre., adj.* بالای bâlâ-ye' برپا bar-pâ بیدار bi-dâr فراز farâz
up(against it) *n.* درگیر dar-gir

up(against) *n.* رو برو با ru be-ru bâ
up(and doing) *n.* مشغول mashqul فعال fa'~âl
up-and-coming *adj.* وارد vâred بااستعداد bâ-este'dâd
up-and-down *adj.* بالا و پایین bâlâ-o pâyin
up-to-date *adj.* تاکنونی tâkonuni باخبرازحال bâ-khabar az-hâl
upbeat *n., adj.* نت بالا not-e' bâlâ کیف کوک keyf-e' kuk
upbraid *vt.* سرزنش کردن sarzanesh kardan
upbringing *n.* پرورش parvaresh تربیت خانوادگی tarbiyat-e' khânevâd
upgrade *n., adj., adv., vt.* بالاتربردن bâlâtar bordan
اصلاح کردن eslâh kardan
upheaval *n.* قیام qiâm بالاآمدگی bâlâ-âmadegi
upheave *vt., vi.* بالاآمدن bâlâ âmadan
upheld *v.* تصدیق شده tasdiq-shodeh
uphill *adv., adj., n.* سربالایی sar-bâlâyi
uphold *vt.* تصدیق کردن tasdiq kardan ابرام کردن ebrâm kardan
upholster *vt.* روی کشیدن ruy-e' keshidan
upholsterer *n.* رویه کش ruyeh-kesh مبل ساز mobl-sâz
upholstery *n.* رویه کشی ruyeh-keshi مبل سازی mobl-sâzi
upland *n., adj.* زمین مرتفع zamin-e' mortafa'
uplift *vt., vi.* بالاکشیدن bâlâ keshidan بالا بری bâlâ-bari
upon *pre., n.* بر bar روی ruy-e' بمحض bemahz-e'
upper *n.* بالاتر bâlâ-tar بالایی bâlâyi بخش نشاط neshât-bakhsh
علیا 'olyâ
upper hand *np.* دست بالا dast-e' bâlâ دارای امتیاز dârâ-ye' emtiâz
upper-class *adj.* طبقه بالا tabaqeh bâlâ
uppercut *v., n.* آپرکات âperkât
uppermost *adj., adv.* بالا ترین bâlâ-tarin
upright *adj., n., adv.* صاف ' sâf عمودی amudi سیخ sikh
uprise *vi., n.* بلندشدن boland shodan مرتفع mortafa'
uprising *v.* قیام qiâm بالاآمدگی bâlâ-âmadegi جنبش jonbesh
uproar *n.* سروصدا sar-o sedâ جنجال jan-jâl هنگامه hen-gâmeh
uproot *vt., vi.* ازریشه کندن az risheh kandan
ups-and-downs *n.* بالا و پایین bâlâ-o pâyin
فرازو نشیب farâz-o nashib
upset *v.* آشوب شده âshub shodeh
upset *n.* پیروزی تیم ضعیفتر piruzi-e' tim-e' za'iftar
upset *v.* ناراحت آشفته کردن nârâhat âshofteh kardan
upset *v.* منقلب کردن chap kardan چپ کردن monqaleb kardan

upshot *n.* نتیجه natijeh
upside-down *n.* وارونه vâruneh معکوس ma'kus
upstage *adv., adj., vt., n.* پشت پرده posht-e' pardeh
upstairs *n.* طبقهٔ بالا tabaqeh-ye' bâlâ
upstanding *adj.* شق و رق shaq-o raq خوش هیکل khosh-heykal
upstart *n., adj., vi., vt.* تازه بدوران رسیده tâzeh be-dorân resideh
upstate *n.* شمال ایالت shomâl-e' eyâlat
upstream *n.* برخلاف جریان bar-khalâf-e' jaryân
upsurge *vi., n.* خروش آب khorush-e' âb
upswing *n.* ترقی taraq~i
uptake *n.* بالا بری bâlâ-bari دودکش dud-kesh
uptown *adv., adj., n.* شمال شهر shomâl-e' shahr
upturned *adj.* سربالا sar-bâlâ
upward(s) *n.* بطرف بالا be-taraf-e' bâlâ
urban *adj.* شهری shahri مدنی madani
urban *adj.* مودب mo'ad~ab موقر movaq~ar
urbanization *n.* شهرسازی shahr-sâzi
urching *n.* بچه شیطان bach~eh sheytân
urethra *n.* مجرای ادرار majrâ-ye' edrâr میزه راه mizeh-râh
urge *vt., n.* اصرار کردن esrâr kardan واداركردن vâdâr kardan هوس havas
urgency *n.* ضرورت zarurat فوریت fori-yat
urgent *adj.* ضروری zaruri فوری fori
urinal *n.* آبریزگاه âbriz-gâh
urinary *n.* ادراری edrâri پیشابی pishâbi
urinate *vi.* ادرارکردن edrâr kardan شاش کردن shâsh kardan
urine *n.* ادرار شاش shâsh edrâr پیشاب pishâb میزه mizeh
urn *n.* خاکستردان khâkestar-dân
us *pro.* ما را mâ râ به ما beh mâ
usable *adj.* قابل استفاده qâbel-e' estefâdeh
usage *n.* استعمال استفاده estefâdeh este'mâl
use *n.* استفاده فایده estefâdeh fâyedeh
use *v.* سوء استفاده کردن su'-e' estefâdeh kardan
use *v.* استفاده کردن estefâdeh kardan بکاربردن be-kâr bordan
useful *adj.* مفید mofid مورداستفاده mored-e' estefâdeh
نتیجه بخش natijeh-bakhsh
useless *adj.* بیفایده bi-fâyedeh بیمصرف bi-masraf بیهوده bi-hudeh
عبث 'abas
user *n.* استفاده کننده estefâdeh-konandeh

usher *v.* آوردن âvardan راهنمایی کردن râh-namâyi kardan
usher *n.* راهنما râh-namâ کنترولچی kontorol-chi
usual *adj.* معمولی ma'muli عادی 'âd~i مرسوم marsum
usually *adv.* معمولاً ma'-mulan
usurer *n.* رباخوار rebâ-khâr
usurp *vt., vi.* غصب کردن qasb kardan بزورگرفتن be-zur gereftan
usurper *n.* غاصب qâseb
usury *n.* رباخواری rebâ-khâri
utensil *n.* ظرف zarf وسیلهٔ آشپزی vasileh-ye' âsh-pazi
uterine *adj.* رحمی rahemi مادری mâdari
uterus *n.* رحم majrâ-ye' rahem مجرای
utilities *pl.* برق و گاز barq-o gâz
utility *n., adj.* سودمندی sud-mandi
utilization *n.* استفاده estefâdeh بکارگیری bekâr-giri
utilize *vt.* مورداستفاده قراردادن mored-e' estefâdeh qarâr dâdan
utmost *n.* منتهای montehây-e'
Utopia *n.* مدینهٔ فاضله madineh-ye' fâzeleh
Utopian *adj., n.* خوشبین khosh-bin ایده آلیست ide-'âlist
utter *n.* کامل kâmel محض mahz
utter *v.* اداکردن adâ kardan گفتن goftan
utterance *n.* ادا adâ گفتار goftâr
utterly *n.* بکلی be-kol~i کاملاً kâmelan
uttermost *adj., n.* منتهای montehâ-ye'
uvula *n.* زبان کوچک zabân kuchek
uvular *adj., n.* ارتعاشی erte'âshi

V V v

vacancy *n.* خالی جای jâ-ye' khâli
vacant *adj., vi.* خالی khâli
vacate *vt., vi.* کردن تخلیه takhlieh kardan
vacation *n., vi.* تعطیلات ta'tilât
vacationer *n.* گذر تعطیلات ta'tilât-gozar مسافر mosâfer
vaccinate *vt., vi.* زدن واکسن vâksan zadan کردن تلقیح talqih kardan
vaccination *n.* زنی واکسن vâksan-zani
vaccine *n., adj.* واکسن vâksan
vacillate *vi.* کردن نوسان na-vasân kardan
بودن وسواسی vas-vâsi budan
vacillating *vi.* وسواسی vas-vâsi دودل do-del
vacillation *n.* نوسان navasân دودلی do-deli
vacum cleaner *n.* جاروبرقی jâru barqi
vacuous *adj.* خالی khâli هدف بی bi-hadaf
vacuum *n., vi.* خلاء khala'
vacuum tube *n.* خلاء لولهٔ luleh-ye' khalâ'
vagabond *adj., n.* ولگرد vel-gard آواره âvâreh
vagarious *adj.* بلهوس bol-havas آواره âvâreh
vagary *n.* بلهوسی bol-havasi غریب qarib
vagina *n.* فرج faraj
vaginal *adj.* فرجی faraji
vagrancy *n.* آوارگی âvâregi
vagrant *n., adj.* آواره âvâreh الاف al~âf ولگرد vel-gard
vague *adj.* مبهم mob-ham
vain *adj.* بیهوده bi-hudeh پوچ puch بیهدر bi-hadar عبث 'abas
vain *adj.* مغروربخود maqrur be-khod
valance *n.* والان vâlân
valediction *n.* خداحافظی khodâ-hâfezi وداع vedâ'
valedictory *n., adj.* وداعی vedâ'i
valentine *n.* صنم sanam
valet *n., vt., vi.* پادو pâdo
valet *n., vt., vi.* خدمتکار khedmat-kâr لباس lebâs
valiant *adj.* دلیر dalir
valid *adj.* معتبر mo'tabar
validate *vt.* معتبرساختن mo'tabar sâkhtan
بااعتبارکردن bâ-e'tebâr kardan
validation *n.* تصدیق tasdiq

validtiy *n.* اعتبار e'tebâr
valise *n.* چمدان chamedân
valley *n.* دره dar~eh بازه bâzeh
valor *n.* دليرى daliri شجاعت shojâ'at
valuable *adj., n.* گرانبها gerân-bahâ باارزش bâ-arzesh
value *n.* ارزش arzesh بها bahâ قدر qadr ارج arj
value *v.* ارزش دادن arzesh dâdan
        قدرشناسى كردن qadr-shenâsi kardan
valued *adj.* پرارزش por-arzesh تخمين زده takh-min-zadeh
valueless *adj.* بى ارزش bi-arzesh
valve *v., n.* دريچه daricheh سوپاپ su-pâp
vamp *adj.* عشوه گر 'eshveh-gar
vamp *n.* وصله vâsleh
vamp *v.* وصله زدن vasleh zadan اغفال كردن eqfâl kardan
vampire *n.* خونخوار khun-khâr
van *n., v., pre.* مينى بوس mini-bus
vandal *n.* خرابكار kharâb-kâr
vandalism *n.* خرابكارى kharâb-kâri ويرانى virâni
vandalize *vt.* خراب كارى كردن kharâb-kâri kardan
        صدمه زدن sadameh zadan
vane *n.* بادنما bâd-namâ
vanguard *n.* پيش قراول pish-qarâvol پيشتاز pish-tâz جلودار jelo-dâr
vanilla *n.* وانيل vânil
vanish *vi., vt., n.* ناپديد nâ-padid غيب شدن qeyb shodan
vanity *n.* پوچى puchi بيهودگى bi-hudegi
vanity *n.* كمد komod اشكاف eshkâf
vanquish *vt.* مغلوب كردن maqlub kardan پيروزشدن piruz shodan
vanquished *n.* مغلوب maqlub مقهور maqhur
vantage *n.* امتياز emtiâz آوانتاژ âvântâzh
vapor *n., vt., vi.* بخار bokhâr
vaporize *vt., vi.* تبخير tabkhir بخارشدن bokhâr shodan
vaporizer *n.* بخوركن bokhâr-kon بخور bakhur
variability *n.* تغييرپذيرى taq-yir-paziri
variable *n.* تغييرپذير taq-yir-pazir متغير moteqay~er
variance *n.* اختلاف ekhtelâf تغير taqay~or
variant *n.* مختلف mokh-talef متغير moteqay~er
variate *n.* مختلف بودن mokh-talef budan
variation *n.* تنوع tanavo' گوناگونى gunâguni

varicose adj. واریس vâris باد کرده bâd-kardeh
varicosis n. ورم رگ varam rag
varied adj., v. گوناگون gunâ-gun مختلف mokh-tâlef
variety adj., n. تنوع tanavo′ نوع no′ انواع anvâ′
variety show n. نمایش متنوع na-mâyesh-e′ motenav~e′
various adj. گوناگون gunâ-gun مختلف mokh-tâlef
varisty n. تیم دانشگاه tim-e′ dânesh-gâh
varnish n., vt. لاک الکل lâk-alkol
vary vt., vi. تغییر کردن taqir kardan فرق کردن farq kardan
vascular adj. مجرایی maj-râyi آوندی âvandi
vase n. گلدان gol-dân
vasectomy n. عقیمی مرد ′aqimi-e′ mard
vaseline n. وازلین vâzelin
vassal n., adj. تابع tâbe′ رعیت ra′yat
vast adj., n. وسیع vasi′ پهناور pahnâ-var
vastitude n. وسعت vos′at
vastly adv. وسیعا vasi′an خیلی kheyli
vat n., vt. حوضچه hoz-cheh بشکه bosh-keh
vault n. سردابه sardâbeh طاق tâq
vault n. گاو صندوق اطاقی gâv-sandoq-e′ otâgi
vault v. پریدن paridan
vaulting adj., n. پرشی pareshi جاه طلبانه jâh-talabâneh
vaunt vt., vi., n. لاف زدن lâf zadan
veal n. گوشت گوساله gusht-e′ gusâleh
vector n. بردار bordâr خط شعاعی khat~-e′ sho′â′i
veer vt. تغییر جهت دادن taq-yir-e′ jahat dâdan ویراژ virâzh
vegetable n., adj. سبزی sabzi گیاه giâh
vegetarian n., adj. گیاه خوار giâh-khâr
vegetate n. رشد گیاهی کردن roshd-e′ giâhi kardan
vegetation n. رشد و نمو گیاهی roshd-o nemov-e′ giâhi
vehemence n. شدت shed~at حرارت harârat
vehement adj. با حرارت bâ-harârat شدید shadid
vehemently adv. شدیدا shadidan
vehicle n. وسیله نقلیه vasileh-ye′ naqli آلت âlat
vehicular adj. نقلیه ای naqlieh-i
veil n., vt., vi. رو بند ru-band نقاب neqâb رونما ru-namâ
مقنعه maqna′eh
veiled adj. باروبند bâ-ruband

vein *n., vt.* رگ rag رگه rageh
velar *n.* ته دهانى tah-dahâni
velocity *n.* سرعت sor'at شتاب shetâb
velum *n.* زبان کوچک zabân kuchek
velvet *n., adj.* مخمل makh-mal
velvety *adj.* مخملى makh-mali نرم narm
vend *vt., vi.* فروختن forukhtan بازار یافتن bâzâr yâftan
vendetta *n.* انتقام خونى enteqâm-e' khuni
vendor *n.* فروشنده forushandeh
veneer *n., vt.* روکش چوبى rukesh-e' chubi
venerable *adj., n.* محترم mohtaram
venerably *n.* محترماً mohtaraman
venerate *n.* احترام گذاشتن eh-terâm gozâshtan
veneration *n.* احترام eh-terâm حرمت hormat
venereal *adj.* مقاربتى moqârebati آمیزشى âmizeshi
vengeance *n.* کینه جویى kineh-juyi انتقام جویى enteqâm-juyi
vengeful *adj.* کینه جو kineh-ju انتقام جو enteqâm-ju
venison *n.* گوشت آهو gusht-e' âhu
venitian blind *n.* کرکره ker-kereh
venom *n., vt.* زهر zahr سم sam
venomous *adv.* زهرآلود zahr-âlud سمى sam~i
vent *n.* دریچه daricheh هواکش havâ-kesh منفذ manfaz
vent *v.* بیرون دادن birun dâdan دل خالى کردن del khâli kardan
ventilate *vt.* تهویه کردن tahvieh kardan هوا دادن havâ dâdan
ventilation *n.* تهویه tahvieh
ventilator *n.* دستگاه تهویه dast-gâh-e' tahvieh
ventricle *n.* دریچهٔ قلبى daricheh-ye' qalbi
venture *adj.* کار پر خطر kâr-e' por khatar اقدام ریسکى eqdâm-e' riski
venture *v.* بخطر انداختن be-khatar andâkhtan
جرعت کردن jor'at kardan
venue *n.* محل رسیدگى mahal~-e' residegi
venus *n.* زهره zohreh ناهید nâhid
Venus *n.* زهره zohreh ناهید nâhid ونوس venus
veracious *adj.* راستگو râst-gu صادق sâdeq
veracity *n.* راستگویى râst-guyi صداقت sedâqat
verb *n.* فعل fe'l
verbal *adj., n.* فعلى fe'li شفاهى shafâhi
verbalization *n.* تکلم takal~om

verbalize *vt., vi.* کلمه بکلمه گفتن kalameh be-kalameh goftan
verbally *adv.* شفاهاً shafâhan کلمه‌ای kalameh-i
verbatim *adv., adj.* کلمه بکلمه kalameh be-kalameh
verdict *n.* رأی ra'y تصمیم tasmim
verge *n., vi., vt.* لب lab لبه labeh شرف shorof
verifiable *adj.* قابل تصدیق qâbel-e' tasdiq
verification *n.* تصدیق tasdiq تعیین صحت ta'yin-e' sehat
verify *vt.* تصدیق کردن tasdiq kardan اثبات کردن esbât kardan
verily *n.* حقیقتاً haqiqatan
veritable *adj.* حقیقی haqiqi واقعی vâqe'i
veritably *adv.* واقعاً vâqe'an
verjuice *n., adj.* آبغوره âb-qureh
vermin *n., pl.* کرم kerm انگل angal
vernacular *adj., n.* زبان عام zabân-e' 'âm لهجه lahjeh
vernal *adj.* بهاری bahâri
vernal equinox *np.* تحویل بهار tahvil-e' bahâr
versatile *adj.* گردان gardân مسلط در صحبت mosal~at dar sohbat
versatility *n.* چرخش char-khesh تسلط در صحبت tasal~ot dar soh-bat
verse *n., adj.* بیت beyt نظم nazm آیه âyeh
versed *adj.* مطلع mot~ale' فهمیده fahmideh متبحر motebah~er
version *n.* نوع no' معروضه ma'ruzeh
version *n.* شرح ویژه sharh-e' vizheh تفسیر tafsir
versus *pre.* ضد zed~-e' در مقابل dar moqâbel-e'
vertebra *n.* مهره mohreh
vertebrate(d) *n.* مهره دار mohreh-dâr ذوالفقار zol-faqâr
vertex *n.* نوک nok قله qol~eh
vertical *adj.* عمودی 'amudi قایم qâ'em
vertically *adv.* بطور عمودی betor-e' 'amudi
vertigo *n.* سرگیجه sar-gijeh
verve *n.* حرارت harârat ذوق zoq
very *adv., adj.* خیلی kheyli بسیار bes-yâr همین hamin همان hamân
vessel *n.* سفینه safineh مجرا maj-râ ظرف zarf
vest *v.* دادن dâdan اختیار دادن ekhtiâr dâdan
vest *n.* جلیقه jeli-qeh
vestal *adj., n.* باکره bâkereh پاک دامن pâk-dâman
vested *adj.* بدون شرط bedun-e' shart قطعی qat'i
vestibule *n., vt.* جلو خوان jelo-khân دهلیز dehliz
vestige *n.* اثر asar نشان neshân

vetch *n.* ماش mâsh
veteran *n., adj.* كهنه كار kohneh-kâr پيش كسوت pish-kesvat
    كار كشته kâr-koshteh
veteran *n.* كهنه سرباز kohneh sar-bâz
veterinarian *n.* دامپزشك dâm-pezeshk
veterinary *n., adj.* دامپزشكى dâm-pezeshki
veto *n.* وتو كردن veto kardan رد كردن rad kardan
vex *vt.* اذيت كردن az-yat kardan آزار رساندن âzâr resândan
via *pre., n.* از طريق az tariq-e'
viability *n.* قدرت زندگى qodrat-e' zendegi
viable *adj.* قادر به زندگى qâder be-zendegi
viaduct *n.* پل روى آب pol-e' ru-ye' âb
vial *n., vt.* شيشهٔ دوا shisheh-ye' davâ
vibrancy *n.* ارتعاش erte'âsh
vibrant *adj.* مرتعش morta'esh سرزنده sar-zendeh
vibrate *vi., vt.* لرزيدن larzidan ارتعاش داشتن erte'âsh dâshtan
vibration *n.* لرزش lar-zesh ارتعاش erte'âsh احساس ehsâs
vicar *n.* جانشين jâneshin نايب nâyeb
vicarious *adj.* نيابتى niâbati
vicariously *adv.* نيابتاً niâbatan
vice *n., vt., pre.* فساد fesâd نسق و فجور fesq-o fejur
vice *n., vt., pre.* بجاى bejâ-ye'
vice squad *np.* پليس مبارزه با فساد polis-e' mobârezeh bâ fesâd
vice versa *np.* بالعكس bel-'aks
vice- *n.* معاون mo'âven نايب nâyeb
vice-admiral *n.* دريابان daryâ-bân
vice-consul *n.* كنسول يار konsul-yâr
vice-presidency *n.* معاونت mo'âvenat
vice-president *np.* معاون رئيس جمهور mo'âven-e' ra'is jomhur
viceroy *n.* فرمانفرما farmân-farmâ
vicinity *n.* نزديكى naz-diki همسايگى ham-sâyegi
vicious *adj.* وحشيانه vahshiâneh پليد pâlid
vicious cycle *n.* دايرهٔ خبيثه dâyereh-ye' khabiseh
vicissitude(s) *n.* تغيير taqyir تحول tahav~ol
victim *n.* قربانى qorbâni مضروب mazrub ستمكش setam-kesh
victimize *vt.* قربانى كردن qorbâni kardan اغفال كردن eqfâl kardan
victor *n.* فاتح fâteh پيروز piruz مظفر mozaf~ar
victorious(ly) *n.* پيروزمندانه piruz-mandâneh فاتحانه fâtehâneh

victory *n.* پیروزی piruzi فتح fat-h ظفر zafar
vie *vi., vt.* رقابت کردن reqâbat kardan
view *n., vt.* نگاه negâh بازدید کردن bâzdid kardan
view *n., vt.* نظر nazar نظریه nazarieh منظره manzareh
view finder *n.* منظره بین manzareh-bin ویزور vizor
viewless *adj.* بی منظره bi-manzareh
viewpoint *n.* نقطۀ نظر noqteh-ye' nazar
viewy *adj.* پر منظره por-manzareh متظاهر motezâher
vigil *n.* پاس pâs مراقبت morâqebat
vigilance *n.* هوشیاری hosh-yâri بیداری bi-dâri
vigilant *adj.* هوشیار hosh-yâr بیدار bi-dâr مراقب morâqeb
vigilante *n.* پلیس سر خود polis-e' sar-khod
vigor *n.* قدرت qodrat شدت shed~at
vigoroso *adj.* پر حرارت por harârat
vigorous *adj.* قوی qavi پر زور por-zur شدید shadid
vile *n.* شنیع shani' پست past
vilification *n.* بد نامی bad-nâmi بهتان boh-tân
vilify *vt.* بدنام کردن bad-nâm kardan بد گفتن bad goftan
villa *n.* ویلا vilâ خانه ییلاقی khâneh-ye' yeylâqi کوشک kushk
village *n., adj.* ده deh روستا rustâ قریه qaryeh
villager *n.* دهقان deh-qân دهاتی dehâti روستایی rustâyi
villain *n.* شرور sharur دزده dozdeh
villainous *adj.* شرارت آمیز sharârat-âmiz شریر sharir
vindicate *vt.* مبراکردن mobarâ kardan توجیح کردن tojih kardan
vindication *n.* الغاء شبهه elqâ-e' shobheh توجیه tojih
vindictive *n.* کینه آمیز kineh-âmiz انتقام جویانه enteqâm-juyâneh
vine *n.* مو mo تاک tâk
vinegar *n.* سرکه serkeh
vinegary *n.* ترش رو torsh-ru
vinery *n.* گرم خانۀ مو garm-khâneh-ye' mo
vineyard *n.* تاکستان tâkestân
vintage *n., adj., vt.* شراب سال sharâb-sâl اعلا a'lâ
vintager *n.* انگور پرور angur-parvar
violate *vt.* تجاوز کردن tajâvoz kârdan تخلف کردن takhal~of kardan
violation *n.* تخلف takhal~of خلاف قانونی khalâf-e' qânuni
تخطی takhât~i هتک hatk
violator *n.* خلاف کار khalâf-kâr متخطی motekhat~i هتاک hat~âk
violence *n.* خشونت khoshunat شدت shed~at

violent *adj.* خشن khashen شدید shadid نجیح fajih
violet *n., adj.* بنفشه banafsheh
violet *n., adj.* بنفش banafsh
violin *n.* ویولن violon
violinist *n.* ویولنیست violonist
violoncello *n.* ویولن سل violon-sel
viper *n.* افعی af'i
viperous *adj.* زهر آلود zahr-âlud
virgine *n.* دوشیزه dushizeh باکره bâkereh
virginity *n.* دوشیزگی dushizegi بکارت bekârat
Virgo *n.* سنبله sonboleh شهریور shahrivar
virile *adj.* مردانه mardâneh کمر قرص kamar-qors
virility *n.* مردی mardi کمر قرصی kamar-qorsi
virtual *adj.* مطلق motlaq واقعی vâqe'i
virtually *n.* مطلقاً motlaqan در واقع dar vâqe'
virtue *n.* پرهیز گاری pahiz-gâri تقوا taq-vâ
virtuosity *n., adj.* علاقه به هنر 'alâqeh be-honar
virtuoso *n.* استاد ostâd
virtuous *adj.* پاکدامن pâk-dâman پرهیز کار parhiz-gâr عفیف 'afif
نجیب najib
virulence *n.* چرکی cherki کدورت kodurat
virulent *adj.* سمی sam~i خصم آلود khasm-âlud
virus *n.* ویروس virus
vis-a-vis *n.* روبرو ruberu در برابر dar barâbare
visa *n., vt.* ویزا vizâ روادید ravâdid
visage *n.* سیما simâ چهره chehreh
viscosity *n.* غلظت qelzat چسبندگی chas-bandegi
vise *n., vt.* گیره gireh
visibility *n.* برد بینایی bord binâyi نمایانی namâyâni
visible *adj.* نمایان namâyân آشکار âshkâr مرئی mar'i
visibly *n.* ظاهراً zâheran بطور معلوم betore ma'lum
vision *n., vt.* بینایی binâyi تصویر خیالی tasvire khiâli
visional *adj.* خیالی khiâli
visionary *adj., n., vi.* خیال بین khiâl-bin رویایی royâyi
visit *n.* ویزیت vizit ملاقات molâqât دیدار didâr
visit *v.* ملاقات کردن molâqât kardan دیدن کردن didan kardan
visitation *n.* ملاقات molâqât عیادت ayâdat
visitor *n.* ملاقات کننده molâqât konandeh ویزیتور vizitor

visor *n., vt.* آفتاب گردان âftâb-gardân سایبان sâyeh-bân
vista *n.* منظره manzareh دور نما dur-namâ نظرگاه nazar-gâh
visual *adj., n.* بینایی binâyi بصرى basari ظاهرى zâheri
visual aids *n.* کمک های بصرى komak-hâye basari
visualization *n.* تجسم tajas~om تصور tasav~or
visualize *vi., vt.* تجسم کردن tajas~om kardan
تصور کردن tasav~or kardan
visually *adv.* بصرى basari بانگاه bâ-negâh
vital *adj.* حیاتی hayâti واجب vâjeb
vitalism *adj.* قدرت حیاتی qodrat hayâti
vitality *n.* شوق زندگی shoq-e' zendegi
vitalize *vt.* حیاتی کردن hayâti kardan
حیات بخشیدن hayât bakhshidan
vitally *adv.* بطور حیاتی betor-e' hayâti
vitamin *n.* ویتامین vitâmin
viva! *n.* زنده باد zendeh bâd!
vivacious *adj.* پر نشاط por-neshât
vivacity *n.* با نشاطی bâ-neshâti نشاط neshât
vivid *adj.* روشن roshan آشکار âshkâr سر زنده sar-zendeh
vividly *adv.* آشکاراً âsh-kâran بطور واضح be-tor-e' vâzeh
vixen *n.* روباه ماده rubâh-e' mâd~eh پتیاره patiâreh
vocabulary *n.* لغت loqat کلمه kalameh
vocal *adj., n.* صوتی soti خود بیان khod-bayân
vocal cords *np.* صوتی تارهای târ-hâ-ye' soti
vocalic *adj.* آوایی âvâyi
vocalist *n.* آوازه خوان âvâzeh-khân
vocalize *vt., vi.* به بیان آوردن be-bayân âvardan
vocally *adv.* شفاهاً shafâhan
vocation *n.* حرفه herfeh پیشه pisheh
vocational *adj.* حرفهایی herfeh-yi صنعتی san'ati
vogue *n.* مد mod محبوبیت mah-bubiyat
voice *n., vt.* صدا sedâ آواز âvâz بناء banâ'
voiced *adj., v.* باصدا bâ-sedâ
voiceless *adj., n., vt., vi.* بی صدا bi-sedâ گنگ gong
void *v.* خالی کردن khâli kardan باطل کردن bâtel kardan
void *n.* خالی khâli عارى 'âri
voidable *adj.* باطل شدنی bâtel-shodani
voided *n.* باطل شده bâtel shodeh خالی khâli

volatile *adj.* نزار farâr مزاج دمدمی damdami mezâj
volcanic *adj.* آتش نشانی âtash-feshâni
volcanize *n.* حرارت زیاد دادن harârat-e' ziâd dâdan
volcano *n.* آتش نشان âtash-feshân
volition *n.* اراده erâdeh تصمیم tasmim
volley *n., vt., vi.* شلیک کردن shelik kardan
توپ پس دادن tup pas dâdan
volleyball *n.* والیبال vâlibâl
volt *n.* ولت volt
voltage *n.* ولتاژ voltâzh
voltammeter *n.* ولت سنج volt-sanj
volume *n.* جلد jeld
volume *n.* گنجایش gonjâyesh ظرفیت zarfiyat حجم hajm
volume *n.* درجۀ صدا darejeh-ye' sedâ
voluminous *adj.* پر حجم por-hajm
voluntary *adj., n.* داوطلبانه dâv-talabâneh ارادی erâdi
volunteer *n., adj., vi., vt.* داوطلب شدن dâvtalab shodan
voluptuous *adj.* سکسی seksi شهوت انگیز shahvat-angiz
vomit *vi., vt.* استفراغ کردن estefrâq kardan بالا آوردن bâlâ âvardan
قی کردن qey kardan
voodoo *n.* جادو کردن jâdu kardan افسون کردن afsun kardan
voracious *adj.* حریص haris پر خور por-khor
voracity *n.* حرص hers پر خوری por-khori
vorn *n.* میخچه mikh-cheh
vortex *n.* گرداب gerd-âb
votable *adj.* رأی دادنی ra'y-dâdani
vote *n., vi., vt.* رأی دادن ra'y dâdan
voter *n.* رأی دهنده ra'y-dahandeh
vouch *vi., vt., n.* ضمانت کردن zemânat kardan
voucher *n., vt., vi.* رسید resid سند sanad ضمانت نامه zemânat-nâmeh
vow *n., vi.* سوگند خوردن sogand khordan نذر کردن nazr kardan
vowel *n., adj.* آوا âvâ مصوت mosav~at اعراب e'râb
vows *n.* سوگند sogand عهد 'ahd پیمان peymân
voyage *n.* سفر دریایی safar-e' daryâyi
voyager *n.* مسافر mosâfer
voyeur *n.* چشم چران cheshm-charân
voyeurism *n.* چشم چرانی cheshm-charâni
vulgar *adj.* رکیک rakik قبیح qabih

vulgarity *n.* قباحت qebâhat رکیکی rakiki
vulnerability *n.* آسیب پذیری âsib-paziri
vulnerable *adj.* قابل نفوذ qâbel-e' nofuz آسیب پذیر âsib-pazir
vulpine *n.* روباه صفت rubâh-sefat روباهی rubâhi
vulture *n.* کرکس karkas لاشخور lâsh-khor
vulturous *n.* لاشخور صفت lâsh-khor-sefat
vulva *n.* فرج farj
vying *adj., v.* رقابت کننده reqâbat-konandeh

W W w

W.C. *n.* مستراح mostarâh
wacko *n.* خل khol عوضى 'avazi
wacky *adj.* خنده دار khandeh-dâr خل مآب khol-maâb
wad *n.* دسته dasteh تکه tek~eh کهنه kohneh
wad *v.* دسته کردن dasteh kardan پنبه گذاشتن panbeh gozâshtan
wadding *n., v.* پنبه کارى panbeh-kâri
waddle *vi., n.* اردک وار راه رفتن ordak-vâr râh raftan
wade *vi., vt., n.* پیش رفتن pish raftan
wade in(to) *n.* دل بدریا زدن del be-daryâ zadan
wadi *n.* واحه vâheh
wafer *n., vt.* بادبزن bâd-bezan
waffle *n., vi., adj.* نون پنجره nun-panjereh
waft *n., vt.* حمل کردن haml kardan وزش vazesh
wag *v.* تکان دادن takân dâdan جنباندن jonbândan
wage *n.* مزد mozd دستمزد dast-mozd کارمزد kâr-mozd اجرت ojrat
wage *v.* دست زدن dast zadan مبادرت کردن mobâderat kardan
wage scale *n.* رتبۀ حقوق rotbeh-ye' hoquq
wage(war) *n.* جنگ کردن jang kardan
wage-earner *n.* حقوق بگیر hoquq-begir
wager *n.* شرط بستن shart bastan
wagon *n.* واگن vâgon گارى gâri ارابه arâbeh
wagoner *n.* واگن چى vâgon-chi گارى چى gâri-chi
waht's what *n.* حقیقت موضوع haqiqat mozu'
waif *n.* ول vel سر راهى sar-e' râhi
wail *vi., vt., n.* شیون کردن shivan kardan زار زدن zâr zadan
waist *n.* کمر kamar
waist-high *np.* تا کمر بالا tâ kamar bâlâ
waistband *n.* کمر بند kamar-band
waistline *n.* کمر kamar
wait *vi., vt.* صبر کردن sabr kardan منتظر شدن montazer shodan
wait(on tables) *n.* گارسونى کردن gârsoni kardan
wait(on/upon) *n.* پیشخدمتى کردن pish-khedmati kardan
wait(up) *n.* بیدار ماندن bidâr mândan
waiter *n.* گارسون gârson پیشخدمت pish-khedmat
waiting room *np.* اطاق انتظار otâq-e' entezâr
waitress *n.* پیشخدمت زن pish-khedmat-e' zan
waive *vt., vi.* صرفنظر کردن sarfe-nazar kardan نخواستن nakhâstan

wake *v.* بیدار کردن bidâr kardan بیدار شدن bidâr shodan
wake *n.* دنبالهٔ آب donbâleh-ye' âb
wake *n.* ختم khatm
wake-up call *n.* تلفن بیدار باش telefon-e' bidâr-bâsh
wakeful *adj.* بیدار bidâr مراقب morâqeb
waken *n.* بیدار شدن bidâr shodan بیدار کردن bidâr kardan
walk *n.* راه râh روی پیاده piâdeh-ravi پیشه pisheh
walk *v.* راه رفتن râh raftan قدم زدن qadam zadan
راه بردن râh bordan
walk(off with) *n.* دزدیدن dozdidan راحت بردن râhat bordan
walk(off) *n.* بیرون آمدن birun âmadan
walk(out on) *n.* گذاشتن و رفتن gozâshtan va raftan
walk(out) *n.* اعتصاب کردن e'tesâb kardan
walk-on *n.* نقش کوچک naqsh-e' kuchek
walkaway *n.* برد راحت bord-e' râhat
walkie-talkie *n.* بی سیم bi-sim
walking *adj., n.* راه رونده râh-ravandeh گردان gardân
walking papers *np.* برگ اخراج barg-e' ekhrâj
walking stick *np.* عصا 'asâ چوب دستی chub-dasti
walkout *n.* اعتصاب e'tesâb
wall *n., adj.* دیوار divâr
walled *n.* داخل دیوار dâkhel-e' divâr محصور mahsur
wallet *n.* کیف جیبی kif-e' jibi
walleyed *adj.* چشم بابا قوری cheshm-e' bâbâ-qori
wallop *vt.* سخت زدن sakht zadan
walloping *n., adj.* خیلی kheyli شکست shekast
wallow *vi., n.* غلطیدن qaltidan
wallpaper *n.* کاغذ دیواری kâqaz-divâri
walnut *n.* جوز گردو gerdu joz
walrus *n.* گراز دریایی gorâz-e' daryâ-yi
waltz *n., adj., vi., vt.* والس vâls
wan *adj.* رنگ پریده rang-parideh
wand *n.* چوب دست جادویی chub-dast-e' jâdu-yi
wander *vi., vt., n.* سرگردان بودن sar-gardân budan
آواره بودن âvâreh budan
wandering *adj., n.* سرگردانی آواره âvâreh sar-gardâni
wane *n.* محاق mohâq زوال zavâl افول oful
wane *v.* رو به زوال رفتن ru beh zavâl raftan

want *vt., n.* خواستن khâstan
want ad *np.* آگهی تقاضا âgahi-e' taqâzâ
want(in) *n.* تقاضای ورود کردن taqâzâ-ye' vorud kardan
want(out) *n.* تقاضای خروج کردن taqâzâ-ye' khoruj kardan
wanting *n.* بدون bedun-e' منهای menhâ-ye'
wanton *adj., n., vi., vt.* بیخودی bikhodi نافرمانی nâ-farmâni
war *adv., v., n., adj.* جنگ jang
war cry *np.* نعرهٔ جنگی na'reh-ye' jangi
war lord *n.* سردار جنگی sardâr-e' jangi
ward *n., vt.* بخش bakhsh
ward(off) *n.* دفع کردن daf' kardan
warden *n.* رئیس زندان ra'is-e' zendân سرپرست sar-parast
wardrobe *n.* لباسها lebâs-hâ البسه albaseh
wardship *n.* قیومیت qoyumiyat
ware *adj., v., n., vt.* جات jât آلات âlât
warehouse *n., vt.* انبار anbâr
warfare *n.* جنگ jang کارزار kâr-zâr
warlock *vt., n.* طلسم بند telesm-band
warm *adj., vt., vi.* گرم کردن garm kardan صمیمانه samimâneh
warm(up to) *n.* نزدیکتر شدن nazdik-tar shodan
رفیق شدن rafiq shodan
warm-blooded *adj.* خونگرم khun-garm
warm-hearted *adj.* دلگرمانه del-garmâneh خوش قلب khosh-qalb
warm-up *n.* گرمکن garm-kon
warmonger *n.* جنگ طلب jang-talab
warmth *n.* گرمی garmi حرارت harârat
warn *vt.* اخطار دادن ekhtâr dâdan آگاه کردن âgâh kardan
warning *n.* اخطار ekhtâr
warp *n.* کجی kaji تاب tâb پیچ pich
warp *v.* کج و کوله کردن kaj-o koleh kardan
منحرف کردن monharef kardan
warpath *n.* عازم جنگ 'âzem-e' jang
warped *n.* کج و کوله kaj-o koleh پیچ خورده pich-khordeh
warrant *n., vt.* اختیار دادن ekhtiâr dâdan
مجوز کردن mojav~az kardan
warrant officer *np.* استوار ostovâr
warranty *n.* ضمانت zemânat
warrent *n.* مجوز mojav~az حکم hokm حواله havâleh

warrior *n.* جنگ مرد jang-mard سلحشور salah-shur
رزمنده raz-mandeh

warship *n.* کشتی جنگی kashti-e' jangi

wart *n.* زگیل zegil

wart hog *np.* گراز وحشی gorâz-e' vahshi

wartime *n., adj.* زمان جنگ zamân-e' jang

wary *adj.* محتاط mohtât

wash *vt., n.* شستن shostan شستشو دادن shosteshu dâdan

wash(down) *n.* با آب شستن bâ âb shostan

wash(out) *n.* شستن shostan

washable *adj.* شستنی shos-tani

washboard *n.* تختۀ رخت شویی takhteh-ye' rakht shu-i

washbowl *n.* دست شویی dast-shuyi

washcloth *n.* کهنۀ رخت شویی kohneh-ye'- rakht-shu-i

washed-out *adj.* رنگ پریده rang parideh

washed-up *adj.* تمام شده tamâm-shodeh

washer *n.* واشر vâsher شوینده shuyandeh

washing *n.* شست و شو shost-o-shu

washing machine *np.* ماشین رخت شویی mâshin-e' rakht-shu-i

washout *n.* آب شست âb-shost

washrag *n.* کهنۀ رخت شویی kohneh-ye' rakht-shu-i

washroom *n.* اطاق دست شویی otâq-e' dast-shuyi

washy *adj.* شل âbaki آبکی shol

wasp *n.* زنبور zanbur

wastage *n.* اتلاف etlâf

waste *v.* تلف کردن talaf kardan ضایع کردن zâye' kardan
تباه کردن tabâh kardan

waste *adj.* پس مانده pas-mândeh بی مصرف bi-masraf مدفوع madfu'

wastebasket *n.* سبد آشغال sabad âshqâl

wasteful *adj.* تلف کن talaf-kon افراطی efrâti

wasteland *n.* بیابان biâbân

wastepaper *n.* کاغذ آشغال kâqaz-e' âshqâl

wasting *adj., v.* ضایعگر zâye'-gar

watch *n.* پاس pâs کشیک keshik

watch *n.* ساعت مچی sâ'at mochi

watch *v.* تماشا کردن tamâshâ kardan مراقبت کردن morâqebat kardan

watch(out) *n.* مواظب بودن movâzeb budan

watch(over) *n.* مراقب بودن morâqeb budan پاییدن pâyidan

watchdog *n.* مراقب morâqeb
watchful *adj.* مواظب movâzeb حواس جمع havâs-jam'
watchmaker *n.* ساعت ساز sâ'at-sâz
watchman *n.* گارد gârd نگهبان negah-bân
watchtower *n.* برج مراقبت borj-e' morâqebat
water *n.* آب âb
water *v.* آب دادن âb dâdan
water closet *np.* مستراح mostarâh
water cooler *np.* آبسرد کن âb-sard-kon
water front *n.* کنار آب kenâr-e' âb بار انداز bâr-andâz
water hole *np.* گودال آب godâl-e' âb حوضچه huz-cheh
water pipe *np.* قليان qal-yân
water snake *np.* مار آبی mâr-e' âbi
water supply *np.* ذخیرهٔ آب zakhireh-ye' âb
water tower *np.* برج آب borj-e' âb
water wheel *np.* چرخ آب charkh-e' âb
water(down) *n.* آبکی کردن âbaki kardan رقیق کردن raqiq kardan
water-color *adj.* آبرنگ âb-rang
water-cool *vt.* با آب خنک کردن bâ-âb khonak kardan
water-logged *n.* آب گرفته âb-gerefteh
water-ski *vi.* اسکی روی آب eski-e' ru-ye' âb
water-soluble *adj.* محلول در آب mahlul dar âb
waterfall *n.* آبشار âbshâr
watergate *n.* آبگیر âb-gir
waterless *adj.* بی آب bi-âb خشک khoshk
waterlight *n.* آب نگیر کیپ kip âb-nagir
watermark *n.* خط آب khat~-e' âb
watermelon *n.* هندوانه hendevâneh
waterproof *adj., n.* ضد آب zed~-e' âb
watershed *n.* آب ریز âb-riz
waterway *n.* آبراه âb-râh
waterworks *pl.* شرکت آب sherkat-e' âb
watery *adj.* خیس khis رقیق raqiq
watt *n.* وات vât
wave *n.* موج moj فر fer
wave *v.* تکان دادن takân dâdan دست تکان دادن dast takân dâdan
wave lenght *n.* طول موج tul-e' moj
waver *n., vi.* تردید کردن tardid kardan

متزلزل بودن .... motezal-zel budan
wavy *adj., n.* موجی moji نرنری fer-feri
wax *n.* موم mum
wax *n.* چرک cherk
wax *v.* برق انداختن barq andâkhtan
کم کم بزرگ شدن kam kam bozorg shodan
wax paper *np.* کاغذ شمعی kâqaz sham'i
way *n.* راه râh طریق tariq طرز tarz سبیل sabil
waybill *n.* بارنامه bâr-nâmeh
wayfarer *n.* راه رونده râh-râvandeh رهگذر rah-gozar
waygoing *adj., n.* روانه ای ravâneh-i
waylay *n.* در کمین نشستن dar kamin neshastan
wayside *n., adj.* کنار راه kenâr râh
wayward *adj.* خود سر khod-sar
wayworn *adj.* خسته از راه khasteh az râh
we *pro.* ما mâ
weak(en) *n.* ضعیف کردن za'if kardan ناتوان کردن nâ-tavân kardan
weak-kneed *adj.* سست sost بی عزم bi-'azm
weak-minded *adj.* سبک مغز sabok-maqz
weakliness *n.* ضعیفی za'ifi
weakling *n., adj.* موجود ضعیف mojud-e' za'if
weakly *adj., adv.* ضعیف المزاج za'ifol mezâj
weakness *n.* ضعف za'f ناتوانی nâ-tavâni
wealth *n.* ثروت servat
wealthy *adj.* ثروتمند servat-mand پولدار puldâr متمول motemav~el
متنعم motena'~em
wean *n., vt.* از شیر گرفتن az shir gereftan
weapon *n.* اسلحه aslaheh سلاح selâh حربه harbeh
wear *v.* پوشیدن pushidan تن کردن tan kardan
wear *v.* سائیدن sâ'idan فرسودن farsudan
wear *v.* شانه کردن shâneh kardan
wear and tear *np.* استهلاک estehlâk فرسایش farsâyesh
wear(down) *n.* خسته کردن khasteh kardan از رو بردن az-ru bordan
wear(off) *n.* کمتر شدن kam-tar shodan
wear(out) *n.* سایدن sâyidan خسته کردن khasteh kardan
wearable *adj., n.* پوشیدنی pushidani
weariness *n.* خستگی khastegi
wearisome *adj.* خسته کننده khasteh-konandeh

weary *adj.* خسته khasteh زده zadeh بیزار bizâr کسل kesel
weasel *n., vi.* راسو râsu موذی muzi
weather *n.* هوا havâ آب و هوا âb-o havâ
weather *v.* جان بدر بردن jân bedar bordan
weather *v.* باد دادن bâd dâdan
weathercock *n.* باد نما bâd-namâ
weathered *adj.* فرسوده farsudeh رنگ رفته rang-rafteh
weathering *n.* فرسایش farsâyesh شیب shib
weatherman *n.* هوا شناس havâ-shenâs
weave *vt., vi.* بافتن bâftan پیچیدن pichidan تنیدن tanidan
weaver *n.* بافنده bâfandeh نساج nas~âj
web *n., vt., vi.* پرده pardeh تار târ رشته reshteh
web-foot(ed) *n.* پا پرده‌ایی pâ-pardeh-i
webbed *adj., v.* پرده ای pardeh-i
webbing *v.* نوار محکم navâr-e' mohkam
wed *vt., vi.* ازدواج کردن ezdevâj kardan
بعقد درآمدن be'aqd dar âmadan
wedded *adj.* مزدوج mozdavaj عقدی 'aqdi
wedding *n.* عقد 'aqd ازدواج ezdevâj
wedge *n., vi.* گوه guh میان شکاف miân-shekâf
wedlock *n.* عقد 'aqd زناشویی zanâ-shuyi
wednesday *n.* چهارشنبه chahâr-shanbeh
wee *adj., n.* کوچولو kuchulu
wee hours *n.* ساعات اول sâ'ât-e' av~al
weed *n., v.* علف هرزه کندن 'alaf harzeh kandan
weed(out) *n.* وجین کردن vejin kardan
weeder *n.* وجین کن vejin-kon
weedy *adj.* پر علف por-'alaf دراز علی derâz-'ali
week *n., adv.* هفته hafteh
weekday *n., adj.* روز هفته ruz-e' hafteh
weekend *n., adj., vi.* آخر هفته âkhar-e' hafteh
weekly *adj., adv., n.* هفتگی haftegi
weenie/weeny *n.* سوسیس sosis دودول dudul
weep *v.* گریه کردن geryeh kardan آب گرفتن âb gereftan
weeper *v.* گریه کن geryeh-kon
weeping willow *np.* بید مجنون bid-e' majnun
weft *n.* پود pud
weigh *vt.* سنجیدن sanjidan سنگین کردن سبک sabok sangin kardan

weigh(in) *n.* وزن کشی کردن vazn-keshi kardan
weight *v.* وزن کردن vazn kardan کشیدن keshidan
weight *n.* وزن vazn سنگینی sangini وزنه vazneh
weights *n.* وزنه vazneh هالتر hâlter
weir *n.* آبگیر âb-gir سد ماهیگیر sad~-e' mâhi-gir
weird *adj.* غریب qarib عجیب 'ajib
weirdo *n.* عوضی 'avazi
welcome *v.* خوش آمد گفتن kosh-âmad goftan
خوشی پذیرفتن be-khoshi paziroftan
welcome *v.* به نیکی گرفتن be-niki gereftan
welcome *adj.* مطلوب matlub مورد پسند mored-e' pasand
weld *n.* جوش دادن jush dâdan
welder *n.* جوشکار jush-kâr
welding *n.* جوشکاری jush-kâri
welfare *n.* رفاه refâh خیر kheyr
welhead *n.* سرچشمه sar-cheshmeh
well *adv., adj., int., n.* خوب khub بخوبی be-khubi خیلی kheyli
well *adv., adj., int., n.* والله vâl~ âh! خب khob
well *adv., adj., int., n.* چاه châh قنات qanât کاریز kâriz
well-balanced *adj.* میزان mizân سالم sâlem
well-behaved *adj.* خوش رفتار khosh-raftâr
well-being *n.* سلامتی salâmati
well-bred *adj.* با تربیت bâ-tarbiyat
well-chosen *n.* حساب کرده hesâb-kardeh
well-doer *n.* نیکو کار niku-kâr
well-done *adj.* کار خوب kâr-e' khub
بارک الله bârekal~ âh!
well-done *adj.* خوب پخته khub-pokhteh
well-fed *adj.* خوب خورده khub-khurdeh فربه farbeh
well-heeled *adj.* پولدار pul-dâr
well-informed *n.* با اطلاع bâ-et~ elâ'
well-intentioned *adj.* بدون منظور bedun-e' manzur
well-known *adj.* معروف ma'ruf شناخته شده shenâkhteh shodeh
well-made *n.* خوش ساخت khosh-sâkht
well-mannered *adj.* با ادب bâ-adab
well-meant *n.* خوش نیت khosh-niyat
well-off *adj.* مرفه moraf~ah پولدار pul-dâr
well-preserved *n.* خوب مانده khub-mândeh

well-proportioned *adj.* متناسب motenâseb موزون mozun
well-read *adj.* کتاب خوانده ketâb-khândeh مطلع mot~ale'
well-spoken *adj.* خوش صحبت khosh-soh-bat
well-thought-of *adj.* مورد پسند mored-e' pasand محبوب mah-bub
well-to-do *adj.* مرفه moraf~ah پولدار pul-dâr
well-wisher *n.* خیرخواه kheyr-khâh
well-wishing *adj., n.* خیرخواهی kheyr-khâhi
well-worn *adj.* کهنه kohneh مبتذل mobtazal
welldoing *n., adj.* نیکو کاری niku-kâri
wellspring *n.* سر چشمه sar-cheshmeh
welsh *vi.* جر زدن jer zadan زیرش زدن ziresh zadan
welt *n., vt.* کتک زدن kotak zadan مغزی maqzi
welter *vi., adj., n.* غلطیدن qaltidan
welterweight *n.* سبک وزن sabok-vazn
wench *n., vi.* دختر dokhtar دختر بازی کردن dokhtar-bâzi kardan
west *n., adj.* غرب qarb باختر bâkhtar مغرب maqreb
westerly *adj., adv., n.* غربی qarbi بطرف غرب be-taraf-e' qarb
western *n.* غربی qarbi کابویی kâbo-i
westerner *n.* غربی qarbi
westernize *vt.* غربی کردن qarbi kardan
غرب زده کردن qarb-zadeh kardan
westward *adj., adv., n.* بطرف غرب be-taraf qarb باختری bâkhtari
wet *adj., n., vt., vi.* خیس کردن khis kardan تر کردن tar kardan
wet-nurse *vt.* دایه dâyeh
wetback *n.* ویزیتور قاچاقچی visitor-e' qâchâq-chi
wether *n.* گوسفند اخته gusfand akhteh
whack *vt., vi., n.* محکم زدن mohkam zadan
whale *n., vt.* نهنگ nahang بالن bâlon
whaleboat *n.* کشتی نهنگ گیر kashti-e' nahang-gir
whaling *n., v.* نهنگ گیری nahang-giri
wharf *n.* بارانداز bâr-andâz اسکله eskeleh
what *pro., n., adj., adv.* آنچه ân-cheh چیزی که chizi-keh
what *pro., n., adj., adv.* هرچه har-cheh
what *pro., n., adj., adv.* چی؟ chi? چه؟ cheh?
what(for) *n.* برای چه barây-e' cheh?
what(have you) *n.* غیره qeyreh هرچی har-chi
what(if) *n.* چی اگر؟ chi agar ?
what(it takes) *n.* چیزیکه لازم است chizi keh lâzem-ast

what(of it) *n.* چی؟ که keh chi?
whatever *pro.* هرچی har-chi هر چه har-cheh هر قدر har-qadr
whatnot *n.* خرت و پرت khert-o pert
whatsoever *pro., adj.* هر چه har-cheh بهیچ وجه behich-vajh
wheat *n.* گندم gandom
wheel *n., vt., vi.* چرخ charkh
wheel chair *n.* صندلی چرخ دار sandali-e' charkh-dâr
wheelbarrow *n.* چرخ دستی charkh dasti
wheelbase *n.* فاصلهٔ دو چرخ fâseleh-ye' do-charkh
wheeler dealer *n.* بساز بفروش be-sâz be-frush
wheels *n.* ماشین mâshin
wheelwright *n.* چرخ ساز charkh-sâz
wheeze *n., vi.* خس خس کردن khes-khes kardan
wheezy *adj.* خس خسی khes-khesi
whell *n.* با چرخ بردن bâ-charkh bordan
when *adv., con., pro., n.* وقتیکه vaqti-keh
when *adv., con., pro., n.* کی key چه وقت ؟ cheh-vaqt
whenas *con.* آنقدر که ânqadr-keh
whence *adv.* از کجا az kojâ
whencesoever *adv., con.* از هر کجا az har-kojâ
whenever *con.* هر وقت که har-vaqt keh هرگاه har-gâh
whensoever *con., pro., n.* هرگاه har-gâh
where *adv., con., pro., n.* کجا kojâ
where *adv., con., pro., n.* جایی که jâyi-keh
whereabouts *n.* حدود تقریبی hodud-e' taqribi
whereas *con., n.* در حالیکه dar hâli-keh حال آنکه hâl ân-keh
whereat *adv., con.* در کجا dar kojâ
whereby *con., adv.* بدان وسیله bedân-vasileh
wherefore *n.* بدان جهت bedân jahat
wherefrom *con., adv.* از کجا az kojâ
wherein *con., adv.* در آنجا dar ân-jâ در کجا dar kojâ
whereinto *con.* در توی آن dar tu-ye' ân
whereof *adv., con.* در کجا dar kojâ در آنجا dar ânjâ
whereon *con., adv.* بر روی چی bar ru-ye' chi
wheresoever *n.* در هرکجا dar har-kojâ
whereto *con., adv.* به کجا beh-kojâ به چی beh-chi
whereupon *con.* که keh در نتیجه dar natijeh
wherever *con., adv.* هر جا که har-jâ keh هر کجا har-kojâ

wherewith *n.* با آن bâ-ân
whet *vt., n.* تیز کردن tiz kardan باز کردن bâz kardan
whether *con., pro.* که آیا keh âyâ خواه khâh چه cheh
whetstone *n.* سنگ چاقو تیزکنی sang-e' châqu tiz-koni
whetter *n.* تیز کن tiz-kon
whew *int., n.* پیف pif!
whey *n.* کشک kashk
which *pro., adj.* کدام یک kodâm yek
which *pro., adj.* که keh
whichever *pro., adj.* هر کدام har-kodâm
whichsoever *pro., adj.* هرکدام که har-kodâm keh
whiff *n., vi., vt.* بو bu پف pof دم dam
while *con., n., pre., vt.* زمانی که zamâni-keh مادامیکه mâdâmi-keh
while *con., n., pre., vt.* زمان zamân مدت mod~at
while(away) *n.* گذراندن gozarândan
whilst *con.* زمانی که zamâni-keh مادامیکه mâdâmi-keh
whim *n.* هوس havas
whimper *vi., vt., n.* ناله کردن nâleh kardan
whimsical *adj.* هوسی havasi بوالهوس bol-havas
whimsical *n.* هوسی havasi
whine *n.* ناله nâleh زوزه zuzeh ضجه zaj~eh
whine *n., vi.* ناله کردن nâleh kardan زوزه کشیدن zuzeh keshidan
whip *n.* شلاق shal~âq تازیانه tâziâneh
whip *n.* ناظم nâzem رئیس ra'is
whip *v.* شلاق زدن shal~âq zadan زدن zadan در آوردن dar âvardan
whip(up) *n.* جمع کردن jam kardan دست و پا کردن dast-o pâ kardan
whipped cream *n.* خامه khâmeh
whipping *n., v.* شلاق زنی shal~âq-zani
whipping boy *np.* کتک خور kotak-khor
whirl *vi., vt., n.* چرخیدن charkhidan چرخاندن charkhândan
whirlpool *n.* گرداب gerd-âb
whirlwind *n.* گردباد gerd-bâd
whish *vi., n.* فش fesh
whisk *n.* گردگیر gard-gir
whisk *v.* قاپ زدن qâp zadan تند بردن tond bordan
whisker(s) *n.* سبیل sebil
whiskered *n.* سبیلو sebilu
whisper *vi., vt.* پچ پچ کردن pech-pech kardan

در گوشی گفتن .... dar-gushi goftan
whispering *n., adj.* نجوایی najvâyi شرشری shor-shori
whistle *n., vi., vt.* سوت زدن sut zadan سوت کشیدن sut keshidan
whistle(for) *n.* سماق مکیدن somâq mekidan
white *adj., n., vt.* سفید sefid سفیدی sefidi سفیده sefideh
white flag *np.* پرچم تسلیمی parcham taslimi
white gold *np.* طلای سفید talâ-ye' sefid
white heat *np.* التهاب hayâjân هیجان eltehâb
White House *n.* کاخ سفید kâkh-e' sefid
white lie *n.* دروغ مصلحتی doruq-e' maslahati
white meat *np.* گوشت سفید gusht-e' sefid
white paper *n.* گزارش رسمی gozâresh-e' rasmi
white-collar *n.* اداره ای edâreh-i کارمند kâr-mand
white-faced *adj.* سفید رو sefid-ru
white-hot *adj.* داغ داغ dâq-e' dâq
whitebread *n.* نان سفید nân sefid
whitecap *n.* موج کف دار moj-e' kaf-dâr
whitefish *n.* سفید ماهی sefid-mâhi
whiten *n.* سفید کردن sefid kardan
whitening *n.* سفید کاری sefid-kâri
whitewash *n., vt.* ماست مالی کردن mâst-mâli kardan
whither *n., adv., con.* بکجا be-kojâ جایی که jâyi-keh
whittle *vt., vi., n.* تراشیدن tarâshidan کم کردن kam kardan
whity *n.* سفید رو sefid-ru برفی barfi
whiz *vi., vt., n.* ماهر mâher نابغه nâbeqeh
whiz(z) *n.* ماهر mâher نابغه nâbeqeh وز کردن qezh kardan
who *pro.* کی ؟ ki? چه کسی؟ che-kasi?
who *pro.* که keh
who('s who) *n.* کی کیه ki kiyeh
whodunit *n.* کی کرده؟ ki kardeh? معمایی mo'am~âyi
whoever *pro.* هرکی har-ki هرکه har-keh هر کس که har-kas keh
whole *adj., n.* تمام tamâm یک تکه yek-tek~eh کل kol قاطبه qâtebeh
whole *adj., n.* کامل kâmel صحیح sahih
whole milk *np.* شیر خامه دار shir-e' khâmeh-dâr
whole-wheat *adj.* تمام گندم tamâm gandom
wholehearted(ly) *n.* از ته دل az tah-e' del
wholeness *n.* کلیت kol~iyat کمال kamâl
wholesale *n., adj., adv., vt.* عمده فروشی 'omdeh-forushi

wholesaler *n.* عمده فروش 'omdeh-forush بنكدار bonak-dâr
wholesome *n.* سالم sâlem
wholly *adv.* تماماً tamâman كاملاً kâmelan
whom *pro.* به كى be-ki كى را ki-râ
whomever *n.* هر كى har-ki هركسى har-kasi
whoop *n., vi.* فرياد كشيدن faryâd keshidan جيغ كشيدن jiq keshidan
whoopee! *n.* آخ جون âkh jun!
whooping cough *n.* سياه سرفه siâh-sorfeh
whoops! *n.* اى واى ey-vây!
whop *n., vt.* زدن zadan
whopper *n.* بزرگ bozorg گنده gondeh
whopping *adj., v.* خيلى بزرگ kheyli bozorg سرسام آور sar-sâm-âvar
whore *n., vi., vt.* جنده jendeh فاحشه fâhesheh
whorehouse *n.* جنده خانه jendeh-khâneh
whose *pro.* مال كى mâl-e' ki
whosesoever *pro.* مال هر كى mâl-e' har-ki
why *adv., con., n., int.* چرا cherâ چى chi براى barâ-ye' chi
wick *n.* فتيله fetileh
wicked *adj.* پست past لييم la'im
wickedness *n.* پستى pasti شرارت sharârat دنائت denâ'at
wide *adj., adv., n.* پهن pahn عريض 'ariz فراخ farâkh گشاد goshâd
wide *adj., adv., n.* وسيع vasi مختلف mokh-talef
wide *adj., adv., n.* باز bâz گشاد goshâd
wide-angle *adj.* زاويۀ پهن zâvieh-ye' pahn
wide-awake *n.* بيدار بيدار bidâr-e' bidâr
wide-eyed *adj.* با چشم باز bâ cheshm-e' bâz
wide-open *adj.* باز باز bâz-e' bâz
widely *adv.* بطرز وسيع betarz-e' vasi'
widen *vt., vi.* پهن كردن pahn kardan گشاد كردن goshâd kardan
widespread *adj.* متداول motedâvel همه جايى hameh-jâyi
widow *n., vt.* زن بيوه zan-e' biveh
widower *n.* مرد بيوه mard-e' biveh
width *n.* پهنا pahnâ عرض 'arz
wield *vt.* در دست داشتن dar-dast dâshtan اعمال كردن e'mâl kardan
wiener *n.* سوسيس sosis
wife *n., vi., vt.* زن zan همسر hamsar زوجه zojeh عيال 'ayâl
wig *n., vt.* كلاه گيس kolâh-gis
wiggle *n., vi., vt.* وول خوردن vul khordan قر دادن qer dâdan

wiggly *adj.* وول ووللی vul-vuli
wigwag *vt., vi., n.* ارتباط پرچمی ertebât-e′ parcham
wigwam *n.* چادر مخروطی châdor-e′ makhruti
wild *adj., adv.* وحشیانه vahshiâneh
wild *adj., adv.* وحش vahsh
wild *adj., adv.* وحشی vahshi جنگلی jangali خود رو khod-ro
wild boar *np.* گراز وحشی gorâz-e′ vahshi
wild fire *n.* آتشزا âtash-zâ
wild rue *n.* اسپند espand
wild thyme *n.* کاکوتی kâkuti
wild-eyed *adj.* نگاه هراسان negâh-e′ harâsân
wild-goose chase *np.* دنبال نخود سیاه donbâl-e′ nokhod siâ
wildcat *n.* گربه وحشی gorbeh-ye′ vahshi
wildcat strike *n.* اعتصاب غیر قانونی e′tesâb-e′ qeyr-e′ qânuni
wilderness *n.* طبیعت وحش tabi′at-e′ vahsh بیابان biâbân
wile *n., vt.* کلک زدن kalak zadan
will *n.* اراده erâdeh نیت niyat خواست khast مشیت mashiyat
will *n.* وصیت نامه vasiy~at-nâmeh
will *v.* اراده کردن erâdeh kardan وصیت کردن vasiyat kardan
willful *adj.* ارادهای erâdeh-i قصدی qasdi
willies *pl.* دل شوری del-shuri
willing *adj.* مایل mâyel حاضر hâzer
willingness *n.* میل meyl رضایت rezâyat
willow *n.* بید bid
wilt *n., v., vi.* پژمرده شدن pazh-mordeh shodan وا رفتن vâ raftan
wily *adj.* ناقلا nâ-qolâ موذی muzi
win *vi., vt., n.* بردن bordan پیروز شدن piruz shodan
win(over) *n.* بدست آوردن be-dast âvardan
wince *vi., n.* جا خوردن jâ khordan
wind *n.* باد bâd بادی bâdi نفس nafas
wind *v.* پیچیدن pichidan کوک کردن kuk kardan
wind(down) *n.* آرامتر شدن ârâm-tar shodan
    کوک در رفتن kuk dar raftan
wind(off) *n.* باز کردن bâz kardan
wind(up) *n.* تمام کردن tamâm kardan کوک کردن kuk kardan
windbag *n.* پر حرف por-harf
windbreak *n.* باد شکن bâd-shekan باد گیر bâd-gir
windbreaker *n.* ژاکت باد گیر zhâkat-e′ bâd-gir

winded *vt.* بی نفس bi-nafas
winder *n.* کوک کن kuk-kon پیچ pich
winding *n., vt., adj.* پیچ پیچی pich-pichi
windmill *n., vt.* آسیای بادی âsiâ-ye' bâdi
window *n.* پنجره panjereh
window *n.* ویترین vitrin
window shade *n.* آفتاب گیر âftâb-gir پرده pardeh
window-shopping *vi.* ویترین تماشایی vitrin-tamâshâyi
windshield *n.* شیشۀ جلو shisheh-ye' jelo
windshield wipers *n.* برف پاک کن barf pâk-kon
windstorm *n.* طوفان باد tufân-e' bâd
wine *n., adj., vt., vi.* شراب sharâb می mey باده bâdeh نبیذ nabiz
wineglass *n.* لیوان شراب livân-e' sharâb
winery *n.* کارخانۀ شراب سازی kâr-khâneh-ye' sharâbsâzi
winfall *n.* باد آورده bâd-âvardeh
wing *v.* زخمی کردن zakhmi kardan
wing *n., vt., vi.* بال bâl پره pareh
wing *n.* بخش bakhsh جناح jenâh
winged *adj.* بالدار bâl-dâr
wingless *adj.* بی بال bi-bâl
wink *vi., vt., n.* چشمک زدن chesh-mak zadan
winning *n., v., adj.* برد bord پیروزی piruzi برنده barandeh
winnow *vt., vi., n.* باد دادن bâd dâdan
wino *n.* باده نوش bâdeh-nush می خواره mey-khâreh
گدای مست gedây-e' mast
winsome *adj.* دلکش del-kash خوش ادا khosh-adâ
winter *n., adj., vi.* زمستان zemestân
winterkill *v., n.* سرما زدگی sarmâ-zadegi
wintertime *n.* فصل زمستان fasl-e' zemestân
wipe *n.* پاک کردن pâk kardan خشک کردن khoshk kardan
wipe(out) *n.* ازبین بردن az beyn bordan
wiper *n., adj., vt.* پاک کن pâk-kon
wire *v.* سیم کشی کردن sim-keshi kardan
wire *v.* تلگراف کردن telegrâf kardan
wire *n., adj., vt., vi.* سیم sim مفتول maftul
wire cutter *np.* سیم بر sim-bor
wireless *n.* بی سیم bi-sim
wireman *n.* سیم کش sim-kesh

wiring *n., adj.* سیم کشی sim-keshi
wiry *n.* جالاک باریک bârik châlâk
wisdom *n.* دانایی dânâ-yi عقل 'aql خرد kherad
wisdom tooth *n.* دندان عقل dandân-e' 'aql
wise *adj., vt.* دانا dânâ عاقل 'âqel خردمند kherad-mand
　　　　فرزانه farzâneh
wise guy *n.* بچه پر رو bach~eh por-ru مردم آزار mardom-âzâr
wise(up) *n.* آگاه شدن âgâh shodan
wisecrack *n., vi., vt.* متلک گفتن mat~alak goftan
　　　　مزه انداختن mazeh andâkhtan
wisely *n.* عاقلانه 'âqelâneh
wish *vt., vi., n.* آرزو داشتن ârezu dâshtan آرزو کردن ârezu kardan
wishbone *n.* جناغ jenâq
wishful *adj.* آرزومند ârezu-mand خواهان khâhân
wishful thinking *np.* خوش خیالی khosh-khiâli
wishy-washy *n.* شل و ول shol-o vel آبکی âbaki
wisp *n., vt.* ذره zar~eh دسته dasteh
wispy *adj.* نازک nâzok
wistful *adj.* مشتاق moshtâq
wit *n.* عقل 'aql هوش hush مشعر mash'ar
wit and wisdom *n.* عقل و شعور 'aql-o sho'ur
witch *n., vt., adj., vi.* جادوگر jâdu-gar عجوزه 'ajuzeh
witch doctor *n.* جادوگر قبیله jâdu-gar-e' gabileh
witchcraft *n.* جادوگری jâdu-gari سحر sehr
with *n., pre.* با bâ بوسیله bevasileh-e'
withdraw *vt.* عقب نشینی 'aqab-neshini برداشت bar-dâsht
withdrawn *v., adj.* کناره گرفته kenâreh gerefteh
　　　　توخودرفته tu-khod rafteh
wither *n.* پژمرده pazh-mordeh ضعیف شدن za'if shodan
withhold *vt., vi.* پیش خود نگهداشتن pish-e' khod negah dâshtan
within *adv., n.* درظرف dar-zarf-e'
within *adv., n.* در dar توی tu-ye' درحدود dar-hodud-e' داخل dâkhel
without *pre.* بدون bedun-e' بی bi بیرون birun
withstand *vt., vi.* تحمل کردن taham~ol kardan
　　　　طاقت آوردن tâqat âvardan
witness *adj.* شاهد shâhed گواه gavâh
witness *v.* شهادت دادن shahâdat dâdan گواهی دادن gavâhi dâdan
witticism *n.* بانمکی bâ-namaki بذله گویی bazleh-guyi

wittily *adv.* شوخی شوخی shukhi shukhi
witty *adj.* زیرک zirak بانمک bâ-namak نکته سنج nokteh-sanj
wiz *n.* نابغه nâbeqeh اعجوبه o'jubeh
wizard *n., adj.* جادوگر jâdu-gar
wobble *n.* لنبر دادن lanbar dâdan مردد بودن morad~ad budan
wobbly *adj.* بالنبر bâ-lanbar
woe *n., int.* غم qam محنت mehnat
woeful *adj.* غمگین qam-gin
wolf *n., vt., vi.* گرگ gorg زن باز zan-bâz
wolf dog *np.* سگ گله sag-e' gal~eh
woman *v., n., adj.* زن zan
womanhood *n.* زنانگی zanânegi زنان zanân
womanish *adj.* زن صفت zan-sefat
womanize *vt., vi.* زن بازی کردن zân-bâzi kardan
womanly *adj., adv.* زنانه zanâneh
womb *n.* رحم rahem
women *n., v.* زنان zanân زنها zan-hâ
womenfolk(s) *n.* زن جماعت zan jamâ'at فامیل زن fâmil-e' zan
ناموس nâ-mus
wonder *v.* درحیرت بودن dar heyrat budan
تعجب کردن tâ'aj~ob kardan
wonder *n.* شگفتی shegefti حیرت heyrat
wonder-stricken *adj.* متحیر motehay~er
wonderful *adj.* عالی 'âli شگفت انگیز shegeft-angiz
wondering *adj.* متعجب mote'aj~eb
wonderland *n.* سرزمین عجایب sar-zamin-e' 'ajâyeb
wonderment *n.* تعجب ta'aj~ob حیرت heyrat
wonderwork *n.* معجزه mo'jezeh
wont *adj., n., vt., vi.* عادت کردن 'âdat kardan
wood *n., adj., vt., vi.* چوب chub
woodcraft *n.* چوب سازی chub-sâzi
woodcutter *n.* چوب بر chub-bor هیزم شکن hizom-shekan
woodcutting *n.* چوب بری chub-bori
wooded *adj.* پردرخت por-derakht
wooden *n.* چوبی chubi بیجان bi-jân
woodland *n.* جنگل jangal
woodpecker *n.* دارکوب dâr-kub
woodpecker *n.* دارکوب dâr-kub هدهد hod-hod

woodshed *n., vi.* انبارچوب anbâr-e' chub
woodsman *n.* جنگل نشین jangal-neshin
woody *adj., n.* پردرخت por-derakht
wool *n., adj.* پشم pashm صوف sof
woolen *n.* پشمی pashmi
woolgathering *n.* خیال بافی khiâl-bâfi قازچرانی qâz-charâni
woozy *adj.* شنگول shangul
word *n.* کلمه kalameh لغت logat واژه vâzheh
word association *np.* تداعی معانی tadâ'i-e' ma'âni
word of God *n.* کلام الله kalâmol~âh
word of honor *np.* قول شرف qol-e' sharaf
word of mouth *n.* دهن بدهنی dahan be-dahani
word order *np.* ترتیب لغات tartib-e' loqât
wordage *n.* لغات loqât
wordbook *n.* لغت نامه loqat-nâmeh
wording *n.* کلمه بندی kalameh-bandi جمله بندی jomleh-bandi
wordless *adj.* بیجواب bi-javâb زبان گرفته zabân-gerefteh
wordplay *n.* بازی باکلمات bâzi bâ kalamât
wordy *adj., vi., vt.* پرکلمه por-kalameh
work *n., adj., vi., vt.* کارکردن kâr kardan
بکارانداختن be-kâr andâkhtan
work of art *np.* شاهکارهنری shâh-kâr-e' honari
work off *n.* باکارکم کردن bâ kâr kam kardan
work sheet *np.* کارنامه kâr-nâmeh
work(out) *n.* حل کردن hal kardan درست کردن dorost kardan
work(out) *n.* تمرین کردن tamrin kardan
work(up) *n.* ترقی کردن taraq~i kardan تحریک کردن tahrik kardan
workable *adj.* عملی 'amali
workbook *n.* کتاب کار ketâb-e' kâr
کتاب دستور عمل ketâb-e' dastur-e' 'amal
workday *n., adj.* روزکار ruz-e' kâr
worker *n.* کارگر kâr-gar
working *n.* کاری kâri اجرایی ejrâyi
working class *np.* طبقهٔ کارگر tabaqeh-ye' kâr-gar
working papers *np.* پروانهٔ کار parvâneh-ye' kâr
workingman *n.* کارکن kâr-kon کارگر kâr-gar
workingwoman *n.* زن کارگر zan-e' kâr-gar
workmanship *n.* استادی ostâdi هنردستی honar-e' dasti

workout *n.* تمرین tamrin
workroom *n.* اطاق کار otâq-e' kâr
workshop *n.* کارخانه kâr-khâneh تعمیرخانه ta'mir-khâneh
worktable *n.* میزکار miz-e' kâr
workweek *n.* هفتهٔ کار hafteh-ye' kâr
world *n.* دنیا donyâ جهان jahân عالم 'âlam
world power *np.* قدرت جهانی qodrat-e' jahâni
world-wide *n.* تمام جانی tamâm-jahâni سراسردنیا sarâ-sar-e' donyâ
worldly *n.* دنیوی donyavi مادی mâd~i
worldlywise *n.* دنیادیده donyâ-dideh
worm *n.* کرم kerm
worm *v.* لولیدن lulidan باکلک تورفتن bâ-kalak tu raftan
worm-eaten *adj.* کرم خرده kerm-khordeh
wormy *n.* کرمدار kerm-dâr کرمکی kermaki
worn *v.* رفته rafteh خورده شده khordeh-shodeh
worn-out *v.* ساییده شده sâ'ideh-shodeh فرسوده farsudeh
worriment *n.* ناراحتی nârâhati
worrisome *adj., vt., n.* ناراحت کننده nârâhat-konandeh
غصه خور qos~eh-khor
worry *vi., vt., n.* ناراحت بودن nârâhat budân
غصه خوردن qos~eh khordan
worse *adj., adv.* بدتر bad-tar
worsen *vt., vi.* بدتر کردن bad-tar kardan
worship *n., vt., vi.* پرستیدن parastidan عبادت کردن 'ebâdat kardan
worshipper *n.* پرستنده parastandeh عابد 'âbed
ستایش کننده setâyesh-konandeh
worst *adj., adv., n., vt.* بدترین bad-tarin
worth *pre., vi.* ارزش arzesh بها bahâ
worth-while *n.* ارزشدار arzesh-dâr
worthily *adv.* بطورشایسته be-tor-e' shâyesteh
worthiness *n.* شایستگی shâyestegi لیاقت liâqat
worthless *adj.* بی ارزش bi-arzesh ناچیز nâ-chiz
worthy *adj., n.* شایسته shâyesteh درخور dar-khor لایق lâyeq
قابل qâbel
worthy of praise *n.* شایان تمجید shâyân-e' tamjid
would *v.* کوک kuk
would-be *n.* احتمالی ehtemâli امکانی emkâni
wound *vt., vi.* زخم zakhm زخمی کردن zakhmi kardan جراحت jarâhat

woven *v.* بافته bâfteh
wow! *n.* وای vây !
wrack *n., vi.* لا یه lâyeh فنا fanâ
wrangle *vi., vt., n.* مشاجره کردن moshâjereh kardan
گله کردن geleh kardan
wrap *v.* پوشاندن pushândan پیچیدن pichidan
wrap *n.* پوشش pushesh بسته basteh لفافه lafâfeh
wrapper *n.* پوشش pushesh
wrapping *n., v.* پوششی pusheshi
wrapping paper *n.* کاغذ بسته بندی kâqaz-e' basteh-bandi
wrath *n., adj.* خشم khashm غضب qazab
wrathful *adj.* خشمناک khashm-nâk
wreak *vt.* موردقراردادن mored qarâr dâdan باعث شدن bâ'es shodan
wreak havoc *n.* خرابی ببارآوردن kharâbi be-bâr âvardan
wreath *n., vt., vi.* حلقهٔ گل halqeh-ye' gol
wreck *v.* شکستن shekastan خراب کردن kharâb kardan
wreck *n.* تصادف tasâdof خرابی kharâbi
wreckage *n.* خرابی kharâbi باقیمانده bâqi-mândeh
wrecker *n.* خرابکار kharâb-kâr مخرب mokhar~eb
wrecking *n.* تخریب takh-rib اوراق orâq
wrecking crew *n.* گروه اوراقچی goruh-e' orâq-chi
wrecking yard *n.* دکان اوراقچی dokân-e' orâq-chi
اسقاط خانه esqât-khâneh
wren *n.* گنجشگ gonjeshg سسک sesk
wrench *vt., vi., n.* آچار âchâr پیچ pich دادن کش kesh dâdan
wrest *n.* پیچاندن pichândan بزورگرفتن be-zur gereftan
wrestle *vi., vt., n.* کشتی گرفتن koshti gereftan
wrestler *n.* کشتی گیر kosthi-gir
wrestling *n.* کشتی koshti
wretch *n.* بدبخت bad-bakht مفلس mofles
wretched *n.* پست past نکبت بار nekbat-bâr
wriggle *n.* وول خوردن vul khordan لولیدن lulidan
wriggly *adj.* وولولی vul-vuli مارپیچ mâr-pich
wring *vt., vi., n.* چلاندن chalândan نشردن feshordan
wringer *n.* آبگیر âb-gir
wrinkle *n.,v.* چین خوردن chin khordan چروک دادن choruk dâdan
آژنگ âzhang
wrinkly *adj.* چین دار chin-dâr چروک خورده choruk-khordeh

wrist *n.* مچ moch
wrist watch *np.* ساعت مچی sâ'at mochi
wristband *n.* مچ بند moch-band سرآستین sar-âstin
writ *n., v.* حکم hokm
write *vt., vi.* نوشتن neveshtân
write(down) *n.* ثبت کردن یادداشت yâd-dâsht sabt kardan
write(off) *n.* قلم زدن qalam zadan
write(out) *n.* تمام نوشتن tamâman neveshtan
write(up) *n.* بحساب نوشتن be-hesâb neveshtan
write-in *adj., n.* رأی دلخواه rây-e' del-khâh
write-up *n.* ستایش نامه setâyesh-nâmeh
writer *n.* نویسنده nevisandeh نگارنده negârandeh
writhe *n.* بخود پیچیدن be-khod pichidan
writing *n., v.* نوشته neveshteh
writing-desk *n.* میزتحریر miz-e' tahrir
wrong *adj., n., adv., vt.* اشتباه eshtebâh غلط qalat نادرست nâ-dorost
عوضی 'avazi
wrong-headed *adj.* خیره سر khireh-sar
wrongdoer *n.* آدم نادرست âdam-e' nâ-dorost
wrongdoing *n.* نادرستی nâ-dorosti
wrongful *adj.* خطا khatâ غلط qalat
wrought *v., adj.* ساخته kufteh کوفته sâkhteh
wrought-iron *adj.* آهن صنعتی âhan-e' san'ati

X X x

X-mas *n.* کریسمس keris-mas
X-ray *n.* اشعهٔ ایکس asha'eh-ye' iks
xenophile *n.* بیگانه پرست bigâneh-parast
xenophobia *n.* ترس ازبیگانه tars az bigâneh
بیگانه هراسی bigâneh-harâsi
Xerxes *n.* خشایارشاه khashâyâr shâh
xylophone *n.* سنتورچوبی santur-e' chubi

Y Y ʏ

yacht *n., vi.* قایق مجلل qâyeq-e' mojal~al
yachting *n.* قایق سواری qâyeq-savâri
yachtsman *n.* قایق دار qâyeq-dâr
yahoo *n.* یابو yâbu
yak *n., vi.* گاومیش gâv-mish
yank *vt., vi., n.* یکهوکشیدن yek-ho keshidan
yap *vi., vt., n.* شر و ور گفتن sher-o ver goftan
چاک دهن châk-e' dahan
yard *n.* حیاط yayât
yard *n.* یارد yârd
yardage *n.* اندازهٔ یاردی andâzeh-ye' yârdi
yardman *n.* کارگر kâr-gar
yardstick *n.* خطکش یک یاردی khat-kesh-e' yek-yârdi
yarn *vt., vi.* کانوا kân-vâ قصه بافی qese~h-bâfi
yawn *v.* خمیازه کشیدن kham-yâzeh keshidân
دهن دره کردن dahan-dar~eh kardan
yea *adv., n.* اینقدر in-qadr
yea(h) *n.* آره âreh
year *n.* سال sâl
yearbook *n.* سالنامه sâl-nâmeh
yearling *n.* یکساله yek-sâleh
yearlong *adj.* یکسال تمام yek-sâl tamâm
yearly *adj., adv., n.* سالانه sâlâneh
yearn *vi.* آرزو کردن ârezu kardan مشتاق بودن moshtâq budan
yearning *n.* آرزو ârezu اشتیاق eshtiâq
yeast *n., vi.* خمیرترش khamir torsh
yell *vi., vt., n.* فریادزدن faryâd zadan دادزدن dâd zadan
yellow *adj., n., vt., vi.* زرد zard زرده zardeh
yellow fever *n.* تب زرد tab-e' zard
yellow-skin *n.* زردپوست zard-pust
yellowish *adj.* زردرنگ zard-rang
yelp *vi., vt., n.* واق کردن vâq kardan
yen *n., pl.* علاقه شدید 'alâqeh-ye' shadid
yeoman *n., adj.* افسر جزء afsar-e' joz'
yes *adv., n.* بله baleh آره âreh آری âri
yes man *np.* بله قربان baleh-qorbân چاپلوس châplus
yester *adj.* دیروزی diruzi

yesterday *adv., n., adj.* ديروز diruz
yesteryear *n., adv.* پارسال pâr-sâl
yet *adv., con.* هنوز hanuz بااين همه bâ in hameh باز bâz منتها montehâ
yield *v.* تسليم شدن taslim shodan
yield *n.* بار bâr محصول mâhsul
yield *v.* حق تقدم دادن haq~-e' taqad~om dâdan
yield *v.* باردادن bâr dâdan حاصل دادن hâsel dâdan
yipe! *n.* آخ! âkh! واى! vây!
yo-yo *n.* يويو yoyo خنگ kheng
yodel *vt., vi., n.* چهچه زدن chah-chah zadan
yogurt *n.* ماست mâst
yoke *n., vt., vi.* يوغ yoq سلطه salteh
yolk *n.* زرده zardeh
yonder *adj., adv.* آنطرف تر ân-taraf tar
you *pro.* شمارا shomâ râ تورا to râ
you *pro.* شما shomâ
young *n., adj.* جوان javân برنا bornâ
young blood *np.* نيروى جوان niru-ye' javân
youngster *n.* جوانک javânak پسربچه pesar-bach~eh
yours *pro.* مال شما mâl-e' shomâ مال تو mâl-e' to
yours truly *np.* چاکر châker مخلص شما mokhles-e' shomâ
yourself *n.* خودت khodat خودتان khodetân
youth *n.* جوانى javâni جوانان javânân شباب shabâb
youthful *adj.* جوان javân
yule *n.* فصل کریسمس fasl-e' keris-mas

Z Z z

zany *adj., n.* خل khol مشنگ mashang
zeal *n.* شوق shoq غیرت qeyrat تعصب ta'as~ob
zealot *n.* غیرتی qeyrati متعصب mote'as~eb
zealous *adj.* غیور qayur باشوق bâ-shoq
zebra *n.* گورخر gur-e' khar
zenith *n.* سمت الرأس samtol-ra's اوج oj
zephyr *n.* نسیم nasim بادصبا bâd-e~ sabâ
zero *n., adj.* تمرکزکردن tamarkoz kardan
zero *n., adj.* صفر sefr
zero hour *np.* ساعت موعود sâ'at-e' mo'ud
zest *n., vt.* مزه mazeh اشتیاق eshtiâq
zestful *adj.* بامزه bâ-mazeh بااشتیاق bâ-eshtiâq
zigzag *n., adj., adv., vt.* زیگزاگ رفتن zigzâg raftan
　　　　　ماربیچ رفتن mâr-pich raftan
zinc *n., vt.* روی ruy
zip *n., vi., vt.* زیپ کردن zip kardan تندرفتن tond raftan
zipper *n., vt., vi.* زیپ zip
zodiac *n.* دائرهٔ برجی dâyereh-ye' borji
　　　　　منطقة البروج mentaqatol boruj
zombi(e) *n.* مرده نما mordeh-namâ
zonal *adj.* منطقه ای mantaqeh-i
zone *n., vt., vi.* منطقه mantaqeh
zoning *adj.* منطقه بندی mantaqeh-bandi
zoo *n.* باغ وحش bâq-e' vahsh
zoology *n.* جانورشناسی jânevar-shenâsi
Zoroaster *n.* زرتشت zartosht
Zoroastrian *n.* زرتشتی zartoshti
zucchini *n.* کدو kadu

OTHER TITLES OF INTEREST FROM IBEX PUBLISHES

A LITERARY HISTORY OF PERSIA / EDWARD G. BROWNE
The classic history of Persian literature
2,323 pages / cloth / 0-936347-66-x

AN INTRODUCTION TO PERSIAN / W. M. THACKSTON
A comprehensive guide and grammar to the language
326 pages / softcover / 0-936347-29-5

MILLENNIUM OF CLASSICAL PERSIAN POETRY / W. THACKSTON
A guide to the reading and understanding of Persian poetry from the tenth to the twentieth century
212 pages / softcover / 0-936347-50-3

A PERSIAN READER / LILY AYMAN
Persian first grade reader
104 pages / softcover / 0-936347-34-1

1001 PERSIAN-ENGLISH PROVERBS / SIMIN HABIBIAN
1001 Persian proverbs and idioms with corresponding English proverb and a literal translation in English. Illustrated.
256 pages / softcover / 0-936347-92-9

THE EYE OF AN ANT: PERSIAN PROVERBS & POEMS / F. AKBAR
Persian wisdom rendered into English verse along with the original.
104 pages / softcover / 0-936347-56-2

THE LITTLE BLACK FISH / SAMAD BEHRANGI
Translation and Persian text of mahi siah kuchulu. Translated by Hooshang Amuzegar. In English & Persian.
64 pages / softcover / 0-936347-78-3

MODERN PERSIAN PROSE LITERATURE / HASSAN KAMSHAD
Classic on the subject and Hedayat with new introduction.
xvi + 226 pages / softcover / 0-936347-72-4

PERSIAN STUDIES IN NORTH AMERICA / MEHDI MARASHI, ED.
32 articles by leading scholars on the state of the study of Persian literature.
Four of the articles are in Persian.
xx + 556 pages / cloth / 0-936347-35-X

THE DIVAN-I HAFIZ / H. WILBERFORCE CLARKE TRANSLATOR
Complete literal translation of Hafez's divan with copious notes.
1,180 pages / cloth / 0-936347-80-5

IN WINESELLER'S STREET / THOMAS RAIN CROWE, TRANS.
Renderings of Hafez by American poet.
88 pages / softcover / 0-936347-67-8

AN INTRODUCTION TO KORANIC ARABIC / W. M. THACKSTON
An elementary grammar of the language of the Koran
360 pages / softcover / 0-936347-40-6

AN IRANIAN IN NINETEENTH CENTURY EUROPE,
Translated into English by the grand daughter of the
author with an introduction by Peter Avery.
379 pages / cloth / 0-936347-93-7

PERSIAN COOKING: TABLE OF EXOTIC DELIGHTS / N. RAMAZANI
Comprehensive cookbook and guide to Persian cooking
xxii + 296 pages / softcover / 0-936347-77-5

FROM DURHAM TO TEHRAN / MICHAEL HILLMANN
Recollections of a Persian literature specialist.
128 pages / cloth / 0-936347-18-X

To order the above books or to receive
our catalog, please contact
IBEX Publishers / Post Office Box 30087 / Bethesda, MD 20824
Phone 301 718-8188 / Fax 301 907-8707 / www.ibexpub.com

این فرهنگ با دیگر فرهنگ های موجود در کتابخانه ها دو تفاوت متمایز دارد:

در درجهٔ اول، این فرهنگ به جای اینکه روی تلفظ کلمات انگلیسی تأکید کند، تلفظ کلمات فارسی را به زبان بین المللی «فونتیـک» phonetic به نگـارش در آورده است، تا اگر خوانندهٔ کتاب، با الفبای فارسی آشنایی نداشته باشد با خواندن و تلفظ کلمات فارسی بحروف لاتیـن، قـادر بـه صحبت باشـد. همچنیـن ایـن شیوهٔ نگـارش فرهنگ، میتواند به آن دسته از نسل جدیـد ایرانی در کشـورهای خـارج از ایـران، کـه بدلیلی از فراگیری نحوهٔ نوشتن زبان فارسی بدور افتاده اند کمک های شایسته بنماید.

فرق دوم اینست که بخاطر محدودهٔ استفاده از زبان phonetic، یعنـی بـا پیـش فرصّ اینکه بعضی از خوانندگان این کتاب قادر به خواندن الفبای فارسی نیستند و یـا دسـتور زبان فارسی را خوب نمیدانند، گرد آورندهٔ این فرهنـگ مجبـور بـوده اسـت کلمـات انگلیسی را فقط ترجمهٔ مستقیم کند و نتوانـد معـانی ایـن لغـات را در حاشیه توضیـح بدهد. به این علت ترجمه دقیق بسیاری از کلمات انگلیسی در این چهار چـوب بسیار مشکل و حتی غیر ممکن بوده است.

— داریوش بهنام گیلانی

اگر مردم دنیا، با زبانهای مختلف و دیدگاه های گوناگون، می توانستند راز جـادوئی کلمات را در شعر حافظ دریابند و لذت ببرند مسلماً شیفته او مـی شدند و بـه معرفی این نابغهٔ ادبی و فلسفی و دیگر برجستگان ادب و فرهنگ فارسی، به سـایر مـلـل، هـم صدا و همگام می شدند.

پس شناسائی و آموزش زبان فارسی به دنیا، گامی مؤثر در معرفی فرهنگ و ادب ایران به جهانیان است و این فرهنگ نامه، در کنار دیگر کتابهای مشابه، در مسیر این تـلاش عظیم ملی می تواند همگام و یاور ارزنده ای برای شما باشد.

البته می دانیم که زبان، مانند همه علوم بشری، همیشه در حال تکامل بوده و هسـت. هر سال واژه های نو، با معانی جدیدتری بر گنجینهٔ کلمات خود اضافه میکند و یا این که کلمات تازه تری را جایگزین لغات مشکل و یا پیش پا افتاده مینماید. جمع آورنـده این فرهنگ نامه سعی در این داشته است که مصطلـح ترین کلمـات و لغـات رایـج در میان مردم ایران را صرفاً بنا بر تقدم آنها نسبت بـه کلمـات مـترادف، بـدون هیـچ نـوع تعصب زبانی در ترجمهٔ واژه های انگلیسی بکار ببرد.

با اینکه لغات این فرهنگنامه و معانی این واژه هـا بـا دقت کـامل انتخـاب و تصحیـح شده اند ولی میدانیم که این فرهنگ باز هم دارای اشـتباهات لغـوی و معنـوی و چاپـی میباشد. ما از همهٔ ایرانیان و فارسی زبانان علاقمند دعوت مینماییم که عقاید و نظرات و انتقادات خود را در رابطه با این فرهنگ و اشکلاتی که در آن ملاحظه میکنند بـرای ما ارسال داشته و ما را در انجام این امر یعنی ارتباط زبان فارسی بـا انگلیسـی و دیگر زبانهای دنیا یاری نمایند.

پیشگفتار

زبان فارسی ای که ما امروز از آن استفاده می کنیم پس از فروپاشی سلسله ساسانیان و واژگون شدن تخت و تاج کیانی بتدریج شکل گرفته و تکامل یافته است. هجوم و سلطه، اعراب و دیگر اقوام همسایه، ایران موقتاً در رشد و تکامل این زبان باستانی وقفه ای ایجاد نمود. ولی در طی قرنهای بعد، با همت مردم ایران و کوشش شاعران و نویسندگان گرانمایه اش، بخصوص فردوسی، زبان فارسی زنده شد و با اینکه هزاران لغات جدید خارجی وارد این زبان شده بود. این زبان زیر بنا و دستور زبان (هند و آریایی) خود را حفظ نمود و در شکل زبان (فارسی نو) مورد استفاده کشور ایران و سرزمینهای همسایه قرار گرفت.

در اینکه چه مقدار از لغات مورد استفاده زبان امروز فارسی، از زبان عربی و چه مقدار از زبان ترکی و سایر گویشها گرفته شده در این مقال مورد بحث ما نیست. آنچه مورد نظر ماست بار آوری، گسترش، تفهیم و معرفی آن به دنیای گسترده صنعتی امروز است. اگر از سده های گذشته، برای شناسایی زبان فارسی به دنیای غرب، تلاشی صورت گرفته بود اینک علاوه بر آشنائی بیشتر دنیای امروز با زبان فارسی، بسیاری از شاهکارهای گنجینه غنی و پر بار ادب ایران به زبانهای زنده دنیا ترجمه شده بود. در حالی که تعداد آثاری که از ادب دیروز و امروز فرهنگ پر بارمان به زبانهای مختلف دنیا ترجمه شده، در قیاس با گنجینه غنی دریای ادب ایران چشمگیر نیست.

البته این عقب افتادگی از قافله فرهنگی و ادب جهانی، علل مختلفی دارد که یکی از آنها آشنا نبودن دنیای غرب با زبان فارسی و رمز و راز و پیچیدگی های آن است.

فرهنگ
انگلیسی ـ فارسی

داریوش بهنام گیلانی

چاپ پاژن

فرهنگ انگلیسی - فارسی